This **TIMELINE ACTIVITY** examines other close-call elections in our history.

PRE-TESTS, POST-TESTS, CHAPTER EXAMS and **STUDY GUIDES** for each chapter of your book help students prepare for exams.

This **SIMULATION** ACTIVITY helps students judge whether a police officer who is breaking and entering is violating civil rights.

Available in CourseCompass,™ Web CT, & Blackboard

mypoliscilab™

Where participation leads to action!

with LongmanParticipate.com 3.0 inside!

From **simulations** that place students in the role of campaign manager to **timeline activities**, from **pre- and post-chapter tests** to a fully integrated **Ebook**, MyPoliSciLab brings together an amazing collection of resources for both students and instructors. See a demo now at **www.mypoliscilab.com**!

Here's what's in MyPoliSciLab—

Pre-Test, Post Test, and Chapter Exam.
For each chapter of the text, students will navigate through a pre-test, post-test, and a full chapter exam—all fully integrated with the online Ebook so students can assess, review, and improve their understanding of the material in each chapter.

Ebook.
Matching the exact layout of the printed textbook, the Ebook contains multimedia icons in the margins that launch a wealth of exciting resources.

Chapter Review.
For each chapter, students will find additional resources, such as a complete study guide, learning objectives, a summary, and Web explorations.

Research Navigator™.
This database provides thousands of articles from popular periodicals like *Newsweek* and *USA Today* that give students and professors access to topical content from a variety of sources.

New York Times Online Feed & The New York Times Search by Subject™ Archive.
Both provide free access to the full text of *The New York Times* and articles from the world's leading journalists of the *Times*. The online feed provides students with updated headlines and political news on an hourly basis.

LongmanParticipate.com 3.0
Our well-known and highly respected online tool is now fully updated. Students will find over 100 simulations, interactive timelines, comparative exercises and more—all integrated with the online ebook. Available inside MyPoliSciLab or as a website alone.

LongmanParticipate.com 3.0 *Inside!*

Go to mypoliscilab.com for a free demo.

LONGMAN Participate.com 3.0

www.longmanparticipate.com

LongmanParticipate.com version 3.0 inside MyPoliSciLab or as a website alone!

Within the margins of your textbook you will find these icons directing students to the LongmanParticipate.com activities, which will correspond to the chapter content. Now fully updated with brand new activities!

Longman Participate Activities:

 SIMULATION. Students are given a role to play —such as Congress member, lobbyist, or police officer—and experience the challenges and excitement of politics firsthand.

 VISUAL LITERACY. Students interpret and apply data about intriguing political topics. Each activity begins with an interactive primer on reading graphics.

 TIMELINE. With an abundance of media and graphics, students can step through the evolution of an aspect of government.

 PARTICIPATION. Bringing the importance of politics home, these activities appear as three types: 1.) Debates, 2.) Surveys, and 3.) Get Involved activities.

 COMPARATIVE. Students compare the U.S. political system to that of other countries.

INSTRUCTORS:

Course Management System—

MyPoliSciLab is available in different versions to fit your needs:
- MyPoliSciLab in CourseCompass™
- MyPoliSciLab in Blackboard
- MyPoliSciLab in WebCT

Website alone—
If you do not want a course management system, the LongmanParticipate.com 3.0 activities are available in a website-alone version.

STUDENTS:

If your text did not come with an access code to MyPoliSciLab, you can still get this amazing resource to help you succeed in the course. Just go to www.mypoliscilab.com and click on "How do I get access to mypoliscilab?"

Go to mypoliscilab.com for a free demo.

mypoliscilab™
Where participation leads to action!

THE STRUGGLE
FOR DEMOCRACY

Seventh Edition

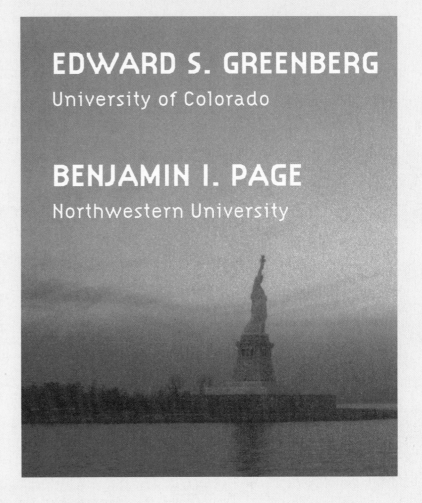

EDWARD S. GREENBERG
University of Colorado

BENJAMIN I. PAGE
Northwestern University

PEARSON
Longman

New York   San Francisco   Boston
London   Toronto   Sydney   Tokyo   Singapore   Madrid
Mexico City   Munich   Paris   Cape Town   Hong Kong   Montreal

EXECUTIVE EDITOR	Eric Stano
DEVELOPMENT EDITOR	Nancy Crochiere
SENIOR MARKETING MANAGER	Elizabeth Fogarty
MEDIA AND SUPPLEMENTS EDITOR	Kristi Olson
MEDIA EDITOR	Patrick McCarthy
PRODUCTION MANAGER	Donna DeBenedictis
PROJECT COORDINATION, TEXT DESIGN, ART RENDERING, AND ELECTRONIC PAGE MAKEUP	Elm Street Publishing Services, Inc.
COVER DESIGNER / MANAGER	Wendy Ann Fredericks
COVER PHOTOS	© SuperStock and © Eliot Crowley/Index Stock Imagery
PHOTO RESEARCHER	Photosearch, Inc.
SENIOR MANUFACTURING BUYER	Dennis J. Para
PRINTER AND BINDER	Quebecor World Taunton
COVER PRINTER	Phoenix Color Corporation

For permission to use copyrighted material, grateful acknowledgment is made to the copyright holders on pages C-1–C-2, which are hereby made part of the copyright page.

Library of Congress Cataloging-in-Publication Data

Greenberg, Edward S., 1942–
    The struggle for democracy / Edward S. Greenberg, Benjamin I. Page.—7th ed.
      p. cm.
    Includes bibliographical references and index.
    ISBN 0-321-24352-8 (alk. paper)—ISBN 0-321-21738-1 (pbk. : alk. paper)
    1. United States—Politics and government. 2. Democracy—United States. I. Page, Benjamin I. II. Title.

    JK276.G74 2005
    320.473—dc22
                                         2004057662

Please visit us at http://www.ablongman.com/greenberg

ISBN 0-321-21738-1 (softcover)
ISBN 0-321-24352-8 (hardcover)

2 3 4 5 6 7 8 9 10—QWT—07 06 05

Brief Contents

Detailed Contents

Note: Each chapter ends with the following sections: Summary, Suggestions for Further Reading, and Internet Sources. Blue bullets designate special features within the chapter.

Preface

Critical Thinking and *The Struggle for Democracy*

This seventh edition of *The Struggle for Democracy* carries forward and strengthens the extensive changes we made in the fifth and sixth editions that contributed to their widespread popularity among teachers and students. Following the well-known adage "If it ain't broke, don't fix it," we decided to confine major changes in this edition to those that would enrich and sharpen its critical thinking focus. In addition to a general updating and freshening of materials throughout the text—including the Bush presidency; the 2004 presidential and congressional election campaigns; the impact of heightened homeland security; the war and occupation in Iraq; the 9/11 Commission Report; the debate over same-sex civil unions and marriage; Supreme Court rulings in the areas of gay rights, affirmative action, and enemy combatants; the return of annual budget deficits; prescription drug coverage under Medicare; and rising tensions with our European allies—our most significant change in this regard is the addition of a new feature we call "The Rise of Partisan Conflict," which addresses the intensification of partisan conflict in American politics and asks students to think about whether this development helps or hinders democracy in the United States. We will say more about this feature later.

The watchword for the seventh edition of *The Struggle for Democracy*, much as it was for the fifth and sixth, is "critical thinking." Critical thinking has always been at the heart of this book, of course, but its sharp edge had gradually, if almost unconsciously, become blunted slightly with each revision as material was added to answer first one perceived need then another. Beginning with the fifth edition and carried on in the sixth, we have sharpened the critical thinking edge, getting it back to where it was supposed to be. Every element in this version of *The Struggle for Democracy* is designed to serve the "critical thinking" objective. We have continued to pare away any and all materials that do not help students think critically about American government and politics and about their role as citizens. In moving in this direction, we are returning to our original vision from when we first decided to write this book, responding to what we learned from a multitude of instructors and students about what they want in an introductory textbook, and conforming to what we, as experienced teachers of the introductory course, know works in the classroom. We have created a textbook that treats students as adults, engages their intellectual and emotional attention, and encourages them to be active learners.

The critical thinking orientation of this edition of *The Struggle for Democracy* is organized around two principal themes: *Using the Democracy Standard* and *Using the Framework*. The first helps students come to grips with American government and politics in normative or value terms. The second helps students cut through the jumble of information about government and politics and bring some order out of the confusion, helping them make sense of why things happen. We have also created a rich set of Web Explorations in which students do assignments on the Internet where they hone their evaluative and analytical critical thinking skills and, at the same time, have some fun.

New to this edition, as we suggest above, is "The Rise of Partisan Conflict," a feature we believe will help students think more carefully about the quality of democracy in the United States. We have also added to and updated the "By the Numbers" exercises, a very popular feature that not only helps students think more critically about published numbers and statistics but also asks them to use the insights they have garnered from using this feature to think about current political problems and issues. We hope this feature will help students become more analytical—and therefore more effective—citizens.

Using the Democracy Standard

Throughout the pages of this textbook, we help students think about the system as a whole, as well as particular political practices and institutions, using a clearly articulated, evaluative democracy "yardstick" for reaching judgments about the degree to which we have become, or are becoming, more or less democratic.

We develop this "evaluating democracy" theme in a number of places:

● Democracy is carefully defined in Chapter 1, and students learn there how they might use democracy to evaluate the performance of the American political system. The definition of democracy is broad and inclusive, built on the concepts of popular sovereignty, political equality, and liberty.

● In the opening pages of each chapter, students are reminded about the democracy "yardstick" and how it might be used to think critically about the subject matter to follow.

● Discussion of the relative democratic performance of the American political system, using the Chapter 1 definition as the yardstick, is laced throughout the text narrative.

● A chapter-ending "How Democratic Are We?" box helps students think through the democracy issue once again, only this time they have the capacity to bring information and insights to bear that they have gained from reading the chapter, attending class and joining its discussions, and doing the Web Explorations. This feature is organized in the following way: It opens with a strongly stated proposition about the relative democratic character of the particular political or governmental institution under consideration in the chapter. The proposition is answered by two opposing views—brief but fairly stated "agree" and "disagree" statements. Finally, we ask students to think carefully about the opposing views, offering some guidelines on how to subject the statements to critical scrutiny. This feature helps students understand the complexity of many of the issues addressed in the book and learn how to formulate intellectually compelling arguments.

Using the Framework

In Chapter 1 we also provide a simple but powerful analytical framework that helps students understand how our complicated political system works. The framework makes clear that government, politics, and the larger society are deeply intertwined in recognizable patterns; that understanding what is going on requires a holistic focus; and that what might be called "deep structures"—the economy, society, political culture, and the constitutional rules—are particularly important for understanding how our system works. These deep structures have a great deal to do with the creation of the problems to which government must attend, the level of resources that is available to solve problems, the ideas that citizens and elected officials have in their heads as they go about using government to address problems, and the distribution of political power in society among individuals, groups, and organizations.

The framework appears in *The Struggle for Democracy* in the following places:

- The framework is discussed in detail in Chapter 1, and students are shown how it can be used to organize the large amounts of material they will encounter in the course of their reading. A powerful graphic associated with the discussion makes the framework more understandable and compelling.

- In the opening pages of each chapter, students are reminded about the framework and how it can be used to understand how government and politics work in the United States.

- Chapters in Part Two examine the nature of American society, political culture, and economy; the United States's position in the world; and our constitutional rules—and why these issues matter for how government and politics work.

- Concepts and insights from the framework, as well as materials from the chapters in Part Two, are used throughout the text narrative.

- A "Using the Framework" box appears in each chapter. The purpose of the box is to show students how the framework might be used to answer questions they might have about why things happen in American government and politics. Concepts and insights from the framework, as well as a graphical reminder, are used to provide the tools to answer questions that students are interested in, such as "Why is out-of-state tuition more costly than in-state tuition?" and "Why can't we seem to get big money out of politics?" Teachers and students have told us repeatedly that this feature, which first appeared in the fifth edition, made the analytical framework come alive for them and helped them appreciate how the framework can be used to understand what is going on in American government and politics.

Web Explorations

We have designed a series of what we call "Web Explorations," where students can explore and use the many riches of the Internet to put their critical thinking skills to work and have some fun at the same time. In these Web Explorations, we do not simply identify a Website for students to visit but give them a question or issue to investigate and ask that they report the results. These reports, tangible products of their investigations and analyses, may be for students' own edification, enriching their experiences in the text, or may be assigned as a class activity. The Explorations are active and interactive in nature, never passive. Students are not casual visitors, browsing a site, but investigators and analysts using their critical thinking skills.

By the Numbers

As teachers of the introductory course, we have grown increasingly concerned over the years by the inability of many students to understand the statistical information on government, politics, economy, and society that they encounter—including statistics such as the gross domestic product, the crime rate, voting turnout in presidential elections, and the level of poverty in the United States—or to distinguish between good and bad statistical information. Partly, this is the result of their general discomfort with statistics and numbers. Partly, this is the product of the failure of statistical reporting agencies and organizations to openly describe their operating assumptions and methods. All too often, moreover, interest and advocacy groups use statistics as instruments of political combat, leaving the impression that all statistics are "lies and damn lies," with one statistic no better than another. The news media are not all that helpful either, with their tendency to report social, economic, and political statistics in a haphazard, noncritical, and out-of-context fashion. Finally, statistics from the federal government, though generally more reliable and sensible than those calculated by interest groups, are themselves often the product of political negotiation and compromise—the poverty-line calculation is a good example. Although government statistics are incredibly useful, the consumer of such statistics must remain alert.

The "By the Numbers" feature appears throughout the text. Two new ones have been added to this seventh edition. The goal of the feature is to help students become better consumers of statistical information and more analytical readers of social, economic, and political statistics reported by government, interest and advocacy groups, and academic researchers. Each box describes a particular statistic and tells why the statistic is important—examples include voting turnout, the poverty line, the crime rate, the size of the federal government, interest group scoring of the performance of senators and representatives, and more. We then tell the story behind the statistic—why the statistic was first calculated, let us say, or what assumptions are embedded in it. We then show how the statistic is calculated and examine what critics and supporters say about its usefulness and validity. Finally, we ask students what they think, thus encouraging them to think in more depth about issues addressed by the statistic, whether it be poverty, voting turnout, or how the U.S. Census Bureau goes about doing the decennial census. If the "By the Numbers" feature works as we hope it does, students should become more sophisticated users of statistical information, but not cynical ones. We believe that in a world increasingly described by numbers, students who are armed with these skills can be better and more effective citizens.

The Rise of Partisan Conflict

This feature, new to the seventh edition, focuses on the increased partisanship in American politics, the tendency of more and more issues to become the stuff of interparty conflict and for the competition between Democrats and Republicans to become more intense. We trace these developments to the dead-even split in the country between Republicans and Democrats at every level in the political system: among party identifiers, among voters in presidential elections (roughly 50–50 in 2000), in Congress, and on the Supreme Court. The closeness of the party division contributes to the intensification of interparty conflicts and, we suggest, to increasing incivility in our political life, because it compels each party to mobilize its base as a first order of business, depending heavily on ideological appeals to do so.

Because, like most people, students are drawn to stories of conflict and competition, they are likely to pay attention to this new feature. Once their attention is drawn, we use the feature to teach some important lessons about American politics and ask students to consider t he impact of rising partisanship on both American democracy and their own willingness and enthusiasm to become active participants in the political process.

Organization and Coverage

Part One contains the introduction to the textbook and focuses primarily on describing the critical thinking tools to be used throughout: democracy and the analytical framework. Part Two covers the structural foundations of American government and politics and also addresses subjects such as the economy, culture, and international system; the constitutional framework of the American political system; and the development of the federal system. Part Three focuses on what we call *political linkage* institutions, such as parties, elections, public opinion, social movements, and interest groups, that serve to convey the wants, needs, and demands of individuals and groups to public officials. Part Four concentrates on the central institutions of the national government, including the presidency, Congress, and the Supreme Court. Part Five describes the kinds of policies the national government produces and analyzes how effective government is in solving pressing social and economic problems.

Although all of the standard topics in the introductory course are covered in the text, our focus on using democracy as a measuring rod to evaluate our system of government, and on using an analytical framework for understanding how things work, allows us to take a fresh look at traditional topics and to pay attention to topics that are not covered in detail in other textbooks:

- We pay much more attention to *structural factors*—which include the American economy, social change in the United States, technological innovations and change, the American political culture, and changes in the global system—and examine how they affect politics, government, and public policy. These factors are introduced in Chapter 4—a chapter unique among introductory texts—and are brought to bear on a wide range of issues in subsequent chapters. For example, our discussion of interest group politics includes relevant information about how the distribution of income and wealth affects the ability of different groups to form effective lobbying organizations.

- We attend very carefully to issues of *democratic political theory*. This follows from our critical thinking objective, which asks students to assess the progress of and prospects for democracy in the United States, and from our desire to present American history as the history of the struggle for democracy. For instance, we examine how the evolution of the party system has improved democracy in some respects in the United States but hurt it in others.

- We also include more *historical information* than is common among introductory texts, because the best way to understand the struggle for democracy and evaluate the progress of democracy in the United States benefits from a historical perspective. We show, for example, how the expansion of civil rights in the United States has been associated with important historical events and trends.

- We also include substantial *comparative information* because we believe that a full understanding of government and politics and the effect of structural factors on them is possible only through a comparison of developments, practices, and institutions in the United States with those in other nations. We understand better how our system of social welfare works, for example, when we see how other rich democratic countries deal with the problems of poverty, unemployment, and old age.

- Our approach also means that the subjects of *civil liberties* and *civil rights* are not treated in conjunction with the Constitution in Part Two, which is the case with many introductory texts, but in Part Five, on public policy. This is because we believe that the real-world status of civil liberties and civil rights, while partly determined by specific provisions of the Constitution, is better understood as the outcome of the interaction of structural, political, and governmental factors. Thus, the status of civil rights for gays and lesbians depends not only on constitutional provisions but also on the state of public opinion, degrees of support from elected political leaders, and the decisions of the Supreme Court. (Instructors who prefer to introduce their students to civil liberties and civil rights immediately after considering the Constitution can simply assign the liberties and rights chapters out of order.)

What's New in This Edition

A number of important changes have been made in this edition. They include the following:

- To reiterate a point already made: The most important change in this seventh edition of *The Struggle for Democracy* is the extension of the focus on critical thinking as the central organizing template. To get there, we have further refined and strengthened our discussions of democracy as a tool of evaluation and of the framework as a tool of analysis and understanding, paid special attention to drawing out these themes in every chapter, and included a series of Web Explorations to enable students to be active critical thinkers.

- This edition of *The Struggle for Democracy* includes two new exercises for the "By the Numbers" feature, described earlier in more detail. This feature is unique among introductory American government and politics textbooks and adds to the critical thinking tools available to students.

- This edition pays more attention to "marginalized" groups in American society, including Hispanics and gays and lesbians. Combining this enhanced attention to marginalized groups with *The Struggle for Democracy*'s traditionally strong coverage of African Americans and women means that the current edition of this textbook reflects much of the cultural richness, diversity, and complexity of American society itself. These new materials are found throughout in the text narrative, in chapter-opening stories, and in boxed features. For example, Chapter 4 describes the rapid rise in the number of Americans of Hispanic origin and explores what this might mean for American politics. Chapter 15 considers the status of civil liberties protections for Arab Americans in the United States in the aftermath of 9/11. Chapter 16 discusses the current status of gay rights in the United States following the Supreme Court's landmark decision *Lawrence* v. *Texas* (2003) and the Massachusetts's high court ruling allowing same-sex marriage.

- We have expanded our coverage of Websites in the Internet Sources sections and integrated them even more tightly with *The Struggle for Democracy* home page. This is in addition to the very strong Internet presence found in the Web Exploration features distributed throughout.

Together, these will allow both students and instructors to have better access to timely information and alternative perspectives.

- We have added a new feature, "The Rise of Partisan Conflict," to explore the implications of rising partisanship in American political life. This feature, described earlier, adds importantly to the critical thinking focus of this textbook.

- In addition to expanded coverage of Websites and the Web Explorations feature, we have made further strides to integrate the Web. Throughout the text, icons can be found in the margins referring readers to the interactive exercises that are available in both *MyPoliSciLab* and *LongmanParticipate.com* 3.0, Longman's two interactive Websites for American government. Each icon appears next to a particular topic and indicates that a simulation, visual literacy exercise, interactive timeline, participation activity, or comparative government exercise related to that topic exists on either site. (The same activities are available on both sites.) Each activity provides feedback, helps the reader better understand the concepts presented in the text, and makes learning fun. Students will know which Website to visit—*MyPoliSciLab* or *LongmanParticipate.com* 3.0—for these exercises by looking at the access code card bundled with this text.

- Information has been updated throughout. There is not a single page in the text without fresh information. Timely subjects, such as the 2004 presidential and congressional elections; the actions and policies of the George W. Bush administration; the continuing impact on American politics of developments in the war on terrorism and homeland security; important Supreme Court decisions involving federalism, civil liberties, and civil rights; emerging foreign policy problems in the Middle East and among our traditional allies in Europe; and much more are covered throughout.

- We have continued our effort to make the text more user-friendly for students by paying more attention to the layout of text and the highlighting of key points, better defining of technical terms, presenting more detailed captions that explain tables and graphs, and providing more information in photo captions. Most importantly, we have tied the chapters together with critical thinking guideposts and exercises.

Supplements

Longman Publishers provides an impressive array of text supplements to aid instructors in teaching and students in learning. Each item in this extensive package works together to create a fully integrated learning system. Great care was taken to provide both students and professors with a supportive supplements package that accurately reflects the unique spirit of *The Struggle for Democracy*.

Instructor Supplements for Qualified College Adopters

Digital Media Archive CD-ROM   This complete multimedia presentation tool for instructors includes more than 150 maps, graphs, and charts; 100 photos; and 50 video clips—all on one CD-ROM and ready for inclusion in an instructor's online course, *PowerPoint*® presentations, and Websites. It was developed in consultation with Kurt Cline, California State University, Fresno; Martin S. Edwards, Texas Tech University; Scott R. Furlong, University of Wisconsin, Green Bay; James M. Lutz, Indiana University Purdue University, Fort Wayne; and John David Rausch, Jr., West Texas A&M University.

***The Struggle for Democracy* Companion Website (http://www .ablongman.com/greenberg)**   Designed to support instructors and students who are using *The Struggle for Democracy*, this Website includes summaries, Web Explorations, and practice tests for each chapter for students. For instructors, there is a *PowerPoint®* presentation created by Terri Wright of California State University, Long Branch, and Mary Carns of Stephen F. Austin State University, to support and enhance lectures; downloadable art and images for each chapter; the Instructor's Manual; and a group of teaching links.

Instructor's Manual   Written by Debra St. John of Collin County Community College District and Mary Carns of Stephen F. Austin State University, this comprehensive manual is designed to help instructors prepare lectures, classroom activities, and assignments. The manual features chapter outlines and summaries, a broad range of teaching suggestions, ideas for student research, and suggestions for discussion that complement text themes.

Test Bank   Prepared by Robert Yowell of Stephen F. Austin State University, this manual is designed to reinforce and test students' knowledge of the themes and concepts of the text. The test bank contains hundreds of multiple-choice, short-answer, true/false, and essay questions with an answer key.

TestGen-EQ Computerized Testing System   This flexible, easy-to-master computerized test bank includes all the test items in the printed test bank. The software allows professors to edit existing questions and to add their own items. Tests can be printed in several different formats and can include features such as graphs and tables. It is available for Windows and Macintosh computers.

***PowerPoint®* Presentations**   Available to download on the textbook's Companion Website at **www.ablongman.com/greenberg**. Written by Mary Carns at Stephen F. Austin State University and Terri Wright of California State University, Long Beach, these slides can also be easily modified using *PowerPoint®* software.

Transparencies   This acetate package is comprised of 40 images taken from the text.

***Supplements Central*™ (www.ablongman.com/suppscentral)**   A helpful Website where instructors can download supplements including: Instructor's Manuals, Test Banks, TestGens, and *PowerPoint®* presentations, as well as CourseCompass®, WebCT, and Blackboard materials. Instructors will need to request a password from their sales representative to gain access.

Faculty Guide to Accompany *MyPoliSciLab* and *LongmanParticipate .com* 3.0   Written by Scott Furlong of the University of Wisconsin, this guide contains chapter-by-chapter detailed summaries for each of the sites' interactive activities, as well as a list of concepts covered, recommendations about how to integrate the sites into coursework, and discussion questions and paper topics for every exercise. Instructors may use the table of contents in the front of the guide to locate information on a given activity icon that appears in the margin of this textbook. This guide also provides instructors with detailed instructions and screen shots showing how to register on the sites and how to set up and use the administrative features.

Quick Start Guide to Accompany *MyPoliSciLab* in CourseCompass® Contains instructor access code and step-by-step instructions for using *MyPoliSciLab*'s features in the CourseCompass® course management system. To order, contact your local Allyn & Bacon/Longman representative and request a copy.

Interactive American Government Video Contains 27 video segments on topics ranging from the term limit debate, to Internet porn, to women in the Citadel. Critical thinking questions accompany each clip, encouraging students to "interact" with the videos.

***Politics in Action* Video** Eleven "lecture launchers," covering broad subjects such as social movements, conducting a campaign, and the passage of a bill, are examined through narrated videos, interviews, edited documentaries, original footage, and political ads.

Longman Political Science Video Program Qualified adopters can peruse our list of videos for the American government classroom. Contact your local Allyn & Bacon/Longman representative for more information.

Student Supplements for Qualified College Adopters

MyPoliSciLab This state-of-the-art, interactive, and instructive online solution for the American government course, fully integrated in the course management system of your choice—CourseCompass®, WebCT, or Blackboard—is available for free with every new copy of *The Struggle for Democracy* and contains the following features:

- **Assessment**. For each chapter of the text, students will navigate through a pre-test, post-test, and a full chapter exam all fully integrated with an online, e-book version of this text so students can assess, review, and improve their understanding of the text chapters.

- ***LongmanParticipate.com* 3.0 interactive exercises**. Developed and revised by a team of more than 12 political science faculty, *LongmanParticipate.com* 3.0 features more than 100 highly interactive activities—including visual literacy exercises, comparative activities, interactive timelines, participation exercises, and more than 30 simulations—for all of the major topics in the course. (These exercises are also available on a separate Website for adopters who do not use a course management system. See the description of *LongmanParticipate.com* 3.0 on the next page for more information.)

- **Research Navigator**™. The EBSCO ContentSelect Academic Journal Database content is collected from thousands of articles organized by discipline and fully searchable. Articles in popular periodicals such as *Newsweek* and *USA Today* are included as well, giving students and professors access to topical content from a variety of sources.

- **Link Library**. Offers editorially selected "best of the Web" sites. Libraries are continually scanned and kept up-to-date, providing the most relevant and accurate links for research assignments.

- **Guidance for the Research Process**. Topics include Finding Sources, Using Your Library, Start Writing, Internet Research, and Citing Sources.

- **Online e-book**. Matching the exact layout of the printed textbook, the online e-book contains multimedia icons in the margins that launch to exciting resources (e.g., *LongmanParticipate.com* 3.0 exercises), which expand on key topics students encounter as they read through the text.

- **Online Administration**. Instructors can easily track student work on the site and monitor students' progress on each activity. The *Instructor Gradebook*, which includes upgraded functionality to ensure a truly seamless experience for users, provides maximum flexibility allowing instructors to sort by student, activity, or to view the entire class in spreadsheet view.

- **The Tutor Center**. On-call qualified tutors answer questions and provide help for *MyPoliSciLab*. Services include starting homework assignments and nonediting help with reviewing papers and assignments for organization, flow, argument, and consistent grammar errors.

- *The New York Times* **Online Feed**. Updated hourly, this feed provides students with free, full access to the full text of *The New York Times* homepage and politics articles.

See the advertisement at the front of this text for more information.

LongmanParticipate.com **3.0**   A subscription to this popular Website is available for free with every new copy of *The Struggle for Democracy*. *LongmanParticipate.com* 3.0, the most interactive and comprehensive Website for the American government, offers more than 100 exciting, in-depth activities—all fully revised and updated from Version 2.0—covering all the major concepts in the course. The site continues to offer five types of exercises designed to engage students in the course material like nothing else can:

- **Simulations**. Students are given a role to play—such as Congress member, lobbyist, or police officer—experiencing the challenges and excitement of politics firsthand. All simulations have been updated and revised for maximum relevance and student appeal. Plus, *LongmanParticipate.com* 3.0 includes 12 all-new simulations—more than 30 simulations in all!

- **Timelines**. With an abundance of media and graphics, students can step through the evolution of an aspect of government. All fully revised and updated.

- **Visual Literacy**. Students interpret data and work with graphs and charts dealing with intriguing political topics. Each activity begins with an interactive primer on reading graphics.

- **Participation**. Bringing the importance of politics home, and designed to encourage student participation, these activities appear in 3 types: (1) "Debates," (2) "Surveys," and (3) "Get Involved" activities. All fully revised and updated.

- **Comparative**. Students compare the U.S. political system with those of other countries. All fully revised and updated.

- **"Test Yourself" quizzes.** These 10-question, multiple-choice quizzes at the end of every activity give instructors a quantifiable way to evaluate student performance. Student answers are e-mailed to the instructor. (To have the Test Yourself grades captured automatically in a gradebook, instructors must adopt *MyPoliSciLab,* which contains these tests in a course management system.)

For more information, see the advertisement at the front of this book.

MyPoliSciLab and *LongmanParticipate.com* 3.0 Student Workbook

This workbook gives students an opportunity for additional analysis, review, and testing based on the exciting exercises found on these Websites. Free when packaged with a new copy of *The Struggle for Democracy*.

Companion Website (www.ablongman.com/greenberg)

This text-specific, online study guide includes: practice tests with feedback (multiple-choice, true/false, fill-in-the-blank, and essay questions), Web exploration exercises, chapter summaries, and more.

Study Wizard CD-ROM

This interactive tutorial program helps students master concepts in the text through practice tests, chapter and topic summaries, and an interactive glossary. Students receive immediate feedback in the form of answer explanations and page references in the text to go to for review.

Study Guide

Written by George Gonzalez of the University of Miami and Mary Carns of Stephen F. Austin State University, this printed study guide includes chapter outlines, key terms, practice tests, and critical thinking questions.

Research Navigator and Research Navigator Guide

Research Navigator is a comprehensive Website comprising three exclusive databases of credible and reliable source material for research and for student assignments: EBSCO's ContentSelect Academic Journal Database, the *New York Times* Search by Subject Archive, and "Best of the Web" Link Library. The site also includes an extensive help section. The Research Navigator Guide provides your students with access to the Research Navigator Website and includes reference material and hints about conducting online research. Free to qualified college adopters when packaged with the text.

New York Times Discount Subscription

A 10-week subscription for only $20! Contact your local Allyn & Bacon/Longman representative for more information.

Voices of Dissent: Critical Readings in American Politics, Fifth Edition

Edited by William F. Grover, St. Michael's College, and Joseph G. Peschek, Hamline University, this collection of critical essays goes beyond the debate between mainstream liberalism and conservatism to fundamentally challenge the status quo. Available at a discount when ordered packaged with the text.

Ten Things That Every American Government Student Should Read

We asked American government instructors across the country to vote for 10 things beyond the text that they believe every student should read and put them in this brief and useful reader edited by Karen O'Connor, American University. Free when ordered packaged with the text.

Choices: An American Government Database Reader   This customizable reader allows instructors to choose from a database of more than 300 readings to create a reader that exactly matches their course needs. Go to **www.pearsoncustom.com/database/choices.html** for more information.

Discount Subscription to *Newsweek* **Magazine**   Students receive 12 issues of *Newsweek* at more than 80 percent off the regular price. An excellent way for students to keep up with current events.

Penguin-Longman Value Bundles   Longman offers 25 Penguin Putnam titles at more than a 60 percent discount when packaged with any Longman text. A totally unique offer and a wonderful way to enhance students' understanding of concepts in American government. Please go to **www.ablongman.com/penguin** for more information.

Writing in Political Science, **Third Edition**   Written by Diane Schmidt, this guide takes students step-by-step through all aspects of writing in political science. Available at a discount when ordered packaged with any Longman textbook.

Getting Involved: A Guide to Student Citizenship   Written by Mark Kann, Todd Belt, Gabriela Cowperthwaite, and Steven Horn, this unique and practical handbook guides students through political participation with concrete advice and extensive sample material—letters, telephone scripts, student interviews, and real-life anecdotes—for getting involved and making a difference in their lives and communities.

Texas Politics Supplement, **Third Edition**   Written by Debra St. John, this is a 90-page primer on state and local government and issues in Texas. Free when shrink-wrapped with the text.

California Politics Supplement, **Third Edition**   Written by Barbara Stone, this is a 70-page primer on state and local government and issues in California. Free when shrink-wrapped with the text.

Florida Politics Supplement   Written by John Bertalan, this is a 50-page primer on state and local government and issues in Florida. Free when shrink-wrapped with the text.

Acknowledgments

Writing and producing an introductory textbook is an incredibly complex and cooperative enterprise in which many people besides the authors play roles. We would like to take the opportunity to thank them, one and all. We start with the many wonderful people at Longman who worked on this edition, including development editor Nancy Crochiere, production manager Donna DeBenedictis, Sue Nodine and her colleagues at Elm Street Publishing

Services for design and production work, photo researcher Sherri Zuckerman, and senior marketing manager Elizabeth Fogarty. Special thanks go to Eric Stano who has always believed in this book project and in us, and whose guidance helped make the sixth edition the most successful one yet. We hope that his wise counsel on revisions for the seventh edition will have a similar result.

We would also like to thank our students for helping to shape this book. The undergraduates in our introductory courses in American government and politics at the University of Colorado, Boulder, and Northwestern University had much to say about what they liked and didn't like in the book, and they were more than willing to tell us how it might be improved. Our many graduate student TAs in these introductory courses, moreover, were extremely helpful in advising us about how the sixth edition was working or not working as a teaching tool in the classroom.

Over the years, Longman enlisted the help of many political scientists on various aspects of this project. Their advice was especially valuable, and the final version of the book is far better than it would have been without their help. We would like to extend our appreciation to the following political scientists, who gave so generously of their time and expertise through the editions of *The Struggle for Democracy* and its supplements:

Gordon Alexandre, *Glendale Community College*

John Ambacher, *Framingham State College*

Sheldon Appleton, *Oakland University*

Jeffrey M. Ayres, *Lake Superior State University*

Ross K. Baker, *Rutgers University*

Manley Elliott Banks II, *Virginia Commonwealth University*

Ryan Barrilleaux, *University of Miami*

Ken Baxter, *San Joaquin Delta College*

Stephen Bennett, *University of Cincinnati*

Bill Bianco, *Duke University*

Melanie J. Blumberg, *University of Akron*

Joseph P. Boyle, *Cypress College*

Richard Braunstein, *University of South Dakota*

Evelyn Brodkin, *University of Chicago*

James Bromeland, *Winona State University*

Barbara Brown, *Southern Illinois University–Carbondale*

Charles R. Brown, Jr., *Central Washington University*

Joseph S. Brown, *Baylor University*

Mark Byrnes, *Middle Tennessee State University*

David E. Camacho, *Northern Arizona University*

Mary Carns, *Stephen F. Austin University*

Jim Carter, *Sam Houston State University*

Gregory Casey, *University of Missouri*

Carl D. Cavalli, *North Georgia College and State University*

James Chalmers, *Wayne State University*

Paul Chardoul, *Grand Rapids Community College*

Mark A. Cichock, *University of Texas at Arlington*

Alan J. Cigler, *University of Kansas*

David Cingranelli, *State University of New York at Binghamton*

Natale H. Cipollina, *CUNY Baruch College*

Dewey M. Clayton, *University of Louisville*

John Coleman, *University of Wisconsin*

Ken Collier, *University of Kansas*

Lee Collins, *Monmouth College*

Edward Collins Jr., *University of Maine*

Richard W. Crockett, *Western Illinois University*

Lane Crothers, *Illinois State University*

Landon Curry, *University of Texas*

Paul B. Davis, *Truckee Meadows Community College*

Christine Day, *University of New Orleans*

Alan Draper, *St. Lawrence University*

Euel Elliott, *University of Texas*

Bob England, *Oklahoma State University*

Robert S. Erikson, *University of Houston*

Thomas Ferguson, *University of Massachusetts, Boston*

M. Lauren Ficaro, *Chapman University*

Brian J. Fogarty, *University of North Carolina, Chapel Hill*

John Geer, *Arizona State University*

Scott D. Gerber, *College of William and Mary*

Thomas Gillespie, *Seton Hall University*

Gregory Goldey, *Morehead State University*

Doris A. Graber, *University of Illinois*

John Green, *University of Akron*

Daniel P. Gregory, *El Camino Community College*

Eric E. Grier, *Georgia State University*

Mark F. Griffith, *The University of West Alabama*

Bruce E. Gronbeck, *University of Iowa*

Maria Guido, *Bentley College*

Robert Gumbrecht, *Merritt College*

Russell L. Hanson, *Indiana University*

Kevin R. Hardwick, *Canisius College*

Valerie Heitshusen, *University of Missouri*

Peter B. Heller, *Manhattan College*

Richard Herrara, *Arizona State University*

Roberta Herzberg, *Indiana University*

Seth Hirshorn, *University of Michigan*

Eugene Hogan, *Western Washington University*

John W. Homan, *Boise State University*

Marilyn Howard, *Columbus State Community College*

Ronald J. Hrebnar, *University of Utah*

David Hunt, *Triton College*

Jon Hurwitz, *University of Pittsburgh*

James Hutter, *Iowa State University*

Gary C. Jacobson, *University of California at San Diego*

William Jacoby, *University of South Carolina*

Willoughby Jarrell, *Kennesaw State College*

Jodi Jenkin, *Fullerton College*

Christopher B. Jones, *Eastern Oregon State University*

Mark R. Joslyn, *University of Kansas*

William Kelly, *Auburn University*

Fred Kramer, *University of Massachusetts*

Richard Lehne, *Rutgers University*

Jan E. Leighley, *Texas A&M University*

Joel Lieske, *Cleveland State University*

R. Philip Loy, *Taylor University*

Stan Luger, *University of Northern Colorado*

Dean E. Mann, *University of California*

Joseph R. Marbach, *Seton Hall University*

Michael D. Martinez, *University of Florida*

Peter Mathews, *Cypress College*

Louise Mayo, *County College of Morris*

Steve Mazurana, *University of Northern Colorado*

Michael W. McCann, *University of Washington*

Carroll R. McKibbin, *California Polytechnic State University*

William P. McLauchlan, *Purdue University*

Michael E. Meagher, *University of Missouri*

Stanley Melnick, *Valencia Community College*

Charles K. Menifield, *Murray State University*

Norma H. E. Miller, *South Carolina State University*

Neil Milner, *University of Hawaii*

Paul Moke, *Wilmington College*

Kristen R. Monroe, *Princeton University*

Mike Munger, *University of Texas*

Laurel A. Myer, *Sinclair Community College*

Albert Nelson, *University of Wisconsin, La Crosse*

David Nice, *Washington State University*

Charles Noble, *California State University at Long Beach*

Maureen Rand Oakley, *Mount St. Mary's College*

Colleen M. O'Connor, *San Diego Mesa College*

Daniel J. O'Connor, *California State University at Long Beach*

David J. Olson, *University of Washington*

Laura Katz Olson, *Lehigh University*

John Orman, *Fairfield University*

Marvin Overby, *University of Mississippi*

Elizabeth M. H. Paddock, *Drury College*

Kenneth T. Palmer, *University of Maine*

Toby Paone, *St. Charles Community College*

David Paul, *The Ohio State University–Newark*

Arthur Paulson, *Southern Connecticut State University*

Joseph Peschek, *Hamline University*

Mark P. Petracca, *University of California*

Larry Pool, *Mountain View College*

Amy Pritchett, *Cypress College*

John D. Redifer, *Mesa State College*

Richard Reitano, *Dutchess Community College*

Curtis G. Reithel, *University of Wisconsin, La Crosse*

Russell D. Renka, *Southeast Missouri State University*

Richard C. Rich, *Virginia Polytechnic Institute and State University*

Leroy N. Rieselbach, *Indiana University*

Sue Tolleson Rinehart, *Texas Tech University*

Phyllis F. Rippey, *Western Illinois University*

David Robinson, *University of Houston–Downtown*

David W. Romero, *University of California*

Francis E. Rourke, *Johns Hopkins University*

David C. Saffell, *Ohio Northern University*

Donald L. Scruggs, *Stephens College*

Jim Seroka, *University of North Florida*

L. Earl Shaw, *Northern Arizona University*

John M. Shebb, *University of Tennessee*

Mark Silverstein, *Boston University*

Morton Sipress, *University of Wisconsin, Eau Claire*

Henry B. Sirgo, *McNeese State University*

David A. Smeltzer, *Portland State University*

Neil Snortland, *University of Arkansas, Little Rock*

David Tabb, *San Francisco State University*

C. Neal Tate, *University of North Texas*

James Lance Taylor, *University of San Francisco*

Robert Thomas, *University of Houston*

Richard J. Timpone, *State University of New York at Stony Brook*

Eric Ulsaner, *University of Maryland*

José M. Vadi, *California State Polytechnic University, Pomona*

Elliot Vittes, *University of Central Florida*

Charles Walcott, *University of Minnesota*

Benjamin Walter, *Vanderbilt University*

Susan Weissman, *St. Mary's College of California*

Jonathan P. West, *University of Miami*

Nelson Wikstrom, *Virginia Commonwealth University*

Leonard A. Williams, *Manchester College*

Daniel Wirls, *Merrill College*

Eugene R. Wittkopf, *Louisiana State University*

James Woods, *University of Toledo*

Teresa Wright, *California State University–Long Beach*

Jay Zarowitz, *Muskegon Community College*

Michele Zebich-Knos, *Kennesaw State University*

Finally, we thank you, the instructors and students who use this book. May it bring you success.

EDWARD S. GREENBERG
BENJAMIN I. PAGE

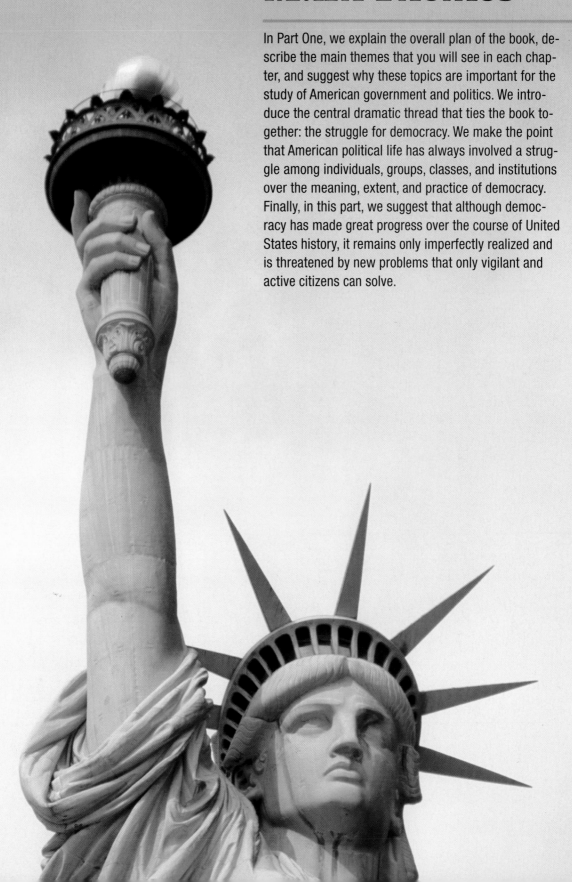

Part One

Introduction: Main Themes

In Part One, we explain the overall plan of the book, describe the main themes that you will see in each chapter, and suggest why these topics are important for the study of American government and politics. We introduce the central dramatic thread that ties the book together: the struggle for democracy. We make the point that American political life has always involved a struggle among individuals, groups, classes, and institutions over the meaning, extent, and practice of democracy. Finally, in this part, we suggest that although democracy has made great progress over the course of United States history, it remains only imperfectly realized and is threatened by new problems that only vigilant and active citizens can solve.

Chapter 1
Democracy and American Politics

In This Chapter

- An introduction to how government and politics work

- What democracy means, and how it can be used as a standard to evaluate American government and politics

Robert Moses and the Struggle for African American Voting Rights

The right to vote in elections is fundamental to democracy. But many Americans won the right to vote only after long struggles. It took more than 30 years from the adoption of the Constitution, for instance, for most states to allow people without property to vote. Women gained the right to vote in all U.S. elections only in 1920, and young people ages 18 to 20 did so only beginning in 1971. As the following story indicates, African Americans in the South were not able to vote in any numbers until after 1965 despite the existence of the Fifteenth Amendment—which says that the vote cannot be denied to American citizens on the basis of race, color, or previous condition of servitude—adopted in 1870.

In Mississippi in the early 1960s, only 5 percent of African Americans were registered to vote, and none held elective office, although they accounted for 43 percent of the population. In Amite County, Mississippi, only one African American was registered to vote out of approximately 5,000 eligible voters; in Walthall County, not a single black was registered, although roughly 3,000 were eligible to vote.[1] What kept them away from the polls was a combination of biased voting registration rules, economic pressures, and physical intimidation and violence directed against those brave enough to defy the prevailing political and social order. In Ruleville, Mississippi, Mrs. Fannie Lou Hamer was forced out of the house she was renting on a large plantation; fired from her job; and arrested, jailed, and beaten by police after she tried to register to vote.[2]

The Student Non-Violent Coordinating Committee (widely known by its initials, SNCC) launched its Voter Education Project in 1961 with the aim of ending black political isolation and powerlessness in the Deep South. Composed primarily of African American college students from both the North and the South, SNCC aimed to increase black voter registration and to challenge exclusionary rules like the poll tax and the literacy test. SNCC also wanted to enter African American candidates in local elections. Its first step was to create "freedom schools" in some of the most segregated counties in Mississippi, Alabama, and Georgia to teach black citizens about their rights under the law and to encourage them to register to vote. Needless to say, SNCC volunteers tended to attract the malevolent attentions of police, local officials, and vigilantes.

The first of the freedom schools was founded in McComb, Mississippi, by a remarkable young man named Robert Parris Moses who quit his job as a teacher in order to work with other young people in SNCC. Despite repeated threats to his life and more than a few physical attacks, Moses traveled the back roads of Amite and Walthall counties, meeting with small groups of black farmers and encouraging them to attend the SNCC freedom school. At the school, he showed them not only how to fill out the registration forms but also how to read and interpret

the constitution of Mississippi for the "literacy test" required to register to vote. Once people in the school gathered the courage to journey to the county seat to try to register, Moses went along with them to lend support and encouragement.

Moses suffered for these activities. Over a period of a few months, he was arrested several times for purported traffic violations; attacked on the main street of Liberty, Mississippi, by the county sheriff's cousin and beaten with the butt end of a knife; assaulted by a mob behind the McComb County courthouse; hit by police and dragged into the station house while standing in line at the voting registrar's office with one of his students; and jailed for not paying fines connected with his participation in civil rights demonstrations.

Despite the efforts of Bob Moses and other SNCC volunteers and the bravery of African Americans who dared to defy the rules of black political exclusion in Mississippi, African American voting registration barely increased in that state in the early 1960s. Black Americans in Mississippi would have to await the passage of the 1965 Voting Rights Act, which provided powerful federal government protections for all American

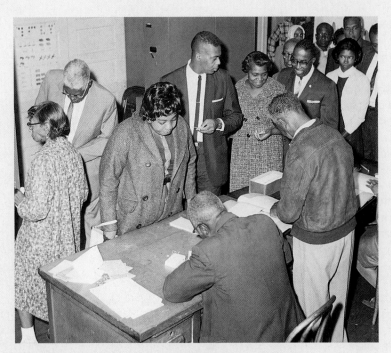

Discriminatory registration restrictions and intimidation heavily curbed African American voting in the Deep South for almost a century after the end of slavery. It was not until the passage of the 1965 Voting Rights Act that literacy tests, poll taxes, and other devices designed to keep blacks away from the polls were outlawed and African Americans were able to turn out at the polls in record numbers.

civil rights
Guarantees by government of equal citizenship to all social groups.

citizens wishing to exercise their right to vote. The Voter Education Project, however, was one of the key building blocks of a powerful civil rights movement (see Chapter 8) that would eventually force federal action in the 1960s to support the citizenship rights (or **civil rights** of African Americans in the South.

Robert Moses and many other African Americans in Mississippi were willing to risk all they had, even their lives, to gain full and equal citizenship in the United States. Likewise, throughout our history, Americans from all walks of life have joined the struggle to make the United States a more democratic country. The same thing is happening in many parts of

the world today. We live in an age of democratic aspiration and upsurge; people the world over are demanding the right to govern themselves and control their own destinies. Americans are participants in this drama, not only because American political ideas and institutions have often provided inspiration for democratic movements in other countries but also because the struggle for democracy continues in our own society. Although honored and celebrated, democracy remains an unfinished project in the United States. The continuing struggle to expand and perfect democracy is a major feature of American history and a defining characteristic of our politics today. It is a central theme of this book.

Democracy

Why should there not be a patient confidence in the ultimate justice of the people? Is there any better, or equal, hope in the world?

—ABRAHAM LINCOLN, FIRST INAUGURAL ADDRESS

When people live together in groups and communities, it is generally understood that a governmental entity of some sort is needed to provide law and order; to protect against external aggressors; and to provide essential public goods such as roads, waste disposal, and clean water. If government is both necessary and inevitable, certain questions become unavoidable: Who is to govern? How are those who govern to be encouraged to serve the best interests of society? How can governments be induced to make policies and laws that citizens consider legitimate and worth obeying? In short, what is the best form of government? For most Americans—and for increasing numbers of people in other places—the answer is clear: democracy.

The intrinsic attractiveness of democracy's central ideas—that ordinary people want to rule themselves and are capable of doing so—is only one reason democracy is so popular. For many political thinkers, democracy is simply superior to every other form of political organization. Some have argued, for example, that democracy is the form of government that best protects human rights because it is the only one based on a recognition of the intrinsic worth and equality of human beings. Others believe that democracy is the form of government most likely to reach rational decisions because it can count on the pooled knowledge and expertise of a society's entire population. Other thinkers have claimed that democracies are more stable and long-lasting because their leaders, elected by their citizens, enjoy a strong sense of legitimacy. Still others suggest that democracy is the form of government most conducive to economic growth and material well-being, a claim that is strongly supported by research findings. Others, finally, believe that democracy is the form of government under which human beings, because they are free, are best able to develop their natural capacities and talents.[3] There are many compelling reasons, then, why democracy has been preferred by so many people.

Americans prefer democracy to other forms of government, and they have helped make the nation more democratic over the course of our history. Nevertheless, democracy remains a work in progress in the United States, an evolving aspiration rather than a finished product. Our goal in this book is to help you think carefully about the quality and progress of democracy in the United States. We want to help you reach your own independent judgments about the degree to which politics and government in the United States make our country more or less democratic. We want to help you draw your own conclusions about which political practices and institutions in the United States encourage and sustain democracy and which ones discourage and undermine it. To do this, we must be clear about the meaning of democracy.

The Democratic Idea

Many of our ideas about democracy originated with the ancient Greeks. The Greek roots of the word *democracy* are *demos,* meaning "the people," and

Web Exploration
The Diffusion of Democracy

Issue: Around the world, over the course of the twentieth century, democracy has both advanced and receded in a series of waves.

Site: Go to the Historical Atlas of the Twentieth Century on our Website at **www.ablongman.com/greenberg.** In the "Web Explorations" section for Chapter 1, open the "diffusion of democracy" link, then click on "Historical Atlas." Under "General Trends," select Government, then look at each decade of the twentieth century.

What You've Learned: What conclusions can you make about the spread of democracy over the course of the century? When and where were the greatest gains made? What factors do you think explain the patterns you have discovered?

HINT: World wars, the rise and fall of fascism and communism, and the spread of mass communications have all played important roles.

democracy

A system of rule by the people, defined by the existence of popular sovereignty, political equality, and political liberty.

tyranny

The abuse of power by a ruler or a government.

Comparing Political Landscapes

direct democracy

A form of political decision making in which the public business is decided by all citizens meeting in small assemblies.

representative democracy

Indirect democracy, in which the people rule through elected representatives.

kratein, meaning "to rule." **Democracy,** then, is "rule by the people" or, to put it another way, self-government by the *many,* as opposed to the *few* or the *one.*

Most Western philosophers and rulers before the eighteenth century were not friendly to the idea of rule by the *many.* Most believed that governing was a difficult art, requiring the greatest sophistication, intelligence, character, and training—certainly not the province of ordinary people. Most preferred rule by a select *few* (such as an aristocracy, in which a hereditary nobility rules) or by an enlightened *one* (such as a king or a military chieftain). In practice, most governments were quite undemocratic. The idea that ordinary people might rule themselves represents an important departure from such beliefs.[4]

Also crucial to the concept of democracy is the idea that it is the purpose of a government to serve *all* of its people and that ultimately none but the people themselves can be relied on to know and hence to act in accordance with their own values and interests. Power in any other hands will eventually lead to **tyranny,** a society where leaders abuse their power.

Interestingly, democracy in the sense described here is more a utopian idea than a description of real societies. Athens of the fifth century is usually cited as the purest form of democracy that ever existed. There, all public policies were decided upon in periodic assemblies of Athenian citizens—but many people, including women, slaves, and immigrants, were still excluded from such assemblies. Nevertheless, the existence of a society in Athens where "a substantial number of free, adult males were entitled as citizens to participate freely in government"[5] proved to be a powerful example of what was possible for those who believed that rule by ordinary people was the best form of government.

A handful of other cases of popular rule kept the democratic idea alive across the centuries. In pre-imperial Rome, for example, all male citizens elected the consuls, the chief magistrates of the powerful city-state. Also, in the Middle Ages in Europe, many cities were governed directly by the people (at least by men who owned property) rather than by nobles, church, or crown. Further, the Russian village, largely self-governing from the early Middle Ages to modern times, inspired democratic reformers in that autocratic society ruled by all-powerful czars. The short-lived but self-governing utopian communities founded by Robert Owen and Charles Fourier in the United States and France in the early nineteenth century also helped spread the democratic idea. And finally, the New England town meeting, where local people rule their communities directly, has inspired many democrats, as has the success of the Israeli Kibbutz.

Direct Versus Representative Democracy

To the ancient Greeks, democracy meant rule by the common people exercised *directly* in open assemblies. They believed that democracy implied face-to-face deliberation and decision making about the public business. **Direct democracy** requires, however, that all citizens be able to meet together regularly to debate and decide the issues of the day. Such a thing was possible in fifth-century B.C. Athens, which was small enough to allow all male citizens to gather in one place. In Athens, moreover, male citizens had time to meet and to deliberate because women provided household labor and slaves accounted for most production.

Because direct, participatory democracy is possible only in small communities where citizens with abundant leisure time can meet often on a face-to-face basis, it is an unworkable arrangement for a large and widely dispersed society such as the United States.[6] Democracy in large societies must take the representative form, since millions of citizens cannot meet in open assembly. By **representative democracy** we mean a system in which the people select others, called *representatives,* to act in their place.

The essence of the classical Greek idea of democracy was face-to-face deliberations among citizens in open assemblies. This is difficult to achieve in societies with large populations where democracy depends instead on the election of representatives.

Although representative (or indirect) democracy seems to be the only form of democracy possible in large-scale societies, some political commentators argue that the participatory aspects of direct democracy are worth preserving as an ideal and that certain domains of everyday life—workplaces and schools, for instance—could be enriched by more direct democratic practices.[7] It is worth pointing out, moreover, that direct democracy can and does flourish in some local communities today. In many New England towns, for example, citizens make decisions directly at town meetings. Some observers believe that the Internet will enable more people to become directly involved in political deliberations and decision making in the future.[8]

Democracy and the Internet

Fundamental Principles of Representative Democracy

In large societies such as our own, then, democracy means rule by the people, exercised indirectly through representatives elected by the people. Still, this definition is not sufficiently precise to use as a standard by which to evaluate the American political system. To help further clarify the definition of democracy, we add three additional benchmarks drawn from both the scholarly literature and popular understandings about democracy. These benchmarks are *popular sovereignty, political equality,* and *political liberty.* A society in which all three flourish, we argue, is a healthy representative democracy. A society in which any of the three is absent or impaired falls short of the representative democratic ideal. Let us see what each of them means.

Popular Sovereignty   **Popular sovereignty** means that the ultimate source of all public authority is the people and that government does the people's bidding. If ultimate authority resides not in the hands of the *many* but in the hands of the *few* (as in an aristocratic order), or of the *one* (whether a benevolent sovereign or a ruthless dictator), democracy does not exist.

popular sovereignty
The basic principle of democracy that the people ultimately rule.

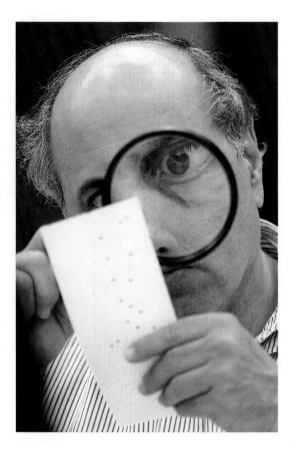

Most Americans believe that all ballots are counted, when, in fact, many go uncounted because of intentional or accidental mistakes by the voter or voting machine errors. Here an election official examines a ballot for "hanging chads" and "dimples" to try to determine voter intentions during the vote recount in Broward County, Florida, in 2000. The recount was eventually stopped by the U.S. Supreme Court, leaving George W. Bush the winner of Florida's electoral college votes and the presidency.

How can we recognize popular sovereignty when we see it? The following six conditions are especially important:

Government Policies Reflect the Wishes of the People

The most obvious sign of popular sovereignty is the existence of a close correspondence between what government does and what the people want it to do. It is hard to imagine a situation in which the people rule but government officials make policies contrary to the people's wishes.

This much seems obvious. However, does the democratic ideal require that government officials always do exactly what the people want, right away, responding to every whim and passing fancy of the public? This question has troubled many democratic theorists, and most have answered that democracy is best served when representatives and other public officials respond to what might be called the "deliberative will" of the people: what the people want after they have deliberated about an issue with others.[9] We might, then, want to speak of democracy as a system in which government policies conform to what the people want over some period of time.

Government Leaders Are Elected

The existence of a close match between what the people want and what government does, however, does not necessarily prove that the people are sovereign. In a dictatorship, for example, the will of the people can be consciously shaped to correspond to the wishes of the leadership. For the direction of influence to flow from the people to the leadership, some mechanism must exist for forcing leaders to be responsive to the people's wishes and to be responsible to them for their actions. The best mechanism ever invented to achieve these goals is the election in which

You Are the Director of Economic Development for the city of Baltimore, MD

both existing and aspiring government leaders must periodically face the people for judgment.

Elections Are Free and Fair If elections are to be useful as a way to keep government leaders responsive and responsible, they must be conducted in a fashion that is free and fair. By free, we mean that there is no coercion of voters or election officials and that virtually all citizens are able to run for office and vote in elections. By fair, we mean, among other things, that election rules do not favor some over others, and that ballots are accurately counted.

People Participate in the Political Process Although government leaders may be elected in a balloting process that is free and fair, such a process is useful in conveying the will of the people and keeping leaders responsive and responsible only if the people participate. If elections and other forms of political participation only attract a minority of the eligible population, they cannot serve as a way to understand what the broad public wants or as an instrument forcing leaders to pay attention to it. Widespread participation in politics—including voting in elections, contacting public officials, working with others to bring matters to public attention, joining associations that work to shape government actions, and more—is necessary to ensure not only that responsive representatives will be chosen, but that they will have continuous incentives to pay attention to the people. Because widespread participation is so central to popular sovereignty, we can say that the less political participation there is in a society, the weaker the democracy. (See "By the Numbers: Is voting turnout declining in the United States?" to get a sense of how much Americans participate.)

Timeline

The Initiative and Referendum

Democracy requires broad citizen participation in public affairs. Special efforts have been made in recent years—much like these at the University of Texas at Austin—to increase voting registration and turnout among young people, a group with especially low participation rates in American elections.

By the Numbers

Is voting turnout declining in the United States?

Commentators have been decrying the declining rate of voting in the United States for many years now. All sorts of explanations have been advanced to explain the decline; all sorts of remedies for the problem have been proposed. But what if there really hasn't been a decline in voting at all?

Why It Matters: We have argued in this chapter that widespread participation in voting and other civic activities is one measure of the health of democracy in any society. If the way we measure participation is inaccurate, we cannot do a good job of assessing the quality of democracy in the United States, or identify what problems and shortcomings in our political system need to be addressed to make it more democratic.

Behind the Traditional Voting Turnout Measure: Voter turnout in American elections is determined by a very simple calculation: the number of people who vote in a national election divided by the number of people in the United States who are of voting age, that is, 18 years of age and older. The denominator for this equation—voting age population, or VAP—is provided by the Census Bureau. But there is a problem: The denominator may be

misleading. The Census Bureau includes in its VAP numbers millions of people who are not eligible to vote at all: noncitizens, felons (some states), people with past felonies (some states), and the mentally incompetent. If we calculated voting turnout as the number of voters divided by the number of people in the United States who are eligible to vote—the voting eligible population, or VEP—turnout would always be higher than is now reported because the denominator would be smaller.

Calculating a VEP-based Measure of Turnout: Two political scientists, Michael McDonald and Samuel Popkin, have done us the great service of transforming the Census Bureau's VAP (voting age population) number to a VEP (voting eligible population) number for every national election from 1948 to 2000, pulling out noncitizens, ineligible felons, and former felons. Using the voting eligible population rather than the resident population over the age of 18 as the denominator in the voting turnout equation, McDonald and Popkin found the following:

- Voting turnout is actually 4 or 5 percentage points higher in recent elections than usually reported.
- Voting turnout declined between 1960 and 1972 regardless of which method was used. However,

High-Quality Information Is Available If people are to form authentic and rational attitudes about public policies and political leaders, they must have access to accurate political information, insightful interpretations, and vigorous debate. These are the responsibility of government officials, opposition parties, opinion leaders, and the mass media. If false or biased information is provided, if policies are not challenged and debated, or if misleading interpretations of the political world (or none at all) are offered, the people cannot form opinions in accordance with their values and interests, and popular sovereignty cannot be said to exist.

The Majority Rules How can the opinions and preferences of many individual citizens be combined into a single binding decision? Since unanimity is unlikely—so the insistence that new policies should require unanimous agreement for them to be adopted would simply enshrine the status quo—reaching a decision requires a decision rule. If the actions of government are to respond to all citizens, each citizen being counted equally, the only decision rule that makes sense is **majority rule,**[10] which means that the government adopts the

majority rule
The form of political decision making in which policies are decided on the basis of what a majority of the people want.

voting turnout appears to decline further after 1972 only when using the traditional VAP method; the VEP method shows no decline in voting turnout over the past 30 years.

The main reason that voting turnout has declined in recent elections using the traditional VAP method is that the number of people who are residents of the United States but who are not eligible to vote in American elections has increased at every election, mostly due to the number of noncitizens living here.

Criticism of the VEP-based Measure of Turnout: Some critics suggest that the old way of calculating voting turnout has useful purposes. The Constitution does not exclude noncitizens from voting, for example; nor does it exclude felons or former felons, so a measure that includes these people as part of the voting population might tell us more about how far we have come as a democracy.

What to Watch For: When you come across voter turnout numbers, pay attention to whether the figure has been calculated based on the voting age population or on the voting eligible population. The latter will always be higher than the former. It is important to be aware that both methods of calculating turnout make sense in their own way; each has a slightly different story to tell.

What Do You Think? Do you think we can and should try to increase the rate of voting turnout in the United States, which is low in comparison to

other democratic countries, regardless of which method of calculation we use? What do you think about making noncitizens—who pay taxes and are subject to U.S. laws—eligible to vote? How about former felons who have paid their debt to society?

Source: Michael P. McDonald and Samuel L. Popkin, "The Myth of the Vanishing Voter," *The American Political Science Review*, 95, no. 4 (December 2001), pp. 963–974.

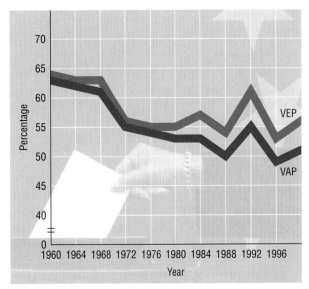

Voting Turnout in Presidential Elections, by Year

policy that the *most* people want. In practical terms, what this means is that the popular will, formed in the best circumstances after careful deliberation, is discovered by ascertaining the positions on public issues of the majority of citizens. The only alternative to majority rule is minority rule, which would unacceptably elevate the *few* over the *many*.

Political Equality The second fundamental principle of democracy is **political equality,** the idea that each person carries the same weight in voting and other political decision making. Imagine, if you will, a society in which one person could cast 100 votes in an election, another person 50 votes, and still another 25 votes, while many unlucky folks had only 1 vote each—or none at all. We would surely find such an arrangement a curious one, especially if that society described itself as democratic. We would react in this way because equality of citizenship has always been central to the democratic ideal. Democracy is a way of making decisions in which each person has one, and only one, voice.

Most people know this intuitively. Our sense of what is proper is offended, for instance, when some class of people is denied the right to vote in a society

political equality
The principle that says that each person carries equal weight in the conduct of the public business.

Although political equality is a cornerstone of American democracy, the nation's understanding of who is entitled to equal status has changed over the years. The right to vote was granted to all men regardless of race in 1870, although stringent registration rules made it very difficult for nonwhites to exercise that right. It wasn't until 1920 that the Nineteenth Amendment extended the right to vote to women; in 1971, a constitutional amendment lowered the voting age from 21 to 18.

that boasts the outer trappings of democracy. The denial of citizenship rights to African Americans in the South before the passage of the 1965 Voting Rights Act is such an example. We count it as a victory for democracy when previously excluded groups win the right to vote.

Political equality also involves what the Fourteenth Amendment to the Constitution calls "equal protection," meaning that everyone in a democracy is treated the same by government. Government programs, for example, should not favor one group over another or deny benefits or protections to identifiable groups in the population, such as racial and religious minorities. Nor should people be treated better or worse than others by law enforcement agencies and the courts.

Does democracy require that inequalities in the distribution of income and wealth not be too extreme? While many do not think this to be the case, thinkers as diverse as Aristotle, Rousseau, and Jefferson thought so, believing that great inequalities in economic circumstances are almost always translated into political inequality. Political scientist Robert Dahl describes the problem in the following way:

> *If citizens are unequal in economic resources, so are they likely to be unequal in political resources; and political equality will be impossible to achieve. In the extreme case, a minority of rich will possess so much greater political resources than other citizens that they will control the state, dominate the majority of citizens, and empty the democratic process of all content.*[11]

In later chapters, we will see that income and wealth are distributed in a highly unequal way in the United States and that this inequality is sometimes translated into great inequalities among people and groups in the political arena. In such circumstances, the norm of political equality is violated.

political liberty

The principle that citizens in a democracy are protected from government interference in the exercise of a range of basic freedoms, such as the freedoms of speech, association, and conscience.

Political Liberty   The third element of democracy is **political liberty.** Political liberty refers to basic freedoms essential to the formation and expression of majority opinion and its translation into public policies. These essential liberties include the freedoms of speech, of conscience and religion, of the press, and of assembly and association, embodied in the First Amendment to the U.S. Constitution.

Without these liberties (and a few more, including freedom from arbitrary arrest and imprisonment), the other fundamental principles of democracy could not exist. Popular sovereignty cannot be guaranteed if people are prevented from participating in politics or if opposition to the government is crushed by the authorities. Popular sovereignty cannot prevail if the voice of the people is silenced and if citizens are not free to argue and debate, based on their own ideas, values, and personal beliefs, and form and express their political opinions.[12] Political equality is violated if some people can speak out but others cannot.

For most people today, democracy and liberty are inseparable. The concept of *self-government* implies not only the right to vote and to run for public office but also the right to speak one's mind, to petition the government, and to join with others in political parties, interest groups, or social movements.

Over the years, a number of political philosophers and practitioners have viewed liberty as *threatened* by democracy rather than as essential to it. We will have more to say about this subject later as we consider several possible objections to democracy. But it is our position that self-government and political liberty are inseparable, in the sense that the former is impossible without the latter.[13] It follows that a majority cannot deprive an individual or a minority group of its political liberty without violating democracy itself.

Objections to Majoritarian Representative Democracy

Not everyone is convinced that majoritarian, representative democracy is the best form of government. Here are the main criticisms that have been leveled against democracy as we have defined it.

"Majority Tyranny" Threatens Liberty   James Madison and the other Founders of the American republic feared that majority rule was bound to undermine freedom and threaten the rights of the individual. They created a constitutional system (as you will see in Chapter 2) that was in fact designed to protect certain liberties against the unwelcome intrusions of the majority. The fears of the Founders were not without basis. What they called the "popular passions" have sometimes stifled the freedoms of groups and individuals who have dared to be different. Until quite recently, for instance, a majority of Americans were unwilling to allow atheists or communists the same rights of free speech that they allowed others, and conscientious objectors were treated harshly during both world wars. In the 1950s, many people in the movie industry, publishing, and education lost their jobs because of the anti-left hysteria whipped up by Senator Joseph McCarthy and others.[14]

Although there have been instances during our history of **majority tyranny,** in which the majority violated the citizenship rights of a minority—the chapter-opening story is a good example—there is no evidence that the *many* consistently threaten liberty more than the *few* or the *one*. To put it another way, the majority does not seem to be a special or unique threat to liberty. Violations of freedom seem as likely to come from powerful individuals and groups or from government officials as from the majority.

Liberty is essential to self-government, and threats to liberty, whatever their origin, must be guarded against by all who value democracy. But we must firmly reject the view that majority rule inevitably or uniquely threatens liberty. Majority rule is unthinkable, in fact, without the existence of basic political liberties.

majority tyranny
Suppression of the rights and liberties of a minority by the majority.

Political hysteria has periodically blemished the record of American democracy. Fear of domestic communism, and anarchism, captured in this editorial cartoon, was particularly potent in the twentieth century and led to the suppression of political groups deemed threatening by the authorities.

The People Are Irrational and Incompetent

Political scientists have spent decades studying the attitudes and behaviors of citizens in the United States, and some of the findings are not encouraging. For the most part, the evidence shows that individual Americans do not care a great deal about politics and are rather poorly informed, unstable in their views, and not much interested in participating in the political process.[15] These findings have led some observers to assert that citizens are ill-equipped for the responsibility of self-governance and that public opinion (the will of the majority) should not be the ultimate determinant of what government does.

We will see in Chapter 5, however, that this evidence about individuals has often been misinterpreted and that the American public taken collectively is more informed, sophisticated, and stable in its views than it is generally given credit for.

Majoritarian Democracy Threatens Minorities

We have suggested that when rendering a decision in a democracy, the majority must prevail. In most cases, the minority on the losing side of an issue need not worry unduly about its well-being because many of its members are likely to be on the winning side in future decisions about other matters. Thus, people on the minority and losing side of an issue such as welfare reform may be part of the majority and winning side on an issue such as educational spending. What prevents majority tyranny over a minority in most policy decisions in a democracy is that the composition of the majority and the minority is always shifting, depending on the issue.

However, what happens in cases that involve race, ethnicity, religion, or sexual orientation, for example, where minority status is fixed? Does the majority pose a threat to such minorities? Many people worry about that possibility. The worry is that unbridled majority rule leaves no room for the claims of minorities. This worry has some historical foundations, for majorities have trampled on minority rights with alarming frequency. Majorities long held, for instance, that Native Americans and African Americans were inferior to whites and undeserving of full citizenship. Irish, Eastern European, Asian, and Latin American immigrants to our shores, among others, have all been subjected to periods of intolerance on the part of the majority, as have Catholics and Jews. Gays and lesbians have been discriminated against in housing and jobs and have sometimes been violently victimized.

As Robert Dahl points out, however, there is no evidence to support the belief that the rights of minorities are better protected under alternative forms of political government, whether rule by the *few* or by the *one* (fascism, communism, authoritarian dictatorship, theocracy, and the like),[16] and that given the other benefits of majority rule democracy, it is to be preferred.

In any case, democracy, as we have defined it, requires the protection of crucial minority rights. Recall that majority rule is only one of the defining conditions of popular sovereignty and that popular sovereignty is only one of the three basic attributes of democracy, the others being political equality and political liberty. The position of minorities is protected in a fully developed democracy, in our view, by the requirements of equal citizenship (the right to vote, to hold public office, to be protected against violence, and to enjoy the equal protection of the law) and access to the full range of civil liberties (speech, press, conscience, and association). To the extent that a majority violates the citizenship rights and liberties of minorities, society falls short of the democratic ideal.

★ Democracy as an Evaluative Standard: How Democratic Are We?

After this discussion, it should be easy to see how and why the democratic ideal can be used as a measuring rod with which to evaluate American politics. We have learned that the fundamental attributes of democracy are popular sovereignty, political equality, and political liberty. Each suggests a set of questions that will be raised throughout this book to encourage critical thinking about American political life.

- *Questions about popular sovereignty.* Does government do what citizens want it to do? Do citizens participate in politics? Can citizens be involved when they choose to be, and are political leaders responsive? Do political linkage institutions, such as political parties, elections, interest groups, and social movements, effectively transmit what citizens want to political leaders? What is the quality of the public deliberation on the major public policy issues of the day? Do the media and political leaders provide accurate and complete information?

- *Questions about political equality.* Do some individuals and groups have persistent and substantial advantages over other individuals and groups in the political process? Or is the political game open to all equally? Do government decisions and policies benefit some individuals and groups more than others?

- *Questions about political liberty.* Are citizens' rights and liberties universally available, protected, and used? Are people free to vote? Can they speak openly and form groups freely to petition their government? Do public authorities, private groups, or the majority threaten liberty or the rights of minorities?

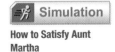

Simulation

How to Satisfy Aunt Martha

These questions will help us assess where we are and where we are going as a democracy. We do not believe that popular sovereignty, political equality, and political liberty are attainable in perfect form. They are, rather, ideals to which our nation can aspire and standards against which we can measure everyday reality.

A Framework for Understanding How American Politics Works

In addition to helping you answer questions about the quality of democracy in the United States, our goal in this textbook is to help you understand how American government and politics work. To help you do so, we describe in this section a simple way to organize information and to think about how our political system works.

Organizing the Main Factors of Political Life

If we are to understand why things happen in government and politics—for example, the passage of the 1965 Voting Rights Act that Robert Moses and his SNCC colleagues did so much to bring about—we must begin with what biologists call *taxonomy:* placing things in their proper categories. We believe that each and every actor, institution, and process that influences what our politics are like and what our national government does can be placed into four main categories: structure, political linkage, government, and government action.

- *Structure.* This category includes the economy and society, the constitutional rules, the political culture, and the international system: the most fundamental and enduring factors that influence government and politics. They form the foundation upon which all else is built. They determine, to a very large extent, what issues become a part of the political agenda, how political power is distributed among the population, what rules structure how government works, and what values Americans bring to their political deliberations.

- *Political linkage.* This category includes all of the political actors, institutions, and processes that transmit the wants and demands of people and groups in our society to government officials and that together help shape what government officials do and what policies they adopt. These include public opinion, political parties, interest groups, the news media, and elections.

- *Government.* This category includes all public officials and institutions (Congress, the president, the federal bureaucracy, and the Supreme Court) that have formal, legal responsibilities for making public policy.

- *Government action.* This category includes the wide range of actions carried out by government: making laws, issuing rules and regulations, waging war and providing national defense, settling civil disputes, providing order, and more.

This textbook is organized around these four categories. The chapters in Part Two focus on structural level factors. The chapters in Part Three are about political linkage processes and institutions. The chapters in Part Four attend to government institutions and leaders. Finally, the chapters in Part Five examine what government does.

Connecting the Main Factors of Political Life

To understand how government and politics work in the United States, we must appreciate the fact that the structural, political linkage, and governmental categories interact with one another in a particular kind of way to determine what actions government takes (see Figure 1.1). The best way to see this

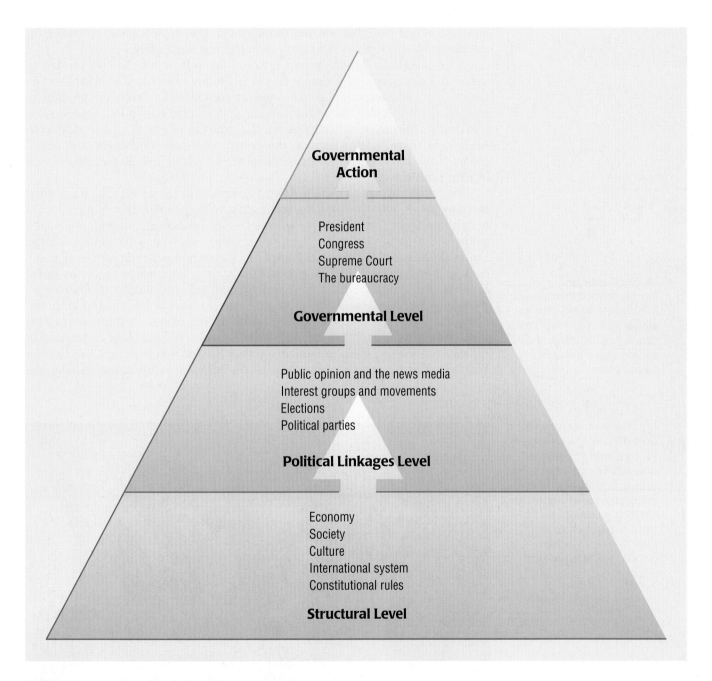

**Governmental
Action**

President
Congress
Supreme Court
The bureaucracy

Governmental Level

Public opinion and the news media
Interest groups and movements
Elections
Political parties

Political Linkages Level

Economy
Society
Culture
International system
Constitutional rules

Structural Level

FIGURE 1.1 • The Analytical Framework

Various actors, institutions, and processes interact to influence what government does in the United States. Structural factors such as the economy, the political culture, the international system, and constitutional rules play a strong role in political events. They may influence the government directly, or, as is more often the case, through political linkages such as elections, parties, and interest groups. In a democratic society, the policies created by the government should reflect these influences.

is to look at these categories in action, using the passage of the 1965 Voting Rights Act as an example. The main point of the exercise is to show how connecting and considering together the main factors of political life—structure, political linkage, and government—can help explain why government takes certain actions.

To understand passage of the landmark legislation, we might begin with *government,* focusing our attention on Congress and its members, President Lyndon Johnson (who was the most vigorous proponent of the voting rights legislation) and his advisers, and the Supreme Court, which was becoming increasingly supportive of civil rights claims in the mid-1960s.

Knowing these things, however, would not tell us all that we needed to know. To understand why Congress, the president, and the Court behaved as they did in 1965, we would want to pay attention to the pressures brought to bear on them by *political linkage* actors and institutions: public opinion (increasingly supportive of civil rights), the growing electoral power of African Americans in the states outside the South, and most important, the moral power of the civil rights movement inspired by people like Robert Moses and Martin Luther King.

Even knowing these things, however, would not tell us all that we needed to know about why the 1965 Voting Rights Act happened. Our inquiry would have to go deeper to include *structural* factors: economic, cultural, and social change; constitutional rules; and the international position of the United States. For example, economic changes in the nation over the course of many decades triggered a "great migration" of African Americans from the rural South to the urban North. Over the long run, this population shift to states with large blocks of **electoral college** votes, critical to the election of presidents, increased the political power of African Americans. Cultural change increased the number of Americans bothered by the second-class citizenship of African Americans, even as combat service in World War II and the Korean War led many black Americans to insist on full citizenship rights. Finally, the

electoral college

Representatives of the states who formally elect the president; the number of electors in each state is equal to the total number of its senators and congressional representatives.

African American combat service in World War II and in Korea helped transform white attitudes about racial equality in the United States and contributed to the emergence of a supportive environment for the civil rights movement. Shown here are six gunners from the 17th Bomb Wing night interdiction team that saw heavy action in Korea.

Cold War struggle of the United States against the Soviet Union played an important role. Many American leaders, recognizing the contradiction between asking for the support of people of color in Third World countries in the struggle against communism while treating African Americans in the United States as second-class citizens, sought an end to the system of official segregation in the South (known as **Jim Crow**).[17]

We see, then, that a full explanation of why the 1965 Voting Rights Act happened (government action) requires that we take into account how governmental, political linkage, and structural factors interact with one another to bring about significant change in American politics.

Understanding American Politics Holistically

This way of looking at things—that what government does can only be understood by considering structural, political linkage, and governmental factors—will be used throughout this book and will help bring order to the information presented. We will suggest throughout that action by public officials is the product not simply of their personal desires (although these are important) but also of the influences and pressures brought to bear by other governmental institutions and by individuals, groups, and classes at work in the political linkage sphere. Political linkage institutions and processes, in turn, can often be understood only when we see how they are shaped by the larger structural context, including such things as the national and global economies and the political culture. This way of understanding how American government and politics work is illustrated in the "Using the Framework" feature on the next page. This feature appears in each chapter.

You should also keep in mind that, as in all complex systems, feedback also occurs. That is to say, influences sometimes flow in the opposite direction, from government to political linkage actors and institutions to structural factors. For example, federal tax laws influence the distribution of income and wealth in society, government regulations affect the operations of corporations, and decisions by the courts may determine what interest groups and political parties are able to do. We will want to pay attention, then, to these sorts of influences in our effort to understand how the American political system works.

You need not worry about remembering exactly which actors and influences belong to which of the four categories. That will become obvious because the chapters of the book are organized into sections corresponding to them. Nor do you need to worry about exactly how the people and institutions in the different levels interact with one another. This will become clear as materials are presented and learned and as you become more familiar with the American political process.

Cold War
The period of tense relations between the United States and the Soviet Union from the late 1940s to the late 1980s.

Jim Crow
Popular term for the system of legally sanctioned racial segregation that existed in the American South until the middle of the twentieth century.

Using the Framework

Background: The Voting Rights Act of 1965 transformed the politics of the American South. Under federal government protection, the Act permitted African Americans to vote and run for elected office in states where a combination of violence, economic pressure, and state and local government rules made political participation difficult if not impossible prior to 1965. We can understand how such a momentous transformation happened by examining structural, political linkage, and governmental factors.

Governmental Action

The Voting Rights Act of 1965

Governmental Level

The Supreme Court prepared the ground by steadily expanding the reach of the "equal protection" clause of the Constitution's Fourteenth Amendment. ➡ A pro–civil rights majority in Congress was responsive to the voting rights issue. ➡ President Lyndon Johnson pushed hard for federal protection of African American voting rights.

Political Linkages Level

The votes of African Americans proved decisive in several large electoral vote states in the 1960 and 1964 presidential elections. ➡ Dramatic civil rights demonstrations highlighted the denial of the vote to black Americans in the Deep South. ➡ Public opinion and the mass media grew more supportive of demands by African Americans for full citizenship. ➡ Unions and business organizations endorsed voting rights legislation.

Structural Level

Industrialization and the rise of large manufacturing corporations spurred the "Great Migration." ➡ Relocation of African Americans to large states outside the Deep South improved their political, social, and economic standing. ➡ World War II generated pressures to integrate the armed forces. ➡ The struggle against the Soviet Union for the "hearts and minds" of Third World peoples made segregation problematic for the United States in world affairs.

Summary

The struggle for democracy has played an important role in American history and remains an important theme in our country today, as well as in many other parts of the world. The struggle has involved the effort to make popular sovereignty, political equality, and political liberty more widely available and practiced. Because democracy holds a very special place in Americans' constellation of values and is particularly relevant to judging political processes, it is the standard used throughout this text to evaluate the quality of our politics and government.

The materials about politics and government are organized in a way that will allow us to make sense of the confusing details of everyday events and see *why* things happen the way they do. The organizing framework presented in this chapter visualizes the world of American politics as a set of interrelated *actors* and *influences*—institutions, groups, and individuals—that operate in three interconnected realms: the *structural, political linkage,* and *governmental* sectors. This way of looking at American political life as an ordered, interconnected whole will be used throughout the remainder of the book.

Suggestions for Further Reading

Dahl, Robert A. *Democracy and Its Critics.* New Haven, CT: Yale University Press, 1989.
> *A sweeping defense of democracy against its critics by one of the most brilliant political theorists of our time.*

Dahl, Robert A. *On Democracy.* New Haven, CT: Yale University Press, 1998.
> *A brief yet surprisingly thorough examination of classical and contemporary democracy, real and theoretical.*

Held, David. *Models of Democracy.* Stanford, CA: Stanford University Press, 1987.
> *A highly accessible review of the many possible meanings of democracy.*

Putnam, Robert D. *Making Democracy Work: Civic Traditions in Modern Italy.* Princeton, NJ: Princeton University Press, 1993.
> *A brilliant and controversial argument that the success of democratic government depends on the vitality of a participatory and tolerant civic culture.*

Shapiro, Ian. *The State of Democratic Theory.* Princeton, NJ: Princeton University Press, 2003.
> *After an incisive examination of alternative understandings of democracy, Shapiro argues that democracy is a form of political society in which domination is minimized.*

Zakaria, Fareed. *The Future of Freedom: Illiberal Democracy at Home and Abroad.* New York: Norton, 2004.
> *The author suggests that majority rule democracy can only happen and be sustained in societies where individual freedom and the rule of law already exist, suggesting that democracy is unlikely to take hold in places such as Russia and Iraq.*

Internet Sources

A number of sites on the World Wide Web serve as "gateways" to vast collections of material on American government and politics. In subsequent chapters, we will indicate the location of sites on the Web to begin searches on the specific subject matter of the chapters. Here we concentrate on the general gateways, the starting points for wide-ranging journeys through cyberspace, geared to governmental and political subjects. Here are the gateways:

The Internet Public Library
http://www.ipl.org/div/subject/browse/law00.00.00/

New York Times, Political Points
www.nytimes.com/library/politics/polpoints.html

Political Resources on the Web
www.politicalresources.net

Weblinks: A Guide to Internet Resources in Political Science
www.abacon.com/internetguides/pol/weblinks.html

Yahoo/Government
http://www.yahoo.com/Government/

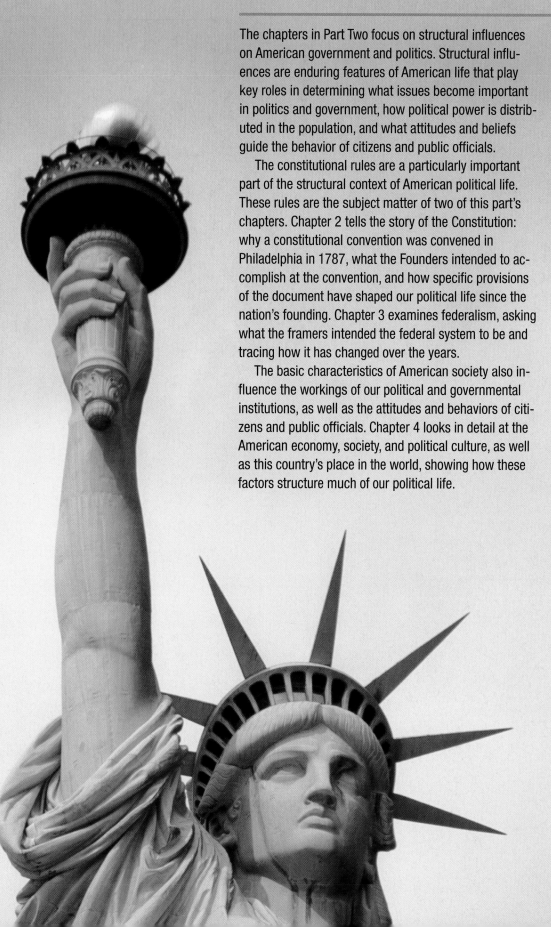

Part Two

Structure

The chapters in Part Two focus on structural influences on American government and politics. Structural influences are enduring features of American life that play key roles in determining what issues become important in politics and government, how political power is distributed in the population, and what attitudes and beliefs guide the behavior of citizens and public officials.

The constitutional rules are a particularly important part of the structural context of American political life. These rules are the subject matter of two of this part's chapters. Chapter 2 tells the story of the Constitution: why a constitutional convention was convened in Philadelphia in 1787, what the Founders intended to accomplish at the convention, and how specific provisions of the document have shaped our political life since the nation's founding. Chapter 3 examines federalism, asking what the framers intended the federal system to be and tracing how it has changed over the years.

The basic characteristics of American society also influence the workings of our political and governmental institutions, as well as the attitudes and behaviors of citizens and public officials. Chapter 4 looks in detail at the American economy, society, and political culture, as well as this country's place in the world, showing how these factors structure much of our political life.

Chapter 2
The Constitution

In This Chapter

- The enduring legacies of the American Revolution and the Declaration of Independence
- Our first constitution: The Articles of Confederation
- The Constitutional Convention
- What kind of constitution the framers created
- How the Constitution structures the rules of American politics

Shays's Rebellion

Artemas Ward, commander of American forces at Bunker Hill, a Revolutionary War hero, and a state judge, could not convince the crowd of several hundred armed farmers to allow him to enter the Worcester, Massachusetts, courthouse. For nearly two hours that day in September 1786, he pleaded and threatened, but to no avail. Unable to convince the local militia to come to his assistance, Ward left Worcester in a fury and carried word of the rebellion to Boston. Other judges trying to hold court in western Massachusetts in the summer and fall of 1786 had no better luck.[1]

The farmers of western Massachusetts were probably not a rebellious lot by nature, but desperate times pushed many of them to desperate actions. The end of the Revolutionary War in 1783 had brought the collapse of prices for agricultural products and widespread economic distress among farmers all over the new nation. Poor farmers sought relief from state governments, and for the most part, political leaders responded. Several states lent money (in the form of scrip, or paper money) to farmers to pay their taxes and debts. Other states passed stay laws, which postponed tax and mortgage payments for hard-pressed farmers.

In Massachusetts, however, the state legislature refused to help. Worse yet, the legislature and the governor had decided that all state debts must be paid in full to establish the creditworthiness of the state. The state's debt, accumulated to pay its share of the war costs, was owed primarily to a handful of the wealthiest Massachusetts citizens. To repay this debt, the legislature levied heavy taxes that fell disproportionately on farmers, especially those in the western part of the state. When the farmers could not pay their taxes—a distressingly common circumstance—the state collected its money through foreclosure: the public sale of farmers' lands, buildings, and livestock. Those who could not pay their debts, then, faced tax foreclosures and imprisonment under harsh conditions. Responding to these dire circumstances, many western Massachusetts farmers took up arms to close down the courts—the situation Artemas Ward faced in 1786.

By September 1786, Governor James Bowdoin had seen enough. He issued a proclamation against unlawful assembly and called out the militia to enforce it. Six hundred soldiers were sent to Springfield to ensure that the state supreme court could meet and issue the expected indictments against the leaders of the insurrection. The soldiers were met there by more than 500 armed farmers led by a former Revolutionary War officer, Captain Daniel Shays. After a long standoff, the militia withdrew, leaving the rebels in charge and the court unable to meet.

These events only hardened the governor's resolve to break the rebellion. He sent armed forces from Boston, which soon proved too much for the hastily organized and ill-equipped force under Shays. By the spring of 1787, the Boston militia

had defeated the rebels in two pitched battles, and Shays's Rebellion (as it was soon called) ended.

Although the insurrection was put down, most of the new nation's leading citizens were alarmed by the apparent inability of state governments to maintain public order under the Articles of Confederation. Shays's Rebellion realized the worst fears of national leaders about the dangers of ineffective state governments and popular democracy spinning out of control, unchecked by a strong national government. As George Washington said, "If government cannot check these disorders, what security has a man?"[2] It was in this climate of crisis that a call was issued for a constitutional convention to meet in Philadelphia to correct the flaws in our first Constitution. Rather than amend the Articles of Confederation, however, the men who met in Philadelphia in the summer of 1787 wrote an entirely new constitution.

Thinking Critically About This Chapter

This chapter is about the founding of the United States (see Figure 2.1) and the formulation of the constitutional rules that structure American politics to this day.

Using the Framework   You will see in this chapter how structural factors such as the American political culture, economic developments, and the composition of the Constitutional Convention shaped the substance of our Constitution. You will also see how the Constitution is itself an important structural factor that helps us understand how American government and politics work today.

Using the Democracy Standard   Using the conception of democracy you learned about in Chapter 1, you will be able to see how and why the framers were uneasy about democracy and created a republican form of government that, although based on popular consent, placed a number of roadblocks in the path of popular rule.

The Political Theory of the Revolutionary Era

Initially, the American Revolution (1775–1783) was waged more to preserve an existing way of life than to create something new. By and large, American colonists in the 1760s and 1770s were proud to be affiliated with Great Britain

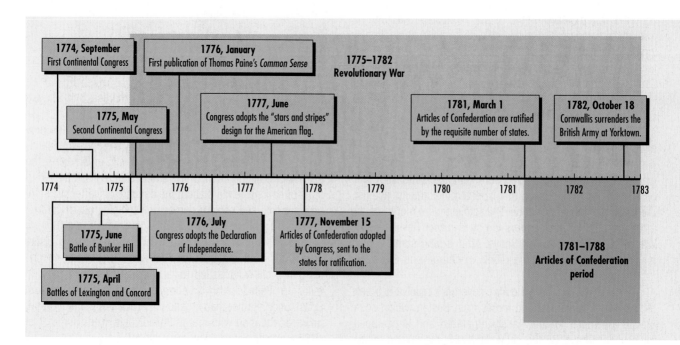

FIGURE 2.1 • **Time Line of the Founding of the United States, 1774–1791**

and satisfied with the general prosperity that came with participation in the British commercial empire.[3] When the revolution broke out, the colonists at first wanted only to preserve the English constitution and their own rights as British subjects. These traditional rights of life, liberty, and property seemed to be threatened by British policies on trade and taxation. Rather than allowing the American colonists to trade freely with whomever they pleased and to produce whatever goods they wanted, for instance, England was restricting the colonists' freedom to do either in order to protect its own manufacturers. To pay for the military protection of the colonies against raids by Native Americans and their French allies, England imposed taxes on a number of items, including sugar, tea, and stamps (required for legal documents, pamphlets, and newspapers). The imposition of these taxes without the consent of the colonists seemed an act of tyranny to many English subjects in America.

Although the initial aims of the Revolution were quite modest, the American Revolution, like most revolutions, did not stay on the track planned by its leaders. Although it was sparked by a concern for liberty—understood as the preservation of traditional rights against the intrusions of a distant government—it also stimulated the development of sentiments for popular sovereignty and political equality. As these sentiments grew, so did the likelihood that the American colonies would split from their British parent and form a system of government more to the liking of the colonists.

The Declaration of Independence

When the Second Continental Congress began its session on May 10, 1775—the First had met only briefly in 1774 to formulate a list of grievances to submit to the British Parliament—the delegates did not have independence in mind, even though armed conflict with Britain had already begun with the battles of Lexington and Concord. Pushed by the logic of armed conflict, an unyielding British government, and Thomas Paine's incendiary call for American independence in his wildly popular pamphlet *Common Sense,* however, the

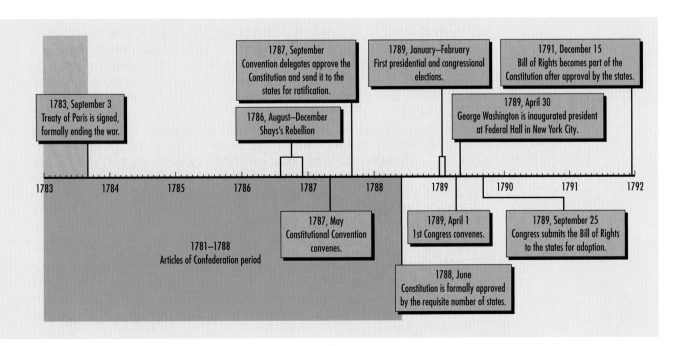

American leaders were reluctant at first to declare independence from Great Britain. One of the things that helped change their minds was Thomas Paine's wildly popular and incendiary pamphlet *Common Sense,* which mercilessly mocked the institution of monarchy.

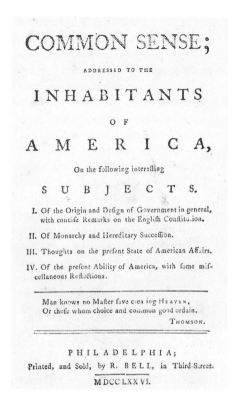

delegates concluded by the spring of 1776 that separation and independence were inescapable.[4] In early June, the Continental Congress appointed a special committee, composed of Thomas Jefferson, John Adams, and Benjamin Franklin, to draft a declaration of independence. The document, mostly Jefferson's handiwork, was adopted unanimously by the Second Continental Congress on July 4, 1776.

Key Ideas in the Declaration of Independence   The ideas in Jefferson's Declaration of Independence are so familiar to us that we may easily miss their revolutionary importance. In the late eighteenth century, most societies in the world were ruled by kings with authority purportedly derived from God, subject to little or no control by their subjects. Closely following John Locke's ideas in *The Second Treatise on Government,* Jefferson's argument that legitimate government can be established only by the people and can govern only with their consent seemed outrageous at the time. However, these ideas sparked a responsive chord in people everywhere when they were first presented, and they remain extremely popular all over the world today. Ideas articulated in the Declaration influenced the French Revolution of 1789, the 1991 "velvet revolution" in Czechoslovakia, and many revolutions in between. The argument as presented in the Declaration of Independence goes as follows:

- Human beings possess rights that cannot be legitimately given away or taken from them. *"We hold these truths to be self-evident, that all men are created equal, that they are endowed by their Creator with certain unalienable Rights, that among these are Life, Liberty, and the Pursuit of Happiness."*

- People create government to protect these rights. *"That to secure these rights, Governments are instituted among Men, deriving their just powers from the consent of the governed."*

- If government fails to protect people's rights or itself becomes a threat to them, people can withdraw their consent from that government and create a new one. *"That whenever any Form of Government becomes destructive of these ends, it is the Right of the People to alter or to abolish it, and to institute new Government, laying its foundation on such principles, and organizing its powers in such form, as to them shall seem most likely to effect their Safety and Happiness."*

Important Omissions in the Declaration The Declaration of Independence carefully avoided several controversial subjects, including what to do about slavery. Jefferson's initial draft denounced the Crown for violating human rights by "captivating and carrying Africans into slavery," but this was considered too controversial and was dropped from subsequent versions. The contradiction between the institution of slavery and the Declaration's sweeping claims for self-government, "unalienable" individual rights, and equality ("all men are created equal") was obvious to many observers at the time and is glaringly apparent to us today. The Declaration was also silent about the political status of women, Native Americans, and African Americans who were not slaves. Indeed, it is safe to assume that neither Jefferson, the main author of the Declaration, nor the other signers of the document had women, Native Americans, free blacks, or slaves in mind when they were fomenting revolution and calling for a different kind of political society. Interestingly, free blacks and women would go on to play important roles in waging the Revolutionary War against Britain.[5]

The Articles of Confederation: The First Constitution

The leaders of the American Revolution almost certainly did not envision the creation of a single, unified nation. At most, they had in mind a loose **confederation** among the states. This should not be surprising. Most Americans in the late eighteenth century believed that a government based on popular consent and committed to the protection of individual rights was possible only in small, homogeneous republics, where government was close to the people and where fundamental conflicts of interest among the people did not exist. Given the great geographic expanse of the colonies, as well as their varied ways of life and economic interests, the formation of a single unified republic seemed unworkable.

confederation
A loose association of states or territorial units formed for a common purpose.

Provisions of the Articles

Our first **constitution,** passed by the Second Continental Congress in the midst of the Revolutionary War in 1777 but not ratified by the requisite number of states until 1781, created a nation that was hardly a nation at all. The Articles of Confederation created in law what had existed in practice from the time of the Declaration of Independence: a loose confederation of independent states with little power in the central government, much like the United Nations today. Under the Articles, most important decisions were made in state legislatures.

The Articles provided for a central government of sorts, but it had few responsibilities and virtually no power. It could make war or peace, but it had no power to levy taxes (even customs duties) to pursue either goal. It could not regulate commerce among the states, nor could it deny the states the right to

constitution
The basic framework of law that prescribes how government is to operate.

collect customs duties. It had no independent chief executive to ensure that the laws passed by Congress would be enforced, nor had it a national court system to settle disputes between the states. There were no means to provide a sound national money system. The rule requiring that all national laws be approved by 9 of the 13 states made lawmaking almost impossible. And, defects in the new constitution were difficult to remedy because amending the Articles required the unanimous approval of the states.

Shortcomings of the Articles

The Articles of Confederation did what most of its authors intended: to preserve the power, independence, and sovereignty of the states and ensure that the central government would not encroach on the liberty of the people. Unfortunately, there were also many problems that the confederation was ill-equipped to handle.

Most important, the new central government could not finance its activities. The government was forced to rely on each state's willingness to pay its annual tax assessment. Few states were eager to cooperate. As a result, the bonds and notes of the confederate government became almost worthless, and the government's attempts to borrow were stymied.

The central government was also unable to defend American interests in foreign affairs. Without a chief executive or a standing army, and with the states holding a veto power over actions of the central government, the confederation lacked the capacity to reach binding agreements with other nations or to deal with a wide range of foreign policy problems. These included the continuing presence of British troops in western lands ceded to the new nation by Britain at the end of the Revolutionary War, violent clashes with Native Americans on the western frontier, and piracy on the high seas.

The government was also unable to prevent the outbreak of commercial warfare between the states. As virtually independent nations with the power to levy customs duties, many states became intense commercial rivals of their neighbors and sought to gain every possible advantage against the products of other states. New York and New Jersey, for instance, imposed high tariffs on goods that crossed their borders from other states.

Factors Leading to the Constitutional Convention

Historians now generally agree that the failings of the Articles of Confederation led most of the leading citizens of the confederation to believe that a new constitution was desperately needed for the fledgling nation. What is left out of many accounts of the convening of the Constitutional Convention in Philadelphia, however, is the story of the growing concern among many of the most influential men in the confederation that the passions for democracy and equality among the common people set loose by the American Revolution were getting out of hand. During the American Revolution, appeals to the people for the defense of freedom and for the spread of the blessings of liberty were often translated by the people to mean their right to better access to the means of government and to the means of livelihood.[6] The common people were convinced that success would bring substantial improvements in their lives.[7]

The Republican Beliefs of the Founders

This fever for popular participation and greater equality is not what most of the leaders of the American Revolution had in mind.[8] The Founders were believers in a theory of government known as **republicanism.** Like all republicans of the eighteenth century, the framers were seeking a form of government that would not only be based on the consent of the governed but that would also make tyranny—the abuse of the inalienable rights of citizens by government—unlikely or impossible, whether the threat of tyranny came from the misrule of a single person (a king or military dictator, let us say), a small group of elites (an aristocracy, a clerical theocracy, or moneyed merchant class), or even the majority of the population. Their solution was threefold: to elect government leaders, to limit the power of government, and to place roadblocks in the path of the majority. The election of representatives, in their view, would keep potentially tyrannical kings and aristocratic factions from power while ensuring popular consent. Limiting the power of government, both by stating what government could and could not do in a written constitution and by fragmenting governmental power, would prevent tyranny no matter who eventually won control, including the majority. Limiting the influence of the majority was accomplished by making only one part of one branch of government subject to direct election of the people—the House of Representatives—leaving the other offices to indirect election (the Senate and the president) or appointment (the Supreme Court).

Although eighteenth-century republicans believed in representative government—a government whose political leaders are elected by the people—they were not sympathetic to what we might today call popular democracy. For the most part, they thought that public affairs ought to be left to men from the "better" parts of society; the conduct of the public business was, in their view, the province of individuals with wisdom and experience, capacities associated mainly with people of social standing, substantial financial resources, and high levels of education. Nor did eighteenth-century republicans believe that

republicanism, eighteenth century
A political doctrine advocating limited government based on popular consent, protected against majority tyranny.

The republican ideas of the framers were greatly influenced by the writings of Cicero and Cato on the Roman republic. They especially admired the Roman republic's commitment to the idea that the actions of rulers must be bound by laws created by an assembly. Here members of the Roman senate debate an important public policy issue.

TABLE 2.1 ● Comparing Eighteenth-Century Republicanism and the Democratic Idea	
18th-Century Republicanism	**The Democratic Ideal**
Government is based on popular consent.	Government is based on popular consent.
Rule by the people is indirect, through representatives.	Rule by the people may be direct or indirect.
The term *people* is narrowly defined (by education, property holding, and social standing).	The term *people* is broadly defined.
Office holding confined to a narrow and privileged stratum of the population.	Broad eligibility for office-holding.
Elected representatives act as "trustees" (act on their own to discover the public good).	Elected representatives act as "delegates" (act as instructed by the people; accurately reflect their wishes).
Barriers to majority rule exist.	Majority rule prevails.
Government is strictly limited in function.	Government does what the people want it to do.
Government safeguards rights and liberties, with a special emphasis on property rights.	Government safeguards rights and liberties, with no special emphasis on property rights.

elected representatives should be too responsive to public opinion. Once in office, representatives were to exercise independent judgment about how best to serve the public interest, taking into account the needs and interests of society rather than the moods and opinions of the people.

Eighteenth-century republicans, then, did not believe that the people could or should rule directly. While they favored a system that allowed the common people to play a larger role in public life than existed in other political systems of the day, the role of the people was to be a far more limited one than we find acceptable today. They worried that too much participation by the people could only have a bad outcome. As James Madison put it in *The Federalist Papers,* "[Democracies] have ever been spectacles of turbulence and contention; have ever been found incompatible with personal security or the rights of property; and have in general been as short in their lives as they have been violent in their deaths."[9] (See Table 2.1 on the differences between democracy and eighteenth-century republicanism.)

Why the Founders Were Worried

An Excess of Democracy in the States Worries that untamed democracy was on the rise were not unfounded.[10] In the mid-1780s, popular assemblies (called conventions) were created in several states to keep tabs on state legislatures and to issue instructions to legislatures concerning what bills to pass. Both conventions and instructions struck directly at the heart of the republican conception of the legislature as a deliberative body shielded from popular opinion.[11]

The constitution of the state of Pennsylvania was also an affront to republican principles. Benjamin Rush, a signatory to the Declaration of Independence, described it as "too much upon the democratic order."[12] This constitution replaced the property qualification to vote with a very small tax (thus allowing many more people to vote), created a unicameral (single-house) legislative body whose members were to be elected in annual elections, mandated that legislative deliberations be open to the public, and required that proposed legislation be widely publicized and voted on only after a general election had been held (making the canvassing of public opinion easier).

To many advocates of popular democracy, including Tom Paine, the Pennsylvania constitution was the most perfect instrument of popular sovereignty. To others, like James Madison, the Pennsylvania case was a perfect example of popular tyranny exercised through the legislative branch of government.[13]

The Threat to Property Rights in the States   One of the freedoms that republicans wanted to protect against the intrusions of a tyrannical government was the right of the people to acquire and enjoy private property. Developments toward the end of the 1770s and the beginning of the 1780s seemed to put this freedom in jeopardy. For one thing, the popular culture was growing increasingly hostile to privilege of any kind, whether of social standing, education, or wealth. Writers derided aristocratic airs; expressed their preference for unlettered, plain-speaking leaders; and pointed out how wealth undermined equal rights.[14] Legislatures were increasingly inclined, moreover, to pass laws protecting debtors. For example, Rhode Island and North Carolina issued cheap paper money, which note holders were forced to accept in payment of debts. Other states enacted **stay acts,** which forbade farm foreclosures for nonpayment of debts. Popular opinion, while strongly in favor of property rights (most of the debtors in question were owners of small farms), also sympathized with farmers, who were hard-pressed to pay their debts with increasingly tight money, and believed—with some reason—that many creditors had accumulated notes speculatively or unfairly and were not entitled to full repayment. Finally, Shays's Rebellion in western Massachusetts, where armed rebels tried to prevent the state courts from seizing farms for the nonpayment of debts, greatly alarmed American notables.

stay acts
Enactments postponing the collection of taxes or mortgage payments.

The Constitutional Convention

Concerned about these developments and shortcomings in the design of government under the Articles, most of America's economic, social, and political leaders were convinced by 1787 that the new nation and the experiment in self-government were in great peril. These concerns helped convince leaders in the states to select 73 delegates to attend the Constitutional Convention in Philadelphia (only 55 actually showed up for its deliberations). The goal was to create a new government capable of providing both energy and stability.

The convention officially convened in Philadelphia on May 25, 1787, with George Washington presiding. It met in secret for a period of almost four months. By the end of their deliberations, the delegates had hammered out a constitutional framework that has served as one of the structural foundations of American government and politics to the present day.

Who Were the Framers?

The delegates were not common folk. There were no common laborers, skilled craftspeople, small farmers, women, or racial minorities in attendance. Most

Members of the convention sign their names to the Constitution on September 17, 1787. The Constitution did not become the law of the land, however, until the ninth state, New Hampshire, ratified it nine months later.

delegates were wealthy men: holders of government bonds, real estate investors, successful merchants, bankers, lawyers, and owners of large plantations worked by slaves. They were, for the most part, far better educated than the average American and solidly steeped in the classics. The journal of the convention debates kept by James Madison of Virginia shows that the delegates were conversant with the great works of Western philosophy and political science; with great facility and frequency, they quoted Aristotle, Plato, Locke, Montesquieu, and scores of other thinkers. They were also a surprisingly young group, averaging barely over 40 years of age. Finally, they were a group with broad experience in American politics, and many were veterans of the Revolutionary War.

Judgments about the framers, their intentions, and what they produced vary widely. Historian Melvin Urofsky wrote that "few gatherings in the history of this or any other country could boast such a concentration of talent."[15] Supreme Court Justice Thurgood Marshall, on the other hand, once claimed that the Constitution was "defective from the start" because the convention at which it was written did not include women or blacks.[16]

The most influential criticism of the framers and what they created was mounted in 1913 by the Progressive historian Charles Beard in his book *An Economic Interpretation of the Constitution*.[17] Beard boldly claimed that the framers were engaged in a conspiracy to protect their immediate and personal economic interests. Those who controlled the convention and the ratification process after the convention, he suggested, were owners of public securities who were interested in a government that could pay its debts, merchants interested in protections of commerce, and land speculators interested in the protection of property rights.

Beard has had legions of defenders and detractors.[18] Historians today generally agree that Beard overemphasized the degree to which the framers were driven by the immediate need to "line their own pockets," failed to give credit to their more noble motivations, and even got many of his facts wrong. So a simple self-interest analysis is not supportable. But Beard was probably on the mark when he suggested that broad economic and social-class motives were at work in shaping the actions of the framers. This is not to suggest that they were not concerned about the national interest, economic stability, or the preservation of liberty. It does suggest, however, that the ways in which they understood these concepts were fully compatible with their own positions of economic and social eminence. In conclusion, it is fair to say that the Constitutional Convention was the work of American leaders who were authentically worried about the instability and economic chaos of the confederation as well as the rise of a democratic and equalitarian culture among the common people.

That being said, we must also acknowledge that the framers were launched on a novel and exciting adventure, trying to create a form of government that existed nowhere else during the late eighteenth century. The success of their efforts was not guaranteed. They were, in effect, sailing in uncharted waters, guided by their reading of history and of the republican philosophers, their understanding of the nature of the English constitution, and their experience with colonial governments before the Revolution and state governments after.

Consensus and Conflict at the Convention

The delegates to the convention were of one mind on many fundamental points. Most importantly, they agreed that the Articles of Confederation had to be scrapped and replaced with a new constitution.

Most of the delegates also agreed about the need for a substantially strengthened national government to protect American interests in the world, provide for social order, and regulate interstate commerce. Such a government would diminish the power and sovereignty of the states. Supporters of the idea of a strong, centralized national government, such as Alexander Hamilton, had long argued this position. By the time of the convention, even such traditional opponents of centralized governmental power as James Madison had changed their minds. As Madison put it, some way must be found "which will at once support a due supremacy of the national authority, and leave in force the local authorities so far as they can be subordinately useful."[19]

But the delegates also believed that a strong national government was potentially tyrannical and should not be allowed to fall into the hands of any particular interest or set of interests, particularly the majority of the people, referred to by Madison as the "majority faction." The delegates' most important task became that of finding a formula for creating a republican government based on popular consent but a government not unduly swayed by public opinion and popular democracy. As Benjamin Franklin put it, "We have been guarding against an evil that old states are most liable to, excess of power in the rulers, but our present danger seems to be a defect of obedience in the subjects."[20]

The Great Compromise   By far the most intense disagreements at the convention concerned the issue of representation in Congress, especially whether large or small states would wield the most power in the legislative branch. The **Virginia Plan,** drafted by James Madison, proposed the creation of a strong central government controlled by the most populous states: Virginia, Massachusetts, and Pennsylvania. The Virginians wanted a national legislature with seats apportioned to the states on the basis of population size and with the power to appoint the executive and the judiciary and to veto state laws. The smaller states countered with a set of proposals drafted by William Paterson of New Jersey (thereafter known as the **New Jersey Plan**), whose

Virginia Plan
Proposal by the large states at the Constitutional Convention to create a strong central government with power in the government apportioned to the states on the basis of population.

New Jersey Plan
Proposal of the smaller states at the Constitutional Convention to create a government based on the equal representation of the states in a unicameral legislature.

central feature was a unicameral national legislature whose seats were apportioned equally among the states. The New Jersey Plan envisioned a slightly more powerful national government than the one that existed under the Articles of Confederation, but one that was to be organized on representational lines not unlike those in the Articles, in which each of the states remained sovereign. The Virginia Plan, by contrast, with its strong national government run by a popularly elected legislature, represented a fundamentally different kind of national union, one in which national sovereignty was superior to state sovereignty.

Debate over this issue was so intense that no decision could be reached on the floor of the convention. As a way out of this impasse, the convention appointed a committee to hammer out a compromise. The so-called Committee of Eleven met over the Fourth of July holiday while the convention was adjourned. It presented its report, sometimes called the Great Compromise and sometimes the **Connecticut Compromise** (because it was drafted by Roger Sherman of that state), on July 5, 1787. Its key feature was a bicameral (two-house) national legislature in which each state's representation in the House of Representatives was to be based on population (thus favoring the large states), while representation in the Senate was to be equal for each of the states (thus favoring the small states). The compromise, adopted on July 16, broke the deadlock at the convention and allowed the delegates to turn their attention to other matters.

Connecticut Compromise
Also called the *Great Compromise;* the compromise between the New Jersey and Virginia plans formulated by the Connecticut delegates at the Constitutional Convention; called for a lower legislative house based on population size and an upper house based on equal representation of the states.

Slavery   Despite great distaste for the institution of slavery among many delegates—it is said that Benjamin Franklin wanted to insert a provision in the Constitution condemning slavery and the slave trade but was talked out of it for fear of splintering the convention[21]—slavery was ultimately condoned in the Constitution, although only indirectly; the word "slavery," in fact, does not appear in the Constitution at all. Rather, the legal standing of "involuntary servitude" is affirmed in three places. First, the delegates agreed, after much heated debate, to count three-fifths of a state's slave population (referred to as "three-fifths of all other Persons") in the calculation of how many representatives a state was entitled to in the House of Representatives (Article I, Section 2,

Web Exploration
Delegates to the Convention

Issue: The Constitution was made by people who were not much like the average inhabitant of the United States in 1787.

Site: Find out more about the delegates to the Convention by going to the National Archives on our Website at **www.ablongman.com/greenberg**. In the "Web Explorations" section for Chapter 2, open "delegates to the convention," then "delegates." Select a state and read the biographies of the delegates.

What You've Learned: How would you describe the average delegate? How representative do you believe them to have been of the American people of the time?

HINT: There were no women; few artisans and small farmers; and no free blacks, indentured servants, slaves, or Native Americans at the proceedings. These groups together comprised the vast majority of the American population.

One of the great shortcomings of the framers was their inability or unwillingness to abolish slavery in the Constitution. It would take a great and terrible civil war to rectify their mistake.

paragraph 3). Much harm was done by this; counting noncitizen slaves for purposes of representation in the House increased the power of the slave states in Congress as well as the number of their electoral votes in presidential elections. This imbalance would continue until 1865, when the Civil War and the Thirteenth Amendment, ratified after the war, ended slavery in the United States. Second, it forbade enactments against the slave trade until the year 1808 (Article I, Section 9). Third, it required nonslave states to return runaway slaves to their owners in slave states (Article IV, Section 2, paragraph 3).

Many Americans today are no doubt bothered by the fact that a significant number of the delegates to a convention whose goal was to build a nontyrannical republic were themselves slaveholders (although a few, including George Washington, had provisions in their wills freeing their slaves upon their death). To understand more fully why the delegates did not abolish slavery, see the "Using the Framework" feature on the next page.

It would finally take a terrible civil war to abolish slavery in the United States. At the convention, Virginia delegate George Mason had a foreboding of such an outcome when he observed about slavery that "providence punishes national sins by national calamities."[22]

The Presidency   The Virginia Plan called for a single executive, while the New Jersey Plan called for a plural executive. In the spirit of cooperation that pervaded the convention after the Great Compromise, the delegates quickly settled on the idea of a single executive. They could not agree, however, on how this executive should be selected. Both sides rejected direct election by the people of the chief executive, of course, because this would be "too much upon the democratic order," but they locked horns over and could not agree to the Virginia Plan's method of selection: by the vote of state legislatures. The compromise that was eventually struck involved a provision for an **electoral college** that would select the president. In the electoral college, each state would have a total of votes equal to its total number of representatives and senators in Congress. Members of the electoral college would then cast their votes for president. Should the electoral college fail to give a

electoral college
Elected representatives of the states whose votes formally elect the president; the number of electors in each state is equal to the total number of its senators and representatives in the House.

Using the Framework

Slavery in the Constitution
Why was slavery allowed in the Constitution of 1787?

Background: Slavery was allowed in the Constitution until passage, after the Civil War, of the Thirteenth Amendment, which ended involuntary servitude in the United States. Although the words "slave" or "involuntary servitude" never appear in the document, slavery is given constitutional standing in the original document in Article I, Section 2, paragraph 3; Article 2, Section 9; and Article IV, Section 2, paragraph 3. For Americans today, it seems almost inconceivable that such a thing could have happened. Taking a broader and more historical view makes the story clearer, though hardly more acceptable.

Governmental Action

The framers allowed the institution of slavery to continue in Article I, Section 2; Article II, Setion 9; and Article IV, Section 2 of the Constitution.

Governmental Level

Slaveholders and merchants involved in the slave trade were well represented among the convention delegates. ➡ Many other delegates, although personally opposed to slavery as an institution, feared that the introduction of a provision to end slavery would cause those states with high numbers of slaves to leave the convention and doom the effort to create a United States of America.

Political Linkages Level

Slaves and free blacks played no significant political role in America during the Articles of Confederation period. Their concerns about slavery had no political weight. ➡ Few private organizations—interest groups, churches, or newspapers—were actively pressing for an end to slavery at the time of the constitutional convention.

Structural Level

The slave trade was a profitable business. ➡ For the most part, individuals of European descent in America during the time of the constitutional convention did not believe that people of African descent were equal to whites in any respect, nor did they believe they were beings who possessed basic human rights.

majority to any person, which most framers assumed would usually happen, the House of Representatives would choose the president, with each state having one vote (Article II, Section 1, paragraphs 2 and 3).

What the Framers Created

What kind of government did the framers create? Let us examine the fundamental design for government laid out in the Constitution.

A Republican Form of Government

Recall that eighteenth-century republican doctrine advocated a form of government that, while based on popular consent and some popular participation, places obstacles in the path of majoritarian democracy and limits the purposes and powers of the government in order to prevent tyranny.

Election of Government Leaders

Republican government is based on the principle of representation, meaning that public policies are made not by the people directly but by the people's elected representatives acting in their stead. Under the rules created by the Constitution, the president and members of Congress are elected by the people, though in the case of the presidency and the Senate, to be sure, they are elected only indirectly (through the electoral college and the state legislatures, respectively). The upshot, then, is that government policies at the national level are mostly made by either directly or indirectly elected officials. This guarantees a degree of popular consent and some protection against the possibilities of tyrannical government arising from misrule by the *one* or by the *few,* given the electoral power of the *many.*

Federalism

The Articles of Confederation envisioned a nation structured as a loose union of politically independent units with little power in the hands of the central government. The Constitution fashioned a **federal** system in which some powers are left to the states, some powers are shared by the component units and the central government, and some powers are granted to the central government alone.

The powers in the Constitution tilt slightly toward the center, however.[23] This recasting of the union from a loose confederation to a more centralized federal system is boldly stated in Article VI, Section 2, commonly called the **supremacy clause**:

> *This Constitution and the Laws of the United States which shall be made in Pursuance thereof; and all Treaties made, or which shall be made, under the Authority of the United States, shall be the supreme Law of the Land; and the Judges in every State shall be bound thereby, any Thing in the Constitution or Laws of any State to the Contrary notwithstanding.*

The tilt toward national power is also enhanced by assigning important powers and responsibilities to the national government: to regulate commerce, to provide a uniform currency, to provide uniform laws on bankruptcy, to raise and support an army and a navy, to declare war, to collect taxes and customs duties, to provide for the common defense of the United States, and more. (See Article I, Section 8.) Especially important for later constitutional history is the last of the clauses in Section 8, which states that Congress has the power to "make all laws which shall be necessary and proper" to carry out its specific powers and responsibilities. We shall see later how this **elastic clause** became one of the foundations for the growth of the federal government in the twentieth century.

federal
Describing a system in which significant governmental powers are divided between a central government and smaller territorial units, such as states.

supremacy clause
The provision in Article VI of the Constitution that states that the Constitution and the laws and treaties of the United States are the supreme law of the land, taking precedence over state laws and constitutions.

elastic clause
Article I, Section 8, of the Constitution, also called the *necessary and proper clause;* gives Congress the authority to make whatever laws are necessary and proper to carry out its enumerated responsibilities.

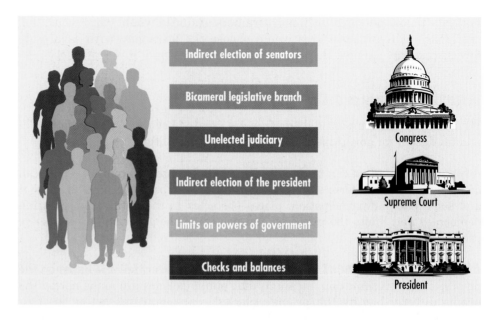

FIGURE 2.2 ● Limiting the Power of the Majority

The framers of the Constitution were concerned that the unreflective and unstable opinions of the majority might overwhelm the considered judgments of government leaders and lead to tyranny. One antidote was to create mechanisms in the Constitution that, while preserving "the consent of the governed," ensured that the voice of the people would be muted in the councils of government.

The Constitution left it up to each of the states, however, to determine qualifications for voting within their borders. This left rules in place in all the states that denied the right to vote to women, slaves, and Native Americans; it left rules untouched in many states that denied the vote to free blacks and to white males without substantial property. Most states removed property qualifications by the 1830s, establishing universal white male suffrage in the United States. It would take many years and constitutional amendments to remove state restrictions on the voting rights of women and racial minorities.

Limited Government   The basic purpose of the U.S. Constitution, like any written constitution, is to define the purposes and powers of the government. Such a definition of purposes and powers automatically places a boundary between what is permissible and what is impermissible. By listing the specific powers (as in Article I, Section 8) of the national government and specifically denying others to the national government (as in Article I, Section 9, and in the first ten amendments to the Constitution, known as the **Bill of Rights**), the Constitution carefully limited what government may legitimately do.

Bill of Rights
The first ten amendments to the U.S. Constitution, concerned with basic liberties.

Checks on Majority Rule   Afraid of unbridled democracy, the framers created a constitution by which the people rule only indirectly, barriers are placed in the path of majorities (see Figure 2.2), and deliberation is prized over conformity to majority opinion. As political philosopher Robert Dahl puts it, "To achieve their goal of preserving a set of inalienable rights superior to the majority principle . . . the framers deliberately created a framework of government that was carefully designed to impede and even prevent the operation of majority rule."[24] Let us see what the framers did to try to dilute the power of the majority in the national government.

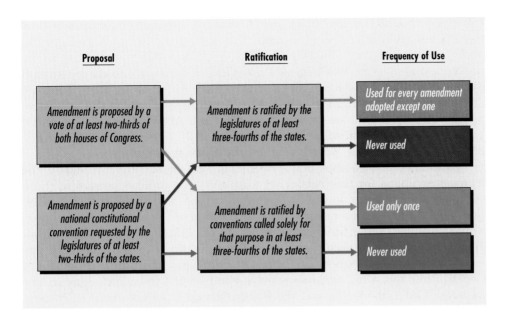

Proposal	Ratification	Frequency of Use
Amendment is proposed by a vote of at least two-thirds of both houses of Congress.	Amendment is ratified by the legislatures of at least three-fourths of the states.	Used for every amendment adopted except one
		Never used
Amendment is proposed by a national constitutional convention requested by the legislatures of at least two-thirds of the states.	Amendment is ratified by conventions called solely for that purpose in at least three-fourths of the states.	Used only once
		Never used

FIGURE 2.3 • Amending the Constitution

With two ways of proposing a constitutional amendment and two ways of ratifying one, there are four routes to changing the Constitution. In all but one case (the Twenty-First Amendment, which repealed Prohibition), constitutional amendments have been proposed by Congress and then ratified by the state legislatures.

Of the three branches of government, only a part of one of them is selected by the direct vote of the people: the House of Representatives (Article I, Section 2, paragraph 1). As for the rest of the national government, the president is elected by the electoral college; the members of the Senate are elected by the state legislatures; and judges are appointed by the president and confirmed by the Senate. Representatives, senators, and presidents are elected, moreover, for different terms (two years for representatives, four years for presidents, and six years for senators), from different constituencies, and (often) at different times. These noncongruencies in elections were intended to ensure that popular majorities, at least in the short run, would be unlikely to overwhelm those who govern. Finally, the framers rejected the advice of radical democrats, such as Thomas Paine, Samuel Adams, and Thomas Jefferson, to allow the Constitution to be easily amended. Instead, they created an amending process that is exceedingly cumbersome and difficult (see Figure 2.3).

Thus, the framers designed a system in which majority opinion, though given some play (more than anywhere in the world at the time), was largely deflected and slowed, allowing somewhat insulated political leaders to deliberate at their pleasure.

You Are Trying to Amend the Constitution

Separation of Powers; Checks and Balances   During the American Revolution, American leaders worried mainly about the misrule of executives (kings and governors) and judges. As an antidote, they substituted legislative supremacy in state constitutions and in the Articles of Confederation, thinking that placing power in an elected representative body would make government effective and nontyrannical. The men who drafted the Constitution, however, though still leery of executive and judicial power, were more concerned by 1787 about the danger of legislative tyranny. To deal with this problem, the

The American System of Checks and Balances

framers turned to the ancient notion of balanced government, popularized by the French philosopher Montesquieu. The central idea of balanced government is that concentrated power of any kind is dangerous and that the way to prevent tyranny is first to fragment governmental power into its constituent parts—executive, legislative, and judicial—then place each into a separate and independent branch. In the U.S. Constitution, Article I (on the legislative power), Article II (on the executive power), and Article III (on the judicial power) designate separate spheres of responsibility and enumerate specific powers for each branch. We call this the **separation of powers.**

To further ensure that power would not be exercised tyrannically, the framers arranged for the legislative, executive, and judicial powers to check one another in such a way that "ambition . . . be made to counteract ambition."[25] They did this by ensuring that no branch of the national government would be able to act entirely on its own without the cooperation of the others. To put it another way, each branch has ways of blocking the actions of the others. For instance, Congress is given the chief lawmaking power under the Constitution, but a bill can become a law only if the president signs it. The Supreme Court, moreover, has the power (though it is not specifically mentioned) to reject a law formulated by Congress and signed by the president if it is contrary to the Constitution. What is at work here was described nicely by Thomas Jefferson: "The powers of government should be so divided and balanced among several bodies of magistracy, as that no one could transcend their legal limits, without being effectually checked and constrained by the others."[26] We call the provisions that accomplish this objective **checks and balances.** Figure 2.4 shows in detail how each separate branch of the federal government can be checked by the other two. In this constitutional scheme, each branch has power, but none is able to exercise all of its powers on its own.

The Foundations for a National Free Enterprise Economy   The framers believed that the right to accumulate, use, and transfer private property was one of the fundamental and inalienable rights that governments were instituted to defend, so they looked for ways to protect it. They also believed that the obstacles to trade allowed under the Articles of Confederation were threatening to block the emergence of a vibrant national economy in which most of them were involved.

Property rights are protected in several places in the Constitution. Article I, Section 10, forbids the states to impair the obligation of contracts, to coin money, or to make anything but gold and silver coin a tender in payment of debts. In other words, the states could no longer help debtors by printing inflated money, forgiving debts, or otherwise infringing on the property of creditors, as had happened in such places as Rhode Island and North Carolina under the Articles of Confederation. Article IV, Section 1, further guarantees contracts by establishing that the states must give "full faith and credit" to the public acts, records, and judicial proceedings of every other state, which means that one could no longer escape legal and financial obligations in one state by moving to another. In addition, the Constitution guaranteed that the U.S. government would pay all debts contracted under the Articles of Confederation (Article VI, Section 1). Article IV, Section 2, paragraph 3, even protected private property in slaves by requiring states to deliver escaped slaves back to their owners.

Besides protecting private property, the framers took additional steps to encourage the emergence of a national free enterprise economy. Article I, Section 8, grants Congress the power to regulate interstate commerce (thus

separation of powers
The distribution of government legislative, executive, and judicial powers to separate branches of government.

checks and balances
The constitutional principle that government power shall be divided and that the fragments should balance or check one another to prevent tyranny.

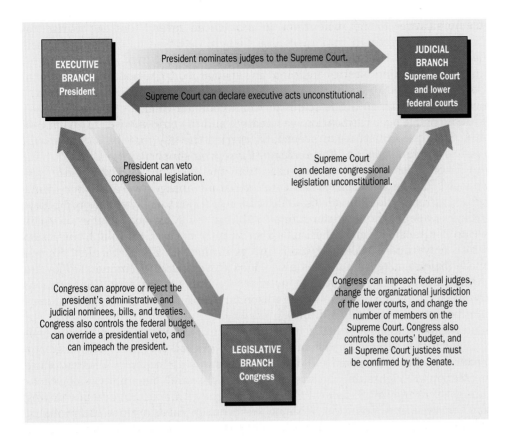

FIGURE 2.4 • Checks and Balances

The framers of the Constitution believed that tyranny might be avoided if the power of government were fragmented into its executive, legislative, and judicial components and if each component were made the responsibility of a separate branch of government. To further protect against tyranny, they created mechanisms by which the actions of any single branch could be blocked by either or both of the other branches. This system of checks and balances is highlighted in this drawing.

ending the chaos of individual states' regulations), to coin money and regulate its value (thus establishing a uniform national currency), to establish uniform laws of bankruptcy, and to protect the financial fruits of invention by establishing patent and copyright laws. At the same time, Article I, Sections 9 and 10, broke down barriers to trade by forbidding the states to impose taxes or duties on other states' exports, to enter into foreign treaties, to coin money, or to lay any imposts or duties on imports or exports.

The Struggle to Ratify the Constitution

Congress had instructed the delegates to the convention to propose changes to the Articles of Confederation. Under the provisions of the Articles of Confederation, such alterations would have required the unanimous consent of the 13 states. To follow such a course would have meant instant rejection of the new constitution, because Rhode Island, never friendly to the deliberations in Philadelphia, surely would have voted against it, and one or two additional states may well have joined Rhode Island. Acting boldly, the framers simply stated that ratification would be based on guidelines specified in Article VII of the unratified document they had just written, namely, approval by nine states meeting in special constitutional conventions. Congress agreed to this procedure, voting on September 28, 1787, to transmit the Constitution to the states for their consideration.

The battle over ratification was heated, and the outcome was far from certain. That the Constitution eventually carried the day may be partly attributed to the fact that the **Federalists** (those who supported the Constitution) did a better job of making their case than the **Anti-Federalists** (those who opposed the Constitution). Their intellectual advantages were nowhere more obvious than in the 85 articles written in defense of the Constitution for New York newspapers, under the name "Publius," by Alexander Hamilton (who wrote the most), James Madison (who wrote the best), and John Jay (who wrote only three). Collected later and published as *The Federalist Papers,* these articles strongly influenced the debate over ratification and remain the most impressive commentaries ever written about the U.S. Constitution. (Numbers 10 and 51, written by Madison, are reprinted in the Appendix, as is number 78, written by Hamilton.)

Anti-Federalist opposition to the Constitution was based on fear of centralized power and concern about the absence of a bill of rights.[27] Although the Federalists firmly believed that a bill of rights was unnecessary because of the protection of rights in the state constitutions and the many safeguards against tyranny in the federal Constitution, they promised to add one during the first session of Congress. Without this promise, ratification would probably not have happened. The Federalists kept their word. The 1st Congress passed a bill of rights in the form of ten amendments to the Constitution (see Table 2.2 and the Appendix), and the amendments were eventually ratified by the required number of states by 1791.

Federalists
Proponents of the Constitution during the ratification fight; also the political party of Hamilton, Washington, and Adams.

Anti-Federalists
Opponents of the Constitution during the fight over ratification.

TABLE 2.2 • The Bill of Rights

Amendment	
Amendment I	Freedom of religion, speech, press, and assembly
Amendment II	The right to bear arms
Amendment III	Prohibition against quartering of troops in private homes
Amendment IV	Prohibition against unreasonable searches and seizures
Amendment V	Rights guaranteed to the accused: requirement for grand jury indictment; protections against double jeopardy and self-incrimination; guarantee of due process
Amendment VI	Right to a speedy and public trial before an impartial jury, to cross-examine witnesses, and to have counsel
Amendment VII	Right to a trial by jury in civil suits
Amendment VIII	Prohibition against excessive bail and fines and against cruel and unusual punishment
Amendment IX	Traditional rights not listed in the Constitution are retained by the people
Amendment X	Powers not denied to them by the Constitution or given solely to the national government are retained by the states

Note: See the Appendix for the full text.

Ratification of the Constitution was a close call. Most of the small states quickly approved, attracted by the formula of equal representation in the Senate. Federalists organized a victory in Pennsylvania before the Anti-Federalists realized what had happened. After that, ratification became a struggle. Rhode Island voted no. North Carolina abstained because of the absence of a bill of rights and did not vote its approval until 1790. In the largest and most important states, the vote was exceedingly close. Massachusetts approved by a vote of 187–168; Virginia, by 89–79; and New York, by 30–27. The struggle was especially intense in Virginia, where prominent, articulate, and influential men were involved on both sides. The Federalists could call on George Washington, James Madison, John Marshall, and Edmund Randolph. The Anti-Federalists countered with George Mason, Richard Henry Lee, and Patrick Henry. Patrick Henry was particularly passionate, saying that the Constitution "squints towards monarchy." Although New Hampshire technically put the Constitution over the top, being the ninth state to vote approval, the proponents did not rest easily until approval was narrowly voted by Virginia and New York.

Simulation

You Are James Madison

The Changing Constitution, Democracy, and American Politics

The Constitution is the basic rule book for the game of American politics. Constitutional rules apportion power and responsibility among governmental branches, define the fundamental nature of the relationships among governmental institutions, specify how individuals are to be selected for office, and tell how the rules themselves may be changed. Every aspiring politician who wants to attain office, every citizen who wants to influence what government does, and every group that wants to advance its interests in the political arena must know the rules and how to use them to their best advantage. Because the Constitution has this character, we understand it to be a fundamental *structural* factor influencing all of American political life.

Like all rules, however, constitutional rules can and do change over time. Their tendency to change with the times is why we sometimes speak of the "living Constitution." Constitutional changes come about in three specific ways: formal amendment, judicial interpretation, and political practices.

The Constitution may be formally amended by use of the procedures outlined in Article V of the Constitution (again, refer to Figure 2.3). This method has resulted in the addition of 27 amendments since the founding, the first ten of which (the Bill of Rights) were added within three years of ratification. That only 17 have been added in the roughly 200 years since suggests that this method of changing the Constitution is extremely difficult. Nevertheless, formal amendments have played an important role in expanding democracy in the United States by ending slavery; extending voting rights to African Americans, women, and young people ages 18 to 20; and making the Senate subject to popular vote.

Timeline

The History of Constitutional Amendments

The Constitution is also changed by decisions and interpretations of the U.S. Supreme Court. For instance, in *Marbury* v. *Madison* (1803), the Court claimed the power of **judicial review**—the right to declare the actions of the other branches of government null and void if they are contrary to the Constitution—even though such a power is not specifically mentioned in the Constitution. In *Griswold* v. *Connecticut* (1965), and later in *Roe* v. *Wade*

judicial review

The power of the Supreme Court to declare actions of the other branches and levels of government unconstitutional.

How Democratic Are We?

A Republic or a Democracy?

PROPOSITION   The Constitution created a republic, not a democracy, and we remain a republic today.

AGREE The framers created a republic because they were worried about the possibility of majority tyranny in the new nation. Consequently, they wrote a number of provisions into the Constitution to control the purported excesses of democracy. These include the separation of powers into executive, legislative, and judicial branches; checks and balances to prevent any of the branches from governing on its own; federalism to fragment government powers between a national government and the states; an appointed federal judiciary with life tenure; selection of the president by the electoral college; and election of members of the Senate by state legislatures. Although some of these provisions have not worked precisely as the framers intended, the American system of government remains essentially "republican" in nature, with the majority finding it very difficult to prevail.

DISAGREE Although the framers had every intention of creating a republic and holding democracy in check, they were unable to do so. Over the years, as the nation became more egalitarian in its cultural, economic, and social life, the tide of democracy transformed the original constitutional design. By formal amendment, judicial interpretations, and changing political practices, government has been fashioned into a highly responsive set of institutions, heeding the voice of the people. For example, the Seventeenth Amendment created a Senate whose members are directly elected by the people. The Supreme Court, moreover, has extended civil rights protections to racial and ethnic minorities. And, the presidency has become both more powerful and more attentive to majority opinion. Today, the national government does pretty much what the American people want it to do, even if it sometimes takes a while for it to do so.

CONSIDER   • Which of the above arguments makes the most sense to you? • Does it appear to be the case that the American people pretty much get what they want from government?   • Can you think of issues where the majority does not, in fact, get its way with elected officials?   • If you can think of such cases, how would you explain the disconnect between people and government? • Is it best explained by lack of responsiveness on the part of elected leaders or by the constitutional system designed by the framers? • On the other hand, can you think of other areas of public life where elected leaders seem too responsive to the public? • In these cases, why is it that the constitutional protections designed by the framers don't seem to be deflecting the influence of majority opinion?

The material in the remainder of this book will help you answer these questions more confidently, to be sure, but a preliminary consideration of them here will serve you well as you learn more about how American politics and government work.

(1973), to take another example, the Court supported a claim for the existence of a fundamental right of privacy even though such a right is not explicitly mentioned in the Constitution.

The meaning of the Constitution also changes through changing political practices, which end up serving as precedents for political actors. Political parties and nominating conventions are not cited in the Constitution, for example,

The Constitution has evolved over the years in three ways: through the amendment process, through evolving political practices, and through the Supreme Court's changing interpretation of the Constitution's meaning. Here antiabortion protesters demonstrate in front of the Supreme court building on the anniversary of the Court's *Roe* v. *Wade* decision to demand a reversal of that landmark decision.

Comparative

Comparing Constitutions

but it would be hard to think about American politics today without them. It is also fair to say that the framers would not recognize the modern presidency, which is now a far more important office than they envisioned, a change that has been brought about largely by the political and military involvement of the United States in world affairs.

The story of how formal amendment, judicial interpretations, and political practices have changed the constitutional rules in the United States will be told in more detail throughout this text.

Summary

The first constitution joining the American states was the Articles of Confederation. Under its terms, the states were organized into a loose confederation in which the states retained full sovereignty and the central government had little power. Because of a wide range of defects in the Articles of Confederation and fears among many American leaders that democratic and egalitarian tendencies were beginning to spin out of control, a gathering was called in Philadelphia to amend the Articles of Confederation. The delegates chose instead to formulate an entirely new constitution, based on the principles of republicanism (federalism, limited government, the separation of powers, checks and balances, and limitations on majority rule).

The Constitution was ratified in an extremely close vote of the states after a hard-fought struggle between the Federalists and the Anti-Federalists. The Federalists were supported primarily by those who believed in a more centralized republicanism; the Anti-Federalists were supported primarily by those who believed in small-scale republicanism. Despite its "close shave," the

Constitution became very popular among the American people within only a few years of the ratification fight. Because of the continuing struggle for democracy by the American people, the Constitution has become far more democratic over the years than was originally intended by the framers.

Suggestions for Further Reading

Ellis, Joseph J. *Founding Brothers: The Revolutionary Generation.* New York: Alfred Knopf, 2001.
> *An entertaining and accessible look at the intertwined lives of the men who wrote the Declaration of Independence, fought the Revolutionary War, fashioned the Constitution, and launched the new American government.*

Rossiter, Clinton, ed. *The Federalist Papers.* New York: New American Library, 1961.
> *Classic commentaries on the Constitution and its key provisions, written by Alexander Hamilton, John Jay, and James Madison.*

Storing, Herbert J. *What the Anti-Federalists Were For.* Chicago: University of Chicago Press, 1981.
> *The most complete collection available on the published views of the Anti-Federalists. Includes convincing commentary by Storing.*

Wills, Gary. *Explaining America: The Federalist.* New York: Doubleday, 1981.
> *A fresh look at the writing of the Constitution by one of America's most provocative intellectuals.*

Wood, Gordon S. *The Creation of the American Republic.* New York: Norton, 1972.
> *The most exhaustive and respected source on America's changing ideas during the period 1776–1787, or from the start of the American Revolution to the writing of the Constitution.*

Wood, Gordon S. *The Radicalism of the American Revolution.* New York: Knopf, 1992.
> *Examines and rejects the argument that the American Revolution was merely a political and not a social and economic revolution.*

Internet Sources

Annotated Constitution
www.gpoaccess.gov/constitution/index.html
> *An annotation of the Constitution in which each clause is tied to Supreme Court decisions concerning its meaning; done by the Library of Congress.*

Biographical Sketches of the Delegates to the Constitutional Convention
www.archives.gov/national_archives_experience/ constitution_founding_fathers.html
> *Profiles of the delegates to the Constitutional Convention.*

Cornell University Law School
http://www.law.cornell.edu/
> *Pathways to the full text of U.S. Supreme Court decisions and opinions, articles on constitutional issues, and much more.*

Political Science Resources: Political Thought
http://www.psr.keele.ac.uk/
> *A vast collection of documents on democracy, liberty, and constitutionalism.*

The U.S. Constitution On-Line
www.usconstitution.net
> *A very rich site that presents material on every aspect of the history and development of the Constitution.*

Chapter 3
Federalism: States and Nation

In This Chapter

- What federalism is and why we have it
- Conflicts over the meaning of federalism in the United States
- How our federal system differs from other systems of government
- Advantages and disadvantages of federalism
- The impact of terrorism on the national–state balance
- Federalism and democracy

State Attorneys-General Stretch the Boundaries

State attorneys-general have traditionally focused their attention on issues pertaining to their own states. In Colorado in 2003, for example, Attorney General Ken Salazar responded to consumer complaints lodged against state agencies or private companies, brought action against firms violating the state's "no call' list, ruled that police records on the Columbine massacre be deposited in the state archives, sponsored a report on youth violence, brought legal action against companies violating Colorado pollution laws, and warned the public about bank check scams. Attorneys-general in each of the states are now and have long been engaged in similar sorts of activities. However, in the last decade or so, state attorneys-general, including Ken Salazar, have dramatically expanded the scope of their activities, taking on broad national issues and forcing policy changes well beyond the borders of their own states. Here are a few examples:[1]

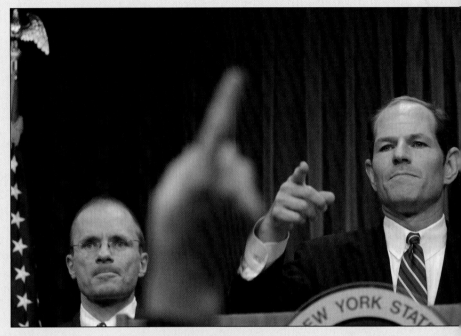

- In 2002, the Ford Motor Company paid a settlement of $52 million to settle claims about false advertising about the safety of its sport utility vehicles. The settlement was not in response to action by federal authorities but to action brought in unison by the 50 state attorneys-general.
- In the same year, and in response to the actions of the attorneys-general of all the states, Household International paid a settlement of $484 million for predatory mortgage lending.
- State attorneys-general were the major players in the antitrust suit brought against Microsoft.
- The attorneys-general from California, Massachusetts, Pennsylvania, New Hampshire, New Jersey, and New York jointly filed a suit against the Environmental Protection Agency (EPA) for its decision to ease restrictions on power plant emissions.
- Connecticut's attorney general led the antitrust investigations into Oracle's attempt to take over rival PeopleSoft.
- The landmark tobacco settlement—in which American tobacco companies agreed to pay the states a sum of $246 billion over 25 years—was engineered by a coalition of attorneys-general from 46 states.
- The most visible and successful of the new, activist attorneys-general is Eliot Spitzer of New York. Spitzer recently brought to light and reached settlements in cases involving predatory lending practices, unsavory hedge-fund policies, drug pricing, conflicts of interest on Wall Street, and, most famously, unethical (and possibly illegal) practices in the mutual fund industry. He has also taken on e-mail spammers, polluting power companies, and gun manufacturers operating outside his own state.

Why have state attorneys-general become so active in a wide range of activities that have come to be considered the business of the national government? Observers offer a number of possible explanations. To critics of this new activism, state attorneys-general have discovered new ways of cooperating with one another that are advantageous to their political careers. Critics have also suggested that the effort to achieve huge monetary settlements is propelled by states' needs to balance their own budgets in a time of fiscal crisis. To others (more neutral observers perhaps), the emergence of a new style of behavior among attorneys-general is better explained by shifts in federal government policies, particularly the effort to download a number of former federal responsibilities to the states—the details of which we will cover in this chapter—and a decline in the regulatory efforts of federal agencies such as the EPA and the SEC, propelled by the deregulation atmosphere that has prevailed in Washington for some time now. The evidence is not yet in. All that we know for certain is that state attorneys-general are venturing into new territory.

This story highlights several things about federalism. First, it suggests that the nature of federalism is always changing; the particular balance of national and state powers and responsibilities is never set in concrete but is constantly in flux, responding to changing times, the calculations of political leaders, and the wishes of the American people. Second, it suggests that even in a time when the national government has become extremely powerful relative to the states, the states remain important players in American politics and government.

Thinking Critically About This Chapter

The mixture of state and national action on this issue, and the state experimentation that affected policymaking in the nation as a whole, is characteristic of American federalism. So, too, is the conflict between national standards and local flexibility.

Using the Framework   In this chapter, you will learn how and why federalism is one of the most important structural factors that affect American politics and government and shape public policy. You will learn how federalism influences our entire system: from the kinds of political parties we have and the workings of Congress to how domestic programs are affected. You will also learn how federalism itself has changed over time.

Using the Democracy Standard   Using the evaluative tools you learned in Chapter 1, you will be able to judge for yourself whether federalism enriches or diminishes democracy in the United States.

Federalism as a System of Government

The United States is full of governments. We have not only a federal government in Washington, D.C. (which, to avoid confusion, we will refer to in this chapter as the *national* or *central* government), but also governments in each of 50 states and in each of thousands of smaller governmental units, such as counties (about 3,000 of them), cities, towns and townships, school districts, and special districts that deal with such matters as parks and sanitation.

All these governments are organized and related to each other in a particular way. The small governments—those of counties, cities, towns, and special districts—are legal creations of state governments. They can be created, changed, or abolished by state laws, at the state's convenience. But state governments themselves have much more weight and permanence because of their prominent place in the Constitution. Together with the national government in Washington, D.C., they form what is known as a federal system. The *federal system* is part of the basic structure of U.S. government, deeply rooted in our Constitution and history. It is one of the most important features of American politics, since it affects practically everything else.

Federations are not necessarily forever. The Yugoslav federation of republics, in which each republic was formed primarily on the basis of nationality, could not withstand the dramatic rise in ethnic tensions after the death of Yugoslav leader Marshall Tito. Here ethnic Serb soldiers and militia escort an elderly Croat from his basement shelter during the battle for Vukovar in 1991.

The Nature of Federalism

Federalism is a system under which significant government powers are divided between the central government and smaller units, such as states or provinces. Neither one completely controls the other; each has some room for independent action. A federal system can be contrasted with two other types of government: a confederation and a unitary government. In a **confederation,** the constituent states get together for certain common purposes but retain ultimate individual authority and can veto major central governmental actions. The United Nations, the European Union, and the American government under the Articles of Confederation are examples. In a **unitary system,** the central government has all the power and can change its constituent units or tell them what to do. Japan and France have this kind of government, as do a substantial majority of nations around the world. These three different types of governmental systems are contrasted in Figure 3.1.

The Roots of Federalism

Some of the elements of federalism go back in history at least as far as the Union of Utrecht in the Netherlands in 1579, but federalism as it exists today is largely an American invention.[2] Including the United States, 24 nations, with roughly 40 percent of the world's population, have federal systems today.[3]

Historical Origins American federalism emerged from the particular way in which the states declared independence from Britain—becoming, in effect, separate countries—and then joined together to form a confederation and then a single nation, as discussed in Chapter 2. Recall that the framers of the Constitution turned to federalism as a middle-ground solution between a confederation form of government—which was deemed a failed model based on the experience of the United States under the Articles of Confederation—and a unitary form of government—which a majority of states, jealous of

federalism
A system in which significant governmental powers are divided between a central government and smaller units, such as states.

confederation
A loose association of states or territorial divisions in which very little power is lodged in the central government.

unitary system
A system in which a central government has complete power over its constituent units or states.

Comparing Federal and Unitary Systems

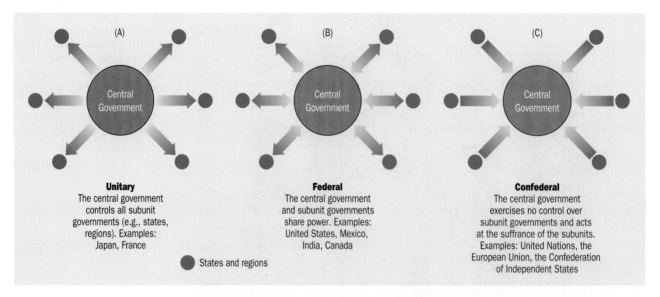

Unitary
The central government controls all subunit governments (e.g., states, regions). Examples: Japan, France

Federal
The central government and subunit governments share power. Examples: United States, Mexico, India, Canada

Confederal
The central government exercises no control over subunit governments and acts at the suffrance of the subunits. Examples: United Nations, the European Union, the Confederation of Independent States

● States and regions

FIGURE 3.1 • Types of Political Systems

A majority of countries have unitary systems (A), in which the central government controls the state and local governments, which in turn exert power over the citizens. The United States, however, has a federal system (B), in which the central government has power on some issues, the states have power on other issues, and the central and state governments share power on yet others. In a confederation (C), the central institutions have only a loose coordinating role, with real governing power residing in the constituent states or units.

their independence and prerogatives, found unacceptable. Federalism was also a form of government that was consistent with the eighteenth-century republicanism of the framers because it helps fragment government power. But we can gain further insight into *why* the United States adopted and has continued as a federal system if we look at what other countries with similar systems have in common.

Role of Size and Diversity   Most federal systems around the world are found in countries that are geographically large and have regions that differ from one another in various important ways: economic activity, religion, ethnicity, and language. In Germany, for example, the conservative Catholics of the south have traditionally been different from the liberal Protestants of the north and east. In Canada, the farmers of the central plains are not much like the fishers of Nova Scotia, and the French-speaking (and primarily Catholic) residents of Quebec differ markedly from the mostly English-speaking Protestants of the rest of the country. Such diverse groups often want the local independence that federalism allows, rather than submitting to a unified central government.

The United States, too, is large and diverse. From the early days of the Republic, the slave-holding and agriculture-oriented South was quite distinct from the merchant Northeast, and some important differences persist today. Illinois is not Louisiana; the farmers of Iowa differ from defense and electronics workers in California. States today also vary from one another in their approaches to public policy, their racial and ethnic composition, and their political cultures.[4] In *The Federalist Papers*, the Founders argued that this size and diversity made federalism especially appropriate for the new United States.

Comparing State and Local Governments

Federalism in the Constitution

Federalism is embodied in the U.S. Constitution in two main ways: (1) Power is expressly given to the states, as well as to the national government, and (2) the states have important roles in shaping, and choosing officials for, the national government itself, and in amending the Constitution.

Independent State Powers

Although the Constitution makes the central government supreme in certain matters, it also makes clear that the state governments have independent powers. The **supremacy clause** in Article VI states that the Constitution, laws, and treaties of the United States shall be the "supreme law of the land," but Article I, Section 8, enumerates what kinds of laws Congress has the power to pass, and the Tenth Amendment declares that the powers not delegated to the central government by the Constitution or prohibited by the Constitution to the states are *"reserved to the states* [emphasis added] respectively, or to the people." This provision is known as the **reservation clause.**

In other words, the U.S. Constitution specifically lists what the national government can do. Its powers include authority to levy taxes, regulate interstate commerce, establish post offices, and declare war, plus make laws "necessary and proper" for carrying out those powers. The Constitution then provides that all other legitimate government functions may be performed by the states, except for a few things, such as coining money or conducting foreign policy, that are forbidden by Article I, Section 10. This leaves a great deal in the hands of state governments, including licensing lawyers, doctors, and dentists; regulating businesses within their boundaries; chartering banks and corporations; providing a system of family law; providing a system of public education; and assuming the responsibility for building roads and highways, licensing drivers, and registering cars. The reservation clause is unique to the United States, and shows how important states are in American federalism. Other federal systems, such as Canada's and Germany's, reserve to the national government all functions not explicitly given to the states. Having said this, it remains the case that the Constitution is not crystal clear about the balance of powers and responsibilities between the state and national governments, leaving ample room for the meaning of federalism to change with the times.

supremacy clause
The provision in Article VI of the Constitution that the Constitution itself and the laws and treaties of the United States are the supreme law of the land, taking precedence over state laws and constitutions.

reservation clause
The Tenth Amendment to the Constitution, reserving powers to the states or the people.

The States' Roles in National Government

Moreover, the Constitution's provisions about the formation of the national government recognize a special position for the states. The Constitution declares in Article VII that it was "done in Convention by the unanimous consent of the *states* present" (emphasis added) and provides that the Constitution would go into effect not when a majority of all Americans voted for it but when the conventions of nine *states* ratified it. Article V provides that the Constitution can be amended only when conventions in or the legislatures of three-quarters of the states ratify an amendment. Article IV, Section 3, makes clear that no states can be combined or divided into new states without the consent of the state legislatures concerned. Thus, the state governments have charge of ratifying and amending the Constitution, and the states control their own boundaries.

The Rise of Partisan Conflict

Texas Legislators on the Lam

The Story: It was an unusual day in Texas state politics, to say the least. On May 11, 2003, Democratic state senators fled the state. Some boarded a private plane in the dead of night to slip quietly into New Mexico. Narrowly avoiding the Texas Rangers sent to keep them within the state borders—not to mention the Department of Homeland Security officials who had been asked to track their flight by Texas Republican congressman Tom DeLay—they made good their escape in a plane owned by Pete Laney, a former Texas Democratic House Speaker.

Why this Great Escape? Why would Democratic state senators exile themselves to another state just when the Texas legislature was scheduled to hold a special session to redraw House district lines? The answer is desperation. Even in the face of possible arrest for thwarting a quorum in the legislature, the Democrats were determined to undermine the special legislative session designed by the Republican majority to redistrict the state and thereby gain several Republican seats in the U.S. House of Representatives.

The Background: After the 2000 census, Texas Republican and Democratic state legislators could not reach an agreement on redistricting—that is,

how to draw the boundaries of House districts in such a way that each district ended up with equal numbers of people in them—and a federal judicial panel was forced to adopt its own redistricting map. However, when Republicans gained control of Texas state government after the 2002 elections, they decided to redistrict again. They were encouraged and assisted in this effort by Tom DeLay, the powerful majority leader of the U.S. House of Representatives who was, himself, from Texas. DeLay is widely credited not only with raising the possibility of a second Texas redistricting but also with drawing the new redistricting map, mediating disputes among Republican legislators over the plan, and channeling campaign funding to state legislators to help along the undecided in his own party.

Although Republican Governor Rick Perry had threatened to arrest the fleeing Democratic senators, when the exiles returned after the special session ended, they were—much to their relief—not arrested. However, when Governor Perry almost immediately called another special session to consider

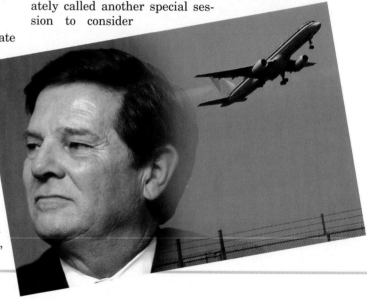

The Constitution also provides special roles for the states in the selection of national government officials. The states decide who can vote for members of the U.S. House of Representatives (Article I, Section 2), and draw the boundaries of House districts. (See "The Rise of Partisan Conflict" for a story that illustrates how contentious the drawing of House district lines has become.) Each state is given two senators (Article V) who were, until 1913, to be chosen by the state legislatures rather than by the voters (Article I, Section 3; altered by the Seventeenth Amendment). And the states play a key part in the complicated electoral college system of choosing a president in which each state has votes equal to the number of its senators and representatives combined, with the president elected by a majority of *electoral* votes, not a majority of popular votes (Article II, Section 1).

the same redistricting plan, Democrats fled the state once more. This second exile did not last very long. Faced with mounting public ridicule and negative news media commentary, the senators returned, first in a trickle, then in a wave. With a quorum no longer at issue, and the legislature solidly in their hands, Texas Republicans passed a new redistricting plan that experts predict will result in the gain in the 2004 elections of at least five Republican seats in the Texas delegation to the U.S. House of Representatives.

What's at Stake? Tom DeLay had a strong incentive to intervene in a process that is a state responsibility under the U.S. Constitution and one in which federal officials have generally feared to tread; the party balance in Congress has been so close in recent national elections that the gain or loss of but a handful of seats in the House and Senate in a congressional election means the difference between controlling Congress and the national legislative agenda and watching from the sidelines as the minority party. In such an environment, each party feels that it must do what it has to do to gain an advantage over the other party. Drawing district lines in a way that enhances the electoral chances of your party's candidates is an especially powerful and commonly used tool in each party's arsenal—as you will see in more detail in Chapter 11—and each party tends to use it rather ruthlessly when it controls the state government. What is unusual in the Texas case is that redistricting had just been completed prior to the 2002 elections. Normally, redistricting is done only once each decade in the period immediately following the release of census results. However, Republicans went ahead and did it a second time. If the practice is allowed by the courts, we may eventually reach the point where redistricting occurs each time that party control of state government changes.

Is This Good for Democracy? It is fairly unusual for national party leaders to intervene in matters that are the province of the states under the Constitution. Nevertheless, given the enormous national stakes that are involved in redistricting decisions—because redistricting can have profound effects on the party balance in the House of Representatives—it is hardly surprising. • Do you believe that changing House district boundaries is a reasonable thing to do, or do you think it undermines people's faith in the legitimacy of elections? • Do you think there are better ways to draw district lines that do not involve the parties? In Iowa, for example, a nonpartisan commission makes these decisions. • Does this appeal to you? • Why?

> **Partisanship** refers to the tendency in American politics to strongly favor the candidates, elected officials, and policies of one's own party and to strongly disfavor those of the opposing party. We believe that partisanship has dramatically increased in recent years in the United States and has had important impacts on the way politics is practiced and the policies that the federal government produces. This is the first of several boxed features titled **The Rise of Partisan Conflict** that examine these issues and ask about their effects on democracy in the United States.

Sources: Headline from the Associated Press, May 14, 2003. Additional information from "A New Low in the Abuse of Rules for Partisan Advantage," *The Economist*, October 18, 2003, p. 34; Ralph Blumenthal, "Texas Democrats Look at New Map and Point Out Victims," *The New York Times*, October 14, 2003, p. A12.

Relations Among the States

The Constitution also regulates relations among the states (these state-to-state relations are sometimes called **horizontal federalism**). Article IV of the Constitution is particularly important in this regard (see Table 3.1). For example, each state is required to give "full faith and credit" to the public acts, records, and judicial proceedings of every other state. This means that private contractual or financial agreements among people or companies in one state are valid in all the other states and that civil judgments by the courts of one state must be recognized by the others. Because of this constitutional provision, people in one state cannot evade financial obligations—for example, credit card or department store debts, alimony and child-support payments—by moving to another state.

horizontal federalism
Term used to refer to relationships among the states.

TABLE 3.1 • Constitutional Underpinnings of Federalism

Provisions	Where to Find Them in the Constitution	What They Mean
Supremacy of the national government in its own sphere	Supremacy clause: Article VI	The supremacy clause establishes that federal laws and the Constitution take precedence over state laws and constitutions.
Limitations on national government powers and reservation of powers to the states	Enumerated national powers: Article I, Section 8; Limits on national powers: Article I, Section 9; Article IV, Section 3; Eleventh Amendment Bill of Rights: First through Tenth Amendments Reservation clause: Tenth Amendment	The powers of the federal government are laid out specifically in the Constitution, as are strict limitations on the power of the federal government. Powers not specifically spelled out are reserved to the states or to the people.
Limitations on state powers	Original restrictions: Article I, Section 10 Civil War Amendments: Thirteenth through Fifteenth Amendments	The Constitution places strict limitations on the power of the states in particular areas of activity.
State role in national government	Ratification of Constitution: Article VII Amendment of Constitution: Article V Election of representatives: Article I, Section 2 and Section 4 Two senators from each state: Article I, Section 3 No deprivation of state suffrage in Senate: Article V Choice of senators: Article I, Section 3 (however, see Seventeenth Amendment) Election of president: Article II, Section 1 (however, see Twelfth Amendment)	The states' role in national affairs is clearly laid out. Rules for voting and electing representatives, senators, and the president are defined so that state governments play a part.
Regulation of relations among states	Full faith and credit: Article IV, Section 1 Privileges and immunities: Article IV, Section 2	Constitutional rules ensure that the states must respect each other's legal actions

Web Exploration
Regional Variation and Federalism

Issue: Federalism seems most appropriate where there is substantial variation among regions of a nation.

Site: You can examine how much variation exists in the United States by going to the *Statistical Abstracts of the United States* on our Website at **www.ablongman.com/greenberg**. In the "Web Explorations" section for Chapter 3, open "Regional Variation and Federalism," then open "states." Select "state rankings." Compare your own state with three or four others from different geographical regions of the United States on issues such as education, income, population growth, immigration, crime, and the like.

What You've Learned: Given the profile of your state compared with others, are the differences great enough to support the need for greater autonomy for your state government, or would national rule making and policies make more sense?

HINT: If the differences are significant, from your point of view, federalism would make a lot of sense. Religious differences seem especially important to many people.

The "full faith and credit" provision raises some intriguing questions. Currently, one of the most explosive concerns same-sex marriages. If one state legalizes same-sex marriages, does the married status of couples hold when they move to another state? In other words, do all the states have to recognize same-sex marriages if one state makes them legal? After it appeared that the state of Hawaii might approve same-sex marriages in the mid-1990s (Hawaii voters and its state legislature and high court, however, subsequently rejected this possibility), 30 states passed laws to immunize themselves against such a fundamental transformation in marriage law. Then, in 1996, Congress passed the Defense of Marriage Act, which denied federal benefits (such as Medicaid and Medicare) for spouses in same-sex marriages and authorized states that wished to do so to enact legislation barring recognition of same-sex marriages from other states. In 2003, the Massachusetts Supreme Court ruled that same-sex marriages were legal in the state, setting off alarm bells in many other states and in Washington. The issue of whether same-sex marriages performed in Massachusetts must be recognized under the "full faith and credit" provision of the Constitution will no doubt eventually find its way to the U.S. Supreme Court.

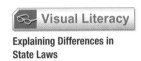

Visual Literacy

Explaining Differences in State Laws

Article IV also specifies that the citizens of each state are entitled to all the "privileges and immunities" of the citizens in the several states. That means that whatever citizenship rights a person has in one state apply in the other states as well. For example, because of this provision, out-of-state residents have the same access to state courts as in-state residents, as well as an equal right to own property and to be protected by the police.

Agreements among a group of states to solve mutual problems, called **interstate compacts,** requires the consent of Congress. The framers inserted this provision (Article I, Section 10) into the Constitution as a way to prevent the emergence of coalitions of states that might threaten federal authority or the union itself. Interstate compacts in force today cover a wide range of cooperative state activities. For example, New York and New Jersey created and Congress approved a compact to create the Port of New York Authority. Other compacts among states include agreements to cooperate on matters such as pollution control, crime prevention, transportation, and disaster planning.

interstate compacts

Agreements among states to cooperate on solving mutual problems; requires approval by Congress.

The Evolution of American Federalism

It took a long time after the adoption of the Constitution for the present federal system to emerge. There were and continue to be ebbs and flows in the nature of the relationship between the states and national government and in the relative power of the states and the federal government as they interacted with one another.[5] Eventually, however, the national government gained ground. There are many reasons why this happened:

- Economic crises and problems generated pressures on the government in Washington to do something to help fix the national economy. The Great Depression in the 1930s is the primary example, but even today, we expect the president, Congress, and the Federal Reserve to competently manage national economic affairs, something the states cannot do for themselves.

- War and the preparation for war are also important spurs to national-level actions, rather than state-level ones, because it is only the government in Washington that can raise an army and a navy, generate sufficient revenues to pay for military campaigns, and coordinate the productive resources of the nation to make sustained war possible. It is no accident, then, that each of our major wars has served to enhance the power of government in Washington: the Civil War, World Wars I and II, the Korean War, the Vietnam War, and the new war on terrorism.

• Finally, a number of problems emerged over the course of our history that most political leaders and the public believed could be solved most effectively by the national government rather than by 50 separate state governments: air and water pollution; unsafe food, drugs, and consumer products; the denial of civil rights for racial minorities; anti-competitive practices by some large corporations; poverty; and more.

The Perpetual Debate About the Nature of American Federalism

From the very beginnings of our nation, two political philosophies have contended with one another over the nature of American federalism and the role to be played by the national government. These are generally referred to as the nationalist position and the states' rights position.

nationalist position
The view of American federalism that holds that the Constitution created a system in which the national government is supreme, relative to the states, and that granted to it a broad range of powers and responsibilities.

The Nationalist Position Nationalists believe that the Constitution was formed by a compact among the people to create a single national community, pointing to the powerful phrase that opens the preamble: "We the People of the United States" (not "We the States"). Nationalists also point to the clear expression in the preamble of the purposes for which "we the people" formed a new government, namely to "create a more perfect union . . . and to promote the General Welfare." Also important in the nationalist brief are provisions in the Constitution that point toward a strong central government with expan-

How to control illegal immigration across the U.S.–Mexican border, and what to do about those who make it across, have become contentious issues between several states and the federal government.

sive responsibilities, namely, the "supremacy clause" in Article VI and the "elastic" or **"necessary and proper" clause** in Article I, Section 8. Not surprisingly, proponents of the nationalist position have advocated an active national government with the capacity and the will to tackle whatever problems might emerge to threaten the peace and prosperity of the United States or the general welfare of its people. Alexander Hamilton, Chief Justice John Marshall, Abraham Lincoln, Woodrow Wilson, the two Roosevelts, and most modern liberals are generally associated with the nationalist position.

The States' Rights Position Proponents of the states' rights position argue that the Constitution was created as a compact among the states and that the framers meant for the states to be coequal with the national government. They base their argument on a number of foundations. They note, for instance, that the Constitution was written by representatives of the states; that it was ratified by the states and not by a vote of the public; and that the process for amending the Constitution requires the affirmative votes of three-fourths of the states, not three-fourths of the people. They also point out that the Constitution mandates equal representation of states in the Senate and requires that the president be elected by the electoral votes of the states. States' rights proponents say that the prominent role of the states in our system of government is also indicated in Article IV, Section 3 (which says that states are inviolate), and in the Tenth Amendment (the "reservation" clause, discussed above).

Not surprisingly, proponents of the states' rights position have argued that the Constitution created a form of government in which the national government is strictly limited in size and responsibility and in which states retain broad autonomy in the conduct of their own affairs. Popular among states' rights proponents is the concept of **dual federalism,** which suggests that there are distinct, nonoverlapping areas of responsibility for the national government and the state governments, and that each level of government is sovereign in its own sphere. Thomas Jefferson, John C. Calhoun, the New England and Southern secessionists, the southern resistors to the civil rights revolution, and many contemporary conservatives are associated with this view of federalism.

We shall see in the pages ahead that the nationalist view has prevailed over the long haul of American history (see Figure 3.2). However, the states' rights view has always been and remains today a vital position from which to oppose too much power and responsibility in the government in Washington.

Federalism Before the Civil War

In the late 1790s, during the administration of John Adams, Thomas Jefferson's Republicans deeply resented the Alien and Sedition Acts, which the Federalists used to punish political dissent by followers of Jefferson. In response, Jefferson and Madison secretly authored the Virginia and Kentucky Resolutions, which declared that the states did not have to obey unconstitutional national laws and left it to the states to decide what was unconstitutional. In this case, the Republicans, representing the more agricultural South, were advocating states' rights against a national government run by the more merchant-oriented Federalists of the Northeast. About a decade later, however, the merchants of New England used the southerners' own arguments to oppose President Madison's War of 1812 against Britain, which they felt interfered with their trade. Neither of these efforts at **nullification** prevailed.

necessary and proper clause
Article I, Section 8, of the Constitution, also known as the *elastic clause*; gives Congress the authority to make whatever laws are necessary and proper to carry out its enumerated responsibilities.

states' rights position
The view of American federalism that holds that the Constitution created a system of dual sovereignty in which the national government and the state governments are sovereign in their own spheres.

dual federalism
Federalism in which the powers of the states and the national government are neatly separated like the sections of a layer cake.

nullification
An attempt by states to declare national laws or actions null and void.

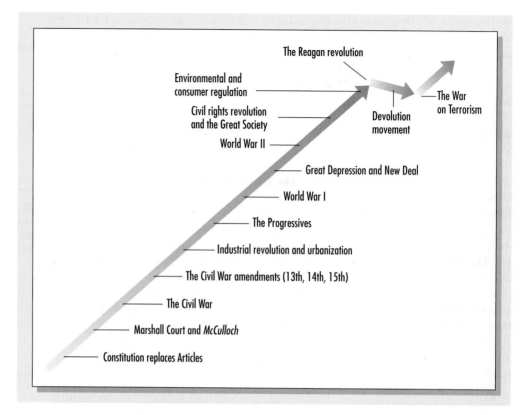

FIGURE 3.2 • Landmarks on the Road of Rising Federal Power and Responsibilities

Over the course of American history, power and responsibilities in our federal system have flowed to the national government. The trend toward devolution of the 1980s and 1990s most likely has been reversed somewhat by the events of Nine-Eleven and the subsequent war on terrorism at home and abroad.

The Pre-Civil War Supreme Court on Federalism   One crucial question about federalism in the early years of the United States concerned who, if anyone, would enforce the supremacy clause. Who would make sure that the U.S. laws and Constitution were actually the "supreme law of the land," controlling state laws? The answer turned out to be the U.S. Supreme Court, but this answer emerged only gradually and haltingly as the Court established its power within the federal system. Only after the strong-willed and subtle John Marshall became chief justice and, in 1803, established the Supreme Court's authority to declare *national* laws unconstitutional did the Supreme Court turn to the question of national power over the states. In *Fletcher* v. *Peck* (1810), it established the power of judicial review over the states, holding a state law unconstitutional under the U.S. Constitution.[6] Chief Justice Marshall cleverly avoided explicit discussion of the Court's power of judicial review over state laws. He simply took it for granted and used it.

The Supreme Court also provided crucial legal justification for the expansion of national government power in the important case of *McCulloch* v. *Maryland* (1819). The *McCulloch* case arose because the state of Maryland had imposed a tax on notes issued by the Bank of the United States, which had been incorporated by Congress in 1816. The U.S. government argued that such a tax on a federal entity was invalid. Maryland replied that the incorporation of the bank had been unconstitutional, exceeding the powers of Congress, and that, in any case, the states could tax whatever they wanted within their own borders. But Chief Justice Marshall upheld the constitutionality of the bank's incorporation and its immunity from taxation, and in the process made a major statement justifying extensive national authority.[7]

In the Court's decision, Marshall declared that the Constitution emanated from the sovereign people. The people had made their national government supreme over all rivals within the sphere of its powers, and those powers must be construed generously if they were to be sufficient for the "various crises" of the age to come. Congress had the power to incorporate the bank under the clause of Article I, Section 8, authorizing Congress to make all laws "necessary and proper" for carrying into execution its named powers. Moreover, Maryland's tax was invalid because "the power to tax involves the power to destroy," which would defeat the national government's supremacy. Justice Marshall's broad reading of the *necessary and proper* clause laid the foundation for an expansion of what the national government could do in the years ahead. He made it clear that states would not be allowed to interfere.

The Supreme Court also ruled that provisions of the U.S. Constitution *excluded* the states from acting in certain areas where they might interfere with federal statutes or authority. According to this doctrine known as **preemption,** which remains in place today, states cannot act in certain matters when the national government has done so.

preemption
Exclusion of the states from actions that might interfere with federal authority or statutes.

In the first half of the nineteenth century, then, the Supreme Court played an important role in affirming the power of the national government relative to the states found in the supremacy clause. The Civil War accelerated this trend toward growing national power.

The Civil War and the Expansion of National Power

The Civil War profoundly affected the relationship between the states and the national government. First, the complete northern victory and unconditional southern surrender decisively established that the Union was indissoluble; states could not withdraw or secede. Hardly any American now questions the permanence of the Union, although it is interesting to compare this attitude with our present-day support for the right of new countries to secede from existing countries, such as the secession of Croatia, Slovenia, and Bosnia from Yugoslavia.

One important principle of American federalism was settled by the Civil War: The nation is indissoluble; no state or group of states can decide on its own to withdraw from it. Establishing that principle required a bloody contest of arms. Here, union dead litter the field at Gettysburg.

Civil War Amendments
The Thirteenth, Fourteenth, and Fifteenth Amendments to the Constitution adopted immediately after the Civil War.

due process clause
The section of the Fourteenth Amendment that prohibits states from depriving anyone of life, liberty, or property "without due process of law," a guarantee against arbitrary or unfair government action.

equal protection clause
The section of the Fourteenth Amendment that provides equal protection of the laws to all citizens.

Second, passage of what has become known as the **Civil War Amendments** resulted in constitutional changes that subordinated the states to certain new national standards, enforced by the central government. For example, the Thirteenth Amendment abolished slavery, and the Fifteenth gave former male slaves a constitutional right to vote. (This right was enforced by the national government for a short time after the Civil War; it was then widely ignored until the 1965 Voting Rights Act.)

Moreover, the Fourteenth Amendment (1868) included broad language going well beyond the slave issue: it declared that *no state* shall "deprive any person of life, liberty, or property, without due process of law; nor deny to any person within its jurisdiction the equal protection of the laws." The **due process clause** eventually became the vehicle by which the Supreme Court ruled that many civil liberties in the Bill of Rights, which originally protected people only against the national government, also provided protections against the states. And the **equal protection clause** eventually became the foundation for protecting the rights of blacks, women, and other categories of people against discrimination by state or local governments.

Expanded National Activity Since the Civil War

Since the Civil War, and especially during the twentieth century, the activities of the national government expanded greatly, so that they now touch on almost every aspect of daily life and are thoroughly entangled with state government activities.

The Late Nineteenth Century to World War I

During the late nineteenth century, the national government was increasingly active in administering western lands, subsidizing economic development (granting railroads enormous tracts of land along their transcontinental lines), helping farmers, and beginning to regulate business, particularly through the Interstate Commerce Act of 1887 and the Sherman Antitrust Act of 1890. The national government became still more active with Woodrow Wilson's New Freedom domestic legislation in 1913 and 1914, and with the great economic and military effort of World War I. During that war, for example, the War Industries Board engaged in a form of economic planning whose orders and regulations covered a substantial number of the nation's manufacturing firms.

The New Deal and World War II

Still more important, however, was Franklin Roosevelt's New Deal of the 1930s. In response to the Great Depression, the New Deal created many new national regulatory agencies to supervise various aspects of business, including communications (the Federal Communications Commission, or FCC), airlines (the Civil Aeronautics Board, or CAB), financial markets (the Securities and Exchange Commission, or SEC), utilities (the Federal Power Commission, or FPC), and labor-management relations (the National Labor Relations Board, or NLRB). The New Deal also brought national government spending to such areas as welfare and relief, which had previously been reserved almost entirely to the states, and established the Social Security pension system.

World War II involved a total economic and military mobilization to fight Germany and Japan. Not surprisingly, directing that mobilization, as well as collecting taxes to support it, planning for production of war materials, and bringing on board the employees to accomplish all of this, was centered in Washington, D.C., not in the states.

The Works Project Administration (WPA), created by Franklin Roosevelt as part of the New Deal, put many unemployed Americans to work on federal building projects during the Great Depression.

The Post-War Period   Ever since World War II, the federal government has spent nearly twice as much per year as all of the states and localities put together. Much of the money has gone in direct payments to individuals (through such items as Social Security benefits), and for national defense, especially during the height of the Cold War and during the years of the Vietnam conflict.

Two other trends in the last third of the twentieth century enhanced the role of the national government relative to the states. The first was the civil rights revolution (discussed in Chapters 8 and 16), and the second was the regulatory revolution, especially regulation related to environmental protection (discussed in Chapter 17). With respect to both, national standards, often fashioned by bureaucrats under broad legislative mandates and watched over by federal courts, were imposed on both states and localities. The civil rights revolution also had a great deal to do with the creation of Lyndon Johnson's Great Society program designed both to alleviate poverty and politically empower the poor and racial minorities. The Great Society not only increased the level of domestic spending but also increased the federal role in the political lives of states and localities.

The Supreme Court's Support for Nationalism   For several decades, beginning in the late nineteenth century, the U.S. Supreme Court resisted the growth in national government power to regulate business. In 1895, for example, it said that the Sherman Antitrust Act could not forbid monopolies in manufacturing, since manufacturing affected interstate commerce only "indirectly." In 1918, the Court struck down as unconstitutional a national law regulating child labor. During the 1930s, the Supreme Court declared

Timeline

Federalism and the Supreme Court

unconstitutional such important New Deal measures as the National Recovery Act and the Agricultural Adjustment Act.[8]

After 1937, perhaps chastened by President Roosevelt's attempt to enlarge the Supreme Court and appoint more friendly justices, the Court became a nationalizing force, immediately upholding essential elements of the New Deal, including the Social Security Act and the National Labor Relations Act. Since that time, and until quite recently, the Court has upheld virtually every piece of national legislation that has come before it.

An important example is the Civil Rights Act of 1964, which rests on a very broad interpretation of the Constitution's commerce clause. In the 1964 act, the national government asserted a power to forbid discrimination at lunch counters and other public accommodations on the grounds that they are engaged in interstate commerce: They serve food imported from out of state. State economies are so closely tied to each other that by this standard, practically every economic transaction everywhere affects interstate commerce and is therefore subject to national legislative power.

Resurgence of the States in the 1990s

During the 1990s, there were a number of indications that the states were becoming more important in the American federal system. First, the states accounted for an ever-increasing share of public spending in the United States, suggesting that they were becoming more active in providing the wide range of government services the public demands. Second, the states accounted for an ever-increasing share of public employees in the United States; while state (and local) government employment grew during the 1990s, federal government employment shrank, suggesting that government service delivery was shifting to the states. Moreover, according to many scholars and political observers, state governments began to capture a rising share of the talented people who enter government service, both in elected office and in state bureaucracies.[9] None of this would have happened unless the states were becoming increasingly important as locations for policy innovations and delivery of government services.

Behind the new vitality of the states within American federalism was the growing national consensus during the 1980s and 1990s about the virtues of **devolution,** the idea that more power in the federal system should be in the hands of the states. Public opinion surveys, for example, showed that a substantial majority of Americans believed that state governments were more effective and more trustworthy than the government in Washington and more likely to be responsive to the people. And Americans said that they wanted state governments to do more and the federal government to do less.[10]

The Rehnquist Court has been especially enthusiastic about increasing the power of the states and decreasing that of the national government. It overruled a number of federal actions and laws on the ground that the federal government had exceeded its constitutional powers, reversing more than half a century of decisions favoring an increased federal government role. In 1995, for example, the Court overturned federal legislation banning guns from the area around schools and legislation requiring background checks for gun buyers, arguing that both represented too broad a use of the commerce power in the Constitution. The Court used similar language in 2000 when it invalidated part of the Violence Against Women Act and in 2001 when it did the same to the Americans with Disabilities Act. The Court also decided two cases in which it ruled that states could not be sued for violating federal rules and laws. It based the decision on a concept of "state sovereign immunity" that most constitutional scholars had never heard of and that considerably increased the autonomy of the states. In a 5–4 decision in the case *Federal Maritime Commission* v. *South Carolina* (2002), the court reaffirmed this controversial doctrine.

devolution

The delegation of power by the central government to state or local bodies.

You Are a Federal Judge

During the 1990s, responsibility for several traditional federal programs was shifted to the states. The most important of these involved welfare. Working under broad federal guidelines and partially subsidized by welfare block grants, each of the states instituted its own "welfare to work" program.

President Clinton was also an enthusiastic devotee of devolution, freely granting waivers from federal regulations to the states for experimenting with new forms of welfare, boasting of cuts in federal government employment, and touting the benefits of state government. And the Republican majority in the 104th Congress, working with President Clinton (but few from his party), passed legislation restricting "unfunded mandates" (about which we will have more to say later) and transferring welfare responsibility to the states.

Terrorism and the Resurgence of the Federal Government The terrorist attacks of September 11, 2001, and the subsequent war on terrorism helped refocus the nation's attention on national leaders in Washington, D.C. As in all wartime situations during our country's history, war and the mobilization for war require centralized coordination and planning. This tendency toward nationalism during war will probably be further exaggerated by the perceived need for homeland security, with the national government in Washington playing a larger role in areas such as law enforcement, intelligence gathering, bank oversight (to track terrorist money), public health (to protect against possible bioterrorism), and more.

Changing American Federalism Over the course of our history, there has been a perceptible shift of power and responsibility to the national government in Washington.[11] We summarize that history in Figure 3.3. Imagine, if you will, a continuum of forms of government ranging from the pure unitary form on one end to the pure confederational form at the other end, with the federal form as a midpoint between the two. We suggest that our original Constitution, though fundamentally federal in its design, was tilted slightly

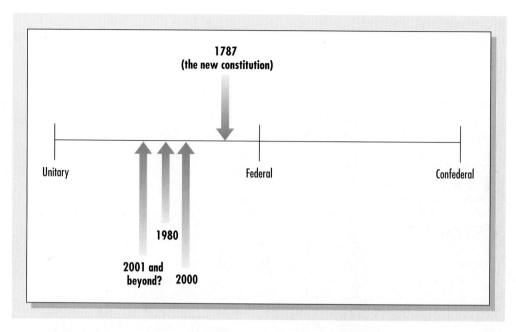

FIGURE 3.3 ● The Evolution of American Federalism

Over the years, American federalism has become more centralized in power and responsibilities, meaning that the nation has shifted slightly toward the unitary end of the Unitary-Confederal continuum. The war on terrorism may move the United States even further toward the unitary end.

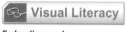

Federalism and Regulations

toward central government power. By 1980, we also suggest, the United States had shifted even further toward centralized government power. In the 1990s, states regained some lost ground. In all probability, the war on terrorism at home and abroad is likely to rekindle the long-term trend toward national government preeminence. Note, however, that the 2001 arrow on the continuum is still placed well to the right of unitary government, suggesting that the states still play, and will continue to play, a very important role in the way Americans govern themselves.

Today's federalism is very different from what it was in the 1790s or early 1800s. One major difference is that the national government is dominant in many policy areas; it calls many shots for the states. Another difference is that state and national government powers and activities have become deeply intertwined and entangled. The old, simple metaphor for federalism was a "layer cake": a system of **dual federalism** in which state and national powers were neatly divided into separate layers, with each level of government going its own way, unencumbered by the other. If we stay with bakery images, a much more accurate metaphor for today's federalism is a "marble cake," in which elements of national and state influence swirl around each other, without very clear boundaries.[12] Much of this intertwining is due to financial links among the national and state governments, which we address in the next section.

dual federalism

An interpretation of federalism in which the states and the national government have separate jurisdictions and responsibilities.

National Grants-in-Aid to the States

One of the most important elements in modern American federalism is the grant of money from the national government to state and local governments, which has been used to increase national government influence over what the states and localities do. These grants have grown from small beginnings to form a substantial part of government budgets.

Origin and Growth of Grants

National government grants to the states began at least as early as the 1787 Northwest Ordinance. The U.S. government granted land for government buildings, schools, and colleges in the Northwest Territory and imposed various regulations, such as forbidding the importation of any new slaves. During the early nineteenth century, the national government provided some land grants to the states for roads, canals, and railroads, as well as a little cash for militias; after 1862, it helped establish agricultural colleges. Some small cash-grant programs were begun around 1900 for agriculture, vocational education, and highways.[13]

However, it was during the 1950s, 1960s, and 1970s, under both Republican and Democratic administrations, that federal grants to the states really took off. Such programs as President Dwight Eisenhower's interstate highway system and President Lyndon Johnson's Great Society poured money into the states.[14] After a pause during the Reagan presidency, grants began to increase again in the 1990s (see Figure 3.4). National grant money to the states increased because Congress sought to deal with many nationwide

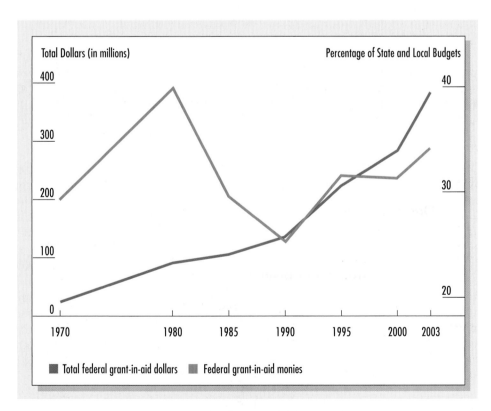

FIGURE 3.4 • The Growth in Federal Grants-in-Aid to States and Localities

Federal grants-in-aid to state and local governments grew throughout the 1960s and 1970s. During the Reagan presidency in the 1980s, the rate of increase in total grant dollars slowed a bit, and federal grants covered an ever-shrinking proportion of state and local budgets. After that, grants-in-aid began growing again at a healthy clip.

Lyndon Johnson visits Job Corps sites. The Job Corps was part of Johnson's Great Society of the 1960s, which relied heavily on categorical grants to state and local governments.

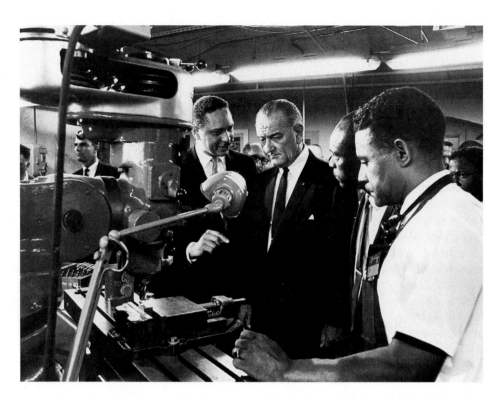

problems—especially interstate highways, poverty, crime, and pollution—by setting policy at the national level and providing money from national tax revenues while having state and local officials carry out the policies.

Categorical Grants

categorical grants
Federal aid to states and localities clearly specifying what the money can be used for.

Many of the new programs were established through **categorical grants**, which give the states money but clearly specify the category of activity for which the money has to be spent and often define rather precisely how the program should work. For example, the Clean Air Act of 1970 and the Medicaid program of 1965 provided large amounts of money along with specific instructions on how to use it.

As the new programs were developed and enacted, there was much talk about a new system of **cooperative federalism.** Soon, however, conflicts between the national and the state governments emerged. In some cases, when national rules and guidelines were vague, state and local governments used the money for purposes different from those Congress intended. When the rules were tightened up, some state and local governments complained about "red tape." And if state and local governments were bypassed, they complained that their authority had been undermined.

cooperative federalism
Federalism in which the powers of the states and the national government are so intertwined that public policies can happen only if the two levels of government cooperate.

Block Grants and Revenue Sharing

block grants
Federal grants to the states to be used for general activities.

The Republican Nixon and Ford administrations eased national control, first instituting **block grants** (which give money for more general purposes and with fewer rules than categorical grant programs), then **general revenue sharing**,

general revenue sharing
Federal aid to the states without any conditions on how the money is to be spent.

which distributed money to the states with no federal controls at all. President Nixon spoke of a "New Federalism" and pushed to increase these kinds of grants with few strings attached. They often provided money under an automatic formula related to the statistical characteristics of each state or locality, such as the number of needy residents, the total size of the population, or the average income level.

Disputes frequently arise when these formulas benefit one state or region rather than another. Because statistical counts by the census affect how much money the states and localities get, census counts themselves have become the subject of political conflict. Illinois, New York, and Chicago sued the Census Bureau for allegedly undercounting their populations, especially the urban poor, in the 1990 census. (See "By the Numbers" for more information about how population counts are done and why it matters.)

Block grants—and especially revenue sharing—reached a peak at the end of the 1970s, when they constituted about one-quarter of the total **grants-in-aid.** But then they fell out of favor. Increasing numbers of strings were attached to the money, and general revenue sharing was completely ended in 1987. Although block grants are still important, a good deal more of federal government money distributed to the states is in the form of categorical grants (see Figure 3.4).

grants-in-aid
Funds from the national government to state and local governments to help pay for programs created by the national government.

Debates About Federal Money and Control

Most contemporary conflicts about federalism concern not just money but also control.

Conditions on Aid   As we have seen, many categorical grant-in-aid programs require that the states spend federal money only in certain restricted ways. Increasingly, even general block grants have carried **conditions.** In theory, these conditions are "voluntary" because the states could refuse to accept the aid. But in practice, there is no clear line between incentives and coercion. Because the states cannot generally afford to give up federal money, they have to accept the conditions attached to it.

conditions
Provisions in federal assistance requiring that state and local governments follow certain policies in order to obtain federal funds.

The states depend on federal aid, often based on formulas based on census figures, to help them take care of the homeless. But when 2000 census takers failed to count a large number of homeless people, cities received less money in national grants.

By the Numbers

How do we know how many people there are in each of the states?

Utah officials were angry. Convinced that the counting method used for the 2000 census had undercounted the number of people residing in the state, thereby "robbing" them of a congressional seat, they sued the U.S. Census Bureau.

How can something as simple as counting people become so controversial? And why are these census figures so important to states, anyway?

Why It Matters: The Constitution specifies that every ten years, a census will be taken of the population of the United States. One purpose of the census is to determine how the finite number of seats in the House of Representatives (435) will be divided among the states, based on the size of their populations. A state's population also determines how much federal money (for example, highway money) it will get. Moreover, counts of certain categories of people, like the poor, determine how much aid (for example, Medicaid) the state will receive.

The Story Behind the Number: For most of our nation's history, the Census Bureau hired people to go door-to-door all across the United States—from isolated farms to packed apartment buildings—to conduct a direct count of the population. Many people were missed in this process. Some were not home when the census takers came by; others lived in high crime neighborhoods where census takers did not want to venture; some had no home other than a crude shelter under a highway overpass. Recent im-

migrants had trouble communicating in English, and illegal aliens did not necessarily want to be found by census takers.

Indeed, the undercounted population in every recent census has been comprised mainly of racial minorities, recent immigrants, the homeless, and the undocumented. This pattern has generated complaints from a wide range of people and organizations: advocates of the poor who want more federal government monies directed to the problem of poverty in each state; civil rights organizations that believe that racial minorities are underrepresented in the House of Representatives; and Democratic Party politicians who believe that a more accurate count would benefit their party (the assumption being that lower income people, racial minorities, and recent immigrants tend to vote for Democrats).

In an attempt to remedy these undercount problems, the Census Bureau wanted to use "statistical sampling" of the population to fill in the gaps. However, the Supreme Court ruled in 1999 that the Bureau could not do so for purposes of reapportioning congressional seats, and President Bush announced that sampling could not be used to determine how much federal money the states would get. As an alternative, the Bureau has increasingly relied on a statistical procedure called "imputing."

Calculating Population Size and Characteristics: Although Census Bureau statisticians have been using "imputing" in limited ways since the 1940s to fill in the gaps left by the inevitable undercounting, they relied much more on it for the 2000 census. In imputing, estimates are made about the characteristics of people living in a household where the Bureau has been unable to collect information. The estimates are based on what their neighbors are like (whether they are poor or rich, white or African American, and so on).

Some of the most important provisions of the 1964 Civil Rights Act, for example, are those that declare that no federal aid of any kind can be used in ways that discriminate against people on grounds of race, gender, religion, or national origin. Thus, the enormous program of national aid for elementary and secondary education, which began in 1965, became a powerful lever for forcing schools to desegregate.

The national government uses its money to influence many diverse kinds of policies. During the energy crisis of the 1970s, all states were required to

In the 2000 census, using imputing, almost 6 million people who had not actually been counted were included in the nation's population total. In some states, most notably in those with large numbers of racial minorities and immigrants (including California, Arizona, New Mexico, and Texas), more than 3 percent of the state's total population was imputed.

This brings us back to the state of Utah. Utah's suit claimed that the Census Bureau had illegally imputed tens of thousands of additional people to the state of North Carolina, resulting in North Carolina receiving the congressional seat that properly should have gone to Utah. Unfortunately for Utah, the Supreme Court approved imputing in 2002.

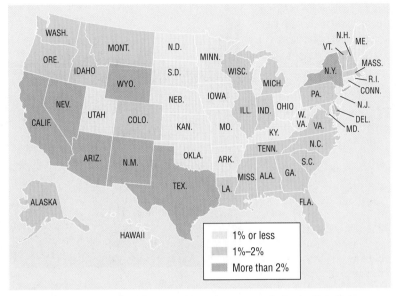

Percentage of People Imputed by the U.S. Census Bureau in Its Population Totals, by State

Source: The Wall Street Journal, August 30, 2001.

Imputing Criticized: Although most statisticians believe that imputing is a reasonable way to solve the problem of under-counting, the technique has its critics:

- The Utah suit claimed, and others agree, that imputing—much like more standard sampling—makes statistical inferences about parts of the population rather than counting people directly, as implied by the wording in the Constitution (Article I, Section 2).
- Imputing assumes that neighborhoods are homogenous; it is based on the assumption that a household's characteristics can be estimated from the characteristics of its neighbors. Members of several minority groups who tend to live in less segregated circumstances—Asians and Pacific Islanders, for example—may find themselves undercounted.

What to Watch For: Official statistics are often published in both "adjusted" and "unadjusted" forms. "Adjusted" means that the raw information has been corrected in one way or another. Usually, the reasons for doing so are very reasonable and defensible. You might want to look at the documentation that is associated with all government statistical information to learn how the numbers have been "adjusted."

What Do You Think?   In your view, does it make sense to depend on the census for methods of enumerating that were fashioned by the framers of the Constitution? Is there a reason to keep to traditional methods? Or does the greater accuracy introduced by advances in statistical computing—either imputing or sampling—argue for a different method for conducting the census?

impose a 55-mile-per-hour speed limit or lose a portion of their highway assistance funds. The requirement was finally repealed in 1995. Similarly, in 1984, all states were required to set a minimum drinking age of 21 or have their highway aid cut by 15 percent.

Mandates   The national government often imposes a **mandate,** or demand, that the states carry out certain policies even when little or no national government aid is offered. (An "unfunded" mandate involves no aid at all or less

mandate
A formal order from the national government that the states carry out certain policies.

Industrial pollution often affects the people of more than one state and requires the participation of the national government to clean up the mess and prevent recurrences.

aid than compliance will cost.) Mandates have been especially important in the areas of civil rights and the environment. Most civil rights policies flow from the equal protection clause of the Fourteenth Amendment to the U.S. Constitution or from national legislation that imposes uniform national standards. Most environmental regulations also come from the national government, since problems of dirty air, polluted water, and acid rain spill across state boundaries. Many civil rights and environmental regulations, therefore, are enforced by the federal courts.

Federal courts have, for example, mandated expensive reforms of overcrowded state prisons, most notably in Texas. National legislation and regulations have required state governments to provide costly special facilities for the disabled, to set up environmental protection agencies, and to limit the kinds and amounts of pollutants that can be discharged. The states often complain bitterly about federal mandates that require state spending without providing the money.

Cutting back on these "unfunded mandates" was one of the main promises in the Republicans' 1994 Contract with America.[15] The congressional Republicans delivered on their promise early in 1995 with a bill that had bipartisan support in Congress and that President Clinton signed into law. Because it does not apply to past mandates, however, and because it does not ban unfunded mandates but only regulates them (requiring cost-benefit analyses, for example), it is not yet clear how much effect the legislation is having.

U.S. Federalism: Pro and Con

Participation

Is Federalism Dead and Should It Be?

Over the years, from the framing of the U.S. Constitution to the present day, people have offered a number of strong arguments for and against federalism, in contrast to a more unitary system. Let us consider some of these arguments.

Using the Framework

Out-of-State Tuition

I thought that attending a public university would save a lot of money, but it hasn't because I have to pay out-of-state tuition. Why do I have to pay so much money?

Background: All over the United States, students who choose to attend out-of-state public universities pay much higher tuition than state residents. Some educational reformers have suggested that the system be reformed so that students might attend public universities wherever they choose, without financial penalty. They have suggested that, over the long-haul and on average, such a reform would not have much impact on state budgets because students would randomly distribute themselves across state borders. Such proposals have never gotten very far. Taking a broad view of how structural, political linkage, and governmental factors affect this issue will help explain the situation.

Governmental Action

State legislatures decline to pass uniform tuition legislation.

The Supreme Court decides that different tuition rates for in-state and out-of-state residents do not violate the "privileges and immunities" section of Article IV, Section 2, of the Constitution.

Governmental Level

Elected leaders know that voters want access to low cost higher education for state residents. ➡

Elected leaders are not subject to political pressures to change tuition policy. ➡

Elected leaders are concerned with short-term budget issues; high out-of-state tuition allows them to raise part of the higher education budget out of such revenues.

Political Linkages Level

Voters in each state insist on access for their children and the children of their neighbors to low-cost public higher education. ➡

There is little political pressure on elected leaders within the states to lower or eliminate out-of-state tuition, whether from
– Public opinion and voters.
– Parties.
– The mass media.
– Interest groups.
– Social movements. ➡

Out-of-state students rarely vote in the states where they go to school; politicians have no incentive to think seriously about their tuition concerns.

Structural Level

The states are mainly responsible for education in our federal system; national tuition reform would require agreements among all the states.

75

Pro: Diversity of Needs

The oldest and most important argument in favor of decentralized government is that in a large and diverse country, needs and wants and conditions differ from one place to another. Why not let different states enact different policies to meet their own needs? (See the "Using the Framework" feature on why states can set their own tuition levels, including those for out-of-state students.)

Con: The Importance of National Standards

However, the needs or desires that different states pursue may not be worthy ones. Political scientist William Riker has pointed out that, historically, one of the main effects of federalism was to let white majorities in the southern states enslave and then discriminate against black people, without interference from the North.[16] Perhaps it is better, in some cases, to insist on national standards that apply everywhere.

You Are a Restaurant Owner

Pro: Closeness to the People

It is sometimes claimed that state governments are closer to the ordinary citizens, who have a better chance to know their officials, to be aware of what they are doing, to contact them, and to hold them responsible for what they do.

Con: Low Visibility and Lack of Popular Control

However, others respond that geographic closeness may not be the real issue. More Americans are better informed about the *national* government than they are about state governments, and more people participate in national than in state elections. When more people know what the government is doing and more people vote, they are better able to insist that the government do what they want. For that reason, responsiveness to ordinary citizens may actually be greater in national government.

Pro: Innovation and Experimentation

When the states have independent power, they can try out new ideas. Individual states can be "laboratories." If the experiments work, other states or the nation as a whole can adopt their ideas, as has happened on such issues as allowing women and 18-year-olds to vote, fighting air pollution, reforming welfare, and dealing with water pollution.[17] To take another important example, welfare reform at the national level followed innovations by several states, with Wisconsin under Governor Tommy Thompson playing a particularly important role.

Likewise, when the national government is controlled by one political party, federalism allows the states with majorities favoring a different party to compensate by enacting different policies. This aspect of diversity in policymaking is related to the Founders' contention that tyranny is less likely when government's power is dispersed. Multiple governments reduce the risks of bad policy or the blockage of the popular will; if things go wrong at one governmental level, they may go right at another.

Con: Spillover Effects and Competition

Diversity and experimentation in policies, however, may not always be good. Divergent regulations can cause bad effects that spill over from one state to another. When factories in the Midwest spew out oxides of nitrogen and sulfur that fall as acid rain in the Northeast, the northeastern states can do nothing about it. Only nationwide rules can solve such problems. Similarly, it is very difficult for cities or local communities in the states to do much about poverty or other social problems.

FIGURE 3.5 ● **Women Legislators in the United States, 2003**

There has been a steady increase in the number of women legislators in the United States over the past three decades or so. Wide variations exist among the states, however, on what proportion of their legislatures are accounted for by women.

Source: National Conference of State Legislatures, 2003.

If a city raises taxes to pay for social programs, businesses and the wealthy may move out of town, and the poor may move in, impoverishing the city.[18]

Pro: Training Ground for Women and Racial Minorities   It is often in politics at the local and state levels that talented women and minority group members have been identified, recruited, and trained for public office (see Figure 3.5). And it is frequently their performance on the job and the visibility provided by state and local offices that launches women and minorities into national politics. Former Congresswoman Barbara Jordan, an African American, made her start in Texas politics. Senator Carol Moseley-Braun was a player in Illinois politics before she made her successful run for the Senate (she lost her bid for a second term, however). Loretta Sanchez was active in Orange County, California, politics before she won a seat in Congress in 1996. J. C. Watts (R–OK), an African American now retired from politics, was elected Oklahoma Corporation Counsel before he won election to the House of Representatives.

What Sort of Federalism?

As the pros and cons indicate, a lot is at stake. It is not likely, however, that Americans will ever have a chance to vote yes or no on the federal system or to choose a unitary government instead. What we can decide is exactly *what sort* of federalism we will have—how much power will go to the states and how much will remain with the national government. Indeed, we may want a fluid system in which the balance of power varies from one kind of policy to another.

How Democratic Are We?

Federalism, Majority Rule, and Political Equality

PROPOSITION: Federalism undermines democracy by getting in the way of majority rule and political equality.

AGREE: Federalism adds complexity to policy-making and makes it difficult for citizens to know which elected leaders to hold responsible for government actions. For example, it is not entirely clear whom citizens ought to hold responsible—state officials or federal government officials—when nothing is done to stop firms from polluting local air and water supplies. Also, citizens are much less informed about what goes on in state governments where many important policies are made. This is hardly surprising, because local news telecasts are more likely to carry news about the national government than state governments. In state-level politics, moreover, popular participation tends to be lower, politics tends to be less visible, and interest groups may have an easier time getting their way—precisely because media attention to such groups is limited. Because the well organized and the affluent have extra influence, political equality is impaired.

DISAGREE: Federalism promotes popular democracy rather than undermining it. It does so by allowing a majority of citizens in each state to exercise control over a range of policies that directly affect them. This is especially important in a country where the populations of the states vary as widely as they do. With diverse populations, with their diverse needs and interests, federalism allows for diverse policies. This is especially true in those many states where citizens can bypass uncooperative legislatures and governors by using the initiative process to put into place new policy and constitutional changes they want. Citizens in many states, for example, forced term limits on officials, even though elected officials were mostly hostile to this reform. In other states, citizens forced changes in affirmative action policies in state colleges and universities.

CONSIDER: • Where do you stand on these two competing positions? • Which level of government do you know the most about? • Which public officials are you most familiar with, state or national? • Which kinds of elected officials, state or national, do you think you might have the most influence with? • Have you ever contacted your member of Congress or your local representative or senator in the state legislature? • If so, which of them, national-level legislators or state-level legislators, were most responsive to your concerns. • If you have never been in touch with such officials, which level of government do you think would be most responsive to you or to a group to which you belong, perhaps on increasing college scholarship assistance in the future?

The balance of power between states and nation has been a very hot issue in recent years, with most Republicans favoring increasing the power of state governments and Democrats favoring retention of national government programs and standards. Over the long term of American history, of course, the nationalist position on federalism rather than the states' rights position has generally prevailed. While some devolution of governmental power oc-

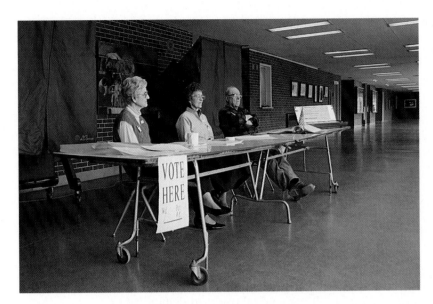

A shift of power and responsibility from the federal level to the states and localities, given low voting turnout in state and local elections, may mean a decrease in the quality of American democracy.

curred in the 1990s, the terrorist attacks on the United States in 2001 and the subsequent war on terrorism may have tilted the balance once again toward the center.

It is important to keep in mind that arguments about federalism do not concern just abstract theories; they affect who wins and who loses valuable benefits. People's opinions about federalism often depend on their interests, their ideologies, and the kinds of things they want government to do.

Summary

Federalism, a system under which political powers are divided between the state and national governments, is a key structural aspect of American politics. Federalism is most frequently found in large, diverse countries. Arguments in favor of federalism have to do with diversity of needs, closeness to the people, experimentation, and innovation. Arguments against federalism involve national standards, popular control, and needs for uniformity.

The U.S. Constitution specifies the powers of the national government and reserves all others (except a few that are specifically forbidden) to the states. The Constitution also provides special roles for the states in adopting and amending the Constitution and in choosing national officials. The precise balance of federalism has evolved over time, with the national government gaining ground as a result of U.S. Supreme Court decisions, the Civil War, expanding national domestic programs, two world wars, and the war against terrorism.

Contemporary federalism involves complex "marble cake" relations among the national and state governments, in which federal grants-in-aid play an important part. Grants for many purposes grew rapidly for a time but have now slowed down. The national government also influences or controls many state policies through mandates and through conditions placed on aid. Federalism has mixed implications for democracy.

Suggestions for Further Reading

Derthick, Martha. *Keeping the Compound Republic: Essays in American Federalism.* Washington, D.C.: Brookings, 2001.

> *An examination of the enduring features of federalism, as well as its most important changes, in light of the framers original design, in Madison's words, of a compound republic.*

Hero, Rodney E. *Faces of Inequality: Social Diversity in American Politics.* New York: Oxford University Press, 1998.

> *An impressive argument with strong empirical evidence that the racial and ethnic composition of states matters for patterns of state politics.*

Nagel, Robert. *The Implosion of American Federalism.* New York: Oxford University Press, 2002.

> *Argues that American federalism has largely disappeared as power in the United States has flowed steadily to Washington, D.C.*

Peterson, Paul E. *The Price of Federalism.* Washington, D.C.: Brookings Institution, 1995.

> *Describes modern federalism and argues that the national government is best at redistributive programs, while the states and localities are best at economic development.*

Riker, William H. *The Development of American Federalism.* Boston: Kluwer Academic, 1987.

> *An influential discussion of what American federalism is and how it came about.*

Walker, David B. *The Rebirth of Federalism,* 2nd ed. New York: Chatham House/Seven Bridges Press, 2000.

> *Examination of the revitalization of the states and why it has happened.*

Internet Sources

Assessing the New Federalism
www.urban.org/Content/Research/NewFederalism/AboutANF/AboutANF.htm

> *News, essays, and research on the New Federalism and devolution.*

National Center for State Courts
www.ncsconline.org

> *Links to the home pages of the court systems of each of the states.*

National Conference of State Legislatures
http://www.ncsl.org

> *Information about state governments and federal relations, including the distribution of federal revenues and expenditures in the states.*

Publius
http://ww2.lafayette.edu/~publius/

> *Home page of the leading academic journal on federalism.*

State Constitutions
www.findlaw.com/

> *A site where the constitutions of all the states may be found.*

Chapter 4
The Structural Foundations of American Government and Politics

In This Chapter

- How population size, location, and diversity affect American politics
- How the free enterprise economy shapes American political life
- Income and wealth distribution and why they matter
- How globalization affects the United States and its people
- What Americans believe about people, politics, government, and the economy

"B-1 Bob" Learns About His District

Bob Dornan and the political establishment were stunned. The nine-term Republican member of Congress from Orange County, California's 46th district had lost his House seat to political newcomer Democrat Loretta Sanchez by a mere 984 votes. Known widely as either "B-1 Bob," because of his staunch support for increased military spending, or "sound-bite Bob," because of the former talk-show host's tendency to attack immigrants, gays, feminists, and liberals with short, savage remarks, Dornan played on his traditional themes during the 1996 congressional election. This tactic had always worked in the past. He saw no reason to change his long-term strategy in his district, especially against an opponent who had lost her only previous try for elective office.

What Bob Dornan and others learned was that the 46th district, like many others in California and in other states, had experienced enormous demographic changes, and these changes were inevitably going to play themselves out in the political arena. A bastion of the white middle class for much of the post-war period, the district by the mid-1990s had become mostly working class and minority in composition. In fact, fully 50 percent of the district was Hispanic and 12 percent was Asian. The non-Hispanic whites who remained were mainly blue collar and service workers, having migrated to the southern suburbs of Los Angeles during the previous decade. Bob Dornan's oft-repeated campaign themes—increasing military spending, banning abortion, and bashing gays and immigrants—not only failed to resonate with people more concerned about jobs, crime, and education but actively alienated the largest ethnic group in his district.

Loretta Sanchez understood the new math, even if Dornan did not. A former Republican and business consultant, she was also the daughter of Mexican immigrants to the United States and a former Head Start child. She switched her party affiliation because she was angry with the Republican Party, as were many other Hispanics, for sponsoring state ballot initiatives attacking affirmative action, bilingual education, and immigrant rights. A moderate Republican turned moderate Democrat, she focused her door-to-door, low-budget campaign on issues more attuned to the interests of potential voters in her district and spent precious campaign time attending festivities in the Hispanic and Asian communities. Striking back in a way that was typical of his previous campaigns, Dornan attacked Sanchez as "the champion of homosexuals."

Lorretta Sanchez defeated Bob Dorman in 1996 and has been reelected to Congress four times. In 2002, her sister

Linda also won a seat in the House of Representatives from a district in Southern California. During these years, the number of Hispanic Americans in the California legislature increased by more than 40 percent, while two different Hispanic Americans served as Speaker of the Assembly. Lt. Governor Cruz Bustamante was an important candidate for the governorship in the California contest in the special recall election in 2003 to unseat Governor Gray Davis. These examples suggest that politics in California are changing significantly because of the growing Hispanic population in the state and the increasing tendency for Hispanics citizens to vote (though still at lower rates than other ethnic groups).

The growth of the Hispanic population is but one of the many important demographic changes going on in the United States. And demographic change is but one of many important changes going on in American society, culture, and economy that are shaping and reshaping American politics and government. Tracking these many changes in the structural level of our analytical model, and examining how they are influencing American politics and what government does, is the focus of this chapter.

Thinking Critically About This Chapter

This chapter is about the structural foundations of politics and government in the United States; it is about how the nature of America's society, economy, culture, and place in the world shapes the political system.

Using the Framework In this chapter, you will learn about the demographic characteristics of the American population (race, ethnicity, geographical location, occupation, income, and the like), the U.S. economy and how it is evolving and changing, and the American political culture. Together with the constitutional rules you learned about in previous chapters, you will see how these structural-level factors have a great deal to do with what issues dominate the political agenda, how political power is distributed in the population, and what ideas Americans bring to bear when grappling with complex public policy issues.

Using the Democratic Standard Popular sovereignty, political equality, and liberty require a supportive economic and social environment. These include (but are not confined to) such things as a well-educated population, a sizable middle class with access to resources allowing its members to participate in public affairs, conditions of nondiscrimination against racial and ethnic minorities, and a culture that values and protects liberty. In this chapter you will learn whether or not such an environment exists.

American Society: How It Has Changed and Why It Matters

The typical American today is very different from the typical American of 1950, let alone 1790, when the first census was conducted. Where we live, how we work, our racial and ethnic composition, and our average age and standard of living have all changed substantially. Each change has influenced our political life.

Growing Diversity

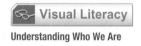

Understanding Who We Are

Ours is an ethnically, religiously, and racially diverse society. The white European Protestants, black slaves, and Native Americans who made up the bulk of the U.S. population when the first census was taken in 1790 were joined by Catholic immigrants from Ireland and Germany in the 1840s and 1850s (see Figure 4.1). In the 1870s, Chinese migrated to America, drawn by jobs in railroad construction. Around the turn of the twentieth century, most emigration was from eastern, central, and southern Europe, with its many ethnic, linguistic, and religious groups. Today most emigration is from Asia and Latin America, with people from Mexico representing the largest single component. There has also been a significant increase in the number of immigrants from the Middle East and other locations with Muslim populations, though this slowed dramatically after Nine-Eleven.

The rate of migration to the United States has accelerated in recent decades. If estimates of illegal entrants are included in the total, from 22 to

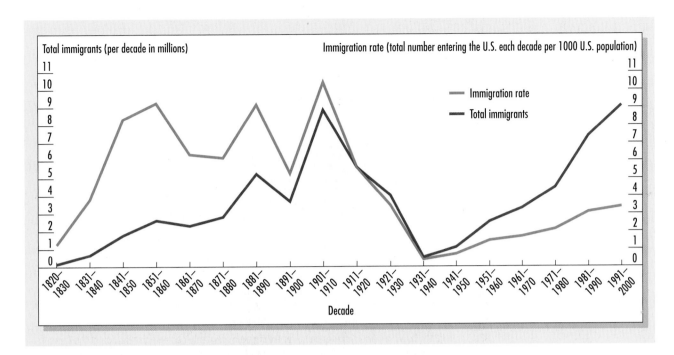

FIGURE 4.1 • **Immigration to the United States, by Decade**

Measuring immigration to the United States in different ways gives rise to quite different interpretations of its scale. Measured in total numbers, the high points of immigration were the 1880s, the decade and a half after 1900, and the 1980s and 1990s. Measured in terms of the total U.S. population, however, immigration was an important factor in population change for much of the nineteenth century and the early part of the twentieth century, but not much after that. Recent immigration, relative to the total U.S. population, remains historically low, although it is has been increasing steadily since its low point in the 1930s.

Source: U.S. Bureau of the Census.

24 million people immigrated to the United States during the 1980s and 1990s, the highest total for any two consecutive decades in American history[1] (see Figure 4.1). As a result of this and other immigration streams, the percentage of foreign-born people resident in the United States has almost tripled since 1970, reaching almost 12 percent of the population in 2003, its highest level since 1970. Although the foreign-born population is concentrated in a handful of states—mainly California, New York, New Jersey, Florida, and Texas—and a handful of cities and localities—mainly Miami, New York, Los Angeles–Long Beach, Orange County, Oakland, and Houston—the presence of new immigrants is being felt almost everywhere in America, including the Midwest and the Deep South. In California, nearly 27 percent of the population is foreign-born.[2]

Although immigration is substantial, it is worth noting that, in a proportional sense, the number of immigrants to the United States today does not approach historical highs. Thus, immigration as a proportion of the total population was much higher between 1840 and 1920 (see Figure 4.1). As a percentage of the population, moreover, the foreign-born population of the United States today is lower than it was in the late nineteenth and early twentieth centuries when it reach almost 15 percent. For most people, of course, it is what has been happening recently that is most important to them, not historical comparisons.

The natural outcome of this history of immigration is substantial racial and ethnic diversity in the American population. Although the United States

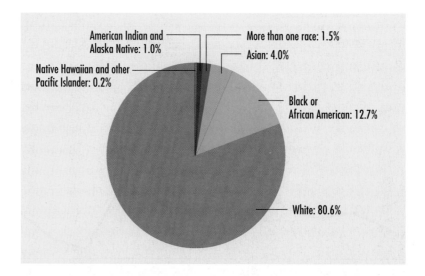

FIGURE 4.2 • **Racial Composition of the United States, 2002**

The United States is a racially diverse society and is becoming more so every year. Whites remain a substantial majority, however, and will remain so for a long time, primarily because the Bureau of the Census classifies Hispanic origin as an ethnic rather than a racial category, and nearly 5 out of 10 Hispanics classify themselves as white. (Non-Hispanic whites were 68 percent of the U.S. population in 2002.) Also, for the first time in 2000, the Census allowed people to identify themselves as more than one race.
Source: U.S. Bureau of the Census.

is still overwhelmingly white (see Figure 4.2), its diversity is growing with every passing year. Most importantly, Hispanics (who can be of any race, with almost one-half of Hispanics categorizing themselves as white in Census Bureau surveys) became the nation's largest minority group in 2002, accounting for 13.5 percent of America's resident population compared with 13.2 percent for non-Hispanic blacks. The Hispanic total grew by almost 3 million between 2000 and 2002 alone, with a little more than half of that growth attributed to immigration to the United States. The Asian-origin population is growing faster than any other group, but it is still relatively small, accounting for about 4 percent of the U.S. population in 2002.

The most recent wave of immigration, like all previous ones, has added to our rich linguistic, cultural, and religious traditions; it has also helped revitalize formerly poverty-stricken neighborhoods in cities such as Los Angeles, New York, and Chicago. But it has also generated political and social tensions. The arrival of immigrants who are different from the majority population in significant ways has often sparked anti-immigration agitation and demands that public officials stem the tide. **Nativist** (anti-foreign) reactions to Irish Catholic migrants were common throughout the nineteenth century. Anti-Chinese agitation swept the western states in the 1870s and 1880s. Alarm at the arrival of waves of immigrants from eastern, southern, and central Europe in the early part of the last century led Congress virtually to close the doors of the United States in 1921 and keep them closed until the 1950s. Wars have also triggered hostile actions against certain immigrant groups: German immigrants during World War I; Japanese Americans during World War II; and people from Middle Eastern and other Muslim countries after the September 11, 2001, terrorist attacks on the United States.

The current wave of Hispanic immigration has caused unease among some Americans. In 1994, for example, California voters approved Proposition 187, which barred welfare, health, and education benefits to illegal immi-

nativist
Anti-foreign; applied to political movements active in the nineteenth century.

grants (the Proposition has since been declared unconstitutional by a federal district court). In 1998, California voters approved another proposition that banned bilingual education. However, though waves of immigration often trigger an initial negative response from the native population (among all races and ethnic groups, it is important to add) and opportunistic politicians, elected officials invariably begin to pay attention to immigrant groups as more of their number become citizens and voters. Indeed, immigrants now represent the fastest growing voting bloc in the American electorate.[3] Those that fail to take note of the change, like Representative Bob Dornan in our chapter-opening

Participation

The Debate Over Immigration

Web Exploration
Immigration and Immigrants

Issue: Immigration, and what to do about it and its social consequences, has become a contentious issue in American politics.

Site: Find out what Americans want to do about immigration by going to Public Agenda On-Line. Access our Website at **www.ablongman.com/greenberg.** In the "Web Explorations" section for Chapter 4, select "Immigration and Immigrants," then "Immigrants." Under Issue Guides, select "immigration." Then look at "people's chief concerns."

What You've Learned: What are Americans most worried about when it comes to immigration? What do they want to do about it? As you look at each survey question, ask yourself what immigration policies you favor. Are your views in line with the majority of Americans, or are you an "outlier?"

HINT: Note that people seem to worry not about immigration, as such, but about illegal immigration. They strongly support policies, moreover, that rapidly assimilate immigrants, including a focus on learning English.

story, court defeat. The upshot of this change is that elected officials at all levels of government are likely to become more responsive to the needs and interests of recent immigrant groups.

The growing political importance of immigrants in the United States, especially Hispanics, is partly a reflection of sheer numbers and partly a reflection of the geographic concentration of immigrants into states with very large or closely contested blocs of electoral votes in presidential elections. Both George W. Bush and John Kerry were conscious of this new math of presidential elections and made special appeals to Hispanic voters during the 2004 presidential contest in such battleground states as Florida, New Mexico, Nevada, and Arizona.

Although the doors to the United States have been relatively wide open for immigrants since the early 1970s, there is some evidence that these doors may be closing a bit in the wake of the terrorist attacks of 2001. A substantial majority of Americans now favors a decrease in the number of people allowed to immigrate to the United States and supports stronger efforts by the government to find and deport illegal immigrants.[4] The federal government has responded to the attacks in a number of ways that may also affect future immigration by making the United States either less attractive as a destination or a harder place to enter. For example, the government has increased the number of civilian and military personnel assigned to protect American borders. It has also strengthened visa requirements for those wishing to visit the United States or study here, especially for people from Muslim countries. A program to interview young men in high Arab Muslim population areas such as Dearborn, Michigan, and Brooklyn, New York, led to a spate of arrests and deportations in 2002 and 2003, triggering a significant out-migration of Arabs Muslims to Canada and Europe.[5]

Changing Location

Where the growing population of the United States is located also matters. Although we began as a country of rural farms and small towns, we rapidly became an urban people. By 1910, some 50 cities had populations of more than 100,000, and three (New York, Philadelphia, and Chicago) had more than 1 million. Urbanization, caused mainly by industrialization—the rise of large manufacturing firms required many industrial workers, while the mechanization of farming meant that fewer agricultural workers were needed—continued unabated until the mid-1940s. After World War II, a massive federal and state road-building program and government-guaranteed home loans for veterans started the process by which the United States became an overwhelmingly suburban nation. Presently, "exurbia"—the areas beyond the older, first-ring of suburbia—is the fastest growing part of America's metropolitan areas (see Figure 4.3).

This shift in the location of the American population has had important political ramifications. The continued drain of population from rural areas, for instance, has diminished the power of the rural voice in state and national politics. For their part, some central cities, burdened with populations of the poor and the less well-to-do, find it difficult to provide the level of public services considered normal only a few years ago. Heavily dependent on the assistance of the federal government, poor central-city populations have become even more consistently Democratic in their voting preferences than in the past. Conversely, people living in the distant suburbs, mainly middle-class and working-class homeowners—who increasingly include among their number many members of minority and immigrant groups—have become less willing

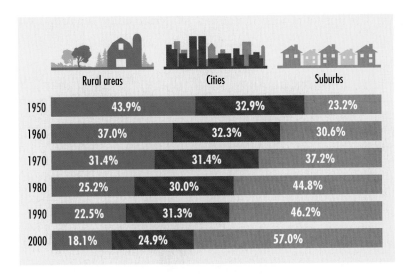

FIGURE 4.3 • Population Shift: From Rural to Urban to Suburban

In a relatively short period of time, the United States has changed from a society in which the largest percentage of the population lived in rural areas to one in which the largest percentage lives in suburbs. This development has produced several important changes in American politics and in the fortunes of our political parties.

Source: U.S. Bureau of the Census.

to support programs for central-city populations. They are more attuned to politicians who promise to pay attention to issues of traffic congestion and sprawl.

The U.S. population has also moved west and south over the course of time. The shift accelerated after World War II as people followed manufacturing jobs to these regions (many companies were attracted to the western and southern states because of their low taxes and anti-union policies). This population shift has led to changes in the relative political power of the states. Following each census from 1950 to 2000, states in the East and the upper Midwest lost congressional seats and presidential electoral votes. States in the West and the South—often referred to as the **Sun Belt** because of their generally pleasant weather—gained at their expense. Figure 4.4 shows the extent of change during the 1990s. Because a majority of Sun Belt states are more conservative than other states, their increasing importance in national politics may have contributed to Republican gains in Congress in the 1990s.

Sun Belt
States of the Lower South, Southwest, and West, where sunny weather and often conservative politics prevail.

Changing Jobs and Occupations

At the time of the first census in 1790, almost three-quarters of all Americans worked in agriculture. Most of the remainder of the population worked in retail trade, transportation, and skilled trades closely connected to agriculture. About 80 percent of the working, male, nonslave population was self-employed, owning small farms, stores, wagons and horses, and workshops.[6]

The American occupational structure was radically transformed by the industrialization of the United States in the late nineteenth century (often called the **Industrial Revolution**). By 1910, the proportion of the labor force in agriculture had dropped to only 32 percent, and individuals working for others for wages and salaries had swelled to more than 69 percent.[7] By 1940,

Industrial Revolution
The period of transition from predominantly agricultural to predominantly industrial societies in the Western nations in the nineteenth century.

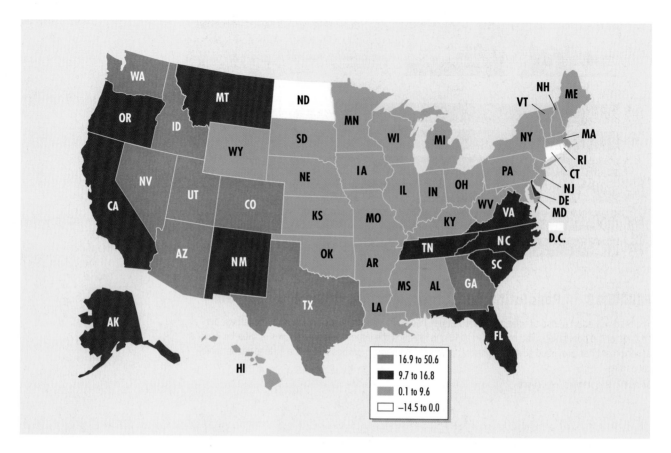

FIGURE 4.4 • **Population Change in the States, 1990–2000**

The U.S. Bureau of the Census reports that the relative population sizes of the states changed substantially in the 1990s, with the bulk of the relative population gains in the states of the Southeast, Southwest, and the West. As a result, many of these states gained seats in the House of Representatives at the expense of states elsewhere.

Source: U.S. Bureau of the Census.

blue-collar worker
A skilled, semiskilled, or unskilled worker in industry.

white-collar worker
A person working at a service, sales, or office job.

the "typical" American was a skilled, semiskilled, or unskilled **blue-collar worker** in manufacturing.

In 1950, the United States became the first nation in the world where **white-collar workers** (in clerical, technical, professional, managerial, services, and sales jobs) were the majority. Throughout the last quarter of the twentieth century and into the first years of the twenty-first, rising productivity in manufacturing (meaning that more could be produced with fewer employees because of technological innovations), the transfer of manufacturing capacity overseas by some companies, the disappearance of the small family farm, and the rapid rise of the high-technology and information sectors accelerated the shift of employment from factory and farm to the office. By 2002, only 2.5 percent of the American population were working in agriculture; only 13 percent were in manufacturing jobs.

Occupational change matters a great deal in our society and in our politics. Here are a few examples. The migration from agriculture has had a devastating effect on small- and medium-sized towns in rural areas across the United States and has decreased the effect of rural voters in American politics. The loss of good-paying manufacturing jobs for those with only a high

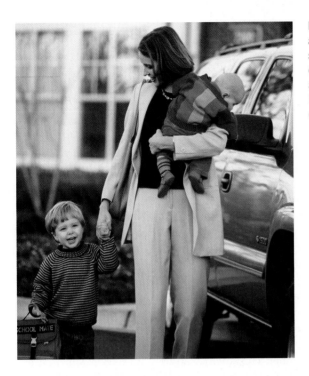

Because fewer and fewer families can afford the luxury of having one parent stay home with the children, pressures on government for a longer school day and increased funding for day care are likely to increase. Here, a mother drops off her children at a day care center.

school education, has meant a decline in living standards for an important part of the African American community.[8] These and other displaced manufacturing workers often ask government to expand welfare and unemployment benefits, job retraining, and programs that encourage economic development. The entrance of women into service, clerical, technical, educational, managerial, and other kinds of white-collar jobs has enhanced the economic position of women, increased their assertiveness and self-confidence in politics, and fueled their demand for the expansion of early education programs and for the extension of the school day.

Income, Wealth, and Poverty

The United States enjoys one of the highest standards of living in the world. The United States usually ranks first or second in the annual world rankings of per-capita gross domestic product (GDP) per capita—Norway is the other country steadily in the running for the top spot. On the U.N.'s Human Development Index—which takes into account education and life expectancy as well as per-capita GDP—the United States in 2003 ranked among the top six nations (with Australia, Canada, France, Norway, and Iceland), with little apparent difference among the members of this group.[9] However, the high standard of living represented by these numbers is not shared by all Americans.

Income   Between 1973 and 1993, **median household income** in the United States hardly changed at all. From 1994 through 2000, spurred by the high-tech economic boom of the 1990s, household income rose steadily among all demographic groups, including the least educated and skilled. Median household income fell every year from 2001 to 2003, however, rocked by the recession of 2001 and the jobless economic growth that followed (See the "By the Numbers" feature for various ways to measure the performance of the U.S.

median household income
Household income number at which one-half of all households have more income and one-half have less income; the midpoint of all households ranked by income.

By the Numbers

How well is the American economy performing?

Is the economy getting better or worse, and by how much? Seem like easy questions to answer, but consider the two examples graphed here from official U.S. government reports.

Why It Matters: Government reports on the state of the American economy are very important. Such reports affect the mood of the public and their sense of confidence in the direction the country is moving and how much they support and trust elected leaders. These reports also influence investors' confidence in the American economy and their willingness to invest, thus shaping the future direction of the economy. These reports also are important pieces of information for government leaders—including the Federal Reserve Board, Congress, and the president—as they fashion policies to keep the economy on course. Finally, the reports trigger automatic changes in a wide range of government benefits and financial instruments, including Social Security checks and inflation-adjusted bonds. So, it is important to get the numbers right and correctly interpret the numbers the government reports.

The Story Behind the Numbers: Let's look at the jobs numbers first. The Bureau of Labor Statistics (BLS)—which reported a drop in nonfarm payrolls of 30,000 in June 2003—bases its payroll numbers on reports by businesses and governments that are compared with unemployment insurance records in the states, which are fairly comprehensive and current. Total employment—which gained 251,000 according to the BLS—is based on a sampling of households that is compared with household employment figures from the census taken every 10 years. Most economists suggest using the nonfarm payroll numbers as the better of the two measures of short-term job gains and losses because of the total employment number's dependence on census numbers as the base for calculations in a society whose household numbers are changing year to year.

The second number—quarterly economic growth—is reported in three ways because the data to make firmer calculations comes only in bits and pieces. Thus, the Commerce Department reports an advance number, a preliminary number, and a final number. The advance and preliminary numbers are particularly troublesome because they depend a

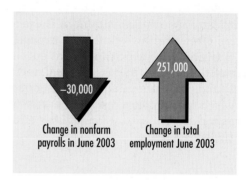

Job Growth or Job Loss? June 2003

economy.) By 2003, median family income in the United States was roughly $42,400.[10] In real dollar terms—that is, adjusted for inflation—median household income was up 25 percent from 1967 when the federal government first began to collect this statistic, but there also have been periods of stagnation and even decline.

Changes in household income can have important political effects. Not surprisingly, when household income is rising, Americans tend to express satisfaction with their situation and confidence in elected leaders. During periods of stagnation and decline, the opposite is evident. During the long 1973–1993 period of stagnation, for example, political observers talked about the rise of an "angry" middle class, manifested during the 1980s and early 1990s in outbursts against taxes, immigrants, and welfare recipients, and a decline in great deal on incomplete information—businesses don't always get their quarterly government reports done on time, and reports in some areas of the economy, most notably the service sector, are not made on a quarterly basis. So, government statistical agencies have to do a substantial amount of statistical guesswork, inferring some numbers from more solid ones. As an example, the total amount of money paid in commissions for financial transactions—a component in the calculation of overall economic activity—is inferred from the total volume of stock market activity.

What to Watch For: It is important to understand how important government statistics are collected and reported. This may seem like a pretty hard thing to do, but each statistical reporting agency in the federal government includes this information in its reports, though you may sometimes have to dig for it. The average person, of course, doesn't necessarily have the time or inclination to perform such investigations. It is probably reasonable to pay attention to professional economists and financial analysts as they discuss the meanings of competing numbers, especially to the ones who have been the most consistently on the mark over the years. It is also worth remembering that many government statistical agencies report preliminary and final numbers, and that the final numbers—taking advantage of the fact that they are based on more complete information—are worth waiting for.

What Do You Think?   In your view, can we depend on government statistical reports to be

accurate reflection of what they purport to measure? Should we depend on statistics that are based on incomplete information and that depend on a great deal of statistical inference? If not, whose statistical reports can we depend on to be more accurate? Industry trade groups? Economic consulting firms? Do we have any other choice but to depend on government trend data, perhaps insisting that they gather the best information available and on a timely basis?

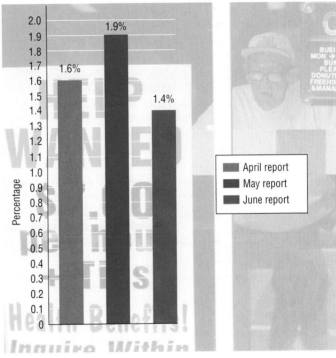

GDP Growth, First Quarter, 2003

trust for government and elected leaders. Middle-class anger also had electoral consequences, playing an important role, for example, in the defeat of incumbent president George H. W. Bush in the 1992 election and in the Republican capture of Congress in 1994.[11]

It is important to point out that median household income varies across demographic groups. African American and Hispanic households have the lowest household incomes—though each made significant strides during the late 1990s—while Asian Americans and non-Hispanic whites have the highest.

Poverty   In 1955, almost 25 percent of Americans fell below the federal government's official **poverty line.** The percentage dropped steadily until it reached 11.6 in 1973. Because of the sustained economic boom in the 1990s,

poverty line
The federal government's calculation of the amount of income families of various sizes need to stay out of poverty.

Poverty and homelessness have persisted in the face of strong economic growth in the 1990s and again after 2003. The contrast between rich and poor is evident on the streets of most large American cities.

poverty fell to 11.3 percent in 2000, its lowest point in American history. Tough economic times in the early 2000s once again pushed the poverty rate upward. By the end of 2002, it stood at 12.1 percent.

The problem of poverty in the United States continues to concern many Americans. Here is why:

- A distressingly large number of Americans still live in poverty, 34.6 million in 2002.
- The official poverty rate is unlikely to fall much unless there is a sustained period of job growth in the next few years.
- The poverty rate in the United States remains substantially higher than in the other rich democracies.

The distribution of poverty is not random. It is concentrated among racial minorities and single-parent, female-headed households and their children.[12] Roughly 24 percent of African Americans and 22 percent of Hispanic Americans live in poverty, for example (although a sizable middle class has emerged in both communities), compared with only 8 percent among non-Hispanic whites and 10 percent among Asians. Almost one in five children under the age of 18 live in poverty as do more than one in three people who live in single-parent, female-headed households.[13]

Obviously, the extent of poverty is politically consequential. Most importantly, poverty often is associated with a range of socially undesirable outcomes, including crime, drug use, and family disintegration,[14] all of which eventually draw the attention of other citizens who want government to do something about these problems. The cause of poverty reduction has also drawn the attention of many Americans who are offended on moral and other grounds by the extent of the poverty that exists in the world's largest economy. (See, the "Using the Framework" feature for insight about why it has been so difficult to further diminish poverty.)

Using the Framework

I keep hearing about how well the economy did during the 1990s. Why then couldn't we seem to do much about poverty?

Background: Although the strong economy in the 1990s caused poverty rates to fall, there is still a surprisingly high number of poor people in the United States. Surveys show that Americans would like to do something to help the poor, although not through the traditional welfare system. But the federal government, with a few exceptions such as the Low Income Tax Credit, has not made the elimination of poverty a major priority. Former Housing and Urban Development Secretary Andrew Cuomo attempted to draw public attention to the plight of the poor in poverty pockets such as Benton Harbor, Michigan, and East St. Louis, Illinois, but this attempt failed to spark a reaction. Taking a look at how structural, political linkage, and governmental factors interact on this issue will help explain the situation.

Governmental Action

The national government provides small safety nets for the poor but does not institute programs to eliminate poverty.

Governmental Level

Proposals to eliminate poverty do not improve the electoral prospects of public officials at the present time.

Elected leaders in both parties tend to support the position that balanced budgets, deregulation, a friendly environment for investors, and encouragement of private enterprise is the best public policy.

Political Linkages Level

The poor are politically invisible; they represent a small minority of the electorate, have few organized groups to push their interests, and have not been able to build a social movement.

Wealthier Americans and large corporations make large contributions to candidates who promise to keep taxes low and government small.

Public opinion opposes big federal government programs to redistribute income.

The Democratic Party, historically the party championing the interests of the poor and near-poor, is often afraid of being tagged with the "liberal" and "tax-and-spend" labels.

Structural Level

American core beliefs about individualism, initiative, and opportunity make it difficult for proposals to assist the poor to gain recognition.

The economic boom of the 1990s, with its record levels of employment, reinforced the belief that anyone who wants to work, can.

Inequality   The degree of income and wealth inequality has always been higher in the United States than in the other rich democracies. Over the past two decades, income and wealth inequality have become even more pronounced; income and wealth inequality actually grew during the economic booms of the 1980s and 1990s. By 2000, the top quintile (the top 20 percent) of households took home almost 50 percent of national income (see Figure 4.5), the highest proportion ever recorded. Wealth (assets such as real estate, stocks and bonds, art, bank accounts, cash-value insurance policies, and so on) in the United States is even more unequally distributed than income. According to a study by economist Edward Wolff, the top 1 percent of households—with a net worth of at least $2.3 million—owned more than 42 percent of the nation's wealth by the mid-1990s, up from only 21 percent in 1975.[15] Inequality of wealth today seems similar to that of the 1920s[16] and is likely to become even more pronounced in the future with the recent repeal of the estate tax. Here are a few additional statistics that show that most of the income and wealth gains from economic growth between 1980 and 2000 went to wealthy and upper-income groups, rather than being evenly distributed across the entire population:

- Between 1983 and 1998, 47 percent of all real income gains in the United States went to the top 1 percent of income recipients.[17]

- Wages among the lowest 20 percent of households has changed hardly at all since 1973.

- In 1980, the average CEO was paid 40 times as much at the average worker; in 2002 the CEO received 400 times more.[18]

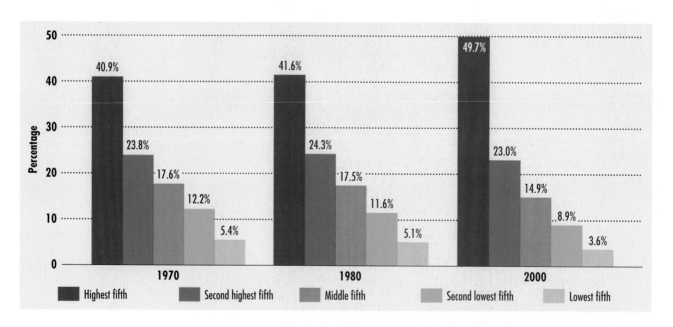

FIGURE 4.5 ● **Household Income Distribution in the United States, by Quintiles, 1970–2000**

Income inequality has been increasing in the United States, reaching levels not seen since the 1920s. A standard way to measure income inequality is to compare the proportion of national income going to each 20 percent (*quintile*) of households in the population. Especially striking is the shrinking share of the bottom 60 percent and the increasing share of the top 20 percent.

Source: U.S. Bureau of the Census.

- Between 1998 and 2001, the net worth of the upper 10 percent of families jumped by 69 percent; that of the lowest 20 percent increased by only 24 percent.[19]

Why worry about income and wealth inequality? Inequality is particularly important in determining how well democracy works. Extensive *material inequality,* as we suggested in Chapter 1, may undermine the possibilities for *political equality*—one of the foundation stones of democracy—because the advantages of high incomes and wealth almost always spill over into political life. People with access to financial resources can use their resources to enhance their political voice and their ease of access to public officials. Poorer Americans, for example, are less likely than those with financial resources to exercise their right to vote and to participate in other ways in politics. People with little money are unlikely to make contributions to political campaigns or to groups that will fight for their interests, as do more advantaged Americans. Those with more income are more likely than others to have computers and Internet access in their homes and are more likely, as a result, to be informed, linked with others into political groups, and in touch with government decision makers. That is why Thomas Jefferson feared that democracy would be at risk in a society with great inequalities in wealth and poverty.

The American Economy

Virtually everything we have discussed so far in this chapter is shaped by the American economy. The growth, diversification, and geographic dispersion of the American population, for example, can be traced directly to changes in the economy. Occupations, standards of living, and the distribution of income and wealth are closely connected to the operations of our economic institutions. Even important elements of the American political culture, as we shall soon see, are associated with our economy and how it works.

The Triumph of the Industrial Corporation

Until the Civil War, the American capitalist economy (except in the slave-holding South) was highly competitive, with many small enterprises, first tied to agriculture and then increasingly to manufacturing. After the Civil War, and partly as a result of it, the economy became increasingly industrialized and concentrated in giant enterprises.[20] By the turn of the twentieth century, the United States was the world's leading industrial power.

Industrial enterprises grew to unprecedented size in the late nineteenth and early twentieth centuries. Workers were gathered into enormous workplaces that required coordination by an army of managers. Partly, this change in scale was related to technology: The steam engine, electrical power, and the assembly line provided the means of bringing thousands of working people together for industrial production. Partly, this change in scale was tied to cost: Most of the new industrial technologies required unheard-of levels of investment capital. Large enterprises were also encouraged by changes in the laws of incorporation, which allowed competing corporations to merge into single, giant enterprises. A wave of mergers between 1896 and 1904 fashioned the corporate-dominated economy familiar to us today.[21]

The American economy and American corporations grew impressively during the first two-thirds of the twentieth century. Although thrown seriously off track for at least a decade by the Great Depression, the economy was pushed

The principles of assembly-line, mass production manufacturing were honed to near perfection by Henry Ford in the early twentieth century at his Highland Park complex in Michigan. Here workers assemble a portion of a Model T, the first car to reach the mass public in the United States.

forward again by World War II and the Cold War that followed; both triggered rapid and substantial increases in government spending, research and development, and technological innovation. In 1975, 11 of the largest 15 corporations in the world were American; in 1981, 40 percent of the world's total foreign direct investment was still accounted for by the United States.[22] This enormous growth in the wealth and reach of the American economy after World War II, fueled by the activities of the major corporations, was the foundation of the rapid improvements in the American standard of living and the growth of the middle class.

The Temporary Fall from Grace

Although the U.S. economy continued to grow in the 1970s and 1980s, its rate of growth began to fall behind that of western Europe and Japan, even as American corporations began to feel the pinch of intense competition from foreign corporations. Between the early 1970s and the late 1980s, the U.S. share of world manufacturing declined. The United States lost ground in steel, autos, machine tools, electronics, computer chips, and finance.

The relative decline in America's manufacturing position had a devastating effect on the wages of blue-collar workers, raised protectionist sentiments, and spurred proposals to shield American industry from foreign competition. The intensity of the fight over the North American Free Trade Agreement (NAFTA) shows how America's changing economic position in the world generated a set of important issues in American politics.

Globalization and the American Economy

In the 1990s, however, the American economy rebounded with a vengeance, with its corporations once again becoming the key players in crucial industries. The economies once seen as the principal threats to America's position—the European Union, Japan, and the so-called Asian tigers—began to lose

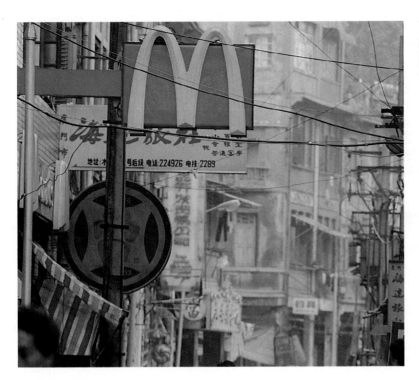

The largest American corporations are also global corporations in the sense that they produce and sell their products all over the world. This McDonald's is in Xiamen, China.

ground. The reason for the turnaround has been the subject of much debate and disagreement among economists and business leaders. Some point to the lighter hand of government and labor unions in the United States, some point to stronger entrepreneurial traditions here, and still others credit the existence of freer markets, but all seem to agree that American corporations were better positioned to succeed in the new global economy that blossomed in the 1990s.

U.S. corporations are proving to be the most important actors in the new global economy. Behind the apparent decline in the competitiveness of the American economy in the 1970s and 1980s, something startling seems to have been going on. Leaving older industries such as mining, steel, and shipbuilding to others, American companies proved to be particularly adept in areas such as computer software, biotechnology, business services (insurance, law, accounting, advertising, and so on), computer chips, Internet services, telecommunications, military and commercial aircraft, and popular entertainment. In this emergent global economy, Microsoft, Intel, Boeing, Disney, Amazon.com, Sun, Google, eBay, and Cisco were (and most still are) the companies that drew attention.

The dynamism of the American economy in the 1990s had several effects that were politically consequential. On the one hand, the steady economic growth, low inflation, and heady stock market performance of that period helped fuel an impressive rate of job creation, low levels of unemployment, and heightened consumer confidence. On the other hand, the new global economy is one in which certain skills are highly sought after and rewarded—software engineers, portfolio managers, Website creators, filmmakers, and business strategists, for example—while others are not—low-skill manual and service workers, for example. For the former, work tends to be both exciting and lucrative. For the latter, work is routine, not very well paid, and characterized by frequent layoffs and part-time status. This may be why a booming economy in the 1990s did not diminish income inequality in the United States.

The heady 1990s were followed by developments that threaten the pace of globalization and America's growing dominant role in it. First, the United States fell into difficult economic times: economic recession in 2001; jobless economic growth in 2002 and 2003; and the collapse of many dot-com, high-tech, and telecommunications companies, the stars of the 1990s boom. Strong economic growth started in the last quarter of 2003, however, so some lost ground was made up. Second, the American business world and consumer confidence were rocked by revelations of financial chicanery among many corporations and accounting firms, most notably Enron, Arthur Andersen, and WorldCom. Third, and perhaps most importantly, terrorism and the war against terrorism at home and abroad threatens the globalization process, though it is too early to tell what the effects of these developments will be. In one scenario, the worry about terrorism will compel the United States to more tightly regulate the flow of people, goods, and finance across our borders, thus choking off the blood flow of globalization. In another scenario, fear that radical Islamic terrorism will target western companies and their employees, suppliers, and outlets might convince some companies to draw back from the world and confine themselves to business in the United States. In yet another scenario, American companies will continue to operate and even expand their activities abroad, either because the war on terrorism proves successful—thus lessening the probability of terrorist attacks—or because companies calculate that business necessity requires that they think in global terms, no matter the risk. Only time will tell which scenario wins out.

The United States in the International System

America's position in the world is another important structural fact that shapes politics and government in the United States. In this section, we sketch the general outlines of that position over the course of U.S. history; in Chapter 18, we examine the foreign policies that have been forged in response to America's position in the world and how such policies are made.

It is often said that the United States is the world's last remaining superpower. If this is true, then it took awhile to reach this status. For most of the nineteenth century, the attention of most Americans and their leaders was focused on the North American continent. Their energies were devoted primarily to filling in a vast, continental-scale nation-state—which required, of course, moving Native Americans aside, buying territories from France and Spain, and seizing our present Southwest from Mexico—and to building an industrial economy. The great expanse of the Atlantic Ocean allowed our domestic growth and development to move forward, unhindered by the European powers. Our foreign policy was **isolationist:** American policy leaders believed in attending to our own affairs and staying out of world affairs, unless directly threatened. Starting toward the end of the nineteenth century, however, our attentions began to turn abroad, and our growing economic power inevitably provided a seat at the table of the world's most important nations. It was World War II, however, that propelled the United States into its position as the world's most important power.

isolationism
The policy of avoiding involvement in foreign affairs.

The United States as a Superpower I

World War II thrust the United States into the leadership position that its economic position in the world had portended since 1900. The war stimulated a

During the Cold War, the United States and the Soviet Union avoided direct military conflict because their respective leaders feared mutual annihilation from a nuclear exchange if the disagreements between them ever turned from "cold" to "hot." Here nuclear missiles are on display at the annual parade celebrating the 1917 Bolshevik Revolution.

massive expansion of the entire industrial economy. At the same time, the financial and manufacturing infrastructures of our prewar economic rivals—Britain, France, Japan, and Germany—were devastated by the war.

The United States emerged from the war with an expanded industrial economy, a large military establishment, and military superiority in most important areas. There was also a new belief among both Americans and their leaders that isolationism was dangerous and contrary to our long-term national interests.

Within a decade of the end of World War II, the United States stood as the unchallenged economic, political, and military power among the Western nations. For the first time in its history, the United States was willing and able to exercise leadership on the world level. It was the United States that pulled together the major capitalist nations for the first time in their history into a political and economic partnership. It provided funds for rebuilding western Europe and for development projects in the Third World. It successfully pushed for free international trade and provided a stable dollar to serve as the basis of the international monetary system. And it organized and largely paid for the joint military defenses of them all. Is it any wonder, then, that *Life* magazine editor Henry Luce was moved to label the period the "American century"?

The fly in the ointment, of course, was the Soviet Union. Although badly crippled by the war (it is said that 20 million of its citizens died in the conflict), the Soviet Union entered the post-war era with the world's largest land army, superpower ambitions of its own, and a strong desire to keep the nations on its periphery in eastern and southern Europe in hands it considered friendly. In the ensuing **Cold War,** which began in the late 1940s and lasted for four decades, the two superpowers faced each other as leaders of conflicting political, economic, and ideological alliances; became engaged in a nuclear arms race; and fought surrogate wars with each other in various locations in the Third World, from the Belgian Congo to Central America to Afghanistan.

America's superpower status had many implications for U.S. politics and government policies. For one thing, superpower status required a large military establishment and tilted government spending priorities toward national defense. For another thing, as we will see in later chapters, it enhanced the role of the president in policymaking and diminished that of Congress.

Cold War

The period of tense relations between the United States and the Soviet Union from the late 1940s to the late 1980s.

The United States as a Superpower II

The 1990s saw startling changes in the world's military, political, and economic systems, all of which, at least nominally, heightened U.S. power in the world. Communism collapsed in eastern Europe. The Soviet Union ceased to exist. China switched to a market economy. Most developing countries rejected the socialist development model, embraced "privatization," and welcomed foreign investment. Moreover, the United States took the lead in the global economy. We use the heading "Superpower II" to capture the notion, widely bandied about, of the United States's emergence as the world's single "superpower," without any real challengers to its preeminence.

Oddly, however, although the last "superpower" in a military sense, the United States has not necessarily had its way on all important matters, either with allies or enemies, nor is it likely to do so in the future. With the threat of the Soviet Union no longer supplying the glue to hold them together, U.S. allies feel freer to go their own way on a wide range of international issues. The United States could not agree with the Europeans for a very long time on what to do about the ethnic conflicts in Bosnia and Kosovo, for example, and was often at odds with them over aspects of the conduct of the war in Afghanistan and the relief effort that followed. It also has differences with the European Union over trade issues, international treaties on the environment, and on the war with Iraq and the recovery effort there. Relations with France, a long-time ally, became particularly strained over the war in Iraq. Disagreements about nuclear proliferation have strained U.S. relations with Russia, while security issues, human rights violations, and protection of intellectual property have been an irritant in our relations with China. Nor has the United States been able, in spite of all of its power, to bring the Palestinians and Israelis together to encourage or force a solution to their decades-long conflict. And, perhaps most importantly, American citizens, officials, and companies, as well as American allies, remain vulnerable to terrorist attacks, with no end in sight to this danger.

Many of America's traditional allies, including Germany and France, refused to support President Bush's decision to invade Iraq in 2003. Here, American marines engage Iraqi troops in the city of Diyala on their way to Baghdad.

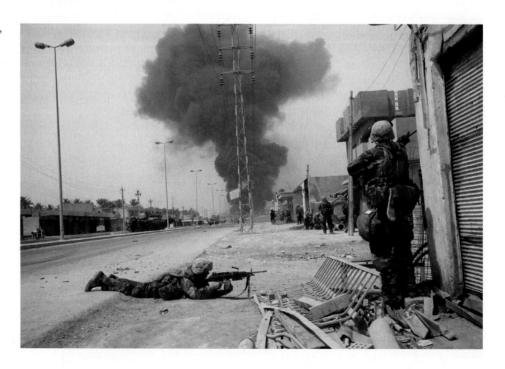

The Foundational Beliefs of American Political Culture

Americans' attitudes and opinions about what policies government should adopt, the performance and responsiveness of elected officials, and what the United States should do internationally are imbedded in more fundamental beliefs about human nature, society, economic relations, and the role of government. Taken together, these fundamental or core beliefs make up the American *political culture*. In the next chapter on public opinion, we will examine the nature of American political attitudes and opinions; here, we will examine the core beliefs that make up the political culture. These core beliefs can be understood as the raw material from which attitudes and opinions are built. Also, in the next chapter, we will examine the processes—called political socialization—by which people come to have particular core beliefs, attitudes, and opinions.

Understanding our political culture is important for understanding American politics and government. Why? Because the kinds of choices Americans make in meeting the challenges posed by a changing economy, society, and post–Cold War world depend a great deal on the core beliefs Americans hold about human nature, society, economic relations, and the role of government.

Evidence strongly suggests that Americans share a common political culture.[23] To be sure, we are a vast, polyglot mixture of races, religions, ethnicities, occupations, and lifestyles. Nevertheless, one of the things that has always struck observers of the American scene, from Tocqueville to Bryce, is the degree to which a broad consensus seems to exist on many of the core beliefs that shape our attitudes and opinions, our ways of engaging in politics, and what we expect of our government. Let's look, then, at the most important of these core beliefs.

Individualism

Compared with people in other countries, Americans tend to believe that an individual's fate is (and ought to be) tied to his or her own efforts. Those with talent, grit, and the willingness to work hard are more likely than not to end up on top, it is believed; those without at least some of these qualities are more likely to wind up on the bottom of the heap. Americans tend to assume that people generally get what they deserve in the long run.

Compared with people in other countries, Americans are also more likely to believe that people are naturally competitive, always striving to better themselves in relation to others. Popular literature in America has always conveyed this theme, ranging from the Horatio Alger books of the late nineteenth century to the many contemporary self-help books with keys to "getting ahead," "making it," and "getting rich."

This core belief in what has been called *competitive individualism* affects American attitudes toward many issues, including inequality and what should be done about it. Americans overwhelmingly endorse the idea of "equality of opportunity" (the idea that people ought to have an equal shot in the competitive game of life), for instance, yet they also overwhelmingly reject the idea that people should be guaranteed equal rewards. Not surprisingly, Americans tend to look favorably on government programs that try to equalize opportunity—Head Start, education programs of various kinds, school lunch programs, and the

Simulation

What Are American Civic Values?

In Japan, commitment to the work team and the company are more important cultural values than they are in the United States.

like—but are generally against programs such as welfare, which seem to redistribute income from the hardworking middle class to individuals who are considered "undeserving."

Because Americans tend to assume that people get different rewards based on their own efforts, a belief in equality of opportunity is consistent with highly unequal outcomes. Another way to say the same thing is to point out that Americans seem to find inequality of income and wealth acceptable, so long as it is the outcome of a process in which individuals compete fairly with one other.[24] Not surprisingly, given this core belief, Americans are less likely to support government efforts to equalize matters than are people in other rich democracies, especially if efforts to equalize outcomes in society involves imposing limits on individual striving and achievement[25] (see Figure 4.6).

Private Property and Private Enterprise

Americans tend to believe in the importance of private property and the efficiencies of the free market. Private property notions, best articulated by the philosopher John Locke, have been reinforced by the experience of fairly widespread property ownership in the United States compared with that in many other countries.[26] Locke argued that the Creator gave the earth and its resources in common to human beings and also gave human beings abilities that they have a right and an obligation to use. When they use these abilities, people turn common property into private property. By mixing their labor with the naturally occurring abundance of the earth, Locke argued, people are justified in taking the product of that effort for their own as private property. Because people are different in their abilities and their willingness to work, this process will always result in inequality. Inevitably, some will end up with more property than others.

The basic theory of the free market was worked out by Adam Smith in his classic work, *The Wealth of Nations*. Smith taught that if the market were left alone to operate naturally, following the laws of supply and demand, it would

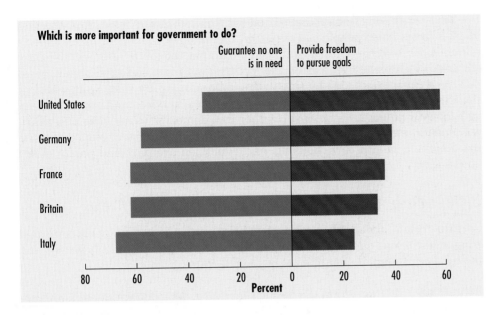

Which is more important for government to do?

FIGURE 4.6 ● **Freedom and Equality, 2003**

American beliefs about equality and individualism are quite different from the beliefs held by people in other rich democracies.

Source: Pew Research Center, reported in *The Economist* (November 8, 2003), p. 4.

coordinate economic life in a nearly perfect fashion. Because the market is efficient and effective if left alone, he suggested, government should not interfere with its operations. Although few Americans now accept this "pure" free market ideal, most Americans today, as in the past, believe that the private sector is usually more effective and efficient than the public sector. Given the esteem in which private property and the market are held, as well as the historical success of the American economy, it is entirely understandable that Americans tend to hold the business system (though not large corporations) in very high regard.

Distrust of Government

From the beginning, Americans have distrusted government. Indeed, as you will recall from the discussion in Chapter 2, the framers created a republican constitutional system precisely because they distrusted government and were trying to create a set of constitutional rules that would deny government the means to act in mischievous or evil ways. Americans have long believed that when governments are imbued with too much power, they are tempted to interfere with private property, individual rights, and economic efficiency. This distrust of government—drawn from the writings of Adam Smith and John Locke, articulated in the words of the Declaration of Independence, and recurring in American political rhetoric throughout our history—still remains attractive to most Americans today, even though most Americans expect government to do far more than the framers ever imagined. This core belief is not universally shared. In countries such as Japan, Sweden, Germany, and France, where governments have always been powerful and have played an important role in directing society and the economy, people are much more likely to trust the intentions and trustworthiness of government.

This set of ideas about individualism, limited government, and the free market (what some people call *classical liberalism*)[27] influences many aspects of public policy in the United States. For example, the eminent economist John Kenneth Galbraith once decried the fact that ours is a society in which great private wealth exists side by side with public squalor. By that, he meant that Americans favor private consumption over public services and amenities and private over public initiatives.[28] In other rich democracies, citizens and political leaders tend to believe that extensive and high-quality public services in mass transit, health care, housing, and education are part and parcel of the good society.

Citizenship and the Nature of the Political Order

Certain beliefs about what kind of political order is most appropriate and what role citizens should play shape the actual daily behavior of citizens and political decision makers alike.

Democracy   At the time of the nation's founding, democracy was not highly regarded in the United States. During our history, however, the practice of democracy has been enriched and expanded, and the term *democracy* has become an honored one.[29] While regard for democracy is one of the bedrocks of the American belief system today, Americans have not necessarily always behaved democratically. After all, African Americans were denied the vote and other citizenship rights in many parts of the nation until the 1960s. It is fair to say, nevertheless, that most Americans believe in democracy as a general principle and take seriously any claim that their behavior is not consistent with it. For example, public opinion surveys done during the past 25 years consistently show that about 60 to 70 percent of Americans want to abolish the Electoral College.

Freedom and Liberty   Foreign visitors have always been fascinated by the American obsession with individual "rights," the belief that in the good society, government leaves people alone in their private pursuits. Studies show that freedom (also called *liberty*) is at the very top of the list of American beliefs and that it is more strongly honored here than elsewhere.[30] From the very beginning, what attracted most people to the United States was the promise of freedom in the New World. Many came for other reasons, to be sure: a great many came for strictly economic reasons, some came as convict labor, and some came in chains as slaves. But many who came to these shores seem to have done so to taste the freedom to speak and think as they chose, to worship as they pleased, to read what they might, and to assemble and petition the government if they had a mind to.

As in many cases, however, to believe in something is not necessarily to act consistently with that belief. There have been many intrusions on basic rights during our history. Later chapters address this issue in more detail.

Populism

The term *populism* refers to the hostility of the common person to concentrated power and the powerful. While public policy is not often driven by populist sentiments (for the powerful, by definition, exercise considerable political influence), populism has always been part of the American core belief system and has sometimes been expressed in visible ways in American politics.

One of the most common targets of populist sentiment has been concentrated economic power and the people who exercise it. Andrew Jackson mobilized this sentiment in his fight against the Bank of the United States in the 1830s. The Populist movement of the 1890s aimed at taming the new corporations of the day, especially the banks and the railroads. Corporations were the target of popular hostility during the dark days of the Great Depression and also in the 1970s, when agitation by consumer and environmental groups made the lives of some corporate executives extremely uncomfortable.

Populism is also hostile to the concentration of power in government. Alabama's segregationist governor, George Wallace, successfully tapped into this sentiment in his run for the Democratic presidential nomination in 1968, when he complained about the "pointy-headed intellectuals in Washington." The populist sentiment is evident today in efforts to impose term limits on public officials and in the popularity during the 1990s of anti-establishment figures such as Ross Perot and Governor Jesse Ventura, the former governor of Minnesota.

Piety

The United States is, by any measure, a strikingly religious society.[31] Polls conducted over the past three or four decades show that more Americans believe in God, regularly attend church, and say that religion is important in their lives, than people in any of the other rich democracies (see Figure 4.7). It has been this way from the beginning of the republic. Religious sentiments have been invoked by most important political leaders in the United States in their public pronouncements, and Americans have come to expect and are not surprised by religious references when leaders talk about public matters.

Religious faith affects politics in important ways. While churches and religious believers have often been on the liberal side of the political divide to be sure—note the substantial involvement of religious leaders, organizations, and believers in the civil rights and anti–Vietnam War movements—

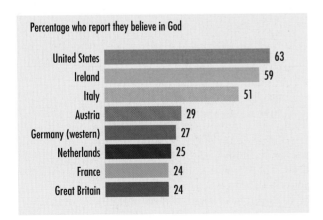

FIGURE 4.7 • **Comparing Nations on Their Strength of Religious Belief**

Compared with people in other rich democracies, a substantially higher proportion of Americans say they believe in God.

Source: International Social Survey, National Opinion Research Center, University of Chicago (1993).

How Democratic Are We?

Is Real Democracy Possible in the United States?

PROPOSITION: The kind of economy, society, and culture we have in the United States makes it difficult to have a real democracy because the key components of a working democracy—popular sovereignty, political equality, and political liberty—cannot flourish.

AGREE: The sort of economic system we have in the United States, though incredibly productive, distributes wealth and income in a highly unequal way, leaving the few at the top with the lion's share. At the same time, the middle class is stuck in place, and poverty prevails at a level unequaled by any of the other rich democracies. This leads to substantial inequalities in political power and influence among different income and wealth groups in the United States, because economic inequality always spills over into political inequality. Matters are made worse by the fact that Americans are dividing into racially and economically homogeneous housing areas, undermining the sense of community and shared sentiments that are the basis for democracy and for the sort of cooperation that is necessary for government to tackle serious social problems. To make matters worse, the American political culture celebrates an extreme form of individualism and anti-government sentiments that makes it hard for Americans to cooperate in a way that makes it possible for the people to use government to serve public purposes.

DISAGREE: American society is open, diverse, and filled with opportunity for those who are ambitious. Economic growth is raising the living standards of the population across the board, which bodes well for democracy; note the evidence that high living standards and democracy seem to go together. Also, economic, technological, and social changes—including the Internet, ease of travel, medical advances, and more—are allowing more and more people to develop their unique abilities and capacities, to become informed, to link together with others who share their public concerns, to get involved in community and political affairs, and to have their voices heard by public officials. Most importantly, perhaps, these developments make it possible for Americans to shape their own lives, improving their situations and those of their families, without the need of government.

CONSIDER: There are two competing arguments discussed here. One focuses on structural developments that contribute to rising inequality, social fragmentation, and contempt for government. The other focuses on rising living standards, expanded opportunities, and the promise of technology for enriching democratic life in the United States.   • Which is the closest to your own experience of life in this country and where you think American society is going?   • Is it possible that there is some truth to each position, that some developments and conditions in American society, economy, culture, and world position are democracy-enhancing, while others are democracy-diminishing?   • And, if the objective is to enrich democratic life in the United States, which of the barriers to democracy you have read about are most amenable to change?

strong religious beliefs are most associated with conservative tendencies in American politics. Public opinion polls show that the most religious Americans (of all denominations) are also the most conservative Americans on issues ranging from abortion to prayer in the schools, social welfare, and military spending. The strength of religious belief in America probably explains why our politics is more open to conservative appeals and tends toward conservative public policies (we will have more to say about this in Chapters 17 and 18) compared with the other rich democracies.[32]

Structural Influences on American Politics

We have now examined a number of structural factors that influence American politics. In Chapters 2 and 3, we examined the constitutional rules; in this chapter, we considered the main features of American society, economy, political culture, and the international system and how each influences important aspects of politics and government in the United States. These structural factors are interrelated. The kind of constitutional rules we have are, to a substantial degree, shaped by our beliefs about the nature of the individual, society, and government that make up our political culture. The political culture, in turn, with its ideas celebrating the market, competitive individualism, and private property, is perfectly attuned to a free enterprise economy. How the economy operates and develops has a lot to do with the life of the American people (where people live, what kind of work they do, and so on), as does the nation's place in the world. The characteristics of the American population trigger their own effects; the populace's level of education and skill has a lot to do with American economic performance, for instance.

These structural factors are used throughout this book to help explain how American politics and government work and what kinds of public policies we have—note especially the "Using the Framework" feature that appears in each chapter—but we want to focus on the importance of specific aspects of these structural factors even more in subsequent chapters. We believe that four structural factors are especially important today in shaping what is going on in the political system. They include the following:

- The threat of terrorism.
- The emergence of the United States as the world's single superpower.
- Rapid technological change.
- Changes in the demographics of the American population.

Each of these changes has altered the agenda of American politics, refashioned political coalitions and alliances, altered the balance of power among competing political interests and government institutions, and pushed public policies in different directions.

Summary

How politics and government work is shaped by such structural factors as the nature of society, the economy, the nation's place in the world, and the political culture.

The most important changes in the American population are its growth; its diversification along ethnic, religious, and racial lines; and its relocation from rural to urban and suburban areas and to the Sun Belt. Americans enjoy a very high standard of living, but inequality is substantial and poverty is surprisingly persistent. These factors affect the agenda of American politics and the distribution of political power.

The American economy is a market economy that has changed over the years from a highly competitive, small-enterprise form to a corporate-dominated one with a global reach. Economic change has had important reverberations in American politics.

The emergence of the United States as a superpower in the twentieth century changed the content of foreign policy, the balance of power between the president and Congress, the size of the federal government, and the priorities of the government's budget. The collapse of socialism in eastern Europe affirmed the position of the United States as the world's most important military power.

Americans believe strongly in individualism, limited government, and free enterprise. Beliefs about democracy, liberty, and the primacy of the common people also help define the political culture. The political culture shapes American ideas about what the good society should look like, the appropriate role for government, and the possibilities for self-government.

Suggestions for Further Reading

Bellah, Robert N., Richard Madsen, William M. Sullivan, Ann Swidler, and Steven M. Tipton. *Habits of the Heart.* Berkeley, CA: University of California Press, 1985.
  A convincing description of competitive individualism and its effects.

Chafe, William H. *The Unfinished Journey: America Since World War II,* 5th ed. New York: Oxford University Press, 2002.
  A history of postwar America, with special attention to how structural transformations have shaped American political life.

Dicken, Peter. *Global Shift: The Internationalization of Economic Activity,* 4th ed. New York: Guilford Press, 2003.
  A comprehensive look at the scope, causes, and consequences of economic globalization.

Hochschild, Jennifer L. *Facing Up to the American Dream.* Princeton, NJ: Princeton University Press, 1995.
  A brilliant examination of the ideology of the American dream and how race and social class affect its interpretation and possibilities.

Hughes, James W., and Joseph J. Seneca, eds. *America's Demographic Tapestry.* New Brunswick, NJ: Rutgers University Press, 1999.
  A collection of research essays on the underlying demographic changes that are transforming the United States.

Page, Benjamin I., and James R. Simmons. *What Government Can Do: Dealing with Poverty and Inequality.* Chicago: University of Chicago Press, 2000.
  An extensive overview of poverty and inequality in the United States, their causes, and what government can do about it.

Phillips, Kevin. *Wealth and Democracy: How Great Fortunes and Government Created America's Aristocracy.* New York: Broadway Books, 2002.
  A hard-hitting analysis of wealth inequality and how it shapes American life and public policies.

Tichener, Daniel. *Dividing Lines: The Politics of Immigration Control in America.* Princeton, NJ: Princeton University Press, 2003.
  A comprehensive history of efforts to control immigration to the United States and the politics behind shifting U.S. policies.

Vaca, Nicolas C. *The Presumed Alliance: The Unspoken Conflict Between Latinos and Blacks and What It Means for America.* New York: Harper Collins/RAYD, 2004.
  An examination of the rise of Latino numbers and political power and an appeal for Latinos to fight for their own interests.

Internet Sources

The Economist
http://www.economist.com/
The home page of one of the world's leading publications on the U.S. and international economies.

Fedstats
http://www.fedstats.gov/
Statistical information on the U.S. economy and society from more than 70 government agencies.

Statistical Abstract of the United States
http://www.census.gov/statab/www
A vast compendium of statistical information on the government, the economy, and society.

Statistical Resources on the Web
www.lib.umich.edu/govdocs/statuniv.html
A vast compendium of statistical information on society, economy, and culture for the United States and other countries, organized by the University of Michigan library in a very user-friendly format.

University of Texas Online, Statistics and Demographics
http://www.lib.utexas.edu/refsites/
statistics.html#intl
A treasure trove of easily accessible U.S. and international statistical information.

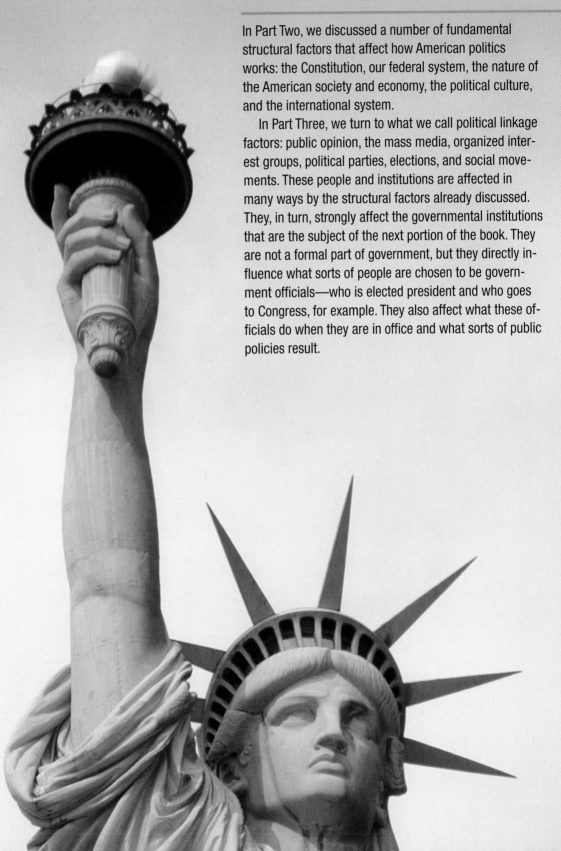

Part Three

Political Linkage

In Part Two, we discussed a number of fundamental structural factors that affect how American politics works: the Constitution, our federal system, the nature of the American society and economy, the political culture, and the international system.

In Part Three, we turn to what we call political linkage factors: public opinion, the mass media, organized interest groups, political parties, elections, and social movements. These people and institutions are affected in many ways by the structural factors already discussed. They, in turn, strongly affect the governmental institutions that are the subject of the next portion of the book. They are not a formal part of government, but they directly influence what sorts of people are chosen to be government officials—who is elected president and who goes to Congress, for example. They also affect what these officials do when they are in office and what sorts of public policies result.

Chapter 5
Public Opinion

In This Chapter

- What public opinion is and how it is related to democracy

- What sorts of government policies Americans favor or oppose

- How people acquire their political attitudes

- How opinions differ according to race, gender, age, income, and other factors

- How much effect public opinion has on what government does

The Vietnam War and the Public

On August 2, 1964, the Pentagon announced that the U.S. destroyer *Maddox,* while on "routine patrol" in international waters in the Gulf of Tonkin near Vietnam, had undergone an "unprovoked attack" by three communist North Vietnamese PT boats. Two days later, the Pentagon reported a "second deliberate attack" on the *Maddox* and its companion destroyer, the *C. Turner Joy.* In a nationwide television broadcast, President Lyndon Johnson referred to "open aggression on the high seas" and declared that these hostile actions required that he retaliate with military force. Air attacks were launched against four North Vietnamese PT boat bases and an oil storage depot.[1]

Years later, the *Pentagon Papers,* a secret Defense Department study leaked to the news media by defense analyst Daniel Ellsberg, revealed that the American people had been deceived. The *Maddox* had not been on an innocent cruise; it had, in fact, been assisting South Vietnamese gunboats make raids on the North Vietnamese coast. The second "attack" apparently never occurred; it was imagined by an inexperienced sonar operator in dark and stormy seas. At the time, however, few skeptics raised questions. On August 7, 1964, by a vote of 88–2, the Senate passed the Tonkin Resolution, which approved the president's taking "all necessary measures," including the use of armed force, to repel any armed attack and to assist any ally in the region. A legal basis for full U.S. involvement in the Vietnam War had been established.

For more than a decade, the United States had been giving large-scale military aid to the French colonialists, and then to the American-installed but authoritarian South Vietnamese government, to fight nationalists and communists in Vietnam. More than 23,000 U.S. military advisers were there by the end of 1964, occasionally engaging in combat. On the other side of the world, the American public knew and cared little about the guerrilla war. In fact, few knew exactly where Vietnam was. Nevertheless, people were willing to go along when their leaders told them that action was essential to resist communist aggression.

After the Tonkin incident, people paid more attention. Public support for the war increased. When asked in August what should be done next in Vietnam, 48 percent said to keep troops there, get tougher, or take definite military action while only 14 percent said negotiate or get out.[2] Through the fall of 1964, more people wanted to step up the war than wanted to pull out, and many endorsed the current policy. In 1965, after the United States had begun the heavy "Rolling Thunder" bombing of North Vietnam, and after large numbers of U.S. troops had gradually engaged in combat in South Vietnam, public support of the war continued. Month after month, pollsters found that only a small minority wanted to withdraw from Vietnam; as many or more wanted

to escalate the war further, and the majority favored continuing the current policy.

But the number of U.S. troops in Vietnam rose rapidly, from 184,300 at the end of 1965 to 536,100 at the end of 1968, and casualties increased correspondingly. A total of 1,369 Americans were killed in 1965; 5,008 in 1966; 9,377 in 1967; and 14,589 in 1968. Many thousands more were wounded, and others were captured or missing.[3] Television news began to display weekly casualty counts in the hundreds, with pictures of dead American soldiers going home in body bags. The war became expensive, as politicians put it, in "American blood and treasure." Senate hearings aired anti-war testimony. Peace marches and demonstrations, though resented by much of the public, nonetheless increased pressure to end the war.

By December 1967, about as many people (45 percent) agreed as disagreed with the proposition that it had been a "mistake" to send troops to fight in Vietnam. A large majority said they favored "Vietnamization," bringing U.S. troops home as South Vietnamese replaced them.

Then catastrophe struck. In January 1968, during Vietnam's Tet holidays, the North Vietnamese army launched what became known as the *Tet Offensive:* massive attacks throughout South Vietnam, including an assault on the U.S. embassy in Saigon. The American public was shocked by televised scenes of urban destruction and bloody corpses, of U.S. soldiers destroying Ben Tre village "in order to save it," of marines bogged down in the rubble of the ancient city of Hue, and of a 77-day siege of the American firebase at Khe Sanh. The chief lesson seemed to be that a U.S. victory in Vietnam, if feasible at all, was going to be very costly in terms of lives and dollars.

After Tet, criticism of the war—by politicians, newspaper editorials, and television commentators such as Walter Cronkite and others—mushroomed, and public support for the war diminished. President Johnson, staggered by a surprisingly strong vote for anti-war candidate Eugene McCarthy in the New Hampshire primary, announced that he would limit the bombing of North Vietnam, seek a negotiated settlement, and withdraw as a candidate for reelection. In March 1968, only 41 percent of Americans described themselves as hawks (supporters of the war), a sharp drop from the 61 percent of early February. Anger over Vietnam contributed to the election defeat of the Democrats the following November.

By January 1969, when the Nixon administration took office, a substantial majority of the public favored monthly reductions in the number of U.S. soldiers in Vietnam: 57 percent approved the idea, while only 28 percent disapproved. In June, Nixon announced the withdrawal of 25,000 troops, followed by announcements of 35,000 more in September, another 50,000 in December, and 150,000 during the following year. Large majorities of the public approved of the withdrawals. Most said they wanted to continue them even if the South Vietnamese government collapsed. There can be little doubt that public opinion influenced U.S. disengagement from the war.

This did not mean that a majority of Americans wanted to get out of Vietnam immediately; most disliked the idea of a communist victory. But anti-war marches and demonstrations continued during 1970 and 1971, and many people wanted a faster pace of withdrawal. Gradually, U.S. troops came out of Vietnam; in January 1973, after the intensive Christmas bombing of North Vietnam, a peace agreement was finally signed. Two years later, the North Vietnamese army took control of Saigon and reunified Vietnam, a nation that had been divided since the end of World War II.

The Vietnam story shows how government officials can sometimes lead or manipulate opinion, especially when it concerns obscure matters in faraway lands, and how opinion is affected by events and their presentation in the mass media. The story also shows that public opinion, even on foreign policy matters, can sometimes have a strong effect on policymaking.

Thinking Critically About This Chapter

This chapter is about public opinion, how it is formed, and what effect it has on American politics and government.

Using the Framework   You will learn in this chapter how public opinion is shaped by a wide range of structural-level factors, including historical events, the political culture, family and community socialization, and economic and social change. You will also learn how public opinion influences the behavior of political leaders and shapes many of the policies of the federal government.

Using the Democracy Standard   Based on the standard of democracy described in Chapter 1, public opinion should be one of the decisive factors in determining what government does. You will see in this chapter, however, that while the influence of public opinion is important, public officials must pay attention to other political forces as well. They sometimes pay close attention to public opinion; at other times, they pay only slight attention to it.

Democracy and Public Opinion

Most Americans have **core beliefs** about the nature of human beings, society, and the political order. These core beliefs—including belief in individualism, limited government, and free enterprise, among others—make up the American political culture, as described in Chapter 4. In addition to their overarching core beliefs, most Americans also have attitudes about the specific political issues of the day, including attitudes about government policies, public officials, political parties, and candidates. When these core beliefs and **political attitudes** are expressed by ordinary people and considered as a whole—particularly as they are revealed by polling surveys—we refer to this as **public opinion.**

Public opinion is particularly important in a democracy if we understand democracy to be fundamentally about the rule of the people. For the people to rule, they must have their voice heard by those in government. To know whether or not the people rule, we require evidence that those in government are responsive to the voice of the people. The best evidence that those in power are responsive to the voice of the people is a strong showing that what government does reflects the wishes of the people. The wishes of the people can be discerned in elections, to be sure, but a particularly powerful way to know what the people want is to ask them directly in a polling survey. In a democracy, there will be a close match between public opinion and government policies and actions, at least in the long run.

Curiously, however, many leading political theorists, including some who say they believe in democracy, have expressed grave doubts about the wisdom of the public. James Madison, Alexander Hamilton, and other Founders of our national government worried that the public's "passions" would infringe on liberty and that public opinion would be susceptible to radical and frequent shifts.[4] Journalist and statesman Walter Lippmann declared that most people do not know what goes on in the world; they have only vague, media-provided pictures in their heads. Lippmann approvingly quoted Sir Robert Peel's reference to "that great compound of folly, weakness, prejudice, wrong feeling, right feeling, obstinacy and newspaper paragraphs which is called public opinion."[5]

Modern survey researchers have not been much kinder. The first voting studies, carried out during the 1940s and 1950s, turned up what scholars considered appalling evidence of public ignorance, lack of interest in politics, and reliance on group or party loyalties rather than judgments about the issues of the day. Repeated surveys of the same individuals found that their responses seemed to change randomly from one interview to another. Philip Converse, a leading student of political behavior, coined the term *nonattitudes:* On many issues of public policy, many or most Americans seemed to have no real views at all but simply offered "doorstep opinions" to satisfy interviewers.[6]

Perhaps even more disturbing, it appears that a substantial majority of federal government officials do not hold the abilities of the public in high regard. One major survey on this issue conducted in 2000 showed that 77 percent of presidential appointees, 80 percent of senior civil servants, and 47 percent of members of Congress did not agree with the statement that "Americans know enough about issues to form wise opinions about what should be done."[7] A study of a broader sample of officials concluded that ". . . two-thirds or more of government officials doubted that the public was sufficiently informed, long-sighted, and emotionally detached to provide sound guidance for government decisions."[8]

core beliefs
Individual's views about the fundamental nature of human beings, society, and economy; taken together, they comprise the political culture.

political attitudes
Individual's views about public policies, political parties, candidates, government institutions, and public officials.

public opinion
Political attitudes expressed by ordinary citizens.

What should we make of this? If ordinary citizens are poorly informed and their views are based on whim, or if they have no real opinions at all, it hardly seems desirable—or even possible—that public opinion should determine what governments do. Both the feasibility and the attractiveness of democracy seem to be thrown into doubt. When we examine exactly what sorts of opinions ordinary Americans have, however, and how those opinions are formed and changed, we will see that such fears about public opinion have been greatly exaggerated.

Before we address the issue of the rationality of public opinion and the degree to which public opinion shapes the actions of government, we need to pay attention to two preliminary but important subjects. First, we must examine how we know what public opinion is. Second, we must learn more about where people's beliefs, attitudes, and opinions come from.

Measuring Public Opinion

Years ago, people who wanted to find out anything about public opinion had to guess, based on what their barbers or taxi drivers said, on what appeared in letters to newspaper editors, or on what sorts of one-liners won cheers at political rallies. But the views of personal acquaintances, letter writers, or rally audiences are often quite different from those of the public as a whole. Similarly, the angry people who called in to radio talk shows at the beginning of the Clinton administration tended to be more conservative and anti-Clinton than most Americans.[9] Listeners could easily get a mistaken impression of what was on their fellow citizens' minds. To figure out what the average American thinks, we cannot rely on unrepresentative groups or noisy minorities.

sample survey
An interview study asking questions of a set of people who are chosen as representative of the whole population.

Public Opinion Polls

A clever invention, the public opinion poll, or **sample survey,** now eliminates most of the guesswork in measuring public opinion. A survey consists of sys-

Exit polls, which survey the opinions of people as they leave the polling place after voting, are a major source of information on who votes and how people make their voting decisions. They are also the basis for network election-night reports on "who won" announcements, made well before all the ballots have been counted.

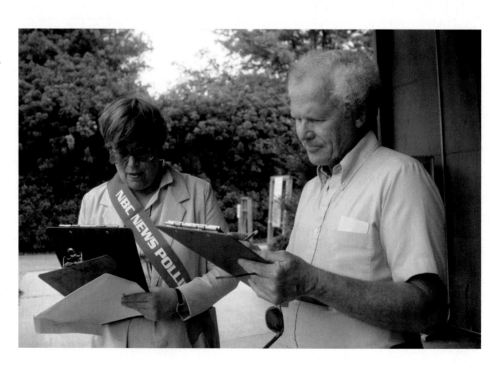

tematic interviews conducted by trained professional interviewers who ask a standardized set of questions of a rather small number of randomly chosen Americans—usually about 1,000 or 1,500 of them for a national survey. Such a survey can reveal with remarkable accuracy what all 260 million or so of us are thinking.

The secret of success is to make sure that the sample of people interviewed is representative of the whole population, that is, that the proportions of people in the sample who are young, old, female, college-educated, black, rural, Catholic, southern, western, and so forth are all about the same as in the U.S. population as a whole. This representativeness is achieved best when the people being interviewed are chosen through **random sampling,** which ensures that each member of the population has an equal chance of being chosen. Then survey researchers can add up all the responses to a given question and compute the percentages of people answering one way or another. Statisticians can use probability theory to tell how close the survey's results are likely to be to what the whole population would say if asked the same questions. Findings from a random sample of 1,500 people have a 95 percent chance of accurately reflecting the views of the whole population within about 3 or 4 percentage points.[10]

Perfectly random sampling is not feasible. Personal interviews have to be clustered geographically so that interviewers can easily get from one respondent to another. Telephone interviews—the cheapest and most common kind—are clustered within particular telephone exchanges. Still, the samples that survey organizations use are sufficiently representative so that survey results closely reflect how the whole population would have responded if everyone in the United States had been asked the same questions at the moment the survey was carried out. Recently, some commercial polling organizations have tried to do polling on the Internet. For the most part, these attempts fall prey to the problem of nonrandom sampling. Not all Americans own computers; not all computer owners regularly use the Internet. So, polling people by Internet is going to capture a sample that is very unrepresentative of the American population.

random sampling
The selection of survey respondents by chance, with equal probability, to ensure their representativeness of the whole population.

**You Are a Polling
Consultant**

Traditional and Emerging Problems in Political Polling

Those who use poll results—including citizens encountering political polls in newspapers and on television—should be aware of the following problems with polls and what competent pollsters try to do about them:

- The wording of questions is important; it often makes a big difference exactly how questions are asked. In one survey, for example, support for a constitutional amendment requiring a balanced budget dropped from 70 percent to 31 percent when the question specified that Medicare would need to be cut to reach that goal.[11] Attaching the name of a popular president or an unpopular one to a survey question—as in "Do you support President X's proposal for medicare reform?"—affects how people respond. Good survey questions try to avoid such "leading" wording.

- "Closed-ended" or "forced-choice" questions, which ask the respondents to choose among preformulated answers, do not always reveal what people are thinking on their own or what they would come up with after a few minutes of thought or discussion. So, in this sense, a survey may not always be capturing what people think is important or what choices they would make. For that reason, "open-ended" questions are sometimes asked in order to yield more spontaneous answers, and small discussion groups or "focus groups" are brought together to show what emerges when people talk among themselves about the topics a

Harry Truman ridicules an edition of the *Chicago Tribune* proclaiming his Republican challenger, Thomas Dewey, president. Opinion polls stopped asking questions too early in the 1948 election campaign, missing Truman's last-minute surge.

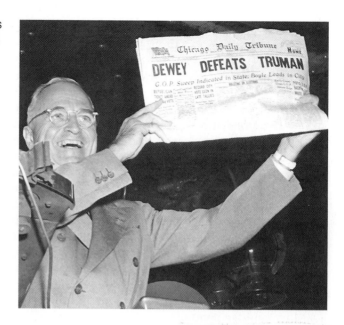

moderator introduces. (See the "By the Numbers" feature on page 122 for more insight into issues in public opinion research.)

Scholars and survey professionals worry about a number of things that can undermine the validity of survey research by making it difficult to draw a sample that is random, meaning representative of the entire population. In some cases, the problems seem to be getting worse. Here are the principal things they are concerned about:

- Because they are inundated by phone calls from advertisers who sometimes try to disguise themselves as researchers, Americans have become less willing to answer pollsters' questions.

- Finding themselves bothered by telephone solicitations that interrupt their lives, Americans are increasingly using answering machines and "caller ID" to screen their calls. Pollsters are finding it increasingly difficult to get past the screening.

- More and more Americans are turning to mobile phones and cutting their reliance on land lines. Because mobile phones are often turned off, survey researchers cannot always get through to people who are part of the prospective random sample.

The top academic and commercial polling firms claim they are taking steps to overcome these problems—using repeated call-backs and statistical methods to fill in for missing people, for example—but the problems are likely to get worse before they get better. For now, we will have to make do with polling results from quality researchers and firms.

Learning Political Beliefs and Attitudes

political socialization
The process by which individuals come to have certain core beliefs and political attitudes.

Political scientists use the term **political socialization** to describe the process by which individuals acquire their core beliefs about human nature, the country, the government, and the economy—which, taken together, form a society's political culture—and their attitudes about government officials, alternative public policies, the parties, candidates for elected office, and other political matters of the day. Agents of socialization—the instruments by which beliefs and attitudes are conveyed to individuals in society—include families, schools, churches, the mass media, and social groups with which individuals are most closely associated. In this section will show how these agents of socialization shape the outlooks of Americans.

Some aspects of political socialization lead Americans to closely resemble one another. This alikeness is particularly striking with regard to the core beliefs of the American people explored in the last chapter: individualism, the sanctity of private property, distrust of government, populism, and piety. Other aspects of political socialization lead Americans to differ from one another in their attitudes and opinions in fairly significant yet understandable ways. We address this matter in a later section of this chapter titled "How People Differ."

Agents of Socialization

Political socialization is a lifetime process in the sense that people engage in political learning throughout the life-course.[12] However, political learning in childhood seems to be particularly important, as childhood is the period when people attain their core beliefs and general outlooks about the political world.

The *family* plays a particularly important role in shaping the outlooks of children. It is in the family—whether in a traditional or nontraditional family—where children pick up their basic outlook on life and the world around them. It is mainly from their family, for example, that children learn to trust or distrust others, something that affects a wide range of political attitudes later in life. It is from the family, and the neighborhood where the family lives, that children learn about which ethnic or racial group, social class or income

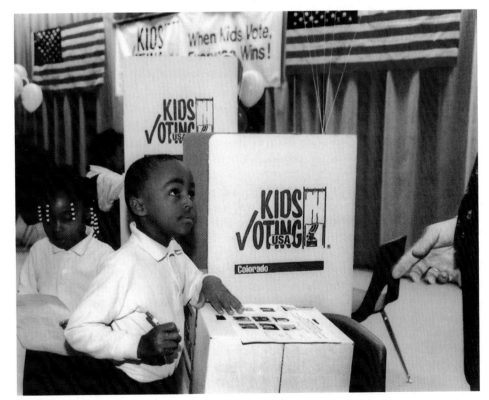

Children gain many of their initial ideas about how the American political system works in their school classrooms. Here, elementary school students take part in a mock election.

By the Numbers

Do Americans support stem cell research? How do we know which survey to believe?

One of the emerging controversies in American politics concerns whether the federal government should encourage or discourage medical research that uses embryonic stem cells. Proponents say the use of such cells, today harvested primarily from unused embryos from fertility clinics, is almost certain to lead to new medical treatments for a wide range of genetically linked diseases, such as Parkinson's and juvenile diabetes. Opponents say the expanded use of stem cells for research will encourage more abortions—aborted embryos being a potentially important source of stem cells—as well as the creation of cloned embryos, both of which, in their view, are morally unacceptable.

Why It Matters: In the long run, government policies tend to follow public opinion on major issues. Whether the federal government will allow research in this emerging biomedical field, and whether it will help pay for basic research, will depend a great deal on how strong the public stance is on the issue.

Behind the Number: At first blush, it certainly looks as if the public strongly supports stem cell re-search. In early 2001, several leading survey organizations reported the public in favor of moving along this path: An NBC News/*Wall Street Journal* poll showed 69 percent in favor; Gallup reported 54 percent in favor; ABC News weighed in with 58 percent in favor; and the Juvenile Diabetes Foundation reported 70 percent in favor. On the other hand, a poll sponsored by the Conference of Catholic Bishops showed only 24 percent in favor of stem cell research.

Calculating the Number: In the surveys reported here, the various polling organizations did not simply ask respondents whether they were in favor of stem cell research or against it, but offered alternative positions for respondents to consider, briefly spelling out the arguments being made for both sides in the debate. So it would seem, given the care with which questions were written and the opinion numbers reported above, that proponents of stem cell research have won the public opinion battle.

Criticisms of the Number: But not so fast! Consider a number of problems raised by academic critics, all of which are related to a concern about whether Americans really have opinions at all about stem cell research:

- High levels of "don't know" responses are a clue that the public has not formed well-grounded

group, and religion they belong to and begin to pick up attitudes that are typical of these groups. In dinner table conversations and other encounters with parents, children start to acquire ideas about the country—ideas about patriotism, for example—and their first vague ideological ideas: whether government is a good or bad thing, whether taxes are a good or bad thing, and whether certain people and groups in society are to be admired or not (welfare recipients, rich people, corporations, and the like). Most importantly, because it represents the filter through which a great deal of future political learning takes place, many children adopt the political party identifications of their parents, especially if the parents share the same party identification. Although the relationship between parent and child party identification is weaker now than it was in the 1940s and 1950s, a majority of adult Americans still identify with the same party as their parents.

   Schools are also important as agents of political socialization. In the early grades, through explicit lessons and the celebration of national symbols—such as the flag in the classroom, recitation of the Pledge of Allegiance, pictures on opinions about the survey issue. Unfortunately, among the surveys cited, only the Gallup organization offered such an option to respondents. The Gallup finding of high numbers of "don't know" responses suggests Americans may be more uncertain about stem cell research than appears on the surface.

- When wide variations in opinion are reported—in this case, between those in the Catholic Bishops' survey and the others—the culprit may be the question wording. Well-established and strongly held opinions are not easily shaken or changed by question wording. Consequently, when question wording leads to wide variations in expressed opinions, public opinion specialists suspect that the public has not yet formed opinions about the issues being addressed in the survey. There is some evidence of this in the Bishops' survey; examination of the survey shows that some fairly loaded language was used, including wording such as "the live embryos would be destroyed in their first week of development." Their questionnaire, moreover, states that the embryos would be used "in experiments," leaving unmentioned possible medical advances arising from research.

What to Watch For: Although respondents in a survey are generally willing to help out survey researchers by saying whether they are "for" or

"against" one thing or another, they may not really have solid, well-formed opinions about the issue being addressed. Three very useful clues are

- A high number of "don't know" responses. Check the original source of the survey results reported in the newspaper or on television to find out the number of these responses.
- Wide variations in the results of opinion surveys on a particular issue. Do not depend on the results of one survey but look at several on the same subject.
- The presence of highly detailed questions that explain the issue to the respondent. Go to the original source and see how the question or questions are worded.

What Do You Think?   Have you formed an opinion about the benefits and drawbacks of stem cell research? If you have an opinion, do you believe it is based on information you have encountered and thought about carefully? If you have formed a solid point of view on stem cell research, you may want to contact various elected officials and let them know where you stand.

Source: Adam Clymer, "The Unbearable Lightness of Public Opinion Polls," *The New York Times* (August 12, 2001), "Week in Review," p. 1; Richard Morin, "Who Knows?" *The Washington Post National Edition* (September 10–16, 2001), p. 34.

the walls of famous presidents, patriotic pageants, and the like—schools convey lessons about American identity and patriotism. In the middle grades, schools teach children about the political process by sponsoring mock presidential elections and elections to student government. In the upper grades, most students in most school districts take courses in American history and American government and continue learning about participation through student government.

Popular culture—movies, music, and advertising—also shapes the budding political outlooks of young people. To be sure, most of the messages coming from the popular culture have more to do with style, fashion, and attitude. But much in popular culture conveys political messages. Many rap-music performers, for example, imbed political messages in their songs. Many Hollywood movies come with a political message; for example, themes of sleazy politicians and untrustworthy or corrupt elected officials are quite common.

Political socialization does not stop when children become adults. Substantial evidence shows that a *college education* affects people's outlooks about public policies and the role of government. People with a college education, for example, are more likely to support government programs to protect the environment. We know, moreover, that people's political outlooks are shaped by *major events* or developments that affect the country during their young adult years. In the past, such events have included the Great Depression, World War II, the civil rights movement and the countercultural revolution of the 1960s, the Reagan Revolution of the 1980s, and the 9/11 terrorist attacks on the United States. The effect of these events and developments seems most pronounced for young people who are just coming to a sense of political awareness. Political scientists identify this phenomenon as a *generational effect.* Thus, young people coming of age politically during the 1960s turned out to be much more liberal throughout their lives than young people coming of age during the 1950s or during the Reagan years.

Finally, a number of socializing agents affect people's attitudes and expressed political opinions throughout adulthood. *Jobs* and experiences at work can affect the confidence that people express about the future for themselves and their families. The *news media* affects people's attitudes by how they select and frame the issues they cover, as you will see in Chapter 6. Getting *married* and buying a home—because they bring with them new concerns with things such as the quality of local schools and neighborhoods, interest rates for consumer goods and home mortgages, and more—cause many people to alter their positions on political parties, candidates, and issues. So too does *retirement,* which often brings a new sense of urgency about government support for retirement and health care benefits.

How People Differ

We have learned that agents of socialization are important in acquiring core beliefs as well as political attitudes about government, the parties, candidates, political leaders, and public policies. To a great extent, as you have seen in this chapter and in Chapter 4's section on the American political culture, the socialization of core beliefs in the United States is common to most Americans. Indeed, a broad range of socialization agents—from the news media and popular entertainment to government leaders and the schools—reinforce one another about what it means to be an American and to live in the United States. However, Americans also grow up and live in a variety of distinctive environments that shape attitudes in distinctive ways. In this section, we explore some of the most significant circumstances that define and divide us in our political views.

Race and Ethnicity

Among the biggest differences are those between white and black Americans. Hispanics and Asian Americans also have some distinctive political opinions. Many white ethnic groups, however, are no longer much different from other members of the population.

African Americans
On most core beliefs about the American system, few differences are discernible between black Americans and other Americans.[13] Similar percentages of each group believe, for example, that people can get ahead by working hard, that providing for equal opportunity is more important than ensuring equal outcomes, and that the federal government should balance its budget. On a range of other political issues, however, the racial divide looms large.[14]

Blacks, who stayed loyal to the Republican party (the party of Lincoln and of Reconstruction) long after the Civil War, became Democrats in large proportions with the New Deal of the 1930s. Most black Americans have remained Democrats, especially since the civil rights struggles of the 1960s. Today African Americans are the most solidly Democratic of any group in the population: Some 64 percent call themselves Democrats, while only about 9 percent call themselves Republicans (see Figure 5.1). In 2004, 88 percent of African

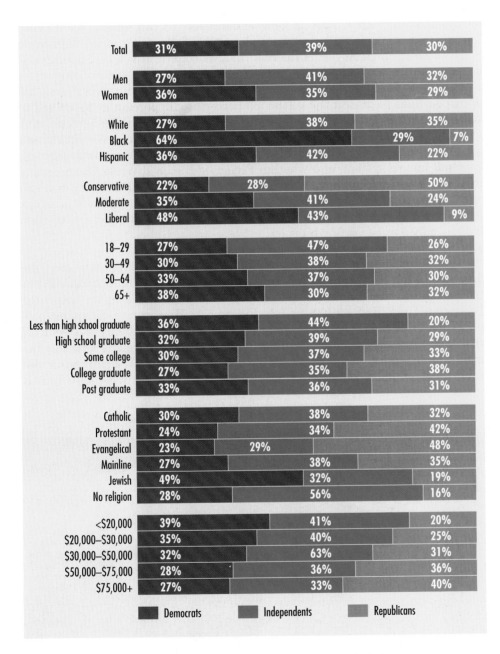

FIGURE 5.1 ● Party Loyalties Among Various Social Groups

Blacks, city dwellers, women, and people of lower-income and educational levels tend to be Democrats, while whites, suburbanites, men, the college-educated, and people with high incomes tend to be Republicans.

Source: The Pew Research Center for the People and the Press, *Evenly Divided and Increasingly Polarized: The 2004 Political Landscape* (Washington, D.C., November 9, 2003).

Americans voted for Democrat John Kerry; only 11 percent supported Republican George W. Bush.[15]

Black Americans also tend to be much more liberal than whites on economic issues, especially those involving government programs to provide assistance to those who need help in the areas of jobs, housing, medical care, education, and so on. This liberalism reflects African Americans' economically disadvantaged position in American society and the still-real effects of slavery and discrimination. On some social issues, however, blacks tend to hold strong religious values and to be rather conservative: More are opposed to abortion, for example, than are whites. In general, however, African Americans are very liberal (that is, favor an activist government to help solve social ills). More blacks identify themselves as liberals than as conservatives or moderates, a pattern that is almost exactly reversed among whites.[16] African Americans also are more likely than Americans in general to favor government regulation of corporations to protect the public (60 percent to 30 percent in 2003) and to favor protection of the environment and the consumer over the need to leave individuals free to act as they want (62 percent to 32 percent).[17] Black and white divisions are most apparent on issues related to affirmative action, the criminal justice system, and whether racism still exists. While 58 percent of African Americans say they favor preferences for blacks in hiring, for example only 13 percent of whites agree.[18] Similarly, large majorities of black Americans believe that blacks receive unfair treatment in society, a position held by only a minority of whites.[19]

Hispanics Hispanics—people of Spanish-speaking background—are the fastest-growing ethnic group in America and the largest minority group in the nation. As a whole, the Hispanic population identifies more with the Democrats than the Republicans (see Figure 5.1). However, the Hispanic population itself is quite diverse. Cuban Americans, many of them refugees from the Castro regime, tend to be conservative, Republican, strongly anti-communist, and skeptical of government programs. The much more numerous Americans of Mexican or Puerto Rican ancestry, by contrast, are mostly

Both major political parties are trying to attract new voters among the rapidly growing Hispanic population. Here, two Hispanic men add their names to the voter rolls at a Democratic party registration drive.

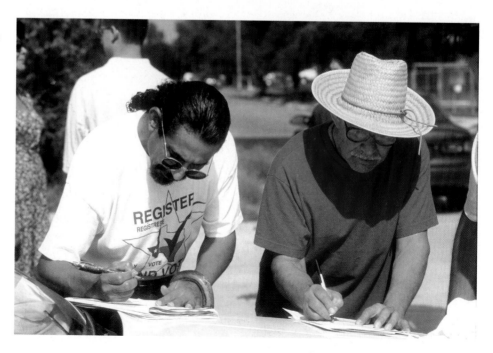

Democrats and quite liberal on economic matters, although rather traditional on social questions—reflecting their predominant Roman Catholicism.

Hispanics have been one of the least politically active groups in the United States, although they have begun to vote in increasing numbers (see the opening story in Chapter 4). Low incomes, suspicion of the authorities, and lack of facility with the English language have long discouraged participation. Now, mobilized by social movement groups and increasingly wooed by both major parties, this sleeping giant of American politics seems to be awakening.[20]

Asian Americans   Asian Americans, a small but growing part of the U.S. population—approximately 4 percent of the population in 2002[21]—come from quite diverse backgrounds in Japan, Korea, Vietnam, Thailand, China, and elsewhere. As a group, Asian Americans have tended to be successful educationally and economically, to participate fairly actively in politics, and to be conservative and Republican. They have also begun to win electoral office at the local level, primarily in large urban areas where the vast majority of Asian Americans live.

White Ethnics   Other ethnic groups are not so distinctive in their political opinions. Irish Americans and people of Italian, Polish, and other southern or eastern European ancestry, for example, became strong Democrats as part of the New Deal coalition. But as they achieved success economically, their economic liberalism faded, and their social conservatism prevailed. By the 1980s, these groups were not much different from the majority of other white Americans.

Religion

Ethnic differences are often interwoven with differences in religious faith and values.[22]

Catholics   Roman Catholics (28 percent of the U.S. population, according to the 2000 census) were heavily Democratic after the New Deal but now resemble the majority of Americans in their party affiliations—pretty evenly split between the Democrats and Republicans. Catholics' economic liberalism has

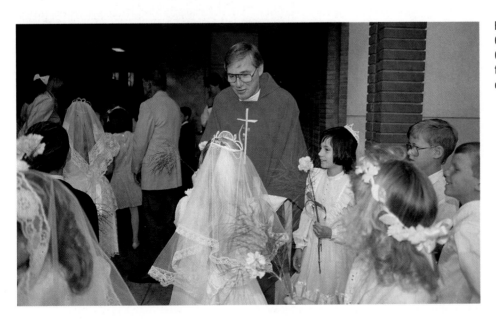

First communion at a Roman Catholic church in Tarzana, California. Practicing Catholics tend to be economically liberal and socially conservative.

faded somewhat with rises in their income, although this liberalism remains substantial. Catholics have tended to be especially concerned with family issues and to espouse measures to promote morality (for example, anti-pornography laws) and law and order. But American Catholics disagree with many church teachings: They support birth control and the right to have abortions in about the same proportions as do other Americans, for example.

Jews American Jews (only about 2 percent of the U.S. population) began to join the Democratic party in the 1920s and did so overwhelmingly in the 1930s, in response to Franklin D. Roosevelt's New Deal social policies and his foreign policy of resisting Hitler. Most Jews have stayed with the party. Next to African Americans, they remain the most Democratic group in the United States: About 49 percent identify themselves as Democrats and only 19 percent as Republicans. In the 2004 presidential election, Jews cast 74 percent of their votes for Kerry and only 25 percent for Bush.

Jews are exceptionally liberal on such social issues as civil liberties and abortion. They also tend to be staunch supporters of civil rights, despite tensions with African Americans over such matters as U.S. policy toward Israel and the Palestinians and anti-Semitic remarks over the years by some black leaders. Rising incomes have somewhat undercut Jews' economic liberalism, but they remain substantially more supportive of social welfare programs than other groups.

Protestants Protestants, who constitute a large majority of Americans, do not differ much from the U.S. average in most respects. But Protestants come in many varieties: relatively high-income (socially liberal, economically conservative) Episcopalians and Presbyterians; generally liberal Unitarian-Universalists and middle-class northern Baptists; conservative and strongly Republican Mormons; and lower-income and quite conservative Southern Baptists and evangelicals of various denominations.

In the early 1980s, evangelical Christians played an important part in the "new right" segment of Ronald Reagan's conservative movement, working hard against abortion, against pornography, for law and order, and for their version of family values. Disappointed by failures to achieve their national goals at that time, some turned toward local and state politics and had considerable success in picketing and disrupting abortion clinics, changing public school curricula, and pushing anti-gay-rights referenda. The Christian Coalition provided much energy and activism for the Republicans' 1994 congressional election victory. Fully 76 percent of white, born-again Christians voted for Republican House candidates in that year, while only 24 percent voted for Democrats.[23] In 2004, they voted for Bush over Kerry by a margin of 78–21.[24]

Region

It is still true that "the South is different," though this is slowly changing. Regional differences have been reduced because of years of migration by southern blacks to northern cities, the movement of industrial plants and northern whites to the Sun Belt, and economic growth catching up with that of the North. But the legacy of slavery and segregation, a large black population, and late industrialization have made the South a unique region in American politics.

Even now, white southerners tend to be somewhat less enthusiastic about civil rights than northerners; only people from the Mountain West are as conservative on racial issues.[25] Southerners also tend to be conservative on social issues, such as school prayer, crime, women's rights, and abortion, and supportive of military spending and a strong foreign policy (although fairly liberal on economic issues, such as job guarantees and health insurance).

These distinctive policy preferences have undercut southern whites' traditionally strong identification with the Democratic party, especially since the 1960s and 1970s, when the national Democrats became identified with liberal social policies and anti-war foreign policy. The white South's switch to the Republican party in the 1994 elections, in fact, is one of the major reasons Republicans were able to win control of Congress. The surge of Republicanism in the South continues up to the present.[26]

On many issues, northeasterners tend to be the most different from southerners, with midwesterners, appropriately, in the middle. Pacific Coast residents resemble northeasterners in many respects, but people from the Rocky Mountain states tend to be quite conservative, with strong majorities opposed to government job guarantees and health insurance assistance, for example.[27] The mountain states' traditions of game hunting in wide-open spaces have led them, like southerners, to cherish the right to bear firearms and to resist gun controls.

Social Class

Compared with much of the world, the United States has had rather little political conflict among people of different income or occupational groupings; in fact, rather few Americans think of themselves as members of a social "class" at all. When forced to choose, about half say they are "working class" and about half say they are "middle class."[28] In Great Britain, on the other hand, where the occupational structure is similar to that of the United States, 72 percent of the population calls itself "working class."[29]

Still, since the time of the New Deal, substantially more low-income people—poor people, as well as blue-collar workers and union members—have identified themselves as Democrats rather than as Republicans. The opposite is true at the top of the income and occupational scales. More business executives, doctors, lawyers, and other highly paid people identify themselves as Republicans. In 2003, those with the lowest incomes were twice as likely to call themselves Democrats as Republicans; those in the highest income brackets were 50 percent more likely to call themselves Republicans (see Figure 5.1).

Although income and occupation have always differentiated Democratic supporters from Republican supporters, the differences seem to be narrowing. In the middle of the 1960s, for example, 70 percent of blue-collar workers supported the Democrats (now down to 55 percent). Support of the Democrats from union members fell from 77 percent to 61 percent during the same time span. In the 2000 election, only 53 percent of those making more than $50,000 a year voted for the Republican candidate, George W. Bush; in 1988, 62 percent of this group had voted for the Republican candidate, George H. W. Bush. A variety of commentators believe that what is happening is that class issues are becoming less salient to voters, and that lifestyle and social issues—abortion, law and order, religion, civil rights, education, gay rights, and more—are becoming more salient. This may help explain why more high-income, high-education congressional districts in places such as California and Connecticut are electing Democrats, and why more white, low-income districts in Kentucky, Tennessee, and West Virginia are sending Republicans to Congress.[30]

Lower-income people have some distinctive policy preferences. Not surprisingly, they tend to favor much more government help with jobs, education, housing, medical care, and the like, whereas the highest-income people, who would presumably pay more and benefit less from such programs, tend to oppose them. To complicate matters, however, some groups of high-income people—especially highly educated professionals—tend to be very liberal on lifestyle issues involving sexual behavior, abortion rights, free speech, and civil rights. They also tend to be especially eager for government action to

The Republican party has been making inroads among blue-collar, unionized workers. Here union members show their support for GOP candidate George W. Bush during the 2000 presidential contest.

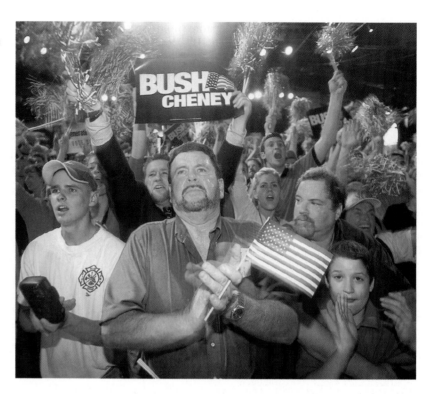

protect the environment. Once again, no simple "liberal" versus "conservative" distinction can accurately sum up all differences in opinions.

Education

The level of formal education that people reach is closely related to their income level because education helps people earn more and also because the wealthy can pay for more and better schooling for their children. But education has some distinct political effects of its own.

As we will see in Chapter 10, education is generally considered the strongest single predictor of participation in politics. College-educated people are much more likely to say that they vote, talk about politics, go to meetings, sign petitions, and write letters to officials than people who have attained only an elementary or a high school education. The highly educated know more about politics. They know what they want and how to go about getting it, joining groups and writing letters, faxes, and e-mail messages to public officials.

People who have earned post-graduate degrees also have some distinctive policy preferences. They are especially protective of the civil rights, civil liberties, and individual freedom of atheists, homosexuals, protesters, and dissenters. Education may contribute to tolerance by exposing people to diverse ideas or by training them in elite-backed norms of tolerance.

Gender

Women were prevented from participating in politics for a large part of our history; they got the vote, by constitutional amendment, only in 1920. Not all women immediately took advantage of this new opportunity. For many years, women voted and participated in politics at lower rates than men—about 10 or 15 percent lower in the elections of the 1950s, for example. And, women are consistently less knowledgeable than men and say they are less interested than men in politics.[31] Only after the women's movement gained force during the 1970s did substantial numbers of female candidates begin to run for high office. Although an office-holding gap remains, the participation gap has virtually disappeared.[32] We will explore this in more depth in Chapter 10.

A partisan "gender gap" first appeared in the 1980s and persists today, with the percentage of women who identify themselves as Democrats about 7 percentage points higher than men (see Figure 5.1). The difference between men and women is primarily a product of declining Democratic Party identification among men, particularly white southerners.[33] The differences show up in elections; in 2004, only 48 percent of women voted for George W. Bush, compared with 55 percent of men.

Women also differ somewhat from men in certain policy preferences. Women tend to be somewhat more supportive of protective policies for the poor, the elderly, and the disabled. Women tend to be more opposed to violence, whether by criminals or by the state. More women over the years have opposed capital punishment and the use of military force abroad and favored arms control and peace agreements.[34] Interestingly, the gender gap on issues like defense spending, the use of military force abroad, and a missile-defense shield disappeared in the wake of terrorist attacks on the United States, as women shifted to a more defense-supportive position similar to that of men.[35] Equal numbers of men and women now endorse the principle of "peace through strength" (62 percent).[36]

Age

The young and the old differ on certain matters that touch their particular interests: the draft in wartime, the drinking age, and, to some extent, Social Security and Medicare. Also, people over the age of 60 tend to be more critical of government, perhaps because their expectations about what government can and should deliver are higher.[37] But the chief difference between old and young

Web Exploration
The Gender Gap

Issue: There has been much talk of a "gender gap" in the United States.

Site: Examine male and female political attitudes and behaviors by accessing the American National Election Study on our Website at **www.ablongman.com/greenberg.** In the "Web Explorations" section for Chapter 5, open "gender gap." Look at a few survey questions about public policies in Section 4. For each question you examine, select "percent among demographic groups who responded," and you will see how men and women have responded over the years to the same questions.

What You've Learned: Is there a "gender gap"? If there is one, does the gap exist in all areas of politics and policy, or is the gap more pronounced on some issues compared with others?

HINT: As a measuring rod to determine the seriousness of the "gender gap," look at the differences between whites and blacks on the same survey questions.

Americans who came of age during the civil rights struggles of the 1960s are more likely than others to favor civil rights protections for African Americans.

has to do with the particular era in which they were raised. Those who were young during the 1960s were especially quick to favor civil rights for blacks, for example. In recent years, young people have been especially concerned about environmental issues. Often social change occurs by generational replacement. Old ideas, like the Depression-era notion that women should stay at home and "not take jobs away from men," die off with old people.

Are the People Fit to Rule?

Now that we know more about how public opinion is measured and why people hold certain core beliefs and political attitudes, we can return to the issue raised in the opening pages of this chapter concerning the place of public opinion in a society that aspires to be a democracy. Recall from the earlier discussion that many observers of American politics in the past and today have had little confidence in the abilities of the average person to understand vital public issues or to rationally engage in public affairs. If, as they have feared, ordinary citizens are uninformed, prone to rapid and irrational changes in their political attitudes, and easily led astray, there is not much reason to assume that public opinion can or ought to play a central role in deciding what government should do. However, as we will see in the next section, further examination of the opinions of ordinary Americans and how they change in response to events and new information will demonstrate that such fears about an uninformed and irrational public have been greatly exaggerated.

What People Know About Politics

Several decades of polling have shown that most ordinary Americans do not know or care a lot about politics.[38] Nearly everyone knows some basic facts, such as the name of the capital of the United States and the length of the president's term of office. But only about two-thirds of adults know which party has the most members in the House of Representatives. About one-half know that there are two U.S. senators from their state, and fewer can name their representative in the House. Only about 30 percent know that the term of a U.S. House member is two years.[39] And barely one in four Americans can explain what is in the First Amendment.[40] Furthermore, people have particular trouble with technical terms, geography, abbreviations, and acronyms like NATO (the North Atlantic Treaty Organization) and SALT (the Strategic Arms Limitations Talks).

The things that most Americans don't know may not be vital to their role as citizens, however. If citizens are aware that arms control talks went on between the United States and the Soviet Union, is it crucial that they recognize the acronym SALT? How important is it for people to know about the two-year term of office for the U.S. House of Representatives, as long as they are aware of the opportunity to vote each time it comes along? Perhaps most people know as much as they need to know in order to be good citizens, particularly if they can form opinions with the help of better-informed cue givers (experts, political leaders, media sources, informed friends, interest groups, and so on) whom they trust or by means of simple rules of thumb.[41]

We do not mean to minimize the consequences of people's lack of political knowledge. It has some extremely important implications. As we will see in Chapter 7, for example, when policy decisions are made in the dark, out of public view, interest groups may influence policies that an informed public would oppose. Nor do we mean to encourage complacency, fatalism, or ignorance. Individuals should take the personal responsibility to be good citizens, and organized efforts to alert and to educate the public are valuable. But low levels of information are a reality that must be taken into account. It is unrealistic to expect everyone to have a detailed knowledge of a wide range of political matters.

By the same token, we should not expect the average American to have an elaborately worked out **political ideology,** a coherent system of interlocking attitudes and beliefs about politics, the economy, and the role of government. You yourself may be a consistent liberal or conservative (or populist, socialist, libertarian, or something else), with many opinions that hang together in a coherent pattern. But surveys show that most people's attitudes are only loosely connected to each other. Most people have opinions that vary from one issue to another: conservative on some issues, liberal on others. Surveys and in-depth interviews indicate that these are often linked by underlying themes and values, but not necessarily in the neat ways that the ideologies of leading political thinkers would dictate.[42]

For the same reasons, we should not be surprised that most individuals' expressed opinions on issues tend to be unstable. Many people give different answers when the same survey question is repeated four years or two years or even a few weeks after their first response. Scholars have disagreed about what these unstable responses mean, but uncertainty and lack of information very likely play a part.

None of this, however, means that the opinions of the public, taken as a whole, are unreal, unstable, or irrelevant. The *collective whole* is greater than its individual parts. Even if there is some randomness in the average individual's expressions of political opinions—even if people often say things off the top of their heads to survey interviewers—the responses of thousands or millions of people tend to average out this randomness and reveal a stable **collective public opinion.** Americans' collective policy preferences are actually very stable over time. That is, the percentage of Americans who favor a particular policy usually stays about the same, unless circumstances change in important ways.

political ideology
A system of interrelated and coherently patterned beliefs and attitudes.

collective public opinion
The political attitudes of the public as a whole, expressed as averages, percentages, or other summaries of many individuals' opinions.

Moreover, even if most people form many of their specific opinions by deferring to others whom they trust (party leaders, television commentators, and the like) rather than by compiling their own mass of political information, the resulting public opinion need not be ignorant or unwise because the trusted leaders may themselves take account of the best available information. Some recent research, moreover, indicates that Americans' collective policy preferences react rather sensibly to events, to changing circumstances, and to new information, so that we can speak of a "rational public."[43]

The Content of Collective Public Opinion

Americans have opinions about many different political matters, including the political system in general, the performance of our government, party identification, and specific policy preferences.

The System in General

At the most general level, Americans are quite proud of their country and its political institutions. In 1998, for example, only 4.8 percent of Americans agreed with the statement that "there are some countries better than the United States." Well over three-quarters of Americans agreed with the statement that the "American system of government is the best in the world."[44] In 2001, about 80 percent of Americans said they were proud to be an American; only 52 percent of British, 36 percent of French, and 19 percent of Germans said the same about their own countries.[45] At the more specific level, however, the picture has not looked so rosy. From the late 1960s to the early 1990s, pollsters, scholars, and journalists all noted a substantial decline in Americans' trust in government and in their regard for public officials[46] (see Figure 5.2).

Americans report very high levels of patriotism compared with people in other rich democracies, as well as higher levels of confidence in their fundamental government and economic institutions (although not necessarily confidence in their present leaders).

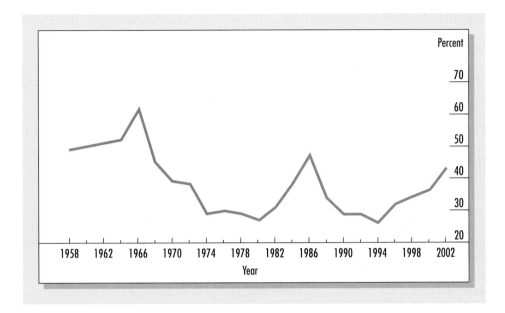

FIGURE 5.2 • Trust in Government, 1956–2002

The graph shows the percentage of Americans who say they "trust the federal government." It is based on the answers to four questions (paraphrased here): Do you trust the federal government to do the right thing most of the time? Do you think that government is run for the benefit of all? Do you think that people in government waste tax money? Do you think that most of the people running government are crooked or not? Note the long decline in trust after the 1960s and the slow but steady increase from the mid-1990s to 2002. Other surveys indicate declines in trust after 2002.

Source: American National Election Studies, 1956–2002.

Americans report that they trust government a bit more these days. The good economic times of the mid- and late 1990s helped restore a modicum of trust, but the real boost came with the 9/11 tragedy (see Figure 5.2). The terrorist attacks and the very popular military effort to punish Osama bin Laden and Al Qaeda and to topple the Taliban regime in Afghanistan enhanced patriotic feelings and a shared sense of danger. According to a *Washington Post*/ABC News poll published in December 2001, for example, roughly two-thirds of Americans said they trusted the government to "do what is right just about always or most of the time"—the first time that a clear majority had felt this way in more than three decades. Although government and government officials almost always gain popular support during war, at least in its earlier stages and as long as things are going well on the battlefield, confidence and trust has never before (at least since the introduction of systematic polling) increased to this degree.[47] By the end of 2002, however, trust in government had dropped back to more normal levels, lower than in the 1950s and 1960s, to be sure, but higher than it has been in awhile. The reason for rising trust in the federal government, according to at least one major study, is that Republicans, the group trusting government least in the past, felt more confident in government with Republicans in control of Congress and the presidency.[48]

Americans' sense of **political efficacy**—their feeling that they can make a difference in what government does and that government will respond to their concerns—has followed a pattern that is similar to that for trust in government, namely, a steady decline, then leveling out, followed by steady improvement beginning in the mid-1990s. In 2002, for example, only 31 percent said that "the federal government doesn't care what people like

political efficacy
The sense that one can affect what government does.

me think," down from 66 percent in 1994; 29 percent agreed with the statement that "people like me don't have a say in what government does" in 2002, way down from 1994 when 56 percent of respondents agreed with the statement.[49]

Government Performance

<u>**presidential approval rating**</u>
A president's standing with the public, indicated by the percentage of Americans who tell survey interviewers that they approve a president's "handling of his job."

One important aspect of happiness or unhappiness with government is a judgment about how well the president has been doing his job. For many decades, pollsters have been asking people whether they approve or disapprove of the president's handling of his job. The percentage of people saying that they approve—the **presidential approval rating**—is taken as a crucial indicator of a president's popularity. Approval tends to fluctuate up and down with particular events—Lyndon Johnson's approval fluctuated with events in Vietnam, and he decided not to run for reelection when his ratings fell to historic lows after the Tet Offensive—but in the current era, most presidents have come on hard times. Richard Nixon, Gerald Ford, and Jimmy Carter all had low approval ratings by the end of their terms. George H. W. Bush reached a then-record 89 percent approval in March 1991 in the aftermath of the Gulf War but fell below 30 percent by the summer, an unprecedented collapse. Oddly, Bill Clinton enjoyed the highest job approval ratings of any recent president for the final two years of the presidential term, in spite of the fact that he was impeached by the House of Representatives. George W. Bush's 90 percent job approval in late 2001 broke his father's record. By summer 2004, however, Bush's approval had dropped below 50 percent, his standing rocked by bad news from Iraq, high gasoline prices, and a slow jobs recovery.

The American public's approval of President Bush's job performance soared to historic highs after 9/11. Here he thanks firefighters and other rescue workers at the devastated World Trade Center. The public's approval fell below 50 percent by summer 2004, however, as partisan bickering, economic uncertainty, and bad news from Iraq undermined his support.

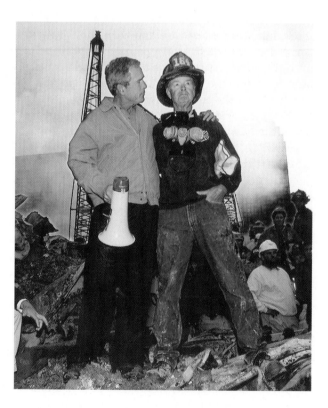

The public's evaluations of presidents' handling of their jobs depend on how well things are actually going. The state of the economy is especially important: When the country is prosperous and ordinary Americans are doing well and feeling confident about the future, the president tends to be popular; when there is high inflation or unemployment or when general living standards remain stagnant, the president's popularity falls. George W. Bush's declining approval offer his post–9/11 high point in 2001 was probably tied, in part, to the economic doldrums of 2002 and 2003. International crises may lead the public to rally and support the president (providing that leaders in both parties are doing so), but that solidarity lasts only a little while unless the crisis works out well. If bad news keeps coming, people begin to disapprove of the president's performance.[50] In 1980, for example, the long drawn-out Iran hostage crisis undermined President Carter's popularity and political influence and cost him the election against Ronald Reagan.

Party Identification

Historically, one of the most important political attitudes in the United States has been identification with a political party. Many Americans still feel such an identification. When survey researchers ask people whether, generally speaking, they consider themselves Republicans, Democrats, independents, or something else, about 60 percent pick one of the two major parties (see Figure 5.3). That sense of belonging to a party is called **party identification.** Among the remainder of Americans, many say they "lean" toward one party or the other and are sometimes included by political scientists among those who identify with that party.

party identification
The sense of belonging to one or another political party.

People use the party label to help organize their thinking about politics: to guide them in voting, in judging new policy proposals, and so on. For example, people who consider themselves Republicans are much more likely than Democrats to vote for Republican candidates and to approve of Republican presidents; they tend to belong to different social and economic groups; and they are somewhat more likely to favor policies associated with the Republican party. Moreover, the evidence suggests that there is a growing tendency for Americans to see things in government and politics through a highly partisan lens. The Pew Research Center reported in 2003 that people who identify as Republicans are much more likely than in the past to vote across the board for Republicans and to hold conservative economic and social beliefs, and that Democratic identifiers are much more likely than in the past to vote for Democrats and to hold liberal economic and social beliefs. Thus, Republicans are much more likely than Democrats to support big business and an assertive national security policy; Democrats are much more likely than Republicans to support government programs to help the poor and help racial minorities get ahead.[51]

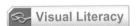 **Visual Literacy**

Who Are Liberals and Conservatives? What's the Difference?

Beginning at the time of Roosevelt's highly popular New Deal in the 1930s and continuing to the late 1980s, the Democratic lead over Republicans among party identifiers was substantial, making them the majority party. The Democrats still maintained a lead among party identifiers for most of the 1990s, but it was a small one indeed, ranging from 2 to 7 percentage points. After 9/11, the Democrats and Republicans were dead even, with each accounting for 30 to 31 percent of the population. The country is now so evenly divided between party identifiers that even very small swings from election to election in Democratic and Republican voting turnout can have big effects on who wins and loses in presidential and congressional contests.

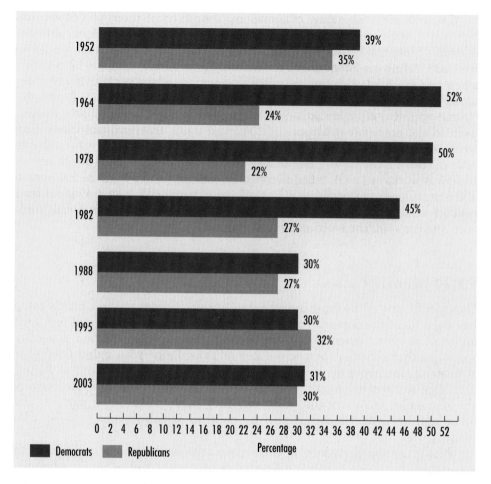

FIGURE 5.3 ● **Trends in Party Identification, 1952–2003**

Over the years, the split in the population between those who call themselves Democrats and those who call themselves Republicans has been getting closer. This is happening because fewer Americans today identify as Democrats and more identify as Independents.

Source: American National Election Studies, 2003.

The party balance among voters has important effects on who rules in Washington, D.C., especially on which party controls Congress. Democrats controlled Congress for most of the time from the New Deal until the end of the 1970s because of their big lead in party identification. As the gap between the parties narrowed, Republicans began to achieve more success, winning majorities in the Senate from 1981 to 1986 and gaining control of both houses of Congress from 1994 through 2000. In 2002, Republicans again won control of both the House of Representatives and the Senate; in 2004, they maintained their control.

The proportion of people who say they are independents—including "leaners," or those who say they are independents but lean slightly to one party or another—has steadily increased, from the low-20s in the 1960s to the mid-30s today (the remainder are respondents who choose "no preference" or "don't know"). Although some scholars maintain that these figures exaggerate the rise of independents because many leaners behave the same way as people who say they consider themselves Republicans or Democrats,[52] there has clearly been a decline in the proportion of Americans who identify with either of the two major parties. Scholars do not agree why this decline has occurred.[53] It is worth remembering, however, that among the 60 percent or so who still identify with one of the two major parties, differences in public policy outlooks between Democrats and Republicans are becoming more and more pronounced, and Democrats and Republicans hold these partisan-organized views more intensely than in the past.[54] Oddly, then, while a growing proportion of the American population is calling itself independent, views about public policies in the United States are becoming increasingly polarized along partisan lines, primarily because partisans vote at higher rates than independents and are more involved in other areas of political life as well. This increased polarization is examined further in "The Rise of Partisan Conflict" feature.

Participation

Are You a Liberal or a Conservative?

Government's Role

Although most Americans do not adhere to a rigid political ideology of the sort beloved by certain political philosophers or adhered to by many people in around the world—for example, Marxism, communism, socialism, fascism, anarchism, political Islam, and the like—they do divide on the role they believe government should play. To complicate matters, Americans generally divide along two dimensions when it comes to government: one related to government's role in the economy, the other related to government's role in society. Some Americans—those we usually label **economic conservatives**—tend to put more emphasis on economic liberty and freedom from government interference; they believe that a free market offers the best road to economic efficiency and a decent society. Others—whom we usually label **economic liberals**—stress the necessary role of government in ensuring equality of opportunity, regulating potentially damaging business practices, and providing safety nets for individuals unable to compete in the job market. Government regulation of the economy and spending to help the disadvantaged are two of the main sources of political disputes in America; they make up a big part of the difference between the ideologies of liberalism and of conservatism. However, this accounts for only one of the two dimensions. It is also useful to distinguish between **social (or lifestyle) liberals** and **social (or lifestyle) conservatives,** who differ on such issues as abortion, prayer in the schools, homosexuality, pornography, crime, and political dissent. Those who favor free choices and the rights of the accused are often said to be liberals, while those preferring government enforcement of order and traditional values are called conservatives.

It should be apparent that opinions on economic and social issues do not necessarily go together, however. Many people are liberal in some ways but conservative in others. A gay activist, for example, would likely be a social liberal but he might also be an economic conservative when it comes to taxes and regulation of business. An evangelical minister preaching in a poor community might be a social conservative on issues such as homosexuality and pornography, but an economic liberal when it comes to government programs to help the disadvantaged.

economic conservatives
People who favor private enterprise and oppose government regulations on spending.

economic liberals
People who favor government regulation of business and government spending for social programs.

social (lifestyle) liberals
People who favor civil liberties, abortion rights, and alternative lifestyles.

social (lifestyle) conservatives
People who favor traditional social values; they tend to support strong law-and-order measures and oppose abortion and gay rights.

Policy Preferences

According to democratic theory, one of the chief determinants of what governments do should be what the citizens *want* them to do, that is, citizens' **policy preferences.**

policy preferences
Citizens' preferences concerning what policies they want government to pursue.

The Rise of Partisan Conflict

Evenly Divided and Increasingly Polarized

The Story: Seasoned observers agree: American politics is becoming nastier and more partisan. Increasingly, incivility is obvious when elected leaders of one party interact with those of the opposing party. Opponents in Congress are accused of being "scoundrels" or "liars" or worse. Presidents are accused by their partisan opponents of being masterminds of plots to undermine civil liberties, squash religious freedom, or enrich their friends. Federal judicial nominees are reviled by partisan opponents in the Senate and subjected to public castigation by advocacy groups associated with the opposition. Partisans eagerly snap up books by writers accusing presidents of the other party of treason, stupidity, malfeasance, and even conspiracy to commit murder. In this environment, it is hardly surprising that cooperation across party lines is increasingly rare, not only in Congress but in state legislatures and city councils as well. There are probably a multitude of causes for this development, but one is surely the increasing tendency for voters to divide themselves fairly evenly along party lines—about half the electorate considers itself Democratic, while half considers itself Republican*—with each party favoring different sorts of candidates and policies, feeling more passionately about these preferences, and finding fewer and fewer areas of agreement with voters who favor the other party.

The Background: The even split among voters in their party preferences is reflected in recent national elections. In 2000, the national presidential vote divided 48.4 percent for Al Gore and 47.9 percent for George W. Bush. In that same year, the national vote for Congress divided 50–50, the result being a Senate with 50 Democratic senators and 50 Republican ones, and a House of Representatives in which the Republicans enjoyed a slim 9-vote advantage over the Democrats. Even in the 2002 congressional elections, when Republicans picked up seats in both the House and the Senate—usual for a president's party in an off-year election, by the way—the electorate split pretty evenly across the nation, with Republicans winning 52 percent of the national vote and the Democrats 48. The same pattern held in elections for representatives and

Spending Programs As Figure 5.4 on page 142 indicates, large and rather stable majorities of Americans (around 70 percent in recent years) think we are spending "too little" on education and fighting crime. The public also gives high and stable support to Social Security, Medicare, and environmental programs. Substantial majorities, moreover, want the federal government to help people pay medical bills and to pay for more research on diseases such as cancer and AIDS. About half of all Americans would increase spending on national defense.[55]

By contrast, few people—only about 1 percent—think too little is being spent on foreign aid; many more think too much is being spent. Except for disaster relief, foreign aid is generally unpopular. (The reason may be, in part, senators in state legislatures. In 2000, Democrats won 52 percent of the votes for these state offices. In 2002, Republicans and Democrats split the votes for state legislators 50–50.

Not only are the voters split evenly with respect to party preferences, but they are also increasingly likely to view the issues in partisan terms. As the authors of the Pew Research Center's report "Evenly Divided and Increasingly Polarized" put it, "American voters are . . . seeing things largely through a partisan prism." Their surveys of American voters in 2003 found that Republican and Democratic voters differ in major ways on the most important issues of public policy. Here is a small sample of their extensive results; the numbers refer to percentage agreeing with the statement:

Partisanship and Issue Positions

Opinion Sought	Democrats	Republicans
Government should make every effort to help blacks and other minorities, even if it means giving them preferential treatment.	55	24
Government should guarantee every citizen enough to eat and place to sleep.	81	46
We have gone too far in pushing equal rights in this country.	34	55
The best way to ensure peace is through military strength.	44	69
We all should be willing to fight for our country, right or wrong.	46	62
Government is really run for the benefit of all the people.	46	70
Business corporations make too much profit.	72	46

What's at Stake? With voters evenly split between the parties and so deeply split on the issues, every election becomes enormously consequential for voters and political leaders in each party camp. Very small differences in turnout, or very small change in the distribution of partisan loyalties in the electorate, can alter which party controls the government from election to election. And, because the parties and their partisans are so deeply divided on the issues, who controls government matters more to leaders and supporters of each of the parties; those who lose elections feel that there is a lot more to lose than in the past when the parties were not so deeply divided and when bipartisanship was more common.

Is This Good for Democracy? Are high-stakes, partisan elections good for democracy? Those who believe that intense competition between political parties is good for democracy feel that it offers voters very clear choices and helps the majority determine what government will do in the future. Those who believe that democracy requires some degree of compromise and a spirit of goodwill between the parties worry about the deepening partisan divisions.

What Do You Think? • As a voter, do you want clear choices between the parties? • Or would you prefer a situation in which the differences between the parties are not so stark, and where compromises might more often be struck?

*Note that the reference here is to the "electorate," those who go to the polls and cast a vote. The distribution of party identification among the electorate is different than the distribution of party identification among American adults. Among all adults, roughly 40 percent identify themselves as independents, and about 60 percent identify with one of the two major parties. But here is the rub: Self-identified independents vote at much lower rates than party identifiers, so they make up a much smaller portion of the electorate, those who eventually cast a vote. So, the electorate is made up overwhelmingly of partisan identifiers, pretty evenly split between Democrats and Republicans.

Sources: The title is from the Pew Research Center for the People and the Press, "Evenly Divided and Increasingly Polarized: The 2004 Political Landscape," Washington, D.C., 2003. Other information is from Stanley B. Greenberg, *The Two Americas: Our Current Political Deadlock and How to Break It* (New York: Thomas Dunne Books, 2004); Office of the Clerk, U.S. House of Representatives, Washington, D.C.

that few realize how little is spent on foreign aid—only about 1 percent of the budget. When this is made clear, support for economic aid rises sharply.)[56] Large majorities of the public oppose military aid or arms sales abroad. The space program wins only slightly greater support.

Social Issues   As Figure 5.5 on page 143 shows, Americans make sharp distinctions among different circumstances when deciding whether they favor permitting abortions. For much of the past 25 years, about 90 percent of Americans have favored allowing legal abortion if a woman's health is endangered. About 75 to 80 percent would permit abortion in cases of serious birth defects. But only about 45 percent approve of abortion if a woman is

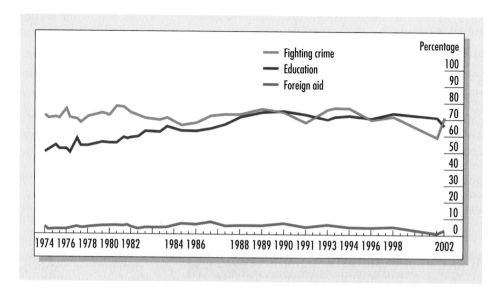

FIGURE 5.4 • Public Support for Spending Programs

Large, fairly stable majorities of Americans have favored increased spending for fighting crime and aiding education, but very few have favored increased foreign aid.
Source: General Social Survey, 1973–2002.

poor or simply wants no more children. This same graph indicates that approval of abortion under each of the different circumstances rose markedly between 1965 and the early 1970s.

Other surveys have revealed steadily growing support for civil liberties protections and for civil rights for women and minorities. Beginning in the 1940s or 1950s, for example, more and more Americans have come to favor having black and white children go to the same schools and integrating work, housing, and public accommodations. (At the same time, however, there is considerable opposition to mandatory busing to integrate schools and affirmative action.) And, there has been a slow but steady increase in support of equal treatment for gays and lesbians. These issues are explored in depth in Chapter 16. More and more members of the public have also favored letting various dissenting groups (communists, socialists, atheists, and others) teach school, speak in public, and have their books in libraries. These trends are discussed further in Chapter 15.

On a number of issues, Americans support positions favored by social conservatives. Large majorities, for example, favor allowing organized prayer in the public schools, banning pornography, preventing flag burning, penalizing drug use, punishing crimes severely, and imposing capital punishment for murder. Yet large majorities favor various types of gun regulations, which are thought of as measures favored by social liberals. (See the "Using the Framework" feature for more on the difficulties of winning more gun control.)

Foreign Policy   In the realm of foreign policy, public opinion sometimes changes rapidly in response to crises and other dramatic events. Major international events affect opinions, as we saw in the chapter-opening story on public reactions to the Tet Offensive during the Vietnam War. But often foreign policy opinions are quite stable. Since World War II, for example, two-thirds or more of those giving an opinion have usually said that the United States should take an "active part" in world affairs. The exact percentage favoring an active

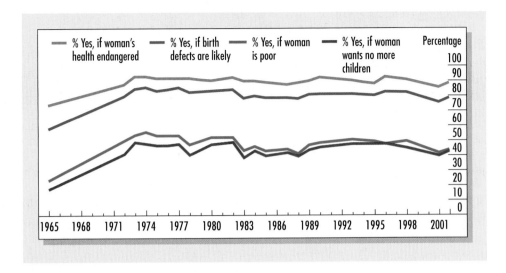

FIGURE 5.5 ● **Public Approval for Allowing Abortions**

Public opinion about abortion varies greatly with the circumstances. Large majorities favor allowing abortions if the woman's health is endangered or in the case of serious birth defects, but less than half the public would allow abortions in cases of poverty or simply wanting no more children.
Source: General Social Survey, 1965–2002.

role has varied somewhat, rising to a peak of about 83 percent in 1965, near the onset of the Vietnam War; dropping to about 62 percent after the failure of that war; and recovering in later years. Today, those believing that the United States should play an active role in world affairs again hovers near 80 percent.[57] The percentage supporting a U.S. role has remained consistently high, not fluctuating much with alleged public moods.[58]

The public has been quite hesitant to use troops abroad, unless the threat to the United States is tangible. Just before U.S. troops were sent as peacekeepers to Bosnia, for example, 78 percent of the public opposed the idea, and only 17 percent were in favor.[59] Opposition faded as the operation began to look less risky, but any substantial casualties abroad arouse large-scale public disapproval. This is probably why President Clinton ruled out the use of ground troops in Kosovo to stop ethnic cleansing by Serb militias and the Yugoslav army. However, the public strongly supported the use of the military to destroy Al Qaeda and the Taliban regime in Afghanistan[60] and initially supported President Bush's decision to invade Iraq in 2003. However, much of this support went away once bad news from Iraq began to dominate the news.

Although not many Americans embrace pure **isolationism**—the view that the United States should not be involved abroad and should only pay attention to its own affairs—the public (and political and economic leaders, as well) is divided over whether its involvement in the world should take a **unilateralist** or a **multilateralist** form. Unilateralists want to go it alone, taking action when it suits our purposes, and not necessarily seeking the approval or help of international organizations such as the United Nations or regional organizations such as NATO. Unilateralists are also uncomfortable with entering into too many international treaties. Multilateralists believe that the protection of American interests requires continuous engagement in the world, but do not think that the United States has the resources or ability to accomplish its ends without cooperating with other nations and with

 Timeline

War, Peace, and
Public Opinion

isolationism
The policy of avoiding involvement in foreign affairs.

unilateralist
The stance toward foreign policy that suggests that the United States should "go it alone," pursuing its national interests without seeking the cooperation of other nations or multilateral institutions.

multilateralist
The stance toward foreign policy that suggests that the United States should seek the cooperation of other nations and multilateral institutions in pursuing its goals.

Using the Framework

Why So Little Gun Control?

If a majority of Americans want gun control, why hasn't the federal government done much about it?

Background: Public opinion surveys have consistently indicated high public support for stricter federal gun control laws. At a general level, around two-thirds of Americans say they want stricter laws. Several specific proposals receive even higher levels of support. For example, 80 percent want a nationwide ban on assault weapons, while 70 percent want the government to ban gun sales by mail-order and over the Internet. Although some laws, such as the Brady Bill–which requires background checks of gun buyers and a waiting period–have passed Congress, proposals for stricter control over the sale and distribution of weapons almost never get very far. Taking a broad look at how structural, political linkage, and governmental factors affect gun control legislation will help explain the situation.

Governmental Action

Most major gun control bills fail to become law.

Governmental Level

The reelection calculations of members of Congress favor doing nothing: voting for stricter laws invites the opposition of intense minorities, such as the NRA; voting against such laws does not alienate many voters.

Republican presidents have generally opposed stricter gun control laws.

Democratic presidents have either had other legislative priorities or have faced daunting GOP opposition in Congress when they have introduced gun control proposals.

Political Linkages Level

A majority of Americans supports gun control, but don't rank it very high among their priorities for government action.

Voters rarely take gun control into account when deciding who they will vote for.

The National Rifle Association funnels substantial amounts of money into congressional, presidential, referenda, and issue campaigns.

Many candidates are reluctant to attract the negative attention of the National Rifle Association; many others want NRA campaign contributions.

Structural Level

The Second Amendment to the Constitution guarantees that "the right of the people to keep and bear arms shall not be infringed."

The gun has long been an important icon of American popular culture.

144

Many Americans—including these demonstrators marching in New York City on March 23, 2003—opposed the decision to go to war in Iraq without the backing of the United Nations or the support of many traditional U.S. allies.

international and regional organizations. According to most surveys, roughly two out of three Americans are in the multilateralist camp, telling pollsters they oppose unilateral U.S. military intervention in most cases and support cooperation with the United Nations and NATO and international treaties on human rights, the environment, and arms control.[61]

The Peoples' "Fitness to Rule" Revisited

This examination of collective public opinion, its evident stability on a wide range of issues over time, and why it sometimes changes on some issues leads us to conclude that confidence in the role of the public in the American political system is warranted. The evidence demonstrates that collective public opinion is quite stable and sensible when it comes to core beliefs and attitudes about government, the parties, and policy preferences. The evidence further shows that when collective public opinion does change, it does so for perfectly understandable reasons: dramatic events, new information, or changes in perspective among American leaders. The conclusion we draw is a simple yet powerful one: The American people are fit to rule. The next question to address is whether the people, in fact, do rule.

Is Government Responsive to Public Opinion?

We have argued that a crucial test of how well democracy is working is how closely a government's policies match the expressed wishes of its citizens. Do the actions of the U.S. government match what collective public opinion says it wants government to do? Some scholars say yes, while some say no. Let's look at both sides.

"Yes, It Is"

Our opening story about the Vietnam War suggests that at least under some circumstances, public opinion does affect policymaking. We have encountered other examples that tell the same "government responsiveness" story in this book. We saw in Chapter 1, for example, that Congress passed the historic Civil Rights Act of 1964 after a period of time when public support for racial segregation was declining.

These stories about government responsiveness to public opinion have been buttressed by important statistical assessments.[62] Looking at many different policy issues—foreign and domestic—one scholar found, for example, that about two-thirds of the time, U.S. government policy coincides with what opinion surveys say the public wants. The same two-thirds correspondence has appeared when other scholars investigated how *changes* in public opinion relate to changes in federal, state, and local policies. Moreover, when public opinion changes by a substantial and enduring amount and the issue is prominent, government policy has moved in the same direction as the public 87 percent of the time within a year or so afterward.[63] Another study shows that substantial swings in the national political mood have occurred over the past half century or so and that public policy has followed accordingly. As the American people have moved first in a liberal direction, then a conservative direction, and back again over the years, elected leaders in Washington have shaped their policies to fit the public mood, being more activist in liberal periods and less activist in conservative periods.[64]

"No, It's Not"

While these studies seem to lend substantial support for the idea that public opinion is a powerful determinant of what government does in the United States, this research has no shortage of critics. Showing a high correlation (that is, a strong statistical relationship) between public opinion and government policy does not prove that public opinion *causes* government policies. There are any number of plausible reasons why a "causal relationship" may not really exist. Here is what the critics say:[65]

- It may be the case that public opinion and government policies move in the same direction because some third factor causes both of them to change. In this example, the true cause of government action is this third factor, not public opinion. There are many instances in the real world where this has happened. For example, the news media often play up a particular incident or situation and persuade both public opinion and government policymakers that action is needed. This is clearly what happened when the Hearst newspaper chain whipped up fervor among both the public and elected leaders for war against Spain in the wake of the sinking of the battleship *Maine* in Havana harbor. Or an interest group or set of interest groups might sway public opinion and government officials in the same direction at the same time, as medical, insurance, and hospital associations did when they launched a successful campaign to sink Bill Clinton's health care initiative in 1994.

- Even if public opinion and government actions are highly correlated, it may be the case that it is government that shapes public opinion. In statistical language, we might say that the causal arrow is reversed, going not from the public to government, but the other way around: that

How Democratic Are We?

The Influence of Public Opinion on American Government

PROPOSITION: Public opinion is not very important in determining what the federal government does in the United States.

AGREE: Although the news media publish polls and talk a great deal about their meaning and effect on politics, public opinion is far less important than interest groups, business firms, large contributors, and periodic elections in determining what policies are enacted. There are simply too many examples of government acting contrary to the views of the public—including, for example, the disconnect between the expressed views of the public and government action on issues such as gun control, the impeachment of Bill Clinton, and health care—to plausibly argue for public opinion as a decisive tool of democracy. On most of the important issues of the day—whether regulating polluting companies or media empires, letting contracts for rebuilding Iraq, or fashioning trade legislation—powerful interest groups and large corporations generally get their way. Government leaders can get away with this because the public has no knowledge of or opinions about broad areas of public policy; with regard to other issues, like gun control, the public does not express very intense feelings; and with regard to still other issues, leaders can shape public opinion to fit what they want to do.

DISAGREE: Political leaders pay very close attention to public opinion when they are in the midst of deciding on alternative courses of action. Some would argue that they do entirely too much of this, in fact, pandering to the whims of the public rather than exercising leadership. This desire to find out what the public thinks and what it wants is why congressional incumbents, candidates for office, presidents, and government agencies spend so much time and money polling their relevant constituencies. And it is no mystery why elected officials do this, as do their challengers: Public opinion is eventually translated into votes at election time. So, staying on the right side of public opinion—giving people what they want in terms of policies, as it were—is how people gain and keep elected offices. The result is that what the public wants generally becomes public policy; political scientists have show that public opinion and government policy match up more often than not.

CONSIDER: • Does the federal government generally do what you want it to do on most major issues? • If it doesn't, why do you think that might be the case? • Is it because your views are different from those of a majority of other Americans who generally get their way with government leaders? • Or is it because elected leaders are not likely to listen to people like you, even if your views are similar to a large majority of Americans, when powerful interest groups want these leaders to do something else? • If powerful interests are getting their way rather than what you and a majority of other Americans want from government, what do you think people like you can do about it? • Are there alternative ways that you and the people who agree with you can be heard by government leaders? • Would more intense participation in electoral politics do the trick? • Or will getting your voice heard require different sorts of actions, perhaps petitions, or mobilizing like-minded people on the Internet, or marches, or disruptive demonstrations?

officials act to gain popular support for policies and actions these officials want.[66] Such efforts can range from outright manipulation of the public—the Tonkin Gulf incident described in the opening story in this chapter is such a case—to the conventional public relations efforts carried out every day by government officials and agencies. This is why both the legislative and executive branches of the federal government are so well equipped with communications offices, press secretaries, and public liaison personnel.

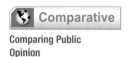

Comparative

Comparing Public Opinion

So where does all of this leave us on the question of public opinion's influence on government? It is probably reasonable to say that public opinion plays an important role in shaping what government does, but so do a range of other political actors and institutions, including parties, interest groups, the news media, and social movements. It is probably reasonable to say, moreover, that the influence of public opinion on government is significantly less than the statistical studies suggest (for example, the "two-thirds" rule) for the reasons given: the impact of third factors on both opinion and government and the significant amount of influence government officials have over popular opinion. And, it is hard to avoid noticing the many times government acts almost exactly contrary to public opinion—Congress's decision to go ahead with the impeachment and trial of Bill Clinton in the face of public opposition being the most recent notable example.

There is one more reason a simple, straightforward answer cannot be given to the question, "How much influence does public opinion have on government policy?" Scholars have reported that opinion plays an important role in shaping government policy under certain conditions, but much less so under others. Public opinion seems to matter the most when issues are highly visible to the public (usually because there has been lots of political conflict surrounding the issue), are about matters that affect the lives of Americans most directly, and concern issues for which people have access to reliable and understandable information. When economic times are tough—during a recession, for example—no amount of rhetoric from political leaders, the news media, or interest groups is likely to convince people "that they never had it so good." People have a reality check in such circumstances. By the same token, many foreign policy questions are distant from people's lives, and involve issues where information is scarce or incomplete. In this circumstance, government officials act with wide latitude and play an important role shaping what the public believes. Additionally, some issues, such as the details of tax legislation or the deregulation of the telecommunications industry, are so obscure and complex that they become the province of interest groups and experts, with the public having but ill-formed and not very intense opinions.

Summary

Public opinion consists of the core political beliefs and political attitudes expressed by ordinary citizens; it can be measured rather accurately through polls and surveys. The democratic ideals of popular sovereignty and majority rule imply that government policy should respond to the wishes of the citizens, at least in the long run. An important test of how well democracy is working, then, is how closely government policy corresponds to public opinion.

People learn their political attitudes and beliefs from their families, peers, schools, and workplaces; they also respond to political events and the mass media. Structural factors in the society, the economy, and the international system strongly affect public opinion. Opinions and party loyalties differ according to race, religion, region, urban or rural residence, social class, education level, gender, and age. Blacks, Jews, city dwellers, women, and low-income people tend to be particularly liberal and Democratic; white Protestants, suburbanites, males, and the wealthy tend to be conservative and Republican.

Whether people are fit to rule depends a great deal on the quality of public opinion. Most people, of course, do not know a lot of facts about politics and do not have well-worked-out ideologies or highly stable policy preferences. Contrary to the fears of the Founders and others, however, the *collective* public opinion of Americans is real and stable, and it takes account of the available information.

For the past four decades, Americans' trust in government and approval of the performance of political leaders have been declining. The public's regard for government and political officials rebounded dramatically in the aftermath of the terrorist attacks on the United States and the war on terrorism, then declined again. Party loyalty, although still widespread, has declined in strength. Most Americans strongly believe in freedom, economic liberty, capitalism, equality of opportunity, and democracy, but they disagree about the role of government in fostering these things. Economic liberals and conservatives disagree about economic regulation, taxes, government spending, and the need for safety nets for the unfortunate. Social liberals and conservatives disagree about the role of religion in American life, abortion, and the rights of gays and lesbians, among other things. Majorities of the public favor government action on crime, education, medical care, and the environment. Support is lower for defense and the space program and lower still for foreign aid. Support for civil rights, civil liberties, and the right to have an abortion has increased, but the public is conservative about patriotism, crime, prayer, and obscenity.

Public opinion has important effects on what federal, state, and local governments do, but so do other political actors and events. And government officials often shape public opinion. When all is said and done, the responsiveness of government to public opinion falls considerably short of the hopes of advocates of strong democracy.

Suggestions for Further Reading

Erikson, Robert S., and Kent L. Tedin, *American Public Opinion*, 6th ed. New York: Longman Publishers, 2003.
  A comprehensive survey of what we know about American public opinion and how we know it.

Garcia, John A. *Latino Politics in America.* Lanham, MD.: Rowman and Littlefield Publishers, 2003.
  Useful chapters on Hispanic public opinion and political socialization.

Jacobs, Lawrence C., and Robert Y. Shapiro. *Politicians Don't Pander: Political Manipulation and the Loss of Democratic Responsiveness.* Chicago: University of Chicago Press, 2000.
  A complex but rewarding argument that carefully describes how government officials manage to deflect and avoid the pressures of public opinion.

Manza, Jeff, Fay Lomax Cook, and Benjamin I. Page, eds., *Navigating Public Opinion: Polls, Policy, and the Future of American Democracy.* New York: Oxford University Press, 2002.
  Leading public opinion scholars examine the question of whether and to what extent public opinion determines the shape of government policies in the United States.

Page, Benjamin I., and Robert Y. Shapiro. *The Rational Public: Fifty Years of Trends in Americans' Policy Preferences.* Chicago: University of Chicago Press, 1992.
  Extensive description of opinion trends, arguing that the public is rational.

Weissberg, Robert, *Polling, Policy, and Public Opinion: The Case Against Heeding the "Voice of the People."* New York: Palgrave, 2002.
  A passionate argument on why government officials should not be too responsive to public opinion.

Internet Sources

Doonesbury
www.doonesbury.com/arcade/strawpoll/index.cfm
A daily online poll on current issues.

Gallup Organization
www.gallup.com/
Access to recent Gallup polls as well as to the Gallup archives. Requires a paid subscription.

General Social Survey
www.icpsr.umich.edu/GSS/index.html
Online access to the National Opinion Research Center's biennial survey of American attitudes.

National Election Studies
www.umich.edu/~nes/nesguide/nesguide.htm
Biennial survey of voters, focusing on electoral issues.

Pew Research Center for the People and the Press
www.people-press.org
Complex, in-depth polls on domestic and foreign issues.

Political Compass
www.politicalcompass.org
Determine where you stand in ideological terms by completing the online survey.

Polling Report
www.pollingreport.com
A compilation of surveys from a variety of sources on politics and public affairs.

Chapter 6
The News Media

In This Chapter

- The role of the news media in a democracy
- How the news is gathered and disseminated
- Why government officials are key news sources
- Whether the news media have a liberal or a conservative bias
- Why some media are more regulated than others
- How the news media affect public opinion and policymaking

News Media Coverage of the War and Occupation in Iraq

Both liberal Democrats and conservative Republicans complained that news media coverage of the war in Iraq was marred by bias favoring the other side of the partisan and ideological divide. Complaints ranged from coverage of events leading up to the invasion of Iraq, the progress of the fighting in Iraq, and the occupation and rebuilding of Iraq after President Bush's declaration of victory aboard the aircraft carrier USS Abraham Lincoln on May 2, 2003. Is there anything to these claims? Are the news media politically biased?

The complaints of liberal Democrats focused on the period leading up to the invasion and coverage of combat during the dash to take Baghdad. Here were their main charges:

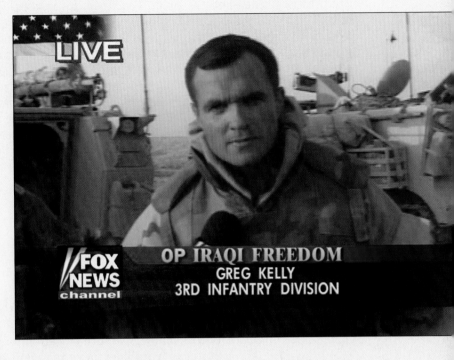

- The news media allowed the Bush administration to dominate the debate about whether to invade Iraq by failing to seriously examine administration arguments for war and the adequacy of the evidence marshaled by the administration to bolster its case. The mainstream news media—network news organizations, news magazines, and major newspapers—were especially deficient, the charge goes, in failing to closely scrutinize Bush administration claims about Iraq's weapons of mass destruction programs and ties to al Qaeda and other terrorist organizations.
- During the run-up to the war, liberal Democrats charged, the news media paid very little attention to evidence showing that the American public was opposed to unilateral military action against Iraq, preferring instead multilateral action sanctioned by the United Nations. The media were especially remiss, critics claimed, when they failed to give much attention to or attribute much importance to the massive worldwide protests on March 15, 2003, against the impending war, which, by most estimates, were the largest set of simultaneous protests in history.
- The Pentagon practice of embedding reporters into combat units distorted information in two important ways, according to liberal critics. First, embedded reporters, sharing the life and dangers of the troops, were bound to grow attached to American soldiers and see the war from their perspective, losing their impartiality and objectiveness. Second, news coverage came to be dominated by the drama of battles in progress—the ul-

timate reality show, if you will—drawing resources and attention away from broader coverage of Iraqi society and the politics of the region, and leaving the interpretation of the overall progress of the war to administration spokespeople.

The complaints of conservative Republicans focused on the news media's coverage of the opening period of the war and the occupation. Here are their main charges:

- One week into the war, critics claimed, when the military's drive to Baghdad was slowed by fierce sandstorms, attacks on a handful of supply convoys, and pockets of resistance by Iraqi fighters, the news media turned defeatist. Lead stories, columnists, and assorted pundits focused on poor planning by Defense Secretary Donald Rumsfeld and the Pentagon, the deployment of too few troops to accomplish the mission, and poor morale among the troops. In the end, the critics suggest, the news media were wrong, and the delay in the military advance was brief and unimportant.
- During the occupation and administration of Iraq after the fall of Baghdad, say conservative Republican critics, the news media focused almost entirely on problems rather than the many significant and tangible achievements of the Occupation Authority. Reports on water

and electricity problems, looting of archaeological trea-sures from the National Museum (which later proved to be largely untrue), demonstrations by angry Iraqis about living conditions, terrorist attacks against Red Cross and U.N. facilities and personnel, hostility toward Americans in the so-called Sunni triangle, attacks on American troops, and the brutalization of Iraqi prisoners dominated the headlines. Almost entirely overlooked, say the critics, were positive developments including the establishment of peace and stable administrations in the north and south of the country, the upgrade of electrical and water treatment systems, the construc-tion of scores of medical clinics and schools, and the creation of an Iraqi Governing Council.

It is hardly surprising, given the intensely partisan times in which we live—with Democrats and Republicans evenly di-vided in government and in the country and with their liberal and conservative partisans locked in ideological combat across a wide range of issues—that sharply different versions exist about the bias of the news media in their coverage of the Iraq war and its aftermath. Clearly, political bias in the news media is one issue with which we, as political consumers, need to concern ourselves. However, we should also be aware of media biases in favor of a range of other things—including, but not confined to, attracting large audiences and making profits. As we shall see in this chapter, such biases result in news cover-age that is more entertainment than news and has questionable usefulness to the American public as a tool of democracy.

Thinking Critically About This Chapter

In this chapter, we turn our attention to the diverse news media in the United States to learn how they are organized, how they work, and what effects they have on the quality of our political life.

Using the Framework   In this chapter you will learn about the role the news media play in influencing significant actors in the political system, including citizens and elected leaders. You also will learn how the media can shape what government does. And you will learn how the media are influenced by changes in technology and business organization and by government regulation and constitutional rules regarding freedom of the press.

Using the Democracy Standard   Using the tools presented in Chapter 1, you will be able to evaluate the degree to which the news media advance democ-racy in the United States or retard it. You will be able to judge whether the media promote popular sovereignty, political equality, and liberty. Finally, you will see how certain changes in the media are cause for concern in terms of the health of democracy.

Roles of the News Media in Democracy

The central idea of democracy is that ordinary citizens should control what their government does. However, citizens cannot hope to control officials, choose candidates, speak intelligently with others about public affairs, or even make up their minds about what policies they favor unless they have good in-formation about politics and policies. Most of that information must come through the news media, whether newspapers, radio, television, or, increas-

PUBLIC WATCHDOG

ingly, the Internet. How well democracy works, then, depends partly on how good a job the news media are doing.

Watchdog Over Government

One role of the media in a democracy is that of **watchdog** over government. The idea is that the press should dig up facts and warn the public when officials are doing something wrong. Citizens can hold officials accountable for setting things right only if they know about errors and wrongdoing.

watchdog
The role of the media in scrutinizing the actions of government officials.

The First Amendment to the Constitution ("Congress shall make no law . . . abridging the freedom . . . of the press") helps ensure that the news media will be able to expose officials' misbehavior without fear of censorship or prosecution. This is a treasured American right that is not available in many other countries. Under dictatorships and other authoritarian regimes, the media are usually tightly controlled. Even in a democratic country such as Great Britain, strict secrecy laws limit what the press can say about certain government activities. In many countries, including France, Israel, and Sweden, the government owns and operates major television channels and makes sure that the programs are not too critical.[1] Although freedom of the press is far from perfect in the United States, the news media enjoy greater freedom than their counterparts in other countries.

Comparing News Media

But how often do the media in the United States fulfill their watchdog role? Even without formal censorship or government ownership of the media, various factors, including the way in which the news media are organized and their routines of news gathering, may limit how willing or able they are to be critical of government policies. In addition, the media may be too quick to blow scandals out of proportion and to destroy political leaders' careers.[2]

Clarifying Electoral Choices

A second role of the news media in a democracy is to make clear what electoral choices the public has: what the political parties stand for and how the candidates shape up in terms of personal character, knowledge, experience, and positions on the issues. Without such information, it is difficult for voters to make intelligent choices.

How much or how little attention do the media pay to candidates' stands on public policies? Do they devote too much coverage to the "horse race" (who is winning? who is losing?) aspect of campaigns instead? In scrutinizing the character and personality of candidates, do the media go overboard in digging up dirt and reporting negative material even when it is very minor?

Providing Policy Information

A third role of the news media is to present a diverse, full, and enlightening set of facts and ideas about public policy. Citizens need to know how well current policies are working, as well as the pros and cons of the alternative policies that might be tried, to formulate sensible preferences. In a democracy, government should respond to public opinion, but that opinion should be reasonably well informed.

How much policy information do the U.S. media actually convey, and how accessible is it? How diverse and how accurate is that information? Is it biased—toward liberalism, for example, or toward conservatism? Are some voices heard and others ignored? We will address such questions in this chapter.

The Media Landscape

Timeline

Three Centuries of American Mass Media

The media have changed greatly over our history and continue to change ever more rapidly. Taken together, they represent, at least potentially, a multitude of ways for the public to gain access to political news, analysis, and commentary.

Newspapers

The first newspapers in the early Republic were not meant for the mass public. Newspapers were expensive and directed at an elite audience. Technological changes and the gradual democratization of American life made newspapers into a "mass" phenomenon. By the mid-1830s, "penny papers" such as the *New York Herald* reached mass audiences of ordinary working people by means of low prices and human interest stories, written in a breezy and often sensational style. The invention of the telegraph allowed news to be gathered and distributed quickly, eventually to millions of people. In the 1840s, several New York newspapers formed the Associated Press (AP) to cooperate in gathering news and distributing it by telegraph. In the late nineteenth century, Joseph Pulitzer of the *New York World* (1883) and William Randolph Hearst of the *New York Journal* invented **yellow journalism,** a new sort of newspaper that combined sensationalism and political crusades with oversized headlines and full-color illustrations and comics. One Hearst crusade in 1898 helped provoke war against Spain over Spanish control of Cuba, a key step in the emergence of the United States as a world power. Today's tabloids, such as the *New York Post,* are less likely to start wars, but their journalistic techniques still resemble Hearst's yellow journalism.

The development of wire services such as the AP, the United Press International, and the Scripps-Howard Service (the last two are now defunct) meant that more political news could be spread much more quickly, to much

yellow journalism
Sensational newspaper stories with large headlines and, in some cases, color cartoons.

William Randolph Hearst's *New York Journal* stirred war fever in 1898 with unsubstantiated charges that the Spanish had destroyed the U.S. battleship *Maine* in Cuba.

bigger audiences, and, inevitably, in a much more nationally uniform way than ever before. Homogenization was accentuated by the development of large "chains" of newspapers, owned by the same company and pursuing uniform editorial policies. Most major metropolitan newspapers today are parts of such chains (which are themselves often parts of larger multimedia companies). They depend mainly on the AP for national and international news, on syndicated columnists for their editorial page, and on their own reporters to cover local affairs.

In addition to the chain-associated metropolitan dailies, newspapers come in three rough categories. First, there are newspapers that give serious, in-depth attention to domestic and international political affairs. Most notable is the *New York Times,* which claims to publish "all the news that's fit to print" and aspires to be America's "newspaper of record." It remains the preeminent U.S. newspaper for reporting on international affairs. It is rivaled only by the *Washington Post* for the extent of its domestic political reporting and by *The Wall Street Journal* for business and financial news. The *Los Angeles Times,* the *Miami Herald,* the *Boston Globe,* and the *Chicago Tribune* also fall on the serious side of the news spectrum. Second, there are newspapers in urban areas that address minority communities of one kind or another and the issues that directly concern them, including gays and lesbians, African Americans, Hispanics, and Asian-Americans. Finally, there are the sensation-driven supermarket tabloids, such as the *National Enquirer,* the *Globe,* and the *Star,* which also include political stories, many of which eventually end up in the more mainstream press.

Today, despite all of the innovations making newspapers accessible and entertaining, Americans are relying less and less on them for their information about the world in favor of television and radio.[3] This may be a problem for democracy because television and radio have traditionally been less comprehensive and more shallow in their news coverage than the nation's top newspapers.

Magazines

Several journals of political opinion and analysis were founded in the nineteenth century. Some of these, such as *The Nation* and the *Atlantic Monthly,* are still published, and a wide range of other journals—liberal, conservative, radical, and reactionary—have entered the political debate.

Beginning in the 1920s, Henry Luce's *Time,* the weekly newsmagazine, brought analysis and interpretation of the week's news, written in a brisk and colorful style, to hundreds of thousands and then millions of readers; it later drew competition from *Newsweek* and *U.S. News & World Report.* Large-circulation magazines such as the *Saturday Evening Post, Life,* and especially *Reader's Digest* gained circulations in the millions. Countless specialized journals appeared, providing information and entertainment of diverse sorts.

Radio

Major Technological Innovations That Have Changed the Political Landscape

Commercial radio stations with broad audiences were established during the 1920s and were soon organized into networks that shared news and other programs. In the depths of the Great Depression of the 1930s, millions of Americans could hear the reassuring voice of President Franklin Roosevelt giving "fireside chats." Later, millions could hear the latest news about the battles with Japan and Nazi Germany during World War II.

Radio, once thought vanquished by the television juggernaut, has been reborn. Besides music, AM and FM stations offer frequent news bulletins and call-in talk shows, on which all manner of political opinions, including the cranky and the outrageous, are voiced. Disproportionately middle-aged, male, and politically conservative (both callers and listeners),[4] syndicated talk shows, hosted by people such as Rush Limbaugh (with an audience of almost 15 million),[5] have become a political force, able to generate a flood of mail to Congress or the White House and even to force decisions on Washington policymakers. In 2004, liberals created a competing network, Air America.

Radio is not all sound and populist fury, however. Public Broadcasting System (PBS) stations provide extended news analysis and commentary, often thoughtful and occasionally unorthodox, on programs such as *Morning Edition* and *All Things Considered.*

Television

The television revolution transformed American media yet again. Television was invented before World War II; it was developed commercially in the late 1940s and entered American households on a large scale in the 1950s. Scores and then hundreds of television stations were established around the country, most eventually affiliating with one of the three major networks—ABC, CBS, and NBC—which provided the bulk of prime-time programming. The networks also produced and distributed national news programs, which in 1963 were expanded from 15 to 30 minutes of early evening time, and became the main source of national news for most Americans. Today, cable all-news networks such as CNN, Fox News, and MSNBC have eaten into the network television news monopoly, while political junkies can turn to C-SPAN for live coverage of Congress and other inside-the-beltway activities. The BET offers news on public affairs that are of particular interest to African Americans.

Talk radio has become a very influential—and decidedly conservative—voice in American politics. Right-wing personality Rush Limbaugh, who often criticizes the mass media as being too liberal, draws a large and loyal audience.

According to a multitude of polls, Americans name television as their most important source of news, and most say they trust television a great deal.[6] (See the "By the Numbers" feature to gain a sense of how accurate television news is in informing people about crime.)

The Internet

Personal computers with modems or broadband connections, appearing in a rapidly increasing number of homes, schools, and offices, create opportunities to gather political and public policy information from a host of sources on the Internet, including libraries, government agencies, online newspapers and magazines, special interest groups, scholars, and public interest organizations. This medium has a ways to go to catch up to traditional mass media, but it is coming fast. During the 1996 election cycle, only 6 percent of the public reported visiting a politically oriented Website. By the 2000 election cycle, 29 percent reported having done so.[7] With candidates and parties, public and private interest groups, and advocacy organizations making huge investments in Websites and e-mail operations, the pace of politically oriented Internet use is expanding rapidly.

The true promise of the Internet, however, is in its capacity to serve as an interactive, two-way communications medium[8] in which citizens can talk back to political leaders and deliberate with one another. Scores of political chat rooms already exist, members of Congress register public opinion via e-mail, citizens communicate and share documents with others in their interest groups, and many online magazines and newspapers encourage reader online feedback and commentary. Howard Dean's campaign, during his run for the 2004 Democratic party presidential nomination, used the Internet very effectively to raise money, encourage grassroots organizers to run their

Participation

Democracy and the Internet

By the Numbers

How much serious crime is there in the United States?

"If it bleeds, it leads" seems to be the mantra of television news. Indeed, we are in danger in this country of being overwhelmed by news stories about crime, and the problem seems to be getting worse. While coverage of public affairs and foreign affairs has been falling, news coverage of crime has flourished. Local news coverage is even more slanted toward crime.

Why It Matters: If television news broadcasts are accurately portraying real trends in crime, then they are doing a public service. If portrayals are inaccurate, then the public is being misled. This is problematic because public and official perceptions about the scale of particular social problems affect politics and government deeply. For example,

- When pressed by the public to address a perceived problem, government officials respond by redirecting resources at the problem and make budget and personnel decisions in light of it. If the problem is a false one, then government attention and resources get used ineffectively.
- Candidates campaign on issues that are most salient to the public. When the public misperceives the scale of a problem, it makes electoral choices based on irrelevant grounds.
- The more threatening the public finds a particular problem, the more it pushes aside other public priorities, such as education and health care.

The Story Behind the Crime Numbers: How accurately are the news media portraying the true state of affairs? To put it bluntly, not very well. Crime in general, and violent crime in particular, declined substantially during the 1990s, at precisely the same time that concerns about crime were at the forefront of media, popular attention, and political saliency. How do we know this to be the case?

The two most widely used measures of the incidence of crime in the United States are the Uniform Crime Report (UCR) of the FBI and the National Crime Victimization Survey (NCVS) of the Department of Justice. Each counts the incidence of crime in a different way. The UCR is based on reports from law enforcement agencies and is meant to help state and local police departments track their own performance and to plan their budgets. The NCVS is based on a survey of victims of crime and is used to assess how crime is experienced by Americans and how it affects them and their families.

Calculating the Crime Rate: The FBI's UCR, based on reports submitted voluntarily by state and local law enforcement agencies, counts the annual incidence of "violent crimes" (murder, forcible rape, robbery, and aggravated assault), "property crimes" (burglary, larceny-theft, motor vehicle theft, and arson), and "serious crimes" (all of the above). However, here is what is most important about the FBI's methodology: *It only counts crimes that come to the attention of police.*

The Justice Department's NCVS is based on an annual survey of roughly 50,000 randomly selected U.S. households. One person over the age of 18 in

own campaigns for Dean, and trade information about public policies and electoral tactics with supporters.

We are also discovering—whether for better or worse is not yet clear—that almost anyone with an Internet connection can become a combination reporter, editor, and publisher. Thousands of Americans are now putting their ideas about a wide range of subjects online in personal weblogs, for example, and many of them are read widely. The most famous of these instant media moguls, if you will, is Matt Drudge, whose "Drudge Report" played each household is interviewed about any crimes that may have been committed against any member of the household during the previous year. The result is annual crime *victimization* information for more than 100,000 people, a very large number for a national survey. Because the NCVS includes crimes experienced by people that are never reported to the authorities, it tends to show higher rates of serious crime than the UCR.

Criticisms of Crime Rate Calculations: The experts generally prefer the NCVS numbers to those of the UCR for understanding the dimensions of the crime problem. The principal problems with the UCR concern the accuracy of recording and reporting crime. For example,

- Many serious crimes, especially rape, go unreported to police.
- Ideas about what constitutes a serious crime may change as social mores change. Domestic violence was treated in the past by police as a family matter; now it tends to get recorded and reported by police.
- A small number of law enforcement agencies do not participate in the UCR reporting system or do not treat it with the seriousness that the FBI hopes for.

What to Watch For: Each way of measuring crime is valid and has its purposes. Although the UCR measure has some problems, it does a fairly good job of telling us what is going on year to year with respect to police encounters with crime. This, in turn, is useful to national, state, and local governments in deciding on budget and staffing issues for law enforcement. The NCVS does a very good job of telling us what is going on year to year with respect

to overall victimization trends, and gives us a handle on the size of the underlying crime problem. The lesson here is to use the statistic that conforms most closely to the purposes of your inquiry.

What Do You Think? Do you believe that television news programs underplay or overplay the incidence of violent crime? Monitor local and national news for the next week or so and try to keep a running count of stories about crime. How does your count match what the UCR and NCVS numbers are telling us about crime?

Serious Violent Crimes
Source: Bureau of Justice Statistics, United States Department of Justice, 2001.

such a large role in the news cycle leading to the Clinton impeachment. Today, suck "blogs" cover virtually every political topic from every point on the ideological compass.

Commentators disagree about the democratic potential of the Internet. To many, the scarcity of editorial gatekeepers with a strong sense of journalistic integrity on the Internet means that citizens cannot be certain about the reliability of information found at most sites.[9] Also, the Internet makes it easier for fringe groups such as the "militia movement" and hate groups such as the

The Vietnam War was the first American war fully covered by television. Footage of American deaths and casualties, as well as visual reminders of the terrible consequences of the conflict on the Vietnamese civilian population, helped turn public opinion in the United States against the war. This still from television footage of children napalmed by an accidental American attack on a village of Trang Bang is a particularly powerful example of the war coming home to American living rooms.

"skinheads" and neo-Nazis to spread their messages and recruit new members. On the other hand, say other commentators, the Internet gives citizens fuller and easier access to information and opinions about government performance, electoral choices, and policy options. And it allows geographically diverse individuals and groups to organize politically and convey their views to policymakers. For example, the Internet was an important tool for organizers of the anti-war demonstrations that took place in scores of cities and towns across the country just prior to the invasion of Iraq in 2003. Some even suggest that the Internet ought to be thought of as a new space for participation in the political process, equal in stature to other participatory spaces in American politics.[10]

How the Media Work

The precise ways in which the news media are organized and function affect whether citizens get the kinds of information they need for democracy to work properly.

Organization of the News Media

Nearly all media in the United States are privately owned businesses. Most are either very large businesses in their own right or, more typically, part of very large corporate empires.

Corporate Ownership   Some television stations and newspapers—especially the smaller ones—are still owned locally, by families or by groups of investors, although they account for a rapidly declining share of the total. Most of the biggest stations and newspapers, however, as well as the television and cable networks, are owned by large media corporations, some of which, in turn, are subsidiaries of enormous conglomerates.

Each media sector is dominated by a few firms. Gannett (*USA Today* and 99 other dailies), Knight-Ridder, and Newhouse dominate the newspaper business. Time Warner dominates both magazine publishing and consumer Internet services. General Electric, Westinghouse, Disney, News Corp., and Viacom dominate television. Six corporations receive more than half of all book-publishing revenues. Clear Channel, with 1,200 stations across the country, dominates radio. And five firms (Warner Communications, Gulf+Western, Disney, Universal-MCA, and Columbia Pictures) get most of the gross box office revenues from movies.[11]

Mergers across media lines have accelerated in recent years. In the late 1990s, Disney bought ABC/Cap Cities, Time Warner acquired Turner Broadcasting (and was later bought by AOL), and Westinghouse Electric bought CBS. Then Viacom and CBS merged, bringing together many familiar media and entertainment names: MTV, Nickelodeon, Showtime, Paramount Pictures, Simon and Schuster Publishers, Blockbuster Video, and CBS TV and radio. In a stunning deal in early 2000, America Online acquired Time Warner, merging news, publishing, entertainment, and Internet resources into a single giant company (troubles at AOL, however, shifted control to the Time Warner part of the corporation in 2003). Familiar companies in this group include AOL; Warner Books; Time-Life Books; HBO; CNN; Warner Bros. Films and Television; *Time, Fortune, Sports Illustrated, People,* and *Money* magazines; Warner Music Group; Turner Network Television; Turner Sports; the Atlanta Braves; and the Atlanta Hawks. In 2003, General Electric acquired Vivendi Universal, combining Vivendi's movie and television assets with those of NBC, which it already owned, in a bid to be more competitive with Disney, Viacom, News Corp, and Time Warner.

Rupert Murdoch's News Corp—whose operations extend throughout North America, Europe, and Asia—owns newspapers, television stations and networks, radio stations, movie studios, and sports teams. His holdings include Fox News, a strongly conservative voice on American television.

Scholars disagree about the effect of corporate ownership and increased media concentration. A few see efficiency gains and an increase in the output and availability of information. But some critics maintain that the concentrated corporate control of our media adds dangerously to the already strong business presence in American politics. Others worry that increased concentration of ownership may lead to less diversity of news and opinion. Still others worry that news organizations may pull their punches when reporting about the activities of their corporate parents or partners. Will MSNBC—a joint news venture of Microsoft and NBC—report fairly and accurately about Microsoft activities, for example? Will ABC News go easy on Disney, which owns ABC?[12]

Uniformity and Diversity   Whoever owns them, most newspapers and television stations depend largely on the same sources for news. Political scientist Lance Bennett points out that while there is a growing diversity of news outlets in the United States—more specialized magazines, television channels, and newspaper home pages on the Web—news sources are contracting. That is to say, much of what comes to us over a multitude of media avenues originates in fewer and fewer centralized sources.[13] Almost all major newspapers in the country now subscribe to the AP wire service. The AP supplies most of the main national and international news stories, even those that are rewritten to carry a local reporter's byline. Most of what appears on network and cable television news, too, is inspired by the AP wire. National and local television news organizations depend on centralized news and video suppliers, with fewer of them using their own reporters. This is why viewers are likely to see the same news (and sports) footage on different stations as they switch channels, although each station adds its own "voiceover" from a reporter or news anchor. In most cases, the person doing the voiceover has no direct relationship to the story.

Along with the centralization and homogenization of the mass media, however, there is also quite a lot of diversity, for anyone who makes the effort to seek it out. People who are especially interested in politics can find special publications that look at the world in a way that they find compatible or interesting, whether it is the *Weekly Standard* or *National Review* (conservative), *The Nation* and *The American Prospect* (liberal), *Commentary* (neoconservative), *Mother Jones* (irreverent), the *New York Review of Books* (intellectual and critical), the *New Yorker, Rolling Stone,* or dozens of others with small circulations. The World Wide Web also provides a wealth of information uncontrolled by government or corporations. And new Internet political magazines such as *Slate* and *Salon* are beginning to appear. African American, Spanish-language, and gay and lesbian newspapers, magazines, and Websites are also increasingly available. The audiences for these news sources, however, represent but a small fraction of the number of people who depend on the mainstream media for its news.

Profit Motives   Media corporations, like other corporations, are in business primarily to make a profit. This fact has important consequences. It means, for example, that the major news media must appeal to large audiences and get many people to buy their publications or the products they advertise. If most people are mainly interested in entertainment and want their news short, snappy, and sensational—what has come to be called **infotainment**—that is what they will get on network and cable television news and in *USA Today*. The process is especially well developed in evening local news broadcasts

infotainment
The merging of hard news and entertainment in news presentations.

where coverage of politics and government have been "crowded out by coverage of crime, sports, weather, lifestyles and other audience-grabbing topics."[14]

Political Newsmaking

The kind of news that the media present is affected by the organization and technology of news gathering and news production. Much depends on where reporters are, what sources they talk to, and what sorts of video pictures are available.

The Limited Geography of Political News   For national news, most reporters are located in two main locations: first, inside the beltway in Washington, D.C., site of the federal government and most of the nation's most influential think tanks and interest group organizations, and second, in New York City, the center of most media operations and the location of key national and global financial institutions. Thus, the national news has a strong Washington–New York orientation.

The major television networks and most newspapers cannot afford to station many reporters outside Washington or New York. The networks usually add just Chicago, Los Angeles, Miami, and Houston or Dallas. When stories break in San Francisco or Seattle, news organizations can rush reporters to the area, or turn to part-time "stringers" to do the reporting. Some significant stories from outside the main media centers simply do not make it into the national news. News-only channels, such as CNN, CNBC, and Fox News, have a big advantage on fast-breaking news, which they are ready to cover (through their own reporters or the purchase of local footage) and to use immediately on their continuous newscasts.

While some newspapers have strong regional bureaus, the majority print mostly wire service reports of news from elsewhere around the country. The television networks' assignment editors also rely on the wire services to decide what stories to cover; during one month that was studied, NBC got the idea for 70 percent of its domestic film stories from the wire services.[15]

Because so much expensive, high-tech equipment is involved, and because a considerable amount of editing is required to turn raw video into coherent stories, most television news coverage is assigned to predictable events—news conferences and the like—long before they happen, usually in one of the cities with a permanent television crew. For such spontaneous news as riots, accidents, and natural disasters, special video camera crews can be rushed to the location, but they usually arrive after the main events occur and have to rely on "reaction" interviews or aftermath stories. This is not always true; occasionally television news organizations find themselves in the middle of an unfolding set of events and can convey its texture, explore its human meaning, and speculate about its political implications in particularly meaningful ways. This was certainly true of television coverage of the September 11, 2001, terrorist attacks on the United States and the public and government response to them.

Dependence on Official Sources   Most political news is based on what public officials say. This fact has important consequences for how well the media serve democracy.

Beats and Routines   A newspaper or television reporter's work is usually organized around a particular **beat,** which he or she checks every day for news stories. Most political beats center on some official government institution

beat
The assigned location where a reporter regularly gathers news stories.

Much national television newsmaking takes place in Washington, D.C., where reporters have access to government officials and to a wide variety of dramatic visual backdrops.

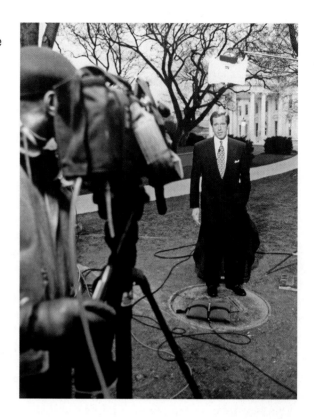

that regularly produces news, such as a local police station or city council, the White House, Congress, the Pentagon, an American embassy abroad, or a country's foreign ministry.

In fact, many news reports are created or originated by officials, not by reporters. Investigative reporting of the sort that Carl Bernstein and Robert Woodward did to uncover the Watergate scandal in the early 1970s is rare because it is so time consuming and expensive. Most reporters get most of their stories quickly and efficiently from press conferences and the press releases that officials write, along with comments solicited from other officials.

One pioneering study found that government officials, domestic or foreign, were the sources of nearly three-quarters of all news in the *New York Times* and the *Washington Post.* Moreover, the vast majority, 70 to 90 percent of all news stories, were drawn from situations over which the newsmakers had substantial control: press conferences (24.5 percent), interviews (24.7 percent), press releases (17.5 percent), and official proceedings (13 percent).[16] The same is true of wire service reports and local newspapers.

Military Actions   Dependence on official sources is especially evident in military actions abroad. Because it is wary of the release of information that might help an adversary or undermine public support for U.S. actions—as happened during the Vietnam conflict—the Defense Department carefully restricts the access of reporters to military personnel and the battlefield and provides carefully screened information for use by the news media. The Pentagon carefully managed the flow of information in the invasion of Grenada in 1983, the Gulf War in 1991, peacekeeping missions in Bosnia and Kosovo, and the campaign in Afghanistan against the Taliban regime and

Osama bin Laden. Information management was especially evident during the Gulf War with its televised news briefings featuring video of "smart" weapons, Defense Department organization of press pools, and tight restrictions on reporters' access to the battlefields in Kuwait and Iraq. Press management was even more highly developed during the conflict in Afghanistan, when reporters found it almost impossible to develop independent information. During phases of the Afghan operation, reporters had little access to military personnel, many of whom were located in scattered and inaccessible locations—often in countries where officials wanted to keep the nature of U.S. involvement out of the public limelight—and involved in special operations that required strict secrecy. Regarding the war in Iraq, as you will recall from the story opening this chapter, the Defense Department encouraged coverage of combat by journalists embedded in combat units, though administration officials continued to exercise control over information about the big picture during the initial stages of the war. In the end, however, the administration was unable to control news about abuse of Iraqi prisoners, American casualties, or difficulties with the handover of power.

Mutual Needs   Reporters and officials work with each other every day. They need each other. Reporters want stories; they have to cultivate access to people who can provide stories with quotes or anonymous leaks. Officials want favorable publicity and want to avoid or counteract unfavorable publicity. Thus, a comfortable relationship tends to develop. Even when reporters put on a show of aggressive questioning at White House press conferences, they usually work hard to stay on good terms with officials and to avoid fundamental challenges of the officials' positions.

The media's heavy reliance on official sources means that government officials are sometimes able to control what journalists report and how they report it. The Reagan administration was particularly successful at picking a

Journalists and government officials often socialize together, raising questions about the media's ability to serve as honest watchdog. Here Federal Reserve Chair Allan Greenspan arrives at a Hollywood party with NBC journalist Andrea Mitchell (his wife) and CNN anchor Judy Woodruff.

"story of the day" and having many officials feed that story to reporters, with a unified interpretation.[17] Reliance on officials also means that when officials of both parties agree, debate tends to be constricted. This was true for the momentous Telecommunications Act of 1996, which helped usher in the current dramatic changes in the business of mass media and telecommunications, but which occasioned little public debate.

newsworthy

Worth printing or broadcasting as news, according to editors' judgments.

You Are the News Editor

Newsworthiness   Decisions about what kinds of news to print or to televise depend largely on professional judgments about what is **newsworthy.** Exactly what makes a story newsworthy is difficult to spell out, but experienced editors make quick and confident judgments of what their audiences (and their employers) want. If they were consistently wrong, they would probably not remain in their jobs very long.

In practice, newsworthiness seems to depend on such factors as novelty (man bites dog, not dog bites man), drama and human interest, relevance to the lives of Americans, high stakes (physical violence or conflict), and celebrity. Some trivial topics are judged newsworthy, such as the hairstyles of O.J. Simpson trial stars Marcia Clark and Kato Kaelin. As the term *news story* implies, news works best when it can be framed as a familiar kind of narrative: an exposé of greed, sex, or corruption; conflict between politicians; or a foreign affairs crisis. On television, of course, dramatic or startling film footage helps make a story gripping. Important stories without visuals are often pushed aside for less important stories for which visuals exist.

Templates   On many important stories, a subtle "governing template" may prevail, a sense among both reporters and editors that news stories must take a generally agreed-upon slant to be taken seriously and to make it into the news broadcast or the newspaper. This is not because of censorship but because of the development of a general agreement among news reporters and editors that the public already knows what the big story looks like on a range of issues—filling in the details is what is important. Take reporting from China as an example. For many years, editors only wanted to hear about economic prosperity, emerging democratic freedoms, and happy peasants liberated from the economic and personal straightjacket of the Maoist collective farm system. After the pro-democracy demonstrations in Tiannanmen Square were brutally repressed by the People's Liberation Army, however, reporters say that it became almost impossible to write anything positive about China, because the prevailing template about China had changed.[18] Now that China has become a very important trading partner, stories about the Chinese economic miracle have proliferated.

Episodic Foreign Coverage   Very few newspapers other than the *New York Times* can afford to station reporters abroad. Even the *Times* and the networks and wire services cannot regularly cover most nations of the world. They keep reporters in the countries of greatest interest to Americans—those that have big effects on American interests or enjoy close economic or cultural ties with the United States, such as Great Britain, Germany, Japan, Israel, Russia, and China—and they have regional bureaus in Africa and Latin America. In many countries, however, they depend on "stringers" (local journalists who file occasional reports). During major crises or big events, the media send in temporary news teams, such as the armies of reporters that swarmed to Bosnia and Kosovo during the conflicts with the Serbs, and

Washington insiders are the main guests on Sunday morning network news shows. Here, *Meet the Press* host Tim Russert leads a discussion on the Abu Ghraib prisoner abuse scandal with Senators John Warner (R–VA), and Lindsey Graham (R–SC) and General Wesley Clarke.

to the countries surrounding Afghanistan during the war to unseat the Taliban and find Osama bin Laden. The result is that most media devote the majority of their attention to limited areas of the world, dropping in only occasionally on others.

Foreign news, therefore, tends to be episodic. An unfamiliar country, such as Rwanda or Haiti, suddenly jumps into the headlines with a spectacular story of a coup, an invasion, or a famine, which comes as a surprise to most Americans because they have not been prepared by background reports. For a few days or weeks, the story dominates the news, with intensive coverage through pictures, interviews, and commentaries. Then, if nothing new and exciting happens, the story grows stale and disappears from the media. Most viewers are left with little more understanding of the country than they began with. Thus, they find it difficult to form judgments about U.S. foreign policy.

Interpreting

Political news does not make much sense without an interpretation of what it means. Under the informal rules of **objective journalism,** however, explicit interpretations by journalists are avoided, except for commentary or editorials that are labeled as such. Thus, even if a reporter knows that an official is lying, he or she cannot say so directly, but must find someone else who will say so for the record. Staged events—such as a news conference held in a national park to announce a bill to protect the environment—cannot be identified by reporters as staged events. In news stories, most interpretations are left implicit (so that they are hard to detect and argue with) or are given by so-called experts who are interviewed for comments. Often, particular experts are selected by print, broadcast, and telecast journalists because the position the experts will take is entirely predictable.

objective journalism
News reported with no evaluative language and with any opinions quoted or attributed to a specific source.

Experts are selected partly for reasons of convenience and audience appeal: Scholars and commentators who live close to New York City or Washington, D.C., who like to speak in public, who look good on camera, and who are skillful in coming up with colorful quotations on a variety of subjects are contacted again and again. They often show up on television to comment on the news of the day, even on issues that are far from the area of their special expertise. In many cases, these pundits are simply well known for being on television often and are not experts on any subject at all.

The experts and commentators featured in the media are often ex-officials. Their views are usually in harmony with the political currents of the day; that is, they tend to reflect a fairly narrow spectrum of opinion close to that of the party in power in Washington, D.C., or to the prevailing "conventional wisdom" inside the beltway. During the 1980s and early 1990s, for example, the experts most frequently quoted on television were a handful of former Reagan or Bush administration officials and others associated with conservative **think tanks,** such as the American Enterprise Institute and the Center for Strategic and International Studies. The commentator "punditocracy" was also quite conservative.[19]

At other times, with different politicians in power, different kinds of experts have been favored. Anti-poverty advocates got a lot of media attention during Lyndon Johnson's administration, for example, and some liberal and centrist voices began to reappear in the media when Bill Clinton replaced George H. W. Bush. Even during the Clinton years, however, the tilt toward liberal experts was quite muted. One scholar reports that a Lexis-Nexis search of political and governmental news stories between January 1999 and October 2000 uncovered 753 references to experts from the Brookings Institution (a centrist think tank), 949 references to experts from the Heritage Foundation and the American Enterprise Institute (conservative think tanks), but only 161 references to the liberal Economic Policy Institute.[20] Independent radical thinkers such as I. F. Stone, whose *Weekly* became influential for a time during the Vietnam War, or Noam Chomsky, a fierce critic of media reporting on U.S. foreign policy today, have rarely penetrated the mainstream news media at all.

Is the News Biased?

Few topics arouse more disagreement than the question of whether the news media in the United States have a liberal or conservative **bias** or a Democratic or Republican one—or any bias at all. For years, a number of journalists and scholars have maintained that the media tend to favor Republicans, the establishment, and conservative views, reflecting their corporate ownership and their dependence on official sources for news. Conservative critics have counterattacked, arguing that liberal media elites favor Democrats and regularly publish and broadcast anti-establishment, anti-authority news with a liberal bias.

Liberal Democratic Reporters Surveys of reporters' and journalists' opinions suggest that these individuals tend to be somewhat more liberal than the average American on certain matters, including the environment and such social issues as civil rights and liberties, affirmative action, abortion, and women's rights.[21] This is especially true of those employed by certain elite media organizations, including the *New York Times,* the *Washington Post,* and

think tanks

Nonprofit organizations that do research on public policy issues and distribute their findings through a variety of outlets. Although formally nonpartisan, most have an identifiable ideological stance.

bias

Deviation from some ideal standard, such as representativeness or objectivity.

Are the Media Biased?

PBS. It is likely that reporters' liberalism has been reflected in the treatment of issues such as nuclear energy, global warming, and toxic waste. In 1990, for example, an exhaustive three-volume government report that found that damage from acid rain had been greatly overestimated was ignored by virtually all the major media, except *60 Minutes* and *The Wall Street Journal.*[22]

But there is little or no systematic evidence that reporters' personal values regularly affect what appears in the media.[23] Journalists' commitment to the idea of objectivity helps them resist temptation, as do critical scrutiny and rewriting by editors. And in any case, the liberalism of journalists may be offset by their need to rely on official sources, by their reliance on experts who are either former officials or associated with centrist or conservative think tanks, and by conservatism among media owners and publishers. It is also difficult to sustain the position that reporters slant their stories in a liberal direction after witnessing the pummeling Bill Clinton received in the media throughout his presidency.

Conservative Republican Owners　　The owners and top managers of most media corporations tend to be conservative and Republican. This is hardly surprising. The shareholders and executives of multibillion-dollar corporations are not very interested in undermining the free enterprise system, for example, or, for that matter, increasing their own taxes, raising labor costs, or losing income from offended advertisers. These owners and managers ultimately decide which reporters, newscasters, and editors to hire or fire, promote or discourage. Journalists who want to get ahead, therefore, may have to come to terms with the policies of the people who own and run media businesses.

One sign of conservatism in the media is newspapers' endorsements of presidential candidates, which are decided mostly by owners and publishers. In all six presidential elections from 1968 through 1988, more newspapers— usually many more—backed the Republican than the Democratic candidate.[24] Newspapers bucked the trend when a majority of them endorsed friendly-to-business-Democrat Bill Clinton in 1992 and 1996, but returned to the fold in 2000 when a majority endorsed Bush over Gore.[25] This is important given evidence that the editorial positions of newspapers are significantly related to how campaigns are covered in the papers, and in turn, to the voting choices made by readers.[26]

The Marketplace　　The question of political bias in the news media is not so easily answered. Both reporters and news media owners have biases, but it is difficult to see that these views consistently move news reports in one direction or another. For another thing, the news media are now so diverse that pinning a political or partisan label on the "news media" as a whole makes no sense. Talk radio has an orientation different from that of network news. Network news organizations—the favorite whipping boys for both liberal and conservative critics—have lost their near monopoly over news distribution and find themselves in fierce competition for audience with cable news operations, Internet news sources, and news radio. Small journals of opinion, for their part, cover the gamut of political views, from extreme libertarian to socialist.

It is impossible, then, to support the claim that the news media is consistently biased in one partisan direction or another; all views can be found there. What can be said, however, is that the news media, being themselves business enterprises or part of larger corporate entities, are in business to make a profit for themselves or their corporate parents. This leads many of them to engage in certain practices in news gathering and presentation that may be harmful to their central role in a democratic society. We examine these practices in much of the remainder of this chapter.

Prevailing Themes in Political News

Even if we cannot be sure whether or how the media are biased, it is easy to identify certain tendencies in media coverage, certain beliefs that are assumed, and certain values and points of view that are emphasized.

Nationalism   Although perhaps not terribly surprising, most news about foreign affairs takes a definitely pro-American, patriotic point of view, usually putting the United States in a favorable light and its opponents in an unfavorable light. This tendency is especially pronounced in news about military conflicts involving U.S. troops, as in Iraq, but it can be found as well in a wide range of foreign affairs news reports, including those concerning conflicts with other governments on trade, arms control, immigration, and intellectual property rights (patents and copyrights).

The news media also focus on subjects that interest and concern ordinary Americans, regardless of their importance in the larger picture. For example, in 1980 U.S. newspapers and television devoted intensive, year-long coverage to the fate of 49 Americans held hostage in the U.S. embassy in Tehran, Iran; in the early 1990s, they exhaustively covered a U.S. pilot, Scott O'Grady, who had been shot down over Bosnia. But much less attention has been paid to the slaughter of millions of people during the same time in Indonesia, Nigeria, East Timor, Cambodia, and Rwanda.

This nationalistic perspective, together with heavy reliance on U.S. government news sources, means that coverage of foreign news generally harmonizes well with official U.S. foreign policy. Thus, the media tend to go along with the U.S. government in assuming the best about our close allies and the worst about official "enemies." When the United States was assisting Iraq in its war against Iran, for example, Saddam Hussein was depicted in a positive light; during the 1991 Gulf War and the Iraq war 12 years later, media characterizations of him changed dramatically.

In foreign policy crisis situations, the reliance on official news sources means that the media sometimes propagate government statements that are false or misleading, as in the announcement of unprovoked attacks on U.S. destroyers in the Gulf of Tonkin at the beginning of the Vietnam War (recall the chapter-opening story in Chapter 5). Secret information can also be controlled by the government. The widely reported "missile gap" that led to a big arms buildup during the Kennedy years and the "window of vulnerability" that preceded the Reagan defense budget increases both turned out to be illusions.[27]

Approval of the American Economic System   Another tendency of the media is to run stories generally approving of free markets, free international trade, and minimal regulation. Our economic system wins approval, while variant or alternative systems, such as European social democracies with comprehensive social welfare programs, are generally portrayed more negatively. Countries whose economic policies mirror those of the U.S. economy, such as Poland, are praised, while countries trying to preserve a vibrant welfare state, such as France or Sweden, are criticized. Individual U.S. corporations are criticized for errors and misdeeds—for example, polluters are likely to be hauled before the court of public opinion, as are large firms such as Enron and WorldCom, who lie about their profits in order to keep their stock prices high—but the economic system itself is rarely challenged. This stance is hardly surprising, since most Americans like the U.S. economic system (see Chapter 4), but it may sometimes discourage the consideration of alternative approaches to enduring problems.

Negativity and Scandal Increasingly, political candidates and officials are being subjected to a relentless barrage of negative coverage. Some of this coverage starts with negative advertisements by opponents, which are then sometimes echoed in media reporting. Research has shown that negative ads increase citizens' anger and alienation and discourage many of them from voting.[28] News stories often picked up and amplified these negative themes.

Incumbent officials also get plenty of negative publicity, especially when even the appearance of wrongdoing in their personal lives creates dramatic human interest stories. "Whitewater" allegations against President Clinton and First Lady Hillary Rodham Clinton—that they had dealt improperly with a real estate investment and a bank's campaign contributions while Clinton was governor of Arkansas and had obstructed justice while in the White House—were doggedly pursued by the *American Spectator,* the *New York Times,* and other media for most of Clinton's first term. Sex scandals dogged Bill Clinton for most of his presidency and contributed to his eventual impeachment hearings. Sex and financial scandals also claimed, among others, Senator Gary Hart, former House Speakers Jim Wright and Newt Gingrich, and House Speaker–elect Bob Livingston. And, until the September 11, 2001, terrorist attacks on the United States shifted the focus of the media, great attention was given to speculations about the affair between Congressman Gary Condit and intern Chandra Levy and her disappearance. (See the "Using the Framework" feature for further examination of this issue.)

In the view of many observers, the news media in the United States have become increasingly mired in scandal and sensationalism. During the Pope's historic visit to communist Cuba, for example, the breaking Monica Lewinsky "White House intern" sex scandal dominated television news, talk radio, and newspapers. Dan Rather even left Havana in the middle of the Pope's visit in order to be on top of what CBS News producers considered to be the more important story.

Using the Framework

Monica All the Time

Why was the Monica Lewinsky story on the TV news for almost a year?

Background: President Clinton's sexual liaison with White House intern Monica Lewinsky dominated the nation's political news from the early summer of 1998 through the end of the Senate impeachment trial of the president in early 1999. It was almost as if nothing else of importance was happening in the nation or around the world. Why is that? Taking a look at how structural, political linkage, and governmental factors affected news coverage will help explain the situation.

Governmental Action

Impeachment hearings and vote in the House provided dramatic news material.

Senate deliberations and vote to remove the president from office provided dramatic news material.

Governmental Level

President Clinton engaged in behavior that was offensive to most Americans. → Many members of Congress believed that President Clinton had obstructed justice in the Paula Jones and Monica Lewinsky affairs. → A bitter partisan atmosphere permeated the 105th Congress. → The Republican Congress and Democratic President Bill Clinton were bitterly deadlocked on a wide range of issues; severe tensions existed between the two branches of government.

Political Linkages Level

Media television executives used "attack journalism," "infotainment," and scandal as a way to attract viewers from a highly fragmented set of media consumers. → The media fell into their "one big story at a time" syndrome, also evident in the O. J. Simpson and JonBenet Ramsey cases. → Web-based and scandal-sheet papers fed leads to major mainstream media. → The Republican Party used the Lewinsky scandal in advertising for the 1998 congressional elections. → Conservative interest groups also saw advantages in a weakened President Clinton and ran ad campaigns highlighting the Lewinsky matter.

Structural Level

Technological innovations multiplied the number of television channels, all of which require content to fill the hours. → As the Internet developed, it became (among other things) a medium for the distribution of information, opinion, and rumors.

Infotainment   One of the most dramatic changes that has occurred in the news is the insertion of entertainment values into political reporting and news presentation. As little as 15 to 20 years ago, news was monopolized by the three major television networks and the big-city daily newspapers, and the audiences for the news were fairly stable. In the intervening years, we have seen, the media have been revolutionized by the growth of cable television and the Internet and the multiplication of news outlets. In this new world, the networks and the big-city dailies have lost audience, leaving each of the fragments of the old and new media to fight for audience share. The best way to do this, media executives have discovered, is to make the news more entertaining, for the worst sin of this brave new media world is to be boring.[29] All too often, "more entertaining" means that sensation and scandal replace consideration of domestic politics, public policies, and international affairs; short and snappy coverage displaces longer, more analytical coverage; dramatic visuals push aside stories that cannot be easily visualized; and stories that feature angry conflict displace stories in which political leaders are trying to make workable compromises.[30]

The current "culture wars" between liberals and conservatives over the various legacies of the 1960s—involving issues such as abortion, affirmative action, religious values, gay and lesbian rights, and more—is perfect grist for the infotainment mill. Thus, a current staple of cable and broadcast television public affairs programming is the gathering of **pundits** from both sides of the cultural and political divide angrily shouting at one other for 30 or 60 minutes: *The Capital Gang* and *Hard Ball* are examples. And, because bringing together shouting pundits is far cheaper than sending reporters into the field to gather hard news, this form of news coverage is becoming more and more common, especially in the world of cable TV. It is highly unlikely that this emergent journalism of assertion and attack improves public understanding of the candidates, political leaders, and public policies.

Conflict and contest are also evident in coverage of campaigns, where the media concentrate on who is winning and who is losing the electoral race and what strategies candidates are using to gain ground or to maintain their lead. When candidates sometimes make a stab at talking seriously about issues, the media almost always treat such talk as a mere stratagem of the long campaign. The perpetual struggle between Congress and the president, built into our constitutional system, is also perfect for the infotainment news industry, especially if the struggle can be personalized, as it was in the years when House Speaker Newt Gingrich was doing battle with President Bill Clinton.

pundits
Somewhat derisive term for print, broadcast, and radio commentators on the political news.

Limited, Fragmented, and Incoherent Political Information   Most communications scholars agree that the media coverage of political news has certain distinctive features that result from characteristics of the mass media themselves, including the prevailing technology and organization of news gathering, corporate ownership, and the profit-making drive to appeal to mass audiences. These characteristics of the media mean that news, especially on television, tends to be episodic and fragmented rather than sustained, analytical, or dispassionate. Information comes in bits and pieces, out of context, and without historical background. Its effect is to entertain more than to inform.

Effects of the News Media on Politics

The old idea that the mass media have only "minimal effects" on politics is now discredited. The contents of the media do make a difference; they affect public opinion and policymaking in a number of ways, including setting the agenda for public debate and framing how issues are understood.[31]

Agenda Setting

agenda setting
Influencing what people consider important.

Several studies have demonstrated the effect known as **agenda setting.** The topics that get the most coverage in the media are the same ones that most people tell pollsters are the most important problems facing the country. This correlation does not result just from the media's printing what people are most interested in; it is a real effect of what appears in the media. In controlled experiments, people who are shown doctored television news broadcasts emphasizing a particular problem (for example, national defense) mention that problem as being important more often than people who have seen broadcasts that have not been tampered with.[32]

Of course, media managers do not arbitrarily decide what news to emphasize; their decisions reflect what is happening in the world and what American audiences care about. If there is a war or an economic depression, the media report it. But some research has indicated that what the media cover sometimes diverges from actual trends in problems. Publicity about crime, for example, may reflect editors' fears or a few dramatic incidents rather than a rising crime rate. When the two diverge, it seems to be the media's emphasis rather than real trends that affects public opinion.[33]

When the media decide to highlight a human rights tragedy in "real time," such as "ethnic cleansing" in Kosovo, public officials often feel compelled to act. When the media ignore equally troubling human tragedies, such as the genocide in Rwanda, public officials can attend to other matters. One scholarly study shows that in the foreign policy area, media choices about coverage shape what presidents pay attention to.[34]

Framing and Effects on Policy Preferences

framing
Providing a context for interpretation.

Experiments also indicate that the media's **framing,** or interpretation of stories, affects how people think about political problems and how they assign blame. Whether citizens ascribe poverty to the laziness of the poor or to the

Web Exploration
Agenda Setting

Issue: Scholarly research shows that the news media help set the political agenda for both political leaders and ordinary citizens.

Site: Access the Center for Media and Public Affairs on our Website at **www.ablongman.com/greenberg.** Go to the "Web Explorations" section for Chapter 6, open "agenda setting," then "studies" so that you can see what kinds of stories have received the most media attention in different years and how they have been covered. Look at the most recent studies.

What You've Learned: Has the emphasis in the news changed over time? Are the same kinds of stories carried year after year or not? Is there more or less substantive news about government and politics? Is there more or less news about scandals and government wrong-doing? How well and fairly have news stories been reported?

Hint: Even a cynic might be surprised to learn how much news coverage is directed at scandal and sensation.

nature of the economy, for example, depends partly on whether the media run stories about poor individuals (implying that they are responsible for their own plight) or stories about overall economic trends such as wage stagnation and unemployment.[35]

What appears in the media affects people's policy preferences as well. One study found that changes in the percentages of the public that favored various policies could be predicted rather accurately by what sorts of stories appeared on network television news shows between one opinion survey and the next. News from experts, commentators, and popular presidents had especially strong effects.[36]

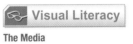

The Media

Affecting Policymaking

By affecting what ordinary Americans think is important, how they understand problems, and what policies they want, the media indirectly affect what government does, because the government tends to respond to public opinion. Heavy support for the North American Free Trade Agreement (NAFTA) by the *New York Times* and other media, for example, probably helped counteract initial public opposition due to fears of job losses. In addition, the media affect who is elected to office. As we will see in Chapter 10, media stories about the character of presidential and other candidates have enormous effects on fundraising and on citizens' judgments of who would make a good leader. Thus, early press portrayal of George W. Bush as a "fresh face" in the Republican Party capable of winning the presidential election helped him raise record-setting amounts of money for his presidential run in 2000.

Moreover, what appears in the media has a direct effect on policymaking. Policymakers learn about the world and about each other's activities from the media. Investigative journalism that exposes problems, for example, often leads local, state, or federal officials to act. Sometimes, journalists and politicians actively work together: The journalists expose problems that the politicians want to solve, and then the politicians' statements, hearings, and bills prolong the story for journalists to continue reporting.[37]

Fueling Cynicism

Americans are quite cynical about the political parties, politicians, and most incumbent political leaders. To some extent, this has been true since the founding of the nation. Nevertheless, scholars and political commentators have noted a considerable increase in negative feelings about the political system over the past two decades or so. Many commentators believe that news media coverage of American politics has a great deal to do with this attitude change.[38] As the adversarial-attack journalism style and infotainment have taken over political reporting, serious consideration of the issues, careful examination of policy alternatives, and dispassionate examination of the actions of government institutions have taken a back seat to a steady diet of charges about personal misbehavior. When President George H. W. Bush, for example, joined a world leader to describe the nature of the agreement they had reached, reporters asked him instead about rumors of an extramarital affair a few years earlier. With the message being delivered by the mass media that political issues are really about special-interest maneuvering, that political leaders and aspiring political leaders never say what they mean or mean what they say, that all of them have something in their personal lives they want to hide, and that even the most admired of the lot have feet of clay, is it any wonder that the American people are becoming increasingly disenchanted with the whole business?

Government Regulation of the Media

Our Constitution protects freedom of the press, and the U.S. government has less legal control over the media than the governments of most other countries do. But our government has the authority to make various technical and substantive regulations on the electronic media, if it wishes.

Print Media

Early in American history, government sometimes interfered with the press in a heavy-handed way. Under the Alien and Sedition Acts of 1798, for example, several Anti-Federalist newspaper editors were jailed for criticizing John Adams's administration. In recent years, however, the Constitution has been interpreted as forbidding government from preventing the publication of most kinds of political information or from punishing its publication afterward. The main exceptions involve national security, especially during wartime.

Prior Restraint   Several U.S. Supreme Court decisions, beginning in the 1920s and 1930s, have ensured the press a great deal of constitutional protection. The First Amendment provision that Congress shall make no law "abridging freedom of speech, or of the press" has been held by the Supreme Court to prevent the federal censorship of newspapers or magazines. Only under the most pressing circumstances of danger to national security can the government engage in **prior restraint** and prevent the publication of material to which it objects (see Chapter 15).

On June 30, 1971, for example, the Supreme Court denied a request by the Nixon administration to restrain the *New York Times* and the *Washington Post* from publishing excerpts from the *Pentagon Papers,* a secret Defense Department history of the United States's involvement in Vietnam. The Court declared that "the Government 'thus carries a heavy burden of showing justification for the enforcement of such a restraint.' . . . The Government had not

prior restraint
The government's power to prevent publication, as opposed to punishment afterward.

Coverage of the Persian Gulf War in 1991, even more than that of previous wars, was carefully controlled and censored by the U.S. military.

met that burden." Justice Hugo Black's concurring opinion has become an important statement on freedom of the press.

Wartime Controls   In a sense, however, the *Pentagon Papers* case was an easy one because it concerned the right to publish a two-year-old history and analysis of past government policy, not information about current military or foreign policy actions that could jeopardize American lives. During wartime, the government has almost always asserted broad powers to control what reporters can see and what they can print. During World War II, for example, the Office of Censorship monitored all news entering and leaving the country, but it focused mainly on news about casualties and troop and ship movements rather than on political matters.

Relatively free media access to the Vietnam War eventually brought a flood of negative stories.[39] U.S. officials, having learned their lesson, restricted access to the 1991 war with Iraq. During that war, the military imposed an elaborate system of control and censorship, requiring reporters to work only in escorted pools, limiting their access to U.S. troops, and censoring their stories. The media went along with these restrictions at the time, and large majorities of the public approved of it, but the result was incomplete and misleading coverage.[40]

Strict controls were also imposed by the Defense Department on press coverage of the war in Afghanistan. These included disseminating information in tightly controlled press briefings, denying access to officers and enlisted personnel engaged in the conflict, strictly limiting access to the battlefield, and successfully requesting that news organizations not print or show bin Laden speeches. In the 2003 war with Iraq, embedded journalists had access to the battlefront—or, more accurately, the battlefront in the south of the country with the invasion launched from Kuwait—but the Pentagon and the administration tried to maintain control over reporting of the wider war and its implications. It was not entirely successful in this effort, however, because European, Asian, and Arabic news organizations also were reporting the war, often from the point of view of the Iraqis. Although few Americans had access to these print and television news reports, many people around the world did, fueling the rise of anti-American feelings in many countries.[41] And, as you have seen, efforts to control bad news from Iraq during the American occupation were not successful.

The Electronic Media

The electronic media are more directly regulated by government than the print media, although such regulation has been diminishing.

Government Licensing of the Airwaves   The federal government has broad powers to regulate the use of the airwaves, which are considered public property. Ever since the passage of the Radio Act of 1927 and the Communications Act of 1934, which established the Federal Communications Commission (FCC), the government has licensed radio and television stations and has required them to observe certain rules as a condition for obtaining licenses.

FCC rules specify the frequencies on which stations can broadcast and the amount of power that they can use, in order to prevent interference among broadcasters of the sort that had brought chaos to radio during the 1920s. Government regulations divide the VHF television band into 12 channels and allocate them in such a way that most major cities have three VHF stations—the main reason for the early emergence of just three major networks. The development of cable television greatly expanded variety and competition.

For a long time, to prevent monopolies of scarce channels, federal rules prohibited networks or anyone else from owning more than five VHF stations around the country. This changed with the passage of the Telecommunications Act of 1996; now a single company can own many radio and television stations in many markets around the country. Needless to say, this encouraged a wave of mergers in the late 1990s and into the new century. The FCC further loosened ownership rules in 2003, permitting the big networks to own local stations and cable operations, thus allowing them to reach 45 percent of the nation's public. Congress later reduced the maximum allowable coverage to 39 percent.

Growing concerns among many Americans about the increased availability of sexually suggestive materials on network and cable television, and on radio, have triggered increased scrutiny of media decency practices and standards by the FCC, as well as congressional investigations. Public officials were especially sensitive to the public outcry over Janet Jackson's televised half-time performance at the Super Bowl in 2004. Worried by the FCC's renewed attention and increased willingness to levy fines for on-air indecency, and by the prospect of new legislation being considered in Congress that would increase allowable fines for indecency to as much as $3 million a day, some media corporations moved quickly to try to stem the tide. The major TV networks announced, for example, moves to beef up their standards departments, and began to delay many live broadcasts for a few seconds so that potentially offensive material might be deleted—famously, Bono's spontaneous expletive at the 2003 Golden Globes and Janet Jackson's exposure. For its part, Clear Channel radio dropped the raunchy "Bubba the Love Sponge" show and did the same for the Howard Stern show in six cities in its network.

Public Service Broadcasting   The FCC was mandated by Congress to regulate the airwaves for the "public interest, convenience, or necessity." This vague phrase has been interpreted as including "the development of an informed public opinion through the public dissemination of news and ideas concerning the vital public issues of the day," with ideas coming from "diverse and antagonistic sources," and with an emphasis on service to the local community.

In practice, this requirement has mainly meant FCC pressure (backed up by the threat of not renewing stations' licenses) to provide a certain number of hours of news and "public service" broadcasting. Thus, government regulation created an artificial demand for news programming, before it became profitable, and contributed to the rise and expansion of network news and to the development of documentaries and news specials. In that way, government regulation presumably contributed to informed public opinion and to democracy. Recently, however, this public service requirement has been eroded and the amount of this kind of programming has declined.

Fairness   For many years, the **fairness doctrine** of 1949 required that licensees present contrasting viewpoints on any controversial issue of public importance that was discussed. This requirement led to efforts at balance—presenting two sides on any issue that was mentioned—and sometimes to the avoidance of controversial issues altogether. It was left mostly up to broadcasters, however, to decide what was important or controversial and what constituted a fair reply and a fair amount of time to give it.

> **fairness doctrine**
> The former requirement that television stations present contrasting points of view.

Fairness is not easy to define: Which of the unlimited number of possible opinions deserves a hearing? The FCC itself long ago made clear that it did not intend to make time available to "communist viewpoints," and both of the "two sides" that the media air are usually quite mainstream.

Equal Time   Similarly, the **equal time provision** of the 1934 Communications Act required that except for news programs, stations that granted (or sold) air time to any one candidate for public office had to grant (or sell) other candidates equal time. This requirement threatened to cause the media great expense when minor party candidates insisted on their share of air time or when opponents wanted to reply to political speeches by incumbent presidents in election years. Contrary to its intent, therefore, this requirement led to some curtailment of political programming.

> **equal time provision**
> The former requirement that television stations give or sell the same amount of time to all competing candidates.

The equal time provision was suspended in 1960 to allow televised debates between candidates John F. Kennedy and Richard M. Nixon, and in 1976 and 1980, the FCC permitted the staging of the Ford–Carter and Carter–Reagan debates as "public meetings," sponsored by the League of Women Voters, to get around the provision. In 1983, the FCC declared that radio and television broadcasters were free to stage debates at all political levels among candidates of their own choosing.[42] Broadcasters and the Commission on Presidential Debates (a nonpartisan corporation created to sponsor presidential debates) decided to allow Independent candidate Ross Perot to join the debates in 1992 (Bush v. Clinton) and 1996 (Clinton v. Dole), but chose not to include Green Party candidate Ralph Nader in 2000 (W. Bush v. Gore), much to the chagrin of Nader and his supporters.

Rate Regulation   Federal and local regulation of the rates charged by cable TV firms (many of them monopoly providers in local areas) has been imposed, removed, and imposed once again. Most recently, the Telecommunications Act of 1996 ended the regulation of cable rates by the FCC in 1999. Congress's thinking was that competition from the telephone companies would keep cable rates down. This remains to be seen, but the evidence so far is not encouraging: cable rates since 1999 have risen three times faster the cost of living.[43]

The Internet

When television and radio were introduced, the industries were regulated by the federal government almost immediately. This has not been the case for the Internet, despite its extraordinary growth and social impact. Although

Election year debates, such as this 2004 debate between presidential candidates George W. Bush and John Kerry, have become a regular feature of presidential campaigns and can have an important effect on the election outcome.

initially a product of government encouragement and financial support—it was first created to link together university and government defense researchers[44]—the Internet has been relatively free from regulation, although there have been calls for government to prevent certain content from appearing on it. The few attempts that have been made have not been successful. Congress, for example, tried to ban obscenity on the Net, but the Supreme Court in 1997 declared the statute an unconstitutional restriction of free speech. When the Clinton administration tried to prevent people from posting encryption codes, a federal court declared the effort as unconstitutional on the same grounds. In the view of the federal courts, at this writing, the Internet is an open medium where people are free to express their views, no different from dissemination of ideas by voice from atop a soap-box or by a pamphlet. Statute and case law in this area is sure to grow, however, as the Internet comes to play an ever larger role in our lives. The story of Internet regulation is not yet finished.[45] For example, Congress revisited the issue of Internet pornography when it passed the Child Online Protection Act of 1998 designed to block access to material on the Web that might be harmful to children. In 2004, however, the Supreme Court upheld a lower court's ruling blocking the law from taking effect, with the majority suggesting that the new law was an unconstitutional restriction on free speech.

Taken as a whole, then, government regulation of the media does not now amount to much. The trend has been toward a free market system with little government interference. Although the 2001 USA Patriot Act allows the federal government to more easily conduct surveillances of Internet and e-mail use by suspected terrorists, the overall conclusion about the light regulatory hand of the government still holds.

How Democratic Are We?

The Media and Democratic Citizenship

PROPOSITION: The news media are an important ingredient in making American politics democratic.

AGREE: Without the information provided by the news media, ordinary citizens would have little hope of learning what is happening abroad; they could not begin to think about what sorts of policies the United States should pursue in foreign affairs. Nor, without the news media, could most Americans learn what their government is doing domestically, what sorts of candidates are running for office, or what kinds of public policies are being considered. For example, in late 2003 the news media extensively reported the battle between Democrats and Republicans over prescription drug benefits under Social Security, the alternative policies proposed by the leaders of each party, and details of the bill that was eventually signed by President Bush.

In these respects, the spread of the news media in the United States, and the penetration of millions of homes by newspapers, radio, television, and computers, has undoubtedly helped democracy. It has made it much easier for ordinary citizens to decide about alternative public policies, to judge the actions of government and elected leaders, and to make decisions about who should be elected to office. News media thus tend to broaden the scope of conflict and contribute to political equality. When citizens, rather than just political leaders or special-interest groups, know what is going on, they can have a voice in politics. Moreover, interactive media and media-published polls help politicians hear that voice.

DISAGREE: Scholars and media critics who want the news media to be highly informative, analytical, and issue oriented are appalled by the personalized, episodic, dramatic, and fragmented character of most news stories, which do not provide sustained and coherent explanations of what is going on. Others worry about ideological biases they think arise from a leftist media elite or from a corporate-owned media industry. Some criticize the media's patriotic and ethnocentric tendencies to support official U.S. foreign policy and even to pass along deliberate untruths stated by government officials. If the news media regularly present one-sided or false pictures of politics, people may form mistaken policy preferences. Government responsiveness to manipulated preferences would not be truly democratic.

Still other critics worry that constant media exposés of alleged official wrongdoing or government inefficiency, and the mocking tone aimed at virtually all political leaders by journalists and talk radio hosts, have fueled the growing political cynicism of the public. If this is true, the media are not serving democracy as well as they might.

CONSIDER: • Which news media sources do you pay most attention to? Network or cable news programs? Talk radio? Websites of news organizations, advocacy groups, or nonpartisan policy organizations? Newspapers or magazines? • Looking back on important recent actions by government leaders—for example, waging war and occupation in Iraq or the struggle in Congress to fashion a new national energy policy—do you think the news sources you most depend on did a good job in keeping you informed? • Do you believe you were well served by the news sources you used? • If not, why do you think this might be the case? • What did these sources miss and why? • What do you think they might do to improve their performance as a source of credible news and information for you and other American citizens?

As Internet usage has expanded in the United States, various and sundry individuals and groups have called for tighter federal regulation of the new medium, primarily to protect children from material with sexual content and to prevent dissemination of hate material. So far, none of the bills passed by Congress to achieve these regulatory goals has passed constitutional muster with the Supreme Court.

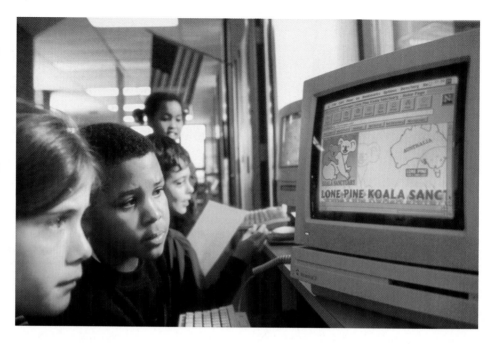

Summary

The shape of the news media in the United States has been determined largely by structural factors: technological developments; the growth of the American population and economy; and the development of a privately owned, corporation-dominated media industry.

The profit motive leads the major media to appeal to large audiences by limiting the quantity and depth of political news, by appealing to patriotism and other mainstream political values, and by emphasizing dramatic stories with visual impact and human interest.

News gathering is organized around New York City, Washington, D.C., and a handful of major cities in the United States and abroad. Most foreign countries are ignored unless there are crises or other big stories to communicate. Most news comes from government officials, who cultivate friendly relations with the press and provide accessible press conferences and information handouts.

Observers disagree about whether the media are biased in a liberal or a conservative direction. Reporters tend to be liberal, especially on social issues, but this tendency may be balanced or reversed by conservative owners and editors. The U.S. media tend to reflect ethnocentrism, support U.S. foreign policy, and celebrate American-style capitalism. They also broadcast negative campaign ads, publicize personal scandals, and sharply criticize officials who have lost popularity.

Media stories have substantial effects on the public's perceptions of problems, its interpretations of events, its evaluations of political candidates, and its policy preferences.

The media, especially the print media, are protected from many kinds of government interference by the First Amendment to the Constitution. But censorship occurs during wars and crises, and officials have indirect ways of influencing the news. The electronic media are legally open to direct regulation, but such regulation, including the fairness doctrine and the equal time provision, has mostly lapsed. The Internet remains relatively free from government regulation.

Suggestions for Further Reading

Alterman, Eric. *What Liberal Media: The Truth About Bias and the News.* New York: Basic Books, 2003.
> An impassioned yet well-documented answer to the charge that the news media are biased against conservatives.

Bagdikian, Ben H. *The New Media Monopoly,* Boston: Beacon Press, 2004.
> An analysis of the corporate structure of the media and its consequences.

Bennett, W. Lance. *News: Politics of Illusion,* 5th ed. New York: Longman, 2003.
> A critique of the news as trivial and uninformative.

Graber, Doris. *Media Power in Politics.* Washington, D.C.: CQ Press, 2000.
> A comprehensive examination of the news media's effect on American politics.

Jamieson, Kathleen Hall, and Paul Waldman. *The Press Effect.* New York: Oxford University Press, 2002.
> A careful but lively discussion of how the news media frame events for the American people.

Kovach, Bill, and Tom Rosenstiel. *Warp Speed: America in the Age of Mixed Media.* New York: The Century Foundation Press, 1999.
> A sober and sometimes somber description of the effect of the rapidly changing mass media industry on American politics and government.

Internet Sources

Almost every television news organization has a Website on the Internet:

ABC News
http://www.abcnews.com

CBS News
http://www.cbsnews.com

CNN Interactive
http://www.cnn.com/

NBC News
http://www.nbcnews.com

The same is true of the major national newspapers:

Chicago Tribune
http://www.chicagotribune.com

Los Angeles Times
http://www.latimes.com

New York Times
http://www.nytimes.com

USA Today
http://www.usatoday.com

Washington Post
http://www.washingtonpost.com

Other sources for studies on media trends and effects on society include

The Center for Media and Public Affairs
www.cmpa.com
> Studies, commentaries, and forums on media and public affairs.

The Columbia Journalism Review
www.cjr.org
> The Website of the leading scholarly monitor of journalism and journalists; loaded with useful information about all aspects of news making and dissemination.

The Pew Research Center for the People and the Press
www.people-press.org/
> The most complete public opinion surveys on citizen evaluations of the quality of media coverage of public affairs.

Chapter 7
Interest Groups and Business Corporations

In This Chapter

- Interest groups in democratic theory
- Why interest groups have proliferated
- How interest groups lobby the government
- How interest groups try to mobilize the grass roots
- Biases in the interest group system
- Why large corporations hold a privileged position

The Energy Industry Pushes an Energy Bill

At the end of 2003, a Republican-sponsored energy bill cleared its conference committee and was approved by the House but failed in the U.S. Senate, falling 2 votes short of the 60 votes needed to break a Democratic filibuster. Republicans promised to reintroduce the bill later. Whatever the ultimate fate of the energy bill—unclear as we go to press—its story illustrates the central role that powerful special interests play in fashioning and pushing forward major bills, and how congressional leaders parcel out rewards to special interests in House districts and states as a way to fashion legislative majorities.

In the 2000 presidential election, the energy and electrical utility industry contributed more than $67 million to congressional candidates and the political parties, 75 percent of that going to Republicans.[1] Not surprisingly, the Bush administration came to office in 2001 promising a new energy policy for the nation that included subsidies for the industry and some loosening of regulatory restrictions. To hammer out the general outlines of a new national energy policy, Vice President Richard Cheney met secretly with a task force made up almost entirely of representatives of large energy corporations and energy trade associations. The bill they proposed didn't get far in the 107th Congress, however, not only because of the public outcry over the plan to drill for oil in the Alaska national wildlife preserve, but because the attention of the country had shifted to the war on terrorism after the 9/11 terrorist attacks.

An energy bill was reintroduced in the 108th Congress following the 2002 elections, partly because of the Bush administration's continuing philosophical commitment to a new energy policy and partly because of the strong push for legislation from large energy and electrical utility companies and trade associations. The fact that these special interests poured almost $58 million into the 2002 congressional elections[2]—73 percent to Republicans and 27 percent to Democrats—helped ensure that the voice of the industry would be heard in the halls and hearing rooms of Congress. Interest in Congress for a major new bill was further heightened by the huge power outage in summer 2003 that hit 70 million Americans, and by the public outcry that followed.

The bill's momentum was increased by a massive lobbying campaign by energy and utility interests, with the Edison Electric Utility Institute—the industry trade association—leading the way. Edison spent a minimum of $25 million in its

lobbying effort on Capitol Hill, and enlisted the help of utility company CEO's in virtually every state to put pressure on representatives and senators. The Southern Company, a utility company covering four states in the South, threw its 12 Washington government affairs people into the battle and hired two lobbying firms to join in the effort. With the exception of a few consumer groups, only a handful of lobbyists from outside the industry were in the mix.[3] Not surprisingly, perhaps, the final energy bill that emerged from the conference committee in 2003 included billions in tax breaks and direct subsidies for energy companies (oil, gas, coal, and nuclear) and electrical utilities and the repeal of an important energy consumer-protection law.

The bill also included a multitude of subsidies, tax breaks, and other encouragement for companies in key states and districts—"pork barrel" is the term traditionally associated with this practice—the result of the efforts of legislative leaders to build support for the bill among representatives and senators. For example, $1 billion in the bill was earmarked for a new nuclear power plant in Idaho, while $800 million was targeted for loan guarantees to coal gasification companies in Minnesota. Another provision protected the Texas producers of MTBE, a gasoline additive, from pollution lawsuits. With Midwest farm states in mind, another provision encouraged an increase in the use of ethanol as a gasoline additive. To secure a few additional votes in western states, subsidies were included for timber companies to help thin forests.

187

In the end, the bill did not pass in 2003. Congressional observers credit a number of things for the failure, including the massive cost of the program at a time of increasing budget deficits and the virtual exclusion of Democrats from legislative deliberations on the bill—the conference committee did not include any Democrats at all. However, the story of the energy bill shows the importance of interest groups in the workings of government in the United States.

Thinking Critically About This Chapter

This chapter is about the important role interest groups play in American government and politics, how they go about achieving their ends, and what effects they have in determining government policies in the United States.

Using the Framework You will see in this chapter how interest groups, in combination with other political linkage institutions, help convey the wishes and interests of people and groups to government decision makers. You will also learn how the kind of interest group system we have in the United States is, in large part, a product of structural factors, including our constitutional rules, political culture, social organization, and economy.

Using the Democracy Standard Interest groups have long held an ambiguous place in American politics. To some, interest groups are "special" interests that act without regard to the public interest and are the instruments of the most privileged parts of American society. To others, interest groups are simply another way by which people and groups in a democratic society get their voices heard by government leaders. Using the democracy standard described in Chapter 1, you will be able to choose between these two positions.

Interest Groups in a Democratic Society: Contrasting Views

interest group
Any private organization or association that seeks to influence public policy as a way to protect or advance some interest.

pressure group
An interest group or lobby; a group that brings pressure to bear on government decision makers.

lobby
An interest or pressure group that seeks to convey the group's interest to government decision makers.

Interest groups are private organizations that try to shape public policy. They are made up of people who share an interest or cause that they are trying to protect or advance with the help of government. To do this, interest groups try to influence the behavior of public officials, such as presidents, members of Congress, bureaucrats, and judges. These efforts are often perceived by officials as pressuring them, so interest groups are often called **pressure groups.** The term **lobby** is also commonly used—because of the practice of interest group representatives' talking to representatives and senators in the lobbies outside committee rooms—as in references to the "dairy lobby" or the "gun lobby."

The Evils of Factions

The danger to good government and the public interest from interest groups is a familiar theme in American politics. They are usually regarded as narrowly self-interested, out for themselves, and without regard for the public good.

In the late nineteenth century, most Americans thought of the Senate as the captive of large corporate trusts and other special-interest groups, as depicted in this popular cartoon, "Bosses of the Senate."

This theme is prominent in *The Federalist,* No. 10, in which James Madison defined **factions** (his term for interest groups and narrow political parties) in the following manner: "A number of citizens, whether amounting to a majority or a minority of the whole, who are united and actuated by some common impulse of passion, or of interest, adverse to the rights of other citizens or to the permanent and aggregate interests of the community."[4] The "evils of faction" theme recurs throughout our history, from the writings of the "muckrakers" at the turn of the twentieth century to the Democratic presidential primary campaign of Howard Dean in 2004.

faction
Madison's term for groups or parties that try to advance their own interests at the expense of the public good.

Interest Group Democracy: The Pluralist Argument

According to many political scientists, however, interest groups do not hurt democracy and the public interest but are an important instrument in attaining both. The argument of these **pluralist** political scientists is shown in Figure 7.1 and goes as follows:[5]

pluralist
A political scientist who views American politics as best understood in terms of the interaction, conflict, and bargaining of groups.

- Free elections, while essential to a democracy, do not adequately communicate the specific wants and interests of the people to political leaders on a continuous basis. These are more accurately, consistently, and frequently conveyed to political leaders by the many groups and organizations to which people belong.

- Interest groups are easy to create; people in the United States are free to join or to organize groups that reflect their interests.

- Because of federalism, checks and balances, and the separation of powers, government power in the United States is broadly dispersed, leaving governmental institutions remarkably porous and open to the entreaties of the many and diverse groups that exist in society.

- Because of the ease of group formation and the accessibility of government, all legitimate interests in society can have their views taken into account by some public official. Because of this, the system is highly democratic.

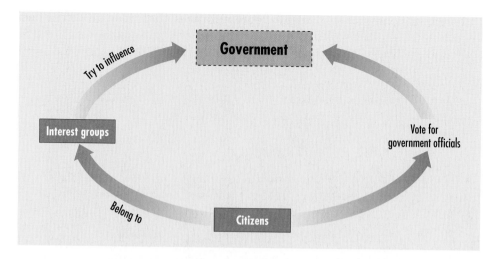

FIGURE 7.1 ● The Pluralist View of American Politics

In the pluralist understanding of the way American democracy works, citizens have more than one way to influence government leaders. In addition to voting, citizens also have the opportunity to participate in organizations that convey member views to public officials. Because of weak political parties, federalism, checks and balances, and the separation of powers, access to public officials is relatively easy.

Pluralists see interest groups, then, not as a problem but as an additional tool of democratic representation, similar to other democratic instruments such as public opinion and elections. We shall explore the degree to which this position is valid in this and other chapters.

Interest Group Formation: Structural, Political Linkage, and Governmental Factors

Nobody knows exactly how many interest groups exist in the United States, but there is wide agreement that the number began to mushroom in the late 1960s, that it has grown steadily ever since, and that it ranges today in the thousands. We have a more precise count, however, of the number of paid lobbyists who work for interest groups in Washington and try to affect government policies. In Washington today, more than 80,000 people work for private associations trying to influence the government.[6] These associations as well as other hired lobbyists, spent about $1.7 billion on lobby efforts in Congress in 2001.[7] Because lobbying Congress is only a part of what interest groups do, so these statistics show only the tip of the iceberg.

Much of the increase in the number of interest groups can be explained by the growing number of public interest or citizen groups organized around some cause or idea, rather than an economic or occupational interest, the traditional basis for forming interest groups. These include environmental, consumer protection, anti-abortion, family values, good government, civil rights, pro-life, and women's organizations. Nevertheless, corporations, business trade associations, and the professions still dominate the scene: One study done during the Reagan years showed that corporations made up 52 percent of all organizations with Washington representatives, that trade and other business associations accounted for another 20 percent, and that professional associations accounted for an additional 8 percent, for a total of 80 percent of the organizations.[8] And, there is no evidence to suggest that the proportion of the total made up by citizen groups has grown much since then.[9]

There are a number of reasons so many interest groups exist in the United States.

Diverse Interests

Being a very diverse society, there are simply lots of interests in the United States. Racial, religious, ethnic, and occupational diversity is pronounced. Our economy is also strikingly complex and multifaceted, and becoming more so. In a free society, these diverse interests usually take organizational forms. Thus, the computer revolution has spawned computer chip manufacturers, software companies, software engineers, computer magazines, Internet services, technical information providers, computer component jobbers, Web designers, and countless others. Each has particular interests to defend or advance before government, and each has formed an association to try to do so. Thus, software engineers have an association to look after their interests. So do software and hardware companies, Internet access providers, digital content providers, industry writers, and so on.

Rules of the Game

The rules of the political game in the United States encourage the formation of interest groups. The First Amendment to the Constitution, for instance, guarantees citizens the right to speak freely, to assemble, and to petition the government, all of which are essential to citizens' ability to form organizations to advance their interests before government. Moreover, the government is organized in such a way that officials are relatively accessible to interest groups. Because of federalism, checks and balances, and the separation of powers, there is no dominant center of decision making, as there is in unitary states such as Great Britain and France. In unitary states (see Chapter 3), most important policy decisions are made in parliamentary bodies. In the United States, important decisions are made by many officials, on many matters, in many jurisdictions. Consequently, there are many more places where interest group pressure can be effective; there are more access points to public officials.

Comparing Interest Groups

The Growth in Government

Government does far more today than it did during the early years of the Republic. As government takes on more responsibilities, it quite naturally comes to have a greater effect on virtually all aspects of economic, social, and personal life. People, groups, and organizations are increasingly affected by the actions of government, so the decisions made by presidents, members of Congress, bureaucrats, and judges are increasingly important. It would be surprising indeed if in response, people, groups, and organizations did not try harder to influence the public officials' decisions that affect them.

Some groups form around government programs in order to take advantage of existing government programs and initiatives. The creation of the Department of Homeland Security, with its large budget for new homeland defense technologies, stimulated the formation of new companies to serve this

New government programs, and the spending associated with such programs, often simulate the formation of new companies to take advantage of opportunities and new organizations to represent these companies. Here, a company representative shows his wares at a homeland security trade show in Washington, D.C.

market, as well as new trade associations—including the Homeland Security Industries Association—to represent them. By mid-September 2003, there were already 108 registered lobbyists for homeland security, and most of the large lobbying firms in Washington had added a homeland security section.

Government sometimes encourages the formation of groups and associations to help carry out and monitor its policies or to achieve other ends. According to political scientist Anne Costain, a commissioner of the Equal Employment Opportunity Commission (EEOC) played an important role in the formation of the National Organization for Women (NOW) because he wanted a counterweight to the overwhelming influence of African American civil rights groups over the EEOC.[10]

Disturbances

The existence of diverse interests, the rules of the game, and the importance of government decisions and policies enable and encourage the formation of interest groups, but formation seems to happen only when interests are threatened, usually by some change in the social and economic environment or in government policy. This is known as the **disturbance theory** of interest group formation.[11] To take one example, the Christian Coalition was formed when many evangelical Christians began to feel threatened by family breakdown, an increase in the number of abortions, the sexual revolution, and the growing voice of gays and lesbians.

disturbance theory
A theory that locates the origins of interest groups in changes in the economic, social, or political environment that threaten the well-being of some segment of the population.

Incentives

Some social scientists argue, however, that people are not inclined to form groups, even when their common interests are threatened, unless the group can offer a selective, material benefit to them.[12] A selective, material benefit is something tangible that is available to the members of an interest group but not to nonmembers. If someone can get the benefit without joining the group, then joining makes no sense as he or she can obtain the same benefit without contributing. This is known as the **free rider** problem, and it generally comes into play when a group is interested in a collective good, such as a government program or action that will be good for all the members of some category whether they belong to a formal organization or not. All women with young children gain when the National Organization for Women helps influence Congress to pass the Family Leave Act and are not required to join the organization to enjoy the benefit. People join, it is argued, when an association has benefits that are available only to its members—for example, discounted life and health insurance programs for the members of the Wheat Growers Association.

This theory emphasizes how difficult and unlikely it is that interest groups will form at all. It cannot account very well, therefore, for the upsurge in group formation during the 1960s and 1970s, especially of the public interest and ideological variety.[13] The proliferation of such groups suggests that groups form not only around selective, material incentives but also around "purposive" (ideological, issue-oriented) incentives and around "solidaristic" (in the sense of being part of something that one values) ones. People often join groups, for instance, because they believe in a particular cause (e.g., nuclear disarmament, civil rights, prayer in the public schools, or an end to legal abortion) or because they enjoy the companionship afforded by belonging to a group.

free rider
One who gains a benefit without contributing; explains why it is so difficult to form social movements and noneconomic interest groups.

What Interests Are Represented

What kinds of interests find a voice in American politics? A useful place to start is with political scientist E. E. Schattschneider's distinction between "private" and "public" interests. Although the boundaries between the two are sometimes fuzzy, the distinction remains important: **Public interests** are connected in one way or another to the general welfare of the community; **private interests,** by contrast, are associated with benefits for some fraction of the community.[14] The latter are mainly economic interests, groups with some tangible stake they wish to protect or to advance by means of government action, but associations that represent the interests of racial and ethnic groups fit in this category as well. The former are mainly noneconomic groups motivated by some ideology, by the desire to advance a general cause—animal rights, let us say, or environmental protection—or by the commitment to some public policy—gun control or an end to abortion.

Private and public interest groups come in a wide range of forms. Some, including the AARP, are large membership organizations with sizable Washington and regional offices. Some large membership organizations have passionately committed members active in its affairs—such as the National Rifle Association—while others have relatively passive members who join for the benefits the organization provides—such as the American Automobile Association with its well-known trip assistance. Other groups are trade associations whose members are business firms. Still others are rather small organizations, without members, run by professionals and sustained by foundations and a sizeable mailing list for soliciting contributions—the Children's Defense Fund and the National Taxpayers Union come to mind.

public interest group
An interest group that advocates for a cause or an ideology.

private interest group
An interest group that seeks to protect or advance the material interests of its members.

Private Interest Groups

Many different kinds of private interest groups are active in American politics.

Business   Because of the vast resources at the disposal of business and because of their strategic role in the health of local, state, and national economies, groups and associations representing business wield enormous power in Washington. Large corporations such as Boeing and Microsoft are able to mount their own lobbying efforts and join with others in influential associations such as the Business Roundtable. Medium-sized businesses are well represented by organizations such as the National Association of Manufacturers and the U.S. Chamber of Commerce. Even small businesses have proved to be quite influential when joined in associations such as the National Federation of Independent Business, which helped stop the Clinton health plan in 1994. Agriculture and agribusinesses (fertilizer, seed, machinery, biotechnology, and food-processing companies) have more than held their own over the years through organizations such as the American Farm Bureau Federation and the Farm Machinery Manufacturer's Association and through scores of commodity groups, including the American Dairy Association and the American Wheat Growers Association. We will look at business power in American politics in more detail later in this chapter.

The Professions   Several associations represent the interests of professionals, such as doctors, lawyers, dentists, and accountants. Because of the prominent social position of professionals in local communities and their ability to make substantial campaign contributions, such associations are very influential in the policymaking process on matters related to their professional expertise and concerns. The American Medical Association (AMA) and the American Dental Association (ADA), for instance, lobbied strongly against the Clinton health care proposal and helped kill it in the 103rd Congress. The Trial Lawyers Association has long been a major financial contributor to the Democratic Party and active in blocking legislation to limit the size of personal injury jury awards.

Labor   Although labor unions are sometimes involved in what might be called public interest activities (such as supporting civil rights legislation), their main role in the United States has been to protect the jobs of their members and to secure maximum wages and benefits for them. Unlike labor unions in many parts of the world, which are as much political and ideological organizations as economic, American labor unions have traditionally focused on so-called bread-and-butter issues. Union lobbying activities are directed at issues that affect the ability of unions to protect the jobs, wages, and benefits of their members and to maintain or increase the size of the union membership rolls. As an important part of the New Deal coalition that dominated American politics well into the late 1960s, labor unions were influential at the federal level during the years when the Democratic party controlled Congress and often won the presidency.

Although organized labor is still a force to be reckoned with in electoral politics, most observers believe that the political power of labor unions has eroded in dramatic ways over the past several decades.[15] Organized labor's main long-range problem in American politics and its declining power relative to business in the workplace is its small membership base; in 2003, only 12.9 percent of American workers—and only 8.2 percent of private-sector workers—were members of labor unions compared with 35 percent in 1954.[16] The long but steady decline in union membership is strongly associated with the

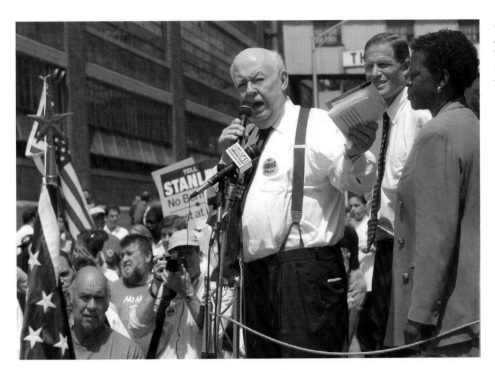

John Sweeney, the president of the AFL-CIO labor federation, has attempted to reinvigorate the organizing efforts and political presence of the labor movement.

decline in the proportion of American workers in manufacturing—the economic sector in which unions have traditionally been the strongest—and has proved resistant to vigorous organizing drives recently mounted by AFL-CIO president John Sweeney.

Racial, Ethnic, and Gender Organizations   In the wake of the civil rights and women's movements (see Chapter 8), it is hardly surprising that a number of associations have been formed to advance the interests of particular racial, ethnic, and gender groups in American society. The National Association for Women advocates policies in Washington that advance the position of women in American society, for example; the League of Latin American Citizens has been concerned, among other things, with national and state policies that affect migrants from Mexico and other Latin American countries. Similarly, the NAACP and the Urban League are advocates for the interests of African Americans.

Public Interest Groups

Public interest groups, sometimes called *citizens' groups,* try to get government to act in ways that will serve the general public and the public interest—as they define the public interest, of course—rather than the direct economic or occupational or social interests of their members.[17] People active in such groups tend to be motivated by ideological concerns or a belief in some cause.

Public interest groups of one kind or another have always been around, but a great upsurge in their number and influence has taken place since the late 1960s.[18] Many were spawned by social movements. The environmental movement created organizations such as the Environmental Defense Fund, the Nature Conservancy, Clean Water Action, and the Natural Resources Defense Council, for example. The evangelical Christian upsurge led to the

You Are an Environmental Activist

Christian conservatives have created several important and influential interest group organizations. Here Gary Bauer, the founder of the Family Research Council, addresses a rally in Washington, D.C., protesting alleged persecution of Christians in China.

creation of such organizations as the Moral Majority, the Christian Coalition, the National Right-to-Life Committee, and the Family Research Council.

Most citizen groups retain a professional, paid administrative staff and are supported by generous donors (often foundations), membership dues, and/or donations generated by direct mail campaigns. While some depend on and encourage grassroots volunteers, and some hold annual membership meetings where members play some role in making association policies, most public interest groups and citizens associations are organizations without active membership involvement (other than check writing), and are run by lobbying and public education professionals.[19]

What Interest Groups Do

Interest groups are in the business of conveying the views and defending the interests of individuals and groups to public officials. There are two basic types of interest group activity: the inside game and the outside game.[20] The inside game—the older and more familiar of the two—involves direct, personal contact between interest group representatives and government officials. The outside game involves interest group mobilization of public opinion, voters, and important contributors in order to bring pressure to bear on elected officials.

The Inside Game

The term *lobbying* conjures up visions of a cigar-chomping interest group representative, his arm around the shoulder of an important senator or representative, advising him on how he ought to vote on some obscure provision of the Tax Code, slipping an envelope, fat with currency, into the politician's jacket pocket. Or it conjures up images of favors given in return for future legislative considerations: paid vacations to exotic locations, honorarium payments for brief speeches at association meetings, and other exchanges verging on bribery.

The images both reveal and confuse. These things surely happened in the past, some continue to happen today, and some will surely happen in the future. In general, however, the images do not help us understand the intricacies of the inside game. This game does not involve bribes. Rather, it is more the politics of insiders and the "old boy" network (although, increasingly, women are also part of the network). It is the politics of one-on-one persuasion, in which the skilled lobbyist tries to get a decision maker to understand and sympathize with the interest group's point of view or to see that what the interest group wants is good for the politician's constituents. Access is critical if one is to be successful at this game.

Simulation

You Are a Lobbyist

Many of the most successful lobbyists are recruited from the ranks of retired members of the House, the Senate, and high levels of the bureaucracy. More than half of the powerful drug industry's registered lobbyists, for example, are former members of Congress, former congressional staffers, or former employees of the executive branch.[21] The promise of lucrative employment based on their skills—and especially on their many contacts—is what keeps so many of them around Washington after they leave office or quit federal employment. The very best of them have been in and out of one office or another in one administration or another for many years, know the D.C. scene as a wine connoisseur knows wine, and are compensated very well for their services.

The inside game seems to work best when the issues are narrow and technical, do not command much media attention or public passion, and do not stir up counteractivity by other interest groups.[22] This is not to say that interest groups play a role only on unimportant matters. Great benefit can come to an interest group or a large corporation from a small change in a single provision of the Tax Code or in a slight change in the wording of a regulation. Enron, for example, was very successful at getting Congress to remove federal oversight on many of its energy-trading and acquisitions activities. These stayed well out of public view until they came to light after Enron's spectacular collapse in 2001.

Lobbyists from citizens groups also play the inside game, often with great skill and effect. Many environmental regulations have been strengthened because of the efforts of skilled lobbyists from the Sierra Club, for example.

Political scientist E. E. Schattschneider has pointed out that the inside game—traditional lobbying—is pretty much outside the view of the public. That is to say, the day-to-day details of this form of lobbying are not the stuff of the evening news, nor the fodder of open political campaigns or conflict; such lobbying takes place behind closed doors. As such, it does not do much to advance democracy.

Lobbying Congress   The essence of the inside game in Congress is the cultivation of personal relationships with people who matter—Senate and House leaders, other influential and well-placed legislators, chairpersons of important committees or subcommittees, and key staff members. Because much of the action in Congress takes place in the committees and because senators and representatives are busy with a wide range of responsibilities, cultivating relationships with important legislative and committee staff members is especially important for successful lobbyists. As one lobbyist put it, "If you have a staff member on your side, it might be a hell of a lot better than talking to the member [of Congress]."[23]

An important part of the job of the lobbyist is to convey the views and concerns of interest group members to representatives and senators. The ability to hire and deploy lobbyists, however, is not randomly distributed among Americans. Those with the greatest economic resources tend to dominate the "inside game" of interest group politics.

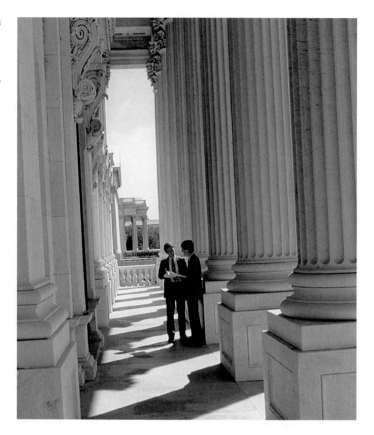

Lobbyists are also expected to attend and make contributions at various congressional fundraisers. The *Washington Post* counted 23 such events on a single day, June 24, 1999, a nonelection year.[24]

Lobbying the Executive Branch

Career civil servants and political appointees in the executive branch have a great deal of discretionary authority because Congress often legislates broad policies, leaving it to bureaucratic agencies to fill in the details. Because of this, interest groups try to establish stable and friendly relationships with the agencies of the executive branch that are most relevant to their interests. The payoffs from these long-term relationships can be quite high. In 2003, for example, Boeing successfully lobbied the Defense Procurement Office in the Pentagon to lease 100 transport planes from the company (the initial deal fell through after unethical behavior by Boeing lobbyists was revealed). In the same year, large media company and news organization leaders and lobbyists met with the top staff of the FCC in a successful effort to get the agency to loosen rules on ownership so that big companies could grow even bigger.

The key to success in lobbying the executive branch is similar to that in lobbying Congress: personal contact and cooperative long-term relationships. Interest group representatives can convey technical information, present the results of their research, help a public official deflect criticism, and show that what the group wants is compatible with good public policy and the political needs of the official.

Lobbying the Courts   Interest groups sometimes lobby the courts, although not in the same way as they lobby the other two branches. A group may find that neither Congress nor the White House is favorably disposed to its interests and will bring a test case to the courts. Realizing that the improvement of the lot of African Americans was very low on the agenda of presidents and members of Congress during the 1940s and 1950s, for example, the NAACP turned to the courts for satisfaction. The effort eventually paid off in 1954 in the landmark *Brown* v. *Board of Education* decision.

Interest groups sometimes lobby the courts by filing *amicus curiae* ("friends of the court") briefs in cases involving other parties. In this kind of brief, a person or an organization that is not a party in the suit may file an argument in support of one side or the other in the hope of swaying the views of the judge or judges. Major controversies before the Supreme Court on such issues as abortion, free speech, or civil rights attract scores of *amicus curiae* briefs.

Interest groups also get involved in the appointment of federal judges. Particularly controversial appointments, such as the Supreme Court nominations of Robert Bork (whom many women's and civil rights interests considered too conservative) in 1987 and Clarence Thomas (who was opposed by liberal and women's groups) in 1992, drew interest group attention and strenuous efforts for and against the nominees.

The Outside Game

The outside game is being played when interest groups try to mobilize **grassroots,** constituency, and public opinion support for their goals and bring them to bear on elected officials. By all indications, the outside game has been growing steadily in importance in recent years compared to more traditional forms of lobbying.[25] This may be a good development for democracy, and here is why. Although groups involved in the outside game often try to hide their true identities—Americans for Fair Drug Prices, for example, may well be funded by the drug industry—and while some groups involved in the outside game have more resources than others, it is still the case that this form of politics has the effect of expanding and heightening political conflict, bringing issues out into the open and subjecting them to public scrutiny—what Schattschneider has called the "socialization of conflict."[26]

grassroots
The constituents, voters, or rank-and-file of a party.

Mobilizing Membership   Those interest groups with a large membership base try to persuade their members to send letters and to make telephone calls to senators and representatives when an important issue is before Congress. They sound the alarm, using direct mail and, increasingly, e-mail. They define the threat to members; suggest a way to respond to the threat; and supply the addresses, phone numbers, and e-mail addresses of the people to contact in Washington. Members are grouped by congressional district and state and are given the addresses of their own representatives or senators. The National Rifle Association (NRA) is particularly effective in mobilizing its considerable membership whenever the threat of federal gun control rears its head. (It is said by the NRA and others that the organization can mobilize roughly 175,000 members to stump for candidates or contact a member of Congress.) Environmental organizations such as the Sierra Club and Friends of the Earth sound the alarm to people on their mailing list whenever Congress threatens to loosen environmental protections.

Participation
Gun Rights and Gun Control

Organizing the District   Members of Congress are especially attuned to the individuals and groups in their states or districts who can affect their reelection

Mass demonstrations, designed to attract public attention through media coverage, are important tools in the arsenals of many interest groups. Here anti-gun groups show their displeasure with the National Rifle Association's opposition to gun control at the NRA's annual meeting in Denver in 1999, only weeks after the massacre at Columbine High School.

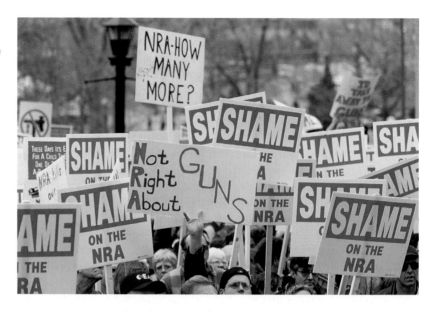

prospects. The smart interest group, therefore, not only will convince its own members in the state and district to put pressure on the senator or congressional representative but will also make every effort to be in touch with the most important campaign contributors and opinion leaders there.

Shaping Public Opinion   "Educating" the public on issues that are important to the interest group is one of the central features of new-style lobbying. The idea is to shape opinion in such a way that government officials will be favorably disposed to the views of the interest group. These attempts to shape public and elite opinion come in many forms. One strategy is to produce and distribute research reports that bolster the group's position. Citizen groups such as the Environmental Defense Fund and the Food Research and Action Center have been very adept and effective in this area.[27]

Another strategy is media advertising. Sometimes this takes the form of pressing a position on a particular issue, such as the Teamsters Union raising the alarm about open borders with Mexico, focusing on the purported unsafe nature of Mexican trucks roaming American highways. Sometimes it is "image" advertising, in which some company or industry portrays its positive contribution to American life.[28]

In the effort to shape public opinion, the well-heeled interest group will also prepare materials that will be of use to radio and television broadcasters and to newspaper and magazine editors. Many produce opinion pieces, magazine articles, television spots and radio "sound bites," and even television documentaries. Others stage events to be covered as news. The environmentalist group Greenpeace puts the news media on full alert, for example, when it tries to disrupt a whaling operation or a nuclear weapons test.

Getting Involved in Campaigns and Elections   Interest groups try to increase their influence by getting involved in political campaigns. Many interest groups, for example, rate members of Congress on their support for the interest group's position on a selection of key votes. The ratings are distributed to the members of the interest group and other interested parties in the hope that the ratings will influence their voting behavior. We show how groups do this in the "By the Numbers" feature in this section.

Interest groups also encourage their members to get involved in the electoral campaigns of candidates who are favorable to their interests. Groups often assist campaigns in more tangible ways—allowing the use of their telephone banks, mailing lists, fax and photocopy machines, computers, and the like. Some interest groups help with fund-raising events or ask members to make financial contributions to candidates.

Interest groups also endorse particular candidates for public office. The strategy may backfire and is somewhat risky, for to endorse a losing candidate is to risk losing access to the winner. Nevertheless, it is fairly common now for labor unions, environmental organizations, religious groups, and liberal and conservative ideological groups to make such endorsements. On the flip side of the coin, some interest group organizations announce their intention to work to unseat an elected official; AFL-CIO chief John Sweeney pledged in early 2003 that his organization was aiming at ousting President Bush in the 2004 election because Bush "favored the rich and hurt working families."[29]

Interest groups are also an increasingly important part of campaign fund-raising. This topic will be explored in more detail in the next section.

Possible Flaws in the Pluralist Heaven

Political scientist E. E. Schattschneider once observed that the flaw in the pluralist (or interest group) heaven is "that the heavenly chorus sings with a strong upper class accent." If his observation is accurate, then political equality is undermined by the interest group system, and democracy is less fully developed than it might be even taking into account the new importance of the outside game (which, as we have said, tends to "socialize conflict"). In this section, we look at inequalities in the interest group system and evaluate their effects.

Representational Inequalities

Not all segments of society are equally represented in the interest group system. The interest group game in Washington, D.C., is dominated, in sheer numbers and weight of activity, by business corporations, industry trade associations, and associations of the professions, although liberal and conservative citizen groups play an important role as well. In addition, among citizen or public interest groups, those whose members are among the better educated and more affluent tend to be more visible and more effective in Washington.[30]

Resource Inequalities

Business corporations and professionals are the most economically well-off parts of American society. It is hardly surprising that interest groups representing them can afford to spend far more than other groups to hire professional lobbying firms, form their own Washington liaison office, place advertising in the media, conduct targeted mailings on issues, mobilize their members to contact government officials, and pursue all of the other activities of old- and new-style lobbying. For example, about 80 percent of all monies spent on lobbying in 1999 was accounted for by business (corporations and trade associations).[31] In 2001, there were 625 registered lobbyists representing the drug

Timeline

Interest Groups and Campaign Finance

By the Numbers

Is there a reliable way to evaluate the performance of our representatives in Congress?

Why It Matters: Having a consistent and reliable way to grade each member of Congress can help voters make more rational electoral choices. Without such grades, each citizen would have to investigate the record of his or her member of Congress, rely on news reports, or depend on information provided by the member.

Imagine you are at the end of the semester and four different teachers give you a grade in your introductory political science course. One looks at your performance and gives you a grade of 100 percent. Your day is made! Teacher number 2 gives you an 83. OK, you might say, "I can live with that." Teachers 3 and 4 slam you with a 20 and a 10. Ouch! How to make sense of all of this? How come two teachers love you and two hate you? Surely they must be biased in some way.

This is exactly what happens to members of Congress when they are graded on their performance by interest groups. Unlike you, the confused student in the example above, Congressional representatives expect the wide disparity in the grades they receive, understand what is going on, and are even proud of most of their grades, whether high or low. Note the wildly contrasting grades for Republican Senator Richard Shelby of Alabama and Democratic Senator Barbara Boxer of California given by four organizations in 2002: the Americans for Democratic Action (ADA), the American Conservative Union (ACU), the League of Conservation Voters (LCV), and the National Taxpayers Union (NTU).

Behind the Numbers: How are members of Congress graded? The answer is pretty straightforward. Each interest group in this example is strongly ideological or committed to a certain set of concerns, and each grades members of Congress in terms of these standards. The ADA is very strongly liberal—interested in civil liberties, civil rights, and economic and social justice—while the ACU is strongly conservative—in favor of capitalism, traditional moral values, and a strong national defense. The LCV supports legislation to protect the environment, while the NTU wants lower taxes, less wasteful government spending, and a balanced budget. So, members of Congress who vote to increase spending on child welfare programs, let us say, are likely to get high grades from the ADA, but low grades from the ACU and the NTU. Members who vote to open the Alaska National Wildlife Reserve for oil exploration would surely receive a low grade from the folks at LCV.

industry, more than the total membership of the House and Senate.[32] (You can learn more about the influence of the drug industry, as well as the insurance industry, in the "Using the Framework" feature on the new Medicare drug prescription law on page 204.)

Corporate, trade, and professional associations also dominate the world of campaign finance. **Political action committees (PACs)** are entities created by interest groups—whether business firms, unions, membership organizations, or liberal and conservative citizen groups—to collect money and make contributions to candidates in federal elections. Corporate, trade, and professional PACs lead other groups in both in sheer numbers (see Figure 7.2 on page 2005) and levels of spending, although labor unions and large and committed citizenship organizations such as the NRA and the Sierra Club are also important in the world of PACs. During the 2001–2002 election cycle, for example, political action committees representing business and the professions

political action committee (PAC)

An entity created by an interest whose purpose is to collect money and make contributions to candidates in federal elections.

Calculating Interest Group Scores: Although each group uses a slightly different method to do its grading, at base, each approaches grading in pretty much the same way. For each interest group, its professional staff, sometimes in conjunction with outside experts, selects a set of key votes on which to assess members of Congress. The particular votes selected by each group will differ—a group interested solely in civil rights issues will not, for example, use a vote on the defense budget for its scorecard—but each identifies a set of votes it considers to be a good indicator of ideological or policy loyalty. On each vote, members of Congress are scored "with the group" or "against the group." The numbers are added up, then transformed to percentage terms, with 100 being the highest score and 0 the lowest.

What to Watch For: Oddly enough, though not terribly sophisticated in either conceptual or computational terms, these are numbers you can trust. You can, as they say, "take them to the bank." Why? Because each interest group is clear about what it stands for, and each makes it clear that it is judging members of Congress from a particular perspective. When you are considering whether to vote for or against an incumbent member of Congress, a good method would be to check member

scores from organizations whose ideology and/or policy views you support.

What Do You Think? How does your representative in Congress score with those groups whose values and policy position come closest to your own? You can investigate this at the Project Vote Smart Website at **www.vote-smart.org** where you can find how your representative is evaluated by different interest groups.

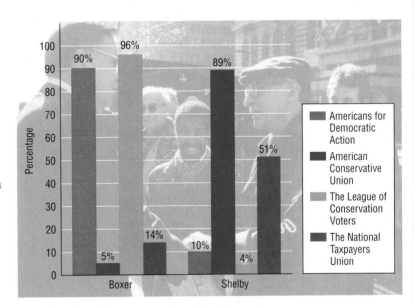

Interest Group Ratings of Senators Boxer and Shelby

Source: Project Vote Smart (**www.vote.smart.org**) for the year 2002.

accounted for 53 percent of the $352 million spent by all PACs on candidates for federal office, while labor unions accounted for only 19 percent.[33] PACs representing the least-privileged sectors of American society are notable for their absence. As former Senator (R–KS) and presidential candidate Bob Dole once put it, "There aren't any poor PACs or food stamp PACs or nutrition PACs or Medicaid PACs."[34]

During the 1990s, PACs became proportionally less important in campaign financing than **soft money** and **independent expenditures**—sometimes called issue campaigns—by private and public interest group organizations. Soft money—banned after the 2002 elections by the Bipartisan Campaign Reform Act (better known as McCain-Feingold, after the names of the law's first sponsors in the Senate)—was money given by interest groups and individuals to the political parties for "party-building" activities that usually found its way into parallel campaigns supporting presidential and

soft money
Unregulated expenditures by political parties on general public education, voter registration, and voter mobilization; often used to indirectly influence campaigns for elective office, until banned after 2002.

independent expenditures
Money spent on behalf of candidates by interest groups and individuals who are not connected to a candidate's campaign organization.

Using the Framework

Prescription Drugs Under Medicare

How did a prescription drug benefit get added to Medicare in 2003 after so many years of failure?

Background: Democratic presidents and members of Congress had tried–but failed–for more then twenty years to add a prescription drug benefit to the Medicare program. In 2003, with Republicans in control of both the House and Senate, President George W. Bush was able to deliver on his campaign promise to the elderly. Although many of the elderly will still have to pay a substantial amount of money for their prescription drugs after the program goes into effect in 2006, most will see a reduction in what they will have to pay. But others gained as well: Drug companies won provisions forbidding the importation of cheaper drugs from abroad and the negotiation of lower prices for drugs by the government, insurance companies were granted subsidies for providing drug benefit policies, and doctors won a provision in the bill loosening some of the restrictions on fees they receive under Medicare. How did all of this happen? Looking at how structural, political linkage, and governmental factors affected the political process will help us explain the outcome.

Governmental Action

The drug benefit under Medicare becomes law, though most of its provisions do not go into effect until 2006.

Seniors receive a drug discount card to partially fill-in the drug coverage gap in 2004 and 2005.

Governmental Level

A Republican president, George W. Bush, was in the White House. His plan for a prescription drug benefit under Medicare was introduced in the House and the Senate.

Republicans controlled both houses of Congress; a slightly different version of the bill passed in each one.

The House easily passed the bill that emerged from the Republican-controlled conference committee.

Senate Republicans won a close vote for the bill, after defeating a Democratic filibuster on the conference report.

President Bush signed the bill in an elaborate ceremony in the White House.

Political Linkages Level

Relative to other groups, the elderly vote in very high proportions in both presidential and congressional elections. These voters have said time and again that they want assistance with rising drug costs.

Drug and insurance companies, as well as the AMA, made very large campaign donations during the 2000 and 2002 election cycles.

Drug and insurance companies, as well as the AMA, mounted major lobbying efforts in the 108th Congress to ensure that the new program would take their interests into account.

During the 2000 presidential election campaign, both Al Gore and George W. Bush promised help to seniors with their rising drug costs. During the 2002 election campaign, many congressional candidates in both parties made similar promises.

Surprisingly, the most important interest group representing seniors, the usually Democratic-leaning American Association for Retired People (AARP), endorsed the plan fashioned by a Republican president and the Republican leaders of Congress.

Structural Level

The number of Americans over the age of 65 has been growing, and their prescription drug costs have been rising much faster than the cost of living.

Scientific innovation has helped create increasingly powerful, effective, and expensive drugs.

The drug industry is dominated by a handful of very large and economically powerful firms.

Insurance in the United States, including health care and medical insurance, is provided by a handful of very large and economically powerful firms.

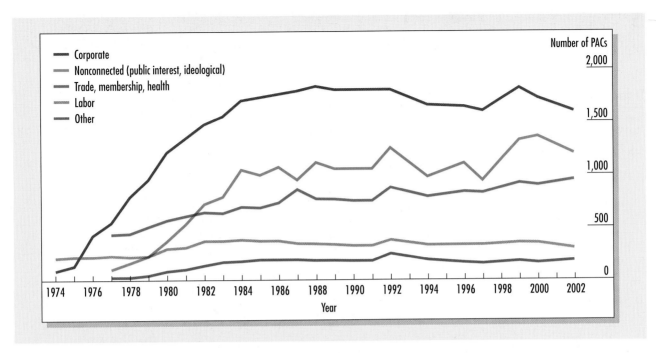

FIGURE 7.2 ● **PACs in the United States, 1974–2002**

Political action committees play an important role in financing congressional elections. The growth in the share provided by corporate, nonconnected (ideological), and trade groups is particularly striking, as is the relatively small share accounted for by organized labor.

Source: Federal Election Commission.

congressional candidates. Because there was no regulatory limit on the size of allowable contributions, or how much could be spent on campaigns, soft money rapidly became a central pillar of the campaign finance system in the United States. Soft money expenditures grew rapidly, more than doubling between each election cycle from 1995–1996 to 2001–2002. Of this total, about 63 percent came from corporations, trade associations, and professional organizations. Or example, Sabin Entertainment gave more than $9 million to the Democratic party in 2001–2002; the American Financial Group gave more than $3 million to the Republicans.[35] Independent expenditures—money spent by interest groups on issue campaigns designed to help or hurt particular candidates—also grew rapidly. The bulk of such independent expenditures on issue campaigns are also accounted for by business, trade, and professional organizations, though many public interest and advocacy groups were also heavily involved.

With passage of the Bipartisan Campaign Reform Act in 2002—and the Supreme Court's ruling in 2003 that the Act's main provisions are constitutional—PACs are likely to regain some of the ground lost in the 1990s to soft money in the affections of parties and candidate campaign organizations. Although McCain-Feingold imposes new limits on corporations' and labor unions' abilities to directly mount issue campaigns that mention candidates or officeholders in the period leading up to primary and general elections, the new law allows corporate and labor PACs to accept larger donations from individual contributors than in the past, contribute more to candidates and parties than under the old law, and run issue campaigns on television and radio

TABLE 7.1 • Interest Group Political Fund-Raising and Spending Rules Under Terms of the Bipartisan Campaign Reform Act		
	Soft Money[a]	**Hard Money**[b]
Corporations and labor unions	• May not use funds from their *general treasuries* to make contributions to federal candidates or national political party organizations. • May not use funds from their *general treasuries* to pay for "electioneering communications" that mention a candidate or officeholder on television or radio 30 days prior to a primary election or 60 days prior to a general election. • Can make unlimited contributions to advocacy organizations.	• Can create Political Action Committees (PACs) to collect and contribute "regulated" money to federal candidates and party committees. • PACs can give up to $5,000 to a candidate for a federal office for each election (primary and general election). • PACs can give up to $15,000 per year to a national party committee. • One PAC can give up to $5,000 per year to another PAC. • No limits on a PAC's total contributions to federal candidates and national party committees. • No limits on a PAC's "electioneering communications" on television and radio.
Public interest/advocacy groups, and other private associations (527s)	• No restriction on the size of individual contributions that the group or association can accept or how much money they can collect in the aggregate. • May not use "unregulated" money to pay for "electioneering communications" on television or radio 30 days prior to a primary election or 60 days prior to a general election. • No limits on "electioneering communications" prior to the pre-election "blackout" dates. • No limits on use of soft money for other electioneering activities including telephoning, targeted mailings, e-mail campaigns, door-to-door contact.	• Can create Political Action Committees to collect and contribute "regulated" money to candidates and party committees. • Same rules on collection and use of "regulated" money as for PACs created by corporations and labor unions.

[a] Money for use in campaigns collected *free of federal rules* limiting the size of allowable contributions; "unregulated" money.

[b] Money for use in campaigns collected *under strict federal rules* limiting the size of allowable contributions; "regulated" money.

right up to the day of primary and general elections, with no limitations on their aggregate or total expenditures (see Table 7.1).

The new law also is likely to enhance the importance of public interest and advocacy groups in presidential and congressional campaigns—called 527 groups because of where they are defined in the Tax Code—because McCain-Feingold places no limits on how much "unregulated" soft money can be contributed to them, but it bans soft money contributions to national party organizations. "Unregulated" money, amounting to almost $500 million in the 2002 election cycle, will now flow to these groups rather than to the parties. These groups can use "unregulated" money to talk about issues, mobilize voters, and praise or criticize candidates and officeholders—the only restriction being the use of television and radio in the period immediately preceding primary and general elections (see Table 7.1 for details). Many new groups devoted to liberal or conservative causes and candidates sprouted up after passage of McCain-Feingold. Particularly noteworthy because of the size of its unregulated money coffers is America Coming Together—an organization committed to the defeat of George W. Bush and the recapture of the House and Senate by Democrats in the 2004 elections—backed by large contributions from billionaire financier and philanthropist George Soros.

Although the campaign finance system is dominated by business, trade associations, and professionals, there are some interesting exceptions. Various public interest groups, for example, have become quite adept at **bundling,** a process for creating extensive donor networks. Here is how it works: An association contacts people on its mailing list suggesting which candidates deserve a contribution; the association collects the checks and bundles them together for each of the candidates on its preferred list; it then passes the checks on the candidate campaigns. EMILY's list—an organization committed to the election of Democratic, pro-choice women to office—was the pioneer in this area and remains among the most effective at this form of fund-raising. Conservative religious organizations and other liberal and conservative ideological groups are also adept at this practice.

Interest groups don't contribute money to campaigns and to candidates without some expectation of a return on their investment. Advocacy groups want attention paid to the issues they care about; private interest groups want attention paid to their material interests. It has been argued that there are so many interest groups around that they tend to neutralize one another; hence, campaign contributions and expenditures don't really matter.[36] This may sometimes be true, in fact, on high-visibility issues in which the public

bundling
A practice in which an interest group asks its supporters to write checks for a preferred list of candidates; the group then sends the checks in a bundle to each of the candidates.

Web Exploration
Corporations and Political Money

Issue: It has been suggested that corporations and business and professional associations dominate the campaign finance system, adding to their political influence.

Site: See who contributed what during the 2004 elections by accessing the Center for Responsive Politics on our Website at **www.ablongman.com/ greenberg**. Go to the "Web Explorations" section for Chapter 7, select "Corporations and Political Money," then "corporate money." Select "Who Gets" then "election overview." Look at "Top Overall Donors." Categorize the contributors in this list and the amounts spent.

What You've Learned: Is the claim of corporate and business dominance supported by the evidence?

Hint: Pay attention to the flow of dollars to each party; while there is some overlap, each has distinct sets of contributors.

and an array of interest groups are engaged. Where interest groups seem to matter the most is in the small details of legislation, forged mainly in the committees and subcommittees of Congress: a small subsidy in a defense spending bill or a waiver of a regulation for a particular industry or company. Enron's successful push for the deregulation of many of its activities followed this well-worn path.

Access Inequality

Inequalities of representation and resources are further exaggerated by the ability of some groups, especially those representing large business corporations, to gain a permanent foothold within the government. Although scholars have not reached a consensus on its exact form and extent, they have identified several basic forms of this phenomenon, which they call **subgovernments.**

What some scholars call **capture** is a form of government–business relationship in which an independent regulatory agency acts in partnership with the industry it is supposed to regulate.[37] **Interest group liberalism** is an arrangement in which aspects of federal government policymaking are turned over to interest groups.[38] Many (though not all) of the most important of these arrangements involve business and the professions. Thus, the private medical community is involved in deciding local payment guidelines in the Medicare program. An **iron triangle** is an alliance of a private interest group (usually, but not always, a corporation or business trade association), an agency in the executive branch, and committees or subcommittees in Congress. The goal of the iron triangle is to advance and protect government programs that work to the mutual benefit of its members. An example is shown in Figure 7.3.

Many political scientists argue that the capture and iron triangle arrangements are no longer very common.[39] Policy, they suggest, is no longer formed in the dark, out of public sight. Many political scientists today are more apt to talk about "issue networks," in which each major policy arena attracts its own broad and diverse set of actors.[40] A set of corporations, bureaucratic agencies, and congressional committees is still involved, to be sure, but so are a broad range of interest groups (including public interest groups) and policy experts. On narrower and less public issues, however, a good many political scientists and Washington observers still believe that subgovernments are alive and well.[41]

subgovernment

Alliances among interest groups, institutions within each house of Congress, and an executive branch agency that work to advance a particular agenda; can take various forms.

capture

A situation in which a regulated industry exercises substantial influence on the government agency regulating it.

interest group liberalism

A political regime in which interest groups help formulate and carry out government policies.

iron triangle

An enduring alliance of common interest among an interest group, a congressional committee, and a bureaucratic agency.

The Special Place of Business Corporations

Economist and political scientist Charles Lindblom has argued that corporations wield such disproportionate power in American politics that they undermine democracy. He closes his book *Politics and Markets* with this observation: "The large private corporation fits oddly into democratic theory. Indeed, it does not fit."[42] Twenty years later, political scientist Neil Mitchell concluded his book *The Conspicuous Corporation,* which reported the results of careful empirical testing of Lindblom's ideas, with the conclusion that "business interests [in the United States] are not routinely countervailed in the policy process. Their political resources and incentives to participate are usually greater than other interests."[43] Let's see why these scholars reached their somber conclusion about business corporations in American politics.

We have already learned about many of the advantages that corporations and business trade associations representing groups of corporations enjoy

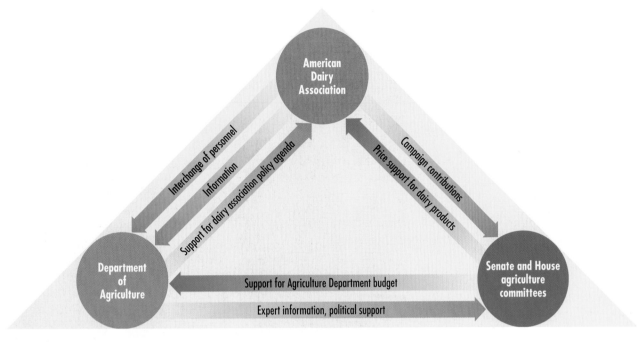

FIGURE 7.3 ● **Iron Triangle**

In an iron triangle, an alliance based on common interests is formed among a powerful corporation or interest group, an agency of the executive branch, and congressional committees or subcommittees. In this example from the dairy industry, an alliance is formed among parties that share an interest in the existence and expansion of dairy subsidies. Most scholars think iron triangles are less common today than in the past.

over others in the political process. The largest corporations are far ahead of their competitors in the number of interest organizations that represent them, the number of lobbyists they employ, the level of resources they can and do use for political purposes, their ability to shape public perceptions and opinions through such instruments as issue advertising and subsidization of business-oriented think tanks like the American Enterprise Institute, and the ease of access they have to government officials. Note that after President George W. Bush assigned Vice President Dick Cheney the task of fashioning a new national energy policy, for example, Cheney met almost exclusively with representatives from large energy companies and energy trade associations, including Enron and the Edison Electric Institute, as well as with members of the Business Round Table, the association comprised of the CEOs of the nation's most important business corporations. Lower-level aides were assigned to meetings with representatives of environmental, labor, and consumer groups, and this happened only after news media stories broke about their exclusion.

An additional source of corporate power is the general regard in which business is held in American society and the central and honored place of business values in our culture. Faith in free enterprise gives special advantages to the central institution of free enterprise, the corporation. Any political leader contemplating hostile action against corporations must contend with business's special place of honor in the United States. To be sure, scandals involving large business enterprises—WorldCom and mutual fund trading irregularities come to mind—can tarnish big business now and then, but in the long run, as President Coolidge once famously said, "the business of America is business."

Because the well-being of many Americans depends on the well-being of American corporations, political leaders often equate the interests of business with the interests of the nation. Here President George H. W. Bush celebrates the opening of a Toys R Us store during a trip to Japan to promote U.S. exports.

Business corporations are also unusually influential because the health of the American economy—and thus the standard of living of the people—is tied closely to the economic well-being of large corporations. It is widely and not entirely unreasonably believed that what is good for business is good for America. Because of their vital role in the economy, government officials tend to interpret business corporations not as "special interests" but as the voice of the national interest and to listen more attentively to their demands than they do to those of other sectors of American society. In this sense, corporations enjoy an especially privileged position in American politics.

Corporations are also powerful because their mobility is an important counterweight to any government effort (local, state, or national) to raise taxes or impose regulations that business deems especially onerous. Increasingly, large corporations are able to design, produce, and market their goods and services all over the world; they are not irrevocably tied to a single location. If government threatens their interests, large corporations can credibly counter with a threat to move all or part of their operations elsewhere. In this new global economic environment, political leaders are increasingly of a mind to maintain a friendly and supportive business climate.

Large corporations do not, of course, run the show entirely. Although they have the most resources, for instance, these resources do not translate automatically into real political influence. One interest group may have enormous resource advantages over other interest groups, for instance, but may use its resources ineffectively. Or an interest group with great resources may find itself opposed by other interest groups that together are able to mobilize impressive resources of their own. A powerful interest group may also find that an elected politician is not cooperative because the voters in the district are of a different mind from the interest group. Politicians may also run from the corporate embrace in times of highly publicized business scandals, like those in 2001 and 2002 involving Enron, Arthur Andersen, WorldCom, and others.

So even with this immense set of resources, business power is not automatically and inevitably translated into political power.[44]

Nor does business always get its way in Washington. There are many issues of great importance on which business in general, or one corporation in particular, loses in the give-and-take of politics. There are times when business finds itself squared off against powerful coalitions of other interest groups (labor, consumer, and environmentalist groups, let us say). On occasion, corporations also find themselves at odds with one another on public policy issues. Thus, Microsoft and Sun Microsystems want very different policies regarding federal anti-trust policy.

Most important, corporate political power is not a constant in American politics; it waxes and wanes over time.[45] Corporate political power was most impressive during the 1920s, the Reagan 1980s, and in the 104th Congress after the 1994 elections, for instance. Corporations were less able to get their way during other periods, such as the early 1970s, when the power of corporations was almost matched by that of the consumer and environmental movements.

Corporate power seems to reach its apex under certain conditions.[46] During bad economic times, for instance, Americans are more interested in getting the economy going again than in undertaking reforms that might cut into corporate profits. Politicians in bad times are more solicitous of corporate interests. In good economic times (e.g., the late 1960s and the late 1990s), politicians are less worried about corporate profits drying up if tax money is used for social purposes.

Corporations are most powerful when they can build alliances among themselves. Most of the time, corporations are in competition with one another; they do not form a unified political bloc capable of moving government to action on their behalf. On those few occasions when corporations feel that their collective interests are at stake, however, they are capable of coming together to form powerful political coalitions. As political scientist David Vogel put it, "When business is both mobilized and unified, its political power can be formidable."[47] During the mid-1970s, corporations felt that they were under assault, and they responded by building broad political coalitions that proved quite effective. These became the foundation of the movement for deregulation, tax cuts, and curtailment of domestic programs, an important part of the conservative trend in American politics that led to the election of Ronald Reagan in 1980 and the Republican capture of Congress in 1994.

In our view, the best way to think about corporations in American politics is to see their power waxing and waning within their overall privileged position. Corporate power may be greater at certain times and weaker at other times, but always in a game in which corporations enjoy advantages over other groups. If corporations feel that their collective interests are at stake—as when labor unions are particularly aggressive or when government's regulatory burden is perceived to be too heavy—and they are able to present a united front, they are simply unbeatable. This cannot be said about any other sector of American society.[48]

Curing the Mischief of Factions

Americans have worried about the "mischief of factions" ever since James Madison wrote about them in *The Federalist,* No. 10 (see the Appendix). Over the years, various things have been tried to control the purported negative

How Democratic Are We?

Interest Groups and American Politics

PROPOSITION: Because they represent narrow and special interests, the proliferation of interest groups has made American politics less and less democratic.

AGREE: The interest group system is by and for the privileged. The democratic principle of "political equality" is violated because powerful interest groups that play the largest role in shaping public policies in the United States represent, by and large, wealthier and better-educated Americans, corporations, and other business interests and professionals, such as doctors and lawyers.

DISAGREE: The interest group system enhances democracy because it gives individuals and groups another tool to keep elected and appointed officials responsive and responsible to their needs, wants, and interests. Political parties are important for making popular sovereignty work, to be sure, but being broad and inclusive umbrella organizations, they often ignore the interests of particular groups. And, although elections are essential for keeping public officials on their toes, they happen only every two to four years. The day-to-day work of popular sovereignty is done by interest groups. Additionally, the rise of citizen groups, supported by thousands of ordinary people with ordinary incomes, has made the interest group system less unequal; a wider range of groups representing a broad swath of the population, is now a key player in the political game.

CONSIDER: There is no doubt that the interest group system plays an important role in shaping what government does in the United States; elected officials pay lots of attention to them, for all the reasons explored in this chapter. Whether the interest group system advances or retards democracy, however, can only be determined by knowing which sectors of the American population are represented by interest groups and how well interest groups represent the people they claim to be representing. After examining the materials in this chapter, consider how you would answer these questions.

• Is any sector left out or underrepresented by interest groups? • How about your personal experience with interest groups? • Have any of them been in contact with you? • Are you involved with any of them, perhaps participating in some activity sponsored by interest groups? • Have you made financial contributions to any of them? • If you have some association with some interest group—perhaps a student government group representing the interests of students at your school before state and national government bodies—how would you rate its effectiveness? • What made this group effective or ineffective?

effects of these special interests. Disclosure has been the principal tool of regulation. In 1946, Congress imposed a requirement (in the Federal Regulation of Lobbying Act) that all lobbyists working in Congress be registered. The Lobby Disclosure Act of 1995 requires a wider range of political actors to register as lobbyists and makes them report every six months on which policies they are trying to influence and how much they are spending to do it. So far, the new law has not been strongly enforced.[49]

Reformers have also tried to regulate some of the most troublesome abuses of the politics of factions. Sections of the Ethics in Government Act (1978) aim at the so-called revolving door in which former government officials become lobbyists for interests with whom they formerly dealt in their official capacity. The act forbids ex-officials from lobbying their former agency for a year or lobbying at all on any issue in which the official was substantially involved. Finally, the 1995 Act says that former U.S. trade representatives and their deputies are banned for life from lobbying for foreign interests.

Reformers have also tried to control the effects of interest group money in politics. The McCain-Feingold bill, passed in 2002 and designed to put limits on the use of soft money, is the latest attempt. It is too soon to tell how effective this reform will be.

While such steps are to be applauded, many observers worry that these reforms have not gone to the heart of the problem. Some political scientists have suggested that we focus our efforts instead on strengthening the institutions of majoritarian democracy. The key institution of majoritarian democracy, at least in theory (as you will see in Chapter 9), is the political party. Parties can, as political scientist Walter Dean Burnham put it, "generate countervailing collective power on behalf of the many individually powerless against the relatively few who are individually—or organizationally—powerful."[50] Others believe that the narrowness of interest group politics might be tempered by strengthening the presidency, our only nationally elected office.[51]

Summary

Americans have long denigrated special interests as contrary to the public good. Some political scientists, however, see interest groups as an important addition to the representative process in a democracy.

The United States provides a rich environment for interest groups because of our constitutional system, our political culture, and the broad responsibilities of our government.

A number of interests are accommodated in our interest group system. The most important private interests include business, agriculture, labor, and the professions. Public interest or citizens' groups try to advance some issue or ideological interest that is not connected to the direct material benefit of their own members. There has been a significant expansion in the number of such groups since 1968.

Interest groups attempt to influence the shape of public policy in a number of ways. In the inside game, interest group representatives are in direct contact with government officials and try to build influence on the basis of personal relationships. In the outside game, interest groups attempt to apply indirect pressure to officials by mobilizing other groups, the members of their own group, public opinion, elite opinion, and the electorate to support their positions on policy matters.

Business, trade, and professional associations dominate the interest group system, although citizens groups are also influential. They enjoy clear advantages over other groups in terms of resources and access to public officials. The business corporation holds an especially privileged place in the interest group system because of the support of business values in our culture and the perceived importance of the corporation to the economic well-being of Americans.

Efforts to control the "mischief of factions" have mainly been regulatory in nature. Some reformers believe that interest groups will only cease to be a problem if the parties and presidency are strengthened.

Suggestions for Further Reading

Ainsworth, Scott H. *Analyzing Interest Groups: Group Influence on People and Policies.* New York: W. W. Norton, 2002.
> *Shows how economic forms of reasoning can be used to better understand how interest groups work and what effect they have on politics and government.*

Berry, Jeffrey M. *The New Liberalism: The Rising Power of Citizen Groups.* Washington, D.C.: Brookings, 1999.
> *A controversial book that argues that liberal citizen groups representing consumer, civil rights, and environmental interests are more influential in the halls of Congress than either business or conservative citizens groups.*

Clawson, Dan, Alan Neustadt, and Mark Weller. *Dollars and Votes: How Business Campaign Contributions Subvert Democracy.* Philadelphia: Temple University Press, 1998.
> *An excellent book about the campaign finance system, based on interviews with corporate personnel responsible for making PAC and soft money contributions to candidates and parties.*

Dahl, Robert A. *A Preface to Democratic Theory.* Chicago: University of Chicago Press, 1956.
> *The leading theoretical statement of the pluralist position and the democratic role of the interest group.*

Kollman, Ken. *Outside Lobbying: Public Opinion and Interest Group Strategies.* Princeton, NJ: Princeton University Press, 1998.
> *The first systematic study of how interest groups try to influence government policies by focusing their efforts on shaping public opinion.*

Lindblom, Charles. *Politics and Markets.* New York: Basic Books, 1977.
> *A controversial and widely commented-on book in which one of the leading pluralist theorists concludes that the modern corporation is incompatible with democracy.*

Skocpol, Theda. *Diminished Democracy: From Membership to Management in American Civic Life.* Norman, OK: University of Oklahoma Press, 2003.
> *An analysis of the decline of mass membership associations and how it hurts American civic life.*

Internet Sources

Center for Responsive Politics
www.opensecrets.org/
> *Follow the money trail—who gets it? who contributes?— in American politics.*

Labor Net
www.labornet.org
> *Access to labor unions and information on labor issues.*

National Organization for Women
www.now.org
> *The women's organization that has long been a "player" in Washington politics.*

National Rifle Association
http://www.nra.org/
> *Home page of one of America's most politically successful interest groups.*

Project VoteSmart
www.vote-smart.org/
> *Information on interest group campaign contributions to and ratings for all members of Congress.*

Rightgrrl
www.rightgrrl.com/
> *Conservative women's issues and organizations.*

Student Environmental Action Committee
http://www.seac.org/
> *A grassroots coalition of student environmental groups.*

Townhall
www.townhall.com/citizens
> *A portal to scores of conservative organizations and citizen groups.*

Yahoo/Organizations and Interest Groups
http://www.yahoo.com/Government/Politics/
> *Direct links to the home pages of scores of public and private interest groups as well as to Washington lobbying firms.*

Chapter 8
Social Movements

In This Chapter

- Why social movements develop
- Where social movements fit in a democratic society
- What social movements do in politics
- How social movements influence what government does

Women Win the Right to Vote

The struggle for women's suffrage (e.g., the right to vote) was long and difficult. The main instrument for winning the struggle to amend the Constitution to admit women to full citizenship was a powerful social movement that dared to challenge the status quo, used unconventional tactics to gain attention and sympathy, and demanded bravery and commitment from many women.[1] One of these women was Angelina Grimké.

Abolitionist Angelina Grimké addressed the Massachusetts legislature in February 1838, presenting a petition against slavery from an estimated 20,000 women of the state. In doing so, she became the first woman to speak before an American legislative body. Because women at this time were legally subordinate to men and shut out of civic life—

the life of home and church were considered their proper domains—Grimké felt it necessary to defend women's involvement in the abolitionist movement to end slavery. She said the following to the legislators:

> Are we aliens because we are women? Are we bereft of citizenship because we are mothers, wives and daughters of a mighty people? Have women no country—no interests staked in public weal—no partnership in a nation's guilt and shame? . . . I hold, Mr. Chairman, that American women have to do this subject [the abolition of slavery], not only because it is moral and religious, but because it is political, inasmuch as we are citizens of the Republic and as such our honor, happiness and well-being are bound up in its politics, government and laws.

Although this bold claim of citizenship for women did not fall on receptive ears—Grimké was derided as ridiculous and blasphemous by press and pulpit—it helped inspire other women who had entered political life by way of the abolitionist movement to press for women's rights as well. Meeting at Seneca Falls, New York, in 1848, a group of women issued a declaration written by Elizabeth Cady Stanton stating that "all men and women are created equal, endowed with the same inalienable rights." The declaration, much like the Declaration of Independence on which it was modeled, then presented a long list of violations of rights.

The Seneca Falls Declaration remains one of the most eloquent statements of women's equality ever written, but it failed to have an immediate effect because most politically active women (and men) in the abolitionist movement believed that their first order of business was to end slavery. Women's rights would have to wait.

After the Civil War destroyed the slave system, women's rights leaders such as Stanton, Susan B. Anthony, and Lucy Stone pressed for equal citizenship rights for all, white or black, male or female. They were bitterly disappointed when the Fourteenth Amendment, ratified after the war, declared full citizenship rights for all males born or naturalized in the United States, including those who had been slaves, but failed to include women. Women's rights activists realized that they would have to fight for rights on their own, with their own organizations.

Women's rights organizations were formed soon after the Civil War. For more than two decades, though, the National Woman Suffrage Association (NWSA) and the American Woman Suffrage Association (AWSA) feuded over how to pressure male politicians. Susan B. Anthony (with the NWSA) and Lucy Stone (with the AWSA) were divided by temperament and ideology. Anthony favored pressing for a broad range of rights and organized dramatic actions to expose men's hypocrisy. At an 1876 centennial celebration of the United States in Philadelphia, Anthony and several other women marched onto the platform, where the emperor of Brazil and other dignitaries sat, and handed over a declaration of women's rights. They then marched off the platform and read the declaration aloud. Stone favored gaining the vote as the primary objective of the rights movement and used quieter methods of persuasion, such as petitions.

In 1890, the two main organizations joined together to form the National American Woman Suffrage Association (NAWSA). They dropped such controversial NWSA demands as divorce reform and legalized prostitution in favor of one order of business: women's suffrage. The movement was now focused, united, and growing more powerful every year.

In 1912, the NAWSA organized a march to support a constitutional amendment for suffrage. More than 5,000 women dressed in white, some on horseback, paraded through the streets of Washington before Woodrow Wilson's inauguration. The police offered the marchers no protection from antagonistic spectators who pelted the marchers with rotten fruit and vegetables and an occasional rock, despite the legal parade permit they had obtained. This lack of protection outraged the public and attracted media attention to the suffrage movement. The NAWSA took advantage of the favorable publicity, launching a petition drive and sending regular delegations to press President Wilson for a national solution.

Almost immediately after the United States entered World War I in April 1916, with the express purpose of "making the world safe for democracy," women began to picket the White House, demanding that full democracy be instituted in America. One demonstrator's sign quoted directly from President Wilson's war message—"we shall fight . . . for the right of those who submit to authority to have a voice in their own government"—and asked why women were excluded from American democracy. As the picketing at the White House picked up in numbers and in intensity, the police began arresting large groups of women. Other women took their place. The cycle continued until local jails were filled to capacity. When suffragists began a hunger strike in jail, authorities responded with forced feedings and isolation cells. By November, public outrage forced local authorities to relent and free the women. By this time, public opinion had shifted in favor of women's right to vote.

In the years surrounding U.S. entry into the war, other women's groups worked state by state, senator by senator, pressuring male politicians to support women's suffrage. After two prominent senators from New England were defeated in 1918 primarily because of the efforts of suffragists and prohibitionists, the political clout of the women's groups became apparent to most elected officials. In June 1919, Congress passed the Nineteenth Amendment, and the necessary 36 states ratified it the following year. By uniting around a common cause, women's organizations gained the right to vote for all women.

Although few social movements have been as effective as the women's suffrage movement in reaching their primary goal, other social movements have also played an important role in American political life. This chapter is about what social movements are, how and why they form, what tactics they use, and how they affect American political life and what government does.

Thinking Critically About This Chapter

This chapter is about the important role of social movements in American government and politics.

Using the Framework   You will see in this chapter how social movements are a response to structural changes in the economy, culture, and society and how they affect other political linkage actors and institutions—parties, interest groups, and public opinion, for example—and government. You will learn, most importantly, under what conditions social movements most effectively shape the behavior of elected leaders and the content of government policies.

Using the Democracy Standard   At first glance, because social movements are most often the political instrument of minorities, it may seem that they have little to do with democracy. You will see in this chapter, however, that social movements play an especially important role in our democracy, principally by broadening public debate on important issues and bringing outsiders and nonparticipants into the political arena.

What Are Social Movements?

Social movements are loosely organized collections of people and groups who act over time, outside established institutions, to promote or resist social change. Today's Christian conservative movement, for example, is a broad collection of people, churches, and other organizations that have come together to resist the **secularization** of American society and to promote religious values in American life.

secularization
The spread of nonreligious values and outlooks.

Although they share some similarities, social movements are different from political parties and interest groups. Unlike political parties, for example, the sole aim of social movements is not to elect their own members to public office, although they may sometimes try to do so. Unlike interest groups, the sole aim of social movements is not to lobby political decision makers about legislative matters, although they may sometimes try to do this as well. What sets social movements apart from parties and interest groups is their focus on broad, societywide issues and their tendency to act outside the normal channels of government and politics, using unconventional and often disruptive tactics.[2] Some scholars call social movement politics "contentious politics."[3] When suffragists disrupted meetings, went on hunger strikes, and marched to demand the right to vote, they were engaged in contentious politics.

This general definition of social movements requires further elaboration if we are to understand their role in American politics. Here we highlight some important things to know about them:

- *Social movements are generally the political instruments of political outsiders.* Social movements often help people who are outside the mainstream gain a hearing from the public and from political decision makers. The women's suffrage movement forced the issue of votes for women onto the public agenda. The civil rights movement did the same for the issue of equal citizenship for African Americans. Gays and lesbians forced the country to pay attention to issues that had long been left "in the closet." Insiders don't need social movements; they can rely instead on interest groups, political action committees (PACs), lobbyists, campaign contributions, and the like to make their voices heard.

- *Social movements are generally mass grassroots phenomena.* Because outsiders and excluded groups often lack the financial and political resources of insiders, they must take advantage of what they have: numbers, energy, and commitment.

- *Social movements often use unconventional and disruptive tactics.* Officials and citizens almost always complain that social movements are ill-mannered and disruptive. For social movements, that is precisely the point. Unconventional and disruptive tactics help gain attention for movement grievances.

 Simulation

You Are the Leader of Concerned Citizens for World Justice

- *Social movements are populated by individuals with a shared sense of grievance.* People would not take on the considerable risks involved in joining others in a social movement unless they felt a strong, shared sense of grievance against the status quo and a desire to bring about social change. Social movements tend to form when a significant number of people come to define their own troubles and problems not in personal terms but in more general social terms (the belief that there is a common cause for all of their troubles) and when they believe that the government can be moved to take action on their behalf. Because this is a rare combination, social movements are very difficult to organize and sustain.

In recent years, many religious Americans have become politically active because of their objection to the general secularization of American life and social trends such as gay rights and abortion, which they consider contrary to traditional family values. Here a group of fundamentalist Christians demonstrates against the legal protection of abortion.

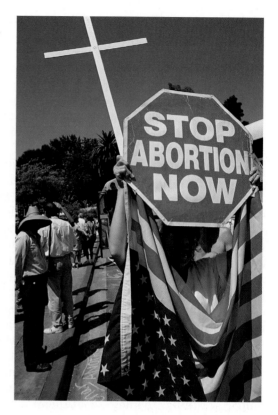

Major Social Movements in the United States

Many social movements have left their mark on American political life and have shaped what government does in the United States. Here we describe some of the most important.

The *abolitionists* aimed to end slavery in the United States. They were active in the northern states in the three decades before the outbreak of the Civil War. Their harsh condemnation of the slave system helped bring on the war that ended slavery.

The *Populist* movement was made up of disaffected farmers of the American South and West in the 1880s and 1890s who were angry with business practices and developments in the American economy that were adversely affecting them. Their aim was to force public ownership or regulation of banks, grain storage companies, and the railroads. For a short time, they were quite successful, winning control of several state legislatures, sending members to Congress, helping to nominate William Jennings Bryan as the Democratic candidate for president in 1896, and forcing the federal regulation of corporations (e.g., in the Interstate Commerce Commission Act).

The *women's suffrage* movement, active in the late nineteenth and early twentieth centuries, aimed to win the right to vote for women. As we saw in the chapter opening story, the movement won its objective when the Nineteenth Amendment to the Constitution was ratified in 1920.

The *labor* movement represents efforts by working people over the years to protect jobs, ensure decent wages and benefits, and guarantee safe workplaces. The periods of greatest militancy—when working people took to the streets and the factory floors to demand recognition of their unions—were in the 1880s, the 1890s, and the 1930s. The labor movement eventually forced the federal government to recognize the right of working people to form labor unions to represent them in negotiations with management.

A *peace* movement in one form or another has been around since the time of World War I, when it tried to encourage resistance to the draft. Its strategy of encouraging Americans to refuse service on religious or moral grounds—known as *conscientious objection*—was carried over to World War II, the Korean War, the Vietnam War, the war in Kosovo, and the campaign against the Taliban in Afghanistan. The movement has also focused on the threat of nuclear war, taking shape as "ban the bomb" protests in the 1950s, "nuclear freeze" demonstrations in the 1980s, and attempts in the 1980s to force local governments to declare their localities "nuclear-free zones," where no nuclear weapons could be manufactured or stored.

The *civil rights* movement began in the late 1950s, reached the peak of its activity in the mid-1960s, and gradually lost steam after that. The movement is one of the most influential on record, having pressed successfully for the end of formal segregation in the South and discriminatory practices across the nation (see Chapters 1 and 16). The main weapons of the movement were non-violent civil disobedience and mass demonstrations.

The *anti–Vietnam War* movement was active in the United States in the late 1960s and early 1970s. Its aim was to end the war in Vietnam. It used a wide variety of tactics in this effort, from mass demonstrations to voting registration and civil disobedience. Fringe elements even turned to violence, exemplified by the Days of Rage vandalism along Chicago's Gold Coast mounted by a wing of Students for a Democratic Society and the bombing of a research lab at the University of Wisconsin in which a graduate student was killed.

The *women's* movement has been important in American life since the late 1960s. Its aim has been to win civil rights protections for women and to

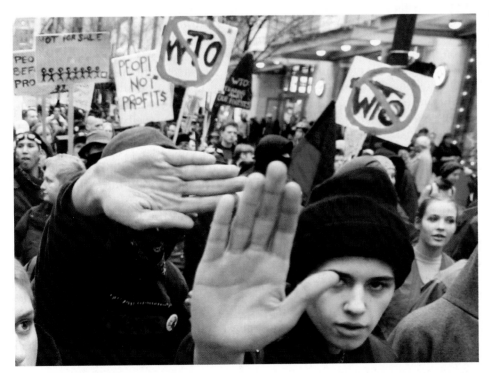

The anti-globalization movement first gained widespread public attention in the United States when demonstrators converged on Seattle in late 1999 to protest at a meeting of the World Trade Organization.

Equal Rights Amendment (ERA)
Proposed amendment to the U.S. Constitution stating that equality of rights shall not be abridged or denied on account of a person's gender.

broaden the participation of women in all aspects of American society, economy, and politics. Although it did not win one of its main objectives—passage of the **Equal Rights Amendment (ERA)** to the U.S. Constitution—the broad advance of women on virtually all fronts in the United States attests to its overall effectiveness.

The *environmental* movement has been active in the United States since the early 1970s. Its aim has been to encourage government regulation of damaging environmental practices and to raise the environmental sympathies of the public. While the vitality of the movement has waxed and waned over the years, the public's strong support for environmental regulation suggests that it has been unusually successful. Although disruptive and even violent tactics have sometimes been used, the movement has depended more on legal challenges to business practices and the creation of organizations to lobby in Washington.

The *gay and lesbian* movement began in earnest in the late 1960s. Its aim was to gain the same civil rights protections under the law enjoyed by African Americans and other minority groups and to gain respect from the public. Ranging from patient lobbying and voting to mass demonstrations and deliberately shocking actions by groups such as ACT-UP, the movement's efforts have been partially successful—anti-discrimination and civil union laws have been passed in many communities; many private corporations have introduced domestic partner benefits for their employees, and the Supreme Court has overturned anti-homosexual sodomy laws at the state level (see Chapter 16)—but have also sparked strong counterattacks by groups such as the Christian Coalition and Focus on the Family that are opposed to their objectives.

Religious fundamentalist movements have occurred at several different moments in American history and have been very influential. These movements have brought together strongly religious people trying to infuse American society and public policies with their values. These movements were particularly vital during the decades preceding the American Revolution and the Civil War; in the late nineteenth and early twentieth centuries, when religious revivals swept across the country; and in our own day. The contemporary movement of Christian conservatives falls within this tradition and has become very important in American politics, especially on the issues of abortion, school prayer, educational curriculum, and censorship of the media. The *pro-life (anti-abortion)* movement is part of the current larger religious fundamentalist movement. Its main objective is to end the legal availability of abortion in the United States.

An emergent *anti-globalization* movement announced itself to the public with demonstrations against the World Trade Organization in Seattle in late 1999. This movement is extremely diverse and includes people who are worried about the effects of globalization on the environment, income inequality in the United States and Third World countries, food safety, labor rights, sweat shops, unfair trade, and national sovereignty.

An *anti-Iraq war* movement quickly formed in the months leading up to the U.S. invasion of Iraq in 2003 and remained an important force for opposition to American foreign policy in the Middle East after the fall of Baghdad. Using the Internet to great advantage—namely, e-mail and Websites to rapidly spread information, raise money, and mobilize people for demonstrations—anti-war activists organized a movement that spanned much of the United States, western Europe, and Asia. The movement's most dramatic political act was the organization of massive demonstrations across the world on February 15, 2003. Rome had a million demonstrators, London more than

700,000, and Madrid 200,000. In the United States, demonstrations took place in 150 cities; in New York, the crowd converging on the U.N. headquarters building filled a space 20 blocks long, along First and Second Avenues.[4] The massive demonstrations did not convince President Bush to put off the Iraq invasion, however.

Social Movements in a Majoritarian Democracy

At first glance, social movements do not seem to fit very well in a democracy. First, social movements usually start out with only a small minority of people, whereas democracy requires majority rule. Second, social movements often use disruptive tactics, when it seems that many channels already exist (e.g., voting, petitioning and writing to policymakers, and writing letters to newspapers) for people to express their grievances. In this section, we talk about how social movements can (and often do) help make American politics more democratic.

Encouraging Participation

Social movements may increase the level of popular involvement and interest in politics. In one sense, this is true simply by definition: Social movements are the instruments of outsiders. Thus, the women's suffrage movement showed many middle-class women that their activities need not be confined exclusively to home, family, church, and charity work and encouraged them to venture into political life by gathering petitions or joining demonstrations demanding the vote for women. The civil rights movement in the 1960s encouraged southern African Americans, who had long been barred from the political life of their communities, to become active in their own emancipation. The Christian conservative movement spurred the involvement of previously politically apathetic evangelicals.

Social movements also encourage popular participation by dramatizing and bringing to public attention a range of issues that have been ignored or have been dealt with behind closed doors. The reason is that their contentious actions make these movements' members highly visible. They offer irresistible fare for the television camera. This ability to make politics more visible—called broadening the **scope of conflict** by political scientist E. E. Schattschneider[5]—makes politics the province of the many rather than the few.

scope of conflict
The number of groups involved in a political conflict; few groups mean a narrow scope of conflict, and many groups mean a wide scope of conflict.

Overcoming Political Inequality

Social movements also sometimes allow individuals and groups without substantial resources to enter the game of politics. Many social movements are made up of people who do not have access to the money, time, contacts, or organizational resources that fuel normal politics.[6] The ability of those without resources to disrupt the status quo by mobilizing thousands to take to the streets to voice their demands—what sociologists call **mass mobilization**—is a powerful political tool for people on the outside looking in. In the right circumstances, the disruptive politics of social groups can become as politically useful as other resources such as money and votes. Seemingly politically powerless women were able to mobilize to win the vote in the early part of the twentieth century; seemingly politically powerless blacks in the Deep South were able to secure full citizenship rights in the 1960s.

mass mobilization
The process of involving large numbers of people in a social movement.

Creating New Majorities

Over time, social movements may also help create new majorities in society. Social movements are the province of minorities, of course, and in a majoritarian democracy, minorities should have their way only if they can convince enough of their fellow citizens that what they want is reasonable. Before the 1930s, for instance, only a minority of Americans may have been convinced that labor unions were a good idea. The **Great Depression** and a vigorous, militant labor movement changed the opinion climate in the nation and created the basis for federal laws protecting the right of working people to form labor unions. Such issues as gender-based job discrimination and pay inequity, to take another example, were not important to the general public until they were brought center stage by the women's movement.

Great Depression

The period of economic crisis in the United States that lasted from the stock market crash of 1929 to America's entry into World War II.

Overcoming Gridlock

Sometimes it takes the energy of a social movement to overcome the antimajoritarian aspects of our constitutional system (see Chapter 2) and get anything done at all. As political scientist Theodore Lowi describes the issue:

> Our political system is almost perfectly designed to maintain an existing state of affairs. . . . Our system is so designed that only a determined and undoubted majority could make it move. This is why our history is replete with social movements. It takes that kind of energy to get anything like a majority. . . . Change comes neither from the genius of the system nor from the liberality or wisdom of its supporters and of the organized groups. It comes from new groups or nascent groups—social movements—when the situation is most dramatic.[7]

It is important to note that many of the social reforms of which most Americans are most proud—women's right to vote, equal citizenship rights for

Web Exploration
Movements and Political Participation

Issue: A common claim for social movements as a democratic instrument is that they increase political participation by outsiders.

Site: Access the American National Election Study on our Website at **www.ablongman.com/greenberg**. Go to the "Web Explorations" section for Chapter 8, select "movements and political participation," then "participation." Select "Political Involvement and Participation in Politics." Choose various questions related to political participation, including voting. At the bottom of the page where you find general results for each question, the results are broken down by racial groups and gender.

What You've Learned: Did the Civil Rights movement and the women's movement increase political participation among African Americans and women? Did participation increase in the period during and immediately after the social movements were at their height?

Hint: For African Americans, the relevant dates are the early 1960s to the present; for women, the relevant dates are the early 1970s to the present.

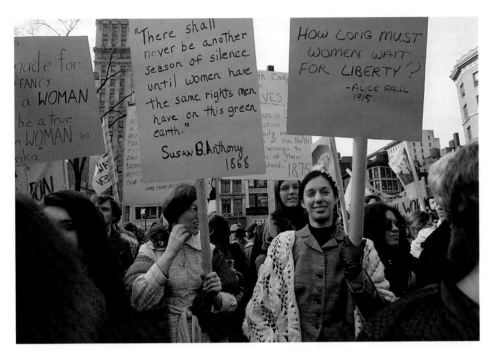

Social movements are a response to a real, immediate social distress or injustice. When women began to enter the job market in increasing numbers during the 1960s and 1970s, discriminatory hiring, barriers to career advancement, and unequal pay were unspoken realities of the business world. As more and more women refused to accept these conditions, the women's movement emerged.

African Americans, Social Security, collective bargaining, and environmental protection—have been less the result of "normal" politics than of social movements started by determined and often disruptive minorities.

Factors That Encourage the Creation of Social Movements

A certain combination of factors, mainly structural, is apparently necessary for a social movement to develop.[8] We review the most important ones here.

The Existence of Social Distress

People who are safe, prosperous, and respected generally have no need of social movements. By contrast, those whose lives are difficult and unsafe or whose way of life or values are threatened, or whose way of life is disrespected, often find social movements an attractive means of calling attention to their plight and of pressing for changes in the status quo.[9]

Social distress caused by economic, social, and technological change helped create the conditions for the rise of most of the major social movements in American history. For example, the Populist movement occurred after western and southern farmers suffered great economic reverses during the latter part of the nineteenth century. The labor movement during the 1930s was spurred by the Great Depression—the virtual collapse of the industrial sector of the American economy, historically unprecedented levels of unemployment, and widespread destitution. The rise of the Christian conservative movement seems to be associated with the perceived threat of the apparent decline in religious and family values in American life. For many women, distress caused by discriminatory hiring, blocked career advancement—in the form of the "glass ceiling" and the "mommy track"—and unequal pay at a time when they were entering the job market in increasing numbers during the 1960s and 1970s made participation in the women's movement attractive.[10] Discrimination, police harassment, and violence directed against them spurred gays and lesbians to turn to "contentious politics."[11] The AIDS epidemic added to their sense of distress and stimulated further political participation.

Availability of Resources for Mobilization

Social strain and distress are almost always present in society. But social movements occur, it seems, only when the aggrieved group has the resources (including skilled leaders) sufficient to organize those who are suffering strain and distress.[12] The grievances expressed by the labor movement had existed for a long time in the United States, but it was not until a few unions developed—generating talented leaders, a very active labor press, and widespread media attention—that the movement began to take off. The women's movement's assets included a sizable population of educated and skilled women, a lively women's press, and a broad network of meetings to talk about common problems[13] (generally called *consciousness-raising groups*). The Christian conservative movement could build on a base of skilled clergy (for instance, Jerry Falwell and Pat Robertson), an expanding evangelical church membership, religious television and radio networks, and highly developed fund-raising technologies. Gay and lesbian activists could depend on a rich assortment of organizations, an active press, and the financial support of gay- and lesbian-owned businesses. The anti-globalization and anti-Iraq war movements, highly decentralized and organizationally amorphous, skillfully used the Internet to spread information, raise money, and organize demonstrations here and abroad.

MoveOn.org is one of several new organizations that have successfully used the Internet as a tool for political fund-raising. MoveOn.org backs liberal causes such as environmental protection and efforts to regain the White House for Democrats. In this picture, Al Gore speaks at a MoveOn.org–sponsored event.

For its part, the 1960s civil rights movement could count on organizationally skilled clergy and close-knit congregations, black-owned newspapers and radio stations, an expanding pool of college-educated African American youth, and blocs of African American voters located in electorally important states. The existence of such experienced, tested, and effective organizations as the Congress of Racial Equality (CORE), the Urban League, and the National Association for the Advancement of Colored People (NAACP) was especially valuable.

A Supportive Environment

The rise of social movements requires more than the existence of resources for mobilization among aggrieved groups. The times must also be right, in the sense that a degree of support and tolerance must exist for the movement among the public and society's leaders.[14] The civil rights movement took place when overt racism among the public was declining (even in the South; see Table 8.1), and national leaders were worried about the bad effects of segregation in the South on American foreign policy. Christian conservatives mobilized in an environment in which many other Americans were also worried

TABLE 8.1 • White Support for Integration, 1942–1963

	Total	South	North
"Negroes should have as good a chance as white people to get any kind of job."			
1944	42%	—	—
1963	83	—	—
"White students and Negro students should go to the same schools."			
1942	30%	2%	40%
1956	49	15	61
1963	62	31	73
There should not be "separate sections for Negroes on streetcars and buses."			
1942	44%	4%	57%
1956	60	27	73
1963	79	52	89
Would not make any difference to them if "a Negro with the same income and education as you moved into your block."			
1942	35%	12%	42%
1956	51	38	58
1963	64	51	70

Source: Stephen Thernstrom and Abigail Thernstrom, *America in Black and White* (New York: Simon & Schuster, 1997), p. 141. Data from William G. Mayer, *The Changing American Mind: How and Why American Public Opinion Changed Between 1960 and 1988* (Ann Arbor, MI: University of Michigan Press, 1993), p. 366; Paul B. Sheatsley, "White Attitudes Toward the Negro," *Daedalus,* 95 (1966), pp. 219, 222.

Gays and lesbians have become much more politically visible and assertive since the "Stonewall" incident and riots in 1969. Here, a gay-pride parade in San Francisco calls attention to the gay and lesbian communities and to the issues the members of these communities want placed on the political agenda.

about changes in social values and practices and when the Republican party was looking for a way to detach traditional Democratic voters from their party. The labor movement's upsurge during the 1930s coincided with the electoral needs of the Democratic party.[15] The women's movement surged at a time when public opinion was becoming much more favorable toward women's equality.[16] In 1972, for example, two out of three Americans reported to pollsters that they supported the proposal for an Equal Rights Amendment; the same proportion said they believed that the issues raised by the women's movement were important.[17] Gays and lesbians have benefited from the more tolerant attitudes toward homosexuality that have developed in recent years. Asked whether school boards should have the right to fire teachers who are homosexuals, only 33 percent of Americans agreed with the statement in 2003, compared with 51 percent as recently as 1987.[18]

A Sense of Efficacy Among Participants

Some scholars believe that to develop an effective social movement, people who are on the outside looking in must come to believe that their actions can make a difference, that other citizens and political leaders will listen and respond to their grievances. Political scientists call this "I can make a difference" attitude a sense of **political efficacy.** Without a sense of efficacy, grievances might explode into brief demonstrations or riots, but they would not support a long-term effort requiring time, commitment, and risk.

It may well be that the highly decentralized and fragmented nature of our political system helps sustain a sense of efficacy, because movements often find places in the system where they will be heard by officials. Christian conservative social movements have had little effect on school curricula in unitary political systems like that of Great Britain, for instance, where educational policy is made centrally, so few try to do anything about it. In the

political efficacy
The sense that an individual can affect what government does.

United States, Christian conservatives know they can gain the ear of local school boards and state officials in regions where religious belief is strong. Gays and lesbians have been able to convince public officials and local voters to pass anti-discrimination ordinances in accepting communities, such as San Francisco, California, and Boulder, Colorado, and to win cases in several state courts.

Some scholars have suggested that a strong sense of common identity among protest groups contributes to efficacy. Knowing that one is not alone, that others see the world in common ways and have common concerns, is often the basis for people's willingness to commit the time and energy and to take the risks that social movements require. Growing gay and lesbian identity seems to be an important component of the rising political self-confidence of this movement.[19]

A Spark to Set Off the Flames

Social movements require, as we have seen, a set of grievances among a group of people, the resources to form and sustain organization, a supportive environment, and a sense of political efficacy among the potential participants in the movement. But they also seem to require something to set off the mix, some dramatic precipitating event (or series of events), sometimes called a *catalyst,* to set them in motion. Passage of the Fourteenth Amendment, protecting the citizenship rights of males, galvanized the early women's suffrage movement, as we saw in the chapter-opening story. The gay and lesbian movement seems to have been sparked by the 1969 "Stonewall rebellion"—three days of rioting set off by police harassment of the patrons of a popular gay bar in Greenwich Village in New York City. The most important catalyst for the civil rights movement was Rosa Parks's simple refusal to give up her seat on a Montgomery, Alabama, bus in 1957.

A number of catalytic events also galvanized the women's movement. There was the 1963 publication of Betty Friedan's *Feminine Mystique,* in which she spoke to women's discontent ("a problem that has no name," as she put it) as no one had done before. The example set by the civil rights movement showed many women that outsiders could gain a hearing in American politics if they were willing to use collective-action tactics. There was also resentment over the failure of the federal government to enforce Title VII of the 1964 Civil Rights Act, which guaranteed women protections in the area of equal employment. Finally, younger women active in the civil rights and anti–Vietnam War movements discovered that they were not well treated within these movements, despite the movements' rhetoric of equality, and concluded that women's problems could be addressed only if women took their own political initiative.

Tactics of Social Movements

Social movements tend to use unconventional tactics to make themselves heard. Such tactics depend on the dramatic gesture and are often disruptive. As you saw in the opening story, the women's suffrage movement used mass demonstrations and hunger strikes to great effect. The labor movement invented **sit-down strikes** and plant takeovers as its most effective weapons in the 1930s. Pro-life activists added to the protest repertoire clinic blockades and the harassment of clinic patients, doctors, employees, and their families.

sit-down strike
A form of labor action in which workers stop production but do not leave their job site.

The sit-down strike was invented by labor movement activists in the American auto industry in the 1930s. Here union members strike but stay put on the job site, daring management to use violence to end the work stoppage.

More extreme elements within these groups have even added violence against clinics and doctors, including murder.

The most effective tool of the civil rights movement was nonviolent **civil disobedience,** a conscious refusal to obey a law that a group considers unfair, unjust, or unconstitutional. A particularly dramatic and effective use of this tactic took place in Greensboro, North Carolina. Four black students from North Carolina Agricultural and Technical State University sat down at a "whites only" lunch counter in a Woolworth's store on February 1, 1960, and politely asked to be served. When requested to leave, they refused. They stayed put and remained calm even as a mob of young white men screamed at them, squirted them with ketchup and mustard, and threatened to lynch them. Each day, more students from the college joined them. By the end of the week, more than 1,000 black students had joined the sit-in to demand an end to segregation. These actions ignited the South. Within two months, similar sit-ins had taken place in nearly 60 cities across nine states; almost 4,000 young people had tasted a night in jail for their actions. Their bravery galvanized other blacks across the nation and generated sympathy among many whites. The student sit-in movement also spawned a new and more impatient civil rights organization, the Student Non-Violent Coordinating Committee (SNCC). (See the story of SNCC in Chapter 1.)

Another particularly effective use of nonviolent civil disobedience was organized in Birmingham, Alabama, by the spiritual leader of the civil rights movement, Dr. Martin Luther King, Jr., who led a series of massive nonviolent demonstrations to demand the **integration** of schools and public transportation. Nonviolent demonstrators, most of them schoolchildren, were assaulted by snarling police dogs, electric cattle prods, and high-pressure fire hoses that sent demonstrators sprawling. Police Commissioner Eugene "Bull" Connor filled his jails to overflowing with hundreds of young marchers, who resisted only passively, alternately praying and singing civil rights songs, including "We Shall Overcome." The quiet bravery of the demonstrators and the palpable sense among public officials and private sector leaders in the nation that

civil disobedience
Intentionally breaking a law and accepting the consequences as a way to publicize the unjustness of the law.

integration
Policies encouraging the interaction between different races in schools or public facilities.

Nonviolent civil disobedience proved the most effective tool of the civil rights movement. By violating unjust laws quietly and nonviolently, protesters alerted outsiders to the injustice of their situation. The sit-in at a "whites only" lunch counter in Greensboro, North Carolina—shown here—sparked similar protests all over the country, and the arrests of the protesters generated sympathetic interest among previously apathetic whites.

matters were quickly spinning out of control convinced President John Kennedy on June 11, 1963, to introduce his historic civil rights bill for congressional consideration.

Why Some Social Movements Succeed and Others Do Not

Social movements have had a significant effect on American politics and on what government does. Not all social movements are equally successful, however. What makes some more successful than others seems to be

- The proximity of the movement's goals to American values.
- The movement's capacity to win public attention and support.
- The movement's ability to affect the political fortunes of elected leaders.

Low-Impact Social Movements

A social movement will have little effect if it has few followers or activists, has little support among the general public, and is unable to disrupt everyday life significantly or to affect the electoral prospects of politicians. The poor people's movement, which tried to convince Americans to enact policies that would end poverty in the United States, failed to make much of a mark in the late 1960s.

A social movement is particularly unlikely to have an effect on policy when it stimulates the formation of a powerful countermovement. The rational politician may find it prudent to take no action at all when he or she has difficulty calculating the relative weight of the two sides in a dispute between movements. This is one of several things that happened to the proposed Equal Rights Amendment banning discrimination on the grounds of gender. The ERA failed to receive the approval of the necessary three-fourths of the states after anti-ERA forces (mainly Christian conservatives) rallied to block action during the 1970s.[20]

Repressed Social Movements

Social movements committed to a radical change in the society and the economy tend to threaten widely shared values and the interests of powerful individuals, groups, and institutions. As a result, they rarely gain widespread popular support and almost always arouse the hostility of political leaders. Such movements very often face repression of one kind or another.[21] In the late nineteenth and early twentieth centuries, for instance, the labor movement was hindered by court injunctions, laws against the formation of labor unions, violence by employer-hired armed gangs, and strikebreaking by the National Guard and the U.S. armed forces. In 1877, 60,000 National Guardsmen were mobilized in 10 states to break the first national railroad strike. The strike against Carnegie Steel in 1892 in Homestead, Pennsylvania, brought the mobilization of 10,000 militiamen, the arrest of 16 strike leaders on conspiracy charges, and the indictment of 27 labor leaders for treason. The Pullman strike of 1894 was abruptly ended by the use of federal troops and by the arrest and indictment of union leaders.

Partially Successful Social Movements

Some social movements have enough power and public support to generate a favorable response from public officials but not enough to force them to go very far. In these situations, government may respond in a partial or half-hearted way. President Franklin D. Roosevelt responded to the social movements pressing for strong antipoverty measures during the Great Depression by proposing the passage of the Social Security Act, which fell far short of movement expectations.[22] The pro-life movement discovered that President Reagan was willing to use movement rhetoric to appoint sympathetic judges but was unwilling to submit anti-abortion legislation to Congress. Christian conservatives enjoyed some legislative successes during the height of their power in the 1990s, but failed to achieve their primary objectives: enactment of a law to ban late-term (in their words, "partial birth") abortions and the removal of Bill Clinton from office through the impeachment process.

Gays and lesbians enjoyed some important successes, but encountered setbacks as well. (For more on gay and lesbian advances and setbacks, see the "Using the Framework" feature.) The AIDS epidemic helped focus public attention on a range of other issues related to gay and lesbian rights, and several local communities across the nation legislated bans on housing and job discrimination, while still other communities passed same-sex domestic partner ordinances. Vermont legislated civil unions for same-sex couples. The Supreme Court ruled in *Lawrence* v. *Texas* (2002) that state anti-homosexual sodomy laws are suspect. And the Massachusetts Supreme Court ruled that the state must allow same-sex marriages. However, the "backlash" created by these successes mobilized opposition groups who were successful winning local and statewide initiatives aimed at ending what its advocates called "special rights" for gays and lesbians, and a number of state legislatures and

Using the Framework

"Don't Ask, Don't Tell"
Why didn't Bill Clinton deliver on his promise to drop all restrictions on gays and lesbians in the military?

Background: Almost immediately after he was elected to office in 1992, Bill Clinton announced that, in his constitutional capacity as Commander-in-Chief, he intended to lift restrictions on gays and lesbians in the armed forces of the United States. In doing so, he was delivering on a campaign promise he had made to gay and lesbian organizations. After only a few weeks, however, he backed off from his promise and instituted a policy that came to be called "don't ask, don't tell, don't pursue." This policy of "turning a blind eye," as it were, satisfied no one. Taking a broad view at how structural, political linkage, and governmental factors affected Clinton's ultimate policy on gays and lesbians in the military will shed light on this situation.

Governmental Action

Bill Clinton announces that he will institute a "don't ask, don't tell" policy for gays and lesbians in the military.

Governmental Level

Members of Congress from both parties strongly oppose lifting restrictions on gays and lesbians in the military.

The Chiefs of each of the branches of the military vehemently and publicly oppose lifting restrictions.

The president, though committed to lifting restrictions on gays and lesbians, realizes that pushing the policy will lead to tension with Congress and the military services, and get his new administration off to a shaky start, so he retreats.

Political Linkages Level

The gay and lesbian movement creates a backlash, particularly among religious conservatives in all denominations.

The Republican Party makes rolling back the so-called gay agenda a major part of its platform.

Public opinion is conflicted; Americans support nondiscrimination against gays and lesbians in principle, but oppose gays and lesbians on a wide range of specific proposals.

Gays and lesbians form and effectively use social protest groups.

Gays and lesbians play an increasingly open role in political campaigns, as candidates, financial contributors, and party activists.

The Democratic Party welcomes gay and lesbian support and participation.

The mass media and entertainment industries become more sympathetic to gays and lesbians.

Structural Level

Higher levels of education among the population increases toleration of alternative lifestyles.

Urbanization creates enclaves where gays and lesbians build communities, create social networks, and develop economic and political resources.

The individualistic component of American culture and the Fourteenth Amendment to the Constitution favor a nondiscriminatory environment.

However, the strongly religious component of American culture is also the foundation for anti-homosexual attitudes.

233

The 2004 decision by the Massachusetts Supreme Court that the state must provide ways for same-sex couples to marry sparked a furious reaction among religious conservatives. Here a group of evangelical Christians prays that the state legislature will reverse the state's high court decision.

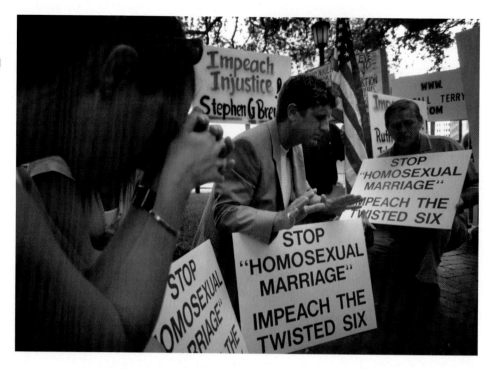

Congress established laws preventing recognition of same-sex marriages. Several states, including Missouri, passed state constitutional amendments defining marriage as a union between a man and a woman. The same-sex marriage decision in Massachusetts was an important stimulant, as well, for the mobilization of conservative evangelicals during the 2004 national elections.

Successful Social Movements

Social movements that have many supporters, win wide public sympathy, do not challenge the basics of the economic and social orders, and wield some clout in the electoral arena are likely to achieve a substantial number of their goals. The women's suffrage movement, described in the chapter-opening story, is one of the best examples. The civil rights movement is another, yielding, after years of struggle, the Civil Rights Act of 1964—which banned segregation in places of public accommodations such as hotels and restaurants—and the Voting Rights Act of 1965—which put the might of the federal government behind efforts to allow African Americans to vote and hold elected office. These enactments helped sound the death knell of the "separate but equal" doctrine enunciated in the infamous *Plessy* decision (1896), engineered the collapse of legal segregation in the South, and made the guarantee of full citizenship rights for African Americans a reality. The Voting Rights Act was particularly important in transforming the politics of the South. Black registration and voting turnout increased dramatically all over the region during the late 1960s and the 1970s. Elected black officials filled legislative seats, city council seats, the mayors' offices in large and small cities, and sheriffs' offices. Between 1960 and 2001—the last year for which this statistic is available—the number of elected black officials in the United States increased from a mere 40 to more than 9,000 (see Figure 8.1).

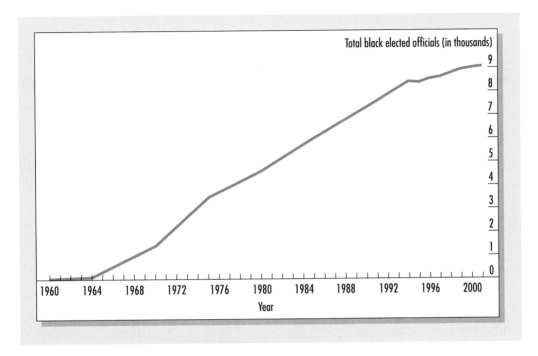

FIGURE 8.1 • **Black Elected Officials in the United States, 1960–2001 (all levels of government)**

One of the success stories of the civil rights movement is the growing number of black officials being elected in the United States.

Source: U.S. Bureau of the Census.

Elected white officials, tacking with the new winds of change, soon began to court the black vote. George Wallace, who first became famous by "standing in the schoolhouse door" to prevent the integration of the University of Alabama and who once kicked off a political campaign with the slogan "Segregation Today, Segregation Tomorrow, Segregation Forever," actively pursued the black vote in his last run for public office.

Movements can be successful even if no new laws are passed. Other measures of success include increased respect for members of the movement, changes in fundamental underlying values in society, and increased representation of the group in decision-making bodies. The women's movement has had this kind of success. Although the Equal Rights Amendment (the movement's main goal) failed, women's issues came to the forefront during these years, and to a very substantial degree, the demands of the movement for equal treatment and respect made great headway in many areas of American life.[23] Issues such as pay equity, family leave, sexual harassment, and attention to women's health problems in medical research are now a part of the American political agenda. Women have made important gains economically and are becoming more numerous in the professions, corporate managerial offices (although there is some evidence that a glass ceiling remains in place), and political office.

How Democratic Are We?

Social Movements and American Politics

PROPOSITION: Social movements make American politics more democratic.

AGREE: Our constitutional system favors the *status quo*. Federalism, separation of powers, and checks and balances make it extremely difficult to institute fundamentally new policies or to change existing social and economic conditions. The primacy of the status quo is further enhanced by the political power of economically and socially privileged groups and individuals who generally resist changes that might undermine their positions. Social movements represent a way—a difficult way, to be sure—by which political outsiders and the politically powerless can become players in the political game. Movements are a way such groups and individuals can gain a hearing for their grievances, work to win over a majority of their fellow citizens, and force elected leaders to take action. Equal citizenship for women and for African Americans, for example, would not have happened at all, or would have been much longer in coming, if not for existence of social movements demanding change.

DISAGREE: Social movements are the tool of small minorities who force elected officials to respond to their demands because of the tangible threat of social disruption. Based on the age-old notion that "the squeaky wheel gets the grease," troublesome and disruptive groups can often get their way, even though the majority does not favor such action. In addition, because social movements often defy the law and social conventions, they tend to tear at the foundations of a stable democracy. A society that depends on social movements to bring needed change, moreover, is in a pretty sorry state; the normal tools for bring change in a democracy are sufficient.

CONSIDER: Think about the most important changes brought about by government action in the United States.

• Which of them do you most admire? Perhaps Social Security and Medicare? Perhaps equal citizenship for disadvantaged minorities? Perhaps the expansion of civil liberties protections?   • Which of the most important changes do you admire the least? Perhaps annual budget deficits? Perhaps domestic programs that don't work?   • As best as you are able to tell, did social movements play an important role in forcing the policies that you most admire? Or in the policies that you least admire?   • Based on your answers to these questions, what do you think the overall role of social movements ought to be in American politics?   • Are they a good thing or a bad thing for American democracy?   • Do leaders listen too much to them or too little?

Summary

Social movements emphasize rather dramatically the point that the struggle for democracy is a recurring feature of our political life. They are mainly the instruments of political outsiders who want to gain a hearing in American politics. Social movements often contribute to democracy by increasing the visibility of important issues, by encouraging wider participation in public affairs, and sometimes by providing the energy to overcome the many anti-majoritarian features of our constitutional system.

Social movements try to bring about social change through collective action. Their rise is tied to the availability of organizational and leadership resources to a group of people who have a strong sense of grievance. Successful social movements happen, moreover, only if the political environment is supportive, in the sense that at least portions of the general population and some public officials are sympathetic to the movements' goals. The decline of particular social movements is associated with a number of things, including goal attainment, factional splits, the exhaustion of movement activists, and the replacement of grassroots activity by formal organization.

Social movements have had an important effect on our political life and in determining what our government does. Some of our most important legislative landmarks can be attributed to them. However, social movements do not always get what they want. They seem to be most successful when their goals are consistent with the central values of the society, have wide popular support, and fit the needs of political leaders.

Suggestions for Further Reading

Branch, Taylor. *Parting the Waters: America in the King Years, 1954–1963*. New York: Simon & Schuster, 1988.
  A detailed and compelling description of the civil rights movement, with a particular focus on Martin Luther King, Jr.; winner of the National Book Award and the Pulitzer Prize.

Chafe, William H. *The Unfinished Journey: America Since World War II*, New York: Oxford University Press, 2003.
  A justly celebrated history of America since 1945, with a particular focus on the civil rights and women's movements.

Dudziak, Mary L. *Cold War Civil Rights*. Princeton, NJ: Princeton University Press, 2002.
  A compelling history of how the Cold War struggle with the Soviet Union provided a supportive environment for the civil rights movement.

Evans, Sarah M. *Born for Liberty: A History of Women in America*. New York: Free Press, 1997.
  A compelling and widely used history of women in America, both substantively rich and a joy to read.

Martin, Mart. *The Almanac of Women and Minorities in American Politics*. Boulder, CO: Westview Press, 2002.
  A detailed, in-depth compendium about every aspect of women's and minorities' places in American political life.

Piven, Frances Fox, and Richard A. Cloward. *Poor People's Movements*. New York: Vintage, 1979.
  A controversial treatment of poor people's movements that argues that they are successful only as long as and to the extent that they remain grassroots, disruptive insurgencies.

Rimmerman, Craig A. *From Identity to Politics*. Philadelphia: Temple University Press, 2002.
  An analysis of the gay and lesbian movement, using social movement theory to clarify how it has developed and changed, and a political agenda for the future.

Tarrow, Sidney. *Power in Movement: Social Movements and Contentious Politics*. Cambridge: Cambridge University Press, 1998.
  The leading academic treatment of social movements; analytically sophisticated and loaded with useful information about a broad range of movements.

Internet Sources

Afronet
www.afronet.com/
  A Website devoted to materials on African American political, social, economic, and cultural life.

Christian Coalition
www.cc.org/
  Information and links from the nation's most influential Christian conservative organization.

The Lesbian and Gay Alliance Against Defamation
www.glaad.org
  News, issues, and links related to the gay and lesbian movement.

The Smithsonian Exhibits: Disability Rights
http://americanhistory.si.edu/disabilityrights/ welcome.html
  A Smithsonian online exhibit featuring the history of the disability rights movement.

Yahoo!Society and Culture
www.yahoo.com/Society_and_Culture/
  A gateway with links to a multitude of social movements, issues, and groups.

Chapter 9
Political Parties

In This Chapter

- Why political parties are important in a democracy
- How American political parties differ from parties elsewhere
- Why we have a two-party system
- How our party system has changed over the years
- What role third parties play
- How the Republican and Democratic parties differ

New Competition for the Party Campaign Machine

"This was not a good decision for the parties."[1] Bob Bauer, a Democratic campaign finance lawyer, was responding to the 2003 Supreme Court decision upholding the most important provisions of the Bipartisan Campaign Reform Act of 2002—commonly known as McCain-Feingold, after the two senators who had first introduced the reform legislation. Other party professionals, both Democrats and Republicans, expressed concern as well, primarily because the law banned soft-money contributions to national party organizations and empowered nonparty organizations to play a larger role in campaigns (see Table 7.1 for details).

Until 2002, Republican and Democratic national party organizations had it good, enjoying the fact that "the money kept rolling in," to quote the well-known song from the musical *Evita*. Although previous campaign finance laws regulated contributions to presidential and congressional campaigns by individuals and PACs, party professionals had discovered a huge loophole through which the Democratic and Republican parties could collect unlimited amounts of soft money to support "party-building" activities. And collect they did. From 1995 to 2002, the American Federation of State, County, and Municipal Workers, for example, gave more than $16 million to the Democratic Party; Philip Morris Tobacco gave almost $9 million to the Republican Party during the same time period, while the American Financial Group added another $6 million.

The parties used the influx of unregulated soft money to build state-of-the-art campaign machines to help party candidates. Both of the national party organizations built shiny new office buildings in Washington, D.C. Out of these buildings come a range of campaign services for party candidates. In-house TV and radio studios provide attack ads aimed against the opposing party and its candidates, tailored to the particular district or state in which the ads will be used. Other ads extol the sponsoring party and its achievements. Direct mail campaigns are mounted to disseminate information and party positions on the issues and to make appeals for campaign

contributions. News releases are prepared for the media, as are campaign-oriented sound and video bites to be used as news clips on local radio and television. Each of the parties also produces training courses for potential candidates, complete with "how-to" manuals and videos. Each of the two parties has a Website where people can access information about the party, get news about the nefarious behavior of the opposition, and make monetary contributions to the party and party candidates.

To carry out these activities, both the Republican and Democratic National Committees steadily increased the number of employees in their national offices, especially in the areas of finance, advertising, information technology, campaign planning, and video specialist and support personnel, and they expanded their budgets to carry out an ever-broader range of campaign activities for party candidates. Each of the national committees became a highly professionalized campaign organization, filled with highly skilled people able to provide party candidates with what they needed to wage first-rate electoral campaigns.

The ban on soft money imposed by McCain-Feingold will hurt the party organizations; less money will pour into party coffers than in the past. To be sure, they will hardly go broke;

the new law actually allows larger hard- or "regulated"-money contributions to the parties than in the past—$25,000 per year from individuals, for example, compared with $20,000. But the days of unlimited contributions to parties is gone. So, where will unregulated political money go? According to most observers, the beneficiaries of the new law will be private, not-for-profit organizations, with no formal affiliation with the political parties, that espouse a cause or ideology or partisan agenda. The new law imposes no restrictions on the size of the contributions these organizations—called "527 organizations" after the section of the Tax Code that created them—can accept from individuals, other private organizations, labor unions, or corporations. As Senator Mitch McConnell (R–KY) put it, "Soft money has not gone; it has just changed its address."[2] The upshot is that the national party organizations will have to compete in the business of financing and organizing campaigns with powerful new groups such as "America Coming Together," funded by large contributions from billionaire George Soros committed to the defeat of George W. Bush and congressional Republicans in the 2004 elections. Or, they will have to compete with traditional interest groups such as the National Rifle Association, whose executive vice president Wayne LaPierre announced that his organization would devote more energies to increasing the size of its PAC treasure chest and finding new ways to use "unregulated" contributions to get its message to voters, perhaps even buying a television or radio station or two.[3]

This new competition from nonparty organizations comes at an interesting time in the evolution of the parties' campaign organizations. During the 1990s, the Republican and Democratic parties became slick campaign machines, lending ever-more sophisticated advertising and marketing help to local, state, and national party candidates in election contests. As they became more proficient in these tasks, oddly enough, public regard for the parties continued to decline: fewer Americans now identify with the parties than in the past (see Chapter 5); turnout for national elections is at an all-time low; vital grassroots party organizations have withered and disappeared in many areas as party leaders turned their attention and resources to feeding the campaign party machines; fewer people today than in the past volunteer to work in candidate campaigns; and regard for both parties has declined, as has confidence in the ability of either one to solve pressing national problems.[4]

The Republican and Democratic parties face a major dilemma, then. Having abandoned their traditional role as community-based organizations with close links to voters in favor of a new role as campaign service organizations for candidates—and perhaps losing some of their legitimacy with voters and potential voters in the process—they now must face competition from new nonparty organizations (with very deep pockets) that will play a larger and larger role in election campaigns. Although these nonparty organizations often are created by people who say they are committed to mobilize party voters and press party ideas, there is no guarantee that party professionals and leaders can keep them entirely under control. These changes may have important implications for how well political parties function as a tool of democracy in the United States. We will examine these issues in this chapter, as well as in the next chapter on elections and political participation.

Thinking Critically About This Chapter

This chapter is about American political parties, how they evolved, what they do, and how their actions affect the quality of democracy in the United States.

Using the Framework　You will see in this chapter how parties work as political linkage institutions connecting the public with government leaders and institutions. You will see, as well, how structural changes in the American economy and society have affected how our political parties function.

Using the Democracy Standard　You will see in this chapter that political parties, at least in theory, are one of the most important instruments for making popular sovereignty and majority rule a reality in a representative democracy, particularly in a system of checks-and-balances and separated powers such as our own. Evaluating how well our parties carry out these democratic responsibilities is one of the main themes of this chapter.

The Role of Political Parties in a Democracy

Political parties are organizations that try to win control of government by electing people to public office who carry the party label. In representative democracies, parties are the principal organizations that recruit candidates for public office, run their candidates against the candidates of other political parties in competitive elections, and try to organize and coordinate the activities of government officials under party banners and programs.

Many political scientists believe that political parties are essential to democracy.[5] They agree with E. E. Schattschneider that "political parties created democracy and . . . modern democracy is unthinkable save in terms of the parties."[6] What Schattschneider and others see in the political party is the main instrument of popular sovereignty and, especially, majority rule: "The parties are the special form of political organization adapted to the mobilization of majorities. How else can the majority get organized? If democracy means anything at all it means that the majority has the right to organize for the purpose of taking over the government."[7]

In theory, political parties can do a number of things to make popular sovereignty and political equality possible:[8]

- *Keep elected officials responsive.* Political parties can provide a way for the people to keep elected officials responsive through competitive elections. Competitive party elections help voters choose between alternative policy directions for the future. They also allow voters to make a judgment about the past performance of a governing party and decide whether to allow that party to continue in office. And, a party can adjust

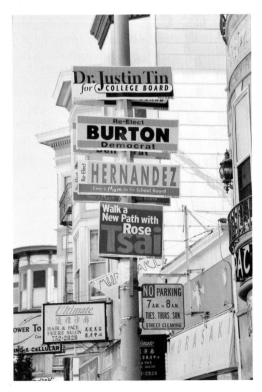

Political parties generally try to broaden their appeal by running candidates from a wide range of ethnic, racial, and religious groups.

party platform

A party's statement of its positions on the issues of the day.

Deciding on a
Political Party

its **party platform**—the party's statement of its position on the issues—to reflect the preferences of the public as a way to win elections. (These three ways in which elections relate to democracy are discussed in Chapter 10.)

- *Include a broad range of groups.* Political parties can enhance political equality in a democracy because they tend to include as many groups as they possibly can. Parties are by nature inclusive, as they must be if they are to create a winning majority coalition in elections. It is customary for parties in the United States to recruit candidates for public office from many ethnic and racial groups and to include language in their platforms to attract a diversity of groups.

- *Stimulate political interest.* When they are working properly, moreover, political parties stimulate interest in politics and public affairs and increase participation.[9] They do this as a natural by-product of their effort to win or retain power in government; they mobilize voters, bring issues to public attention, and educate on the issues that are of interest to the party. Party competition, by "expanding the scope of conflict," attracts attention and gets people involved.[10]

- *Ensure accountability.* Parties can help make officeholders more accountable. When things go wrong or promises are not kept, it is important in a democracy for citizens to know who is responsible. Where there are many offices and branches of government, however, it is hard to pinpoint responsibility. Political parties can simplify this difficult task by allowing for collective responsibility. Citizens can pass judgment on the governing ability of a party as a whole and decide whether to retain the incumbent party or to throw it out of office in favor of the other party.

- *Help people make sense of complexity in politics.* Party labels and party positions on the issues help many people make sense of the political world. Few people have the time or resources to learn about and reach decisions on every candidate on the ballot or the issues before the public at any period in time. Party labels and policy positions can act as useful shortcuts enabling people to cut through the complexities and reach decisions that are consistent with their own values and interests.

- *Make government work.* In a system like ours of separation of powers and checks and balances, designed to make it difficult for government to act decisively, political parties can encourage cooperation across the branches of government among public officials who are members of the same party. Parties can help overcome gridlock, an all too common feature of our constitutional system.

Political parties, then, can be tools of popular sovereignty. Whether our own political parties fulfill these responsibilities to democracy is the question we explore in the remainder of this chapter as well as in Chapter 10.

History of the Two-Party System

The United States comes closer to having a "pure" two-party system than any other nation in the world. Most Western democracies have multiparty systems. In the United States, however, two parties have dominated the political scene since 1836, and the Democrats and the Republicans have controlled the presidency and Congress since 1860. Minor or third parties have rarely polled a significant percentage of the popular vote in either presidential or congressional elections (more will be said later about third parties and independent candidates), although they are sometimes successful at the state and local levels. Jesse Ventura, for example, was elected governor of Minnesota in 1998 as the nominee of the Reform Party.

Although the United States has had a two-party system for most of its history, it has not been static. The party system has, in fact, changed a great deal, both mirroring and playing a central role in the dynamic and sometimes chaotic story of the development of the United States, as described in Chapter 4. There have been six relatively stable periods in the history of the two-party system in the United States, each stretching over 30 or 40 years, interspersed with much shorter periods of transformation or **realignment.** Realignment is a transition period, most notable in our history in 1896 and 1932, when a party system dominated by one of the two major parties is replaced by another system dominated by the other party.[11] Figure 9.1 shows this history in graphic form.

Comparing Political Parties

realignment

The process by which one party supplants another as the dominant party in a political system.

The First Party System: Federalists Versus Democratic Republicans

Although the Founders were hostile to parties in theory, they created them almost immediately. The first was formed in the 1790s by George Washington's energetic secretary of the treasury, Alexander Hamilton. In a successful effort to push through the administration's ambitious legislative program, Hamilton persuaded sympathetic members of Congress to form a loosely organized party that eventually took the name Federalist.

Thomas Jefferson, James Madison, and others formed a party in Congress to oppose the Hamilton domestic program and Federalist foreign policy. They used the label Republican, although the Federalists tried to discredit them by calling them Democratic Republicans (the term *democratic* was a term of derision, not praise, in those days).

The Federalist party gradually disappeared, tainted by its pro-British sympathies during the War of 1812 and its image as a party of the wealthy and the aristocratic in an increasingly democratic America. By 1816, the first two-party system had evolved into a one-party or no-party system, generally known (because of the absence of party competition) as the Era of Good Feelings.

The Second Party System: Democrats Versus Whigs

The Era of Good Feelings gave way in the late 1820s to a strong two-party system that grew out of the disputed presidential election of 1824. In that election, Andrew Jackson won a plurality of the popular and electoral votes but failed to win a majority of either. The House of Representatives chose John Quincy Adams as president. Supporters of Jackson formed an opposition that soon became the Democratic party, while supporters of Adams and his ally in the House, Speaker Henry Clay, organized as the Whig party. Starting in 1828, when Jackson defeated Adams for the presidency, the Democrats won six of the next eight presidential elections.

Each of the parties split apart as the nation drifted toward civil war. The Whig party simply disintegrated and disappeared. Several of its fragments came together with *Free-Soilers* (who opposed the expansion of slavery into the western territories) and antislavery Democrats to form a new Republican party—the ancestor of the present-day Republicans—which ran

First Party System	"Era of Good Feelings"	Second Party System	Realignment	Third Party System

Realignment

First Party System
Federalists vs. Democratic Republicans (Democratic Republican party dominates after 1800)

"Era of Good Feelings" (no parties)

Second Party System
Democrats vs. Whigs (Evenly matched)

Realignment

Third Party System
Democrats vs. Republicans (Evenly matched)

1790   1816   1828   1860   1868   1896

FIGURE 9.1 ● **Party Systems in the United States**

American politics has been characterized by a series of stable political party eras punctuated by brief periods of transition from one party era to another.

its first presidential candidate, John Frémont, in the election of 1856. The Democrats survived but could not agree on a single candidate to run against Republican Abraham Lincoln in 1860, so each wing of the party nominated its own candidate.

From the Civil War to 1896: Republicans and Democrats in Balance

Once the southern states had reentered the Union after Reconstruction, the Republicans and the Democrats found themselves roughly balanced in national politics. Between 1876 and 1896, the Democrats managed to control the presidency for 8 of 20 years, the Senate for 6 years, and the House of

The second party system was characterized by well-organized parties, skilled in the use of methods (such as this parade) to mobilize the "common man" to participate in electoral politics.

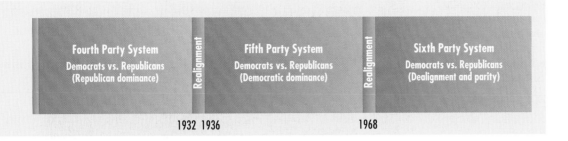

Representatives for 14 years. Each party had a strong regional flavor. The Democratic party was primarily a white southern party, although Catholics and many workers in northern urban areas also supported it. The Republicans (also known as the "Grand Old Party," or GOP) became a party of business, the middle class, and newly enfranchised African Americans.

The Party System of 1896: Republican Dominance

Beneath the apparent calm of a balanced two-party system, however, a storm was brewing. The late nineteenth century was a time of rapid economic and social change and disruption, one effect of which was to spawn a host of protest movements and third parties. The Populist party, the most important of them, garnered 8.5 percent of the total vote in the 1892 election and won four states in the electoral college, running on the slogan, "Wealth belongs to him who creates it." During the 1890s, Populist party candidates also won governorships in eight states and control of at least as many state legislatures.

In 1896, the Populist party joined with the Democratic party to nominate a single candidate for the presidency, the charismatic orator William Jennings Bryan, who urged "free coinage of silver" to help debtors with cheaper currency. The threat of a radical agrarian party, joining blacks and whites, farmers and labor unionists, proved too much for many Americans and contributed to one of the most bitter electoral campaigns in U.S. history. Conservative Democrats deserted their party to join the Republicans. Businesses warned each other and their workers in no uncertain terms about the dangers of a Populist-Democratic victory. Newly formed business organizations, such as the National Association of Manufacturers, spread the alarm about a possible Democratic victory. In the South, efforts to intimidate potential black voters increased dramatically.[12]

The Republicans won handily and dominated American politics until the Great Depression and the election of 1932. Between 1896 and 1932, the Republicans won control of both houses of Congress in 15 out of 18 elections and of the presidency in 7 out of 9.

The New Deal Party System: Democratic Party Dominance

The Great Depression, the **New Deal,** and the leadership of President Franklin D. Roosevelt ushered in a long period of Democratic party dominance. From 1932 through 1964, the Democrats won seven of nine presidential elections, controlled the Senate and the House of Representatives for all but

New Deal

The programs of the administration of President Franklin D. Roosevelt.

Franklin D. Roosevelt, here talking with Georgia farmers during his campaign for the presidency in 1932, fashioned an electoral coalition, based on the urban working class, racial and ethnic minorities, Catholics and Jews, big cities, and the South, that allowed the Democratic party to dominate American politics for almost four decades.

four years, and prevailed in a substantial majority of governorships and state legislatures across the nation. Democratic dominance was built on an alliance of workers, Catholics, Jews, unionists, small- and medium-sized farmers, urban dwellers, white ethnics, southerners, and blacks that came to be known as the **New Deal coalition.** The New Deal coalition supported an expansion of federal government powers and responsibilities, particularly in the areas of old age assistance, aid for the poor, encouragement of unionization, subsidies for agriculture, and regulation of business.

New Deal coalition

The informal electoral alliance of working-class ethnic groups, Catholics, Jews, urban dwellers, racial minorities, and the South that was the basis of the Democratic party dominance of American politics from the New Deal to the early 1970s.

The Sixth Party System: Dealignment and Parity

The New Deal coalition began to slowly disintegrate in the 1968 election (won by Republican Richard Nixon) and finally collapsed in 1980 with the Republican capture of the presidency and the Senate,[13] a process triggered mostly by the civil rights revolution and the subsequent departure of many white southerners and blue collar workers from the Democratic Party.[14] After 1980, the pace of Democratic decline began to pick up; Democrats began to lose their lead in governorships and state legislatures, as well as in party identification among the electorate, lost the Senate to the Republicans from 1981 to 1986, lost both houses of Congress to the Republicans between 1995 and 2001, and after the 2002 congressional elections, and managed to control the presidency for only 12 years between 1968 and 2000. Increasingly during this period, divided government characterized both state government and national government, a situation in which one party controlled the executive and the other party controlled all or part of the legislative branch most of the time.

The transition from the fifth party system to the sixth was not the classic party realignment that occurred after the elections of 1896 and 1932. In those earlier elections, a system dominated by one party was replaced by a system dominated by the other party. This time, instead, the previously dominant party lost preeminence (the Democrats in this case), but no new party took its place as the dominant party. Scholars, journalists, and politicians have come to call this process **dealignment.**[15] The resulting sixth party system is one of near parity in which the Republican and Democratic parties are evenly divided in terms of elected offices held, the distribution of votes among the electorate, and party identification among Americans. The dead-heat between Al Gore and George W. Bush in the 2000 presidential contest, and the near-even split of seats among Democrats and Republicans in Congress following the 2000 and the 2002 elections, exemplified the politics of parity.[16] In party terms, the United States had become a 50–50 nation at the start of the twenty-first century.

This sixth party system, characterized by parity between the parties, declining party identification among the population, but more sharply divided views between the remaining Republican and Democratic party identifiers (see Chapter 5), may mean that we are in for a period of political volatility. Because the parties are so close in the number of elected offices they hold, even small swings in turnout can change which party controls the presidency and Congress. Because Democratic and Republican identifiers are divided so deeply on issues and ideology, partisan voters and party activists and leaders in both parties believe more is at stake in elections, increasing the emotional intensity of elections. And, because there are so many more independent voters than in the past, there are more voters who might swing toward the Democrats in one election then toward the Republicans in the next election. Or, they might now and again support a maverick independent candidate or insurgent third party, upsetting the fine balance between Democrats and Republicans.

> **dealignment**
> A gradual reduction in the dominance of one political party without another party supplanting it.

Why a Two-Party System?

Most Western democracies have multiparty systems, with more than two major parties. Why are we so different from other countries? There are several possible answers.

Electoral Rules

The kinds of rules that organize elections help determine what kind of party system exists.[17] Which rules are chosen, then, has important consequences for a nation's politics.

Proportional Representation   Most other democratic nations use some form of **proportional representation** (PR) to elect their representatives. In PR systems, each party is represented in the legislature in rough proportion to the percentage of the popular vote it receives in an election. In a perfect PR system, a party winning 40 percent of the vote would get 40 seats in a 100-seat legislative body, a party winning 22 percent of the vote would get 22 seats, and so on. In such a system, even very small parties would have a reason to maintain their separate identities, for no matter how narrow their appeal, they would win seats as long as they could win a proportion of the popular vote. Voters with strong views on an issue or with strong ideological outlooks could vote for a party that closely represented their views. A vote for a small party would not be wasted, because it would ultimately be translated into legislative seats and, perhaps, a place in the governing coalition.

Israel and the Netherlands come closest to having a pure PR system, organized on a national basis; most western European nations depart in various

> **proportional representation**
> The awarding of legislative seats to political parties to reflect the proportion of the popular vote each party receives.

A presidential election is decided by which candidate has won a majority in the electoral college, *not* by a majority of the total votes cast. That is why on election night every four years the television networks focus on state-by-state victories and defeats.

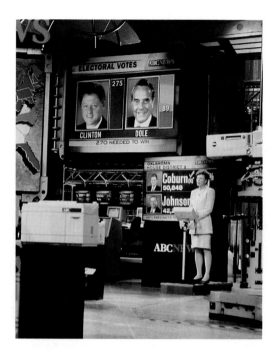

ways from the pure form. Most, for instance, vote for slates of party candidates within multimember electoral districts, apportioning seats in each district according to each party's percentage of the vote. Most also have a minimum threshold (often 5 percent) below which no seats are awarded.

Winner-Take-All, Plurality Election, Single-Member Districts   Elections in the United States are organized on a winner-take-all, single-member-district basis. Each electoral district in the United States—whether it is an urban ward, a county, a congressional district, or a state—elects only one person to a given office and does so on the basis of whoever wins the *most* votes (not necessarily a majority). This is why our way of electing leaders is sometimes called a "first past the post" system, analogous to a horse race. This arrangement creates a powerful incentive for parties to coalesce and for voters to concentrate their attention on big parties. Let's see why.

From the vantage point of party organizations, this type of election discourages minor-party efforts because failure to come in first in the voting leaves a party with no representation at all. Leaders of such parties are tempted to merge with a major party. By the same token, a disaffected faction within a party is unlikely to strike out on its own because the probability of gaining political office is very low.

From the voter's point of view, a single-member, winner-take-all election means that a vote for a minor party is wasted. People who vote for a minor party may feel good, but most voters have few illusions that such votes will translate into representation and so are not inclined to cast them.

Note that the most important office in American government, the presidency, is elected in what is, in effect, a single-district (the nation), winner-take-all election. The candidate who wins a majority of the nation's votes in the electoral college wins the presidency (see Chapter 10). A party cannot win a share of the presidency; it is all or nothing. (The "By the Numbers" feature on page 250 examines the geography of the electoral college.) In parliamentary systems, the executive power is lodged in a cabinet, however, where several parties may be represented.

Restrictions on Minor Parties

Once a party system is in place, the dominant parties often establish rules that make it difficult for other parties to get on the ballot. A number of formidable legal obstacles stand in the way of third parties and independent candidates in the United States. While many of these restrictions have been eased because of successful court challenges by recent minor-party and independent presidential candidates such as Ross Perot, the path to the ballot remains tortuous in many states, where a considerable number of signatures is required to get on the ballot.

The federal government's partial funding of presidential campaigns has made the situation of third parties even more difficult. Major-party candidates automatically qualify for federal funding once they are nominated. Minor-party candidates must attract a minimum of 5 percent of the votes cast in the general election to be eligible for public funding, and they are not reimbursed until after the election. In recent decades, only the Reform Party among the legion of minor parties has managed to cross the threshold to qualify for federal funding. Because the Green Party's candidate, Ralph Nader, won only 2.7 percent of the national vote in the 2000 election, it was not eligible for federal funding for the 2004 election.

Absence of a Strong Labor Movement

The relative weakness of the American labor movement has already been noted in several places in this book. In the western European countries, the organized labor movement was instrumental in the creation of Socialist and Labor political parties that challenged classical Liberal (free enterprise, small government) and traditional Conservative (monarchist, Catholic, and aristocratic) parties. The British Labour party, for instance, was created by trade union officials and Socialists in 1906. Strong Socialist and Labor parties in Europe did not replace traditional Liberal and Conservative parties (except in Great Britain) but spurred them on to more spirited organizing and electioneering of their own. The result has been the creation of a basic three-party system in many European countries—Conservative, Liberal, and Labor or Socialist—with a number of small satellite parties (encouraged by PR electoral systems) clustered about them.

The Role of Minor Parties in the Two-Party System

Minor parties have played a less important role in the United States than in virtually any other democratic nation.[18] In our entire history, only a single minor party (the Republicans) has managed to replace one of the major parties. Only six (not including the Republicans) have been able to win even 10 percent of the popular vote in a presidential election, and only seven have managed to win a single state in a presidential election.

Minor parties have come in a number of forms:

- *Protest parties* sometimes arise as part of a protest movement. The Populist party, for instance, grew out of the western and southern farm protest movements in the late nineteenth century. The Green Party was an offshoot of the environmental and antiglobalization movements.

By the Numbers

Does population movement and change affect the electoral fortunes of the parties?

Two-hundred seventy is the magic number for presidential candidates; it is the number of electoral college votes needed to win the presidency. In 2000, though he lost the national popular vote to Al Gore, George W. Bush won 271 electoral votes and the White House. Like any other winning presidential candidate, Bush put together a package of states with enough electoral college votes to win the only election that counts.

Why It Matters: Because of the magic number 270, presidential campaign strategists always design their campaigns around the states. For the most part, they attempt to build a majority of electoral votes by maintaining their lead in states with solid loyalties to their party, contesting states that might go either way, and generally ignoring states that are safely in the camp of the opposition. As the American population distributes and redistributes itself across the United States, campaign strategists must be alert to changes in the party leanings of the states, and constantly readjust their strategies for winning.

Behind the Number: Over the past half-century or so, the states that each party can count on to put together 270 electoral votes has changed. Much (though not all) of this can be explained by population movements:

- Many African Americans migrated from the deep South to manufacturing centers in the Northeast, the upper Midwest, and far West, bringing their Democratic Party loyalties with them.
- Many other Americans migrated to the South and Southwest to fill jobs in nonunion factories and in defense and high-tech industries, swelling GOP votes in the states of these regions.

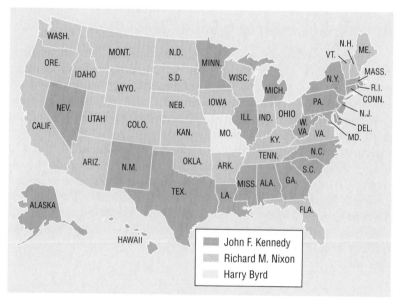

John F. Kennedy
Richard M. Nixon
Harry Byrd

Electoral College Map, 1960

- *Ideological parties* are organized around coherent sets of ideas. The several Socialist parties have been of this sort, as has the Libertarian party. The Green Party ran in the 2000 elections on an anticorporate, antiglobalization platform.
- *Single-issue parties* are barely distinguishable from interest groups. What makes them different is their decision to run candidates for office.

- Immigrants swelled the populations of a wide range of states, making Florida more Republican (its large number of Cuban immigrants favor the GOP), but making California, New York, and Illinois more Democratic (Asian and Hispanic immigrants lean toward the Democrats).
- A substantial number of white Americans migrated to the Mountain states, enhancing their standing as the area with the highest proportion of non-Hispanic whites, anchoring these states even more firmly in the Republican camp.

Counting to 270: We display here two electoral college maps, one showing the distribution of party victories by state in the 1960 presidential election

(John F. Kennedy versus Richard M. Nixon), the other in the 2000 election (George W. Bush versus Al Gore). Democratic states are shown in blue, Republican states in red. Note the geographical pattern of the vote. In 1960, the geographical strength of the Democratic Party was in the South and in the large industrial states of the mid-Atlantic and the upper Midwest; by 2000, states in the South had become bastions of the Republican Party. In 1960, the GOP could count on most of New England, the farm states of the Midwest, the Mountain states, and the Pacific Coast states. By 2000, New England and the Pacific Coast were solidly in the Democratic camp (though, to be sure, the vote in Oregon in 2000 was extremely close).

What to Watch For: Pay attention to where presidential candidates make most of their campaign visits and where the parties spend the most money on advertising and getting out the vote. For the most part, they leave "hopeless" states alone, do enough to maintain their lead in states where they are strong, and focus the bulk of their activities in states that are very close and where the election could go in either direction.

What Do You Think? Do you think that the electoral college distorts political campaigns by encouraging presidential candidates to focus on particular states rather than on Americans everywhere? Or do you think there is something about the electoral college system that is important for the health of our federal system?

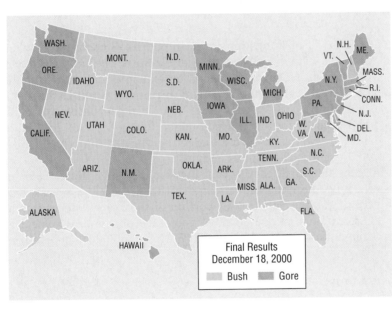

Electoral College Map, 2000

Final Results December 18, 2000
Bush Gore

The Prohibition party and the Free-Soil party fall into this category as did Perot's "balanced budget" Reform Party in 1996.

- *Splinter parties* form when a faction in one of the two major parties bolts to run its own candidate or candidates. An example is the Bull Moose Progressive party of Teddy Roosevelt, formed after Roosevelt split with Republican party regulars in 1912.

Candidates such as Ralph Nader and third parties such as the Green Party often bring up issues the main parties are unable or unwilling to address.

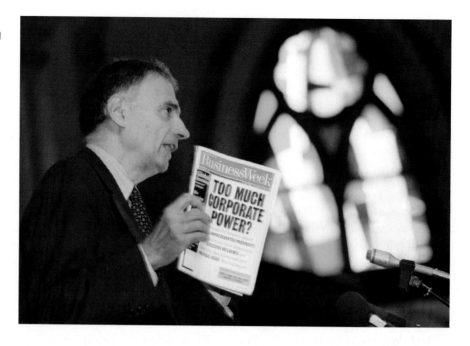

Minor parties do a number of things in American politics. Sometimes they articulate new ideas that are eventually taken over by one or both major parties. The Socialist party under Norman Thomas, for example, advocated public works projects as a way to battle unemployment during the Great Depression, an idea that became part of the Democrats' New Deal legislative package. Ross Perot's popular crusade for a balanced budget during his 1992 campaign helped nudge the major parties toward a budget agreement that, for a while, eliminated annual deficits in the federal budget.

It is also the case that third parties can sometimes change the outcome of presidential contests by changing the outcome of the electoral vote contest in the various states: in 1992, a substantial portion of the Perot vote was comprised of people who otherwise would have voted Republican, allowing Bill Clinton to win enough states to beat George H. W. Bush; in 2000, a substantial

Timeline

Third Parties in American History

Web Exploration
Third Parties in the United States

Issue: We have a two-party system, but many minor parties exist here.

Site: Learn more about these minor, or third, parties at Politics1 on our Website at **www.ablongman.com/greenberg**. Go to the "Web Explorations" section for Chapter 9, select "Third Parties in the United States," then "third parties." Examine the platforms and activities of several minor parties.

What You've Learned: Do any of the parties you examined address issues that neither of the major parties has tackled? Do you find any of them appealing? If you like one of the parties, and that party appears on the ballot, will you vote for that party or not? What are your reasons?

portion of the Nader vote in Florida was comprised of people who otherwise would have voted Democratic, allowing George W. Bush to win Florida's electoral votes and the presidency over Al Gore.

The Parties as Organizations

I don't belong to an organized political party. I'm a Democrat.

—WILL ROGERS

American parties don't look much like the parties in other democratic countries. In most of them, the political parties are fairly well-structured organizations led by party professionals and committed to a set of policies and principles. They also tend to have clearly defined membership requirements, centralized control over party nominations and electoral financing, and disciplinary authority over party members holding political office.

The Ambiguous Nature of American Political Parties

The classic boss-led political machines of American folklore—long identified with such names as Tammany Hall, "Boss Tweed" of New York, Richard J. Daley of Chicago, and Huey Long of Louisiana—have disappeared from the cities and states where they once existed, mainly because of reforms that ended party control over government contracts and jobs. Political machines run by a "boss" have never existed at the national level. There have been leaders with clout, reputation, and vision, to be sure, but never a boss who could issue commands. Even popular, charismatic, and skillful presidents, including George Washington, Abraham Lincoln, Woodrow Wilson, Franklin Roosevelt, Harry Truman, John Kennedy, and Ronald Reagan, have had nearly as much

Richard Daley, mayor of Chicago for more than 20 years, and head of the Cook Country Democratic Party for even longer, was the last in a long line of big-city party bosses in America.

trouble controlling the many diverse and independent groups and individuals within their own parties as they have had dealing with the opposition.

The vagueness of party membership is a good indicator of the ambiguous nature of our parties. Think about what it means to be a Republican or a Democrat in the United States. Americans do not join parties in the sense of paying dues and receiving a membership card. To Americans, being a member of a party may mean voting most of the time for the candidate of a party or choosing to become a candidate of one of them. Or it may mean voting in a party primary. Or it may mean contributing money to, or otherwise helping in, a local, state, or national campaign of one of the party candidates. Or it may just mean a general preference of one party over another most of the time. These are loose criteria for membership, to say the least—looser than for virtually any other organization that might be imagined.

The Organization of American Political Parties

The Republican and Democratic parties are not organizations in the usual sense of the term but rather loose collections of local and state parties, campaign committees, candidates and officeholders, and associated interest groups that get together every four years to nominate a presidential candidate. Unlike a corporation, a bureaucratic agency, a military organization, or even a political party in most other countries, the official leaders of the major American parties cannot issue orders that get passed down a chain of com-

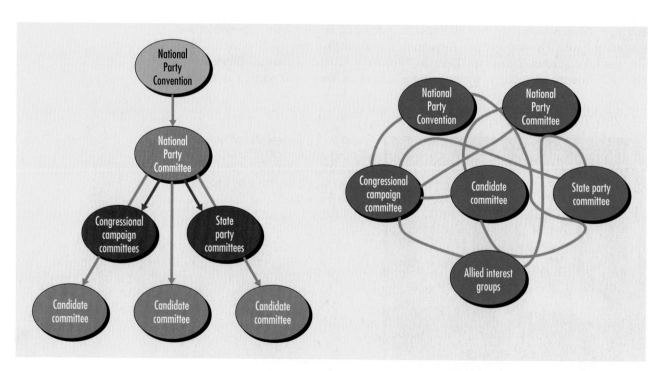

FIGURE 9.2 • Political Party Organization in the United States

The graphic on the left shows a hypothetical organizational chart of the Republican and Democratic parties as if they were structured hierarchically like many other organizations you are familiar with. It would be a mistake, however, to think of our national parties this way. The drawing on the right, which depicts our national parties as network or weblike organizations, where there is neither central authority nor a chain of command, is closer to reality. The ties between elements of the parties include money, ideology, sentiment, and common interests.

mand. The various elements of the party are relatively independent from one another and act in concert not on the basis of orders but on the basis of shared interests, sentiment, and the desire to win elections.[19] Most important, the national party is unable to control its most vital activity—the nomination of candidates running under its party label—or the flow of money that funds electoral campaigns or the behavior of its officeholders. (See Figure 9.2 for a graphical representation of these ideas.)

Party Conventions   This is not to suggest that the parties are entirely devoid of tools to encourage coordination and cooperation among their various levels. The national party conventions are the governing bodies of the parties (see Chapter 10). Convention delegates meet every four years not only to nominate presidential and vice presidential candidates but also to write a party platform and revise party rules.

Although the national convention is the formal governing body of each of the parties, it cannot dictate to party candidates or party organizations at other levels of jurisdiction. The presidential nominee need not adhere to either the letter or the spirit of the party platform, for instance, although most nominees stay fairly close to the platform most of the time (usually because the winning candidate's supporters control the platform-writing committee). State and local party organizations may nominate whomever they choose to run for public office and may or may not support key planks in the national party's platform.

National Party Committees   The Democrats and Republicans each have a national committee whose responsibility is to conduct the business of the party during the four years between national conventions. Although the national committees have little direct power, they provide valuable services for local and state parties and for party candidates at all levels (a subject detailed in the story that opens this chapter). These include production of campaign training materials, issue and policy research, design and maintenance of Websites, assistance in creating radio and TV spots and other campaign materials, and research on the opposition. They also make significant financial contributions to the campaigns of party candidates. The ability of the national party committees to support this range of campaign activities will diminish because they will have less money to use given the ban on soft money contributions to the parties imposed by the Bipartisan Campaign Reform Act (McCain-Feingold). How much it will diminish remains to be seen.

National party conventions serve several purposes for American political parties. Every four years, delegates choose presidential and vice presidential candidates, settle party rules, write the party platform, repair or build political coalitions, and, as shown here, attempt to whip up enthusiasm for their nominees.

The national committees are made up of elected committeemen and committeewomen from each of the states, a sizable staff, and a chairperson. The national committees rarely meet. The real business of the committee is run by the party chair, assisted by the committee staff. The chair exercises little power when a president from the party is in office because the party chair is compelled to take direction from the White House. When the opposition controls the presidency, the party chair exercises more influence in party affairs, although the extent of that power is still not very great.

Congressional Campaign Committees Almost as old as the national party committees, but entirely independent of them, are the congressional campaign committees that aid members of Congress in their campaigns for reelection. They help raise money, provide media services (making short videotapes of the members of Congress for local television news shows, for instance), conduct research, and do whatever else the party members in Congress deem appropriate. These committees are controlled by the party members in Congress, not the party chair, the national committees, or even the president. Much as with the national committees, the congressional campaign committees have become highly professionalized and well funded.[20]

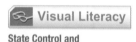

**State Control and
National Platforms**

State Party Organizations As expected in a federal system, separate political party organizations exist in each of the states. Although tied together by bonds of ideology, sentiment, and campaign money and constrained in what they can do by rules set by the national party committees and conventions—rules on how and when to choose delegates to the national convention, for example—the state party organizations are relatively independent of one another and of the national party.

Associated Interest Groups Although not technically part of the formal party organizations, some groups are so closely involved in the affairs of the parties that it is hard to draw a line between them and the political parties. The Christian Coalition, for example, is barely distinguishable from the Republican party; it contributes campaign money almost exclusively to GOP candidates, runs its own candidates in the Republican primaries, and counts many of its members among the delegates to the Republican National Convention. Organized labor has had a similar relationship with the Democratic party since the Great Depression and the New Deal.

Some new interest groups with strong ties to the party have been created as a way to get around the ban on soft money to national party organizations.[21] These 527 groups—described in the chapter-opening story—can accept donations of any size and are free to collect as much money as they can for use in issue and candidate campaigns: making hard money contributions to the parties and candidates, mobilizing voters, and educating the public about issues in ways that are compatible with the views of party candidates. Although theoretically independent of the parties, several have been created by prominent Democrats and Republicans to bolster party electoral fortunes. America Votes, for example, is a liberal campaign organization that works closely with the Democrats; the Club for Growth is a conservative organization that works closely with Republican candidates.

The Primacy of Candidates

American politics is candidate centered, meaning that candidates are primary in our political system and parties are secondary.[22] In the United States, not

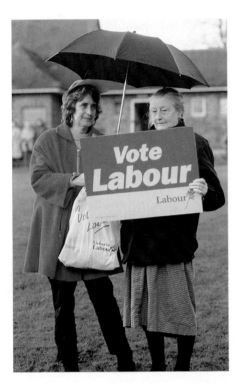

In most European countries, people vote for parties rather than individual candidates. These party activists are urging British voters to cast their ballots for the Labour party, for example, rather than for the rival Conservative party.

only are candidates relatively immune from party pressure but their electoral needs also shape what parties are and what they do.[23] Candidates have independent sources of campaign financing, their own campaign organizations, and their own campaign themes and priorities. And party organizations are becoming but another part, an important part to be sure, of candidates' campaign armament.

In the past, party candidates were usually nominated in district, state, and national conventions, where party regulars played a major role. They are now almost exclusively nominated in primaries or grassroots caucuses, where the party organizations are almost invisible. Nomination comes to those who are best able to raise money, gain access to the media, form their own electoral organizations, and win the support of powerful interest groups (such as the National Rifle Association in the GOP and the National Education Association in the Democratic party).

Nominees are so independent they sometimes oppose party leaders and reject traditional party policies. Republicans were embarrassed, for example, when David Duke, former Grand Wizard of the Ku Klux Klan, was elected to the Louisiana state legislature in 1988 under the Republican banner and ran for the governorship as a Republican in 1990, despite the opposition of state and national Republican officials.

In Germany, by way of contrast, individual candidates for the Bundestag (the equivalent of the House of Representatives) are less important than the political parties. Candidates are nominated by local party committees dominated by party regulars. Party lists for the general election are drawn up by state party organizations. Money for conducting electoral campaigns, moreover, is mostly raised and spent by the party organizations, not individual candidates. Finally, the campaign is waged between the parties and their alternative programs, not between individual candidates, and the electorate tends to make its choices based on feelings about the parties rather than about the candidates. Most of the western European democracies have similar party systems.

The Rise of Partisan Conflict

Democrats Insist Republicans Pull Bush Ad

The Story: The first Republican television ad of the 2003–2004 presidential election season, aired in Iowa during the state's caucus season, had Democrats seeing red. Senate Minority Leader Tom Daschle called the ad—which portrayed President Bush as a heroic foe of terrorism and Democrats as lukewarm supporters of national defense who "are now attacking the president for attacking the terrorists"—"repulsive and outrageous." He demanded that the ad be withdrawn. Terry McAuliffe, Chairman of the Democratic National Committee, was also angry and suggested that he was ". . . tired of seeing the Republicans use the most sophisticated space-age technologies to peddle their Stone Age ideas."

American politics is no stranger to partisan politics and nasty relations between the parties; to one extent or another, Democratic and Republican leaders and activists have always been in the business of making the other party look bad. It's good politics. However, things seem to be getting worse, at least according to most veteran observers of American politics. Most say they have not seen this level of partisan acrimony in a very long time. The editors of the widely respected

magazine *The Economist,* for example, claim that the 2002 congressional elections ranked as "the nastiest campaign of recent memory." And that campaign, they go on to say, was but a part of an emerging pattern of bitter interparty conflict infusing nearly every aspect of political life in the United States, including the relationship between President Bush and Democratic legislative leaders; the relationships among Republican and Democratic members of the House and Senate; the redistricting process in the states; reactions to Supreme Court decisions; and debates over policies regarding affirmative action, same-sex unions and marriage, taxes, civil liberties on the home front, and military action abroad.

The Facts: What accounts for the intense partisanship of American politics today? The consensus of political scientists, journalists, and commentators is that the near–dead heat that exists between the parties across the nation—in expressed party identification among the public, the close party division among the electorate, the close division of seats between

Ideology and Program

Because the Republican and Democratic parties have traditionally organized themselves as broad coalitions, seeking to attract as many voters as possible in order to prevail in winner-take-all, single-member-district elections, there always have been strong pressures on the two major parties to tone down matters of ideology. However, each party also has a core of loyal supporters and party activists, such as delegates to the party convention and caucus attendees, who are more ideologically oriented than the general public. Each

Democrats and Republicans in Congress and in state legislatures, and the very tight vote across the nation in recent presidential elections—is a more compelling explanation because it has led the leaders of each party to conclude that the best strategy for winning elections at all levels in the political system is to unite and mobilize the party's base and get it to the polls. Muting the ideological and policy messages in a bid to win the votes of independents, most of them have concluded, risks alienating their own partisans and decreasing their turnout. Mobilizing key groups in the party's coalition and getting them to the polls is a far easier thing to do than trying to persuade lukewarm independents to vote for party candidates, and the outcome is more certain. So, the first order of business for the parties has become the care and feeding of the party's base. And, what better way to do this than to make appeals that get partisans angry about the plans and deeds of the other party and cause them to worry about the opposition if it were to win power? Democrats try to increase turnout among racial minorities, labor union members, hourly workers, environmentalists, and women by attacking Republicans for opposing affirmative action, rolling back environmental regulation, undermining the right of abortion, supporting unfair tax policies, and being too friendly with large corporations. Republicans, on the other hand, try to mobilize their base of evangelical Christians, social conservatives, farmers, white southerners, people in the Mountain West, and the economically better-off; they appeal to these groups by attacking Democrats for undermining the traditional family; blocking economic prosperity by supporting inefficient regulations and taxes; and sapping American strength abroad, thereby weakening the country in the fight against terrorism.

What's at Stake? Party strategists are not only looking for a win in the next election but for a way to solidify gains in such a way that the party will become the dominant party in the next period of American history. The current thinking among many Democrats is that demographic change favors expansion in the number of Americans who are a solid part of its base. They point to the rapid expansion of the Democratic-leaning Hispanic population in the United States; the growth in the numbers of highly educated women, scientific and technical workers, and professionals who tend to favor Democrats; and in the rapid expansion in the populations of cosmopolitan, socially liberal, metropolitan areas—with universities and high-tech knowledge-based industries—where Democrats hold an edge. Republicans see their hope for dominance among the growing numbers of religiously oriented people, that segment of the Hispanic population that is religious and committed to traditional values, and the continued population growth in the South and Sun Belt, where Republicans fare best. Although party strategists sometimes advise making symbolic appeals to independents—"compassionate conservatism" comes to mind—or using appointments to try to steal a few votes from the other side's base—something that both Bill Clinton and George W. Bush did with great skill—for the most part, mobilizing one's own base is the name of today's game.

Is This Good for Democracy?

● Are we stuck between a rock and a hard place? ● Can we have parties that serve democracy without having partisan conflict? ● Here is the dilemma. When party competition is close and elections are hard fought, partisanship conflict grows and civility and bipartisanship decline. But is party competition that gives people real choices about the future what serves democracy best? ● If we yearn for a peaceful and civil form of politics, must we do without real party conflict over who shall run the government and what policies should be established? ● Is the dominance by a single party—such as the Republican dominance from 1896 to 1932 and the Democrats from 1936 to the early 1970s—the only way to have cooperation, compromise, and comity across party lines?

Sources: Headline and quotes are from Jennifer C. Kerr, "Democrats Insist Republicans Pull Bush Ad," *Associated Press,* November 23, 2003. Material on party strategies is from Matt Bai, "Turnout Wins Elections," *The New York Times Sunday Magazine* (November 14, 2003), pp. 100–102; Dan Balz, "The GOP's Big Plan," *The Washington Post National Edition* (June 30, 2003), pp.13–14; "Politics as Warfare," *The Economist* (November 8, 2003), pp. 15–18; Stanley B. Greenberg, *The Two Americas: Our Current Political Deadlock and How to Break It* (New York: Thomas Dunne Books, 2004).

party, moreover, has a stable core set of voters from groups concerned about particular issues and problems and committed to particular government policies. The result is a party system composed of parties less ideologically focused and identifiable than the parties in other democratic countries, but with significant and growing ideological and policy differences between them nevertheless.[24]

Ideology may be understood as a coherently organized set of beliefs about the fundamental nature of the good society and the role government ought to play in achieving it. Commonly in other Western democracies, the major parties are closely associated with an ideology—an organized set of beliefs about the fundamental nature of the good society and the role government ought to play in achieving it—in the sense that their activists, members, and officeholders identify with it, campaign with themes based on its ideas, and are guided by it in their governmental actions. Socialist and Labor parties often line up in elections against Liberal and Conservative or Catholic parties, with Marxist, Christian Socialist, Monarchist, Neo-Fascist, Nationalist, and other parties entering into the contest as well.

Ideological contests in the European manner are not the norm in U.S. elections because both American parties share many of the same fundamental beliefs: free enterprise, individualism, the Constitution, the Bill of Rights, and so on. Nevertheless, the differences between Democrats and Republicans on many issues—especially on affirmative action, abortion, the environment, taxes, gay rights, and the role of government in the economy—are real, important, and enduring, and are becoming much more distinctive. (See "The Rise of Partisan Conflict" for an examination of party ideological differences and how they help fuel the contest between Democrats and Republicans.)

Let's see how ideological and policies differences manifest themselves in our political parties.

Ideology and Party in Public Perceptions

liberal

The political position that holds that the federal government has a substantial role to play in economic regulation, social welfare, and overcoming racial inequality.

conservative

The political position that holds that the federal government ought to play a very small role in economic regulation, social welfare, and overcoming racial inequality.

Ideology and Party in Public Perceptions   For one thing, the Democratic and Republican parties differ in the electorate's perceptions of them; 64 percent of Americans, for example, report that they see the parties as different on a whole range of issues.[25] Most accurately see the Democrats as the more **liberal** party (in the sense of favoring an active federal government, helping citizens with jobs, education, medical care, and the like) and the Republicans as the more **conservative** party (opposing such government activism and supporting business).[26] Democrats, moreover, are much more likely to say they are liberals; Republicans are much more likely than others to say they are conservative. Additionally, those Americans who classify themselves as liberals overwhelmingly support Democratic candidates; self-described conservatives overwhelmingly support Republicans. This association of liberalism with the Democrats and conservatism with the Republicans is growing stronger all the time.[27]

Ideology in Party Platforms   Our parties also tend to write different political platforms at their conventions. Scholars have discovered persistent differences in the platforms of the two parties in terms of rhetoric (Republicans tend to talk more about opportunity and freedom), issues (Democrats worry more about poverty and social welfare), and the public policies advocated.[28]

The Ideologies of Party Activists   The activists of one party are quite different in their views from activists and voters in the other party, as well as the general public. Republican delegates to the 2004 Republican National Convention, for example, as in all recent conventions, were more conservative than Republican voters and much more conservative than the average registered voter. They were also much more hostile to affirmative action, same-sex marriage, social spending programs, and gun control than Republican voters and registered voters in general. Analogously, delegates to the Democratic National Conven-tion were more liberal than Democratic voters and registered voters and much more favorable to gun control, affirmative action, gay rights, and a woman's right to an abortion than the other two groups.[29]

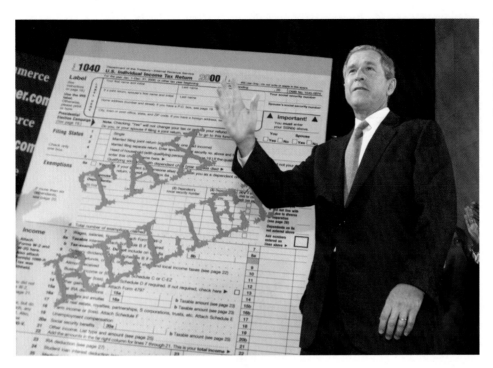

One of the main pillars of Republican party ideology is the idea that federal taxes are too high for efficient economic performance and need to be cut. President George W. Bush has been a strong advocate of this position.

Party Ideologies in Action   Finally, the parties differ in what they do when they win. Republican members of Congress tend to vote differently from Democrats, the former being considerably more conservative on domestic issues. This difference translates into public policy. Republicans and Democrats produce different policies on taxes, corporate regulation, and social welfare when they are in power.[30] These differences will be explored further in Chapter 11 on Congress.

Growing Ideological Differences Between the Parties   The Republican party has become much more ideologically cohesive and conservative since the mid-1970s, advocating free markets and less regulation, low taxes, a halt to most abortions, diminished social spending, opposition to affirmative action, and a hard line on "law and order." The party seems to have settled on an outlook in which government helps create a society where individuals are free to pursue their own happiness and to take the consequences if they fail, without government providing a minimum standard of living below which people cannot fall. This growing conservatism is a product of the increasing influence in the party of the business community, anti-tax and anti-big government advocacy groups, the white South and suburbs, and Christian evangelicals. It is also a product of the declining influence in party affairs of the northeastern states, the traditional breeding ground of GOP moderates (represented in the past by such figures as Nelson Rockefeller of New York and John Chafee of Rhode Island).[31] And, similar to ideological parties in Europe, Republican party leaders in Congress have successfully imposed party discipline on important legislative votes, particularly in the House of Representatives, using ideological appeals and campaign funds as carrots and harsh discipline of dissenters from the party line as the stick.[32]

The Democratic party is split between a very liberal wing—found among Democratic activists, party officeholders in the non-Southern states, and in members of Congress—and a more "centrist" wing—represented by the Democratic Leadership Council (of which Bill Clinton and Al Gore were prominent members). The liberal wing supports traditional Democratic party programs in which government plays a central role in societal improvement, leveling the playing field for all Americans regardless of race or gender, encouraging economic growth, protecting union jobs, providing substantial social safety nets, and protecting civil liberties. The centrist wing of the party opposes racial quotas and set-asides and supports lower taxes, free trade, deregulation, and a crackdown on crime, thus blurring the lines between itself and Republicans. During the Clinton years, the president and congressional Democrats, not surprisingly, often found themselves at loggerheads, especially over the budget, welfare reform, and trade. The trade issue has been particularly divisive for Democrats, with free traders such as Clinton and Gore faced off against organized labor and environmentalists, important parts of the party base.

The Parties in Government and in the Electorate

Fearful of the tyrannical possibilities of a vigorous government, the framers designed a system of government in which power is so fragmented and competitive that effectiveness is unlikely. One of the roles that political parties can play in a democracy such as ours is to overcome this deadlock by persuading officials of the same party in the different branches of government to cooperate with one another on the basis of party loyalty.[33] The constitutionally designed conflict between the president and Congress can be bridged, it has been argued, when a single party controls both houses of Congress and the presidency.

We will learn in considerable detail what parties do in government in later chapters on Congress (Chapter 11), the president (Chapter 12), the executive branch (Chapter 13), and the courts (Chapter 14). In general, we will see that the parties only partially improve the cohesiveness and responsiveness of our government. The parties seem to be the best institutions we have for making government work in a cohesive and responsive fashion—that is, when the same party controls the legislative and executive branches—but they do not consistently do the job very well.

The Problem of Divided Government

For much of the last half century, Republicans controlled the presidency, while Democrats controlled one or both houses of Congress. After the 1994 election, the situation reversed, with Republicans gaining control of Congress and Democrats retaining the presidency (see Figure 9.3). After the 2000 elections, unified government returned for a few months until moderate Vermont Republican Senator James Jeffords quit his party, giving the Democrats control of the Senate. (Republicans retained control of the House and the presidency.) The 2002 congressional elections resulted in a return to unified government when the GOP won both houses of Congress.

Divided party control of the federal government has worried scholars and journalists for many years and has produced a substantial amount of litera-

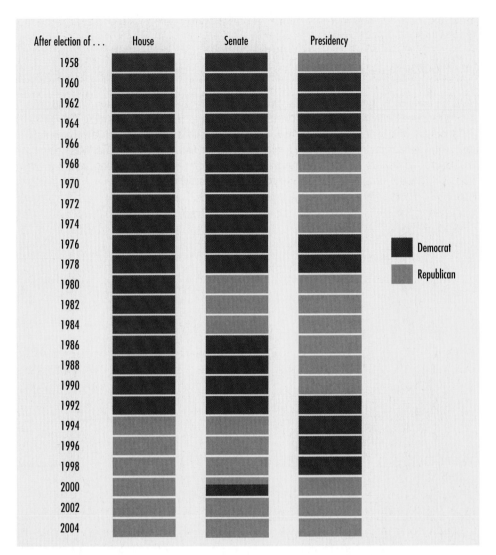

FIGURE 9.3 • **Party Control of Congress and the Presidency**

One of the most striking things about our recent political history was the existence of split party control of the presidency and Congress. Scholars disagree about the effects of this development: Some believe it crippled the government; others say split party control made no difference.

ture that examines its causes and assesses its effects.[34] (See "Using the Framework" feature on why gridlock happens.) Many scholars and journalists believe the effects to be unfortunate. At best, they suggest, divided party control added to the gridlock and paralysis that are built into the constitutional design of our system of government.[35] At worst, they suggest, divided party control gave rise to a state of near civil war between the two branches, in which each tries to damage the other in the interests of advancing the fortunes of its party.[36]

Some scholars have begun to argue, however, that divided party control was not so very important. They point to cases in which unified party control did not produce good results and cases in which divided control did not prevent the fashioning of coherent policy. Unified party control of government under the Democrats after the 1936 election did not guarantee a vigorous

Using the Framework

Gridlock

Why were things so gridlocked in Washington for most of the 1990s?

Background: In the 1990s, official Washington not only seemed to come to a screeching halt, but there was a dramatic decline in the atmosphere of civility in Congress and in the relations between Congress and the president. Fierce partisan warfare broke out over President Clinton's health care proposal, the federal budget (which led to the closure of the federal government at one point), foreign policy issues (Haiti, Bosnia, Kosovo, and the Test Ban Treaty), abortion and, of course, the impeachment and trial of the president. Taking a look at how structural, political linkage, and governmental factors affect party politics and policymaking in Washington will help explain the situation. The role of strong parties in a divided government is especially noteworthy.

Governmental Action

Government inaction on the nation's agenda in the 1990s.

Governmental Level

Democratic President Bill Clinton and the Republican-controlled 104th, 105th, and 106th Congresses battled over most important issues, reaching agreement on only a few of them.

Political Linkages Level

Neither party had a commanding lead in party identification nationally. → Congressional elections became very close and hotly contested, with control of Congress hanging in the balance every two years. → The political parties became more ideological, with the virtual disappearance of conservative Democrats in the South and Mountain West and liberal Republicans in New England. → Partisan warfare and scandals became standard fare in the mass media, making cooperation and civility in public affairs, in general, and between the parties, in particular, less likely.

Structural Level

The Constitution created a system in which tension always exists between the president and Congress. → The end of the Cold War ended the semi-crisis atmosphere that encouraged the political parties in Congress, and the Congress and the president, to cooperate with one another on a wide range of issues.

How Democratic Are We?

Political Parties and Responsive Government

PROPOSITION: American political parties don't ensure that government is responsive and responsible to the people.

AGREE: Our parties are so loose and fragmented in an organizational sense, and often so mushy in an ideological sense, that voters do not know what they are getting when they put a party in office and cannot be assured that the majority party will be able to carry out its program, even if it wanted to do so. Democrat Bill Clinton, for example, campaigned as a liberal in the 1992 presidential campaign but ended up advocating free trade, balanced budgets, and a cautious approach to affirmative action. In addition, parties don't seem to be able to do much to overcome the constraints on bold initiatives created by our system of separation of powers and checks and balances, even when one party is in control of several branches of government. For example, George W. Bush's attempt to fashion a new energy policy for the United States was killed in Congress in 2003, despite the fact that his party—the Republicans—controlled both the House and the Senate. Things are even worse when Republicans control one branch of government and the Democrats control the other. Partisan warfare and gridlock in Washington are the most common result of this division of power between the parties.

DISAGREE: Our parties are the only mechanism we have for allowing voters to decide on a program for the government and to hold a group or team of elected officials responsible for their actions. Though flawed, parties are the only instrument that people have for doing this. Interest groups and social movements are much too narrow; only parties seek to be inclusive and present broad programs for public approval. Moreover, the parties are becoming better organized and more ideologically distinctive, so voters increasingly know what they are getting when they put a party in office. To be sure, divided government often leads to gridlock when strong parties exist, but this is simply an argument that people ought to vote along party lines and have a single party control the entire government.

CONSIDER: Political scientists tend to believe that strong political parties are an essential part of democracy.

- Are you persuaded that political parties are important for democracy?   • If you believe they are important for democracy, how well do you think our existing parties carry out their responsibilities?   • Does the increasing intensity of partisan conflict in the United States appeal to you as a way to simplify electoral and policy choices, or do you find yourself turned off, wishing that the overlap between Democrats and Republicans were greater and that bipartisanship might play a larger part in American politics today?   • If you believe that parties are important in a democracy, but they are not fulfilling their role very well, what would you do to change what they do?   • Are we stuck with parties as they are, or can they be changed to better serve citizens?

and effective federal government in the last years of Roosevelt's New Deal. Democratic presidents Carter and Clinton did not produce impressive periods of government performance even when both enjoyed Democratic majorities in Congress. There is some evidence, moreover, that gridlock is no more prominent in periods of divided party control than in periods of unified control.[37] Having completed their studies before the appearance of intense partisan gridlock in the middle and late 1990s, however, these scholars may have seriously underestimated the detrimental effects of divided government. Anyone witnessing the closing of the federal government during the presidential–congressional budget battles during the Clinton years and the intensely partisan impeachment process to remove President Clinton from office cannot feel sanguine about divided government.

Parties in the Electorate

Parties are not only organizations and officeholders but also images in the minds of voters and potential voters, mental cues that affect the behavior of the electorate. This aspect of the parties was discussed in Chapter 5 and will be considered in greater detail in Chapter 10. We will simply reiterate the points that fewer Americans than in the past are inclined to identify with or to have confidence in a party but that those who still identify themselves as Republicans or Democrats feel more strongly about this identification and divide more clearly along the lines of ideology and policy preferences. This odd combination of growing indifference toward the parties and withdrawal from active participation among one group of Americans (mainly independents), and an intensification of commitment and partisanship among party identifiers and activists, is helping contribute to a more volatile and conflict-ridden politics in the United States, a theme we will return to over the course of this text.

Summary

The American party system is unique among the Western democracies in several respects. First, ours is a relatively pure two-party system and has been so since the 1830s. Second, our major parties are candidate centered, having very little power in their national party organizations to affect the behavior of individual candidates, officeholders, or state and local party organizations. American parties are less ideologically coherent than parties in other democracies, but the enduring and important differences between Democrats and Republicans are very important and becoming more pronounced.

Although American politics has been dominated by the same two parties for almost a century and a half, the two-party system has not been stagnant. It has undergone a series of realignments, spurred by structural changes in society and the economy, in which the relative power of the parties has shifted, as have the voting alignments of the public, the dominant political coalitions, and government policies.

The parties play an important role in government, sometimes contributing to governmental effectiveness and policy coherence. In the era of divided government, however, parties often contribute to gridlock.

Suggestions for Further Reading

Burnham, Walter Dean. *Critical Elections and the Mainsprings of American Politics*. New York: Norton, 1970.
   The classic analysis of the realignment process in the American party system.

Gould, Lewis. *Grand Old Party: A History of the Republicans*. New York: Random House, 2003.
   A comprehensive history of the Republican party in the United States.

Greenberg, Stanley B. *The Two Americas: Our Current Political Deadlock and How to Break It*. New York: Thomas Dunne Books, 2004.
   A bold plan for breaking the politics of parity by one of the Democratic Party's leading strategists.

Hershey, Marjory, and Paul Allen Beck. *Party Politics in America*, 10th ed. New York: Longman Publishers, 2003.
   A new edition of the leading political parties textbook in the United States; comprehensive, detailed, yet engaging.

Mayhew, David R. *Divided We Govern: Party Control, Lawmaking, and Investigations, 1946–1990*. New Haven, CT: Yale University Press, 1991.
   A sophisticated attempt to assess the effect of divided government. Argues that the alarm about divided government has been overstated.

Menefee-Libey, David. *The Triumph of Campaign-Centered Politics*. New York: Chatham House, 2000.
   A vivid description of how the requirements of modern campaign politics have changed the political parties.

Rosenstone, Steven J., Ray L. Behr, and Edward T. Lazarus. *Third Parties in America: Citizen Response to Major Party Failure*. Princeton, NJ: Princeton University Press, 1996.
   A rigorous analysis of the conditions under which third parties and independent candidates emerge in American politics.

Witcover, Jules. *Party of the People: A History of the Democrats*. New York: Random House, 2003.
   A comprehensive history of the Democratic party in the United States.

Internet Sources

Democratic National Committee
www.democrats.org/
   Information about Democratic party candidates, party history, convention and national committees, state parties, stands on the issues, affiliated groups, upcoming events, and more.

The Green Party
www.greenpartyus.org
   News about the Green Party and links to state and local Green-affiliated groups.

National Political Index
http://www.politicalindex.com/
   Links to state and local parties and affiliated organizations and interest group, as well as news and information about the parties.

Political Resources on the Web
www.politicalresources.net/
   Information about political parties in all democratic countries.

Republican National Committee
http://www.rnc.org/
   Information about Republican party candidates, party history, convention and national committees, state parties, stands on the issues, affiliated groups, upcoming events, and more.

The Reform Party
www.reformparty.org/
   Learn about Reform Party candidates, proposals, and issue positions.

Chapter 10
Participation, Voting, and Elections

In This Chapter

- What the role of elections is in a democracy
- How African Americans, women, and young people won the right to vote
- Why many Americans don't vote
- How to run for the presidency
- What part money plays in presidential elections
- How voters decide
- Why elections matter

Bush Wins the 2004 Presidential Election

After a bruising, bitter, and closely contested race with Democrat John Kerry, Republican George W. Bush was reelected to the presidency in 2004. The campaign was one of the most intense in recent American history—and certainly the longest and most expensive. Unlike the disputed election of 2000 (when he received about 500,000 fewer votes than Al Gore), Bush won both Electoral College and popular vote majorities in 2004; roughly 3.5 million more people voted for him than for Kerry.

To many Americans, the campaign seemed to go on forever. Bush and Kerry battled for almost eight months; they opened their campaigns against each other in early March 2004 and carried on through election day on November 2. Typically, presidential contests come up to full speed in the days following the late-summer Republican and Democratic nominating conventions. In this election, however, each of the parties' presidential nominees was known early: Bush because he was running unopposed for the presidential nomination in the Republican Party and Kerry because he had enough primary wins by early March to virtually sew up the Democratic Party nomination. This happened because the Democratic primaries were "front-loaded;" that is, most were squeezed into the period between late January and early March, a strategy decided upon by party professionals as a way to choose their candidate early and avoid intraparty blood-letting. The strategy worked; Kerry locked up the nomination a full four months before the Democratic convention in July. Knowing that Kerry was to be the eventual Democratic nominee, the Bush campaign and associated advocacy groups were concentrating on him by mid-March. Assured of the nomination, Kerry ignored the handful of Democratic presidential hopefuls who remained on primary ballots in states that had not yet voted and turned his full attention to attacking the Bush record.

The two campaigns were able to launch into full-scale attack mode because the official campaign organizations, state and national party organizations, and associated advocacy groups were loaded with money. Bush had amassed a war chest of more than $200 million for his uncontested nomination campaign; Kerry, who had to mortgage his house to keep his campaign going in February, recovered nicely by mid-March and managed to raised more than $100 million for his pre-convention campaign against the president, 30 percent of the total coming from Internet donations. Counting additional funds for the post-convention period, the Bush campaign raised $273 million; Kerry raised almost as much—$249 million—making him the best-financed challenger ever.

In part, the Bush and Kerry campaigns were able to raise these enormous sums because of changes in the campaign finance system under the McCain-Feingold law, which doubled the amount of money individuals could contribute to federal candidates and increased what they could give to party organizations. Each of the candidates' campaign organizations, as well as national, state, and congressional party organizations, used these changes to great advantage, raising more money than had ever been raised before in a presidential election. Adding to the money glut were so-called 527 advocacy organizations, such as Swift Boat Veterans for Truth (anti-Kerry) and MoveOn.com (anti-Bush), able to raise and spend unlimited amounts of money for the expression of political views. Politically committed superwealthy individuals gave staggering amounts to 527s: Ohio businessman Peter Lewis gave $23 million to anti-Kerry organizations, and Texas oil magnate T. Boone Pickens added over $3 million; financier George Soros gave more than $15 million to anti-Bush groups.[1] Union, corporate, and interest group PACs, moreover, raised more money for the campaign than they ever had before, adding to the flood. In the end, spending by all concerned was conservatively estimated to have topped $1.2 billion—30 percent greater than in 2000—making it the most expensive presidential election in American history.[2]

Changes in the campaign finance rules were only part of the reason for the surge in campaign giving. What drove the process more than anything else was the fierce partisanship that has come to characterize American political life, a subject addressed throughout this book. Each side of the partisan divide was convinced that the stakes were very high in the 2004 election. For many Democrats, Bush was an illegitimate president, chosen in 2000 not by the American people, but by the Supreme Court. He was even less worthy of support, in the eyes of many Democrats, because of what they perceived to be the president's unilateralist foreign policy, which had alienated allies; record tax cuts for the wealthy and the return of massive federal government deficits; an unnecessary and botched war in Iraq; and growing dangers to civil liberties by the anti-terrorism steamroller. A Bush victory, moreover, seemed to portend further erosions in the wall separating church and state and a new Supreme Court that would overturn *Roe* v. *Wade.* For many Republicans, a Kerry victory seemed to portend the creation of massive new government programs, increases in taxes, more support for gay rights and abortions, additional regulations hampering business, and, perhaps most important of all, weakness and lack of resolve in the war on terrorism.

It is hardly surprising—given the level of partisan rancor, the widespread sense that the outcome of the election would determine the shape of American domestic and foreign policy for years to come, generous campaign war chests on both sides, and the proliferation of well-funded, single-issue, and ideological 527 organizations—that 2004 proved to be one of the nastiest and most uncivil races in recent memory. Although 2004 would not match the level of vitriol that characterized the elections of 1800, 1860, 1896, and 1932, it was bad enough. Each side attacked not only the policies and qualifications of the other party's candidate, but his basic honesty and integrity, moral character, values, courage, and commitment to constitutional values. It was not a pretty sight, to be sure.

Not surprisingly—given the high level of partisanship; the widespread sense that this election would have important consequences for the future of the nation; and the unprecedented effort by the campaigns, the parties, and 527 organizations to get their base to the polls—voting turnout was very high. More than 120 million Americans cast ballots, roughly 60 percent of voting-age-eligible Americans, the highest percentage since the 1968 election. Most experts assumed that this high turnout—bringing more independent and younger voters to the polls—would benefit the Democratic candidate, John Kerry. In the end, however, the higher turnout failed to deliver a Kerry victory, as new voters were equally likely to vote for Bush as for Kerry.

Finally, the 2004 election demonstrated once again that presidents are chosen by electoral votes, not popular votes, which explains why the campaigns focused almost all their efforts in a handful of so-called battleground states, where the contest between Kerry and Bush was close. States strongly in the camp of one party or the other—California and New York for the Democrats, for example, and Texas, Utah, and Indiana for the Republicans—hardly saw a television campaign ad or had a visit from either of the candidates. Closely contested states, especially Florida, Pennsylvania, Ohio, Michigan, Minnesota, Wisconsin, Iowa, and New Mexico, were inundated. In the end, the 2004 campaign was waged primarily in this handful of states.

Thinking Critically About This Chapter

The story of the 2004 presidential election focuses our attention on the issue of democratic control of the national government through the electoral process and on the degree to which the public participates in this key activity of the representative democratic process.

Using the Framework   You will see in this chapter that elections are affected by the different rates of participation of groups in American society and how structural factors such as constitutional rules, unequal access to resources, and cultural ideas help determine why some groups participate more than others. You will also learn how elections affect the behavior of public officials.

Using the Democracy Standard   We suggest in this chapter that elections are the lynchpin of any discussion about the democratic quality of any system of government because they are, in theory, what makes popular sovereignty possible. You will see in this chapter that while elections in the United States do much to make our system democratic, they fall short of their democratic promise.

Elections and Democracy

Elections are fundamental to democratic politics, the chief means by which citizens control what their government does. Many important struggles for democracy in the United States have involved conflicts over the right to vote. But can elections actually ensure that governments will do what their people want?

Democratic theorists have suggested several ways that elections in a two-party system like that found in the United States can bring about popular control of government. We will briefly discuss three of these ways, indicating how they might work in theory and what might go wrong in practice.[3] The rest of this chapter is concerned with what actually happens in American national elections and with the question of whether these elections really bring about popular control of government.

The Prospective (or Responsible Party) Voting Model

The idea of **responsible party** elections is based on the old commonsense notion that elections should present a "real choice": Political parties should stand for different policies, the voters should choose between them, and the winning party should carry out its mandate. Political scientists call this the **prospective voting model,** meaning that voters are interested in and capable of deciding what government will do in the future.

responsible party
A political party that takes clear, distinct stands on the issues and enacts them as policy when in office.

prospective voting model
A theory of democratic elections in which voters decide what government will do in the near future by choosing one or another responsible party.

Theory   For this system to work perfectly, each of the two parties must be cohesive and unified; each must take clear policy positions that differ significantly from the other party's positions; citizens must accurately perceive these positions and vote on the basis of them; and the winning party, when it takes office, must do exactly what it said it would do. If all these conditions are met, then the party with the more popular policy positions will win and enact its program. In such an electoral system, government will do what the majority of the voters want.[4]

Problems   Even if an election were to work exactly as the responsible party ideal dictates, however, a serious problem arises. There is no actual guarantee that either party would take policy positions that pleased the voters, only that the winning party's stand is less *unpopular* than the loser's. Also, crucial decisions about what the parties stand for and what choices they present to the voters would be made by someone other than ordinary citizens—by party leaders or perhaps by interest groups and big contributors.

Moreover, the conditions under which responsible party government is supposed to work do not fully exist in the United States. American voters, for example, do not vote solely on the issues or on ideology, as the prospective voting model requires them to do, because they take other things into account when casting their ballots, including candidate personalities. Moreover, the parties do not always keep their promises once in office. Even if the parties fully intend to keep their promises, they sometimes fail to do so because they are unable to win control of the entire government in our system of separated powers—a precondition of any effort to transform campaign promises into policies. And, when there is divided government—for example, when there is a Democratic President and a Republican-controlled Congress—the existence of distinctive and highly competitive political parties will almost always lead to gridlock, so that few policies promised in an election campaign can be put into effect.

There is an additional problem with the prospective voting model that its adherents did not anticipate: As the Republican and Democratic parties become more internally coherent in terms of policy preferences and ideology—which we suggested in Chapter 9 is happening—political conflict becomes more intense and impassioned because the stakes for each party in the outcome of elections become much more important. If the other party wins control of the government, even if it does so by a razor-thin margin, the party out of power has more to lose. The party in power can make policies to which the party out of power objects very strongly. This is one of the reasons contemporary politics in the United States increasingly is characterized by intense partisanship and incivility.

Clearly, then, the responsible party idea does not correspond exactly to what happens in American elections. But we will see that it comes close enough to the truth to describe at least a part of reality. Also, theories about responsible parties provide some useful standards for judging what may be wrong with U.S. elections and how they might be improved, particularly with respect to the clarity of stands on issues.

The Electoral Competition Voting Model

electoral competition model
A form of election in which parties seeking votes move toward the median voter or the center of the political spectrum.

median voter
Refers to the voter at the exact middle of the political spectrum.

A very different, and less obvious, sort of democratic control can be found in what political scientists call the **electoral competition** or **median voter model** of democratic elections. In this sort of electoral model, unified parties compete for votes by taking the *most popular* positions they can. They do so by trying to take positions that will appeal to the median voter at the exact midpoint of the political spectrum. Both parties are therefore likely to end up standing for the *same* policies: those favored by the most voters.

Theory   Scholars have proved mathematically that if citizens' preferences are organized along a single dimension (such as the liberal–conservative continuum shown in Figure 10.1), and if parties purely seek votes, both parties will take positions exactly at the *median* of public opinion, that is, at the

FIGURE 10.1 • Electoral Competition Model

This model suggests that in the interest of winning the election, parties will move toward the median voter (where most votes are to be found) as the campaign progresses.

point where exactly one-half the voters are more liberal and one-half are more conservative. If either party took a position even a bit away from the median, the other party could easily win more votes by taking a position closer to the median.[5]

If electoral competition drives parties together in this way, and if they keep their promises, then, in theory, it should not matter which party wins; the winner enacts the policies that the most voters want. Democracy is ensured by the hidden hand of competition, much as efficiency is ensured by competitive markets, according to standard economic theory.

To be sure, electoral competition processes cannot ensure that the parties will educate voters about issues or try to mobilize them to participate, as in the prospective/responsible party model. However, they hold out the promise that popular sovereignty and a perfectly democratic outcome—rather than just the lesser of two evils—may result from elections.

Problems   Again, however, the conditions needed for electoral competition to work perfectly are not likely to be met in the real world. Electoral competition ensures democratic control only if the parties are unified and take stands on the issues for pure and direct vote-seeking reasons; it can break down if the parties are fragmented or ambiguous, if they care about policies for ideological reasons rather than for reasons of securing the most votes, or if they seek contributors' dollars rather than citizens' votes. In order for democratic control to be complete, everyone has to vote. Moreover, the voters must consider nothing but the issues (e.g., not being distracted by candidates' personalities or images) and must know exactly where the parties stand. And the parties have to keep their promises. There are reasons to doubt that any of these things will happen flawlessly.

Still, we will see that these conditions are close enough to the truth so that electoral competition does work, to a significant extent, in real elections. Indeed, electoral competition is probably one of the main reasons that government policy is significantly influenced by public opinion. Also, by looking at how actual elections deviate from the theoretical ideal of electoral competition (e.g., how money and campaign contributions sometimes push parties away from popular policies, or how politicians can sometimes fool the median voter about their real position on the issues[6]), we can see specific ways in which American elections might be improved as instruments of democracy.

The Retrospective (or Reward and Punishment) Voting Model

A third process by which elections might bring about democratic control of government is **electoral reward and punishment,** a form of election in which voters judge how well a group in power has governed and decide if they want this group to continue in office.

electoral reward and punishment
The tendency to vote for the incumbents when times are good and against them when times are bad.

Theory   Here the idea is that the voters simply make **retrospective,** backward-looking judgments about how well incumbent officials have done in the past, rewarding success with reelection and punishing failure by throwing the incumbents out. The result, in theory, is that politicians who want to stay in office have strong incentives to bring about peace and prosperity and to solve problems that the American people want solved. Politicians' ambitions force them to anticipate what the public wants and to accomplish it.[7]

retrospective voting
A form of election in which voters look back at the performance of a party in power and cast ballots on the basis of how well it did in office.

The reward-and-punishment process of democratic control has the advantage of simplicity. It requires very little of voters: no elaborate policy preferences, no study of campaign platforms, just judgments of how well or how badly things have been going. Also, like electoral competition, it relies on politicians'

According to exit polls, voters cast their ballots in the 1980 election to remove President Jimmy Carter from office, rather than to choose the conservative future offered by GOP candidate Ronald Reagan. Their vote of "no confidence" for Carter is an excellent example of "retrospective" voting.

selfishness rather than their altruism. It allows time for deliberation, and it lets leaders try out experimental or temporarily unpopular policies, as long as the results work out well and please the public in time for the next election.

Problems   However, reward and punishment may be a rather blunt instrument. It gets rid of bad political leaders only after (not before) disasters happen, without guaranteeing that the next leaders will be any better. It relies on politicians *anticipating* the effects of future policies, which they cannot always do successfully. Moreover, the reward-and-punishment process focuses only on the most prominent issues and may leave room for unpopular policies on matters that are less visible. It may also encourage politicians to produce deceptively happy but temporary results that arrive just in time for Election Day and then fade away.

Imperfect Electoral Democracy

We will see that each of the three processes of democratic control we have discussed works, to some extent, in American elections. On occasion, even, the three processes converge and help produce an election that is enormously consequential for the direction of the nation. The 1932 election was one of these occasions, and is described in the "Using the Framework" feature on page 276.

But none of the three processes works well enough to guarantee perfectly democratic outcomes most of the time. In certain respects, they conflict: Responsible parties and electoral competition, for example, tend to push in opposite directions. In other respects, all three processes require similar conditions that are not met in reality.

To pin down politicians' responsibility, all three require more unified political parties than we actually have. Similarly, they cannot ensure government responsiveness to all citizens unless *all* citizens have the right to vote and exercise that right. Unfortunately, millions of Americans cannot or do not go to the polls. Their voices are not heard; political equality is not achieved.

Another problem with our system of elections was brought to public attention by the chaos and uncertainty of the 2000 presidential election in Florida: Not all ballots cast by voters are actually counted. For a variety of reasons, ranging from lack of voter education to confusing ballot layouts and malfunctioning voting machines, a number of ballots in every election in the United States are disqualified and not included in the final vote tally. In 2000, from 4 to 6 million votes of the roughly 100 million cast nationally were not counted.[8] Worse yet, especially for the democratic norm of political equality, the votes of poor people and members of racial minorities were three times more likely than those of other Americans to be uncounted in the 2000 election.[9]

Finally, another problem for all three democratic election models is that money, organizational resources, and active campaigning—not just citizens' policy preferences and votes—may influence the stands that parties take and the outcomes of elections. Thus, money givers, activists, and the leaders of organized groups may have more influence than ordinary citizens do; again, political equality is not realized.

The Nature of American Elections

American elections differ quite dramatically from those of most other democratic countries. The differences are the result of rules—mainly found in the Constitution but also in federal statutes and judicial decisions—that define offices and tell how elections are to be conducted. Here are the distinguishing features of elections in the United States:

Comparing Voting and Elections

The United States Has More Elections Than Any Other Democratic Country
In some sense, we are "election happy" in the United States. We not only elect the president and members of Congress (senators and representatives), but

Web Exploration
Party Platforms and Electoral Theory

Issue: According to democratic theorists, elections can ensure popular accountability in representative democracies in three ways: by allowing the public to choose between future courses of action (responsible party government), by allowing voters to render judgments about a party's performance in office (electoral reward and punishment), and by forcing parties and candidates to offer platforms that conform to what the public wants (electoral competition).

Site: Access the Democratic and Republican National Committees on our Website at **www.ablongman.com/greenberg.** Go to the "Web Explorations" section for Chapter 10, open "Party Platforms and Electoral Theory," then the national committee sites for each party. At each party site, look at the official platforms passed at their respective 2004 conventions.

What You've Learned: How did each party present itself during the 2004 national election cycle in terms of the models of electoral democracy described in this chapter? Did Republicans and Democrats ask voters to choose a future direction for government or ask them to simply make a judgment about the party's past performance? Or did the parties simply try to position themselves in terms of where they judged the voters to be?

Hint: You will probably discover that each of the parties shows signs of trying to do all three, although the emphasis will probably be on one.

Using the Framework

Elections Bring the New Deal

Have elections ever changed the course of American government?

Background: Occasionally in American history, a national election is so consequential that it alters the overall direction of government policy and the role of government in the United States. The election of Franklin Delano Roosevelt and an overwhelmingly Democratic Congress in the 1932 elections was just such a moment. In the first 100 days of his administration, Roosevelt launched his New Deal, convincing Congress to pass bills to regulate the banking and securities industries, to bail out failing banks and protect the deposits of the public, to launch public works and relief efforts, and to provide price supports for farmers. This revolution in the role of the federal government was made possible by the 1932 elections, but to fully understand what happened, structural, political linkage, and governmental factors have to be taken into account.

Governmental Action

The New Deal is launched.

Governmental Level

Franklin Roosevelt interpreted the 1932 election as a mandate for immediate and far-reaching actions by the federal government to meet the crisis of the Great Depression.

Roosevelt mobilized business and labor leaders, as well as the public, behind his emergency program.

The Democratic-controlled Congress, aware of Roosevelt's enormous popularity, and concerned about the national crisis, pass all of the president's emergency measures.

Political Linkages Level

Public opinion strongly supported a greater role for the federal government in fighting the depression.

Social disorder was widespread, leading to concerns that the country was near the point of collapse.

Social movements that demanded government action were growing and making their presence felt.

Democrats won big majorities in the House (313 out of 435 total seats) and the Senate (59 of 96 seats).

Roosevelt won an overwhelming victory in the 1932 presidential election, tallying 472 electoral votes to Hoover's 59.

Structural Level

The 1932 election was held in the midst of the Great Depression, with unemployment reaching 33 percent, bank failures at an all-time high, and industrial and farm production at 50 percent of their levels in the mid-1920s.

The preamble to the Constitution says that the Constitution was intended to create a government that would "...insure Domestic tranquility...[and]...promote the general Welfare."

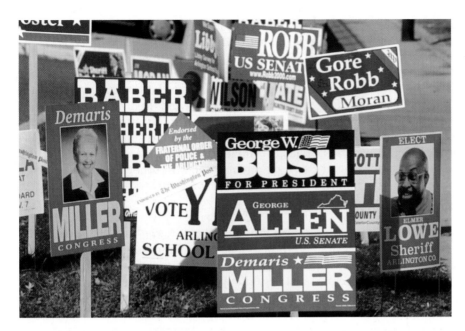

The United States depends more on elections to fill its public offices than other democratic countries, contributing to more frequent elections and longer ballots than elsewhere.

also, being a federal system, we elect governors, state legislators, and (in most states) judges. In addition, state constitutions allow autonomy for counties, cities, and towns, and all of their top officials are elected by the people. We also elect school boards in most places, and the top positions in special districts (e.g., water or conservation districts). And then there are the many state and local ballot initiatives that add to the length and complexity of the ballot at election time.

Elections in the United States Are Separate and Independent from One Another   Not only do we have a multitude of elections, but the election to fill each particular office is separate and independent from the others. In parliamentary systems, one votes for a party, and the party that wins a majority gets to appoint a whole range of other officials. The majority party in the British parliament (the legislative branch), for example, chooses the Prime Minister and cabinet ministers (the executive branch) who run the government. The government, in turn, appoints officials to many posts that are filled by elections here. In the United States, the president and members of Congress are elected independently from one another, as are governors, state legislators, mayors of cities, city councils, and school boards.

Elections Fill Government Positions That Have Fixed Terms of Office   The office of president of the United States is fixed at four years, representatives serve for two years, and senators for six. At the state level, terms of office for all important elected positions are fixed, whether for governors or legislators. The same holds true for county, city, and town elected offices. In parliamentary systems, the government can call an election at any time within a certain number of years (in Britain, it is five years), timing the election to maximize chances for reelection. One implication of fixed elections in the United States is that presidents cannot call for new elections in hopes of changing the party mix in Congress to their advantage. It also means that an unpopular president can stay in office until the next election, since there is no method to remove him other than by impeachment and trial.

National (and Statewide) Elections Are Held on a Fixed Date   The Constitution sets elections for president and members of Congress for the Tuesday after the first Monday in November. States have generally followed suit for election of governors and members of the legislature. One implication, related to the fixed terms of offices described earlier, is that neither presidents nor governors can time elections to their political advantage. Another implication is that Tuesday elections may cut down on participation. In other democracies, elections are held either on the weekend or on days that are declared a national holiday.

Elections in the United States Are Almost Always of the "First Past the Post" Type, in Which Only a Single Person Is Elected   Winners in most elections in the United States are those who win the most votes—not necessarily a majority—in a particular electoral district. This type of election is often called "first past the post," as in a horse race where the winner is the first past the finish line. This includes Congressional elections and presidential contests for electoral votes in each of the states. We do not have proportional representation in national level races, nor do we have "run-off" elections between the top two vote getters in presidential or congressional elections to ensure a majority victor.

Political Participation

In this section, we turn our attention to political participation. For elections to be democratic—whether in the prospective, electoral competition, or retrospective voting models—participation in elections and campaign activities must not only be at high levels, but also must not vary substantially across social groups in the population (i.e., by race, gender, income, occupation, religion, ethnicity, region, and so on), or else the principle of political equality would be violated.

participation
Political activity, including voting, campaign activity, contacting officials, and demonstrating.

unconventional participation
Political activity in the form of demonstrations or protests.

conventional participation
Political activity related to elections (voting, persuading, and campaigning) or to contacting public officials.

Political **participation** is political activity by individual citizens. It includes **unconventional participation,** such as demonstrating, boycotting, and the like (discussed in Chapter 8), and also **conventional participation,** such as writing letters to the editor on political issues, contacting officials, going to public meetings, working in campaigns, and giving money, which we focus on here. The most basic form of conventional political participation, the one that plays the most central part in theories of democratic control through elections, is the act of voting.

Expansion of the Franchise

franchise
The right to vote.

Until passage of the Fourteenth and Fifteenth Amendments after the Civil War, it was up to each state to determine who within its borders was eligible to vote. In the early years of the United States, many of the states limited the legal right to vote—called the **franchise**—quite severely. In fact, a majority of people could not vote at all. Slaves, Native Americans, and women were excluded altogether. In most states, white men without property or who had not paid some set level of taxes were not allowed to vote. In some states early on, white men with certain religious beliefs were excluded.

One of the most important developments in the political history of the United States, an essential part of the struggle for democracy, has been the ex-

Early U.S. elections were poorly organized and hard to get to. In addition, only a small proportion of the population was eligible to vote.

pansion of the right to vote. The extension of the franchise has been a lengthy and uneven process, spanning 200 years.

White Male Suffrage   The first barriers to fall were those concerning property and religion. So strong were the democratic currents during Thomas Jefferson's presidency (1801–1809) and in the years leading up to the election of Andrew Jackson in 1828 that by 1829, property, tax-paying, and religious requirements had been dropped in all states except North Carolina and Virginia. That left universal **suffrage,** or the ability to vote, firmly in place for most adult white males in the United States.[10] Most of Europe, including Britain, did not achieve this degree of democracy until after World War I.

suffrage
The right to vote.

Blacks, Women, and Young People   Despite this head start for the United States compared with the rest of the world, the struggle to expand the suffrage to include African Americans, women, and young people proved difficult and painful. Ironically, universal white male suffrage was often accompanied by the withdrawal of voting rights from black freedmen, even in states that did not permit slavery.[11] It took the bloody Civil War to free the slaves and the Fifteenth Amendment to the U.S. Constitution (1870) to extend the right to vote to all black males, in both North and South. Even so, most blacks were effectively disfranchised in the South by the end of the nineteenth century and remained so until the 1960s civil rights movement and the Voting Rights Act of 1965 (see Chapter 1).

Women won the right to vote in 1920 in all the states with the Nineteenth Amendment to the Constitution, after a long political battle. (See the opening story in Chapter 8 for details of this struggle.) Residents of the District of Columbia were allowed to vote in presidential—but not congressional—elections after 1961, and 18- to 20-year-olds gained the franchise only in 1971.

The result of these changes at the state and national levels was an enormous increase in the proportion of Americans who were legally eligible to vote: from about 23 percent of the adult population in 1788–1789 to nearly 98 percent by the beginning of the 1970s—practically all citizens except people who have recently moved, people in mental institutions, and incarcerated felons. However, the proportion of the voting-age population that is eligible to vote has dropped a bit in recent years, primarily because of the large influx of immigrants into the United States over the past two decades who cannot vote until they become citizens.

Also important in the recent story of the rising ineligibles is the denial of the right to vote for former felons by many states. The rapid rise in the number of felony convictions in recent decades—largely a product of the war on drugs—means that many in the voting-age population are not eligible to vote. To a very large extent, these people tend to be African American and other minority young men. Some critics suggest that people who have paid their debt to society should be able to exercise their full rights as citizens, including voting.[12] Others believe that long-lasting citizenship sanctions against felons are effective deterrents against criminal behavior.

Direct Partisan Elections

A related trend has involved the more direct election of government officials, replacing the old indirect methods that insulated officials from the public. At the same time, the development of a two-party system has clarified choices by focusing citizens' attention on just two alternatives for each office.

electoral college
Representatives of the states who formally elect the president; the number of electors in each state is equal to the total number of its senators and congressional representatives.

The election of the president, even with the existence of the **electoral college,** has become more directly democratic. By the time of the Jefferson–Adams presidential campaign of 1800, which pitted the new Republican and Federalist parties against each other, most state legislatures had stopped picking the presidential electors themselves (as the Constitution permits). Instead, the legislatures allowed a popular vote for electors, most of whom were pledged to support the presidential candidate of one party or the other.

This is the same system we use today: In practically every state, there is a winner-take-all popular vote for a slate of electors—positions usually awarded by each of the political parties to loyal party workers and contributors—who are pledged to a particular presidential candidate. In fact, only the name of the candidate and the party to whom the electors are pledged, not the names of the electors we are actually voting for, appear on the ballot. Thus, when the winning electors meet as the electoral college in their respective states and cast ballots to elect the president, their actions are generally controlled by the popular vote that chose them. This system, odd and cumbersome as it is, almost always ensures that American citizens choose their president more or less directly (though not in the 2000 Bush–Gore election when Bush won the electoral college vote—and thus the presidency—and Gore won the popular vote).

primary election
Statewide elections in which voters choose delegates to the national party conventions; virtually all delegates are pledged to a specific candidate for the party's nomination.

caucus nominating system
A system for selecting delegates to the national party conventions characterized by neighborhood and areawide meetings of party supporters and activists; used in only a handful of states.

By 1840, the parties had started nominating presidential candidates in national conventions instead of congressional caucuses. Later still, the parties began letting voters select many convention delegates directly in state **primary elections** instead of having party activists choose them in political party conventions in each of the states. Today, most delegates to the Republican and Democratic national conventions are selected in primary elections, though a handful of states, including Iowa, use a **caucus nominating system** in which party supporters and activists hold neighborhood and areawide meetings to select delegates. These innovations have probably increased the democratic control of government, although we will see that each of them has anti-democratic features, too.

The direct popular election of U.S. senators did not replace their being chosen by state legislatures until 1913, with the Seventeenth Amendment to the Constitution. Since 1913, all members of the Senate have been subject to direct choice by the voters.

Taken together, the expansion of the franchise and the development of direct, two-party elections have represented major successes in the struggle for democracy. But victory is not yet complete.

Low Voting Turnout

During the first 100 years or so of the United States' existence, not only did more and more people gain the right to vote but also higher and higher proportions of eligible voters actually turned out on election day and voted. It is not easy to be sure of the exact **turnout** percentages because of data inaccuracies and voting fraud, but in presidential elections, the figure of roughly 11 percent of eligible voters who turned out in 1788–1789 jumped to about 31 percent in 1800 (when Thomas Jefferson was first elected) and to about 57 percent in 1828 (Andrew Jackson's first victory). By 1840, the figure had reached 80 percent, and it stayed at about that level until 1896.[13]

The disturbing fact is that today, a much smaller proportion of people vote than did during most of the nineteenth century. Since 1912, only about 50 to 65 percent of Americans have voted in presidential elections (see Figure 10.2) and still fewer in other elections: 40 to 50 percent in off-year (non-presidential-

turnout
The proportion of eligible voters who actually vote in a given election.

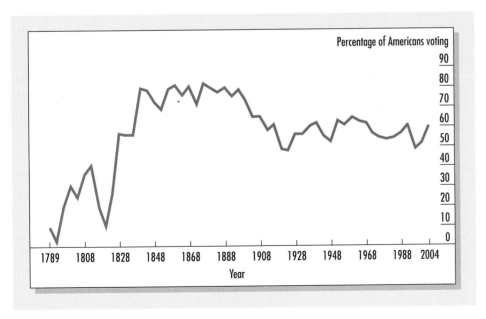

FIGURE 10.2 ● **The Rise and Fall of Turnout in Presidential Elections, 1789–2004**

Turnout in presidential elections rose sharply during the nineteenth century but declined in the twentieth century. In 2004, turnout increased dramatically, but only to levels typical of the 1950s and 1960s.

Sources: U.S. Bureau of the Census; and "Biggest Turnout of Voters Since 1968," The Associated Press, November 3, 2004. From 1920, the Census Bureau has calculated voting turnout as the percentage of the voting age population voting.

In Oregon, voting entirely by mail (or by dropping off ballots in convenient collection boxes) has saved the state money and increased turnout.

Participation

The Prepared Voter Kit

year) congressional elections and as few as 10 to 20 percent in primaries and minor local elections. In recent years, the turnout rate as a percentage of the voting age population has dropped to the lower end of those ranges (it is higher if we calculate turnout in terms of eligible voters), though there was a big jump in 2004. Turnout here is much lower than in most other rich democracies; in western Europe, turnout rates regularly top 75 percent.

Most observers consider low turnout to be a serious problem for democracy in America, particularly because (as we will see) people who vote tend to be different from those who do not.[14] Nonvoters do not get an equal voice in political choices. Political equality, one of the key elements of democracy, is violated.

Causes of Low Turnout Why do so few Americans participate in elections? Scholars have identified several possible factors; most are related to whether they are allowed to vote, whether they are interested in voting, and whether anyone asks them to vote.[15]

Barriers to Voting In the United States, only citizens who take the initiative to register before an election are permitted to vote. People who move from one community to another, for example, must register to vote in their new location. In one presidential election, about 35 percent of the nonvoters, but only 16 percent of voters, said that they had moved in the past two years.[16]

In most European countries with high turnout rates, the government, rather than individual citizens, is responsible for deciding who is listed as eligible to vote and registers them automatically. In some countries, such as Belgium and Italy, moreover, citizens are *required* to vote and may be fined if they don't. Also, in most countries, election days are holidays on which people don't have to go to work.

The United States might increase political equality and popular sovereignty by making voting easier. One way to do so would be to ease registration requirements,[17] perhaps allowing registration by postcard or same-day registration at polling places. It is worth noting that voting turnout in the United States among those who have registered to vote hovers at about 85 percent and that voting participation in states that allow same-day registration is significantly higher than in other states.[18] These findings suggest that the registration requirement for voting is probably a significant barrier to participation, because participation rates go up when such barriers are lowered. The federal "motor voter" law passed in 1993, providing for registration in motor vehicle bureaus and other government offices, represents an important attempt to lower the registration barrier in the United States.

Another way to increase participation would be to ease the voting act itself. Suggestions include making every election day a holiday, as is done in most Western European countries; allowing an extended voting period, such as the two-and-a-half weeks tried in Texas; broadening the right of absentee voting, as in California; or allowing voting by mail over an extended period, as in Oregon.

Lack of Attractive Choices   Some scholars believe that the nature of the political parties and the choices that they offer also affect turnout. Countries with proportional representation and multiparty systems—that is, with diverse and competitive parties from which to choose—have averaged an 83 percent turnout rate, whereas single-district, plurality-vote countries (which usually have just two parties) have had a voter turnout rate that is closer to 70 percent. Many American citizens may not like the candidates of either of the major parties well enough to bother voting for them and see no reason to vote for a third-party or independent candidate who has no chance of winning.

Too Much Complexity   As we suggested earlier, when voters go to the polls in the United States, they must make voting choices for a multitude of federal, state, and local offices and often decide on constitutional and policy measures put on the ballot by state legislatures (called **referenda**) or the public (called **initiatives**), especially in states such as California and Colorado where these are common. Research demonstrates that many potential voters are simply overwhelmed by the complexity of the ballot and stay home.[19]

Alienation   That many Americans felt apathetic toward or alienated from politics and government undoubtedly contributed to the declines in turnout that began in the late 1960s.[20] Such unsettling events as the assassination of popular leaders (John F. Kennedy, Robert Kennedy, Martin Luther King, Jr.), the Vietnam War, urban unrest, and the Watergate and Iran-Contra scandals surely played a role in the decline in voting.[21] More recently, the turn of the mass media to "infotainment" and scandals as staples of what they do has probably discouraged potential voters. Some scholars blame the increase in negative campaign advertising as a leading culprit, although other scholars disagree, saying that such ads sometimes even spur people to vote.[22] One scholar suggests that the recent rise in partisan conflict as our parties become more ideologically coherent is also a part of the low voter turnout story. It seems that a very large number of Americans do not like principled parties and zealous partisan activists and find it more comfortable not to be involved in elections. It is telling that professed independents have lower turnout than those who identify with a party and show the most precipitous declines in voting since the late 1960s.[23]

referenda
Procedures available in some states by which proposed state laws or constitutional amendments are submitted to the voters for approval or rejection.

initiatives
Procedures available in some states for citizens to put proposed laws and constitutional amendment on the ballot for voter approval or rejection.

Lack of General Voter Mobilization by the Parties   Another reason voting turnout is low may be tied to the failure of the political parties to rouse people and get them to the polls to vote. The parties have always been interested, of course, in getting their own supporters to the polls, and doing what they could to keep the opposition away. They have never been in the business of increasing the vote turnout in general as a sort of civic duty. The problem is that aiming at your own voters with highly partisan appeals delivered by mail, telephone, and, increasingly, by e-mail, by highly professionalized but distant party organizations and advocacy groups does not increase turnout among the noncommitted public[24] and may even persuade many of them to stay home, as we suggest in the previous section. As well, old-style, door-to-door canvassing in neighborhoods seems to have been far more effective in raising turnout than modern methods, but it is used less often than in the past (though the parties have recently redoubled their door-to-door convassing efforts).[25]

Campaign Involvement and Contacting Public Officials   Despite the relatively low voter turnout levels in the United States, however, Americans are actually more likely than people in other countries to participate actively in campaigns.[26] During the 1996 presidential campaign, some 7 percent of adults said they gave money to a party or candidate, 9 percent attended political meetings, 10 percent attended a political rally, and 4 percent worked actively in a campaign organization.[27] Much the same thing is true of contacting public officials; about one-third (34 percent) of Americans say they have done so during the past year, most often with local elected officials.[28] Americans are also far more likely than citizens in other democracies to be involved in organizations, of both the private and public variety (see Chapter 7), that play such an important role in our electoral politics.[29]

Who Participates?

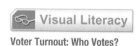

Voter Turnout: Who Votes?

Not all Americans participate equally in politics; the evidence shows that political participation varies a great deal according to people's income, education, age, and ethnicity. This means that some kinds of people have more representation and influence with elected officials than others and, other things being equal, they are more likely to have their preferences and interests reflected in what government does.

Income and Education

For the most part, politically active people tend to be those with higher-than-average incomes and more formal education.[30] These people are also more likely to vote. In 2000, 75 percent of those with incomes of $75,000 or above said they had voted, but only 49 percent of those with incomes under $35,000 said they had done so. In 2000, 75 percent of college graduates reported that they had voted, but only 53 percent of high school graduates and 38 percent of those who had not graduated from high school had done so (see Figure 10.3).

Some statistical analyses have indicated that the crucial factor in voter turnout is level of formal education. When other factors are controlled, college-educated people are much more likely to tell interviewers that they have voted than are the less educated. There are several possible reasons: People with

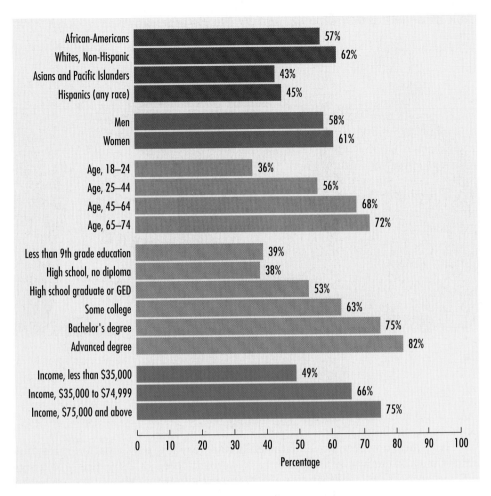

FIGURE 10.3 • **2000 Presidential Election Turnout by Social Group**

Age, education, race, ethnicity, income, and gender all affect voting behavior. Members of certain social groups are more likely to vote in elections than others.

Note: Low income is defined as family income below $25,000; middle income is defined as family income between $25,000 and $75,000; high income is defined as family income above $75,000.

Source: U.S. Bureau of the Census.

more education learn more about politics, are less troubled by registration requirements, and are more confident in their ability to affect political life.

At the same time, citizens with lower incomes are also less likely to work in campaigns, give money, contact officials, and the like. Wealthier Americans, who have more time, more money, and more knowledge of how to get things done, tend to be much more active politically. As a result, they may have more political clout than their fellow citizens.

Race and Ethnicity

In the past, fewer black people than whites voted, but now the proportions are more nearly equal: 62 percent of whites and 57 percent of blacks voted in 2000 (see Figure 10.3). The remaining differences result from blacks' lower average levels of income and education. Blacks are at least equally likely to

Both civil rights organizations and the two major political parties have been increasing their efforts in recent years to register voters from among the rapidly expanding Hispanic population.

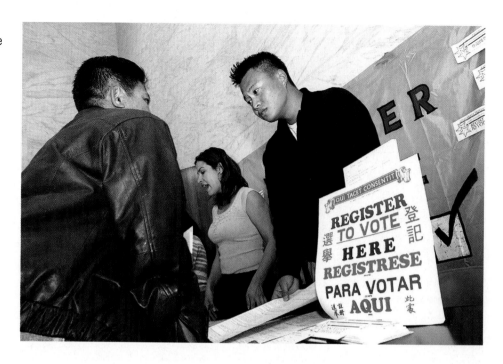

vote, and sometimes more likely, than whites of similar educational and income backgrounds.

Hispanics, however, have historically had very low participation rates, but things may be changing; though only 46 percent voted in 2000, this was a significant jump from 1996 when only 27 reported voting. Many Hispanics are discouraged from participating by low incomes, language problems, or suspicion of government authorities. This recent jump in the turnout rate for Hispanics has made a difference in states where Hispanic voters are concentrated: California, Texas, and Florida. And, both George W. Bush and John Kerry made special efforts to win over this group in their 2004 campaigns, demonstrating its rising importance.

Voting has also been relatively low among Asian Americans; only 43 percent reported voting in 2000. However, Asian American individuals and organizations have become more active in local politics and have increased campaign contributions to candidates and parties.

Age

Age is one of the most important variables explaining why some people vote and others do not. The youngest groups of eligible voters go to the polls much less often than older voters: Only 36 percent of 18- to 24-year-olds did so in 2000, compared with 72 percent of 65- to 74-year-olds. The reasons may be that young people tend to be less rooted in communities, less familiar with registration and voting procedures, less in the habit of voting, and less clear about what stake they have in elections.[31] Or, it may be that no recent candidates have appealed to them. In the 2004 Democratic presidential nomination contest, Howard Dean struck a cord among many young Americans who supported and worked for the Dean campaign, though the extent and durability of this possible increase in youth involvement is unknown at the present time.

Gender

The gender gap in voting and other forms of political participation disappeared in the United States by the end of the 1980s.[32] Indeed, in the 2000 presidential election, women voted at slightly higher rates than men (again, see Figure 10.3). This marks a dramatic change over the past two decades and may be traced to the improvement in the educational attainments of women, the entrance of more women than ever into the paid workforce, and the increased importance of issues such as pay equity and abortion on the American political agenda.

Does It Matter Who Votes?

Some observers have argued that it doesn't matter if many people don't vote because their preferences aren't much different from those who do; the results would be about the same if everyone voted. In some elections, nonvoters have shown support for the same candidate who won, so their votes would apparently have changed nothing,[33] and some surveys have indicated that nonvoters' policy preferences differ little from those of voters.

However, we should not be too quick to accept these arguments, just as few now accept the nineteenth-century view that there was no need for women to vote because their husbands could protect their interests. Even when the expressed preferences of nonvoters or nonparticipators do not look very distinctive, their objective circumstances, and therefore their needs for government services, may differ markedly.[34] Latinos, the young, and those with low incomes might benefit from government programs that are of less interest to other citizens. A political system that included and mobilized these people vigorously might produce quite different government policies. Of course, we cannot be sure, but one sign of what a difference participation can make is that when black Americans won effective voting rights, the number of elected black officials rose sharply and nonblack politicians and officials paid more attention to black constituents (see Chapters 1 and 8).

In any case, broader participation in U.S. elections would increase popular sovereignty and political equality and would thus contribute to democracy. The limited number of Americans who vote and participate in other ways is one major respect in which the struggle for democracy has not fully succeeded.

Campaigning for Office

The ideas we discussed about how elections might ensure democratic policy-making all depend in various ways on what sorts of choices are presented to the voters. It makes a difference what kind of people run for office, whether they take clear policy stands, whether those stands differ from each other, and whether they stand for what the average voter wants. In evaluating how democratic our elections are, therefore, we need to examine what kinds of alternatives are put before the voters in campaigns. In this chapter, we focus on presidential campaigns. Congressional campaigns are addressed in Chapter 11.

Comparing Political Campaigns

Contending for the Party Presidential Nomination

The major party candidates for president of the United States are formally chosen well before the November election and are effectively chosen even before the parties hold nominating conventions. Candidates are drawn from a rather small pool. Despite what some parents tell their children, not every American has a significant chance of becoming president or of being nominated for president by a major party.

Who Has a Chance   In any given presidential election, only a handful of candidates are serious possibilities. So far in American history, these have virtually always been middle-aged or elderly white Protestant men with extensive formal educations, fairly high incomes, and substantial experience as public figures—usually as government officials (especially governors or senators) or military heroes. Movie stars, media commentators, business executives, and others who would be president almost always have to perform lesser government service before they are seriously considered for the presidency. Ronald Reagan, for example, most of whose career was spent acting in motion pictures and on television, served as governor of California before being elected president.

In recent years, the presidency has been practically monopolized by former governors such as Bill Clinton and George W. Bush (who have demonstrated executive ability) and vice presidents (who have had a close look at how the job is done). The single best stepping-stone to becoming president is clearly the vice presidency, which is usually filled by former senators or governors. Since 1900, 5 of the 18 presidents have succeeded from the vice presidency after the president's death or resignation, and two others, Nixon and Bush (the elder), were former vice-presidents elected in their own right.

Serious candidates for president almost invariably represent mainstream American values and policy preferences. Seldom does an "extreme" candidate get very far. Serious candidates are also generally acceptable to the business community and have enthusiastic support from at least some sectors of industry or finance. And they must be considered "presidential" by the news media.

Getting Started   A person who wants to run for the presidency usually begins at least two or three years before the election by testing the waters, asking friends and financial backers if they will support a run, and observing how people react to the mythical "Great Mentioner." A friendly journalist may write that Senator Blathers "has been mentioned" as a smart, attractive, strong candidate; Blathers waits to see whether anyone agrees. The would-be candidate may commission a national survey to check for name recognition and a positive image. He or she may put together an exploratory committee to round up private endorsements, commitments, and financial contributions, perhaps setting up private political action committees to gather money.

You Are a Professional Campaign Manager

If all goes well in the early stages, the presidential aspirant becomes more serious, assembling a group of close advisers, formulating strategy, officially announcing his or her candidacy, forming a fund-raising operation, and putting together organizations ("Draft Blathers" or "Citizens for Blathers" committees) in key states. Early money is crucial to finance organization and advertising and to qualify for federal matching funds later.[35] And it is a clear sign that party big whigs and associated interest groups take the candidacy seriously. For all of these reasons, those who fail to raise early money almost always fail in the first primaries and eventually drop out. By October 1999, months before the first primary, candidate George W. Bush had already gathered $57 million, discouraging several potential rivals, including Elizabeth Dole; running unopposed for renomination as the Republican Party's candidate in the 2004 presidential election, President George W. Bush had collected almost $100 million by the end of 2003 before the primary season had even be-

TABLE 10.1 • The Public Presidential Campaign Financing System		
Rules on campaign spending for candidates who accept federal matching funds.*		
Overall Spending Limits for Candidates in Pre-Convention Nominating Campaigns	Overall Spending Limits for Presidential Candidates in the General Election (Post-Convention)	Maximum Amount of Money from Federal Matching Funds to Candidates in Pre-Convention Nominating Campaigns
$44.6 million	$74.4 million	$18.6 million

*George W. Bush, John Dean, and John Kerry refused preconvention public financing for their campaigns in 2004.

Source: The Federal Election Commission, 2004.

gun. Entering the 2004 primary season, insurgent Democratic candidate Howard Dean had amassed more then $30 million in his war chest; Senator Bob Graham of Florida, considered at one time to be among the most serious candidates for the Democratic nomination, dropped out of the race well before the start of the primaries after he was able to raise only $4.5 million.

Another important early decision is whether to be a part of the public campaign finance system—in which the federal government matches the first $250 from each individual donor on condition that candidates limit pre-convention campaign spending to no more than $44.6 million—or to go it alone, raise hard money contributions from individuals (limited to $2,000) and PACs (limited to $5,000), and spend what they wish. In the 2004 election cycle, Bush, Dean, and John Kerry were able to raise enough money to fund their campaigns outside the public system, so each decided to forgo public money with its attendant spending limits (see Table 10.1).

Those candidates who perform below expectations in the primaries and caucuses drop out of the nomination race well before the party conventions. Dick Gephardt, expected to win or be the runner-up in the Iowa Democratic caucus in 2004, struggled to a fourth-place finish and left the race.

The endorsement of his candidacy for the Democratic Party presidential nomination by former Vice President and Democratic presidential nominee Al Gore didn't do Howard Dean much good. The Vermont governor, the front-runner at the end of 2003, dropped out of the nomination race after suffering a string of stinging primary and caucus defeats to John Kerry early in 2004.

You Are a Media Consultant for a Political Campaign

Another important early decision involves which state primaries and caucus contests to enter. Each entry takes a lot of money, energy, and organization, and any loss is damaging; many candidates drop out after just a few early defeats, as Dick Gephardt, Wesley Clark, and Joe Lieberman did in 2004. To win the nomination, it is generally necessary to put together a string of primary victories.

Deciding on the theme of the campaign and the strategy to deliver the message is increasingly in the hands of hired pollsters and campaign consultants.[36] Alternative approaches to themes, messages, and issues are proposed; tested with the public in focus groups and surveys; and then crafted into stump speeches, television and radio spots, and Web pages. Of course, candidates with strong views on the issues—such as Howard Dean's on the wrongheadedness of the invasion and occupation of Iraq—always have the final word on campaign themes.

convention
A gathering of delegates who nominate a party's presidential candidate.

Primaries and Caucuses   Party nominees for president are officially selected every four years at national party **conventions,** made up of state party delegations from around the country. Since the 1970s, most of the delegates to the conventions have been chosen in state primary elections, with direct voting by citizens. (Some primaries are open to all voters, as in the 2000 GOP primaries in South Carolina and Michigan; others are closed, reserved for those who register with the party whose primary election it is.) The Democrats' popularly elected delegates are supplemented by "superdelegates," usually members of Congress or local officials. A few states use caucuses, where active party members and officials gather in meetings around the state to choose delegates to state conventions, which in turn select the delegates to the national convention.

Because the states and the parties—not the federal government—control this nominating process, the system is a disorganized, even chaotic one, and it changes from one election to the next. Some states have primaries for both parties on the same day (including the all-important <u>New Hampshire</u> primaries); others hold primaries for the parties on separate dates. States are particularly anxious that they are not ignored, so an increasing number of them have moved their primary and caucus dates forward in the calendar. States with late primaries, even very large ones such as California, discovered in recent elections that the winners of early primaries had, for all intents and purposes, sewed up the party nominations, discounting the importance of their own primaries and caucuses. As a result, the primary and caucus season was "front-loaded" in 2004, with the bulk of delegates selected for both parties between the Iowa caucuses and the New Hampshire primaries in late January and the Kansas primaries in mid-March.

It is especially important for a candidate to establish momentum by winning early primaries and caucuses. Early winners get press attention, financial contributions, and better standings in the polls as voters and contributors decide they are viable candidates and must have some merit if people in other states have supported them. All these factors—attention from the media, money, and increased popular support—help the candidates who win early contests go on to win more and more contests.[37]

The impression conveyed by political conventions can have an important impact on elections. The apparent unhappiness of many anti–Vietnam War delegates with their party's selection at the 1968 Democratic convention in Chicago severely damaged the campaign of nominee Hubert Humphrey. In contrast, the 1980 Republican convention that selected Ronald Reagan as its nominee more nearly resembled a coronation and gave Reagan and the GOP a fast start in the fall campaign.

Since 1952, no national party convention has taken more than one ballot to nominate its candidate for the presidency, and the preconvention front-runner has always been the nominee. Now the trick is to win delegates in primaries and caucuses, which, in reality, decide the nomination before the convention ever takes place.[38] In 2004, the nominee for each party was known by early March. For the GOP, George W. Bush ran virtually unopposed, and his nomination was never in doubt. For the, Democrats, John Kerry's sweeping victory in the Super Tuesday primaries, coupled with his earlier primary and caucus victories, all but served up the nomination for the senator from Massachusetts by March 2.

The Convention   Because the front-runner now comes to the national convention with enough delegates to win on the first ballot, the gathering has become a coronation ceremony in which prepledged delegates ratify the selection of the leading candidate, accept that candidate's choice for the vice presidency, and put on a colorful show for the media and the country. Enthusiasm and unity are staged for the national television audience; it is a disaster if serious conflicts break out or the timing goes wrong.

The evidence from polls indicates that at virtually all recent national conventions, the party nominee has been the surviving candidate who has had the most support from rank-and-file party identifiers in the nation as a whole.[39] The candidates who have survived the hurdles of raising money, mobilizing activists, and winning primary votes do not, of course, necessarily include the most popular potential presidents in the country; if they did, Colin Powell would probably have won the Republican presidential nomination in 1996. And the big differences between the delegates of the two parties tend to push the two parties' nominees and issue positions away from each other, in a responsible party rather than a purely electoral competition process. Still, the parties not only use the convention as a gathering of activist partisans to nominate one of their own but usually try to make an appeal for support from more centrist voters around the country. Sometimes this balancing act works; sometimes it doesn't. Conservative Barry Goldwater was the darling of the 1964 Republican convention, but he failed miserably in the general election; liberal and anti-war candidate George McGovern was the favorite of Democratic convention delegates in 1972, but he was badly defeated by Richard Nixon in the general election.

Nomination Politics and Democracy   What does all this have to do with democratic control of government? Several things. On the one hand, as we have indicated, the nomination process has some success in coming up with candidates who take stands with wide popular appeal, much as electoral competition theories dictate. On the other hand, as the sharp differences between Republican and Democratic convention delegates suggest (see Table 10.2), Republican and Democratic nominees tend to differ in certain systematic ways, in responsible party fashion. Party platforms—the parties' official statements of their stand on issues—tend to include appeals to average voters but also distinctive appeals to each party's constituencies.

Both these tendencies might be considered good for democracy. However, the crucial role of party activists and money givers in selecting candidates means that nominees and their policy stands are chosen partly to appeal to party elites, financial contributors, and strong partisans rather than to ordinary voters. Thus, neither party's nominee may stand for what ordinary citizens want, the result being voter dissatisfaction and no ideal democratic outcome.

TABLE 10.2 • Comparing Delegates to the 2004 National Party Conventions with Other Americans*					
	Delegates to Democratic National Convention	Democratic Voters	All Voters	Republican Voters	Delegates to Republican National Convention
Very or somewhat liberal	41	33	20	6	2
Very or somewhat conservative	3	19	35	56	60
Believe government should do more to solve national problems	79	48	42	35	7
Believe gay couples should be allowed to marry	45	36	26	11	3
Believe abortion should be generally available to those who want it	75	49	34	17	13
Believe that when it comes to regulating the environmental and safety practices of business, the federal government should do more	85	71	59	45	15
Believe that it is extremely important for for the United States to work through the United Nations to solve international problems	79	66	49	31	7

Source: *New York Times*/CBS News polls. June 16–July 17, 2004, and August 3–23, 2004.

*All numbers indicate the percentage of people agreeing with the statement.

Incumbents   We have been focusing on how outsiders and political challengers try to win party nominations. Things are very different for incumbent presidents seeking reelection, like Bill Clinton in 1996 or George W. Bush in 2004. These candidates must also enter and win primaries, but they have the machinery of government working for them and, if times are reasonably good, a unified party behind them. . They also have an easier time getting campaign contributions, especially for the primaries when incumbent presidents only occasionally meet serious competition. They campaign on the job, taking credit for policy successes while discounting or blaming others, such as Congress, for failures. Winning renomination as president is usually easy, except in cases of disaster such as the 1968 Vietnam War debacle for Lyndon Johnson.

The Autumn Campaign

Incumbents and challengers alike, having won a party nomination, must face the autumn campaign, which traditionally began in early September (on Labor Day) but now tends to start right after the summer conventions or even earlier. In 2004, for example, George W. Bush and John Kerry were aiming fire at each other by mid-March.

For the general election, if not before, the candidates set up a campaign organization in each state, sending aides to coordinate backers and local party

You Are A Presidential Campaign Consultant

Television and Presidential Campaigns

leaders. Intense money-raising continues, and a new round of public financing kicks in. Candidates plan itineraries to make three or four speeches in different media markets each day, concentrating on big states with large blocs of electoral votes and so-called battleground states where the contest between the presidential candidates is deemed to be very close and could go either way. Small states and states where there is not much of a contest—that is, where the election is a sure bet to go to a particular party—tend to be ignored, with visits and television ads saved for more important contests by presidential campaigns. In all of this, hired pollsters and campaign consultants are deeply involved, playing a role in virtually all tactical and strategic decision making.[40]

A new media blitz begins, with many brief spot commercials on television, including "attack" ads such as Clinton's in 1992 mocking George Bush's "read my lips, no new taxes" pledge (which he did not keep) and Dole's in 1996 pointing to Clinton's flawed character. Political consultants use voter focus groups to identify hot-button emotional appeals. Negative advertising has been heavily criticized as simplistic and misleading, but it has often proved effective and is difficult to control or counteract.

Another element of strategy is to get potential supporters registered and to the polls. Organized labor and 527 organizations such as MoveOn work on turning out Democrats, while conservative Christian groups and business-oriented organizations work on Republican turnout. As we have noted, low-income and minority citizens have sometimes been ignored by both major parties.

Informing Voters   What kinds of information do voters get in presidential campaigns? Among other things, voters get information on the candidates' stands on the issues, their past performances, and their personal characteristics.

Issues   Some of the information voters get concerns issues. In accord with electoral competition theories, both the Republican and the Democratic candidates usually try to appeal to the average voter by taking similar, popular stands on policy, especially foreign policy. Gore and Bush both stayed close to the center in 2000. But as responsible party theories suggest, Republican and Democratic candidates usually do differ on a number of issues, such as medical care, federal aid to education, prescription drug programs, tax cuts, social welfare, civil rights, the environment, abortion, and the use of the military in foreign policy. On these issues, the Democratic candidate tends to take a more liberal stand than the Republican, just as Democratic party identifiers, activists, money givers, and convention delegates tend to be more liberal than their Republican counterparts.

While Democratic and Republican presidential candidates generally differ on a range of issues that are fairly predictable, and that tend to appeal to party identifiers, they also try to appeal to independent voters and a few in the opposition party by using vague and ambiguous "feel good" themes. No one, for example, could object to George H. W. Bush's 1988 promises to be an "education president" and an "environmental president" or to Clinton's 1996 promise to "build a bridge to the twenty-first century." Candidates often emphasize symbolic matters that appeal to virtually everyone, such as George H. W. Bush's invocation of the American flag and the Pledge of Allegiance during his campaign against Bill Clinton in 1992.

In 1988, a Republican group used the case of Willie Horton, a convicted murderer who raped a woman while on furlough from a Massachusetts prison, to imply that Democratic presidential candidate Michael Dukakis, Massachusett's governor at the time, was soft on crime.

© 1997 Dayton Daily News/Tribune Media Services

Past Performance   Often candidates talk about past performance and future goals. The "outs" blame the "ins" for wars, recessions, and other calamities. The "ins" brag about how they have brought peace and prosperity and paint a warm picture of a glorious future, without saying exactly how it will come about.

Incumbent presidents, of course, can do things that accurately or inaccurately suggest successful performance. They can try to schedule recessions for off years, pumping up the economy in time for reelection. Or they can make dramatic foreign policy moves just before election day, like Nixon's 1972 trips to the Soviet Union and China.

Personal Characteristics   Most of all, however, voters get a chance to learn about the real or alleged personal characteristics of the candidates. Even when the candidates are talking about something else, they give an impression of either competence or incompetence. Jimmy Carter, for example, emphasized his expertise as a "nuclear engineer," whereas Gerald Ford was haunted by films of him stumbling on airplane ramps.

Candidates also come across as warm or cold. Dwight D. Eisenhower's radiant grin appeared everywhere in 1952 and 1956, as Reagan's did in 1984, but Richard Nixon was perceived as cold and aloof in 1968, despite clever efforts at selling his personality.

Still another dimension of candidates' personalities is strength or weakness. George H. W. Bush overcame the so-called wimp factor in 1988 with his tough talk about crime and the flag. Merely by surviving many personal attacks in 1992 and 1996, Clinton appeared strong and resilient.

The sparse and ambiguous treatment of policy issues in campaigns, as well as the emphasis on past performance and personal competence, fits better with ideas about electoral reward and punishment than with responsible parties or issue-oriented electoral competition. Candidate personalities are not irrelevant to the democratic control of government. Obviously, it is useful for voters to pick presidents who possess competence, warmth, and strength. And citizens may be more skillful in judging people than in figuring out complicated policy issues.

Voters can be fooled, however, by dirty tricks or slick advertising that sells presidential candidates' personalities and tears down the opponent. Moreover, the focus on personal imagery may distract attention from policy stands. If candidates who favor unpopular policies are elected on the basis of attractive personal images, democratic control of policymaking is weakened. By the purchase of advertising and the hiring of smart consultants, money may, in effect, overcome the popular will.

Money and Elections

Most observers agree that money creates problems in U.S. presidential elections. The main problem is probably not that too much money is spent but that the money comes from private sources that may influence government policymaking after the election is over.

The Cost of Presidential Campaigns

Presidential campaigns cost a great deal of money, though the system is so complex that even seasoned observers can make only educated guesses about the total. Expenditures by the official presidential campaigns and party committees is fairly easy to keep track of, to be sure, because of reporting requirements to the Federal Election Commission. During the 2000 election cycle, candidate committees spent $343 million during the pre-convention stage, and the Gore and Bush campaigns spent an additional $135 million on the general election. In 2004, the Bush campaign spent more than $200 million prior to the GOP convention, while John Kerry spent more than $100 million before the Democratic convention. Together the two candidates spent on additional $150 million in the general election contest. Republican and Democratic national committees spent $650 million during the 1999–2000 election cycle, split between the presidential and congressional contests. Party committees also contributed about $500 million from soft money sources—now illegal under terms of the McCain-Feingold reforms—also split between presidential and congressional contests. Where the numbers get tricky is keeping track of money spent by private associations and advocacy groups on activities that closely parallel presidential, congressional, and party campaigns. It is anyone's guess what these organizations spend on things such as "get out the vote" drives, issue advertising on television and radio, door-to-door campaigning for candidates and issues, appeals to organization members, and more, because most of these expenditures do not have to be reported.

Where Does the Money Come From?

Since 1971, most of the money spent in the fall presidential campaign by the two presidential candidates has come from the federal treasury, paid by the taxpayers. Taxpayers can check off a box on their tax returns to authorize a $3 contribution from public funds. The gov-

TABLE 10.3 ● Contribution Limits to Campaigns of Federal Candidates*

	To a Political Candidate	To a National Party Committee	To a Political Action Committee (PAC)	Maximum Contributions Allowed
Individual	$2,000 per election	$25,000 per year	$5,000 per year	$95,000 for each two-year election cycle
Political Action Committee	$5,000	$15,000	$5,000	No limit

*Often referred to as "hard" money.

Source: The Federal Election Commission, 2004.

ernment uses these taxpayer contributions to provide matches for money contributors give to candidates during the primary and general election campaigns of those candidates who agree to spending limits (see Table 10.3 for the current rules on campaign contributions). In 2004, the Kerry and Bush campaigns each received $74.4 million for the general election in the fall. Although Kerry and Bush refused public money for their nomination campaigns, both accepted public funding for the general election contest. But why would they do such a thing, given that accepting public funding for their campaigns limited what they could spend?

- Because publically provided funds are not inconsiderable.
- Because the two party presidential candidates get lots of free publicity simply by being the standard bearer of one of the two major parties.
- Because various state, local, and national party committees spend generously on the campaigns.
- Because interest groups and advocacy organizations spend lavishly on independent parallel campaigns (see Chapter 7).

Does Money Talk?   Money matters a great deal in the presidential nomination process—aspirants for party nominations who cannot raise sizeable funds always drop out of the race—but not so much during the post-convention run for the White House.[41] As we pointed out earlier, once a presidential campaign is under way, each of the major party candidates has at his or her disposal all of the organizational resources of the party organization and money from traditional party contributors and allied interest groups as well as matching funds from the government; each candidate generally has enough money to run a credible campaign. In the general election, one cannot safely predict the outcome based on who has spent the most money. If that were true, Republicans would almost always win the election.

Money may talk at a later stage, however. It is widely believed, although difficult to prove, that contributors of money often get something back.[42] The point is not that presidential candidates take outright bribes in exchange for policy favors. Indeed, exchanges between politicians and money givers are complex and varied, sometimes yielding little benefit to contributors. Undeniably, however, cozy relationships do tend to develop between politicians

Under the new McCain-Feingold campaign finance rules that bar soft money contributions to national party committees, advocacy groups with close ties to the parties have become increasingly important. Cecile Richards is president of America Votes, an organization that pays for issue campaigns in favor of abortion rights, environmental protection, worker rights and protections, and other issues close to the hearts of Democrats.

and major money givers. Contributors gain access to, and a friendly hearing from, those whom they help to win office.

It is clear that money givers are different from average citizens. They have special interests of their own. As we have indicated, a large amount of campaign money comes from large corporations, investment banking firms, wealthy families, labor unions, professional associations (e.g., doctors, lawyers, or realtors), and issue-oriented groups such as the National Rifle Association, the Christian Coalition, and the National Abortion Rights Action League. The big contributors generally do not represent ordinary workers, consumers, or taxpayers, let alone minorities or the poor. Surveys show that the individuals who give money tend to have much higher incomes and more conservative views on economic issues than the average American.[43]

The result is political inequality. Those who are well organized or have a lot of money to spend on politics have a better chance of influencing policy than ordinary citizens do, and they tend to influence it in directions different from those the general public would want. The role of money in presidential nomination and election campaigns (and in congressional campaigns, as we show in Chapter 11) is a major problem for the working of democracy in the United States.

Election Outcomes

After the parties and candidates have presented their campaigns, the voters decide. Exactly how people make their voting decisions affects how well or how poorly elections contribute to the democratic control of government.

How Voters Decide

Years of scholarly research have made it clear that feelings about the parties, the candidates, and the issues have substantial effects on how people vote.[44]

Social Characteristics People's socioeconomic status, religion, and ethnic background are significantly related to how they vote. Since the 1930s, for example, African Americans, Jews, and lower-income citizens have tended to vote heavily for Democrats, while white Protestants and upper-income Americans have voted mostly for Republicans. In 2004, 88 percent of blacks, but only 41 percent of whites, voted for John Kerry against George W. Bush; 55 percent of people with household incomes under $50,000, but only 41 percent of those with incomes over $100,000, voted for Kerry; and 74 percent of Jews, but only 29 percent of Protestant regular church-goers, voted for him. Recently, women have voted for Democrats in greater numbers than have men, though the differences were not as marked in 2004; 51 percent of women, but only 44 percent of men, voted for Kerry. Older people have traditionally supported Democratic candidates more often, and at higher rates, than other age groups, but this is no longer true. In 2004, 54 percent of those over 65 voted for Bush (see Figure 10.4).

Party Loyalties To some extent, these social patterns work through long-term attachments to, or identification with, political parties. As indicated earlier, a majority of Americans still say they consider themselves Republicans or Democrats. Party loyalties vary among different groups of the population, often because of past or present differences between the parties on policy issues, especially economic and social issues.[45] For this reason, party cues help many people vote for candidates who are close to them on the issues.

Party loyalties are very good predictors of how people will vote.[46] Those who say they consider themselves Republicans tend to vote for Republican candidates in one election after another, and those who consider themselves Democrats vote for Democratic candidates. This is especially true in congressional elections and in state and local races, where most voters know little more about the candidates than their party labels, but the party loyalty factor is extremely important in presidential elections as well. Thus, in 2004, 89 percent of Democratic identifiers voted for Kerry, and 93 percent of Republican identifiers voted for Bush.

Candidates Another reason presidential election outcomes have not simply reflected the party balance and the Democrats have lost so often is that voters pay a lot of attention to their perceptions of the personal characteristics of candidates. They vote heavily for candidates who have experience, appear

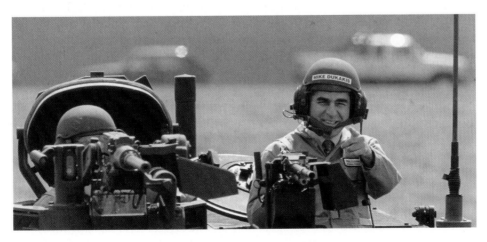

News photos and video of Democratic presidential candidate Michael Dukakis taking a ride in a new M1-A-1 battle tank during the 1988 campaign did not convince very many people that he was strong on national defense, which was his apparent objective. Much to the chagrin of his campaign team, the ride became the butt of jokes by late-night comedians and editorial cartoonists.

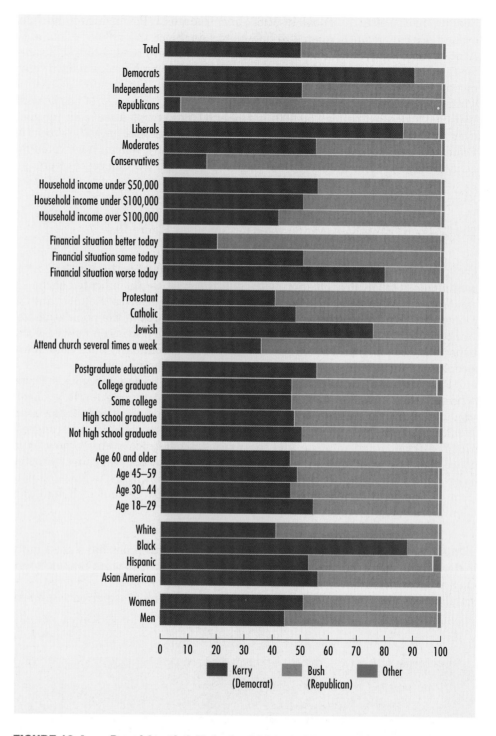

FIGURE 10.4 ● **Presidential Vote in 2004, by Social Group**

Minorities, lower-income voters, and women tended to vote for John Kerry in the 2004 election, while Protestants, regular church-goers, higher-income people, and men tended to favor George W. Bush.

Source: "Edison/Mitofsky Exit Poll, 2004 Presidential Election," CNN.com, **www.cnn.com/ELECTION/2004,** November 2, 2004.

strong and decisive, and convey personal warmth. The Republican candidate in 1952 and 1956, Dwight D. Eisenhower, had a tremendous advantage in these respects over his Democratic opponent, Adlai Stevenson;[47] so did Ronald

Reagan over Walter Mondale in 1984, and George H. W. Bush over Michael Dukakis in 1988. Only in 1964 did the Democratic candidate (Lyndon Johnson) appeal to voters substantially more than the Republican candidate (Barry Goldwater). In elections between 1952 and 1972, the contrast between Republican and Democratic candidates typically gained the Republicans 4 or 5 percentage points—just enough to overcome the Democrats' advantage in what political scientists call the **normal vote:** how votes would be cast if only party identification determined voters' choices for president.

normal vote
The proportion of the votes that each party would win if party identification alone affected voting decisions.

Issues   Voters also pay attention to issues. Sometimes this means choosing between different policy proposals for the future (as in the responsible party voting model), such as Reagan's 1980 promises to cut back federal government activity or Clinton's 1992 pledges of jobs and a middle-class tax cut. More often, however, issue voting has meant retrospective voting (the electoral reward and punishment model), making judgments about the past, especially on major questions about war or peace and the state of the economy. The voters tend to reward the incumbent party for what they see as good times and to punish it for what they see as bad times, though this did not occur in 2000 for reasons that are still being debated by political observers.[48] Several scholars and pollsters believe that cultural issues—such as gay and lesbian rights, abortion, civil rights and affirmative action, law and order, and the like—may have become more important than economic issues in determining voter choices. This may help explain why increasing numbers of affluent and educated Americans are voting Democratic, while lower income, less educated, and church-going whites are increasingly casting their ballots for Republicans.[49]

The Economy   The state of the economy and how Americans feel about their economic well-being and prospects are especially important. After severe economic downturns, Americans tend to vote the incumbent party out of office, as they did the Republicans during the Great Depression in 1932. In 1992, the electorate punished Republican George H. W. Bush for the poor state of the economy and, in 1996, it rewarded Bill Clinton for being president during good economic times. Economic concerns—jobs and gas price in particular—played a part in the 2004 election.

Foreign Policy   Foreign policy can be important. Bitter disillusionment over the Korean War hurt the Democrats in 1952, just as the Vietnam War cost them in 1968, and unhappiness about American hostages in Iran and the Soviet intervention in Afghanistan hurt Jimmy Carter in 1980. During nearly all of the past half-century, in fact, Republican candidates have been seen as better at providing foreign policy strength and at keeping us out of war. In most elections, however, foreign policy concerns take a back seat to domestic ones for most voters, though the war on terrorism and the war in Iraq were factors in 2004.

New Issues   In recent years, new issues have also become important to voters. These include deficit cutting, law and order, the environment, affirmative action, and abortion. Becoming increasingly important are issues related to globalization, including free trade. Certain to be important in future elections is the public's assessment of progress in the war against terrorism, especially if a protracted war brings with it a wide range of problems.

The Impact of Campaigns

Some factors that determine how voters decide are relatively fixed, for example, their social characteristics and party loyalties. As a result, the autumn campaigns for the presidency, despite all the money spent and the excitement generated by them, are unlikely to persuade very large numbers of voters to change their minds. Campaigns mainly reinforce previous voter preferences and activate people to go to the polls.[50] Political scientists have also determined that a number of factors that affect the outcome of an election are known by the close of the nominating party conventions at the end of the summer—for example, whether an incumbent president is in the race (incumbents tend to get reelected) and whether the state of the economy is good or bad (a good economy helps the party in power). Given all of this, it is hard to imagine that the autumn campaign matters much at all. Some political scientists have gone so far as to suggest that most presidential elections can be predicted before the campaign gets under way, and a lively industry has sprung up to publicize these predictions.

As far as we are able to determine, however, the campaign does matter, though not as much perhaps as journalists, candidates, and campaign consultants believe. One very careful recent investigation of this issue concludes that campaigns affect, on average, about 4 percent of the national vote.[51] While this may not seem like much, it is worth noting that the average margin of victory over the years in presidential elections has been only about 5 percentage points. What this means is that over and above relatively fixed factors such as party identification, the state of the economy, and the presence of a sitting president in the race, the impact of the campaign proves decisive in about one in five presidential elections.[52]

The Electoral College

As many Americans learned for the first time in 2000, the outcome of presidential elections is determined not by the number of popular votes cast for each candidate; it depends on the votes in the Electoral College. (See "By the Numbers: Did George W. Bush really win the 2000 presidential vote in Florida?" for more information on the 2000 election.)

electors
Representatives who are elected in the states to formally choose the U.S. president.

When Americans vote for a presidential candidate whose name appears on the ballot, they are actually voting for a slate of **electors** in their—equal to the number of the state's U.S. senators and representatives—who have promised to support a party's presidential candidate. (Very rarely have electors reneged on their promises and cast ballots for someone else; there was one so-called faithless elector in 2000.) Nearly all states now have winner-take-all systems in which the winner of the popular vote wins the state's entire allotment of electoral votes; Maine and Nebraska, in slight variations, choose electors on a winner-take-all basis for each congressional district.

The "college" of electors from the different states never actually meets; instead, the electors meet in their respective states and send lists of how they have voted to Washington, D.C. (see the Twelfth Amendment to the Constitution). The candidate who receives a majority of all the electoral votes in the country is elected president. Not since 1824 has it been necessary to resort to the odd constitutional provisions that apply when no one gets a majority of electoral votes: The House of Representatives chooses among the top three candidates, by majority vote of state delegations.

Participation

The Electoral College

Most of the time, this peculiar Electoral College system works about the same way as if Americans chose their presidents by direct popular vote, though this was not true in 2000 when Bush won the electoral vote while losing the popular vote. The old idea that electors would exercise their independent judgments is long gone. But the system does have certain consequences:

- *It magnifies the popular support of winners.* A candidate who wins in many states, by a narrow margin in each, can win a "landslide" in the electoral college. In 1996, for example, Bill Clinton's 49 percent of the popular vote translated into 379 electoral votes, or 70 percent of the total. Ordinarily, this magnification just adds legitimacy to the democratic choice, especially when the winner has only a **plurality** of the popular vote, that is, more than anybody else but less than a majority of all votes. Many of our presidents have been elected by a plurality but with less than 50 percent of the popular vote—most recently, Clinton (1992 and 1996), Richard Nixon (1968), John Kennedy (1960), and Harry Truman (1948).

- *It may let the less popular candidate win.* A president can be elected who had *fewer* votes than an opponent, if those votes happened to produce narrow margins in many states. Such a result has occurred three times: in 1876, when Rutherford Hayes defeated Samuel Tilden; in 1888, when Benjamin Harrison beat the more popular Grover Cleveland; and in 2000, when George W. Bush defeated Al Gore. (Gore beat Bush by more than a half million votes nationally.) Several early-nineteenth-century presidents were probably chosen with only small fractions of the popular vote, although we cannot be sure because some of the statistics are unreliable. Most notably, in 1824, John Quincy Adams defeated the very popular Andrew Jackson in the House of Representatives.

- *It discourages third parties.* Our constitutional arrangements for a single president and single-member congressional districts (rather than proportional representation) already discourage third parties; if candidates cannot win a plurality, they get nothing. The Electoral College adds symbolically to this discouragement: A third party with substantial support may get no electoral votes at all, if its support is scattered among many states. In 1992, for example, Ross Perot's impressive 19 percent of the popular vote translated into zero electoral votes because he failed to win a plurality in any single state.

People who would like to abolish the Electoral College point to its narrowing of choices and the possibility of undemocratic outcomes. Those who like it claim that it discourages fraud by limiting the votes that any one state can cast, that the two-party system it encourages is good, and that the added legitimacy of electoral college "landslides" is helpful—or at least harmless.

 Timeline

And the Winner Is . . . ?
Close Calls in Presidential Elections

 plurality

More votes than any other candidate but less than a majority of all votes cast.

Visual Literacy

American Electoral Rules: How Do They Influence Campaigns?

By the Numbers

Did George W. Bush really win the 2000 presidential vote in Florida?

George W. Bush was officially certified the winner of the presidential contest in Florida on December 12, 2000, thirty-five days after the November election. Florida's 25 electoral votes brought his national total to 271, just barely enough to win the White House.

Interestingly, however, a comprehensive review of Florida ballots has come up with several other possible outcomes to the Florida vote, depending on different ways the ballots could have been counted. In fact, the outcomes vary from Bush winning by 537 votes, to Gore winning by 200!

Why It Matters: Elections must be fair if they are to play the role assigned to them in democratic theory. Part of a fair election is an accurate count of votes cast. Without an accurate count, voter wishes will not be conveyed to public officials, and the legitimacy of elected officials is at risk, making governance more difficult.

Behind the Vote Count Numbers: A consortium of eight leading news organizations—including *The Wall Street Journal,* the *New York Times, The Washington Post,* the Associated Press, and CNN—recently sponsored a 10-month study by the widely respected National Opinion Research Center at the University of Chicago. Center researchers examined every uncounted "under-vote" ballot (where no vote for president was recorded by the voting machine), with an eye toward determining each voter's intent.

Only ballots that showed evidence of clear voter intention were included in the consortium's recount. These included ballots with "hanging" and "pregnant" chads which the machines failed to record and optical scan ballots where voters indicated their vote with a check mark or an "x" rather than filling in the bubble as instructed.

Calculating the Winner's Margin of Victory: The official tally concluded that Bush won by 537 votes. However, Center investigators found that different counting methods would have yielded the results shown on page 305. There are some incredible ironies in these numbers.

- Had the Gore team gotten everything it asked for from election officials and the courts, Gore still would have lost to George W. Bush.
- The U.S. Supreme Court did not steal the election, as many Gore supporters claimed, for had it allowed the Florida Supreme Court's solution to stand, Bush would have won anyway.
- A majority of Florida voters went to the polls on November 8 to cast a vote for Al Gore for president. The method proposed by the U.S. Supreme Court shows this; recounting all "under-count" disputed ballots on a statewide basis using consistent standards yields a Gore victory. The upshot: Gore was badly advised by his team of lawyers, who insisted on recounts in only certain counties.
- Because of the enormous boost in George W. Bush's popularity following the terrorist attack on the United States and the subsequent "war on terrorism," most Americans ignored the consortium's findings. Most seemed perfectly content to

have Bush as president, no matter what had happened in Florida.

Criticisms of the Florida "Recount": Some have argued that the consortium's recount was flawed in two major ways:

- First, it did not include "overvotes" in its estimates—those ballots where more than one name for president was indicated or where the same name was entered more than once—which were also ruled invalid by election officials in Florida. For the most part, these involved ballots where voters made two punches on very confusing ballots (the infamous "butterfly ballots") or where voters wrote in the same name as the candidate they had punched or marked, presumably to make clear to election officials who they had voted for. A substantial majority of over-vote ballots had Gore as one of the choices.

- Second, there is the issue of absentee ballots from overseas armed forces personnel. Had they been counted in the same way other ballots were counted—that is, not counting ballots kicked out because of "under-vote" or "over-vote" problems—Bush would have lost hundreds of votes to Gore and probably lost Florida and the White House.

What to Watch For: When counting votes, as in all other counts, the rules for doing so matter. This is why the lawyers from the Gore and Bush teams fought so ferociously following the Florida election

If, as the Gore team insisted, "under-votes" were tallied in Palm Beach, Miami-Dade, Broward, and Volusia counties were recounted.

If, as the Florida Supreme Court ruled, "under-votes" were recounted statewide, using standards set by election officials in each county (this solution was rejected by the U.S. Supreme Court).

If all rejected "under-count" ballots were tallied on a state-wide basis using uniform standards across the state, as suggested by the U.S. Supreme Court in *Bush v. Gore* (but the Supreme Court also ruled that there was no time left to make such a recount).

about how to do the recount. Whenever you run across a statistic that involves counting, in one form or another, you might want to look further into what counting rules were used.

What Do You Think? Can you think of any other way to decide the winner of an election when, for all intents and purposes, the race ends up in a dead heat? Some countries use a "run-off" system in which the two top people run against each other to determine who has won a majority of popular votes before a winner is declared. In the 2000 presidential elections, this would have meant a run-off election between Gore and Bush, without Ralph Nader or Pat Buchanan on the ballot.

How Democratic Are We?

Do Elections Matter?

PROPOSITION: Elections don't matter much in determining what government leaders do. It's probably the reason so many Americans don't bother to vote.

AGREE: Elections don't do much to help the people control the government, mainly because U.S. political parties undermine the ability of elections to play the democratic role reserved for them in responsible party government, electoral competition, and electoral reward-and-punishment theories of democratic elections. Each of these democratic election models requires that the parties be cohesive organizations, with clear programmatic and ideological positions that distinguish them from competing parties. U.S. parties are not like this; they are too "candidate centered," sacrificing coherence and unity to the electoral needs of a diverse set of individual candidates. When candidates feel that their election or reelection depends on their own fundraising and campaigning, and that siding with their party may be risky, they all too easily abandon party loyalty. Parties of this sort, internally contradictory and ambiguous, do not allow voters to choose a governing party team that will takes responsibility for government performance. They do not provide the tools by which the public can cut through the confusion and complexity of politics and government, make sense of how things work, and magnify its voice in public affairs. To make matters worse, many Americans are aware that enormous influence is exercised over parties and their candidates by powerful interest groups and large campaign contributors. Feeling that their vote doesn't matter much in the end, potential voters stay away from the polls in droves.

DISAGREE: Scholars have shown that government officials, in the long run, do what the American people want them to do about two-thirds of the time. Although a variety of instruments help convey what the people want to officials—public opinion polls, interest groups, and social movements—it is ultimately the fact that officials must face the voters that keeps them in line. And, it is the political parties that organize electoral contests and help people sort out the candidates and make sense of their electoral promises, allowing people to cast votes in a relatively rational manner. Elections matter, that is to say, and it is the political parties that make elections function in a way that allows the people to control what goes on in government. The problem of nonvoting is exaggerated, moreover. People are free to participate or not participate; it is a free country. If they choose not to, it is probably because they are not terribly unhappy about the direction that government is taking.

CONSIDER: College-age people vote less often than any other age group. Indeed, age is a better predictor of voting than income, education, or gender.

• Why do you think young people participate at such low levels? • Is it because many young people are not yet rooted in a community and job? • Or do you think that young people are turned off by electoral politics, not seeing it as a mechanism for changing the direction of the country in domestic and foreign affairs? • Or do you think that people your age tend to be pretty well satisfied by the way things are going and stay away from the polls because they don't feel that anything is amiss or needs to be changed? • How about you? • Do you vote? • If not, why is that? • And, if not, what would get you to the voting booth? • If you don't vote, are you active in politics in other ways, such as being part of a social movement or advocacy group? • If so, why do you find this to be a more satisfying way to participate in politics?

Summary

Elections are the most important means by which citizens can exert democratic control over their government. Voters can choose *responsible parties* to carry out their distinctive programs. *Electoral competition* forces vote-seeking parties and candidates to appeal to the center of public opinion. *Electoral reward and punishment* gives officials incentives to carry out policies that will win public approval. However, none of these processes guarantees a perfectly democratic outcome.

Political participation can be conventional (voting, helping in campaigns, and contacting officials) or unconventional (protesting or demonstrating). The right to vote, originally quite limited, was expanded in various historical surges to include nearly all adults and to apply to most major offices. Turnout has declined, however, and in recent years only about half the eligible voters have cast ballots for the presidency.

Candidates for president start by testing the waters, raising money, and forming campaign organizations; in a series of state primaries and caucuses, they seek delegates to the national nominating conventions, which generally choose a clear front-runner or the incumbent president. During the campaign, the candidates are generally vague about issues; they concentrate on building personal images and emphasizing past performance.

Money matters most in the struggle for each party's presidential nomination. Much of the money is regulated "hard money" raised by the candidate and party committees, as well as political action committees representing private interests and advocacy organizations. The remainder is unregulated money spent by individuals and associations on independent issue campaigns that favor one candidate or another. Candidates who cannot raise money or have money raised for them by others do not become serious contenders in the party nomination contests. Money differences between the candidates in the presidential contest in the fall is less important in determining the outcome because of public financing and intense and costless press coverage of the election.

Voters' decisions depend heavily on party loyalties, the personal characteristics of the candidates, and the issues, especially the state of the economy and of U.S. foreign policy. After recessions and unsuccessful wars, the incumbent party generally loses. The Electoral College does not always accurately reflect popular votes. Elections matter not only when there is a clear choice but also when electoral reward or punishment occurs or when electoral competition forces both parties to take similar popular stands.

Suggestions for Further Reading

"Anonymous." *Primary Colors: A Novel of Politics.* New York: Random House, 1996.

Journalist Joe Klein's lively and sometimes ribald account of Bill Clinton's campaign for the 1992 Democratic presidential nomination, thinly disguised as fiction.

Burns, Nancy, Kay Lehman Schlozman, and Sidney Verba. *The Private Roots of Public Action: Gender, Equality and Political Participation* (Cambridge, MA: Harvard University Press, 2001).

A comprehensive examination of the differences in the political activity of men and women and the reasons why differences exist.

Ferguson, Thomas. *Golden Rule.* Chicago: University of Chicago Press, 1995.

A highly critical account of the role of money in American elections.

Keyssar, Alexander. *The Right to Vote: The Contested History of Democracy in the United States.* New York: Basic Books, 2001.

A fresh look at the history of the vote as a struggle between those who believe common people are not fully qualified to vote and those who believe that American democracy is enriched by their full participation.

Polsby, Nelson W., and Aaron Wildavsky. *Presidential Elections,* 11th ed. Lanham, MD: Rowman and Littlefield, 2003.

A comprehensive textbook on the presidential nominating process, campaigning, and voting.

Verba, Sidney, Kay Lehman Schlozman, and Henry E. Brady. *Voice and Equality: Civic Volunteerism in American Politics.* Cambridge, MA: Harvard University Press, 1995.
  A comprehensive analysis of inequalities in political participation and their meaning for the quality of democracy in the United States.

Wattenberg, Martin P., *Where Have All the Voters Gone?* (Cambridge, MA: Harvard University Press, 2002).
  A clear-headed and accessible a look at this perennial and complex question.

Internet Sources

The Center for Public Integrity
www.publicintegrity.org/
  An especially good site for following the money trail—how campaign money is gathered and spent.

Democratic National Committee
www.democrats.org/
  Official site of the Democratic party with information on party positions and candidates, how to work as a volunteer or contribute money, and more.

E-Vote
www.evote.com/
  Up-to-the-minute news, commentary, and polls on national campaigns.

The National Archives Electoral College Site
www.archives.gov/federal_register/electoral_college/ index.html
  Everything there is to know about the law and practices of the Electoral College and the process by which it elects the president.

Political Money Line
http://www.tray.com/fecinfo/
  A very useable site for following the political money trail in American elections.

Project Votesmart
www.vote-smart.org/
  A political portal loaded with links to information about candidates, parties, election rules, and issues.

Republican National Committee
www.rnc.org/
  Official site of the Republican party with information on party positions and candidates, how to work as a volunteer or contribute money, and more.

SelectSmart's American Presidential Candidate Selecter
www.selectsmart.com/president
  Unclear about which candidate's position on the issues is closest to your own? This site will help you find out.

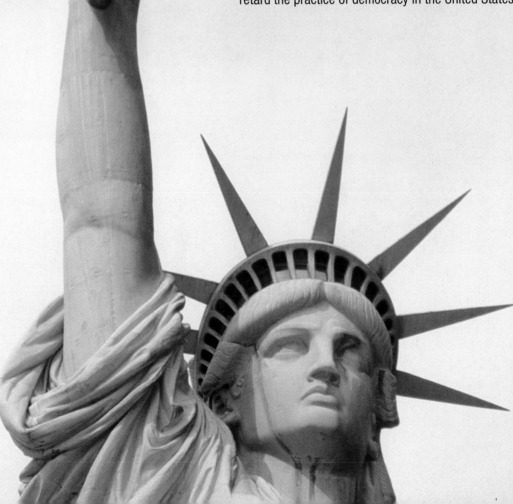

Part Four

Government and Governing

The chapters in Part Four examine how federal government institutions operate and how and why public officials, both elected and appointed, behave as they do in office. Part Four includes chapters on Congress, the presidency, the executive branch, and the Supreme Court.

The chapters in this part assume that government institutions and public officials can be understood only in their structural and political contexts. What government does is influenced strongly by structural factors such as the constitutional rules, the economy, the political culture, society, and the nation's place in the world. What government does is also shaped by political linkage institutions such as elections, parties, interest groups, public opinion, and social movements that transmit the preferences of individuals and groups to public officials.

Democracy is the evaluative thread that runs through each chapter. We ask about the degree to which federal government institutions and public officials advance or retard the practice of democracy in the United States.

Chapter 11
Congress

The Dynamics and Consequences of the 2004 Congressional Elections

In one of the most bitterly partisan congressional election campaigns in recent memory, Republicans increased their majorities in both houses of Congress in 2004, picking up four additional seats in the House of Representatives and four in the Senate. Although the gains were not terribly large in a strictly numerical sense, they were enough to solidify Republican dominance in both houses of Congress. Coupled with the reelection of George W. Bush to the presidency, Republicans managed to extend their unified party control of the federal government for at least two more years. In this long era of divided party government (described in Chapter 9), winning control of the House, the Senate, and the presidency in successive national elections (both houses of Congress in 2002 and 2004, and the presidency in 2000 and 2004) represents a considerable achievement. Unified party government, it is worth noting, existed for only seven years between 1967 and 2002. With a conservative majority on the Supreme Court, moreover, and excellent prospects for additional appointments to the Court during the second Bush administration, Republicans have reason to feel confident about the possibilities for instituting much of their policy agenda in the next several years.

The 2004 congressional elections were noteworthy on a number of grounds. First, and hardly surprisingly, given recent trends in American politics, campaign spending in congressional races reached historic levels. Informed estimates put total spending in congressional races by the candidates, their campaign committees, party committees, PACs, and 527 organizations at roughly $2.7 billion, about 20 percent higher than congressional elections two years before. The average Senate candidate raised about $4.8 million in 2004, up 53 percent from 1998 when these same seats were last contested (one-third of the Senate is elected at each two-year election cycle, meaning that a particular set of seats is contested every six years), and up 19 percent from the Senate average in 2002. In the House, the average winner of a seat raised more than a million dollars, a significant amount when considered in light of the fact that more than three-fourths of all House races were not even mildly competitive, with the winner taking more than 60 percent of the vote.[1]

Also noteworthy in the 2004 congressional elections was the acceleration in the changing geography of representation in the Senate, paralleling a similar change that has been going on for some time now in the House of Representatives. This changing geography of representation is about the historic transformation of the Deep South from a solidly Democratic region at the congressional level to a solidly Republican one. In the 2004 elections, five Republicans were elected to Senate seats previously held by Democrats in the Deep South. Four of these seats were held by southern Democratic moderates—John Breaux of Louisiana, Bob Graham of Florida, Zell Miller of Georgia, and Frizt Hollings of South Carolina, all of whom retired—and one was held by John Edwards of North Carolina, who declined to run for reelection after he joined the Kerry ticket as the vice presidential candidate. The resulting transformation in party regional representation is stunning; in the 109th Congress, there are only four Democrats in the Senate from the 11 states of the former Confederacy.

For the Democrats, there were two additional noteworthy developments in the Senate, one welcome, the other not. In Illinois, the young and charismatic state senator, Barack Obama, the acknowledged speaking star of the Democratic National Convention, won handily, generating early talk about a possible future presidential candidacy. On the other hand, Senate minority leader Tom Daschle, a thorn in the side of the Bush administration since 2001 and a target of national Republicans in this election, was narrowly defeated by John Thune in South Dakota. To say the least, this represented a devastating blow to Democratic Party morale in the Senate and across the country.

Continuing a trend that has been apparent for some time now, incumbents who sought reelection proved to be virtually invincible in 2004. In the Senate, where races are generally more competitive than in the House, only one incumbent (Daschle) was defeated out of a total of 26 races. To be sure, there was some turnover in the Senate's ranks, given eight retirements, but the incumbency reelection rate of 96 percent is impressive, indeed, and higher than normal. In the House, 98 percent of incumbents were successful. There were 401 election contests for House seats that involved an incumbent, and 394 of them were reelected. Importantly, four of the seven losing incumbents in 2004 were Democrats running for reelection in Texas, where House Majority Leader Tom DeLay had engineered a controversial and brilliant redistricting plan in the state legislature that heavily favored Republicans. (You will read more about redistricting and the Texas plan later in this chapter.)

The 2004 congressional elections may prove to be one of the most consequential in recent times because it accelerated a troublesome trend: the development of an evermore partisan and contentious political environment in Washington and across the nation. In the 2004 elections, the moderate center of each party in both houses of Congress was eroded further.[2] In the House, retirements and a handful of electoral defeats reduced the number of moderate voices in the Democratic Party, including long-term congressman Charles Stenholm and three other colleagues in Texas. Democratic representatives now are mostly from New England, the Middle Atlantic States, the upper Midwest, and the Pacific coast. On the Republican side of the House, the addition of four seats to its majority gives even greater power to the strongly conservative leaders of the House—Speaker Dennis Hastert of Illinois and Majority Leader Tom DeLay of Texas—who have already proven themselves masters at maintaining order and discipline on major issues among GOP representatives. In the Senate, as in the House, the retirement and defeat of moderate southern voices in the Democratic Party means that the Democrats have become a more consistently liberal party (though the party's new leader, Harry Reid of Nevada, is a more moderate voice than Tom Daschle, the former leader). For its part, the Republican Party has become a much more fervently conservative party. It is noteworthy that all six new Republican Senators in the 109th Congress first came to Washington in the mid-1990s, elected to the House as strong disciples of Newt Gingrich's combative, conservative revolution. One of these new senators, Tom Coburn of Oklahoma, is generally acknowledged to have been among the most conservative members in the House of Representatives before his successful run for the Senate.

The depletion in the ranks of moderates in each of the two parties in the House and Senate, and the expansion in the ranks of the ideologically committed in both parties in both houses of Congress, suggest that the current, highly partisan period is likely to make it particularly difficult to successfully address a wide range of issues that are highly controversial in the best of times, including Supreme Court appointments, taxes and budget deficits, waging war (in this case, on terrorism and in Iraq), and improving entitlement programs such as Social Security. It remains to be seen how the American people will respond to this development in American politics and whether it enhances or diminishes their confidence in their political and government institutions.

Thinking Critically About This Chapter

In this chapter, we turn our attention to the Congress of the United States, examining how Congress works as both a representative and governing institution.

Using the Framework   In this chapter you will learn how the way in which Congress works is affected by other government actors and institutions; political linkage level factors such as interest groups, public opinion, the media, and elections; and structural factors, such as constitutional rules and economic and social change.

Using the Democracy Standard   Using the concept of democracy developed in Chapter 1, you will be able to evaluate how well Congress acts as a democratic institution. You will see that the story of Congress and democracy is a mixed one: Congress is, at times and under certain circumstances, highly responsive to the American public; at other times and under other circumstances, it is most responsive to special interest groups and large contributors.

Constitutional Foundations of the Modern Congress

As we saw in Chapter 2, the framers of the Constitution were concerned about the possibility of government tyranny. Yet they also wanted an energetic government capable of accomplishing its assigned tasks. These multiple objectives and concerns are reflected in the constitutional design of Congress.

Empowering Congress

The framers began by empowering Congress, making the legislative branch the center of lawmaking in the federal government. In Article I, Section 1, of the Constitution, they gave Congress the power to make the laws: "All legislative power herein granted shall be vested in a Congress of the United States." For the framers, Congress was the main bearer of federal governmental powers. In listing its powers and responsibilities in Article I, Section 8—the **enumerated powers**—they were largely defining the powers and responsibilities of the national government itself.[3] The framers enhanced the enumerated powers by adding the **elastic clause,** granting broad power to Congress to pass whatever legislation was necessary to carry out its enumerated powers.

Constraining Congress

Worried that too strong a legislative branch would lead to tyranny, the framers also limited congressional power. As we learned in Chapter 2, they made Congress a **bicameral** body—divided into two chambers—so that legislation could occur only after patient deliberation. Single-house legislative bodies, they believed, would be prone to rash action. They then added provisions—Article I, Section 9—specifically to prohibit certain kinds of actions: **bills of attainder, ex post facto laws,** the granting of titles of nobility, and the suspension of the right of **habeas corpus.** In the 1st Congress, additional constraints on congressional action were added in the form of the Bill of Rights. Note that the First Amendment, perhaps the most important constitutional provision protecting political liberty, begins with the words "Congress shall make no law . . . ."

We also learned in Chapter 2 that the national government was organized on the basis of a "separation of powers" and "checks and balances" so that "ambition might check ambition" and protect the country from tyranny. This means that although the framers envisioned the legislative branch as the vital center of a vigorous national government, they wanted to make sure that Congress would be surrounded by competing centers of government power. We will see that this fragmentation of governmental power in the United States affects how Congress works and often makes it difficult for it to fashion coherent and effective public policies.

Bicameralism and Representation

Congress is organized into two legislative chambers, each with its own principles of representation and constitutional responsibilities. While we often use the word "Congress" and think of it as a single institution, it is worth remembering that the House and Senate are very different from one another and are "virtually autonomous chambers."[4] In what came to be known as the Great Compromise, the framers decided to apportion the House of Representatives on the basis of population and the Senate on the basis of equal representation of the states (see Chapter 2 for details). The terms of office of the members of the House of Representatives were set at two years. The terms of the members

enumerated powers
Powers of the federal government specifically mentioned in the Constitution.

elastic clause
Article I, Section 8, of the Constitution, also called *the necessary and proper clause;* gives Congress the authority to make whatever laws are necessary and proper to carry out its enumerated responsibilities.

bicameral
As applied to a legislative body, consisting of two houses or chambers.

bill of attainder
A governmental decree that a person is guilty of a crime that carries the death penalty, rendered without benefit of a trial.

ex post facto law
A law that retroactively declares some action illegal.

habeas corpus
The legal doctrine that a person who is arrested must have a timely hearing before a judge.

TABLE 11.1 • Constitutional Differences Between the House and the Senate

	Senate	House of Representatives
Term	6 years	2 years
Elections	One-third elected in November of even-numbered years	Entire membership elected in November of even-numbered years
Number per state	2	Varies by size of state's population (minimum of 1 per state)
Total membership	100	435 (determined by Congress; at present size since 1910)
Minimum age for membership	30 years	25 years
Unique powers	Advice and consent for judicial and upper-level executive branch appointments	Origination of revenue bills
	Trial of impeachment cases	Bringing of impeachment charges
	Advice and consent for treaties	

of the Senate were set at six years, with only one-third of the seats up for election in each two-year election cycle. We learn in this chapter how these differences affect the legislative process.

The Constitution called for the election of senators by state legislatures, not by the people. The objective was to insulate one house of Congress from popular pressures and to make it a seat of deliberation and reflection. As James Madison put it, "The use of the Senate is to consist in its proceeding with more coolness . . . and with more wisdom than the popular branch."[5] The election of senators by the state legislatures could not survive the democratizing tendencies in the country, however. The Seventeenth Amendment, passed in 1913 after years of agitation for reform pressed by labor and farm groups and progressive reformers, gave the people the power to elect senators directly.

In addition to its general grants of power to Congress, the Constitution assigns particular responsibilities to each of the legislative chambers (see Table 11.1). For example, the House of Representatives has the power to impeach the president for "high crimes and misdemeanors," which it did in the case of Bill Clinton; the Senate has the power to conduct the trial of the president and remove him from office, if the impeachment charges are proved to its satisfaction (which they were not for Clinton).

Federalism

Congress is also greatly affected by the federal design of the Constitution. As we learned in Chapter 3, in our federal system, some powers and responsibilities are granted to the national government, some are shared between the national government and the states, and some are reserved for the states. It is inevitable in such a system that conflicts will occur between state governments and the national government and its legislative branch. Such conflicts sometimes reach the Supreme Court for resolution. In *United States* v. *Lopez* (1995), for instance, the Court ruled that Congress had gone too far in the use of its commerce clause powers when it passed a law banning firearms in and around public schools. Although the goal of the law might be worthy, such a matter, in the opinion of the Court, was the business of the states, not Congress.

Federalism also infuses "localism" into congressional affairs.[6] Although Congress is charged with making national policies, we should remember that the members of the Senate and the House come to Washington as the representatives of states and districts. They are elected by and are beholden to the voters at home and have voters' interests and opinions in mind even as they struggle with weighty issues of national importance.

Representation and Democracy

Members of Congress serve as our legislative representatives. But do they carry out this representative responsibility in a way that can be considered democratic?[7] To answer this question, we need to look at several aspects of representation: styles of representation, how closely the demographics of members of Congress match the demographics of the population in general, and the electoral process.

Styles of Representation

In a letter to his constituents written in 1774, English politician and philosopher Edmund Burke described two principal styles of representation. As a **delegate,** the representative tries to mirror perfectly the views of his or her constituents. As a **trustee,** the representative acts independently, trusting to his or her own judgment of how to best serve the public interest. Burke preferred the trustee approach: "Your representative owes you, not his industry

delegate

According to the doctrine articulated by Edmund Burke, an elected representative who acts in perfect accord with the wishes of his or her constituents.

trustee

According to the doctrine articulated by Edmund Burke, an elected representative who believes that his or her own best judgment, rather than instructions from constituents, should be used in making legislative decisions.

Today, candidates for the Senate like Republican Peter Coors of Colorado must hit the campaign trail if they want to be elected or re-elected. Prior to passage of the Seventeenth Amendment in 1913, which mandated that members of the Senate be elected directly by the people, candidates were mainly attuned to members of state legislatures who elected them to office, rather than to the public.

only, but his judgment; and he betrays you, instead of serving you, if he sacrifices it to your opinion."[8]

Campaigning for Congress in Illinois several decades later, Abraham Lincoln argued otherwise: "While acting as [your] representative, I shall be governed by [your] will, on all subjects upon which I have the means of knowing what [your] will is."[9] (If only he had access to public opinion polls!)

Every member of the House and Senate chooses between these two styles of representation. Their choice usually has less to do with their personal tastes than it has to do with the relative safety of their seats and how often they must face the electorate. Senators with six-year terms face the electorate less often than members of the House, so they are generally freer than representatives to assume the trustee style. As they get closer to the end of their term and the prospect of facing the voters, however, senators edge toward the delegate style. Because members of the House must run for reelection every two years, and tend to be in campaign mode at all times, they are pushed almost inexorably toward the delegate style.

You Are an Informed Voter

Race, Gender, and Occupation in Congress

Representation also implies that elected officials are like us in important ways—that they represent us because they are similar to us. Which raises the question: Is the makeup of Congress in a demographic sense similar to that of the nation as a whole? This is often called **descriptive representation.** From the point of view of descriptive representation, the views of significant groups—let us say, women and African Americans—will only be taken into account in policymaking if members of these groups hold seats in a legislative body in rough proportion to their size in the population. From this perspective, a perfectly representative legislative body would be similar to the general population in terms of race, sex, ethnicity, occupation, religion, age, and the like. In this sense, the U.S. Congress is highly *unrepresentative.*

descriptive representation
Sometimes called statistical representation; means that the composition of a representative body reflects the demographic composition of the population as a whole.

Gender and Race   Both women and racial minorities are significantly underrepresented in Congress, particularly in the Senate, despite important recent gains. We can see this in Figure 11.1, which compares the distribution of women and minorities in the 108th Congress (2003–2004) with their distribution in the country as a whole.

Black representation reached its peak during the post–Civil War Reconstruction period, when blacks played an important political role in several southern states. African Americans disappeared from Congress for many years after the reimposition of white supremacy in the South at the end of the nineteenth century. Although a handful of black representatives from northern cities served during the first half of the twentieth century—Oscar De Priest from Chicago's predominantly black South Side and Adam Clayton Powell from New York City's Harlem, for example—very few African Americans were elected to Congress until the late 1960s. While there has been some improvement in representation of African Americans in the House of Representatives—from 26 to 39 between the 102nd (1991–1992) and 107th Congresses (2000–2001)—their numbers are still well below what might be expected, given the proportion of African Americans in the population. All but four twentieth-century African American representatives were Democrats, the most recent of whom was J. C. Watts of Oklahoma.

Hispanics are even more poorly represented than African Americans relative to their proportion of the population, but the increase in their number in recent years has given the Hispanic caucus a greater voice in legislative affairs than in the past. Interestingly, while Hispanics reached parity with African Americans in the population, they are less well represented than

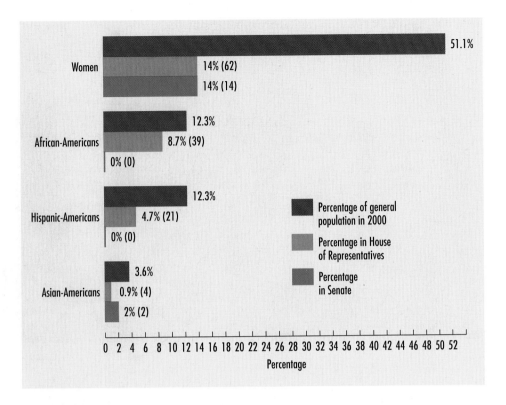

FIGURE 11.1 • **Women and Minorities in the 108th Congress**

Although their numbers in Congress have increased in recent years, women and racial minorities are still substantially underrepresented compared with their proportion in the American population. This graph compares the percentage of women and racial minorities in each house of the 108th Congress with their percentages in the population in 2000.

Source: U.S. Bureau of the Census, 2001; the Website of the U.S. Senate at **www.senate.gov;** and the Website of the House of Representatives at **www.house.gov.**

African Americans in Congress. Twenty-one served in the House (there were no Hispanics in the Senate) in the 108th Congress.

Other minority groups are represented among members of the House. There were seven Arab Americans in the 108th Congress and one Native American. Another Native American, Ben Nighthorse Campbell (R–CO), retired from the Senate at the end of 2004.

The first woman to sit in Congress was Jeannette Rankin of Montana, a suffragist and pacifist, elected in 1916. The number of women in Congress increased during the 1990s, with a big gain coming in the 1992 elections (often called the "year of the woman"), which sent 48 women to the House and 7 to the Senate in the 103rd Congress (compared with only 29 and 2, respectively, in the 102nd Congress). Proportionally, however, female representation in Congress is quite low, given that slightly more than half of all Americans are female; however, the proportion of women in the House of Representatives is about average for national legislative bodies around the world, though it lags seriously behind countries such as Sweden, the Netherlands, and Germany where women hold 45 percent, 37 percent, and 32 percent of legislative seats, respectively.[10] Four women were elected to the Senate in 2000, however, bringing their total to 13, the highest ever. Although leadership posts in Congress are overwhelmingly held by men, a few women have gained committee chairmanships in recent years. In 2003, moreover, Nancy Pelosi of California became the Democratic leader in the House, while Deborah Pryce of Ohio became the chair of the Republican Conference.

Ben Nighthorse Campbell of Colorado—now retired—was the first Native American since 1925 to serve in the U.S. Senate. He surprised both his constituents and colleagues when he switched his party affiliation from Democratic to Republican just a few years after he was first elected to office.

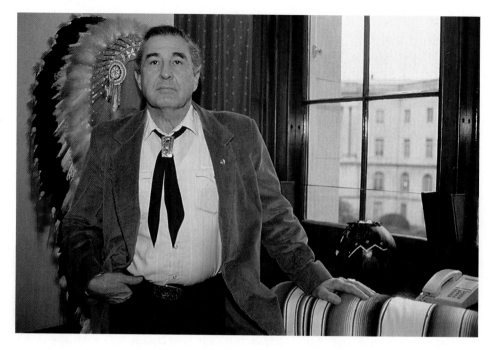

Occupation Members of Congress are far better educated than the rest of the population. They tend to come from high-income families, have personal incomes that are substantially above average, and lean heavily toward legal or business occupations. In 2003, there were 236 lawyers in Congress, or 44 percent (compare this with the late nineteenth century, however, when 60 to 70 percent were lawyers). The next most numerous occupational groups in Congress were in business and banking (together, about 30 percent). Educators made up another 19 percent.[11] Very few representatives and senators come from blue-collar families, traditional blue-collar jobs, or farming.

Does it matter that descriptive representation is so low in Congress, that its members are so demographically unrepresentative of the American people? Some political scientists and close observers of Congress think not. They suggest that the need to face the electorate forces lawmakers to be attentive to all significant groups in their **constituencies.** A representative from a farm district tends to listen to farm **constituents,** for example, even if that representative is not a farmer.

Nevertheless, many who feel they are not well represented—women, African Americans, Asian Americans, Hispanics, blue-collar workers, gays and lesbians, those with disabilities, and the poor—often believe that their interests would get a much better hearing if their numbers were substantially increased in Congress. There is some tentative evidence to support this view: Women members of the House introduce more bills related to women's and children's issues than do their male colleagues.[12] The demographic disparity between the American population and the makeup of Congress, then, suggests a violation of the norm of political equality, an important element of democracy.

constituency
The district of a legislator.

constituent
A citizen who lives in the district of an elected official.

The Electoral Connection

The election is the principal instrument in a democracy for keeping representatives responsive and responsible to citizens. Let's see how congressional elections affect the quality of representation in the United States.

Electoral Districts   Each state is entitled to two senators. Equal representation gives extraordinary power in the Senate to states with small populations. Wyoming, our least populous state, for example, has exactly the same number of senators as California, but it has less than one-seventieth of California's population; two senators in Wyoming represented only 494,000 people, while the two senators from California represented almost 35 million. Hypothetically, a coalition of 41 senators from the 11 smallest populations states, representing a mere 3 percent of the American population, can block any bill in the Senate (because 60 votes are needed to override a filibuster). To say that the Senate enshrines unequal representation is no exaggeration.

Representation in the House of Representatives is determined by a state's population, with the proviso that each state must have a least one congressional district. The House of Representatives decided that, beginning in 1910, its upper limit would be 435 members (the House can change this number at any time, though it is highly unlikely). Because the American population is constantly growing in size and changing where it lives, the 435 House representatives must be periodically redistributed among the states. **Reapportionment,** the technical name for this redistribution, occurs every 10 years, after the national census (see Figure 11.2 for the most recent changes).

reapportionment
The reallocation of House seats among the states, done after each national census, to ensure that seats are held by the states in proportion to the size of their populations.

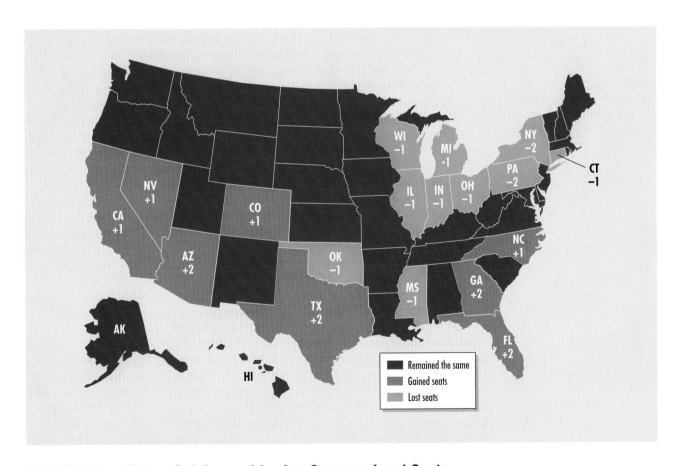

FIGURE 11.2 • States Gaining and Losing Congressional Seats Following the 2000 Census

The number of representatives for each state in the House of Representatives is based on the size of its population. Because the relative sizes of the states' populations change over time while the number of representatives is fixed, the number of representatives from each state is recalculated after each census. This map shows which states gained and lost representatives after the 2000 census.

Source: U.S. Bureau of the Census, 2001.

The term *gerrymander* is derived from this 1812 Elkanah Tinsdale cartoon, which lampoons a Massachusetts district drawn to ensure the election of a Republican candidate. The "Gerrymander" was named after Massachusetts Governor Elbridge Gerry, who signed the bill that created the salamander-shaped district.

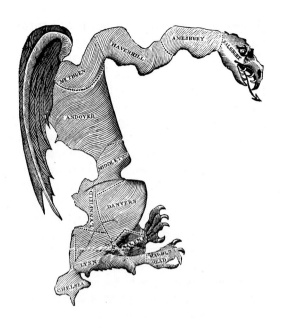

Based on the official census, some states keep the same number of seats; others gain or lose them depending on their relative population gains or losses.

States gaining or losing seats must redraw the boundary lines of their congressional districts so that they are of roughly equal population size. Redrawing district lines within a state is known as **redistricting** and is done primarily by state legislatures, though the courts have been playing a more active role lately in cases where legislatures are unable to decide (redistricting is the job of a nonpartisan commissions in five states). Very often in the past, because it was then legal to do so, legislatures created congressional districts of vastly different population sizes—in New York in the 1930s, some congressional districts had 10 times the population of others—and a significantly overrepresented rural population. The Supreme Court ruled in *Wesberry* v. *Sanders* (1964), however, that the principle of one person, one vote applies to congressional districts, meaning that congressional districts within a state must be of roughly equal population size. Because the distribution of the population changes in many states over the course of 10 years—some people moving from the cities to the suburbs; some people moving from rural areas to cities—many congressional district boundaries must be redrawn even in those states that have neither gained nor lost congressional seats.

Although congressional districts must hold approximately equal numbers of citizens, state legislatures are relatively free to draw district lines where they choose. The party that controls the state legislature and governorship usually tries to draw the lines in a way that will help its candidates win elections.[13] The results are often strange indeed. Rather than creating compact and coherent districts, neighborhoods, towns, and counties can be strung together in odd-looking ways in order to take full partisan advantage of the redistricting process. Taken to an extreme, the process is known as **gerrymandering,** after Governor Elbridge Gerry of Massachusetts, who signed a bill in 1811 that created a district that looked like a salamander. It made wonderful raw material for editorial cartoonists.

The Supreme Court has tried to prevent the most flagrant abuses, especially when some identifiable group of voters—for example, a racial or ethnic

redistricting
The redrawing of congressional district lines within a state to ensure roughly equal populations within each district.

gerrymandering
Redrawing electoral district lines to give an advantage to a particular party or candidate.

group—is disadvantaged, but it has turned a blind eye to partisan redistricting in which parties in power try to draw district lines to their own advantage. The Court, along with most politicians, seems to accept the notion that "to the victor belongs the spoils." This redistricting tends to be easily achieved when the same party controls both houses of the state legislature and the governor's office, though even here there are sometimes conflicts if one or another of the party's incumbent House members feels that he or she has been hurt by the redrawn district lines. But this situation of unified party control existed in only 15 states in 2001 when the states began to redistrict immediately after the Census. So divided party control of the redistricting process was the rule in 30 states—recall that 5 states use nonpartisan commissions—in the period leading up to the 2002 congressional elections. Needless to say, intense partisan conflict and deadlock were often the result, with resolution coming only after the matter was turned over to the courts.

In states with divided party control—a situation characteristic of the vast majority of states—where neither party has sufficient strength to get its way, the two parties have increasingly made redistricting arrangements that protect their incumbents, presumably on the grounds that the best each party can do is to protect hard-won gains. In large states such as California, Illinois, Michigan, New York, and Ohio, there is hardly a district anymore where the incumbent faces serious competition in the general election. Across the nation, incumbent-protection redistricting has become so extensive that no more than about 30 to 40 seats in elections to the House of Representatives are actually competitive; that is, almost every incumbent in the House of Representatives who chooses to run for reelection will win.

Amendments to the 1965 Voting Rights Act passed in 1982 encouraged the states to create House districts in which racial minorities would be in the majority. Sponsors of the legislation hoped that this would lead to an increase in the number of members of racial minority groups elected to the House. The result was the formation of 24 new **majority-minority districts,** 15 with African American majorities and 9 with Hispanic American majorities.[14] The creation of some of these districts has taken great imagination. North Carolina's Twelfth District, for instance, created after the 1990 census, linked a narrow strip of predominantly African American communities along 160 miles of Interstate 85 connecting Durham and Charlotte. After first encouraging the creation of majority-minority districts, the Supreme Court had second thoughts about districts that are highly irregular in form, noncontiguous (not compact), unconnected to traditional political jurisdictions (*Shaw* v. *Reno,* 1993), or drawn with race as the sole criterion (*Miller* v. *Johnson,* 1995). In *Hunt* v. *Cromartie* (2001), and much to the surprise of legal and political observers, the Court approved a slightly redrawn North Carolina Twelfth District map, ruling that race can be a significant factor in drawing district lines "so long as it is not the dominant and controlling one." This ruling suggests that most of the other majority-minority districts will probably survive legal challenges, even if their lines are slightly redrawn in the end. (For more insight into how district lines are drawn, see "By the Numbers: How are congressional districts drawn to include equal numbers of voters?")

The creation of these special majority-minority districts has contributed to the increase in the number of racial minority representatives in Congress; each of the districts has consistently elected a member of a racial minority group to the House. Ironically, however, the creation of such districts has undermined Democratic party strength in other districts by taking traditionally Democratic-oriented minority group voters from them. Naturally, Republicans

Simulation

You Are Redrawing the Districts in Your State

majority-minority districts
Districts drawn to ensure that a racial minority makes up the majority of voters.

By the Numbers

Can congressional districts be drawn to include equal numbers of voters yet favor one party over the other?

will control the House of Representatives, at least until the next census.

Behind Redistricting: In the House of Representatives, seats are apportioned to each state based on the state's population. Thus, after a new census is taken, a state may gain or lose seats based on the current count of people residing there. To gain a seat means that a new congressional district must be carved out of the state; to lose a seat means that lines must be redrawn to fill in the gap. Even in states where the size of its congressional delegation has not changed, lines must always be redrawn because of population shifts within state boundaries (e.g., more people moving to the suburbs). They must make such adjustments because the Supreme Court ruled in *Wesberry* v. *Sanders* (1964) that each congressional district within a state must be of roughly the same population size.

Here is a headline that might have appeared in any city newspaper in late 2001 or early 2002: "Legislature fails to reach agreement on congressional district lines; Issue to be decided by the state courts." What's going on? How difficult can it be to count people and draw congressional district lines? Actually, it is difficult and the issues are important.

Here is what is going on. Every 10 years, immediately after the census is conducted, a complicated process of redrawing congressional district lines goes on in the states. In six of them (Arizona, Hawaii, Idaho, Montana, New Jersey, and Washington), redistricting is done entirely by a special commission;* in the remainder, legislatures and governors must do the job. Agreement becomes especially difficult in states with divided government—those with a legislature controlled by one party and the governorship held by the other party, or those where the two houses of the legislature are controlled by different parties. Often, the courts are called upon to break the deadlock.

Why It Matters: How congressional district lines are drawn has a lot to do with which political party

How District Lines Are Drawn: In theory, as long as district lines create congressional districts of roughly equal size, and as long as district lines do not unduly disadvantage racial and ethnic groups, congressional district lines can be drawn in any way that politicians choose. The politicians can be very imaginative in doing so, as they try to ensure that their own party and favored members of Congress are advantaged by the outcome.

Where the district lines are drawn is extremely important in determining the composition of the congressional delegation from each state. Note the fol-

have been eager to support minority group efforts to form their own districts. Concentrating black voters in homogeneous districts has tipped the balance to Republicans in many congressional districts in the South. One result is that policies favored by a majority of African American citizens are less likely to be enacted because of the decreased strength of Democrats in the House, this despite an increase in the number of African American representatives.[15] In 2003, however, the Supreme Court signaled that it might begin considering the effect of majority-minority districts on the overall political influence of racial minorities in the political process when considering the acceptability of such districts.

lowing hypothetical example, which shows how easily district lines can be used to effect different outcomes. Let "D" stand for 100,000 Democratic voters; let "R" stand for 100,000 Republican voters; and let "A" stand for 100,000 African Americans, most of whom vote for Democrats. Taking the same number and locations of voters, district lines can be drawn to yield three Democratic seats and no Republican seats, and to yield two Republican seats and one Democratic seat.

Comment on the Process for Drawing District Lines: This example is somewhat exaggerated in order to make a point about how politicians strive for maximum flexibility in the redistricting process. In real life, the Court has also demanded that district lines not deviate too much from their historical patterns and that they be relatively compact, putting people who live near each other in the same district. The second example here also shows what happened when African American organizations and leaders, seeking to increase their representation in Congress, and Republicans, seeking to gain an advantage over Democrats, formed an alliance of convenience during the 1990s to create majority-minority districts across a swath of southern states. These majority-minority districts increased the number of African Americans in Congress, but the process of concentrating black voters in these districts made the other districts in these states more homogeneously white and Republican, increasing the GOP advantage.

What to Watch For: Redistricting is one of the most important things that goes on in our political

Result: districts equal in size (1.4 million each); three Democratic seats, zero Republican seats.

Result: districts equal in size (1.4 million each); one Democratic seat carved out to create a position for an African-American and two Republican seats.

D = Democrats   R = Republicans   A = African Americans

Different Congressional District Lines, Different Party Outcomes

system, yet it is virtually invisible to the general public. Pay attention to the debates over redistricting in your state and determine what political alliances appear and what political bargains are being struck.

What Do You Think? Do you think there might be some nonpartisan, scientific method to draw district lines that would avoid the sometimes unseemly process of reshaping congressional districts to suit political parties and interested groups? If there was such a method, do you think it would be better than our current system? Why or why not?

*National Conference of State Legislatures, 2004.

Money and Congressional Elections Running for the House or the Senate is a very expensive proposition, and it keeps getting more expensive. The average Senate race now costs almost $5 million, while the price tag for a House race—where most races are not very competitive, as you've seen—is just under $1 million, double the cost of congressional races just 25 years ago, even taking into account inflation.[16] In total, candidates for Congress spent about $1 billion during the 2001–2002 election cycle.[17] There is nothing particularly surprising about the high cost of political campaigns, given the ever-greater reliance on expensive campaign technologies such as mass and targeted mailings; polling; focus groups; television, radio, and print advertising; Websites; and phone banks.

This spending by the candidate's campaign—called hard money—is but the tip of the iceberg. To the grand total, we must add the dollars raised and spent by national, state, and local political party organizations on congressional campaigns and money spent by private groups on various forms of advertising and get-out-the-vote efforts designed to assist candidates for congressional office. Although new campaign finance rules came into effect after 2002 under terms of the McCain-Feingold legislation that outlawed most soft money contributions to the political parties and restricted some aspects of campaign communications (independent campaigns) by private advocacy groups (see the discussions of the rule changes and their effects in Chapters 7 and 10), individuals and groups have found innovative ways to pump money into congressional campaigns. The doubling of the maximum limit on the amount of money that candidates can accept from individuals under the new law—from $1,000 per election campaign to $2,000—is important. So too is the tendency of advocacy groups to find ways around the restrictions on campaign communications discussed earlier.

Incumbents, especially in the House, have an easier time raising money than their challengers and spend more. **Open-seat election** races, in which no incumbent is involved, also attract and use lots of money (see Figure 11.3). Moreover, being a member of the majority party in Congress serves as a magnet for money because contributors generally want to be able to have access to those in power.[18]

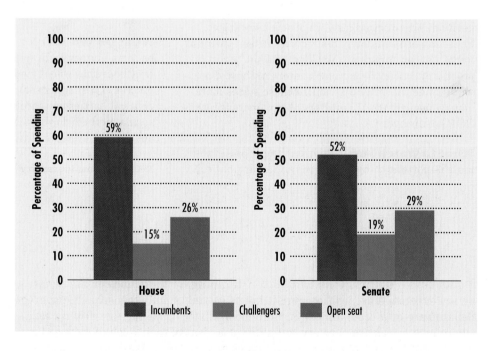

FIGURE 11.3 ● **Campaign Money Spent by Incumbents, Challengers, and Open-Seat Candidates, 2002 Election Cycle**

Because campaign contributors want access to important decision makers in Congress, contributors tend to give a disproportionate share of campaign contributions to incumbents.

Source: Federal Election Commission.

Participation

The Debate Over Campaign Finance Reform

open-seat election

An election in which there is no incumbent officeholder.

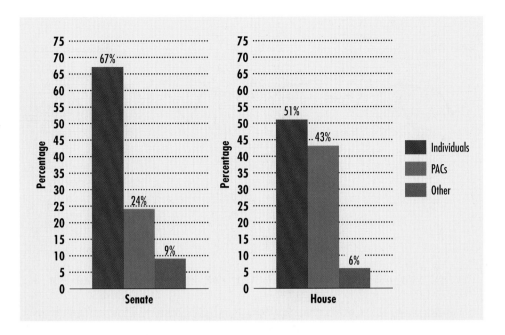

FIGURE 11.4 • **Sources of Congressional Campaign Money, 2002 Election Cycle.**

Although the largest share of hard money campaign contributions comes from individuals, political action committee (PAC) contributions are also very important.

Source: Federal Election Commission.

Congressional campaign hard money comes from four main sources: individuals, political action committees (PACs), political parties, and the candidates themselves (see Figure 11.4). Individuals contribute the largest amount, accounting for 51 percent of contributions to House candidates and 67 percent to Senate candidates in the 2002 election cycle. PACs are the next largest, accounting for 43 percent of campaign contributions in the House contributions and 24 percent in the Senate. PACs are allowed to contribute up to $5,000 per candidate per election, and they can give to as many candidates as they wish. Many especially wealthy candidates support their election campaigns out of their own pockets. In the record to date, John Corzine (D–NJ) spent $62 million in his bid for a Senate seat in 2000. He only barely won.

Congressional candidates also receive campaign money from national, congressional, and state party committees. Party committees are allowed to make a $5,000 contribution per campaign to each House candidate. National and senatorial party committees are allowed to give $17,500 to each candidate for each stage of the electoral process. Many congressional candidates also receive campaign contributions from PACs associated with congressional party leaders such as House Majority Leader Tom Delay of Texas and then–Senate Minority Leader Tom Daschle of South Dakota.

A majority of Americans have been saying for a long time that they wanted to change the system of funding campaigns. Why did it take so long to reform the system? We examine this question in the "Using the Framework" feature.

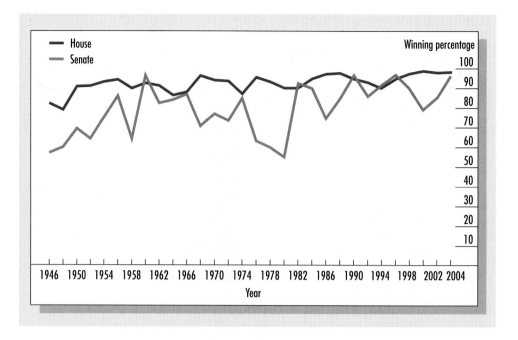

FIGURE 11.5 • Rates of Incumbent Reelection in Congress

The probability that incumbents will be reelected remains at historic highs. This does not mean, however, that the membership of Congress is stagnant. Turnover in membership is substantial because of retirements and the defeat of incumbents in primary elections.

Source: Calculations by the authors from various issues of the *Congressional Quarterly Weekly Report*.

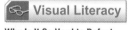

Why Is It So Hard to Defeat
an Incumbent?

The Incumbency Factor   Incumbents—current officeholders—win at much higher rates than in the past, especially in the House (see Figure 11.5). In the 2002 elections, for example, 98 percent of incumbents returned to the House and 85 percent returned to the Senate. In 2004, 98 percent of House and 96 percent of Senate incumbents won reelection. High incumbency reelection rates, especially in the House of Representatives, means that the overwhelming majority of electoral contests for Congress are not really competitive; almost all seats in the House today are considered "safe," with the incumbent facing little serious challenge from the opposition party candidate.

There are several reasons incumbents almost always win when they seek reelection. The most important, of course, is that the redistricting process in many states in recent years—reviewed earlier in this chapter—has been fashioned to protect incumbents in each of the parties. On the face of it, this process has been very effective.

Incumbents also have the advantage of attracting and spending much more campaign money than their rivals. Many contributors look at campaign contributions as an "investment" in access to key members of Congress.[19] To contribute to a challenger is to jeopardize access if the challenger loses, which is most often the case. It may seem odd, at first glance, that incumbents still feel the need to raise and spend so much money on their nomination and election campaigns. They do so, according to most observers, to preempt challenges from within their own party to their renominations and to convince candidates from the other party that they stand little chance in the fall elections.

Using the Framework

Campaign Finance Reform

Why did it take so long to get campaign finance reform when so many Americans wanted it for such a long time?

Background: Campaign finance reform finally happened in 2002 when President George W. Bush signed the Bipartisan Campaign Reform Act. Becoming effective in 2003, the new legislation bans soft-money contributions to the national parties, and limits the ability of independent groups to run television campaign ads in the 30 days before a primary election and 60 days before a general election. The public had long been bothered by the existing campaign finance system, but politicians had not paid much attention. Things began to change only after John McCain made reform the keystone of his campaign to win the Republican nomination for president in 2000. Further impetus to reform came from the Enron collapse in 2001, and revelations of how free it had been with its money in funding parties and candidates. But why did it take so long for reform to happen? Here we take a broad view of the question, considering how structural, political linkage, and governmental factors affected the fortunes of reform.

Governmental Action

Campaign finance reform bills died in the House and Senate.

Governmental Level

The Supreme Court has ruled that government cannot limit the amount of money spent during campaigns by candidates, individuals, and organizations (although it can limit hard-money contributions to candidates).

Incumbent representatives, senators, and presidents were very successful under the existing system of campaign finance; it is not necessarily in their interest to reform the system.

Political Linkages Level

Private groups of all political persuasions worked in Congress and in the states to block campaign finance reform in order to preserve their influence in electoral campaigns.

Voters had not shown much interest in demanding that local, state, or national candidates support campaign finance reform.

Public opinion surveys show that Americans wanted campaign finance reform but cared more about other things, including the state of the economy, crime, terrorism, and education.

Political party committees at all levels found the existing system to be compatible with their interests.

Structural Level

The Bill of Rights protects free expression by all citizens, as well as freedom of association; individuals can support whomever they want in the political arena and can form groups to advance their political causes.

Income and wealth inequality give some Americans, but not others, the means to make substantial contributions to candidate and issue campaigns.

Members of Congress must spend a considerable amount of their time staying in touch with their constituents. Here Representative Rosa DeLauro (D–CT) visits a school in her district.

franking privilege

Public subsidization of mail from the members of Congress to their constituents.

Incumbents also use the congressional machinery to help their reelection chances.[20] Already well known to voters because they garner so much free media coverage, members of Congress have many ways to advertise their accomplishments and keep their names before the public. For example, the **franking privilege** allows them to mail newsletters, legislative updates, surveys, and other self-promoting literature free of charge. The House and the Senate also provide travel budgets for lawmakers to make periodic visits to their states or districts. Because members believe that time spent in their districts helps their electoral chances—a belief supported by a great deal of research[21]—they spend lots of time back home.[22] Some manage to spend three or four days a week in their districts or states, meeting constituents, giving speeches, raising money, and keeping in the public eye. The congressional leadership helps by scheduling important legislative business for the Tuesday-to-Thursday period and cutting down the number of hours Congress is in session.

casework

Services performed by members of Congress for constituents.

Incumbents also use their offices to "service the district." One way is through **casework,** helping constituents cut through the red tape of the federal bureaucracy, whether it be by speeding up the arrival of a late Social Security check or expediting the issuance of a permit for grazing on public land.[23] Generous budgets for establishing and staffing offices in the constituency help representatives and senators do casework. Another way to service the district is to provide **pork**—federal dollars for various projects in the district or state. In 1998, with the federal budget in surplus, members of Congress heightened their prospects in the coming congressional elections by passing a massive highway spending bill that included more than 1,400 "demonstration projects" targeted for specific roads and bridges in 400 congressional districts.

pork

Also called *pork barrel;* projects designed to bring to the constituency jobs and public money for which the members of Congress can claim credit.

How Representative?   Representatives and senators pay a great deal of attention to the interests and the preferences of the people in their districts and states. Because they are worried about being reelected—even incumbents tend to run scared, perhaps afraid of being the exception that proves the rule—they try to see as many people as they can during their frequent visits home, and they pay attention to their mail and the public opinion polls. Moreover, they vote on and pass laws in rough approximation to public opinion. Members of Congress vote in a manner that is consistent with public opinion in their districts about two-thirds of the time[24] (but members also are pretty skilled at influencing public opinion in their districts), and Congress produces laws that are consistent with national public opinion at about the same rate.[25]

In a substantial number of cases, however, Congress does *not* follow public opinion, even on highly visible issues. If members of Congress follow public opinion two-thirds of the time on important bills, that still leaves one-third of the time that they go their own way. The determination of House Republicans to impeach Bill Clinton in 1998 in the face of strong public opinion opposition is the most obvious recent example. Moreover, on many issues of high complexity or low visibility, such as securities and telecommunications regulation, the public may have no well-formed opinions at all. It is in these areas that we can most fully see the influence of money and interest groups at work. The lobbying community, as we have learned, overwhelmingly represents business and the professions. Moreover, legislators, who are almost entirely on their own in organizing and financing their reelection campaigns, are tempting targets for interest groups. To the degree that these influences distort popular sovereignty and undermine political equality, democracy is impaired.

One of the reasons members of Congress have some latitude in representing public opinion in their districts—indeed, in the nation—is that, as we have shown, most come to Congress from relatively "safe" districts where being turned out by the voters is not common. Consequently, House elections do not adequately fulfill the role assigned to elections in democratic theory: as the principle instrument for keeping elected leaders responsive and responsible.

How Congress Works

Congress is a vital center of decision making and policymaking in our national government. It is not a place where the executive's bills are simply rubber-stamped, as it is in legislative bodies in many parliamentary systems. By all accounts, Congress is the most influential and independent legislative body among the Western democratic nations. In this section, we turn our attention to how Congress is organized and how it functions as a working legislative body.

Comparative

Comparing Legislatures

There are a number of very important things to keep in mind as we examine how Congress is organized and operates. First, while they are alike in many ways, the House and Senate are very different institutions. The bodies differ in size, the kinds of constituencies House members and senators represent, the terms of office of their members, and their constitutional responsibilities; together, these differences give each chamber a distinctive character.

Second, both the House and Senate are plagued by what could almost be called centrifugal forces in the sense that things are always on the verge of flying apart, with each representative and senator tempted to go his or her own way. The task of running each body has been likened to "herding cats." The reasons are fairly obvious: Representatives and senators are like independent contractors. Congressional leaders lack the normal tools of organizational

The majority party organizes the House at the beginning of each session of Congress and generally has its way if its members remain disciplined. Here the leadership of the minority Democrats in the 104th Congress protest their exclusion from House deliberations by holding mock sessions outside on the Capitol lawn.

leadership to force compliance with their wishes; they cannot order members about, they cannot hire or fire them (this is the role of voters), nor can they control the size of their paychecks or benefits. Moreover, in our candidate-centered form of politics, congressional leaders have little control over the re-election of representatives and senators who run their own campaigns, from fund-raising to deciding how to pitch their messages to the voters. Because of this, members of Congress come to Washington as relative equals and are not easily pushed about. In this section, we examine ways that Congress tries to pull itself together and work effectively as a legislative body.

Political Parties in Congress

Political parties have a very strong presence in Congress. Its members come to Washington, D.C., as elected candidates of a political party. At the start of each session, they organize their legislative business along political party lines. At the start of each new Congress, each **party caucus** meets to select party committees and leaders. The majority party in the House selects the Speaker of the House, while the majority party in the Senate selects the president pro tempore (usually its most senior member) and the majority leader. The majority party in each house also selects the chairs of the committees and subcommittees and determines the party ratios for each.

party caucus
An organization of the members of a political party in the House or Senate.

The Party Composition of Congress
From the 1932 elections in the midst of the Great Depression until the 1994 elections, with brief interludes of Republican control along the way, Congress was dominated by the Democratic party. The Democratic domination of House elections during this period is especially notable, even surviving GOP landslide wins in the presidential elections of 1980 (Reagan), 1984 (Reagan), and 1988 (Bush). In the Senate, Republicans were in the majority for only 10 years during this same period. Democratic party domination ended with the 1994 elections, however, when Republicans won control of both houses of Congress for the first time in 40 years. Since then,

with the exception of the Senate in 2001–2002, the Republicans have retained control of both houses of Congress, though by small margins.

Party Voting in Congress   The political parties provide important glue for the decentralized fragments of Congress and the legislative process. Party labels are important cues for members of Congress as they decide how to vote on issues before the committees and on the floor of the House and the Senate. We know this from a long tradition of research on party divisions in roll-call voting. This research tells us that party affiliation is the best predictor of the voting behavior of members of the Congress and that it is becoming ever more important.[26] That is to say, both houses of Congress are becoming more **partisan.**

Figure 11.6 shows how often the average Democrat and the average Republican voted with his or her party in partisan votes in Congress.[27] You can see that partisanship is very high—now members vote along party lines in four out of every five votes—and has been steadily increasing. Partisanship was particularly high among Republicans in the 104th Congress, especially in the House, where Newt Gingrich led a partywide effort to legislate the provisions

partisan
A committed member of a party; seeing issues from the point of view of the interests of a single party.

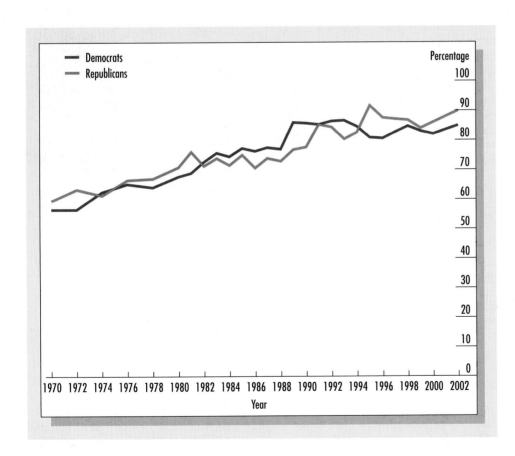

FIGURE 11.6 • **Party Voting in Congress**

Partisanship has been growing in Congress. One indicator is the increase in the percentage of times the average Democrat and Republican in the House and Senate sided with his/her party on partisan votes—those votes when a majority of Democrats voted against a majority of Republicans.

Source: Roger H. Davidson and Walter J. Oleszek, *Congress and Its Members* (Washington, D.C.: CQ Press, 2004), p. 273.

The Rise of *Partisan* *Conflict*

Republican and Democratic Panel Leaders Take Feud to the Senate Floor

The Story: Angry about a draft memo from a Democratic staff member of the Senate Intelligence Committee, Senator Pat Roberts of Kansas, chair of the intelligence panel, blasted the Democrats. He claimed that Democrats were trying to "discredit the committee's work and undermine its conclusions, no matter what these conclusions might be." Republican Whip Roy Blunt of Missouri joined in the condemnation of his Democratic colleagues, saying they were trying to lead the public "down a path of deception to score political points." Senator John D. Rockefeller IV of West Virginia, the ranking Democratic member on the panel rejected the criticism and fought back, saying that "the [Republican] majority has left the Senate minority with two choices. Either abandon what we believe is a fundamental obligation of this body to the American people or reluctantly part

ways and use our rights as a minority to get that job done on our own."

The Facts: In 2003 and 2004, the Senate Intelligence Committee was investigating misuse of intelligence by the Bush administration concerning Iraq's purported chemical, biological, and nuclear programs. The investigation began after Americans forces failed to turn up any evidence of the existence of weapons of mass destruction (WMD) after the fall of Baghdad. The Senate panel's inquiry was vitally important for the country

of the House GOP's congressional campaign platform, the Contract with America. Extraordinary levels of partisanship were also evident in the House on votes to impeach President Clinton in December 1999; in the votes associated with his trial in the Senate in early 1999; and in the House vote in 2001 on President George W. Bush's proposed $1.6 trillion tax cut, when hardly any representative or senator broke ranks with his or her party. In the aftermath of the September 11 attacks on the United States, bipartisanship was the rule in both houses for a few months as Congress tackled legislation connected to the war on terrorism. The honeymoon did not last; Congress adjourned at the end of 2001 torn again by intense party conflict. ("The Rise of Partisan Conflict" feature shows an example of how growing partisanship is affecting the legislative process in Congress.)

There are a number of reasons within-party unity and partisan roll-call voting are increasing. One factor is the changing regional bases of the parties. For example, southern conservative Democrats—frequent allies of because Iraq's possession of such programs was the primary rationale for the invasion of Iraq in spring 2003. Were the stated reasons for going to war caused by bad intelligence? If so, then how might intelligence gathering and interpretation efforts be improved? Or, was intelligence about WMD correct but misused by the administration to firm up public and international support for military action that the president wanted to happen in any event?

It soon became apparent that the partisan stakes in the panel's investigation and report were extraordinarily high. For Democrats, a report from the intelligence panel suggesting that President Bush and members of his administration had misused good intelligence would discredit the president and the Republican party. For Republicans, a report that focused on failures among the intelligence agencies—CIA, FBI, and the National Security Administration—would be preferable, because it would vindicate President Bush's actions in Iraq. It was into this charged partisan atmosphere that the Democratic memo exploded, raising temperatures even higher. The memo suggested that Democrats on the Senate Intelligence Committee should "identify the most exaggerated claims" made by administration officials about WMD in Iraq and "contrast them with the intelligence estimates that have since been declassified." The memo further suggested that the Democrats should be prepared to reject the panel's investigation entirely and insist on the appointment of a special independent prosecutor to conduct an inquiry directed at revealing "the misleading, if not flagrantly dishonest, methods and motives of senior administration officials who made the case for unilateral preemptive war."

What's at Stake? For Democrats, a report stating that the Bush administration had misused intelligence information to further its aims in the Middle East would be a powerful tool to use against the GOP and President Bush in the 2004 elections. For party strategists and leaders, a report that undermined the administration's main rationale for going to war might swing just enough votes to enable the Democrats to regain the presidency and win majorities in the House and Senate. Republicans saw the issues in very much the same terms: A negative report about the administration would put GOP control of the presidency and Congress in jeopardy. Republican panel members were not about to let this happen.

Is This Good for Democracy?

● Does partisan conflict in Congress lead to better government policies? Or has it become so intense lately that it gets in the way of congressional deliberations, and turns off the public to boot? ● In the case here, for example, do you think a report from the deeply divided Senate Intelligence Committee will lead to the better use of intelligence information in the future? Or does partisanship on the committee mean that the investigation was flawed from the start? ● And, if partisan conflict contaminated the Intelligence Committee report, how confident are you that Congress can conduct more investigations of serious problems in the future if the present partisan climate persists?

Source: Headline and quotes are from Douglas Jehl, "Republican and Democratic Panel Leaders Take Feud to the Senate Floor," *New York Times* (November 5, 2003), p. 1.

Republicans in Congress in the past—are fast disappearing, as many politicians and voters have switched over to the Republican party in the rapidly realigning South. In the run-up to the 2004 national elections, five southern Democratic senators—including John Breaux (LA), John Edwards (SC), Ernest Hollings (SC), Bob Graham (FL), and Zell Miller (GA)—announced their retirements, opening the way to further Republican gains in the region. There are also fewer liberal or moderate Republicans in Congress as GOP strength in the northeast—the traditional home of party moderates—has waned. Another reason that partisanship is on the rise in Congress is that partisan conflict and division is happening across the board in the country—a subject we have looked at several times in this book—especially among party activists and voters. Members of Congress, facing an evermore partisan-divided electorate and hearing from increasing numbers of party-associated advocacy groups, are pressured strongly to act as partisans as they go about their legislative tasks.

It is not entirely clear whether party voting differences are caused directly by party affiliation or indirectly by the character of constituencies by ideology. Some scholars have found strong independent party effects regardless of constituency or ideology. Others argue that the tendency of people in the same party to vote together is simply a reflection of the fact that Democratic lawmakers tend to come from districts and states that are similar to one another and that Republican lawmakers come from places that are different from the constituencies of Democrats. Republicans generally come from higher-income districts than Democrats. Democratic districts, in turn, tend to contain more union members and racial minorities. The strongest tie, in this line of argument, is between the member of Congress and the constituency, not between the member and the party.[28]

Increasingly, internal party unity and conflict between the parties seem attributable to ideology. Both in the electorate and among the members of Congress and other political elites, Democrats are becoming more consistently liberal, while Republicans are becoming more consistently conservative.[29] Political scientist and former Democratic representative from Oklahoma Mickey Edwards observes the following about the ideological tendencies of members of Congress: "...most people who run for office have ... [strong] feelings not only about specific issues but about general philosophical concepts, such as the proper role of government, the impact of taxation on investment and savings, and the reasons for crime and poverty."[30]

Congressional Leadership

The political parties work through the leadership structure of Congress because the leaders of the majority political party are, at the same time, the leaders of the House and the Senate.[31] As Congress becomes more partisan, party becomes ever more important in shaping the actions of House and Senate leaders.[32]

Leadership in the House
The leader in the House of Representatives is the Speaker of the House. This position is recognized in the Constitution and stands in the line of succession to the presidency, immediately after the vice president.

Until 1910, the Speaker exercised great power over the House legislative process. The bases of his power were his right to appoint committees and their chairs and his position as chair of the powerful Rules Committee. The revolt of the rank and file against Speaker "Uncle Joe" Cannon in 1910 resulted in the Speaker's removal from the Rules Committee and the elimination of the Speaker's power to appoint committees and their chairs.

From 1910 until the early 1970s, the weakened Speaker competed with a handful of powerful committee chairs for leadership of the House. A few Speakers, such as Sam Rayburn of Texas, were able to lead by sheer dint of their personalities and legislative skills, but power tilted toward the committee chairs most of the time.

The Democratic Caucus staged a revolt against the committee system after 1974 and restored some of the powers of the Speaker, especially in making committee assignments. The Democratic Caucus also gave the Speaker more power to refer bills to committee, control the House agenda, appoint members to select committees, and direct floor debate. This change gave Speakers Tip O'Neill, Jim Wright, and Tom Foley considerable leadership resources.

In 1995, the Republican Caucus gave even more power to control the House legislative process to their first Speaker since 1954, Newt Gingrich.

Timeline

The Power of the Speaker of the House

Some scholars suggest that Gingrich's speakership was the most powerful one since Cannon's.[33] Unexpected losses of Republican House seats in the 1998 elections, after a campaign featuring a Gingrich-designed advertising blitz to impeach the president, led to his resignation of the Speakership and from the House. He was succeeded as Speaker by Dennis Hastert of Illinois, a person much less charismatic than Gingrich and one more tied to the traditional way of doing things in the House.

The majority party in the House also selects a majority leader and **whip** to help the Speaker plan strategy and manage the legislative business of the House. Neither House nor party rules spell out the responsibilities of this office. The nature of these jobs depends very much on what the Speaker wants and on the majority leader's and whip's talents and energy. In the 106th and 107th Congresses (1999–2002), partly because of Hastert's understated style and his apparent aversion to the media spotlight and majority leader Dick Armey's mixed success, it appeared to many observers that Republican Whip Tom DeLay of Texas was the real leader of the House of Representatives.[34] His hard-nosed, "take-no-prisoner" partisanship and his ability to keep his party's representatives in line earned him the nickname "the hammer." Perhaps it was no surprise, then, that DeLay became the House majority leader in the 108th Congress following Armey's retirement at the end of 2002.

The minority party elects a minority floor leader, who acts as the chief spokesperson and legislative strategist for the opposition. The minority leader not only tries to keep the forces together but also seeks out members of the majority party who might be won over against the House leadership on key issues. Like the majority party, the minority party elects a whip to assist the minority leader count and mobilize votes. In 2001, Democrats elected to the post Nancy Pelosi of California, who became the highest-ranking woman in the House.

whip

A political party member in Congress charged with keeping members informed of the plans of the party leadership, counting votes before action on important issues, and rounding up party members for votes on bills.

Web Exploration
Parties and Leaders in Congress

Issue: Much of what Congress does is determined by the parties and the leadership in the House and Senate.

Site: Access the home pages of the Speaker of the House and of the Senate Majority Leader on our Website at **www.ablongman.com/greenberg**. Go to the "Web Explorations" section for Chapter 11. Select "Parties and leaders in Congress," then "leaders" for each house of Congress. For the House, select "leadership offices," then "Office of the Speaker." For the Senate, select "Senators," then "Senate Leadership." At these sites, you will be able to examine not only the biographies of the present leaders, but also the party legislative programs each has fashioned for his institution.

What You've Learned: What do you think of these programs? Where are the major areas of agreement and disagreement between the parties?

Hint: Your answer will probably depend a great deal on whether you identify with one of the parties and its agenda.

Majority leader Tom DeLay of Texas is considered by most close observers to be the real leader of the Republican Party in the House of Representatives, rather than the Speaker, Dennis Hastert.

Leadership in the Senate   Leadership in the Senate is less visible. Senators with formal leadership titles exercise little influence. The presiding officer of the Senate is the vice president of the United States, but he is rarely in evidence and has no power other than the right to break tie votes. On rare occasions, however, this becomes an important power. Because the 2000 elections left the Senate split 50–50, Vice President Cheney's tie-breaking vote allowed the Republicans to control that body. The majority party also elects a president pro tempore (always the member with the most seniority) to preside in the absence of the vice president.

The Senate majority leader is as close as one comes to a leader in this body, but the powers of the office pale before those of the Speaker of the House. The Senate majority leader has some influence in committee assignments, office space designation, and control of access to the floor of the Senate. The majority leader is also important in the scheduling of the business of the Senate. The degree of actual influence is based less on formal powers, however, than on skills of personal persuasion, the respect of colleagues, visibility in the media as majority party spokesperson, and a role at the center of many of the various communication networks.

The power of the position is thus personal and not institutional; it cannot be passed on to the next leader. The Senate remains a body of independent, relatively equal members loosely tied together by threads of party loyalty, ideology, and mutual concern about the next election. It is not an environment conducive to decisive leadership, though a few, such as Lyndon Johnson, managed to transcend the limited powers of the office. Bill Frist (R–TN), the current majority leader, is very much in the traditional mold of Senate leaders.

Congressional Committees

Most of the work of Congress takes place in its many committees and subcommittees. Committees are where many of the details of legislation are hammered out and where much of the oversight of the executive branch takes place.

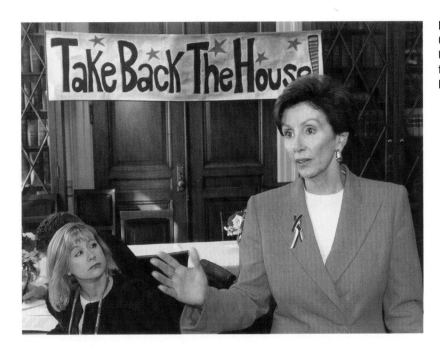

Democratic minority leader Nancy Pelosi of California is the highest-ranking woman in the U.S. House of Representatives. Here she talks to the party activists about the need to recapture the House of the Republicans in the 2004 elections.

Why Congress Has Committees Committees serve several useful purposes. For one thing, they allow Congress to process the huge flow of business that comes before it. The committees serve as screening devices, allowing only a small percentage of the bills put forward to take up the time of the House and the Senate.

Committees are also islands of specialization, where members and staff develop the expertise to handle complex issues and to meet executive branch experts on equal terms. The Ways and Means Committee of the House can go toe-to-toe with the Treasury Department, for instance, on issues related to taxation. Committee expertise is one of the reasons Congress remains a vital lawmaking body.

Members of Congress also use their committee positions to enhance their chances for reelection. Rational lawmakers usually try to secure committee assignments that will allow them to channel benefits to their constituents or to advance an ideological agenda popular in their district or state.

Types of Committees in Congress There are several kinds of committees, each of which serves a special function in the legislative process.

Standing committees are set up permanently, as specified in the House and Senate rules. These committees are the first stop for potential new laws. The ratio of Democrats to Republicans on each committee is set for each house through a process of negotiation between the majority and minority party leaders. The majority party naturally enjoys a majority on each of the committees and controls the chair, as well as a substantial majority on the most important committees, such as the Budget and Finance Committee in the Senate and the Rules Committee and the Ways and Means Committee in the House. The ratio of Democrats and Republicans on committees is a point of considerable contention between the two parties, especially when they are evenly divided, as in the 107th Congress. At the start of that Congress, Senate Democrats threatened to hold up the business of the chamber unless given equal membership on committees in recognition of the 50–50 split in the Senate at the start of the 107th Congress and eventually got their way.

standing committees
Relatively permanent congressional committees that address specific areas of legislation.

Later president of the United States, Lyndon B. Johnson of Texas was one of the most effective majority leaders in the history of the United States Senate. Here he urges Senators Kennedy, Symington, Humphrey, and Proxmire to vote for an important civil rights bill.

hearings

The taking of testimony by a congressional committee or subcommittee.

markup

The process of revising a bill in committee.

select committees

Temporary committees in Congress created to conduct studies or investigations; they have no power to report bills.

joint committees

Congressional committees with members from both the House and the Senate.

conference committees

Ad hoc committees, made up of members of both the Senate and the House of Representatives, set up to reconcile differences in the provisions of bills.

The avalanche of legislative business cannot be managed and given the necessary specialized attention in the full House and Senate standing committees. For most bills, **hearings,** negotiations, and **markup** take place in subcommittees. It is in the subcommittees, moreover, that most oversight of the executive branch takes place.

Select committees are temporary committees created by congressional leaders to conduct studies or investigations. They have no power to send bills to the House or Senate floor. They exist to resolve matters that standing committees cannot or do not wish to handle. Often the issues before select committees are highly visible and gain a great deal of public attention for their members. Select committees investigated the Watergate scandal, the Iran-Contra affair, and the 9/11 Commission's report on intelligence failures.

Joint committees, with members from both houses, are organized to facilitate the flow of legislation. The Joint Budget Committee, for instance, helps speed up the normally slow legislative process of considering the annual federal budget. (The budget process is discussed in Chapter 17.)

Before a bill can go to the president for signature, it must pass in identical form in each chamber. The committee that irons out the differences between House and Senate versions is called a **conference committee,** and one is created as needed for each piece of major legislation. While it is probably an exaggeration to call conference committees the "third house of Congress," as some political observers do, there is no denying their central role in the march of bills through the legislative labyrinth. Although they are supposed to reconcile versions of bills coming out of the House and the Senate, conference committees sometimes add, subtract, or amend provisions that are of great consequence. Much of the power of conference committees comes from the fact that bills reported by them to the House and Senate must be voted up or down; no new amendments are allowed.

How Members of Congress Get on Committees   Because committees are so central to the legislative process, getting on the right one is important for reelection and for achieving policy and ideological goals. Committee assignments are determined by the political parties, guided (but not determined) by the members' **seniority** and preferences. Each party in each chamber goes about the assignment process in a slightly different way. House Democrats use their Steering Committee, chaired by their floor leader, to make assignments. House Republicans have their own Steering Committee on which the Speaker (when Republicans are in the majority) has direct control of one-fourth of the votes. The Speaker also appoints Republican members to the powerful Rules and Ways and Means Committees. In the Senate, both parties use small steering committees made up of party veterans and leaders to make assignments.

seniority
Length of service.

Lawmakers have traditionally tried to land positions on committees that will help them serve their constituents and better their prospects for reelection. Thus, they will try to join a committee that directly serves their constituency—Agriculture if the member is from a farm district or state, or Interior if the member is from a mining or oil district—or one of the elite committees, such as Rules, Ways and Means, Finance, or Appropriations. Appointment to an elite committee gives a lawmaker not only high visibility and a central role in policymaking but also a strategic vantage point from which to help the constituency, advance personal and party policy and ideological goals, and attract campaign contributions—all of which help his or her reelection prospects. There is a long waiting list for assignments to the most powerful committees, so new members are unlikely to be appointed to them. Lawmakers are more likely to gain a position on one of the elite committees if they make significant contributions to the national party committees or to other party congressional candidates from their own campaign funds.[35] For assignments to nonelite standing committees, congressional leaders try to accommodate the wishes of their members, within the constraints of the seniority system.[36]

The Role of Committee Chairs   Not long ago, chairs of committees were the absolute masters of all they surveyed. From 1910, when substantial power was stripped from the Speaker of the House and distributed to committee chairs, until the early 1970s, when the Democrats reined in the autocratic chairs they had created, the heads of congressional committees went unchallenged. Committee chairs hired and assigned staff, controlled the budget, created or abolished subcommittees at will, controlled the agenda, scheduled meetings, and reported (or refused to report) bills to the floor.

Things are different today. Committee chairs now exercise more power over subcommittees and their resources than they did in the 1970s and 1980s, but they have seen much of their power migrate to the party leadership in each house.[37] Republicans in the House and Senate even imposed term limits of six years on committee chairs. The upshot is that decisions that were entirely the province of the chair in the past are now shared with others. Still, committee chairs remain the most influential and active members within their committees. They cannot command obedience, but they are at the center of all of the lines of communication, retain the power to schedule meetings and control the agenda, control the committee staff, manage committee funds, appoint members to conference committees, and are usually the most senior and experienced members of their committees, to whom some deference is owed.

Rules and Norms in the House and Senate

Like all organizations, Congress is guided by both formal rules and informal norms of behavior.[38] Rules specify precisely how things should be done and what is not allowed. Norms are generally accepted expectations about how people ought to behave and how business ought to proceed.

Traditionally, members of the House have been expected to become specialists in some area or areas of policy and to defer to the judgment of other specialists on most bills. This mutual deference is known as **reciprocity.** While reciprocity is still common, deference to specialists—usually chairs or ranking members of committees—is declining in favor of deference to the wishes of party leaders. In the Senate, the norm of reciprocity was always less prevalent than it was in the House. Because there are fewer members in the Senate, because senators are elected on a statewide basis, and because the Senate has been the breeding ground for many presidential candidacies, a senator has more prestige, visibility, and power than a member of the House. As a result, senators are generally unwilling to sit quietly for a term or two, waiting their turn. It is not unusual for a first-term senator to introduce major bills and make important speeches. In the House, such a thing was very unusual in the past. There, the old rule held sway: "To get along, go along."

It is expected in both chambers that lawmakers will respect, or at least tolerate, the reelection motivations of their colleagues. They are expected, for instance, to support a legislative schedule that allows for abundant visits back to the constituency and to vote for funding for campaign-related activities such as the right to send mail to constituents free of charge and for budgets for district offices. They must learn, moreover, to put up with activities that have no specific legislative purpose but allow their fellow lawmakers to advertise, take credit, and take positions—good examples are the insertion of materials into the *Congressional Record* and speeches on the floor tailored to the evening news back home.

At one time, senators and representatives were expected to act with courtesy and civility toward one another, even if they detested one another—hence

reciprocity

Deferral by members of Congress to the judgment of subject-matter specialists, mainly on minor technical bills.

Congressional staff help members of Congress carry out their many legislative responsibilities. Here Representative Speaker of the House Dennis Hastert meets with members of his staff to plan the day's legislative activities.

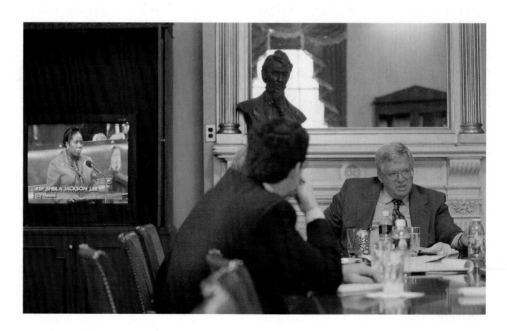

TABLE 11.2 ● Differences Between House and Senate Rules and Norms	
Senate	**House**
Informal, open, nonhierarchical	Rule-bound, hierarchical
Leaders have few formal powers	Leaders have many formal powers
Members may serve on two or more major committees	Members restricted to one major committee
Less specialized	More specialized
Unrestricted floor debate	Restricted floor debate
Unlimited amendments possible	Limited amendments possible
Amendments need not be germane	Amendments must be germane
Unlimited time for debate unless shortened by unanimous consent or halted by invocation of cloture	Limited time for debate
More prestige	Less prestige
More reliance on staff	Less reliance on staff
Minority party plays a larger role	Minority party plays a smaller role

the informal prohibition against the use of names and the elaborate references to the "honorable gentleman from Wisconsin" or the "senior senator from California." This expectation of civility has largely disappeared in recent years, especially in the House, as Congress has become a more partisan and ideological place.[39]

Legislative life is much more rule-bound in the House of Representatives, because of its large size, than in the Senate; it tends to be more organized and hierarchical (see Table 11.2). Leaders in the House have more power, the majority party exercises more control over legislative affairs, the procedures are more structured, and the individual members have a harder time making their mark. It is geared toward majority rule, with the minority playing a lesser role. The Senate tends to be a more open and fluid place, and it lodges less power in its leaders than the House does. Each senator is more of an independent operator than his or her House colleagues. The Senate is a much more relaxed place, one that accommodates mavericks, tolerates the foibles of its members, and pays more attention to members of the minority party. It is a place where the minority and individual senators play important roles in the legislative process.

Differences between the House and the Senate are especially apparent in floor debate. Bills are scheduled for floor debate in the Senate, for instance, not by a powerful committee but by **unanimous consent,** meaning that business can be blocked by a single dissenter. In the Senate, in a growing practice that is beginning to draw criticism, each senator has the power to place a hold on a bill or nomination to delay consideration by the whole body. Unlike the House, where debate on a bill is strictly regulated as to amendments and time limits

unanimous consent
Legislative action taken "without objection" as a way to expedite business; used to conduct much of the business of the Senate.

(determined by the Rules Committee with the agreement of the Speaker), the Senate's tradition allows for unlimited numbers of amendments and unlimited debate. Senators in the minority have periodically used this tolerance of unlimited amendments and debate to good effect. Because limiting debate is so difficult in the Senate, the opponents of a bill can tie up legislative business by refusing to stop debating its merits. This practice is known as the **filibuster.** During a filibuster, senators opposing a bill have been known to talk for hour upon hour, often working in shifts. The only requirement is that they say something; they cannot hold the floor without speaking. During a filibuster, senators need not even talk about the bill itself; Senate rules do not require remarks to be germane. Senators have read from novels or quoted verse, have told stories about their children, and have quoted long lists of sports statistics. The purpose is to force the majority to give up the fight and move on to other business.

When a very strong majority favors a bill or when a bill that has great national import and visibility is before the body, the Senate can close debate by invoking **cloture.** Cloture requires support by three-fifths of those present and voting. It is very rarely tried; it very rarely succeeds. Cloture is so difficult to invoke that the mere threat of a filibuster by a determined minority party, a growing trend in the Senate, often forces the majority to comply with the wishes of the minority. Many observers believe that the increasing use of the filibuster threat circumvents majority rule and therefore undermines democracy.

Legislative Responsibilities: How a Bill Becomes a Law

We can put much of what we have learned to work by seeing how a bill moves through the legislative labyrinth to become a law. The path by which a bill becomes a law is so strewn with obstacles that few bills survive; in fact, only about 6 percent of all bills that are introduced are enacted. To make law is exceedingly difficult; to block bills from becoming laws is relatively easy. At each step along the way (see Figure 11.7), a "no" decision can stop the passage of a bill in its tracks. As one account points out, members of the House or the Senate have "two principal functions: to make laws and to keep laws from being made. The first of these [they] perform only with sweat, patience, and a remarkable skill in the handling of creaking machinery; but the second they perform daily, with ease and infinite variety."[40]

What follows describes how major bills become law most of the time. Minor bills are often considered in each house under special rules that allow shortcuts. Thus, in the House, the "suspension calendar" and the "corrections calendar" set aside certain times for consideration of minor matters. It is also worth noting that bills involving the federal budget—authorization and appropriations bills—have several unique aspects to them, which need not concern us here (but see Chapter 17).

Introducing a Bill   A bill can be introduced only by a member of Congress. In reality, bills are often written in the executive branch. The initial draft of the bill that became the Tax Reform Act of 1986, for instance, was fashioned in the Treasury Department by a committee headed by the department's secretary, James Baker. Bills are also often written by interest groups. Industry trade groups, for example, wrote substantial parts of bills designed to roll back timber and mining regulations in 1995.

With the exception of tax bills (which must originate in the House), a bill may be introduced in either the House or the Senate. In the House, a member

filibuster
A parliamentary device used in the Senate to prevent a bill from coming to a vote by "talking it to death," made possible by the norm of unlimited debate.

cloture
A vote to end a filibuster or a debate; requires the votes of three-fifths of the membership of the Senate.

Simulation
You Are a Member of Congress

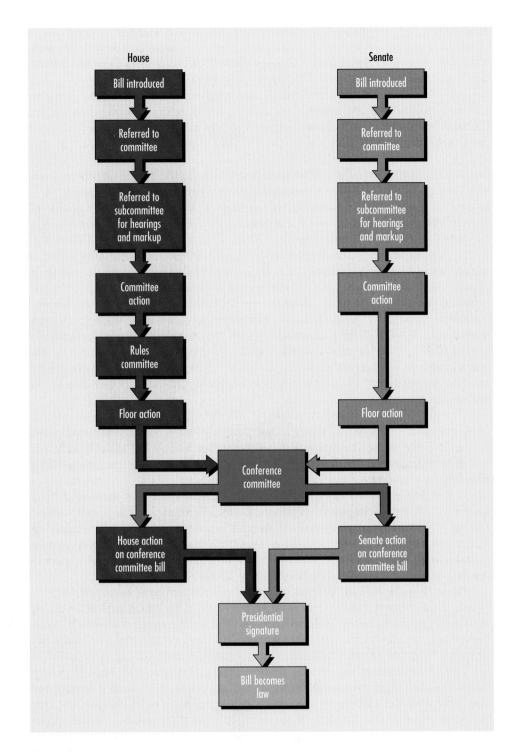

FIGURE 11.7 ● How a Bill Becomes a Law

This diagram shows the path by which major bills introduced in Congress become law. As explained in the text, the road that bills must travel is complex and difficult, and few bills survive it. A bill can be derailed at any stop in its passage. A subcommittee can refuse to report a bill; a bill may be defeated on the floor of each chamber; a conference committee may fail to reach an agreement on a compromise; the conference bill may be defeated in either chamber; or the president may veto the bill.

hopper

The box in the House of Representatives in which proposed bills are placed.

introduces a bill by putting it into the **hopper** (a box watched over by one of the House clerks). In the Senate, a member must announce a bill to the body after being recognized by the presiding officer. The bill is then assigned a number, with the prefix *H.R.* in the House or *S.* in the Senate.

The lawmaker who introduces the bill is known as its *sponsor.* Lawmakers try to build support by signing on as many cosponsors as possible; the bill has an even better chance of surviving if its cosponsors cross party and ideological lines.

Committee Action on a Bill

The presiding officer in the Senate or the Speaker in the House refers the bill to the appropriate standing committee. In about 80 percent of cases, referral to committee is routine; the subject matter of the bill clearly indicates the appropriate committee. Revenue bills go automatically to the Ways and Means Committee in the House and to the Finance Committee in the Senate, for instance. In the other 20 percent of cases, the relevant committee is not so obvious because of overlapping committee jurisdictions. For instance, the House Committee on International Relations is in charge of "international policy," whereas the Commerce Committee is in charge of "foreign commerce generally." In such cases, House leaders can exercise some discretion or send a bill (or parts of a bill) to more than one committee. The practice of multiple referral usually involves the most complex and important bills and has increased substantially since the mid-1970s.[41] The more committee referrals are discretionary and not automatic, of course, the more power House and Senate leaders have.

Committee chairs normally pass the bill on to the appropriate subcommittee for hearings. Many a bill dies at this stage, when either the subcommittee or the full committee declines to consider it further. A bill quietly killed in committee can reach the floor only by a device called a **discharge petition,** which is rarely successful.

If a bill is accepted for consideration, the subcommittee generally holds hearings, taking testimony from people for and against it. Subcommittee staff not only help prepare representatives and senators for the questioning but also often take part in the questioning themselves. The subcommittee may then forward the bill as rewritten by the staff and subcommittee members to the full committee, or it can decide to allow the bill to go no further.

Rewriting the bill in committee is called the *markup* (discussed earlier), which usually occurs amid very intense bargaining and deal making, with an eye toward fashioning a bill that will muster majority support in the full committee and on the floors of the House and the Senate and that will gain the support of the president. The staff plays a central role in the markup.

The subcommittee reports its action to the full committee. The committee chair, in consultation with other important members of his or her committee, may opt for the committee to hold its own hearings and markup sessions, may decide to kill the bill outright, or may simply accept the action of the subcommittee. If the subcommittee has done its job well and has consulted with the most important players on the full committee (especially the chair), the committee will simply rubber-stamp the bill and move it along for floor action.

discharge petition

A petition signed by 218 House members to force a bill that has been before a committee for at least 30 days while the House is in session out of the committee and onto the floor for consideration.

Floor Action on a Bill

If a bill is favorably reported from committee, congressional leaders schedule it for floor debate. In the House, major bills must first go to the Rules Committee, which decides where bills will appear on the legislative calendar and the terms under which bills will be debated by the House. A rule specifies such things as the amount of time for debate and the number (if any) and nature of amendments allowed. The Rules Committee may choose not to issue a rule at all or to drag its feet, as it did with civil rights bills until the mid-1960s. This has happened less often in recent years because both Democratic and Republican Speakers have had more power over Rules Committee appointments. The committee can also grant a "closed rule," allowing only a yes or no vote without amendments, as it generally does with tax bills.

Floor debate in the Senate, where rules do not limit debate as in the House, is much more freewheeling. Floor debate is also more important in the Senate in determining the final form a bill will take because Senate committees are less influential than House committees. Senators are also less likely to defer to committee judgments. Also, the threat of a filibuster means that the minority in the Senate plays an important role in determining the final shape of legislation.

After floor debate, the entire membership of the chamber votes on the bill, either as reported by the committee or (more often) after amendments have been added. If the bill receives a favorable vote, it then goes through the same obstacle course in the other chamber or awaits action by the other house if the bill was introduced there at the same time.

Conference Committee   Even if the bill makes it through both houses, its journey is not yet over. Bills passed by the House and the Senate almost always differ from one another, sometimes in minor ways and sometimes in quite substantial ways. Before the bill goes to the president, its conflicting versions must be rewritten so that a single bill gains the approval of both chambers of Congress. This compromise bill is fashioned in a conference committee made up of members from both the House and the Senate, customarily from the relevant committees.

A bill from a conference committee must be voted up or down on the floors of the House and the Senate; no amendments or further changes are allowed. If, and only if, both houses approve it, the bill is forwarded to the president for consideration.

Presidential Action   Because the president plays an important constitutional role in turning a bill into a law, he or his assistants and advisers are usually consulted throughout the legislative process. If the president approves the bill, he signs it and it becomes law. If he is not particularly favorable but does not want to block the bill, it becomes law after 10 days if he takes no action. He can also **veto** the bill and return it to Congress. A bill can still become law by a two-thirds vote of each house, which will override the president's veto. A president can also kill a bill at the end of a congressional session if he takes no action and Congress adjourns before 10 days pass. This is known as a **pocket veto.** We will have more to say about the presidential veto in Chapter 12.

veto
Presidential disapproval of a bill that has been passed by both houses of Congress. The president's veto can be overridden by a two-thirds vote in each house.

pocket veto
Rejection of a bill if the president takes no action on it for 10 days and Congress has adjourned during that period.

Legislative Oversight of the Executive Branch

Oversight is another important responsibility of Congress. Oversight involves keeping an eye on how the executive branch carries out the provisions of the laws that Congress has passed and on possible abuses of power by executive branch officials, including the president.

Oversight is primarily the province of the committees and subcommittees of Congress, and it is among Congress's most visible and dramatic roles. High-profile examples of legislative probes of alleged administrative misconduct include Watergate, the Iran-Contra affair, Whitewater, the savings-and-loan collapse and bailout, corporate accounting scandals, intelligence failures and prisoner abuse in Iraq, and the Agricultural Department's management of the meat inspection system in the wake of the discovery of "mad cow" disease in the United States.

Hearings are an important part of the oversight process. Testimony is taken from agency officials, outside experts, and congressional investigatory institutions such as the Government Accounting Office and the Office of Technology Assessment. The hearings are not simply information-gathering exercises, however. As often as not, they are designed to send signals from committee members to the relevant part of the bureaucracy. Hearings that focus on the overly aggressive efforts of Internal Revenue Service agents to collect taxes, for example, are a clear signal to IRS officials that they had better rein in their agents before the next round of hearings on the budget. Tough questioning of Attorney General John Ashcroft in 2001 by Senator Patrick Leahy's Judiciary Committee concerning the use of military tribunals, the practice of listening in on conversations between terror suspects and their attorneys, and the detention of suspects and material witnesses for an indeterminant time period was meant as a signal to both Ashcroft and the Bush administration that Congress would be vigilant on how the "war on terrorism" was being waged at home.

Congress's most powerful instrument of oversight of the Executive Branch is impeachment (responsibility of the House) and trial and removal from office (responsibility of the Senate) of high executive officials, including the president. This is a blunt tool, rarely used, except in the most partisan atmosphere or in cases involving truly egregious executive behavior. Over the course of American history, only seven executives have been removed from office by the Senate. No president has ever been convicted and removed from office, but the impeachment processes in the House of presidents Andrew Johnson, Nixon, and Clinton were so divisive that Congress treads very cautiously in this area.

Congress, Public Policy, and the American People

The way Congress is organized and operates greatly influences the kinds of public policies we have, how people feel about government, and the quality of democracy in the United States.

Congress as Policymaker

A frequently heard criticism of Congress is that it is so parochial and fragmented that it cannot fashion coherent national policy.[42] The argument goes like this. First, Congress is filled with members who are judged by the voters on the basis of their individual attributes and service to the district and to interest groups, not on the basis of the performance of Congress as a whole. One result is that lawmakers worry more about themselves than about the stand-

Holding hearings to determine if new laws are needed and if executive branch agencies are properly carrying out their responsibilities under existing laws is one of Congress's most important functions. Here, Defense Secretary Donald Rumsfeld and leaders of the armed forces testify before the House Armed Forces Committee about the abuse of prisoners in Iraq and Afghanistan.

ing and effectiveness of their institution or its collective national policymaking responsibilities.[43]

Second, because lawmakers are responsive to organized interests, serve the constituency as their first order of business, and try to avoid difficult decisions that might put their reelection at risk (or so it is claimed), Congress cannot easily tackle the nation's most difficult problems or think about solutions in general terms. Congress would rather practice "distributive" politics, in which benefits are parceled out to a wide range of constituency and interest group claimants. While this pattern conforms to the self-interested electoral calculations of the individual member, it is, according to many observers, the basis for the overall ineffectiveness and decline of Congress as a national policymaking institution.

It is hard to assess the validity of these criticisms. The evidence is mixed. Congress has, at times, fashioned broad and coherent national policies in response to tangible problems and strong majority opinions. We have also seen that Congress retains a far greater policymaking role than legislative bodies in parliamentary systems and that on domestic issues, it is becoming ever more forceful. Nevertheless, historically, Congress has functioned best as a policymaker when the president, supported by the existence of a national majority in favor of a particular course of action, is able to provide strong leadership. Franklin Roosevelt's New Deal legislative program, Lyndon Johnson's Great Society, and Ronald Reagan's conservative triumphs in 1981 come to mind. For a time, during Newt Gingrich's leadership of the conservative revolution in the House of Representatives in the 104th Congress, it appeared that a major legislative program could be passed without (or against) presidential leadership. Once most bills from the Contract with America failed to become law, however, it became apparent again that the creation of broad and coherent national policies requires presidential leadership.

How Democratic Are We?

Is Congress Out of Touch?

PROPOSITION: Congress is out of touch with the American people and doesn't do what the people want it to do.

AGREE: Although representatives and senators must ultimately face the voters, their reelection prospects are strongly related to how much money they can raise for their campaigns. With a healthy campaign war chest, as well as the advantages they have as incumbents, representatives and senators can get their message to voters and make the case that they should remain in office. Building a healthy campaign war chest also depends heavily on money from special interests and wealthy individuals. It is not surprising, then, that the candidates pay particular attention to what these contributors want. Moreover, the way Congress is organized and works—the power of small states in the Senate, for example, and the power that flows to the minority in the Senate by virtue of the filibuster—makes it very difficult to turn the wishes of the majority into concrete laws, even if members of Congress are inclined to be responsive. Finally, because of redistricting that favors incumbents by creating safe, noncompetitive districts, House members need not worry unduly about elections. This means that one of the most important tools for keeping representatives responsive and responsible to citizens is absent.

DISAGREE: Although they have to attend to the interests of big contributors, representatives and senators are ultimately accountable to the voters. For example, unlike members of the House, Senators cannot create safe districts because their constituency is their entire state. The result is that incumbent reelection rates are much lower in the Senate than in the House, as are voluntary retirements, meaning that there is considerable turnover in the Senate following congressional elections. So the wishes of the electorate are reflected in the composition of the Senate. In the House, though incumbents almost never lose, they act as if their congressional seats are at risk and work hard to retain them. For this reason that they pay a great deal of attention to their constituent mail, spend substantial time in their home districts talking to the voters, and invest heavily in polling to stay in touch. In the end, because senators and representatives pay careful attention to the electorate, they are responsive to the wishes and needs of the people. The result is that Congress legislates in ways that match what the American people want on most major issues.

CONSIDER: If you believe, as the framers did, that Congress ought to be a deliberative body, free from popular pressures, acting in the public interest as representatives and senators define it, then the failure to legislate exactly as the public would want will cause you no great anxiety. If you believe that Congress ought to be democratically responsive, then you might take solace in the evidence that shows that Congress follows public opinion to a substantial degree in the long run.

• What is your position on this issue? • Do you believe that Congress is too responsive or not responsive enough? • What would you do to make Congress fit your conception of the proper role of Congress in the American political system? • Would you further insulate Congress from the voice of the people? • Make it more accessible and responsive to public opinion? • Or leave it as is?

Congress and the American People

Although Americans tend to approve of their own representatives and senators, they have low regard for Congress as an institution. Except in rare instances, fewer Americans say they believe Congress is "doing a good job" than believe that the president is doing a good job. Fewer report having "a great deal of confidence" in Congress as an institution than for the Supreme Court or the president. This pattern has endured for a long time and shows no sign of abating.[44] Approval and confidence ratings, much as those for the president, tend to track the economy and confidence about the future among Americans, being higher in good times and lower in bad times. But it is inescapable that when it comes to national institutions, Congress does not fare well.

Scholars and journalists have advanced a number of reasons for this state of affairs, including rising partisanship, gridlock within Congress and between Congress and the president, and the apparent influence in Congress of special interests. Two scholars have a unique and intriguing alternative explanation: The American people, they suggest, often do not really like the messiness of the democratic process itself, so evident in the give-and-take of the legislative process. As they put it,

> *People do not wish to see uncertainty, conflicting opinions, long debate, competing interests, confusion, bargaining, and compromised, imperfect solutions. They want government to do its job quietly and efficiently, sans conflict and sans fuss. In short . . . they often seek a patently unrealistic form of democracy.*[45]

Summary

The framers of the Constitution wanted to fashion a legislative branch that was both energetic and limited. They granted Congress legislative power, gave it an existence independent of the executive branch, and enumerated an impressive range of powers. They also gave the other branches powers to check legislative excesses, created a bicameral body, and strictly denied certain powers to Congress.

Structural change in the nation has shaped Congress, influencing it to increase in size, expand the volume and complexity of its business, and become more institutionalized and professional.

Congress is a representative institution. Its members are constantly balancing the preferences of the people in their constituencies and important interest groups and contributors. Because elections are the most important mechanism for representation, and because they are the way in which members attain office, elections dominate the time and energy of lawmakers and shape how Congress organizes itself and goes about its business.

To conduct its business, Congress depends on an elaborate set of norms and rules and a web of committees and subcommittees, political parties, legislative leaders, and an extensive staff. Several of these elements encourage fragmentation, decentralization, and occasional gridlock but also allow the development of the specialized expertise that enables Congress to meet the executive branch on equal terms. Other tools help the members coordinate and expedite legislative business.

Suggestions for Further Reading

Caro, Robert. *The Years of Lyndon Johnson.* New York: Knopf, 1982.

This classic and award-winning biography of Lyndon Baines Johnson of Texas reveals more about how Congress worked in the "old days" than virtually any academic treatise.

Davidson, Roger H., and Walter J. Oleszek. *Congress and Its Members,* 9th ed. Washington, D.C.: Congressional Quarterly Press, 2004.

The classic textbook on Congress, now in its ninth edition.

Oleszek, Walter J. *Congressional Procedures and the Policy Process,* 6th ed. Washington, D.C.: Congressional Quarterly Press, 2004.

The most comprehensive compilation yet published of the rules and operations of the legislative process in Congress, written by a scholar who served as the policy director of the Joint Committee on the Organization of Congress.

Sinclair, Barbara. *Unorthodox Lawmaking: New Legislative Processes in the U.S. Congress.* Washington, D.C.: Congressional Quarterly Press, 1997.

Argues that the traditional textbook rendition of "how a bill becomes a law" has dramatically changed over the past two decades.

Specialized newspapers and journals: *The Hill, Roll Call, Congressional Quarterly, National Journal.*

Valuable sources for up-to-the-minute, in-depth coverage of what is happening in Congress.

Internet Sources

CongressLink at the Dirksen Center
www.congresslink.org

Designed for teachers of American government, history, and civics, this is a very rich information site on Congress. Features include access to information on pending legislation, legislative schedules and ways to contact members of Congress, caucuses, committees, rules, histories of the House and Senate, and much more.

Federal Election Commission
www.fec.gov

Information on campaign finance for presidential and congressional elections.

PoliticalMoneyLine
www.tray.com/

Everything you might want to know about campaign fund-raising and spending in congressional races.

Thomas
http://thomas.loc.gov/

Expansive repository of information on the House of Representatives, including the full text and progress of bills, the Congressional Record, legislative procedures and rules, committee actions, and more.

U.S. House of Representatives Home Page
www.house.gov

House schedule, House organization and procedures, links to House committees, information on contacting representatives, and historical documents on the House of Representatives.

U.S. Senate Home Page
www.senate.gov

Similar to the House of Representatives Home Page, focused on the Senate. One exciting new feature is a virtual tour of the Capitol.

Chapter 12
The Presidency

In This Chapter

- Why the presidency grew to be a powerful office
- How presidents play many roles
- Why presidents often disagree with Congress
- How democratic the presidency is—whether presidents listen and respond to the public
- Why different presidents often pursue similar policies

The War Presidency of George W. Bush

George W. Bush's presidency began inauspiciously. He won the presidency over Al Gore in the 2000 election by only four electoral votes, even though he had roughly one-half million fewer votes than Gore nationally. Bush became the first president since Benjamin Harrison in 1889 to assume office under such circumstances. For many Americans, George W. Bush became president under a cloud of illegitimacy and governed without a mandate.

As if that were not enough, Bush administration actions within the first few months of his presidency—overruling Clinton administration rules regulating the amount of arsenic in drinking water, renouncing the Kyoto Treaty on global warming, and refusing to join the new International Criminal Court—brought a cascade of criticism from editorial writers and political leaders both at home and abroad. Congressional Democrats, fuming about the presidential election outcome and the intervention of the Supreme Court in deciding it, were in a decidedly uncooperative mood. By the end of summer 2001, moreover, an economic recession was in full flower and the budget surplus was about to disappear. It is no wonder, then, that Bush's job approval ratings for the first seven months of his presidency hovered in the mid- to upper-50 percent range—quite low in historical terms. Questions about his leadership were being whispered virtually everywhere.

All of this changed dramatically after the terrorist attacks on the United States on September 11, 2001. Responding vigorously and swiftly to the attacks, Bush used the several powers of his office to take the war to the enemy in Afghanistan and elsewhere, form an international coalition against al Qaeda and the Taliban regime in Afghanistan, and initiate measures by executive order[1] to protect the homefront against terrorism. Executive orders were issued, for example, to freeze the financial assets of charitable organizations thought to be tied to terrorism, establish military tribunals for the trial of foreign nationals accused of terrorism, and order the interrogation of thousands of Middle Easterners and Muslims who might conceivably have information about terrorism. The American pub-

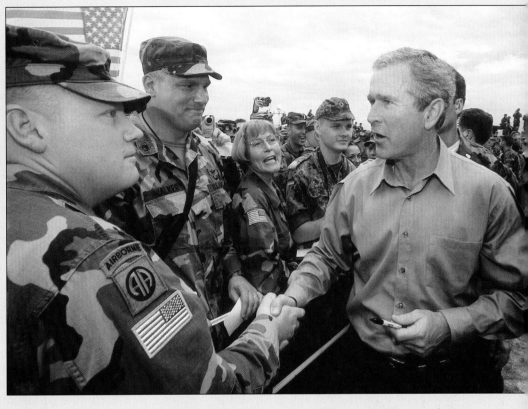

lic responded favorably to these military, diplomatic, homefront measures, giving the president the highest sustained favorable job ratings in the history of public opinion polling.

What had happened? How was a presidency transformed in so short a time? How was George W. Bush, with so many questioning his ability and right to lead, able to act so decisively, with broad popular support and without the usual constraints that presidents face? The answer lies in the fact that both historical precedent and the constitutional responsibilities of the office grant presidents enormous powers when the United States faces a national security crisis and engages in war. The Constitution makes the president the commander-in-chief of the armed forces, in charge of the deployment and use of American military power in defense of the United States. The Constitution also makes the president the chief diplomat of the United States, responsible for conducting relations with other countries, and by extension, for fashioning foreign policy. We need only to look back to the wartime presidencies of Abraham Lincoln, Woodrow Wilson, and Franklin Delano Roosevelt to see that the people and other government officials generally look to presidential leadership during war and national security emergencies, and give presidents enormous latitude to act. But the president's power in these areas is not unlimited, as you shall see.

With the overthrow of the Taliban regime in Afghanistan, President Bush's attention turned to Iraq, a nation he claimed was developing weapons of mass destruction and cavorting with terrorist organizations. Using his enormous standing with the public, the president gradually built support for the invasion of Iraq and the overthrow of Saddam Hussein and his Bathist regime. Although the president's plans were supported only lukewarmly by congressional Democrats, met with skepticism and anger by allied governments and publics around the world, resisted by the U.N. Security Council, and the object of large anti-war demonstrations here and abroad, he nevertheless managed to win a resolution in Congress supporting an attack on Iraq , the support of the American people once the invasion had begun in spring 2003, and a supplemental appropriation of $87 billion from Congress to support the occupation.

Given the president's diplomatic and war powers in the Constitution and the tendency of the public and other government officials to look to the president for leadership in times of national security emergencies, President Bush's ability to act without much consultation or serious opposition for roughly 18 months following the terrorist attacks on the United States is hardly surprising. Nor is it surprising, however, in a political system where there is a government of divided powers, closely and bitterly divided political parties, and a free press, that President Bush's domination of government and hold on the affections of the people would eventually wane. When the immediate threat of terrorism receded as the top public concern, and as the cost of the war in Iraq—in terms of lives and dollars—began to mount in late 2003, the constraints on the president tightened. Many local governments around the country, for example, passed resolutions pledging noncooperation with the USA Patriot Act that gave the federal government new powers of surveillance and detention, and the administration's efforts to strengthen the Act ran into a brick wall in Congress. Federal courts, moreover, began to question the Bush administration's practice of detaining terrorism suspects without formal charges or access to legal counsel and designating American citizens enemy combatants without legal rights. Candidates for the Democratic party's presidential nomination relentlessly attacked the administration's policies in Iraq. Congress held hearings on how contracts were awarded by the Defense Department to Halliburton and other private contractors for work in Iraq, and how prisoner abuse had happened in Iraq and Afghanistan. The 9/11 Commission reported on intelligence failures on the war on terrorism. Inevitably, the president's standing among the public fell below 50 percent. Nevertheless, he won reelection in 2004.

As this story shows, the president has enormous powers under certain circumstances; however, at other times, the president is constrained by the powers of competing branches of government—especially Congress and the courts—news organizations, interest groups, and public opinion. Using this review of the Bush presidency as a backdrop, this chapter will look at the office of the president, with special attention to how it has evolved over time and how the nature of the office at any particular time is the result of the interaction of constitutional rules, historical precedent, the nature of the times, and the qualities of the person who sits in the Oval Office. Because of the constitutional rules and historical precedent, every presidency is, in some respects, similar to every other presidency. On the other hand, because of the importance of contemporary events and the personal qualities of particular presidents in determining how the office operates, every presidency is, to a certain extent, unique.

Thinking Critically About This Chapter

This chapter is about the American presidency, how it has evolved, and what role it plays in American politics and government.

Using the Framework   You will see in this chapter how the presidential office has changed substantially from how the framers envisioned it, primarily because of changes in America's international situation, the nature of its economy, and popular expectations. You will also see how presidents interact with other governmental institutions, such as Congress and the Court, and with political linkage–level actors, such as political parties, public opinion, the mass media, and interest groups, and how these interactions influence what government does.

Using the Democracy Standard   You will see in this chapter how the presidential office, although not envisioned by the framers to be a democratic one, has become more directly connected to and responsive to the American people.

On the other hand, you will be asked to think about whether presidents' growing ability to influence the thinking of the public and shape their perceptions of public events undermines democracy.

The Expanding Presidency

The American presidency has grown considerably since our nation's beginning. The increase has occurred in presidential responsibilities, burdens, power, and impact.

The Earliest and Latest Presidencies Compared

When George Washington took office as the first president, he had a total budget (for 1789–1792) of just over $4 million. Washington had only a handful of federal employees. Even by 1801, there were only about 300 federal officeholders in the capital. Washington's cabinet consisted of only five officials: the secretaries of state, war, and the treasury; a postmaster general; and an attorney general (who acted as the president's personal attorney, rather than as head of a full-fledged Justice Department). The entire Department of State consisted of one secretary, one chief clerk, six minor clerks, and one messenger. In 1790, only about 700 Americans were in uniform, and they had no way to project force around the world. Federal government functions were few. The entire United States consisted of the 13 original eastern and southeastern states, with only 864,746 square miles of land area; the population was only about 4 million persons, most living on small farms.[2]

When George W. Bush was sworn into office more than 200 years later, he presided over a federal budget with more than $1.8 trillion in annual expenditures and a federal bureaucracy with approximately 2.4 million civilian employees. He was commander-in-chief of the armed forces, with about 1.4 million men and women in uniform; hundreds of military bases at home and scattered throughout the world; and perhaps 20,000 deliverable nuclear warheads, enough to obliterate every medium-sized or large city in the world many times over. The United States in 2001 had a population of almost 278 million diverse people; a gross domestic product of more than $9.5 trillion; and a land area of some 3.8 million square miles, stretching from Alaska to Florida and from Hawaii to Maine.[3]

The Founders' Conception of the Presidency

The Founders certainly had in mind a presidency more like Washington's than Bush's. As discussed in Chapter 2, Article II of the Constitution provided for a single executive who would be strong, compared with his role under the Congress-dominated Articles of Confederation, but the Constitution's sparse language barely hinted at the range of things twenty-first-century presidents would do. The Constitution made the president "commander-in-chief" of the armed forces, for example, without any suggestion that there would be a vast standing army that presidents could send abroad to fight without a declaration of war. It empowered presidents to appoint and to "require the opinion in writing" of executive department heads without indicating that a huge federal bureaucracy would evolve. The Constitution provided that presidents could from

The presidency has grown in scale and responsibility. As commander-in-chief of the armed forces, President George Washington commanded an army of just over 700 soldiers and had little to do with affairs outside the United States. Today, the president commands a force of about 1.4 million stationed all over the world.

Source: © Gift of Edgar William, Chrysler & Bernice Garbish/The Metropolitan Museum of Art.

time to time "recommend . . . measures" to Congress without specifying that these proposals would very often (especially in the twentieth century) come to dominate the legislative agenda. Still, the vague language of the Constitution proved flexible enough to encompass the great expansion of the presidency.

The Dormant Presidency

From the time of George Washington's inauguration at Federal Hall in New York City to the end of the nineteenth century, the presidency, for the most part, conformed to the designs of the Founders. The presidency did not, by and large, dominate the political life of the nation. Presidents saw their responsibility as primarily involving the execution of policies decided by Congress. Congress was a fully equal branch of government, or perhaps more than equal. But the office changed after that.

Structural Factors   Why does the early presidency seem so weak in comparison with the contemporary presidency? Surely it is not because early presidents were less intelligent, vigorous, or ambitious; some were and some were not. A more reasonable answer is that the nation did not often require a very strong presidency before the twentieth century, particularly in the key areas of foreign policy and military leadership. Only in the twentieth century did the United States become a world power, involved in military, diplomatic, and economic activities around the globe. With that *structural* development came a simultaneous increase in the power and responsibility of the president.

It was not until the late nineteenth century, moreover, that the economy of the United States was transformed from a simple free market economy of farmers and small firms to a corporate-dominated economy, with units so large and interconnected that their every action had social consequences. This transformation eventually led to demands for more government supervision of the American economic system. As this role of government grew, so did that of the president.

Although the presidency was largely dormant until the end of the nineteenth century, events and the actions of several presidents during the early period anticipated what was to happen to the office in our own time. Precedents were set; expectations were formed; rules were changed.

Important Early Presidents   The war hero George Washington solidified the prestige of the presidency at a time when executive leadership was mistrusted. Washington also affirmed the primacy of the president in foreign affairs and set a precedent for fashioning a domestic legislative program. Thomas Jefferson, although initially hostile to the idea of a vigorous central government, boldly concluded the Louisiana Purchase with France, which roughly doubled the size of the United States and opened the continent for American settlement. Rough-hewn frontiersman Andrew Jackson, elected with broader popular participation than ever before, helped transform the presidency into a popular institution, as symbolized by his vigorous opposition to the Bank of the United States (which was seen by many ordinary Americans as a tool of the wealthy).

James Polk, although often ignored in textbook accounts of "great" presidents, energetically exercised his powers as commander in chief of the armed forces; he provoked a war with Mexico and acquired most of what is now the southwestern United States and California. Abraham Lincoln, in order to win the Civil War, invoked emergency powers based on his broad reading of the Constitution: He raised and spent money and deployed troops on his own initiative, with Congress acquiescing only afterward; he temporarily suspended the right of **habeas corpus** and allowed civilians to be tried in military courts; and he unilaterally freed the slaves in the Confederate states by issuing the Emancipation Proclamation.

habeas corpus
The legal doctrine that a person who is arrested must have a timely hearing before a judge.

The Twentieth-Century Transformation

More enduring changes in the presidency came only in the twentieth century, when new structural conditions made an expanded presidency both possible and necessary.

Theodore Roosevelt   Theodore Roosevelt vigorously pushed the prerogatives and enhanced the powers of the office as no president had done since Lincoln. Roosevelt was happiest when he was deploying the troops as commander-in-

Teddy Roosevelt was a strong advocate for a vigorous presidency, one that would exercise leadership in both domestic and foreign affairs.

chief or serving as the nation's chief diplomat to protect American economic and political interests. On the domestic front, Roosevelt pushed for regulation of the new and frightening business corporations, especially by breaking up **trusts**, and he established many national parks. In Teddy Roosevelt, we see the coming together of an energetic and ambitious political leader and a new set of structural factors in the United States, particularly the nation's emergence as a world power and an industrialized economy. The interplay of these three factors expanded the power and responsibilities of the presidency.

trusts
Large combinations of business corporations.

Woodrow Wilson

Woodrow Wilson's presidency marked further important steps in the expansion of the federal government and the presidency. Wilson's "New Freedom" domestic program built on the Progressive Era measures of Teddy Roosevelt, including further regulation of the economy by establishment of the Federal Reserve Board (1913) and the Federal Trade Commission (1914). Under Wilson, World War I brought an enormous increase in activity: a huge mobilization of military personnel and a large, new civilian bureaucracy to oversee the production and distribution of food, fuel, and armaments by the American "arsenal of democracy."

Franklin D. Roosevelt

It was Franklin D. Roosevelt, however, who presided over the most significant expansion of presidential functions and activities in American history. In a very real sense, the founding of the modern American presidency occurred during Roosevelt's administration, in response to the Great Depression and World War II.

In response to the Great Depression, Roosevelt and the Democratic majority in Congress pushed into law a series of measures for economic relief that grew into vast programs of conservation and public works, farm credit, business loans, and relief payments to the destitute. Roosevelt's New Deal also established a number of independent commissions to regulate aspects of business (the stock market, telephones, utilities, airlines) and enacted programs such as Social Security, which provided income support for retired Americans,

By staying in touch with and responding to the people during the crisis of the Great Depression, Franklin Delano Roosevelt helped define the modern presidency.

and the Wagner Act, which helped workers join unions and bargain collectively with their employers.

Even bigger changes, however, resulted from World War II when the government mobilized the entire population and the whole economy for the war effort. With the end of World War II, the United States was established as a military superpower. Since the time of Franklin Roosevelt, all U.S. presidents have administered a huge national security state with large standing armed forces, nuclear weapons, and bases all around the world.

Similarly, World War II brought substantial government involvement in the economy, with temporary war agencies regulating prices, rationing necessities, monitoring and stimulating industrial output, and helping develop human resources for domestic production. These agencies were dismantled after the war, but they trained a large cadre of officials in an activist view of what the federal government could and should do, and they set precedents for presidential and governmental actions that continue to the present day. All presidents since Roosevelt have presided over a huge government apparatus that has been active in domestic policy as well as in foreign policy.

John F. Kennedy   Although he accomplished little on the legislative front during his brief time in office—he did introduce the 1964 Civil Rights Act, passed after his death—John F. Kennedy was the first president to appreciate the importance of television as both a campaign tool and as an instrument for influencing the public and political actors in Washington, the states, and other countries. His televised speeches and press conferences, where his charm, intelligence, and sense of humor were clearly evident, became one of his most effective governing tools. Presidents after him tried to follow his lead, but only Ronald Reagan and Bill Clinton came close to Kennedy's mastery of the medium.

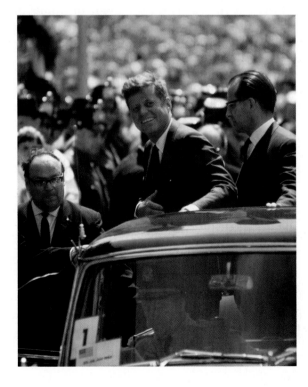

President John F. Kennedy was a master of public performance, particularly on television. This skill enhanced the formal powers of his office, increasing his influence with other government leaders.

Ronald Reagan   Only occasionally does the word "revolution" become associated with the name of a president, and rarely does it mean very much, but in the case of Ronald Reagan, the phrase "Reagan revolution" fits like a glove. In policy terms, Ronald Reagan was largely responsible for bringing the main items of the conservative agenda to fruition: a massive tax cut to stimulate the economy, cutbacks in the number of regulations that affect business, cuts in a wide range of domestic social programs, and a substantial buildup of U.S. armed forces. Perhaps more importantly, he showed the American people and others around the world that a vigorous and popular presidency was still possible after the failed presidencies of Richard Nixon, Gerald Ford, and Jimmy Carter. He maintained his impressive public standing until the end of his term, despite foreign missteps, such as the Iran-Contra Affair, and the appearance of large and persistent budget deficits.

How Important Are Individual Presidents?

We cannot be sure to what extent presidents themselves caused this great expansion of the scope of their office. Clearly, they played a part. Lincoln, Wilson, and Franklin Roosevelt, for example, not only reacted vigorously to events but also helped create events; each had something to do with the coming of the wars that were so crucial in adding to their activities and powers. Yet these great presidents were also the product of great times; they stepped into situations that had deep historical roots and dynamics of their own.

Lincoln found a nation in bitter conflict over the relative economic and political power of North and South and focused on the question of slavery in the western territories; war was a likely, if not inevitable, outcome. Wilson and Franklin Roosevelt each faced a world in which German expansion threatened the perceived economic and cultural interests of the United States and in which U.S. industrial power permitted a strong response. The Great Depression fairly cried out for a new kind of presidential activism. Kennedy faced an international system in which the Soviet Union had become especially strident and menacing. George W. Bush was president when the 9/11 terrorist attacks on the United States occurred. Thus, the great upsurges in presidential power and activity were, at least in part, a result of forces at the *structural* level and the result of developments in the economy, American society, and the international system.

We see, then, that it is this mixture of a president's personal qualities (personality and character) and deeper structural factors (such as the existence of military, foreign policy, or economic crises) that determines which presidents transform the office.

The Powers and Roles of the President

Simulation

Presidential Leadership:
Which Hat Do You Wear?

The American presidency has assumed powers and taken on roles unimaginable to the Founders. Each touches on the daily lives of everyone in the United States and affects tens of millions of people around the world as well.

Ceremonial Responsibilities

The president is both the chief executive of the United States—responsible for the executive branch of the federal government—and the chief of state, a symbol of national authority and unity. In contrast to European parliamentary

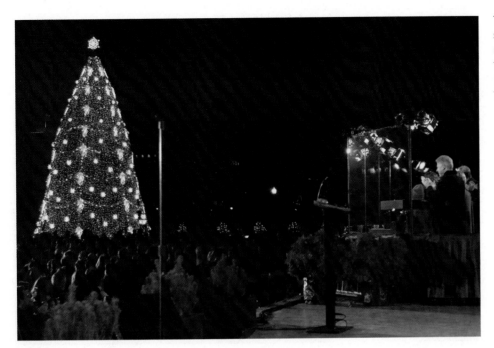

The president's role as chief of state involves many seemingly mundane tasks—such as lighting the national Christmas tree—that nevertheless add to the prestige of the office.

democracies such as Britain or Norway, where a monarch acts as chief of state while a prime minister serves as head of the government, in the United States the two functions are combined. It is the president who performs many ceremonial duties (attending funerals, proclaiming official days, honoring heroes, celebrating anniversaries) that are carried out by members of royal families in other nations. Jimmy Breslin, an irreverent New York newspaper columnist, once wrote, "The office of President is such a bastardized thing, half royalty and half democracy, that nobody knows whether to genuflect or spit."[4] Because it adds to their prestige and standing with other government officials and the public, presidents have always found the chief of state role to be a useful tool in their political arsenal, enabling them to get their way on many important issues.

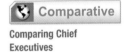

Comparing Chief Executives

Domestic Policy Leader

The president has taken on important responsibilities on the domestic front that were probably not anticipated by the framers. These include his role as the nation's legislative leader and manager of the economy.

Legislative Leader   While the Constitution seems to give responsibility for the legislative agenda to Congress, over time, the initiative for public policy has partly shifted to the president and the executive branch. The bases of this change may be found in the Constitution, statutes passed by Congress, and the changing expectations of the American people. The Constitution, for example, specifies that the president must, ". . . from time to time give the Congress information on the state of the union, and recommend to their consideration such measures as he shall judge necessary and expedient." Until Woodrow Wilson's presidency, the "state of the union" took the form of a written report sent every year or every two years to Congress for its consideration. These reports often gathered dust in the House and Senate clerks' offices. Wilson, a

Presidents use the annual State of the Union address to outline their legislative agenda for the nation.

strong believer in the role of the president as chief legislative leader similar to the prime minister in a parliamentary system, began the practice of delivering the state of the union to Congress in an address to a joint session of the House and Senate, in which the president sets out his agenda for congressional legislation. Wilson correctly sensed that the American people were in the mood for vigorous legislative leadership from the president, given the enormous technological, economic, and social changes that were happening in the United States and the problems that were being generated by these changes. In modern times, the state of the union address has become the most important tool by which presidents gain the attention of the public and other public officials for what they want to accomplish. The state of the nation is now a very dramatic and visible event, delivered before a joint session of Congress, with members of the Supreme Court, the president's cabinet, and the military joint chiefs in attendance, and a national television audience. In the state of the union, presidents, much as Wilson did, set out what issues they hope Congress will address, with a promise that detailed proposals for legislation will be forthcoming. In doing so, presidents now have the biggest say in defining the political agenda for the nation.

The president's legislative role also was enhanced by the Budget Act of 1921 which requires the president to submit an annual federal government budget to Congress for its consideration, accompanied by a budget message setting out the president's rationale and justifications. We will have more to say about the budget process in Chapter 17.

Although the House and Senate often take action on their own with regard to the nation's legislative agenda, what is striking is the degree to which Congress waits for and acts in response to presidential state of the union addresses, budgets, and legislative proposals to meet various national problems. Indeed, the twentieth century is dotted with presidential labels on broad legislative programs: Wilson's New Freedom, Roosevelt's New Deal, Truman's

Fair Deal, Kennedy's New Frontier, and Johnson's Great Society. Ronald Reagan pushed through major changes during his presidency. And George W. Bush pushed through three tax cuts in the first years of his administration.

Manager of the Economy   We now expect presidents to "do something" about the economy when things are going badly. The Great Depression taught most Americans that the federal government has a role to play in fighting economic downturns, and the example of Franklin Roosevelt convinced many that the main actor in this drama ought to be the president. Congress recognized this in 1946 when it passed the Employment Act, requiring the president to produce an annual report on the state of the economy, assisted by a new Council of Economic Advisors, with a set of recommendations for congressional action to maintain the health of the American economy. The role is now so well established that even conservative presidents, such as Ronald Reagan and George H. W. Bush, felt compelled to involve the federal government in the prevention of bank failures, the stimulation of economic growth, and the promotion of exports abroad.

In the rapidly expanding global economy, moreover, presidents have become increasingly engaged in the effort to open world markets on equitable terms to American goods and services. President Reagan pressured Japan into import quotas on automobiles, and President Bush helped push through an agreement with Japan on semiconductors. President Clinton was especially active as a spokesperson for the benefits of the American way of doing business and pushed hard to expand a global free trade regime, negotiating and gaining congressional approval for the North American Free Trade Agreement (NAFTA) treaty and the creation of the World Trade Organization.

Foreign Policy and Military Leader

Although the framers gave a role to Congress in fashioning foreign and military policies—note congressional control of the federal purse strings, its role in declaring war, and the Senate's "advice and consent" responsibilities with respect to treaties and appointment of ambassadors—it fully expected the president to be the major player in these areas. What they could not have anticipated was that the United States would develop into the world's superpower, with global responsibilities and commitments, a development that enormously expanded the power of the presidency in the federal government.

Foreign Policy Leader   In a case decided in 1936, the Supreme Court confirmed the president's position as the nation's preeminent foreign policy maker, saying: ". . . the president is the sole organ of the federal government in the field of international relations."[5] The president's role as foreign policy leader is rooted in the diplomatic and treaty powers sections of Article II of the Constitution, as well as in his role as commander-in-chief of the armed forces.

The Constitution specifies that the president shall have the power to appoint and receive ambassadors and to make treaties. Although these formal constitutional powers may seem minor at first glance, they confer on the president the main responsibility for fashioning American foreign policy. Take the power to appoint and receive ambassadors. From the very beginning of the American republic, presidents have used this provision as a tool for recognizing or refusing to recognizing foreign governments. In 1793, for example, George Washington refused to accept the credentials of the French ambassador Citizen Edmond Genet, signaling that the United States did not recognize the legitimacy of the French revolutionary government. In the twentieth

Richard Nixon scored a number of foreign policy successes during his presidency, including reestablishing friendly U.S. relations with mainland China after a 23-year break.

century, Woodrow Wilson refused to recognize or have dealings with the revolutionary government of Mexico. Presidents Wilson, Harding, Coolidge, and Hoover refused to recognize the revolutionary communist government of the Soviet Union, a policy that was reversed by Franklin D. Roosevelt. The Chinese communist government went unrecognized by the United States for 25 years after it came to power, a policy that was eventually reversed by Richard Nixon. The president's sole power to proclaim U.S. policy in this area is suggested by the following: Neither Franklin D. Roosevelt nor Richard Nixon required the permission of any other government institution or public official—whether Congress or the courts or state legislatures, for example—to change American policy with respect to the Soviet Union or Communist China. The decision was the president's alone to make.

The power to initiate the treaty-making process is also a powerful tool of presidential diplomacy and foreign policymaking. By virtue of this power, the president and the foreign policy officials in the state, treasury, commerce, and defense departments that report to him consult, negotiate, and reach agreements with other countries. Sometimes the agreements with other countries take the form of treaties—the Paris Treaty ending the revolutionary war is an example, as are the various arms control, human rights, trade, and environmental treaties to which the United States is a party. More often, however, international agreements take the form of **executive agreements** entered into by the president and one or more foreign governments. Originally understood to be agreements about minor or technical details associated with a treaty—for example, how to regulate truck loads and safety standards under NAFTA—executive agreements have evolved to the point where they include some of the most important matters of foreign policy. During the Vietnam War, for example, presidents Lyndon Johnson and Richard Nixon entered into secret yet legally binding executive agreements making U.S. commitments to the governments of Laos, Cambodia, and Thailand.

executive agreement
An agreement with another country signed by the president that has the force of law, like a treaty; does not require Senate approval; originally used for minor technical matters, now an important tool of presidential power in foreign affairs.

Commander-in-Chief   Article II, Section 2, of the Constitution specifies that the president is the commander-in-chief of U.S. armed forces—without saying anything at all about what this actually means. On the other hand, Article I, Section 8, specifies that Congress has the power to declare war. What the framers seemed to have in mind was a distinction between defensive war and offensive war, with the president the primary decision maker with respect to the former and Congress preeminent with respect to the latter. Thus, the president was given the power to deploy and use the armed forces in order to protect the United States against external invasions and internal insurrections; Congress was given the power to declare war against another country.[6] Over the years, this distinction between offensive and defensive war has been blurred; American forces increasingly have been sent into hostilities abroad, deployed by presidents without a formal declaration of war by Congress (the last such declaration, in fact, came in December 1941 after the Japanese attack on Pearl Harbor), in the name of defending the United States. Here is what seems to have been going on: As the United States became a global power, presidents, other American leaders, and the public came to believe that defending the United States required more than simply defending against cross-border invasions from other countries. Other threats seemed to many to be equally dangerous, including communism, nationalist threats to American economic interests, drug trafficking, and, most recently, terrorism.

Presidents have used American military power, without an explicit declaration of war, to protect the United States against each of these threats. Thus, in the early 1950s, Harry Truman fought a bitter war in Korea against North Korean and Chinese forces, without a declaration of war from Congress, in the name of halting communist aggression. Presidents Eisenhower, Kennedy, Johnson, and Nixon did the same in Vietnam. Ronald Reagan used American forces in Grenada and Nicaragua to fight communism and launched an air attack against Libya to punish it for its involvement in terrorism. George H. W. Bush launched an invasion of Panama to capture its president and alleged drug lord Manuel Noriega, and in 1991 used more than 500,000 U.S. troops in Operation Desert Storm to push Iraq out of Kuwait. President Bill Clinton

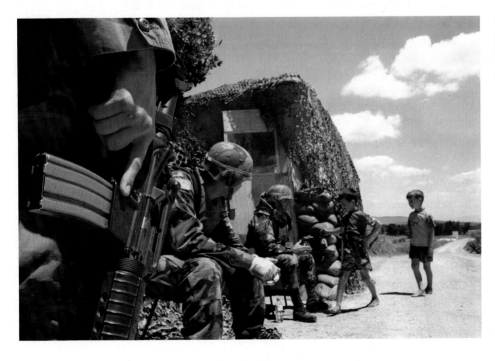

President Bill Clinton, acting in his role as commander-in-chief, sent U.S. armed forces to Kosovo in 1999 to help maintain the peace after a bloody civil war there.

claimed the power to send several thousand American troops as peacekeepers to Bosnia in 1995, Haiti in 1996, and Kosovo in 1999 and to wage an air war against Serbia to try to prevent "ethnic cleansing." For his part, George W. Bush, in the months after the September 11 attacks on the United States, launched a military campaign against the Taliban regime and the al Qaeda terrorist network in Afghanistan, then invaded and occupied Iraq in 2003 to protect the country against weapons of mass destruction. In none of these or related cases was Congress called upon to pass a formal declaration of war.

To be sure, when presidents choose to use American military power, they ordinarily consult widely with Congress and other government and opinion leaders. They do everything they can, moreover, to enlist the support of the public. They may even at times ask that Congress pass a resolution of support authorizing presidential use of the armed forces to defend the national security of the United States, though they are not legally bound to do so. Thus, President George H. W. Bush asked Congress to pass a resolution supporting Desert Storm in 1991, which it did. Likewise, in 2002, his son, President George W. Bush, asked Congress for a resolution supporting military action against Saddam Hussein's Iraq, which it did. Tellingly, each of the Bush presidents let it be known that military action would be forthcoming no matter the outcome of congressional deliberations.

In an effort to regain some of its own power in decisions about waging war in the aftermath of the Vietnam debacle, Congress passed the **War Powers Act** in 1973 (amended in 1983), allowing the president to engage the military in hostile actions for up to 60 days without permission but requiring congressional approval after that. The War Powers Act has not been used very much, however, because every president since 1973 has believed the Act to be an unconstitutional intrusion on the president's war powers (i.e., powers as commander-in-chief). Nor has Congress forced the issue, with most of its members unwilling, perhaps, to face a presidential veto on a war powers resolution or to venture a test of the Act in the courts.

War Powers Act
A resolution passed by Congress in 1973 in an effort to constrain presidential war-making powers because of excesses during the Vietnam War; requires the president to consult with Congress before committing troops and to report to Congress within 48 hours when he has done so, and to terminate the use of U.S. armed forces within 60 days unless Congress gives approval for an extension.

The President's Staff and Cabinet

Each of the president's functions is demanding; together, they are overwhelming. "Passive" presidents such as Chester Arthur or Calvin Coolidge may well be a vanishing breed. Of course, presidents do not face their burdens alone; they have gradually acquired many advisers and helpers. The number and responsibilities of these advisers and helpers have become so extensive, and the functions they perform so essential, that they have come to form what some call the **institutional presidency**.[7]

institutional presidency
The permanent bureaucracy associated with the presidency, designed to help the incumbent of the office carry out his responsibilities.

The White House Staff

The White House staff, for example, which is specially shaped to fit the particular needs of each president, includes a number of close advisers.

One top adviser, usually designated **chief of staff**, tends to serve as the president's right hand, supervising other staff members and organizing much of what the president does. Presidents use their chiefs of staff in different ways. Franklin Roosevelt kept a tight rein on things himself, granting equal but limited power and access to several close advisers in a *competitive* system. Dwight Eisenhower, used to the *hierarchical* army staff system, gave overall responsibility to his chief of staff, Sherman Adams. In the early Reagan White

chief of staff
A top adviser to the president who also manages the White House staff.

House, James Baker shared power *collegially* with Assistant to the President Michael Deaver and Counselor to the President Edwin Meese.

Another important staff member in most presidencies is the **national security adviser**, who is also head of the president's National Security Council, operating out of the White House. The national security adviser generally meets with the president every day to brief him on the latest events and to offer advice on what to do. Several national security advisers, including Henry Kissinger (under Nixon) and Zbigniew Brzezinski (under Carter), have been strong foreign policy managers and active, world-hopping diplomats who sometimes clashed with the secretaries of state and defense. Most recent presidents, however, have appointed team players who have closely reflected the president's wishes and quietly coordinated policy among the various executive departments. Condoleezza Rice followed this pattern in George W. Bush's first administration.

Most presidents also have a top domestic policy adviser who coordinates plans for new domestic laws, regulations, and spending, although this role is often subordinate to that of the chief of staff and is not usually very visible. Close political advisers, often old comrades of the president from past campaigns, may be found in a number of White House or other government posts (James Baker served as George H. W. Bush's secretary of state, for example, while Karen Hughes served as White House Counselor to the younger Bush) or may have no official position at all, such as Republican consultant Dick Morris, who crafted Clinton's 1996 reelection strategy. Prominent in every administration is the press secretary, who holds press conferences, briefs the media, and serves as the voice of the administration. Nearly all presidents have a legal counsel (a hot seat for Bill Clinton's counsel given the Whitewater, campaign finance, and Monica Lewinsky inquiries and his impeachment and trial in Congress). There are also a special assistant to act as a liaison with Congress, another to deal with interest groups, another for political matters, and still another for intergovernmental relations. In George W. Bush's administration, political strategist Karl Rove wore all these hats at the same time.

However, the exact shape of the White House staff changes greatly from one presidency to another, depending on the preferences and style of the president. What is particularly striking about President George W. Bush's management style is his penchant for setting overall goals and policies but giving his staffers a great deal of freedom and latitude in getting the job done.

The Executive Office of the President

One step removed from the presidential staff, and mostly housed in the Executive Office Building next door to the White House, is a set of organizations that forms the **Executive Office of the President (EOP)**.

Most important of these organizations is the **Office of Management and Budget (OMB)**. The OMB advises the president on how much the administration should propose to spend for each government program and where the money will come from. The OMB also exercises legislative clearance; that is, it examines the budgetary implications of any proposed legislation and sometimes kills proposals it deems too expensive or inconsistent with the president's philosophy or goals.

The **Council of Economic Advisers (CEA)** advises the president on economic policy. Occasionally, the head of the council exercises great influence, as Walter Heller did during the Kennedy administration. More often, the head of the CEA is inconspicuous.

national security adviser
A top foreign policy and defense adviser to the president who heads the National Security Council.

Executive Office of the President (EOP)
A group of organizations that advise the president on a wide range of issues; includes the Office of Management and Budget, the National Security Council, and the Council of Economic Advisers.

Office of Management and Budget (OMB)
An organization within the Executive Office of the President that advises on the federal budget, domestic legislation, and regulations.

Council of Economic Advisers (CEA)
An organization in the Executive Office of the President made up of a small group of economists who advise on economic policy.

National Security Council (NSC)

An organization in the Executive Office of the President made up of officials from the State and Defense Departments, the CIA, and the military, who advise on foreign and security affairs.

The Executive Office of the President also includes the **National Security Council (NSC)**, a body of leading officials from the State and Defense Departments, the Central Intelligence Agency (CIA), the military, and elsewhere who advise the president on foreign affairs. The NSC has been particularly active in crisis situations and covert operations. The NSC staff, charged with various analytical and coordinating tasks, is headed by the president's national security adviser. At times, the NSC staff has gone beyond analysis to conduct actual operations, the most famous of which was the Iran-Contra affair, under the direction of Lieutenant Colonel Oliver North, when weapons were secretly sold to Iran in the hope of freeing U.S. hostages and some of the proceeds were illegally diverted to the Nicaraguan Contra rebels.

In recent years, the Executive Office of the President has also included the Office of Science and Technology Policy, the Council on Environmental Quality, and the Office of the U.S. Trade Representative. Again, however, the makeup of the EOP changes from one administration to another, depending on which national problems seem most pressing and on the preferences and operating styles of individual presidents. President George W. Bush, for example, created the Office of Homeland Security directed by Tom Ridge—later made into a cabinet-level department—to coordinate governmental efforts to protect against further terrorist attacks.

The Vice Presidency

Vice presidents find themselves in an awkward position because their main job is simply to be available in case something happens to the president. This happened several times in the twentieth century; Theodore Roosevelt, Calvin Coolidge, Harry Truman, Lyndon Johnson, and Gerald Ford each stepped up from the vice presidency after the death or resignation of the president.

The vice presidency itself, however, has not always been highly regarded. John Nance Garner, Franklin Roosevelt's first vice president, has been quoted as saying in his earthy Texan way that the office was "not worth a pitcher of

Richard Cheney plays a more important role in fashioning administration policy and strategy than any other vice president in American history. Here Cheney confirms with then–Senate majority leader Trent Lott on George W. Bush's 2002 budget proposal.

warm piss."[8] Within administrations, vice presidents used to be fifth wheels, not fully trusted (since they could not be fired) and not personally or politically close to the president. Vice presidents used to spend much of their time running minor errands of state, attending funerals of foreign leaders not important enough to demand presidential attention, or carrying out limited diplomatic missions. Some vice presidents were virtually frozen out of the policymaking process. Harry Truman was never informed of the existence of the Manhattan Project, which built the atomic bomb, for example. He learned of the bomb only months before he was obligated to make a decision on using it to close out the war against Japan.

Recent presidents, however, have involved their vice presidents more.[9] Ronald Reagan included the elder George Bush in major policy meetings and put him in charge of anti-drug efforts. Bill Clinton gave Al Gore important responsibilities, including the formulation of environmental policy, coping with Ross Perot's opposition to NAFTA, and the ambitious effort to "reinvent government." More than any vice president in recent memory, Dick Cheney is at the center of the policymaking process in the George W. Bush White House, serving as one of the president's principal advisors on both domestic and foreign policy.

In 1804, the Twelfth Amendment fixed the flaw in the original Constitution under which Aaron Burr, Thomas Jefferson's running mate in 1800, had tied Jefferson in electoral votes and tried, in the House of Representatives, to grab the presidency for himself. Since then, vice presidents have been elected specifically to that office on a party ticket with their presidents. But now there is also another way to become vice president. The Twenty-Fifth Amendment (ratified in 1967) provides for the succession in case of the temporary or permanent inability of a president to discharge his office. It also states that if the vice presidency becomes vacant, the president can nominate a new vice president, who takes office on confirmation by both houses of Congress. This is how Gerald Ford became vice president in 1973, when Spiro Agnew was forced to resign because of a scandal, and how Nelson Rockefeller became vice president in 1974, when Ford replaced Richard Nixon as president.

The Cabinet

The president's cabinet is not mentioned in the Constitution. No legislation designates the composition of the cabinet, its duties, or its rules of operation. Nevertheless, all presidents since George Washington have had one. It was Washington who established the practice of meeting with his top executive officials as a group to discuss policy matters. Later presidents continued the practice, some meeting with the cabinet as often as twice a week, and others paying it less attention or none at all. Today, the cabinet usually consists of the heads of the major executive departments, plus the vice president, the director of the CIA, and whichever other officials the president deems appropriate.

Rarely, if ever, though, have presidents actually relied on the cabinet as a decision-making body. Presidents know that they alone will be held responsible for decisions, and they alone keep the power to make them. According to legend, when Abraham Lincoln once disagreed with the entire cabinet, he declared, "Eight votes for and one against; the nays have it!"

Most recent presidents have convened the cabinet infrequently and have done serious business with it only rarely. Ronald Reagan held only a few cabinet meetings each year, and those were so dull and unimportant that Reagan was said to doze off from time to time. Bill Clinton, with his "policy wonk" mastery of details, thoroughly dominated cabinet discussions.

President George H. W. Bush makes a point to members of his cabinet. Although the cabinet occasionally meets as a body, most presidents do not rely on it for making important decisions.

One reason for the weakness of the cabinet, especially in recent years, is simply that government has grown large and specialized. Most department heads are experts in their own areas, with little to contribute elsewhere. It could be a waste of everyone's time to engage the secretary of housing and urban development in discussions of military strategy. Another reason is that cabinet members occupy an ambiguous position: They are advisers to the president but also represent their own constituencies, including the permanent civil servants in their departments and the organized interests that their departments serve. They may have substantial political stature of their own, somewhat independent of the president's.

Most presidents also try to include in the cabinet some people with whom they have close personal and political ties. Thus, John Kennedy appointed his brother Robert attorney general. When criticized, Kennedy replied (tongue in cheek): "I can't see that it's wrong to give him a little legal experience before he goes out to practice law."[10] Likewise, President George W. Bush appointed long-time confidant Donald Rumsfeld to be Secretary of Defense.

The President and the Bureaucracy

Many people assume that the president, because he is the chief executive of the United States, has firm control over the federal bureaucracy, the system of departments and agencies that make up the executive branch of the federal government (and which will be discussed in more detail in the next chapter). They assume that he can simply order departments and agencies to do something and they will do it. But Richard Neustadt, in his important book *Presidential Power and the Modern Presidents,* showed that that is far from the whole truth.[11]

Giving Orders

Sometimes presidents get federal bureaucrats to act by issuing **executive orders**—formal directives to executive branch departments and agencies that have the force of law. The legitimacy of such orders are based on the constitutional position of the president as chief executive and commander-in-chief, sometimes on discretionary authority granted to the president by Congress in statutes, and often on precedents set by past presidents. Executive orders are not only about minor administrative matters; many have been issued by presidents to institute important federal policies and programs.[12] For example, George Washington issued the very first executive order, declaring U.S. neutrality in the war between Great Britain and France and ordering all diplomatic and military personnel to act accordingly. Later, Franklin Roosevelt ordered the internment of Japanese Americans during the Second World War. Harry Truman ordered loyalty oaths for all federal employees during the Red Scare in the late 1940s and early 1950s. Lyndon Johnson and Richard Nixon used executive orders to launch the first federal affirmative action programs in the late 1960s and early 1970s. President George W. Bush established the Office of Homeland Security by executive order and issued new rules for airline passenger and baggage screening after the 9/11 attacks on the United States.

In the day-to-day operation of government, direct command is seldom feasible, however. Too much is going on. Presidents cannot keep personal track of each one of the millions of government officials and employees. The president can only issue general guidelines and pass them down the chain of subordinates, hoping that his wishes will be followed faithfully. But lower-level officials, protected by civil service status from being fired, may have their own interests, their own institutional norms and practices, that lead them to do something different. President Kennedy was painfully reminded of this during the Cuban Missile Crisis of 1962, when Soviet Premier Khrushchev demanded that U.S. missiles be removed from Turkey in return for the removal of Soviet missiles from Cuba: Kennedy was surprised to learn that the missiles had not already been taken out of Turkey, for he had ordered them removed a year earlier. The people responsible for carrying out this directive had not followed through.[13]

executive order

A rule or regulation issued by the president that has the force of law, based either on the constitutional powers of the presidency or on congressional statutes.

 Timeline

"With the Stroke of a Pen"—The Executive Order Over Time

Persuasion

To a large extent, a president must *persuade* other executive branch officials to do things. He must bargain, compromise, and convince others that what he wants is in the country's best interest and in their own interest as well. Neustadt put it strongly: "Presidential power is the power to persuade."[14]

Of course, presidents can do many things besides persuade: appoint top officials who share the president's goals; put White House observers in second-level department positions; reshuffle, reorganize, or even—with the consent of Congress—abolish agencies that are not responsive; influence agency budgets and programs through OMB review; and stimulate pressure on departments by Congress and the public.

Still, the president's ability to gain bureaucratic acquiescence is limited. The federal bureaucracy is not merely a creature of the president but is itself a partly independent governmental actor. It is also subject to influences from the political linkage level—especially by public opinion and organized interests, often working through Congress. Congress, after all, appropriates the money. This constrains what presidents can do and helps ensure that the executive branch will respond to broad forces in society rather than simply to the wishes of one leader.

It's never too late for presidential persuasion. Here Ronald Reagan tries to win one more vote for a bill in the Senate before heading off to a White House reception.

The President and Congress: Perpetual Tug-of-War

The president and Congress are often at odds. This is a *structural* fact of American politics, deliberately intended by the authors of the Constitution.[15]

Conflict by Constitutional Design

The Founders created a system of checks and balances between Congress and the president, setting "ambition to counter ambition" in order to prevent tyranny. Because virtually all constitutional powers are shared, there is a potential for conflict over virtually all aspects of government policy.

Shared Powers   Under the Constitution, presidents may propose legislation and can sign or veto bills passed by Congress, but both houses of Congress must pass any laws and can override presidential vetoes. Presidents can appoint ambassadors and high officials and make treaties with foreign countries, but the Senate must approve them. Presidents nominate federal judges, including U.S. Supreme Court justices, but the Senate must approve the nominations. Presidents administer the executive branch, but Congress appropriates funds for it to operate, writes the legislation that defines what it is to do, and oversees its activities.

Presidents cannot always count on the members of Congress—even members of their own political party—to agree with them. The potential conflict written into the Constitution becomes real because the president and Congress often disagree about national goals, especially when there is **divided government**, that is, when the president and the majority in the House and/or the Senate belong to different parties.

divided government
Control of the executive and the legislative branches by different political parties.

Separate Elections   In other countries' parliamentary systems, the national legislatures choose the chief executives so that unified party control is ensured. But in the United States, there are separate elections for the president and the members of Congress. Moreover, our elections do not all come at the same time. In presidential election years, two-thirds of the senators do not have to run and are insulated from new political forces that may affect the choice of a president. In nonpresidential, "off" years, all members of the House and one-third of the senators face the voters, who sometimes elect a Congress with views quite different from those of the president chosen two years earlier. In 1986, for example, halfway through Reagan's second term, the Democrats recaptured control of the Senate and caused Reagan great difficulty with Supreme Court appointments and other matters. The Republicans did the same thing to Clinton in 1994 after they gained control of Congress.

Outcomes   In all these ways, our constitutional structure ensures that what the president can do is limited and influenced by Congress, which in turn reflects various political forces that may differ from those that affect the president. At its most extreme, Congress may even be controlled by the opposing party. This divided government situation always constrains what presidents can do and may sometimes lead to a condition called "gridlock"[16] in which a president and Congress are locked in battle, neither able to make much headway.

What Makes a President Successful with Congress?

A number of political scientists have studied presidents' successes and failures in getting measures that they favor enacted into law by Congress and have suggested reasons some presidents on some issues do much better than others.

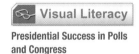

Presidential Success in Polls and Congress

Web Exploration
Impeachment

Issue: Although rarely used, Congress's ultimate weapon in its perpetual struggle with the president is its power to impeach the president and remove him from office.

Site: Access the Jurist Website at the University of Pittsburgh Law School on our Website at **www.ablongman.com/greenberg**. Go to the "Web Explorations" section for Chapter 12 and open "impeachment." Scroll down to "Impeachments in History" and select "Articles of Impeachment Against Richard M. Nixon." Then scroll down to the "Clinton Controversy" and select "Proposed Articles of Impeachment." Compare the articles of impeachment brought against each president.

What You've Learned: How serious do you judge the accusations to be against each president? Did Nixon and/or Clinton, in your view, violate their oaths of office? Had you been a senator at the time, would you have voted for removal of the president from office? Why?

HINT: Pay special attention to the "obstruction of justice" charges against the two presidents, and judge their relative seriousness.

Presidents must cultivate good working relationships with Congress if they are to have any success with their legislative program. Here, President George W. Bush consults with congressional leaders about pending legislation.

Party and Ideology
The most important factor is a simple one: the number of people in Congress who agree with the president in ideology and party affiliation. When the same political party controls both the presidency and Congress, presidents are more likely to get their way. When the opposite party controls one or the other house in Congress, or both, presidents tend to be frustrated. The bigger the majority a president's party has, the better the president does (see Figure 12.1).[17]

This success does not necessarily mean that presidents exercise party discipline, actively whipping their fellow partisans into line. But party members do tend to be like-minded; they tend to vote together because they share the same values and policy preferences, and for the same reason, they tend to go along with a president of their own party.[18] (See "The Rise of Partisan Conflict" feature for more on how partisanship and ideology affect presidential success.)

Foreign Policy and National Security Issues
Presidents tend to do better on foreign policy issues than on domestic ones. Political scientist Aaron Wildavsky went so far as to refer to "two presidencies," domestic and foreign, with the latter president much more dominant. Wildavsky found that during the 1948–1964 period, 59 percent of presidents' proposals on foreign policy were passed, but only 40 percent of their domestic proposals.[19] The reason is that political leaders generally want to show a unified face to a potentially hostile world.

This difference between domestic and foreign policy success by the president has decreased since the Vietnam War, but it remains significant. Although there was significant dissent, Congress voted in January 1991, despite many misgivings, to authorize President George H. W. Bush to use force against Iraq, once again illustrating presidential primacy in foreign affairs. Congress eventually supported Clinton's decision to send U.S. forces to Haiti, Bosnia, and Kosovo as part of multinational peacekeeping operations, despite considerable initial grumbling. The generalization about presidents having an easier time with Congress on foreign policy issues than on domestic ones does

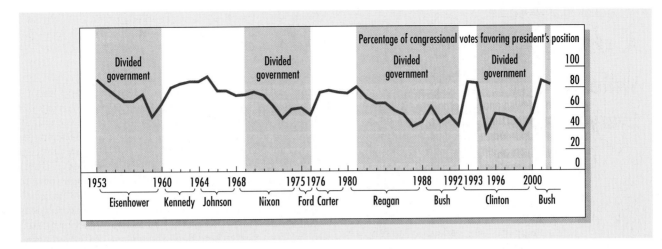

FIGURE 12.1 • Presidential Success in Congress

The party in control of Congress can have a strong effect on a president's success. In periods of divided government (see shaded areas), when the opposing party has a majority in Congress, policies favoring the president's position receive fewer votes. Note the anomalies in 2001. For the first half of the year, President Bush enjoyed a Republican-controlled Congress. When Senator Jeffords left the GOP, Democrats gained control of the Senate, and divided government returned. President Bush continued to have success with Congress, however, because the country rallied around the president's leadership in the aftermath of the September 11 terrorist attacks.

Source: Calculated by the authors from various issues of the *Congressional Quarterly Weekly Report.*

not hold, however, when foreign policy concerns trade and other global economic issues that directly affect constituents.

In a national defense crisis, of course, presidents almost always get their way. After the attack on Pearl Harbor, Congress swiftly approved bills on military mobilization submitted by Franklin Roosevelt. After Nine-Eleven, Congress quickly approved the USA Patriot Act on homeland security and passed emergency military budget supplements as the president requested.

Vetoes   When the issue is a presidential veto of legislation, the president is again very likely to prevail. Vetoes have not been used often, except by certain "veto-happy" presidents, such as Franklin Roosevelt, Truman, and Ford. But when vetoes have been used, they have seldom been overridden—only 5 percent of the time for Truman and only 1.5 percent for Roosevelt. Bill Clinton did not use the veto at all during his first two years in office, when he had a Democratic majority in Congress, but then used it 11 times in 1995 alone during his budget battles with the Republican-controlled 104th Congress. Because Republicans committed to the president's agenda controlled the House from 2001 through 2004 and the Senate after the 2002 elections, George W. Bush did not resort to the veto at all during this period.

The percentage of veto success among presidents may be misleadingly high. The truth is that because presidents like to preserve an image of invulnerability, they generally avoid casting vetoes that might be overridden. Conversely, the mere *threat* of a veto—without any need to carry it out—is often enough to discourage Congress from passing laws that the president will

The Rise of Partisan Conflict

Writer Says, "He Hates Everything About Bush."

The Story: *The Economist* magazine noted in late 2003 that "Bush-hatred is now something that civilized people [mainly Democrats and liberals] wear as a badge of honor."* The magazine was especially taken with Jonathan Chait's cover story in *The New Republic* in which he announced that "he hates everything about Bush," his policies and politics, as well as his personal demeanor and character, and even the way he talks: "...blustery self-assurance masked by a pseudo-populist twang." *The Economist* also pointed to the great popularity among Democrats and liberals of recent books by Michael Moore—*Dude, Where's My Country?*—and

Al Frankin—*Lies and the Lying Liars Who Tell Them: A Fair and Balanced Look at the Right*—with contempt for Bush very close to the surface in each. *The Bush-Hater's Handbook: A Guide to the Most Appalling Presidency of the Past 100 Years* by Jack Huberman, published by Nation Books, carried the genre even further.

The Background: Why were Democrats and liberals so contemptuous of President George W. Bush? Why did many of the most partisan among them reject not simply Bush's policies but the man himself? One reason may be that they feel "turnabout is fair play." Most partisan Democrats believe that Republican President Bush is getting some of the same medicine dished out to Democratic President Bill Clinton from 1993 to 2000. Republicans steadily attacked Clinton; accusations rained down about supposedly nefarious behavior related to the Whitewater land deal, the suicide of Clinton assistant Vince Foster, billing at Hillary Clinton's law office, and

not approve. Clinton was quite successful using this approach with the 105th and 106th Congresses.

Popularity   Although political scientists have had little luck confirming it statistically,[20] most scholars and observers of Washington politics agree that presidential effectiveness with Congress is significantly affected by how popular a president is with the American people.[21] This is probably because of fear among many members of Congress that opposing a highly visible proposal from a popular president might jeopardize their electoral future.

Legislative Skills   Again, although statistical studies of roll-call votes reveal little effect of presidents' legislative skills (this may be the result of poor measures of legislative skills), most longtime observers of Washington politics believe that such skills make a difference. Lyndon Johnson's famous wheeling and dealing surely picked up votes for his favored legislation, as did Ronald Reagan's efforts on the 1981 tax and budget measures that began the so-called Reagan Revolution.

more—most of which was not supported in the end by the report of Special Prosecutor Ken Starr. Then there was the impeachment and trial of Bill Clinton, an action carried out by a united and determined Republican majority against Democratic opposition and popular opinion. One commentator describes the GOP attitude toward Clinton in the following way: "The Republicans have waited eight years excruciating years to get him out of Washington—him with his junk food and his cigars, his big-haired babes and his scary-smart wife, his overwrought empathizing and his pulpit-thumping oratory, his political brilliance and inexplicable popularity ... The Republicans hate Bill Clinton as they have never hated anyone, even Ted Kennedy. He was never just an adversary for Gingrich, Trent Lott, Tom Delay, and the like. He represents everything they despise about the 1960s, they decade they think ruined America."[†]

What's at Stake: At one level, the only thing at stake is a party's prospects for winning or losing national elections. With the country now so evenly divided between the parties, and with each party looking for ways to get an electoral leg up on the opposition, many Republican and Democratic strategists and activists have turned to a strategy of attacking the president if he carries the label of the other party. Rather than opposing the president on policy grounds—that is, opposing him because he stands for policies that they consider wrong-headed—the preferred formula for the party out of power seems to have shifted to a strategy of demeaning the character, intelligence, and decency of the presidential incumbent. Who knows? Doing so might win the party a few extra votes and determine the outcome of a national election.

At another level, the stakes may be much higher, namely, the ability of political leaders in the United States to govern at all, and to do so in a way that satisfies most Americans and takes their interests and concerns into account. Although a president under fierce personal attack may well have the skills and fortitude to be effective—both Clinton and Bush, for example, were successful on a number of fronts during their presidencies—future presidents may not be so blessed.

Is It Good for Democracy?

- Do you think it is possible to disagree with someone without disliking the person? • Why, then, on a national level do partisans increasingly malign or demonize political opponents rather than simply disagreeing with them? • Are the public policy stakes so high at the national level and the parties so closely divided that the drift toward partisan hatred is all but inevitable? • Or is it possible to keep political disagreement from spinning out of control? • In your opinion, where should the line be drawn between legitimate criticism of a president and his policies and over-the-top attacks that may be unfair, unseemly, and uncivil? • If you think current trends are problematic, what do you think can be done about it?

Notes:
[*]Lexington, "The Politics of Rage," *The Economist* (November 22, 2003), p. 34.
[†]Diane Roberts, "Bill Clinton Will Go on Annoying the Republicans," *St. Petersburg Times* (January 14, 2001), p. A21.

The President and the People: An Evolving Relationship

The complicated relationships among the president, the executive branch as a whole, and Congress also interact with public opinion, the political parties, and organized interests to shape the presidency. Particularly important in this interaction is the special relationship between the president and the general public, which has evolved over many years to make the presidency a more democratic office. Let's look at several aspects of this relationship.

Getting Closer to the People

The Founders thought of the president as an elite leader, relatively distant from the people, interacting with Congress often but with the people only rarely. Most nineteenth-century presidents and presidential candidates thought the same. They seldom made speeches directly to the public, for example, generally averaging no more than 10 such speeches per year.[22] In the earli-

As Senate Majority Leader, Lyndon Johnson was famous for exerting strong personal pressure on legislators, a skill he carried with him to the presidency.

est years of the American Republic, presidents were not even chosen directly by the voters but by electors chosen by state legislators or, in case no one got an Electoral College majority, by the House of Representatives. The Constitution thus envisioned very indirect democratic control of the presidency.

As we have also seen, however, this system quickly evolved into one in which the people played a more direct part. The two-party system developed, with parties nominating candidates and running pledged electors and the state legislators allowing ordinary citizens to vote on the electors. Presidential candidates began to win clear-cut victories in the Electoral College, taking the House of Representatives out of the process. Voting rights were broadened as well. Property and religious qualifications were dropped early in the nineteenth century. Later, slaves were freed and given the right to vote; still later, women, Native Americans, and 18-year-olds won the franchise.

By the beginning of the twentieth century, presidents began to speak directly to the public. Theodore Roosevelt embarked on a series of speech-making tours in order to win passage of legislation to regulate the railroads. Woodrow Wilson made appeals to the public a central part of his presidency, articulating a new theory of the office that highlighted the close connections between the president and the public. Wilson saw the desires of the public as the wellspring of democratic government: "As is the majority, so ought the government to be."[23] He argued that presidents are unique because only they are chosen by the entire nation. Presidents, he said, should help educate the citizens about government, interpret their true will, and faithfully respond to it.

Wilson's theory of the presidency has been followed more and more fully in twentieth-century thought and practice. All presidents, especially since Franklin Roosevelt, have attempted to both shape and respond to public opinion; all, to one degree or another, have attempted to speak directly to the people about policy.[24]

More and more frequently, presidents go public, using television to bypass the print media and speak to the public directly about policy. They have held fewer news conferences with White House correspondents (where awkward questions cannot be excluded).[25] Richard Nixon pioneered prime-time television addresses, at which Ronald Reagan later excelled. Bill Clinton was more interactive with citizens, appearing on radio and TV talk shows and holding informal but televised "town hall meetings."

More and more, presidents have traveled outside the White House to make public appearances. Often the settings convey a visual message: George W. Bush used appearances with "typical" American families in their homes to dramatize his tax cut proposals. Most spectacular is travel abroad, which portrays the chief executive as *presidential,* a head of state, and highlights his foreign policy achievements: Kennedy speaking at the Berlin Wall in 1963; Nixon raising his glass in toast at the Great Hall of the People in Beijing in 1972; Reagan strolling through Red Square in Moscow with Mikhail Gorbachev in 1988.

Leading Public Opinion

Especially since the rise of television, modern presidents have enhanced their power to shape public opinion. Some studies have indicated that when a popular president takes a stand in favor of a particular policy, the public's support for that policy tends to rise. A determined president, delivering many speeches and messages over a period of several weeks or months, may be able to gain 5 to 10 percentage points in support of that policy in the polls.[26] This is not an enormous effect, but it tends to confirm Theodore Roosevelt's claim that the presidency is a "bully pulpit."

The power to lead the public also implies a power to *manipulate* public opinion, if a president is so inclined—that is, to deceive or mislead the public so that it will approve policies that it might oppose if it were fully informed.[27] Especially in foreign affairs, presidents can sometimes control what information the public gets, in at least in the short run. Lyndon Johnson, for example,

Modern presidents make concerted efforts to stay in touch with public opinion. Pollster Stanley Greenberg played this role during the first years of the Clinton administration.

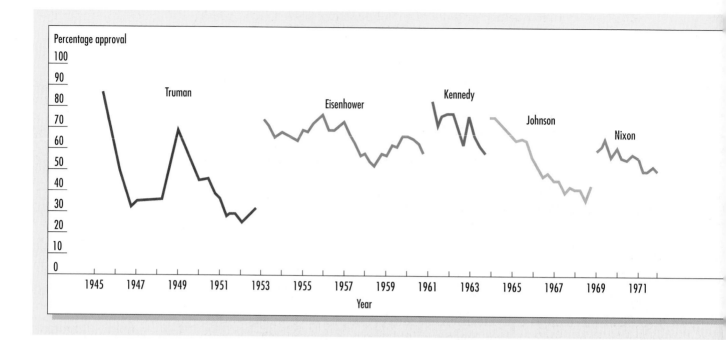

FIGURE 12.2 ● **Trends in Presidential Popularity, 1945–2004**

Popularity ratings of presidents rise and fall in response to political, social and economic events.
Source: Gallup surveys.

purposely misstated the facts about the Gulf of Tonkin incident at the beginning of the Vietnam War (recall the story in Chapter 5).

Champions of energetic presidential leadership must face the possibility that that leadership will go wrong and result in demagoguery or manipulation. The dilemma cannot be resolved. The power to do good is the power to do evil as well. But some safeguards may exist, including the capacity of the public to judge character when it is choosing a president, as well as the ability of other national leaders to counteract a deceitful president. Johnson and Nixon learned this bitter lesson—the former declined to run for a second term; the latter resigned.

Responding to the Public

In any case, the relationship between presidents and the public is very much a two-way street. Besides trying to lead the people, presidents definitely tend to respond to public opinion. Electoral competition produces presidents who tend to share the public's policy preferences. Moreover, most presidents want to be reelected or to win a favorable place in history, and they know that they are unlikely to do so if they defy public opinion on many major issues. Usually, they try to anticipate what the public will want in order to win electoral reward and avoid electoral punishment.

What presidents *want* to do so often resembles what the public wants—that is one reason they were elected in the first place—that there is no conflict to observe. Only occasionally does a modern president get so badly out of touch with the public that the full power of public opinion is revealed.

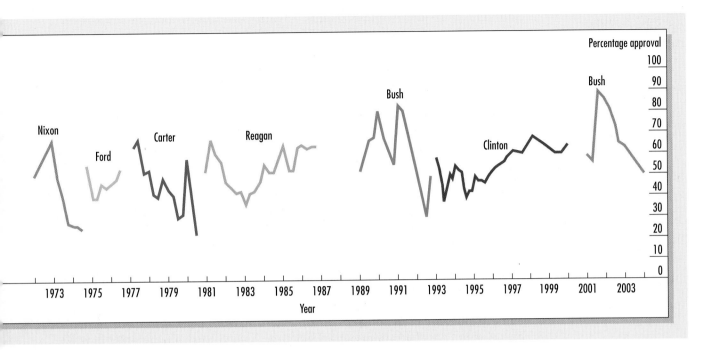

More often, in day-to-day politics, it simply turns out that what the president does is largely in harmony with what the general public wants. When public opinion moved toward favoring a buildup of defense during the late 1970s, Carter and Reagan followed suit. When the public wanted something done about the welfare problem, Clinton acted in concert with Congress. As a general matter, when polls show that public opinion has changed, presidents have tended to shift policy in the same direction.[28]

There is plenty of evidence that presidents pay attention to what the public is thinking. At least since the Kennedy administration, presidents and their staffs have carefully read the available public opinion surveys and now have full-blown polling operations of their own.[29] President Clinton employed several of the best pollsters in the business—including Stanley Greenberg (the author's brother)—to chart his electoral campaigns and legislative agenda. Although such polling is often deplored, it helps presidents choose policies that the American public favors and change or discard those that are unpopular.

Presidential Popularity

The public also influences presidents through its judgments about presidential performance: that is, through **presidential popularity** or unpopularity. Since the 1930s, Gallup and other poll takers have regularly asked Americans whether they approve or disapprove of "the president's handling of the job." The percentage of people who approve varies from month to month and year to year, and as time passes, these varying percentages can be graphed in a sort of fever chart of how the public has thought the president was doing (see Figure 12.2).

A number of factors seem to be especially important in determining presidential popularity, including time, the state of the economy, and foreign policy crises.

Historically, most presidents have begun their terms of office with a majority of Americans—usually 60 percent or more—approving of how they are

presidential popularity
The percentage of Americans who approve a president's handling of his job.

Participation

Rate the Presidents

handling their job. Most presidents have tended to lose popularity as time passes. But this loss of popularity does not represent an inexorable working of time; Eisenhower, Reagan, and Clinton actually gained popularity during their second terms. Those who lose popularity do so in response to bad news. Good news generally makes presidents more popular.[30]

One of the most serious kinds of bad news involves economic recession. When the economy goes sour, fewer Americans approve of the president. This happened to George H. W. Bush in mid-1991, as the economy faltered. On the other hand, the spectacular performance of the American economy in the mid- and late-1990s greatly benefited Bill Clinton, whose historically high approval numbers were sustained even as Congress was attempting to remove him from office.

Successful military actions tend to add to presidential popularity, as Ronald Reagan happily discovered after the U.S. invasion of Grenada in 1982. The senior Bush's approval rating soared on the successful conclusion of the war with Iraq, while the junior Bush's success in Afghanistan sustained his high popularity. Conversely, an unsuccessful war is bad news for a president, especially a limited war that drags on with high casualty rates, such as the Korean War (which detracted from Truman's already low popularity in 1950 and 1951) or the Vietnam War. Rising casualties in Iraq and news of prisoner abuse at the Abu Ghraib prison in Bagdahd eroded Bush's popularity in 2003 and 2004.

The Influence of Interest Groups, Political Parties, and Social Movements on the Presidency

As we saw in Chapter 7, interest groups' relationships with presidents, like other aspects of interest group politics, are a sort of unexplored continent. Much of what goes on is probably kept hidden from scholars and observers. But we can be reasonably sure, from various hints and fragments of evidence, that organized groups exert important kinds of influence.[31]

Interest group and other special-interest money helps candidates win presidential nominations and elections, so those who take office do not simply reflect the preferences of ordinary citizens; they tend to share, or at least sympathize with, the goals of their benefactors. At the least, presidents give special access to those who helped get them into office.

Precisely which interest groups have the most influence on policy depends partly on which party controls the presidency, because some groups are much more closely allied with one party than with the other. Since the 1930s, for example, organized labor and certain businesses have been closely tied to the Democratic party; more recently, civil rights advocates, women's rights advocates, trial lawyers, teachers' unions, and environmental groups have joined this alliance. The Republican party, for its part, has had much closer ties to most manufacturing and energy corporations, small businesses, agribusiness, and organizations of well-to-do professionals, such as doctors and lawyers.[32] The policies of the parties in office tend to reflect these differences. George W. Bush's energy policy, for example, was apparently fashioned in conjunction with large energy companies, including representatives from Enron—not surprising, perhaps, in light of the president's and vice president's long association with the oil industry and the oil industry's sizeable contributions to the 2000 Bush campaign.[33]

Political parties are also important in shaping presidential behavior. Because of their loyalty to the values and policy preferences of their own political party, Republican presidents tend to do things differently from Democratic presidents. Consequently, changes in which party controls the presidency produce significant changes in policy. As a result of party influence, there tend to be partisan cycles of presidential action, with different policies, depending on which party holds office. Democratic presidents tend to fight unemployment,[34] to favor civil rights and environmental measures, and to promote domestic social welfare programs; Republicans tend to worry about inflation, to cut taxes and domestic expenditures, and to take conservative stands on social issues such as abortion.

Social movements occasionally provide yet another political-level influence on presidents. They do so in at least two different ways: (1) Mass demonstrations and protests cause disruptions that are inconvenient or dangerous to ignore, forcing presidents to take action to defuse them. Thus, the massive march on Washington in 1963 convinced President Kennedy to send an historic civil rights bill to Congress. Or (2) mass movements may produce changes in general public opinion that in turn affect presidents. Either way, presidents and other political leaders have to pay attention. The anti–World Trade Organization (WTO) demonstrations in Seattle in late 1999, for example, helped convince Bill Clinton to push the organization to include environmental and labor protections in its rules (see the "Using the Framework" feature).

Structural Influences on the Presidency

Some of the political linkage influences on presidents that we have discussed—especially public opinion—provide substantial continuity from one president to the next. So do a range of governmental factors, including Congress and the courts. Continuity is also provided by the Constitution, which sets the rules of the political game, and the American political culture, which shapes the outlooks of presidents, other political leaders, and the people. Thus, we can speak of an *enduring* presidency, a presidency that does not merely fluctuate with the whims of whoever holds office, but also reflects the goals and preferences of the people, groups, and institutions that make up American society. The enduring presidency is also a product of two structural factors: the international system and the economy.

The International System

From the end of World War II to the end of the Cold War, all presidents, Republicans and Democrats alike, pursued a broadly similar set of foreign policies. Although post-war presidents differed in their means, they fundamentally agreed on the ends: containment of the influence of the Soviet Union, solidification of the Western alliance, encouragement of open economies in which American business might compete, and opposition to leftist or nationalist movements in the developing world. The reason for this continuity is that U.S. foreign policies reflected the basic features of the international system (particularly its bipolarity, with two superpowers); the U.S. position in that system as the dominant superpower; and the nature of U.S. economic interests in markets, raw materials, and investment opportunities.

Using the Framework

Clinton and Free Trade

How could Bill Clinton support free trade, yet also support many ideas of anti-free-trade activists?

Background: In late November 1999, the Seattle meetings of the World Trade Organization were disrupted by large anti-WTO street demonstrations. The labor, human rights, and environmental organization demonstrators were demanding that the WTO be more open to public scrutiny and accountability and that it write into trade rules protections against child and slave labor and standards for work and environmental protections. President Clinton, one of the nation's leading free traders and a strong proponent of the WTO (he believed the world trading system needed a set of agreed-upon rules to make it safe and fair), nevertheless sided with most of the arguments pushed by the demonstrators. How could he be for both sides in this dispute? Taking a broader look at how structural, political linkage, and governmental factors affected President Clinton's views on global trade issues will help explain this situation.

Governmental Action

The president proposes in his speech to WTO delegates that the organization be more accountable and pay attention to demands for labor and environmental protections in its rules.

Governmental Level

President Clinton was a strong believer in both free trade and labor and environmental protections. → The president also felt pressure from interest groups on both sides of the issue; these political pressures accentuated the conflict between his own beliefs. → President Clinton wanted Al Gore to follow him as president and did not want to alienate the Democratic Party base (which includes labor union members and environmentalists).

Political Linkages Level

Many business firms involved in the global economy have lobbied Congress and the President for a world trade regime that emphasizes free and open trade, protection of intellectual property rights, and access to markets. → Labor and environmental organizations are against a free-trade system without protections for labor and environmental protections in less developed nations; these groups were very important parts of President Clinton's Democratic Party. → Social movement demonstrators in the streets of Seattle brought the issues of labor and the environment, and the nature of the WTO, to public attention. → The mass media, although mainly attending to the conflict in the streets of Seattle, also covered the issues raised by the protesters.

Structural Level

Since the end of World War II, the United States has been the leading proponent of global free trade. → Globalization of the world economy, pushed by technological revolutions in telecommunications, computers, and transportation, was and is advancing at a rapid rate. → The United States is the leading nation in the globalizing economy and, overall, has been benefiting from it. → However, some groups in the population are hurt by globalization and by rapid technological change. → The United States has in place a strong set of environmental, labor, and consumer protection laws that some believe will be threatened if the WTO gains too much authority.

How Democratic Are We?

Presidents and the American People

PROPOSITION: The presidency has evolved into a highly democratic institution that is responsive to the American people.

AGREE: The framers did not conceive of the office in very democratic terms, but it has become the most democratic institution in the American federal system. It is, after all, the only office directly elected by the American people as a whole. Members of the Supreme Court are not elected by the people, for example, and members of the House and Senate, although elected by the people, represent only congressional districts and states, not the entire nation. Being elected by the whole people, it is only the president who can claim a national mandate for his programs and actions. Thus, it is only the president who can overcome the inherent stasis of the constitutional system and move the government to action in the interests of and in response to the American people as a whole.

DISAGREE: Although presidents often claim mandates from the people, they are more likely to lead and shape public opinion than to respond to it, especially in the area of foreign and military affairs, so the institution cannot be said to be democratic. For example, Lyndon Johnson first got his way in escalating the war in Vietnam because of the inaccurate information that was released on the Gulf of Tonkin incident. President George W. Bush gained support for the invasion of Iraq because of his warnings about Saddam Hussein's weapons of mass destruction. Presidents can pretty much go their own way in foreign policy, knowing that the people will eventually follow their lead. Because elections happen only every four years, moreover, and assuming that the public has a short memory, presidents have plenty of time to follow their own agendas early in their term without regard to the public. Because presidents can only serve two terms, then, there is no compelling reason they need to pay close attention to the public during their second term.

CONSIDER: If you believe that the United States ought to be as democratic as possible, then you will be heartened by the evidence suggesting that modern presidents are highly responsive to the wishes of the public. If you believe, as the framers did, that political decision makers ought to be insulated from direct pressures from the public, then you will be discouraged by such evidence.

- What about your own sense of presidential responsiveness to public opinion? • Thinking about recent presidents, to what extent did they seem to follow public opinion? • To what extent did they seem to ignore public opinion? • And, to what extent did they seem to be shaping—even manipulating—public opinion? • How about your own stand on important issues? • Have recent presidents acted in ways that support your preferences? • Or have they generally ignored or acted contrary to your positions on the issues?

When the international system changes, presidential policy tends to change, no matter who is president. Thus, when it became painfully evident by the 1970s that the United States had declined in international economic competitiveness and relative economic strength, Democratic President Carter and Republican President Reagan introduced similar measures to reduce taxes, to lighten the burden of regulation, to subsidize high-technology industries, and to encourage exports. When the Soviet Union began to move in conciliatory directions and then collapsed, Reagan and the elder Bush responded in friendly fashion, despite their history of fierce anti-communism. After the terrorist attacks of Nine-Eleven, George W. Bush enunciated a new military doctrine stressing preemptive strikes against terrorist groups and countries.

The Economy

Similarly, all presidents, Republican or Democratic, must work to help the economy grow and flourish while keeping unemployment and inflation low. A healthy economy is essential to a president's popularity and continuation in office, to tax receipts that fund government programs, and to the maintenance of social peace and stability. A healthy economy in turn requires that investors continue to have confidence in the future. This has tended to create a set of presidential policies that favor such investors regardless of whether a Democrat or a Republican is in the White House.

Summary

The American presidency began small; only a few nineteenth-century presidents (among them Jefferson, Jackson, Polk, and Lincoln) made much of a mark. In the twentieth century, however, as a result of industrialization, two world wars and the Cold War, and the Great Depression, presidential powers and resources expanded greatly. The presidency attained much of its modern shape under Franklin Roosevelt.

Presidents have varied in personality and style, with significant consequences. Despite the enormous resources and large staffs available to presidents, they are constrained in what they can do, especially concerning domestic policy. Presidents cannot always control their own executive branch. They engage in tugs-of-war with Congress, pushing their programs with varying success, depending on their party's strength in the legislature, their popularity and legislative skills, and the nature of the issue.

The presidency has become a far more democratic office than the Founders envisioned. Presidents listen to public opinion and respond to it, in addition to leading (and sometimes manipulating) the public. But presidents are also influenced by interest groups, party activists, and financial contributors in ways that may diverge from what the public wants. Further, presidents are affected by such structural factors as the nature of the American economic and social systems and the U.S. position in the world.

Suggestions for Further Reading

Barber, James David. *The Presidential Character: Predicting Performance in the White House,* 4th ed. Englewood Cliffs, NJ: Prentice Hall, 1992.
A fascinating, but controversial, analysis of the nature and effect of presidential personalities on the office.

Cronin, Thomas E., and Michael A. Genovese. *The Paradoxes of the American Presidency.* New York: Oxford University Press, 1998.
Examines the implications of our often conflicting and unrealistic expectations about the office of president.

Howell, William G. *Power Without Persuasion: The Politics of Direct Presidential Action.* Princeton, NJ: Princeton University Press, 2003.
Rejecting the common view among political scientists that presidential power is based primarily on the president's ability to persuade, Howell suggests instead that presidents have many tools for taking unilateral action to get their way.

Morris, Edmund. *Theodore Rex.* New York: Random House, 2001.
A fascinating account of the presidency of Theodore Roosevelt and how the intersection of his personality with a particular moment in American history helped transform the presidential office.

Pfiffner, James, and Roger H. Davidson, eds. *Understanding the Presidency,* 3rd ed. New York: Longman Publishers, 2003.
A comprehensive anthology of recent scholarship on all aspects of the presidency and its place in the American political system.

Skowronek, Stephen. *The Politics Presidents Make.* Cambridge, MA: Harvard University Press, 1993.
An in-depth historical look at the ways in which the political context of the times shapes the nature of the presidency.

Tulis, Jeffrey K. *The Rhetorical Presidency.* Princeton, NJ: Princeton University Press, 1987.
Traces how presidents have moved from the Founders' conception of a distant relationship with the public to the modern closeness.

Internet Sources

The Center for the Study of the Presidency
www.thepresidency.org
Access to research on the presidency sponsored by the Center for the Study of the Presidency.

U.S. Government Information/Executive Orders
http://usgovinfo.about.com/library/weekly/aa121897 .htm
Information about presidential executive orders, from George Washington to George W. Bush.

Potus
www.potus.com
Biographies and other information about American presidents.

National Archives Presidents Site
http://www.archives.gov/presidential_libraries/ addresses/addresses.html
Access to presidential addresses, libraries, and other information about the office.

Roper Center
http://www.lib.uconn.edu/RoperCenter/
Reports on all major presidential job performance and popularity polls.

Watergate Site
www.washingtonpost.com/wp-srv/national/longterm/watergate/front.htm
Complete information on the Watergate affair: background, congressional testimony, official statements, press coverage, speeches, court rulings, biographies of the leading players, and more.

White House Home Page
www.whitehouse.gov/
Information on the first family, recent presidential addresses and orders, text from news conferences, official presidential documents, and ways to contact the White House.

Chapter 13
The Federal Bureaucracy

In This Chapter

- How our bureaucracy compares with those in other countries
- Who bureaucrats are and what they do
- How the executive branch is organized
- What's wrong and what's right with the federal bureaucracy
- Who and what influences bureaucratic decision making

The Return of Big Government After 9/11

President George W. Bush came to office imbued with a conservative philosophy, committed to reducing the size, reach, and cost of the federal government. Although he often talked of "compassionate conservatism" during the 2000 election campaign—which implied to many people that the federal government would need to do more in the future—he simultaneously promised to cut taxes, reduce the size and cost of government in Washington, cut back intrusive regulations, and return more responsibilities to the states. Echoing the words of President Ronald Reagan, Bush told a group of California Republicans during the campaign that "You can't be for big government and big bureaucracy and still be for the little guy."[1]

Rather than shrinking, however, during Bush's watch the federal government grew in important ways: in the number of its civilian employees and active-duty military personnel, the size of its budget, and the degree of its intrusiveness in everyday life. The main reason for this dramatic turnabout is fairly straightforward: the attack on the United States on September 11, 2001, and the particular strategies President Bush settled on for protection against future attacks.

The president's response to Nine-Eleven included both domestic and foreign policies; each contributed to the growth of the federal government's size, cost, and reach. On the domestic protection front, President Bush supported two major changes in Congress. First, although initially reluctant to federalize this function, he strongly supported the creation of the Transportation Security Administration to take over all baggage and passenger screening at U.S. airports. This agency now employs approximately 48,000 screeners. Second, he agreed to the creation of the Department of Homeland Security, the largest reorganization of the federal government in more than half a century. The new department brought together two dozen existing federal agencies, and employs roughly 180,000 government employees, making it the third-largest Cabinet department. The mandate of the new department is sweeping: the oversight and coordination of virtually all agencies responsible for homeland security, including border and transportation security, emergency preparedness and response, national communications and infrastructure protection, and coordination of intelligence. To meet these goals, the new department is authorized, among other things, to collect more information than in the past about people living in or traveling to the United States, impose tighter rules regarding transportation and shipping, and more intensely regulate the flow of people across the nation's borders. To head the new department, the president appointed Tom Ridge, the former governor of Pennsylvania.

President Bush also supported Attorney General John Ashcroft's aggressive use of the Department of Justice for counterterrorism. Bolstered by the authority granted to the Justice Department by the USA Patriot Act and several presidential directives, the Justice Department broadly expanded its use of wire-taps and checks of e-mail communications, detained suspected terrorists and terrorist supporters, registered and questioned men from Middle Eastern and Muslim countries, monitored library checkouts for suspicious material, and issued scores of federal indictments for terrorism-related activities. In the end, the Ashcroft-led Justice Department is considerably more active than recent Justice Departments in investigating, indicting, detaining, and prosecuting citizens and noncitizens alike. Needless to say, as the Justice Department's responsibilities expanded, so did its budget and the number of its employees.

To fight the threat of terrorism abroad, President Bush initiated a number of policies that resulted in a dramatic increase in the budget of the Department of Defense, a slight increase in the size of the active duty armed forces (though not big enough for critics of the administration, who believed that the United States's new commitments and responsibilities around the world required a much larger military), and renewed efforts to beef up the combat readiness and logistical support for U.S. military forces. The first policy was to topple the Taliban regime in Afghanistan and go after the al Qaeda terrorist organization rooted in that country. The second policy was to mount a series of small military operations to root out terrorist organizations around the world, including actions in Yemen, the Philippines, and Somalia. The third policy was the war in Iraq, waged—in the president's view—to rid the world of one leader of the "axis of evil," countries he believed capable and willing to supply weapons of mass destruction to terrorist organizations.

Nine-Eleven and the war on terrorism contributed greatly, then, to the growth in the size, cost, and scope of responsibilities of the federal bureaucracy. Although somewhat surprising that this growth occurred during the presidency of an avowed small-government conservative, the general pattern is consistent with the history of growth of the executive branch of the federal government. When problems appear that seem solvable only at the national level—be they external security threats, financial crises, racial conflict, or environmental deterioration—the American public and its political leaders have repeatedly turned to the national government for solutions, for it is primarily the government in Washington that has the ability to mobilize and coordinate the vast human and material resources to tackle such big problems. Invariably, the result grants more power to the federal government, increases the cost of government, and expands the size of the bureaucratic machinery in the executive branch. This chapter will examine the federal bureaucracy—its history, its form, and how it works with other government institutions and actors.

Thinking Critically About This Chapter

This chapter is about the federal bureaucracy—the executive branch of the federal government responsible for carrying out policies fashioned by Congress, the federal courts, and the president—how it is organized, what it does, and what effects its actions have on public policies and American democracy.

Using the Framework You will see in this chapter how the federal bureaucracy has grown over the years, primarily as a result of structural transformations in the economy and international position of the United States, but also because of the influence of political linkage level actors and institutions, including voters, public opinion, and interest groups. Primary responsibility for many of the enduring features of the federal bureaucracy will be shown to be associated with our political culture and the Constitution.

Using the Democracy Standard You will see in this chapter that the federal bureaucracy in general, despite much speculation to the contrary, is fairly responsive to the American people, reacting in the long run to pressures brought to bear on it by the elected branches, the president, and Congress. On the other hand, bureaucrats in specific agencies, in specific circumstances, can be relatively immune from public opinion, at least in the short and medium run. You will be asked to think about what this means in terms of our democratic evaluative standard.

A Comparative View of the American Bureaucracy

federal bureaucracy
The totality of the departments and agencies of the executive branch of the national government.

The **federal bureaucracy** in America is different from bureaucracies in other democratic nations. Structural influences such as the American political culture and the constitutional rules of the game have a great deal to do with these differences.

Hostile Political Culture

Americans generally do not trust their government, nor do they think it can accomplish most of the tasks assigned to it. They believe, on the whole, that the private sector can usually do a better job and, most of the time, want responsibilities lodged there rather than with government.

This generally hostile environment influences the American bureaucracy in several important ways. For one thing, our public bureaucracy is surrounded by more legal restrictions and is subject to more intense legislative oversight than bureaucracies in other countries. Because **civil servants** have so little prestige, moreover, many of the most talented people in our society tend to stay away; they do not generally aspire to work in government, though this may be changing, as suggested above. In many other democratic countries, by way of contrast, civil servants are highly respected and attract talented people. In France, Britain, and Germany, for example, the higher **civil service** positions are filled by the top graduates of the countries' elite universities and are accorded enormous prestige. Finally, the highest policy-making positions in the U.S. executive branch are closed to civil servants; they are reserved for presidential political appointees. This is not true in other democracies.

civil servants
Government workers employed under the merit system; not political appointees.

civil service
Federal government jobs held by civilian employees, excluding political appointees.

Incoherent Organization

Our bureaucracy is an organizational hodgepodge. It does not take the standard pyramidal form, as bureaucracies elsewhere do. There are few clear lines of control, responsibility, or accountability. Some executive branch units have no relationship at all to other agencies and departments. As one of the leading students of the federal bureaucracy once put it, other societies have "a more orderly and symmetrical, a more prudent, a more cohesive and more powerful bureaucracy," whereas we have "a more internally competitive, a more experimental, a noisier and less coherent, a less powerful bureaucracy."[2] Our bureaucracy was built piece by piece over the years in a political system without a strong central government. Bureaucracies in other democratic nations were often created at a single point in time, by powerful political leaders, such as Frederick the Great in Prussia and Napoleon in France.[3]

 Comparative

Comparing
Bureaucracies

Divided Control

Adding to the organizational incoherence of our federal bureaucracy is the fact that it has two bosses—the president and Congress—who are constantly vying with one another for control. In addition, the federal courts keep an eye on it. This situation is created by the separation of powers and checks and balances in our Constitution, which give each branch a role in the principal activities and responsibilities of the other branches. No other democratic nation has opted for this arrangement. Civil servants in parliamentary democracies are accountable to a single boss, a minister appointed by the prime minister.

Transformation of the Bureaucracy

The Constitution neither specifies the number and kinds of departments to be established nor describes other bureaucratic agencies. The framers apparently wanted to leave these questions to the wisdom of Congress and the president.

 Timeline

Evolution of the
Federal Bureaucracy

bureaucracy

A large, complex organization characterized by a hierarchical set of offices, each with a specific task, controlled through a clear chain of command, and where appointment and advancement of personnel is based on merit.

Over the years, they created a large and complex **bureaucracy** to meet a wide range of needs. The most immediate causes for the transformation of the role of the federal government and the scale of the bureaucracy are political linkage sector pressures—from public opinion, voters, parties, interest groups, and social movements—on government decision makers. The more fundamental causes are changes in such structural level factors as the U.S. economy, the nation's population, and the role of the United States in the world, including involvement in war.

Late Nineteenth- and Early Twentieth-Century Changes

Until the Civil War, the federal government had few responsibilities, and the administrative apparatus of the executive branch was relatively undeveloped. Rapid population growth, westward expansion, the Industrial Revolution, and economic uncertainty in the last quarter of the nineteenth century gradually changed people's thinking about the appropriate responsibilities of government and the size of the bureaucracy.[4] The Department of the Interior, created in 1849, was given responsibility for Indian affairs, the census, and the regulation of public lands and mining. The Department of Justice was created in 1870 to handle the federal government's growing legal burden in the fields of civil and criminal, anti-trust, tax, and natural resources law. The Department of Agriculture became a full-fledged cabinet department in 1889 in response to economic crisis in the farm economy and the demands of farm groups. The Department of Labor was created in 1913 in an effort to ease the rising tensions between workers and owners. The Department of Commerce was created in the same year to foster technological development, standardization, and business cooperation.

The Corporation and the Progressives

The rise to prominence of the large corporations in the late nineteenth and early twentieth centuries, and the problems they caused, also contributed to a rethinking of the role of the federal government. Monopoly practices in the railroad, manufacturing, oil, and banking industries triggered reform movements that resulted in new federal regulatory laws, of which the most important were the Interstate Commerce Act (1887) and the Sherman Antitrust Act (1890). Progressive reformers and farsighted business leaders, who were worried about the growing public hostility to big business, helped convince Congress to pass such landmark legislation as the Federal Reserve Act (passed in 1914 to stabilize the banking industry), the Pure Food and Drug Act (1906), the Meat Inspection Act (passed in 1906 in response to the horrors reported in Upton Sinclair's "muckraking" book *The Jungle*), and the Federal Trade Commission Act (1914).[5] Each piece of legislation was a response to a set of problems, each expanded the federal government's responsibilities, and each created a new executive branch agency to carry out the law.

The Great Depression

The Great Depression forever changed how Americans thought about their government. Economic collapse, widespread social distress, and serious threats of violence and social unrest impelled President Franklin Roosevelt and Congress to respond with a range of new programs: work programs for the unemployed, relief for the poor, Social Security, regulation of the banking and the securities industries, agricultural subsidy programs, collective bargaining,

Certain problems that cross state boundaries—such as the production of unsafe and unwholesome food by companies for a national market—are probably best solved by the federal government. Upton Sinclair's description of a meat-packing plant like this one in his novel *The Jungle* helped swing public opinion behind the Pure Food and Drug Act, passed in 1906.

and programs to encourage business expansion. Each program added new bureaucratic agencies to the executive branch.

World War II and Its Aftermath

World War II, America's new role as a superpower, and the long Cold War with the Soviet Union also brought a substantial increase in the federal government's responsibilities and in the size of the executive branch. Some old-line departments, such as the Department of State, grew substantially after World War II. The Department of Defense was created by merging the old Army and Navy departments and adding an Air Force component. New administrative units such as the Central Intelligence Agency, the National Security Agency, the National Security Council, the Agency for International Development, and the U.S. Arms Control and Disarmament Agency were created to fill new needs and missions. The Atomic Energy Commission was created both to regulate and to encourage atomic power and weapons production. The Internal Revenue Service expanded its operations so that it could collect the revenues to pay for these new responsibilities. By 1950, a federal bureaucracy of substantial size and effect was firmly in place.[6]

The Regulatory State

During the 1960s and 1970s, successful social reform movements and important changes in public opinion convinced political leaders to take on new responsibilities in the areas of civil rights, urban affairs, environmental and consumer protection, workplace safety, and education. Important among these initiatives was the formation of the Department of Health, Education, and Welfare (now split into the Department of Health and Human Services and

During World War II and the Cold War that followed, the increased responsibilities of a superpower were thrust on the U.S. federal government. The executive branch grew so rapidly during World War II that temporary buildings were constructed along the mall in Washington, D.C., to house such new bureaucratic entities as the Atomic Energy Commission.

the Department of Education). The Environmental Protection Agency was created to monitor compliance with federal environmental laws and to regulate business activities that might pollute the nation's air and water. The Occupational Safety and Health Administration keeps its regulatory eye on potentially dangerous workplace practices. Each expansion of responsibility, as in the past, brought an expansion in the size of the bureaucracy. Although the Reagan Revolution slowed the growth in the federal government's responsibilities, it was unable to roll back most of the programs and agencies created since the Great Depression.

Devolution and Rollback

On taking control of Congress after their 1994 landslide electoral victory, Republicans began to pare down the size of the federal government, roll back many of its regulatory responsibilities, and shift a number of functions to the states. For instance, Congress made it more difficult to identify and protect wetlands. It also shifted much of the responsibility for providing public assistance to the states. Finally, Congress made deep slashes in the federal budget, which forced substantial "downsizing" in a broad range of executive branch agencies. Increasingly, Republicans especially, but many Democrats as well, have been asking what essential services the federal government should provide. Bill Clinton echoed this "devolution and rollback" theme in his 1996 State of the Union address, when he announced that "the era of big government is over." Nevertheless, the federal government's size and reach remain quite substantial in historical terms.

Devolution and rollback may be related to changes in the global economy, where success seems to go to business enterprises that are "lean and mean," nimble and entrepreneurial and to countries that allow their major companies to succeed by lowering regulatory and tax burdens. Whether this is cause or excuse is too early to tell. It may well be that globalization forces are not the cause of these changes, as some analysts suggest, but merely a rhetorical device used by the business community to lighten the burden of government regulation on corporations. Whether cause or rhetorical weapon, political leaders in the United States have been paying attention recently to globalization processes and have acted to diminish the role and size of the federal government and its bureaucracy.

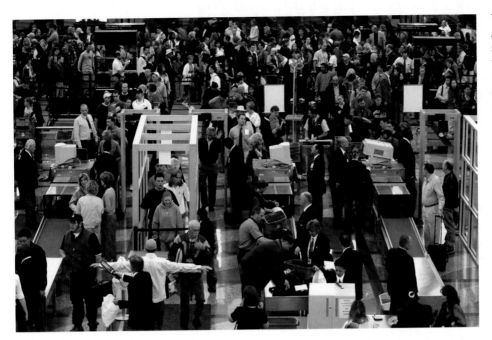

The Transportation Security Administration was created to screen passengers and luggage at the nation's airports as part of a heightened effort by the federal government to improve homeland security against further terrorist attacks.

The War on Terrorism

Because waging war requires the organization and mobilization of vast material and human resources, it has always led to an expansion in the size and reach of the executive branch of government. This looks to be true for the war on terrorism, as well. Soon after September 11, for example, virtually every federal police and intelligence agency—including the FBI, the CIA, and the NSA—was authorized to hire more people, as was the Department of Defense, funded by emergency budget authorizations. The 9/11 Commission, moreover, recommended that a new agency be created to coordinate the evaluation of domestic and foreign terrorism intelligence.[7] There is every indication, then, that bureaucratic expansion, at least in those areas associated with the war on terrorism, is here to stay as long as the threat of terrorism remains a reality.

So, although there have been more than a few fits and starts, the general picture over the course of American history has been toward a growth in the size and responsibilities of the national government. However, determining just how big the government has grown depends on what measures one uses. (See "By the Numbers: How big is the federal government?")

How the Executive Branch Is Organized

The executive branch is made up of several different kinds of administrative units, which make the federal bureaucracy a very complicated entity.

- The most familiar are *departments,* which are headed by cabinet-level secretaries, appointed by the president and approved by the Senate. Departments are meant to carry out the most essential government functions, as suggested by the first three to be established—War, State,

By the Numbers

How big is the federal government? Is it really shrinking, as some people say?

When Bill Clinton proclaimed in 1996 that "the era of big government is over," he was sharing a vision of government espoused by his two conservative predecessors: Ronald Reagan and George H. W. Bush. The notion that the government in Washington is too big and ought to be cut down to size is a recurring theme in American political discourse. Recently, the call to "downsize" or "right size" government has taken an especially strong turn, with recent presidents committed to this vision of a "leaner" and theoretically more efficient government.

What should we make of all these calls to downsize? Just how big is government?

Why It Matters: A significant number of Americans want a smaller government that does less; a significant number of Americans want a bigger government that does more. Whichever camp you fall into, it makes sense that we have accurate measures of what is actually going on.

Calculating the Size of the Federal Government: In addition to using the size of the federal budget as a measure of the size of government—we do this in Chapter 17—it is fairly common among academics, journalists, and politicians to use the number of federal government employees as a

simple, straightforward measure. Using this metric, the size of the government in Washington is not only relatively small at 1.9 million employees (only one-sixth the size of the manufacturing sector in 1996 in terms of employees, and one-thirty-sixth the size of the service sector), but shrinking.

Criticism of the Measure of Government Size: Critics point out that the number of federal civilian employees measures only a portion of the total number of employees who produce goods and services for the federal government. The following, they say, should be included (all figures are for 1996, based on research by Paul Light):

- Employees who work in government contract-created jobs, such as employees working for defense contractors on federal projects (5.6 million).
- Employees who work in government grant-created jobs, such as employees working on federally funded road construction grants or on federally funded research projects (2.4 million).
- Employees hired by state and local governments to meet federal mandates in areas such as child health and nutrition, safe schools, and pollution control (4.6 million).
- U.S. Postal workers, who are not counted as federal civilian employees (0.8 million).
- Uniformed military personnel (1.4 million).

Adding these categories together, we have a total of direct and indirect federal government employ-

and Treasury. Departments vary greatly in size and internal organization. The Department of Agriculture, for example, has almost 50 offices and bureaus, whereas the Department of Housing and Urban Development has only a few operating agencies. Over the years, departments (and employees) were added as the need arose, as powerful groups demanded them, or as presidents and members of Congress wished to signal a new national need or to cement political alliances with important constituencies. As you saw in the chapter-opening story, the Department of Homeland Security was created in the wake of the terrorist attacks on the United States to take on the important role of coordinating anti-terrorism activities on the homefront.

- Subdivisions within cabinet departments are known as *bureaus* and *agencies*. In some departments, such as the Department of Defense, ment of almost 17 million people in 1996, almost as many as work in the American manufacturing sector.

How about the question of whether government is shrinking? The following graph shows what is happening. (Unfortunately, there is no information available for "mandate-created jobs" prior to 1996, so it cannot be included.)

The picture is pretty clear: Although the overall size of government is considerably larger than it first appears using only the numbers of federal civilian employees, the size of government shrank during the period 1984 to 1996. One other fact is worth noting: Most of the shrinkage of government in this period was related to decreases in the size of the defense sector, including cuts in the number of uniformed military personnel and decreases in defense contracting to the private sector. Considering only the domestic side of the equation, the total size of the federal government actually increased by about 15 percent between 1984 and 1996.

What to Watch For: Numbers that are reported by government, journalists, and academics about government may often be correct, yet incomplete. Always try to expand your search to include multiple measures of the phenomenon or institution you are trying to understand.

What Do You Think?   In formulating an opinion about the appropriate size for government, consider what responsibilities and tasks should be the responsibility of the federal government. Are these responsibilities and tasks being accomplished to your satisfaction? Are there too many people working either directly or indirectly for the federal government in

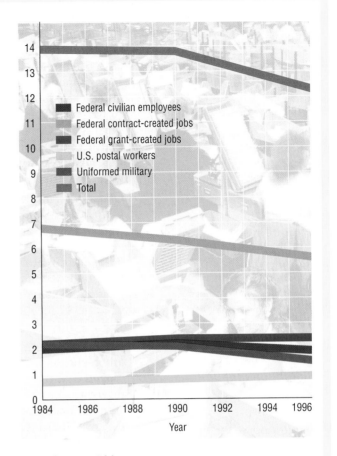

Federal Government Jobs

terms of the responsibilities and tasks? Too few? Or just about the right number?

Source: Paul C. Light, *The True Size of Government* (Washington, D.C.: The Brookings Institution, 1999).

these subdivisions are closely controlled by the department leadership, and the entire department works very much like a textbook hierarchical model. In other cases, where the bureaus or agencies have fashioned their own relationships with interest groups and powerful congressional committees, the departments are little more than holding companies for powerful bureaucratic subunits.[8] During the long reign of J. Edgar Hoover, for example, the FBI did virtually as it pleased, even though it was (and remains) a unit within the Justice Department.

- *Independent executive agencies* report directly to the president rather than to a department- or cabinet-level secretary. They are usually created to give greater control to the president in carrying out some executive function or to highlight some particular public problem or issue that policymakers wish to address. The Environmental Protection

Agency was given independent status to focus government and public attention on environmental issues and to give the federal government more flexibility in solving environmental problems.

- *Government corporations* are agencies that operate very much like private companies. They can sell stock, retain and reinvest earnings, and borrow money, for instance. They are usually created to perform some crucial economic activity that private investors are unwilling or unable to perform. The Tennessee Valley Authority, for example, was created during the Great Depression to bring electricity to most of the upper South; today it provides about 6 percent of all U.S. electrical power. The U.S. Postal Service was transformed from an executive department to a government corporation in 1970 in the hope of increasing efficiency.

- *Quasi-governmental organizations* are hybrids of public and private organizations. They allow the federal government to be involved in a particular area of activity without directly controlling it. They are distinguished from government corporations by the fact that a portion of the boards of directors are appointed by the private sector. The Corporation for Public Broadcasting fits into this category, as does the Federal Reserve Board, responsible for setting the nation's monetary policy (see Chapter 17 for more on the "Fed").

- *Independent regulatory commissions,* such as the Securities and Exchange Commission and the Consumer Product Safety Commission, are responsible for regulating sectors of the economy in which it is judged that the free market does not work properly to protect the public interest. The commissions are "independent" in the sense that they stand outside the departmental structure and are protected against direct presidential or congressional control. A commission is run by commissioners with long, overlapping terms, and many require a balance between Republicans and Democrats.

- *Foundations* are units that are separated from the rest of government to protect them from political interference with science and the arts. Most prominent are the foundations for the Arts and for the Humanities and the National Science Foundation.

The Bureau of Immigration and Customs Enforcement, an agency in the Department of Homeland Security, is responsible for slowing the flow of illegal immigration and screening for possible terrorists, but it must operate within guidelines and budgets determined by Congress.

What Do Bureaucrats Do?

Bureaucrats engage in a wide range of activities that are relevant to the quality of democracy in the United States and affect how laws and regulations work. Let's look at the more prominent and significant of these activities.

bureaucrat
A person who works in a bureaucratic organization.

Executing the Law

The term *executive branch* suggests the branch of the federal government that executes or carries out the law. The framers of the Constitution assumed that Congress would be the principal national policymaker and stipulated that the president and his appointees to administrative positions in the executive branch "shall take care that the laws be faithfully executed" (Article II, Section 2). For the most part, this responsibility is carried out routinely; mail is delivered, troops are trained, and Social Security checks are mailed on time.

Sometimes, executing the law is not so easy, however, because it is not always clear what the law means. Often (all too often, according to some critics[9]), Congress passes laws that are vague about goals and short on procedural guidelines. It may do so because its members believe that something should be done about a particular social problem but are unclear on specifics about how to solve it or disagree among themselves. The Office of Economic Opportunity, for example, was created in 1965 as part of Lyndon Johnson's War on Poverty, with a mandate to "eliminate poverty," but it received virtually no guidance about what time frame was contemplated or what specific things it ought to do. Vaguely written statutes and directives, then, leave a great deal of discretion to bureaucrats.

Congress identifies tasks and creates agencies to complete them using their own expertise. For example, the Environmental Protection Agency was created by Congress to clean up and prevent pollution in the nation's air and water; the EPA creates and implements environmental standards without much direct congressional involvement.

cost-benefit analysis

A method of evaluating rules and regulations by weighing their potential costs against their potential benefits to society.

Regulating (Rule Making)

Congress often gives bureaucratic agencies the power to write specific rules. Because of the complexity of the problems that government must face, Congress tends to create agencies and to specify the job or mission that it wants done and then charges the agency with using its expertise to do the job. Congress created the Environmental Protection Agency (EPA), for instance, and gave it a mission—to help coordinate the cleanup of the nation's air and water—but it left to the EPA the power to set the specific standards that communities and businesses must meet. The standards set by the EPA have the force of law unless they are rescinded by Congress or overruled by the courts. The Food and Drug Administration (FDA) writes rules about the introduction of new drugs that researchers and pharmaceutical companies are obliged to follow. (See the "Using the Framework" feature for more on the FDA.)

Some critics believe that Congress delegates entirely too much lawmaking to the executive branch, but it is difficult to see what alternative Congress has. It cannot micromanage every issue. And in the end, Congress retains control; it can change the rules written by bureaucrats if they drift too far from congressional intent or constituent desires.

Other critics simply believe that there are too many rules and regulations. When candidates promise to "get government off our backs," the reference is to the purported burdens of regulation. Several attempts have been made to roll back executive branch rule making. Under Ronald Reagan, required **cost-benefit analysis** was introduced as a way to slow the rule-making process, for example. And all recent presidents have used the Office of Management and Budget (OMB) to review "excessive" rule making.

Adjudicating

Congress has given some executive branch agencies the power to conduct quasi-judicial proceedings in which disputes are resolved. Much as in a court of law, the decisions of an administrative law judge have the force of law, unless appealed to a higher panel. The National Labor Relations Board, for instance, adjudicates disputes between labor and management on matters concerning federal labor laws. Disputes may involve claims of unfair labor practices, for example—firing a labor organizer falls into this category—or disagreements about whether proper procedures were followed in filing for a union certification election.

It is quite clear that bureaucrats exercise a great deal of discretion. They do not simply follow a set of orders from Congress or the president, but find many opportunities to exercise their own judgment. Because bureaucrats make important decisions that have consequences for many other people, groups, and organizations, we can say that they are policymakers. They are *unelected* policymakers, however, and this fact should immediately alert us to some potential problems with regard to the practice of democracy.

Who Are the Bureaucrats?

Participation

Who Wants to Be a Bureaucrat?

Because bureaucrats exercise substantial discretion as policymakers, we want to know who they are. How representative are they of the American people? In a democracy, we would probably want to see a pretty close correspondence between

Using the Framework

Bureaucratic Rule Making

How can a bureaucratic agency such as the Food and Drug Administration (FDA) make rules on important things like genetically engineered food? The members of the FDA aren't even elected by the people!

Background: One of the emerging conflicts that will be playing itself out over the next few years, both in the United States and in the global economy, concerns the safety of genetically engineered food and the rules that will apply for protecting the public from its possible harmful effects. In the United States, unless Congress chooses to act in its own right, the rules will be made by the Food and Drug Administration. We can better understand why the FDA can make rules on genetically engineered foods by using a broad perspective that takes into account structural, political linkage, and governmental level factors.

Governmental Action

The FDA issues rules on genetically engineered food products.

Governmental Level

The FDA scientific staff pressed the FDA's leadership to become active in this area of rulemaking.

The FDA leadership, attentive to the growing interest in rules to regulate in the area of genetically engineered food, held a series of hearings on the subject in 1999.

The FDA issued rules in 2000 specifying how genetically engineered food is to be tested for safety and wholesomeness and requiring packaging to carry a warning label for consumers.

Congress created the Food and Drug Administration, defined its overall mission, but left room for the FDA to make rules in its areas of responsibility.

The Court has allowed bureaucratic agencies to make rules within the boundaries set by Congress.

No laws specifically addressing genetically engineered food have been enacted, leaving rulemaking in this area to the FDA.

Political Linkages Level

Public opinion polls show that some Americans are beginning to worry about genetically engineered food and want some action.

Interest groups, for and against genetically engineered food, have pressed their positions on public officials, using both "inside" and "outside" forms of lobbying.

Demonstrators at the WTO protests in Seattle targeted genetically engineered food, putting further pressure on public officials to take action.

Structural Level

The Constitution says little about the organization and operations of the Executive Branch and leaves the details to be filled in by Congress.

Scientific researchers have made dramatic breakthroughs in plant and animal genetics, causing some segments of society to call for regulations.

Global agribusiness corporations are always looking for the most efficient forms of production, and genetically engineered products help them do this.

the people and bureaucrats. There are several different personnel systems in the executive branch: career civil service, separate merit services in specific agencies, and political appointees.

The Merit Services

Merit services choose employees on the basis of examinations and educational credentials. These services have evolved in size and complexity, in tandem with the federal bureaucracy, and are of two general types.

Career Civil Service   From the election of Andrew Jackson in 1828 until the late nineteenth century, the executive branch was staffed through what is commonly called the **spoils system.** It was generally accepted that the "spoils of victory" belonged to the winning party. Winners were expected to clear out people who were loyal to the previous administration and to replace them with their own people. Also known as **patronage,** this system of appointment caused no great alarm in the beginning because of the small and relatively unimportant role of the federal government in American society. The shortcomings of the War Department and other bureaucratic agencies during the Civil War, however, convinced many people that reform of the federal personnel system was required. Rampant corruption and favoritism in the government service during the years after the Civil War gave an additional boost to the reform effort, as did the realization that the growing role of the federal government required more skilled and less partisan personnel. The final catalyst for change was the assassination in 1881 of President James Garfield by a person who, it is said, badly wanted a government job but could not get one.

The Civil Service Act of 1883, also known as the Pendleton Act, created a bipartisan Civil Service Commission to oversee a system of appointments to

spoils system
The practice of distributing government offices and contracts to the supporters of the winning party; also called patronage.

patronage
The practice of distributing government offices and contracts to the supporters of the winning party; also called the spoils system.

Most federal government employees are in the civil service and are selected on the basis of competitive examinations.

certain executive branch posts on the basis of merit. Competitive examinations were to be used to determine merit. In the beginning, the competitive civil service system included only about 10 percent of federal positions. Congress has gradually extended the reach of the career civil service; today, it covers about 60 percent of federal employees. In 1978, Congress abolished the Civil Service Commission and replaced it with two separate agencies, the Office of Personnel Management and the Merit Systems Protection Board. The former administers the civil service laws, advertises positions, writes examinations, and acts as a clearinghouse for agencies that are looking for workers. The latter settles disputes concerning employee rights and obligations, hears employee grievances, and orders corrective action when needed.

The civil service system took an important hit when President Bush convinced Congress that the normal civil service rules would not apply in the newly created Department of Homeland Security. The president and Tom Ridge claimed that the new department needed greater flexibility in hiring and firing employees and assigning jobs, in establishing a system of pay-for-performance, and in limiting labor union bargaining rights over working conditions if it was to do the best job possible in defending the nation against terrorism. Critics claimed that this move was but the first step in rolling back other civil service pay and personnel procedures across the entire federal bureaucracy.[10]

Agency Merit Services   Many federal agencies require personnel with particular kinds of training and experience appropriate to their special missions. For such agencies, Congress has established separate merit systems administered by each agency itself. The Public Health Service, for instance, recruits its own doctors. The State Department has its own examinations and procedures for recruiting foreign service officers. The National Aeronautics and Space Administration (NASA) recruits scientists and engineers without the help of the Office of Personnel Management. About 35 percent of all federal civilian employees fall under these agency-specific merit systems.

How Different Are Civil Servants?   Civil servants are very much like other Americans.[11] Their educational levels, regional origins, average incomes, and age distribution match almost exactly those of the adult population. Civil servants' political beliefs and opinions also match almost exactly those of the general American public, although they tend to favor the Democrats a bit more than the general public and are slightly more liberal on social issues than the national average.[12] Women and minorities are very well represented (the latter are actually overrepresented), with women holding 45 percent of all nonpostal jobs and racial and ethnic minorities 30 percent.[13] It is worth noting, however, that women and minorities are overrepresented in the very lowest civil service grades and are underrepresented in the highest. They also are far less evident in the special-agency merit systems (such as the Foreign Service and the FBI) and in the professional categories (scientists at the National Institutes of Health; doctors in the Public Health Service).

In addition, the demographic representativeness of the bureaucracy is far greater in the United States than in virtually any other democratic nation.[14] In Britain and France, for example, people of aristocratic background have long dominated the upper levels of the civil service in the former; graduates of the elite *grandes écoles,* like the École Nationale d'Administration, dominate in the latter.

Political Appointees

The highest policymaking positions in the federal bureaucracy (e.g., department secretaries, assistants to the president, leading officials in the agencies) enter government service not by way of competitive merit examinations but by presidential appointment. About 1,200 of these top appointments require Senate confirmation and about 2,000 more do not. These patronage positions, in theory at least, allow the president to translate his electoral mandate into public policy by permitting him to put his people in place in key policymaking jobs. Top appointees who have the confidence of the president tend to become important policy makers and public figures in their own right. Thus, John Ashcroft, President Bush's Attorney General during his first administration, enhanced the Justice Department's federal law enforcement powers following 9/11—including increased surveillance of e-mail, telephone messages, and library records and detention of terrorism suspects. Defense Secretary Donald Rumsfeld also exercised broad discretion in the reorganization of the military and in the way wars were fought in Afghanistan and Iraq.

Most presidents use patronage not only to build support for their programs but also to firm up their political coalition by being sensitive to the needs of important party factions and interest groups. Ronald Reagan used his appointments to advance a conservative agenda for America and made conservative beliefs a prerequisite for high bureaucratic appointments.[15] President Clinton, by contrast, promised to make government "look more like America" and did so by appointing many women and minorities to top posts in his administration. George W. Bush combined the Reagan and Clinton approaches by making quite conservative but racially and ethnically diverse appointments. Particularly notable conservative Bush appointments included John Ashcroft as Attorney General; Eugene Scalia, son of Supreme Court justice Antonin Scalia and a prominent anti-labor, corporate lawyer, as the solicitor at

Web Exploration
Who Are the Bureaucrats?

Issue: Although women are well represented in the federal bureaucracy, their presence in the upper-most, politically appointed, decision-making positions in the Executive Branch may be less than equitable. Or, they may be well represented in decision-making positions in some agencies and not others.

Site: Access the Plumbook, which lists all federal politically appointed offices, on our Website at **www.ablongman.com/greenberg**. Go to the "Web Explorations" section for Chapter 13. Select "Who are the bureaucrats?" and then open "how representative?" Select three Executive Branch Departments and review the names of the people who hold top offices in the Departments.

What You've Learned: How well are women represented in the Executive Branch departments you selected? If women are better represented in some as compared with others, why do you think that is the case?

Hint: Because women professionals in American society are most heavily represented in education, welfare, the health professions, and in the law, the Departments with their principal missions in these areas are likely to have the most women available for appointment.

Among President George W. Bush's first appointees (to the post of National Security Adviser) and closest advisers was Condoleezza Rice, here leaving a meeting with Prime Minister Tony Blair in 2003, accompanied by Secretary of State Colin Powell. Like other members of the White House staff and the Executive Office of the President, her appointment did not require Senate confirmation.

the Department of Labor; and Harvey Pitt to head the Securities and Exchange Commission. Prominent minorities and women included Colin Powell as Secretary of State, Condoleezza Rice as National Security Adviser and then Secretary of State following Powell, Elaine Chao as Secretary of Labor, Rod Paige as Secretary of Education, Mel Martinez as Secretary of Housing and Urban Development, and Alberto Gonzales as Attorney General.

Presidents also reserve important appointments for people they trust and who bring expertise and experience. George W. Bush has been particularly eager and successful in filling both cabinet posts and his inner circle with people with much experience in the upper reaches of the federal government, including several who had served in his father's administration; namely, Donald Rumsfeld (Secretary of Defense), Colin Powell (Secretary of State), and Condoleezza Rice.

Top political appointees are not very representative of the American people. They tend to be much better educated and wealthier than other Americans. They also tend to be professionals, independent businesspeople, or executives from large corporations and financial institutions. Using this narrow and privileged pool of appointees has important ramifications for the practice of democracy, because it is these officials who exercise the most discretion and make the most important policy decisions. To be sure, background is not everything in the determination of the outlook and behavior of political appointees, but it cannot be discounted either.

Despite having been appointed to their posts by the president, political appointees cannot automatically be assumed to do the president's bidding. High-level political appointees are subject to many influences in addition to the president, including Congress, the courts, personnel in their own departments and agencies, the press, and public opinion. The result is sometimes unpleasant. President Clinton could not have been happy, for example, when Attorney General Janet Reno agreed to allow Special Prosecutor Kenneth Starr to investigate allegations of sexual misconduct against the president.

Top political appointees do not last very long on the job. On average, they stay in office only 22 months; political scientist Hugh Heclo called them "birds of passage."[16] They leave for many reasons. Most are accomplished people from the private sector who see government service as only a short-term commitment. Most make financial sacrifices to become top bureaucratic officials. Many don't find the public notoriety appealing. Some find themselves the target of partisan campaigns that later prove groundless but leave them with damaged reputations. Finally, many become frustrated by how difficult it is to change and implement public policy.

Political and Governmental Influences on Bureaucratic Behavior

Rather than there being a single chain of command with clear lines of authority, the bureaucracy in general (and bureaucrats in particular) must heed several important voices, among the most important of them, the public, the president, Congress, and the courts. Figure 13.1 gives an overview of these several influences on bureaucratic behavior.

The Public

Most Americans pay little attention to bureaucratic agencies as such. The public focuses mainly on the *content* of public policies rather than on the bureaucratic agencies or the bureaucrats who carry them out. Americans have opinions about Social Security—level of benefits, eligibility, taxes, and so on—but do not concern themselves much with the Social Security Administration per

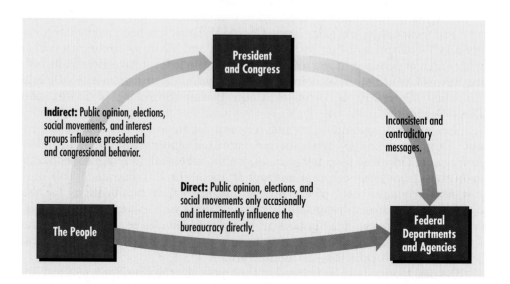

FIGURE 13.1 ● **Popular Control of the Bureaucracy: Imperfect Popular Sovereignty**

Popular control of the federal bureaucracy is complex, indirect, and only partially effective. The public does not elect government bureaucrats, and public opinion has little direct effect on their behavior. However, the members of Congress and the president, all of whom are answerable to the electorate and attentive to public opinion, exercise an important influence on bureaucratic behavior. Because elected officials often send mixed signals, however, some of the effectiveness of such controls is diminished.

se. In general, then, the public does not directly know or think much about bureaucratic agencies.

There are exceptions to this generalization, however. Some agencies are constantly in the public eye and occasion the development of opinions. Because taxes are a constant irritant for most people, Americans tend to have opinions about the Internal Revenue Service. Foul-ups can often focus public attention on an agency, as well. Thus, the Securities and Exchange Commission came to public attention in the aftermath of the collapse of Enron and Arthur Andersen because of its lax enforcement of accounting practices. The CIA came under fire for intelligence failures relating to Nine-Eleven and Iraq's purported weapons of mass destruction.

Interest Groups

Because bureaucratic agencies make important decisions that affect many people, interest and advocacy groups pay lots of attention to what they do, and use a variety of lobbying tools (see Chapter 7) to influence these decisions. Groups lobby Congress, for example, to shape the missions of executive branch departments and agencies, as environmental organizations did to give the EPA authority over development in wetland areas. Groups also lobby bureaucratic agencies directly, as when they appear before them to offer testimony on proposed rules. (Public comment is required in many agencies before binding rules can be issued.) Although various environmental, labor, and consumer advocacy associations regularly offer formal comment on rules, this process is dominated by associations that represent business and the professions who often get their way.[17] It is hardly surprising, then, to learn that livestock producers for years were able to prevent the Department of Agriculture from imposing stringent rules for tracking cattle products as they made their way from the ranch to the dinner table, something that came to light only after "mad cow" disease was discovered in several cows in the state of Washington in late 2003.

The President

The president, as the nation's chief executive, is the formal head of the executive branch. But as we saw in Chapter 12, the president's ability to control the executive branch is limited. Virtually every modern president has been perplexed by the discovery that he cannot assume that bureaucrats will do what he wants them to do.[18]

Richard Nixon was so frustrated by his inability to move the federal bureaucracy that he came to think of it as an alien institution filled with Democratic party enemies. His strategy was to intimidate bureaucrats or bypass them. He created the notorious "plumbers" unit in the White House to act as his personal domestic surveillance and espionage unit. Revelation of its activities was one of the factors leading the House Judiciary Committee to recommend approval of three articles of impeachment in the Watergate scandal.

Why Presidents Are Often Stymied by the Bureaucracy
The sheer size and complexity of the executive branch is one reason presidents are frustrated by it. There is so much going on, in so many agencies, involving the activity of tens of thousands of people, that simply keeping abreast of it all is no easy task. Moreover, because of civil service regulations, presidents have no say about the tenure or salary of most bureaucrats. When presidents want something to happen, they are unlikely to get instantaneous acquiescence from bureaucrats, who do not fear them as they would fear a private employer. Presidents also find that

Popular presidents can use the office, in Teddy Roosevelt's words, as a "bully pulpit" to move the nation to action on a broad range of fronts, even in noncrisis times. Roosevelt was very effective in using the "bully pulpit" to establish the national park system, build a more powerful navy, and move vigorously against the powerful "trusts" that dominated the American economy in the early years of the twentieth century.

they are not the only ones trying to control the actions of bureaucrats; they must always share executive functions with Congress and sometimes with the courts. Finally, bureaucratic agencies are heavily insulated against presidential efforts to control them because of agency alliances with powerful interest groups.

Tools of Presidential Leadership   Presidents are not entirely helpless, of course. They have a number of ways to encourage bureaucratic compliance.[19] Occasionally, because of a crisis or a widely shared national commitment, decisive bureaucratic action is possible, as during Roosevelt's New Deal era, Lyndon Johnson's first years as president, Ronald Reagan's first administration, and George W. Bush's war on terrorism.

Even during ordinary times, however, the president is not helpless. First, although it is difficult to measure precisely, the president's prestige as our only nationally elected political leader makes his wishes hard to ignore. When Teddy Roosevelt called the presidency a "bully pulpit," he meant that only the president can speak for the nation, set the tone for the government, and call the American people to some great national purpose. A popular president, willing and able to play this role, is hard to resist. Bureaucrats are citizens and respond like other Americans to presidential leadership. When a president chooses to become directly involved in some bureaucratic matter—for example, with a phone call to a reluctant agency head or a comment about some bureaucratic shortcoming during a press conference—most bureaucrats respond.

The power of appointment is also an important tool of presidential leadership. If a president is very careful to fill the top administrative posts with people who support him and his programs, he greatly increases his ability to have his way. Although the Senate must advise on and consent to many of his choices, it rarely interferes, recognizing, perhaps, that a coherent administration requires that a president have his own people in place.

The president's power as chief budget officer of the federal government is also a formidable tool of the administration. No agency of the federal bureaucracy, for instance, can make its own budget request directly to Congress; its budget must be submitted to Congress as part of the president's overall budget for the U.S. government. The president's main budgetary instrument, the Office of Management and Budget, also has the statutory authority to block proposed legislation coming from any executive branch agency if it deems it contrary to the president's budget or program.

Congress

Congress also exercises considerable influence over the federal bureaucracy by legislating agency organization and mission, confirming presidential appointments, controlling the agency budget, and holding oversight hearings.

Legislating Agency Organization and Mission

The president and Congress share control over the executive branch. The congressional tools of control, in fact, are at least as formidable as those of the president.[20] Congress legislates the mission of bureaucratic agencies and the details of their organization and can change either one. The creation of the Department of Homeland Security in 2002, for example, required congressional action. Congress can also alter agency policy or behavior. For example, it recently passed a bill requiring the Census Bureau to do the 2000 census by direct count, disallowing the use of statistical sampling.

Confirming Presidential Appointments

Although the Senate almost always approves presidential appointments to top positions in the executive branch, it will sometimes use the "advice and consent" process to shape policies in bureaucratic departments and agencies. It occasionally turns down presidential nominations, as it did in the case of George H. W. Bush's nominee for the post of defense secretary, John Tower. At other times, it can simply draw out and delay the process in a bid to gain concessions from the president and the nominee on future policies. Former Senate Foreign Relations Committee Chairman Jesse Helms was a master at this, gaining concessions on policies concerning Cuba, foreign aid, and funding for international population control agencies. Defeat of nominees and long delays are most likely to happen during periods of divided government, when the atmosphere in the Senate is highly partisan.[21]

Controlling the Agency Budget

Congress can also use its control over agency budgets to influence agency behavior. In theory, Congress uses the budget process to assess the performance of each agency each year, closely scrutinizing its activities before determining its next **appropriation,** the legal authority for the agency to spend money. Congress has neither the time nor the resources actually to do such a thing and usually gives each agency some small increment over what it had in the previous year.[22] Of course, if a particular agency displeases Congress, its budget may be cut; if a new set of responsibilities is given to an agency, its budget is usually increased. Sometimes these agency budget actions are taken with the full concurrence of the president; often they are not. Congress sometimes lends a sympathetic ear and increases the budgets of agencies that are not favored by the president. In the 1980s, Congress consistently gave more money than President Reagan wanted given to the EPA, the National Institutes of Health, and the National Science Foundation.

appropriation
Legal authority for a federal agency to spend money from the U.S. Treasury.

Then–Attorney General John Ashcroft ponders an answer to a question posed by a member of the Senate Judiciary Committee in 2003 on the effect of Justice Department policies on civil liberties in the United States. This kind of oversight is one of the most important congressional tools for influencing the behavior of executive branch agencies and officials.

Holding Oversight Hearings   Oversight hearings are an important instrument for conveying the views of the members of Congress to bureaucrats. There is a great deal of evidence that agency heads listen when the message is delivered clearly.[23] The head of the Internal Revenue Service, for example, recently responded to Senate Finance Committee hearings on the agency's harassment of taxpayers by apologizing to taxpayers and promising changes in IRS behavior and policies. The SEC took a tougher line on accounting practices in public corporations after its leaders underwent hours of congressional grilling in the aftermath of the collapse of Enron and WorldCom in 2002.

Congress does not always speak with a single voice, however. Congress is a highly fragmented and decentralized institution, and its power is dispersed among scores of subcommittees. Often the activities of a particular bureaucratic agency are the province of more than a single committee or subcommittee, and the probability of receiving mixed signals from them is very high. A skilled administrator can often play these competing forces off of each other and gain a degree of autonomy for his or her agency.

Using Inspectors General   Starting in 1978, Congress has established the office of inspector general in nearly every executive branch department and agency. These inspectors general report directly to Congress and are charged with keeping an eye out for waste, fraud, and bureaucratic abuses of power. The inspectors general in the Department of Education, for example, recently reported widespread fraud in several department grant and loan programs. Inspectors general issue periodic formal reports to the relevant congressional committees and many meet with congressional staffers on a regular basis, giving Congress a good handle on what is going on in the bureaucracy.

Reforming the Federal Bureaucracy

How can we improve the federal bureaucracy? The answer depends on what a person thinks is wrong with it and what needs improving. Let's look at some possibilities.

Scaling Back Its Size

If the problem with the federal bureaucracy is perceived to be its size, there are two ways to trim government activities: slimming them down and transferring control of their activities away from the government.

Cutting the Fat

For observers who worry that the federal bureaucracy is simply too big and costly, the preferred strategy is what might be called the "meat ax" approach. Virtually every candidate seeking office promises to "cut the fat" if elected. Bill Clinton made such a promise during the 1992 presidential campaign, and he carried through after his election. In the early weeks of his administration, he ordered that 100,000 federal jobs be eliminated within four years, that freezes be placed on the salaries of government workers, that cost-of-living pay adjustments be reduced, and that the use of government vehicles and planes be sharply restricted.

Privatizing

A much discussed strategy for scaling back the federal bureaucracy is to turn over some of its functions and responsibilities to the private sector.[24] The **privatization** approach is based on two beliefs:

- Private business can almost always do things better than government.
- Competitive pressure from the private sector will force government agencies to be more efficient.

Privatization has actually been happening for many years. For example, the Defense Department does not produce its own weapons systems but uses an elaborate contracting system to design, build, and purchase fighter planes, submarines, and missiles from private corporations. In Iraq, moreover, the Defense Department depended on private contractors such as Halliburton and its subsidiary Kellogg Brown and Root to feed and house soldiers, fight oil field fires and rebuild oil pipelines, build telephone networks, maintain the military's high-tech weapons, make gasoline deliveries to Iraqi consumers, train local police, and more. Advocates of privatizing simply want to expand the process, turning over to private companies functions such as the postal system, the federal prisons, and air traffic control.

Critics worry that privatizing government carries significant costs.[25]

- Some matters seem so central to the national security and well-being that citizens and officials are unwilling to risk that the private sector will necessarily do the job well or at all. A good recent example is the transfer of the responsibility for screening airline passengers and baggage from private companies to a new government agency, the Transportation Security Administration.
- Private business firms might not be willing to provide services if they do not generate a profit. Delivering mail to remote locations is something that the Postal Service does, for instance, but that a private company might decide not to do.

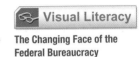

Visual Literacy

The Changing Face of the Federal Bureaucracy

privatization

The process of turning over certain government functions to the private sector.

One strong argument against the privatization of government agencies is that private corporations might discontinue or increase the price of services that are costly or marginally profitable. For example, the U.S. Postal Service provides mail delivery to remote and less populous areas, such as the Alaskan outback, for the same cost as it does for the rest of the country. A private, profit-motivated company might be less inclined to do so.

- A private business under government contract is several steps removed from political control, and the normal instruments of democratic accountability, however imperfect, might not be as effective in controlling private business as they are in controlling government agencies. The voice of the public, expressed in public opinion polls or elections, might not be heard with much clarity by private companies, particularly if they are the only supplier of some essential service. Cable TV customers may have an inkling of the meaning of "nonaccountability."

Reinventing Government

red tape
Overbearing bureaucratic rules and procedures.

If the problem with the federal bureaucracy is perceived to be the inefficiencies of its operations and excessive **red tape,** then the key to reform might be to reinvent governmental bureaucracy along businesslike lines. President Clinton turned over the responsibility for "reinventing government" to Vice President Al Gore at the beginning of his administration. The term "reinventing government" comes from a popular and influential book by that name written by David Osborne and Ted Gaebler,[26] although the ideas for these reforms come from advocates of what is called "the new public management."[27] "Reinventing" advocates propose transforming the federal bureaucracy not only by cutting the fat and privatizing (as discussed in the preceding section), but also by introducing business principles into the executive branch. They believe that government agencies will provide better public services if they are run like private businesses: using pay-for-performance to determine salaries, for example, or focusing more on customer needs. When Gore took on this project, he issued a report that closely followed the proposals made by Osborne and Gaebler and other reinventing government advocates.[28] Although Congress was unwilling to cooperate with Gore's proposals, many changes were made in the agencies by presidential executive order. The most notable change was the dramatic streamlining of the drug approval process at the FDA.[29]

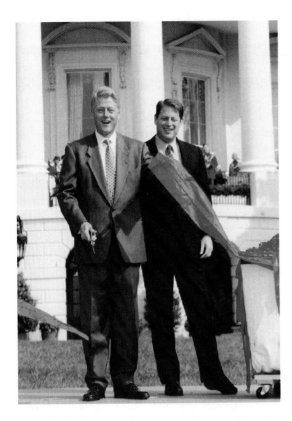

President Clinton and Vice President Al Gore cut "red tape" as a dramatic way to introduce Gore's plan to reinvent government by introducing business principles into the operations of the executive branch. Congress approved only a few of the plan's provisions.

Protecting Against Bureaucratic Abuses of Power

Many people believe that the problem with a bureaucracy of the size, shape, and power of our present one is that it is potentially unresponsive to the public and a dangerous threat to individual liberty. The preferred solution has been closer control over the bureaucracy by elected political bodies and by clear legislative constraints. Accordingly, many legislative enactments have tried to keep bureaucratic activity within narrow boundaries. The Freedom of Information Act of 1966 was designed to enhance the ability of the press and private citizens to obtain information about bureaucratic policies and activities. The Ethics in Government Act of 1978 strengthened requirements of financial disclosure by officials and prohibitions against conflicts of interest.

Some reformers would like to see greater protection provided for **whistle-blowers**—bureaucrats who report corruption, financial mismanagement, abuses of power, or other official malfeasance. All too often, these courageous people, acting in the public interest, are fired or harassed on the job. This happened to Ernest Fitzgerald, a civilian cost accountant at the Pentagon, who lost his job after he revealed $2 billion cost overruns on the C5A military transport plane (he eventually won reinstatement through the courts, but it took 14 years to do so).

whistle-blowers
People who bring official misconduct in their agencies to public attention.

Increasing Presidential Control

One suggestion for reform of the federal bureaucracy is to have it more closely controlled by elected representatives of the people. This suggestion follows directly from the principle of popular sovereignty, which requires that the elected representatives of the people closely control the bureaucracy. Popular

How Democratic Are We?

The Bureaucracy and Democracy

PROPOSITION: The federal bureaucracy is inherently undemocratic because it is filled with unelected people who make important government decisions that affect the lives of Americans.

AGREE: The bureaucracy is out of control. Although the number of federal civil servants is not much different from what it was 10 or 15 years ago, the federal government and its unelected bureaucrats seem to be intruding further and further into our lives. Career civil servants at the Environmental Protection Agency issue rules on how farmers can use wetlands and on which animal species are endangered and protected from hunters. Employees of the Bureau of Land Management make rules for grazing on public lands that ranchers must follow. And the people who work for the new Department of Homeland Security, in the name of protecting us against terrorism, are gathering information about our private lives and living habits and are making travel inconvenient and unpleasant.

DISAGREE: Civil servants are merely carrying out the missions defined for them by elected public officials, namely, Congress and the president. And, since they are especially sensitive to the wishes of the public because of their desire to be effective and to be reelected, the president and members of Congress pay close attention to what civil servants in the bureaucratic agencies are doing and intervene to force changes in bureaucratic behavior when civil servants go astray and act contrary to the public interest and the wishes of the public. A further safeguard against civil servants running amok is the fact that we have a pretty representative federal bureaucracy; civil servants are pretty much like other Americans and have similar concerns, interests, and values.

CONSIDER: It is certainly the case that members of the federal bureaucracy make important decisions and that they exercise considerable discretion when carrying out the missions defined by Congress and the president.

• To what extent do you believe this to be problematic for democracy in the United States today?   • Are you confident that the president and Congress practice enough oversight to ensure that bureaucrats conform to the general wishes of the public when they issue rules or make other important decisions?   • Are you reassured that civil servants who work for the federal government are enough like the rest of us that we can trust them to make rulings and decisions that fit our interests and values?   • If not, what do you think we can do to keep bureaucrats responsive and responsible to the American people?

sovereignty implies that administrative discretion should be narrowed as much as possible and that elected officials should communicate clear directions and unambiguous policies to bureaucratic agencies. (Note that this goal is very different from the one envisioned by the advocates of privatization and reinventing government.) Some advocates of popular sovereignty have argued that the president is the only public official who has an interest in seeing that the bureaucracy *as a whole* is well run and coherently organized. Accordingly, one suggestion for reform is to increase the powers of the president so that he can be the chief executive, in fact and not just in name.[30]

Summary

The executive branch has grown in size and responsibility. This growth is a consequence of a transformation in the conception of the proper role of government because of structural changes in the economy and society. Although *bureaucracy* is not a popular concept in the American political tradition, we have created a sizable one. The reason is partly that bureaucratic organizations have certain strengths that make them attractive for accomplishing large-scale tasks.

Bureaucrats are involved in three major kinds of activities: executing the law, regulating, and adjudicating disputes. In each of these, they exercise a great deal of discretion. Because they are unelected policymakers, democratic theory demands that we be concerned about who the bureaucrats are. In the merit services, they are very much like other Americans in terms of background and attitudes. Political appointees, however, the most important bureaucratic decision makers, are very different from their fellow citizens.

Several political and governmental actors and institutions affect bureaucratic behavior, including the president, Congress, and the courts as well as public opinion and interest groups. Bureaucratic pathologies, while real, are either exaggerated or the result of forces outside the bureaucracy itself: the constitutional rules and the struggle between the president and Congress. Proposals to reform the executive branch are related to what reformers believe is wrong with the federal bureaucracy. Those who worry most about size and inefficiency propose budget and personnel cuts, privatization, and the introduction of business principles into government. Those who want to make democracy more of a reality propose giving more control over the bureaucracy to the president and diminishing the role of interest groups.

Suggestions for Further Reading

Goodsell, Charles T. *The Case for Bureaucracy,* 4th ed. Washington, D.C.: CQ Press, 2003.
   A well-written polemic that suggests that most criticisms of bureaucracy are not well-founded.

Kerwin, Cornelius M. *Rulemaking: How Government Agencies Write Law and Make Policy.* Washington, DC: CQ Press, 2003.
   A comprehensive treatment of rule making by executive branch agencies.

The 9/11 Commision Report: Final Report of the National Commission on Terrorist Attacks Upon the United States. New York: W. W. Norton, 2004.
   An exhaustive study of how 9/11 happened and a set of recommendations—including reorganization of the executive branch—for better homeland defense and security.

Peters, B. Guy. *American Public Policy: Promise and Performance,* 6th ed. New York: CQ Press, 2004.
   A review of American public policies with a particularly informative discussion of the role of the federal bureaucracy in policy implementation.

Sobel, Robert, and David B. Sicilia. eds. *The U.S. Executive Branch: A Biographical Directory of Heads of State and Cabinet Officers.* Westport: CT: Greenwood Press, 2003.
   Biographical sketches of heads of cabinet departments from the beginning of the republic to today.

Stone, Bob, and Tom Peters. *Confessions of a Civil Servant: Lessons in Changing American Government and the Military.* Lanham, MD: Rowman & Littlefield Publishers, 2003.
   An inside look at the accomplishments and failures of the reinventing government movement.

Washington Monthly.
   Washington's leading journal of "bureaucracy bashing"; filled with outrageous and (sometimes) illuminating stories.

Internet Sources

The Federal Register
www.archives.gov/federal_register
All rules issued by federal agencies can be found here.

Fedworld
http://www.fedworld.gov/
The gateway to the federal government's numerous Websites and Gophers; connections to virtually every federal department, bureau, commission, and foundation, as well as access to government statistics and reports.

Office of Personnel Management
www.opm.gov/
The best site to find statistics and other information about federal government employees.

Yahoo: Executive Branch
http://dir.yahoo.com/Government/U_S_Government/ Executive_Branch/
Similar to Fedworld; which one to use depends on personal taste.

Chapter 14
The Courts

In This Chapter

- How the court system is organized and how it operates
- What judicial review is and how it came to be
- How the Supreme Court works
- How and why judicial interpretations of the Constitution have changed
- The role of the Supreme Court in a democratic society

The Supreme Court Stops the Florida Recount

Relatively early in the evening of election night, November 7, 2000, the major television networks proclaimed that Al Gore had won the state of Florida, giving him a major advantage in the race for the presidency against George W. Bush. Later in the evening, the networks pulled Florida from the Gore win column, calling the contest in Florida "too close to call." At 3:00 A.M. on Wednesday, the networks announced a Bush win in Florida and declared him the winner of the presidential election. By 7:00 A.M., however, they again called the race in Florida "too close to call" and said they could not yet declare a winner of the presidential contest. Meanwhile, first reports of voting irregularities and inaccurate vote counting had begun to surface. Responding to these reports, Democrats demanded—and county election officials agreed to—hand recounts in Miami-Dade, Broward, and Palm Beach counties, where the voting returns seemed most suspect. Immediately, a statewide machine recount began as required by the state election code in extremely close elections. On November 13, Florida Secretary of State Katherine Harris announced that her November 14 deadline for certifying election results from each county would not be extended, leaving insufficient time for completion of hand counts. At the end of the day on the 14th, depending entirely on machine recount results from the various counties, Harris declared George W. Bush the winner of Florida's 25 electoral votes. But this hardly settled the affair.

From November 14 until the U.S. Supreme Court ruled on December 12, Americans lived through a period of intense and bitter political and legal combat the likes of which had not been seen here since the disputed Hayes-Tilden presidential election of 1876. Election officials in several counties continued with their hand recounts despite Harris's decision. Lawsuits were filed by candidates and party organizations in various county, state, and federal district courts to have recounts started or stopped. Republican Party activists descended on Florida to mount demonstrations against hand recounts, and local Gore and Bush partisans shouted at each other across police barricades. Republican and Democratic national committees and congressional committees mounted public relations campaigns to support their respective sides in the dispute, while various liberal and conservative citizen groups joined the fray on the ground and on the airwaves. The Florida legislature went into special session to consider

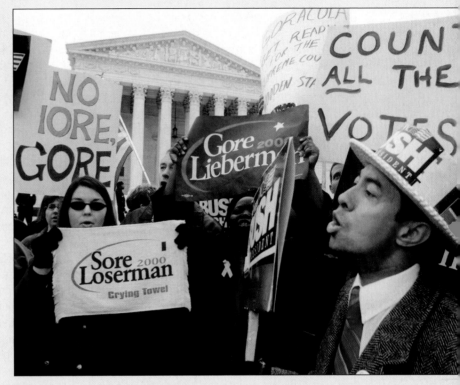

whether it ought to award the state's electoral votes to Bush, whatever the outcome of the hand recounts.

The drama came to a head on December 8, when the Florida Supreme Court, responding to a request from the Gore campaign, ruled that hand recounts could continue in three counties, setting December 12 as the deadline for reporting results to the Florida Secretary of State. On December 9, responding to an appeal by the Bush campaign, the U.S. Supreme Court ordered that the hand recount be temporarily suspended. On December 12, after considering legal briefs and oral arguments from each side, a closely divided U.S. Supreme Court overturned the Florida Supreme Court in *Bush v. Gore,* saying the Florida Court's order to recount in only three counties violated "equal protection" of the laws. Furthermore, according to a majority of the justices, December 12 was the absolute deadline for settling the election contest in Florida. Thus, with no time left to mount a recount in a way that would address the Court's "equal protection" concerns, Secretary of State Harris's previous certification of Bush as the winner in Florida prevailed. On December 13, seeing the handwriting on the wall, Al Gore conceded the presidential election to George W. Bush.

The U.S. Supreme Court's decision in *Bush* v. *Gore* was remarkable for many reasons, not least of which was the degree to which its actions contradicted what scholars, jurists, historians, and journalists have taken to be iron-clad rules and traditions of the Court:

- *The Court has generally avoided becoming involved in "political" and "partisan" issues. Bush* v. *Gore is the first and only decision that decided the outcome of a presidential election.*

- *The Court has generally avoided cases that might hurt its reputation or that of the courts in general.* As Justice John Paul Stevens put it in his dissent, "The endorsement of [plaintiff's position] by the majority of this Court can only lend credence to the most cynical appraisal of the work of judges throughout the land . . . . Although we may never know with complete certainty the identity of the winner of this year's presidential election, the identity of the loser is perfectly clear. It is the nation's confidence in the judge as an impartial guardian of the law."

- *The Court generally tries to avoid 5–4 votes on controversial issues.* While this was less true for the Rehnquist Court than earlier ones, the 5–4 vote in *Bush* v. *Gore* undermined the legitimacy of its decision in the eyes of many Americans, especially since the majority was comprised of the same conservative majority that has recently dominated the Court on other controversial decisions.

- *The Court almost always intends that its decisions will serve as precedents for all other courts to follow.* The Court clearly did not want *Bush* v. *Gore* to serve as a legal precedent with broader meaning. Not wishing to bring the possible harsh light of "equal protection" to other aspects of American elections, the Court made the following incredible point in its opinion: "Our consideration is limited to the present circumstances, for the problem of equal protection in election processes generally presents many complexities."

- *The Court usually tries to be consistent with its previous rulings in a particular domain of the law.* On federalism, the Court has moved decisively to limit federal government power in deference to state autonomy. In *Bush* v. *Gore* it reversed direction (but probably for this case only), something that caught Justice Stevens by surprise. As he put it in his dissent: "When questions arise about the meaning of state laws, including election laws, it is our settled practice to accept the opinions of the highest courts of the States as providing the final answers. On rare occasions, however, either federal statutes or the Federal Constitution may require federal judicial intervention in state elections. This is not such an occasion."

Although the *Bush* v. *Gore* story is probably best understood as the "exception that proves the rule" in terms of how the Court normally behaves, it still gives us insight into many things about the Supreme Court that will be elaborated on in this chapter. Like the president and Congress, the Court makes decisions that have important consequences for the American people. Unlike the president and Congress, it does not pass new laws; it merely interprets the meaning of laws and, especially, the Constitution. In doing so, however, the Court cannot help but make law. In this sense, the Court is a national policymaker. This chapter will explore these issues in depth.

Thinking Critically About This Chapter

Using the Framework   You will see in this chapter that the Court is embedded in a rich governmental, political linkage, and structural environment that shapes its behavior. The other branches of government impinge on its deliberations; political linkage institutions such as elections, interest groups, and social movements matter; and structural factors such as economic and social change influence its agenda and decisions.

Using the Democracy Standard   You will see in this chapter that an unelected Court makes important decisions about public policies, raising fundamental questions about the degree to which popular sovereignty and majority rule prevail in our system. You will also see that the Court often turns its attention to cases that involve issues of political equality and liberty, so essential to the existence of a healthy representative democracy.

The Structural Context of Court Behavior

The judicial Power of the United States shall be vested in one supreme Court, and in such inferior Courts as the Congress may from time to time ordain and establish.
—U.S. Constitution, Article III, Section 1

We are under a Constitution, but the Constitution is what the judges say it is, and the judiciary is the safeguard of our liberty and our property under the Constitution.
—Chief Justice Charles Evans Hughes (1907)

Constitutional Powers

The Constitution speaks only briefly about the judicial branch and doesn't provide much guidance about what it is supposed to do or how it is supposed to go about its job. The document says little about the powers of the judicial branch in relationship to the other two federal branches or about its responsibilities in the area of constitutional interpretation. Article III is considerably shorter than Articles I and II, which focus on Congress and the president. It creates a federal judicial branch, it creates the office of "chief justice of the United States," it states that judges shall serve life terms, it specifies the categories of cases the Court may or must hear (to be explained later), and it grants Congress the power to create additional federal courts as needed. Article III of the Constitution is virtually devoid of detail.

Comparative

Comparing Judiciaries

The Power of Judicial Review

Extremely interesting is the Constitution's silence about **judicial review,** the power of the Supreme Court to declare state and federal laws and actions null and void when they conflict with the Constitution. Debate has raged for many years over the question of whether the framers intended that the Court should have this power.[1]

judicial review
The power of the Supreme Court to declare actions of the other branches and levels of government unconstitutional.

The framers surely believed that the Constitution ought to prevail when other laws were in conflict with it. But did they expect the Supreme Court to make the decisions in this matter? Jefferson and Madison thought that Congress and the president were capable of rendering their own judgments about the constitutionality of their actions. Alexander Hamilton, however, believed that the power of judicial review was inherent in the notion of the separation of powers and was essential to balanced government. As he put it in *The Federalist,* No. 78 (see Appendix), the very purpose of constitutions is to place limitations on the powers of government, and it is only the Court that can ensure such limits in the United States. The legislative branch, in particular, is unlikely to restrain itself without the helping hand of the judiciary.

Hamilton's view was undoubtedly the prevailing one among the framers. They were firm believers, for instance, in the idea that there was a "higher law" to which governments and nations must conform. Their enthusiasm for written constitutions was based on their belief that governments must be limited in what they could do in the service of some higher or more fundamental law, such as that pertaining to individual rights. The attitudes of the time, then, strongly supported the idea that judges, conversant with the legal tradition and free from popular pressures, were best able to decide when statutory and administrative law were in conflict with fundamental law.[2]

Although the Constitution is silent on the issue of judicial review, most of the Founders probably agreed with Alexander Hamilton (left), who argued that the Supreme Court's power to interpret the Constitution and declare state and federal laws and actions unconstitutional is inherent in the notion of the separation of powers. However, it was not until the Supreme Court's 1803 *Marbury* v. *Madison* decision that Chief Justice John Marshall (right) affirmed the Court's power of judicial review.

Marbury* v. *Madison Chief Justice John Marshall boldly claimed the power of judicial review for the U.S. Supreme Court in the case of *Marbury* v. *Madison* in 1803.[3] The case began with a flurry of judicial appointments by President John Adams in the final days of his presidency, after his Federalist party had suffered a resounding defeat in the election of 1800. The apparent aim of these so-called midnight appointments was to establish the federal courts as an outpost of Federalist party power (federal judges are appointed for life) in the midst of Jeffersonian control of the presidency and the Congress.

William Marbury was one of the midnight appointments, but he was less lucky than most. His commission was signed and sealed, but it had not been delivered to him before the new administration took office. Jefferson, knowing what Adams and the Federalists were up to, ordered Secretary of State James Madison not to deliver the commission. Marbury sued Madison, claiming that the secretary of state was obligated to deliver the commission, and he asked the Supreme Court to issue a **writ of mandamus** to force Madison to do so.

Marshall faced a quandary. If the Court decided in favor of Marbury, Madison would almost surely refuse to obey, opening the Court to ridicule for its weakness. The fact that Marshall was a prominent Federalist political figure might even provoke the Jeffersonians to take more extreme measures against the Court. But if the Court ruled in favor of Madison, it would suggest that an executive official could defy without penalty the clear provisions of the law.

Marshall's solution was worthy of Solomon. The Court ruled that William Marbury was entitled to his commission and that James Madison had broken the law in failing to deliver it. By this ruling, the Court rebuked Madison. However, the Court said it could not compel Madison to comply with the law because the section of the Judiciary Act of 1789 that granted the Court the power to issue writs of mandamus was unconstitutional. It was unconstitutional, he said, because it expanded the **original jurisdiction** of the Supreme

writ of mandamus
A court order that forces an official to act.

original jurisdiction
The authority of a court to be the first to hear a particular kind of case.

Court as defined in Article III, which could not be done except by constitutional amendment.

On the surface, the decision was an act of great modesty. It suggested that the Court could not force the action of an executive branch official. It suggested that Congress had erred in the Judiciary Act of 1789 by trying to give the Supreme Court too much power. Beneath the surface, however, was a less modest act: the claim that judicial review was the province of the judicial branch alone. In Marshall's words in his written opinion, "It is emphatically the province and duty of the judicial department to say what the law is." In making this claim, he was following closely Hamilton's argument in *The Federalist,* No. 78.

Until quite recently, the Supreme Court used the power of judicial review with great restraint, perhaps recognizing that its regular use would invite retaliation by the other branches. Judicial review of a congressional act was not exercised again until 54 years after *Marbury* and was used to declare acts of Congress unconstitutional only about 150 times since then until the late 1990s. (In the past few years, however, it has been less reluctant to review and overturn congressional actions, especially in cases involving the nature of federalism.) The Court has been much less constrained about overruling the laws of the states and localities; it has done so more than 1,000 times.

Judicial Review and Democracy   Judicial review involves the right of a body shielded from direct accountability to the people—federal judges are appointed, not elected, and serve for life (barring impeachment for unseemly, unethical, or illegal behavior)—to set aside the actions of government bodies whose members are directly elected. Some observers believe that this is the only way to protect the rights of political and racial minorities, to check the potential excesses of the other two government branches and the states, and to preserve the rules of the democratic process. Others believe that judicial review has no place in a democratic society. We come back to this issue later in this chapter.

The U.S. Court System: Organization and Jurisdiction

Our country has one judicial system for the national government (the federal courts) and another in each of the states. In each state, courts adjudicate cases on the basis of the state's own constitution, statutes, and administrative rules.[4] In total, the great bulk of laws, legal disputes, and court decisions (roughly 99 percent) are located in the states. Most important political and constitutional issues, however, eventually reach the federal courts. In this chapter, our focus is on these federal courts. In the following sections, we'll look at the source of the federal court's power and the organization of its system.

Constitutional Provisions

The only court specifically mentioned in the Constitution's Article III is the U.S. Supreme Court. The framers left to Congress the tasks of designing the details of the Supreme Court and establishing "such inferior courts as the Congress may from time to time ordain and establish." Beginning with the Judiciary Act

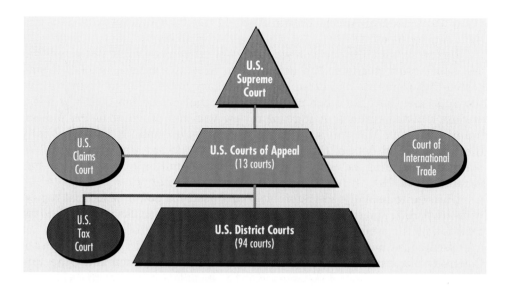

FIGURE 14.1 ● **The U.S. Federal Court System**

The federal court system is a three-tiered pyramidal system, with the Supreme Court at the top. Below it are 13 federal courts of appeal and 94 district courts, with at least one district in each state. Additional courts exist to hear cases in highly specialized areas, such as taxes, international trade, and financial claims against the U.S. government.

Source: Administrative Office of the U.S. Courts.

constitutional courts

Federal courts created by Congress under the authority of Article III of the Constitution.

legislative courts

Highly specialized federal courts created by Congress under the authority of Article I of the Constitution.

You Are a Young Lawyer

of 1789, Congress has periodically reorganized the federal court system. The end result is a three-tiered pyramidal system (see Figure 14.1), with a handful of off-shoots. At the bottom are 94 U.S. federal district courts, with at least one district in each state. In the middle are 13 courts of appeal. At the top of the pyramid is the Supreme Court. These courts are called **constitutional courts** because they were created by Congress under Article III, which discusses the judicial branch. Congress has also created a number of courts to adjudicate cases in highly specialized areas of concern, such as taxes and maritime law. These were established under Article I, which specifies the duties and powers of Congress, and are called **legislative courts.**

Article III does not offer many guidelines for the federal court system, but the few requirements that are stated are very important. The Constitution requires, for instance, that federal judges serve "during good behavior," which, in practice, means for life. Because impeachment by Congress is the only way to remove federal judges, the decision about who will be a judge is an important one. Article III also states that Congress cannot reduce the salaries of judges once they are in office. This provision was designed to maintain the independence of the judiciary by protecting it from legislative intimidation.

Article III also specifies the subject matter of cases that are solely the province of the federal courts:

- The Constitution (e.g., disputes involving the First Amendment or the commerce clause).
- Federal statutes and treaties (including disputes involving ambassadors and other diplomats).
- Admiralty and maritime issues (disputes involving shipping and commerce on the high seas).
- Controversies in which the U.S. government is a party.

- Disputes between the states.
- Disputes between a state and a citizen of another state.
- Disputes between a state (or citizen of a state) and foreign states or citizens.

Federal District Courts

Most cases in the federal court system are first heard in one of the 94 district courts. District courts are courts of original jurisdiction, that is, courts where cases are first heard; they do not hear appeals from other courts. They are also trial courts; some use juries—either **grand juries,** which bring indictments, or **petit (trial) juries,** which decide cases—and in some, cases are heard only by a judge.

Most of the business of the federal courts takes place at this level. About 300,000 cases are filed annually; roughly 80 percent of them are civil cases, and 20 percent are criminal cases. Civil cases include everything from antitrust cases brought by the federal government (as in the recent Justice Department action against Microsoft) to commercial and contract disputes between citizens (or businesses) of two or more states. Criminal cases include violations of federal criminal laws, such as bank robbery, interstate drug trafficking, and kidnapping.

Most civil and criminal cases are concluded at this level. In a relatively small number of disputes, however, one of the parties to the case may feel that a mistake has been made in trial procedure or in the law that was brought to bear in the trial, or one of the parties may feel that a legal or constitutional issue is at stake that was not taken into account at the trial stage or was wrongly interpreted. In such cases, one of the parties may appeal to a higher court—a Court of Appeals.

U.S. Courts of Appeal

The United States is divided into 12 geographic **circuits** (see the map in Figure 14.2) that hear appeals from the district courts. There is also a 13th appeals court, called the U.S. Court of Appeals for the Federal Circuit, located in Washington, D.C., that hears cases on patents and government contracts. More than 60,000 cases are filed annually in the federal appeals courts, although only about 5,000 reach the formal hearing stage (most of these end in negotiated settlements without going to trial). Cases cannot originate in these courts but must come to them from district courts. Because they exist only to hear appeals, they are referred to as **appellate courts.** New factual evidence cannot be introduced before such courts; no witnesses are called or cross-examined. At the appellate level, lawyers do not examine witnesses or introduce new evidence; instead, they submit **briefs,** which set out the legal issues at stake. Judges usually convene as panels of three (on important cases, there are more—sometimes seven members) to hear oral arguments from the lawyers on each side of the case and to cross-examine them on points of law. Weeks or even months later, after considerable study, writing, and discussion among the judges, the panel issues a ruling. In important cases, the ruling is usually accompanied by an **opinion** that sets forth the majority side's reasoning for the decision.

Once appellate decisions are published, they become **precedents** that guide the decisions of other judges in the same circuit. Although judges do not slavishly follow precedents, they tend to move away from them only when

grand juries
Groups of citizens who decide whether there is sufficient evidence to bring an indictment against accused persons.

petit (trial) juries
Juries that hear evidence and sit in judgment on charges brought in civil or criminal cases.

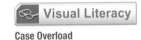
Visual Literacy
Case Overload

circuits
The 12 geographical jurisdictions and one special court that hear appeals from the federal district courts.

appellate courts
Courts that hear cases on appeal from other courts.

briefs
Documents setting out the arguments in legal cases, prepared by attorneys and presented to courts.

opinion
The explanation of the majority's reasoning that accompanies a court decision.

precedents
Rulings by courts that guide judicial reasoning in subsequent cases.

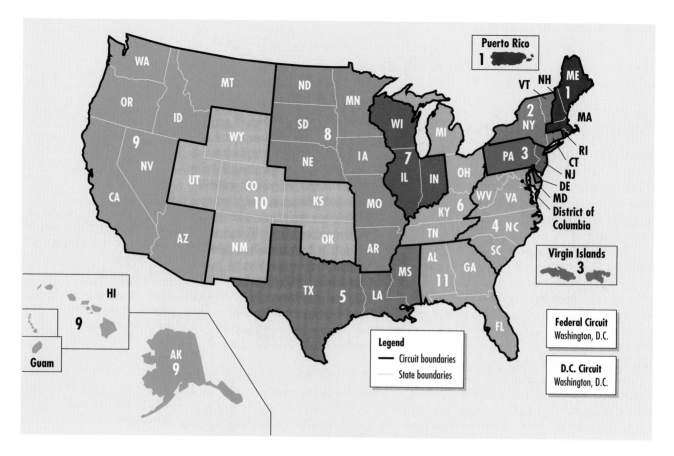

FIGURE 14.2 • U.S. Federal Circuit Courts

The United States is divided into 12 geographic regions (including the D.C. Circuit Court), each housing a federal circuit court of appeals. One additional circuit court of appeal, the Federal Circuit Court, is located in Washington, D.C.

Source: Administrative Office of the U.S. Courts.

stare decisis

The legal doctrine that says precedent should guide judicial decision making.

necessary and only in very small steps. This doctrine of closely following precedents as the basis for legal reasoning is known as **stare decisis.**

Sometimes, particular circuits play a particularly important role in changing constitutional interpretation. Currently, the Fourth Circuit Court, based in Richmond, Virginia, has been a leader in the trend toward reasserting the power of the states in the federal system.[5]

The Supreme Court

Congress decides how many judges sit on the Supreme Court. The first Court had six members. The Federalists, however, reduced the number to five in 1801 to prevent newly elected president Thomas Jefferson from filling a vacancy. In 1869, Congress set the number at its present nine members (eight associate justices and the chief justice). It has remained this way ever since, weathering the failed effort by President Franklin Roosevelt to "pack" the Court with more politically congenial justices by expanding its size to 15.

The Supreme Court is both a court of original jurisdiction and an appellate court. That is, some cases must first be heard in the Supreme Court. Disputes involving ambassadors and other diplomatic personnel, or one or more states, start in the Supreme Court rather than in some other court.

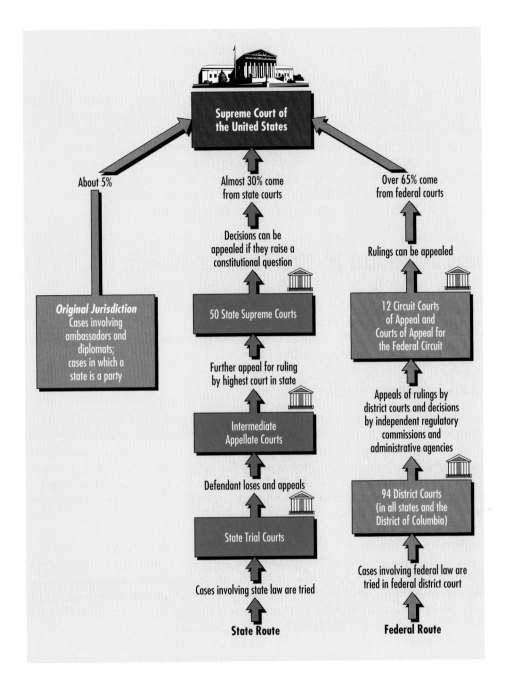

FIGURE 14.3 • How Cases Get to the Supreme Court

The vast majority of cases that reach the Supreme Court come to it from the federal court system. Most of the others come on appeal from the highest state courts. A handful originate in the Supreme Court itself.

Source: Adapted from David O'Brien, *Storm Center: The Supreme Court in American Politics,* 5th ed. (New York: Norton, 2000).

The Supreme Court also, in its most important role, serves as an appellate court for the federal appeals courts and for the highest courts of each of the states. Cases in which a state or a federal law has been declared unconstitutional or in which the highest state court has denied the claim of one of the parties that a state law violates federal law or the Constitution (see Figure 14.3) are eligible to be heard by the Supreme Court.

Congress determines much of the appellate jurisdiction of the Court. In 1869, following the Civil War, a Congress controlled by radical Republicans removed the Court's power to review cases falling under the Reconstruction program for the South. Responding to a plea from Chief Justice Rehnquist to lighten the Court's caseload, Congress dropped the requirement that the Supreme Court *must* hear cases in which a state court declares a federal statute unconstitutional. It can choose, but is not obligated, to do so.

Because it is the highest appellate court in the federal court system, the decisions and opinions of the Supreme Court become the main precedents on federal and constitutional questions for courts at all other levels of jurisdiction. It is for this reason that Supreme Court decisions receive so much attention from other political actors, the media, and the public.

Appointment to the Federal Bench

Because federal judges are appointed for life and make important decisions, it matters in a democratic society who they are and how they get to the bench. If they are isolated from popular influence, democracy is at risk. If they are too responsive, they ignore their judicial role.

Who Are the Appointees?

Appointees to the federal bench must (by custom, not law) be lawyers, but they need not have judicial experience. Almost one-half of all Supreme Court justices during this century have had no prior experience as judges. Among the ranks of the "inexperienced" are some of the most prominent and influential justices in our history, including John Marshall, Louis Brandeis, Harlan Stone, Charles Evans Hughes, Felix Frankfurter, Earl Warren, as well as long-time chief justice, William Rehnquist.[6]

Because federal judges are lawyers, they tend to come from privileged backgrounds. Moreover, federal judges, and particularly Supreme Court justices, come from the most elite parts of the legal profession. For the most part, they have been white male Protestants from upper-income or upper-middle-class backgrounds, who attended the most selective and expensive undergraduate and graduate institutions.[7] During the history of the High Court, through 2004, there have been only two African American justices (Thurgood Marshall and Clarence Thomas), two women (Sandra Day O'Connor and Ruth Bader Ginsburg), seven Jews, and seven Catholics. The representativeness of judicial appointees at the circuit and district court levels is better, but it is still a long way from reflecting the composition of the legal profession, much less the American people as a whole.

The Appointment Process

You Are Appointing a Supreme Court Justice

Federal judges assume office after they have been nominated by the president and approved by the Senate. Presidents pay special attention to judicial appointments, because they are a way for presidents to affect public policy long after they leave office.

Presidents take many things into consideration besides merit. No president wants a nomination rejected by the Senate, for example, so he and his advisers consult with key senators, especially those on the Judiciary Committee, before nominations are forwarded. Nominations for district court judgeships are sub-

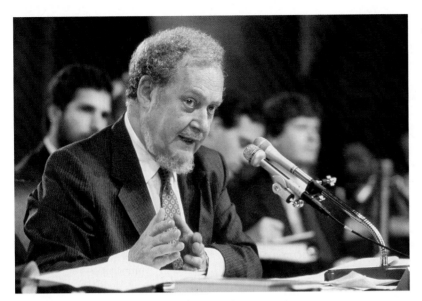

Robert Bork, one of Ronald Reagan's nominees for the Supreme Court, was turned down by a historic margin after lengthy committee hearings and a bruising debate on the floor of the Senate. Many Americans and a majority of senators considered his views too extreme.

ject to what is called **senatorial courtesy,** the right of the senior senator from the president's party in the state where the district court is located to approve the nominee. Senatorial courtesy does not operate, however, in appointments to the circuit courts, whose jurisdictions span more than a single state, or to the Supreme Court, whose jurisdiction is the entire nation. Nevertheless, presidents must be extremely attentive to the views of key senators.

On occasion, despite presidential efforts to placate it, the Senate has refused to give its consent. Of the 143 nominees for the Supreme Court since the founding of the Republic, the Senate has refused to approve 28 of them, although only 5 in the twentieth century. Rejection of nominees has usually happened when the president was weak or when the other party was in control of the Senate. The defeat of Ronald Reagan's nominee, Robert Bork, was the

senatorial courtesy
The tradition that judicial nominations for federal district court appointments be cleared by the senior senator of the president's party from the relevant state.

Web Exploration
Who Is Appointed to the Supreme Court?

Issue: Appointees to the Supreme Court come from a very select group of Americans, not at all representative of the general population either in terms of demographic background or achievement and training.

Site: Access the Cornell Law School home page on our Website at **www.ablongman.com/greenberg**. Go to the "Web Explorations" section for Chapter 14 and open "who is appointed. . . ," then open "biographies." Read the short biographies of each of the present members of the Supreme Court.

What You've Learned: What kinds of people become justices? What can you say about their occupational and educational backgrounds and their other experiences?

HINT: While they are all lawyers, not all have served as judges. And politics and public service have been part of the equation as well.

The Rise of Partisan Conflict

Senate Fails to Overcome Democratic Filibusters on Bush Judicial Nominations

The Story: On November 14, 2003, senators were weary from lack of sleep and hurried meals, and tempers were frayed and short. After almost 40 hours of continuous debate in the Senate, Republicans fell 7 votes short of the 60 votes needed to end Democratic filibusters blocking Senate votes on several Bush federal judicial nominations. Three times, by identical 53–43 votes, cloture motions failed, dooming the nominations of Carolyn Kuhl to the 9th circuit court of appeals, Priscilla Owen for the 5th circuit, and Janice Rogers Brown to the federal appeals court for the District of Columbia circuit.

Although not surprised by the outcome, Republicans were nevertheless furious. Senate Judiciary Chairman Orrin Hatch (R–UT) fumed, saying "this is petty politics . . . cheap politics . . . and can lead to more partisan division in the Senate." Senate Majority Leader Bill Frist (R–TN) called the use of the filibuster to block Senate consideration of judicial nominees "intolerable." President Bush issued a statement after the vote saying that "the Democrats' obstructionist tactics are shameful, unfair, and . . . all too common." Thomas Sowell, the conservative economist and commentator, lamented Charles Schumer's "shameful tactics" as leader of the filibuster effort in the Senate, while several Republican leaders called Schumer anti-Catholic, anti-

feminist, and anti-black, given the demographic characteristics of the rejected judicial nominees. Democrats were not impressed. Senator Ted Kennedy (D–MA) said that his party "would continue to resist any Neanderthal that is nominated by this president" for the federal judiciary. Schumer was equally unapologetic, claiming that the president's nominations showed that he wanted to return constitutional law "not just to the 1930s, but to the 1890s."

The Background: The Constitution grants the Senate the power and responsibility for giving its "advise and consent" to presidential nominees for positions as federal court judges, including nominees for the Supreme Court. Although not stated directly in the Constitution, it has long been assumed—and it has long been Senate practice—that "advise and consent" requires but a simple majority vote, or 51 votes in the current 100 seat Senate. With 53 solid votes—all 51 Republican senators and 2 Democrats—the Republicans would seem to have been in good shape for confirming the nominations of Kuhl, Owen, and Brown. However, as you learned in Chapter 11, the filibuster—which gives the minority a powerful tool for pre-

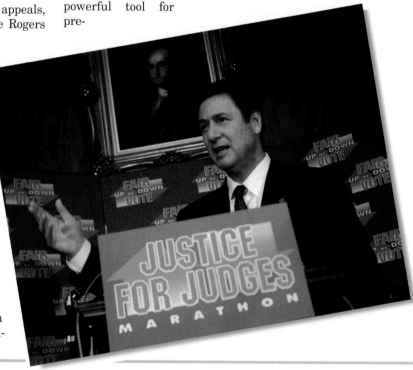

product of deep ideological differences between a Republican president and a Democratic-controlled Senate. There have also been several near defeats. Bush's nominee, Clarence Thomas, was confirmed by a margin of only four votes after questions were raised about his legal qualifications and about sexual harassment charges brought by law professor Anita Hill.

Confirmation of judicial nominees for the federal district and circuit courts recently have been much more contentious. During the Clinton years, Republicans in the Senate bottled up many of the president's nominees in the venting the majority from prevailing on a bill before the Senate—is an old and honored Senate tradition, used by both Democrats and Republicans over the years. The filibuster is so much a part of the upper chamber's traditions that Democrats and Republicans in the Senate over the years have agreed that a motion to invoke cloture to end a filibuster ought to require a supermajority, now standing at 60 votes.

But why would Democratic senators resort to such a blunt instrument, using the filibuster to block action by the majority in the Senate? Republicans, after all, didn't use the filibuster to deny Bill Clinton his judicial nominations, did they? No they didn't, but they blocked many of Clinton's nominations nonetheless. Republicans simply had a more effective tool for accomplishing this objective: quiet death in the Judiciary Committee. Being in the majority in the Senate during the last six years of the Clinton presidency (1995–2000), Republicans controlled all Senate committees, including the powerful Judiciary Committee responsible for reviewing all judicial nominees. Chaired by the very same Orrin Hatch who complained about the Democrat's use of the filibuster in 2003, the Judiciary Committee simply bottled up many Clinton nominees in committee, never allowing the nomination to come to the floor of the Senate for a vote. Hatch refused to hold hearings at all for several nominees, delayed hearings for other nominees for up to 18 months (causing several nominees to withdraw), and engineered negative votes on his committee for still others.

From the Democrat's point of view, Republicans complaints about the filibuster were disingenuous; Republicans reached the same goal during the Clinton years using different tools, blocking nominees before their candidacy ever reached the floor of the Senate for a vote. For Democrats, the filibuster was the only tool they had to pay back Republicans for their behavior during the Clinton years and was an effective strategy for preventing what they believed to be a Republican conservative takeover of the federal courts.

What's at Stake? Journalists and political scientists agree that the party affiliation of federal court judges—whether at the district court, circuit court, or Supreme Court levels—is a pretty good (though far from perfect) predictor of how they will decide cases. One recent study by Cass Sunstein and his colleagues, for example, reports that Republican judicial appointees vote very differently than Democratic judicial appointees on affirmative action, campaign finance, federalism, environmental issues, abortion, and capital punishment cases. This and other research suggest that the party that is able to appoint and confirm a majority of federal judges will be able to have its views of the Constitution and its preferred public policies prevail for a considerable period of time. This didn't matter a great deal when the differences between the parties were not as great as they are today and when there was a great deal of overlap between the parties. With ideological and policy preferences becoming more homogeneous within each of the parties, and with the differences between the parties on ideology and policy becoming more apparent every day, however, each of the parties in the Senate is likely to fight long and hard to keep the federal judiciary out of the hands of the other party. This suggests that the nasty judicial confirmation battles in the Senate of the Clinton and Bush years, rather than being exceptional, may become the normal way of conducting the confirmation business.

Is This Good for Democracy? It has been suggested that the role of the judiciary in a democracy is to act as a fair interpreter of the rules, an impartial judge in settling constitutional disputes, and the protector of the rights of minorities.

- Can judges who are appointed through a highly contentious partisan process be counted on to do these things? • Do you worry that partisan federal judges will do what is best for their party rather than what is fair or best for all? • Or do you think that this concern is overblown and that we can count on judges to act properly? • If you are worried about rising partisanship in the confirmation process, what do you think can be done about it? • Is there some way that presidents can be convinced to appoint judges who are in the mainstream, and that senators can be convinced to confirm them?

Sources: David Rogers, "Gloves Come Off in Fight For the Courts," *The Wall Street Journal* (October 30, 2003), p. 1; Helen Dewar, "Senate Democrats Sustain Filibuster on Judicial Nominations," *The Washington Post* (November 15, 2003), p. 1.

Judiciary Committee; during the Bush years, Democrats in the Senate use the filibuster and the threat of filibuster to block several of the president's nominees (see "The Rise of Partisan Conflict" feature for more information).

Although presidents must be concerned about the merit of their candidates and their acceptability to the Senate, they also try by their appointments to make their mark on the future. Presidents go about this in different ways.

Many presidents have been interested in nominating judges who shared their ideological and program commitments. John Adams nominated John

Marshall and a number of other judges to protect Federalist principles during the ascendancy of the Jeffersonians. Franklin Roosevelt tried to fill the courts with judges who favored the New Deal. Ronald Reagan favored conservatives who were committed to rolling back affirmative action and other civil rights claims, abortion rights, protections for criminal defendants, and broad claims of **standing** in environmental cases. Both George H. W. Bush and his son George W. Bush carried on the Reagan tradition of nominating very conservative judges to the federal courts.

Bill Clinton, eager to avoid a bitter ideological fight in the Senate, where he was trying to forge a bipartisan coalition to support the North American Free Trade Agreement and a national crime bill, nominated two moderates for the High Court—Ruth Bader Ginsburg and Stephen Breyer—in the first years of his administration. The Ginsburg nomination was also indicative of Clinton's apparent commitment to diversifying the federal court system. More than one-half of federal court nominees during his presidency were women and minorities.

Presidents are often disappointed in how their nominees behave once they reach the Court. Dwight Eisenhower was dumbfounded when his friend and nominee, Earl Warren, led the Court to transform constitutional law with regard to civil rights and criminal procedure. Nixon was stunned when Chief Justice Warren Burger voted with a unanimous Court to override the president's claim of **executive privilege** and forced him to give up the documents that would seal his fate in the Watergate affair. The elder George Bush was surprised when his nominee, David Souter, refused to vote for the overturn of *Roe* in *Planned Parenthood* v. *Casey* (1992). Finally, the legal community and veteran Court observers were surprised by the odyssey of the late justice Harry Blackman. A conservative nominated by Richard Nixon in 1970, Blackman became one of the most liberal justices on the court by the time of his retirement in 1994. Despite these dramatic examples, the past political and ideological positions of federal court nominees are a fairly reliable guide to their later behavior on the bench.[8]

The Supreme Court in Action

The Supreme Court meets from the first Monday in October until late June or early July, depending on the press of business. Let's see how it goes about deciding cases.

—Norms of Operation

A set of unwritten but clearly understood rules of behavior—called *norms*—shapes how the Court does things. One norm is *secrecy,* which keeps the conflicts between justices out of the public eye and elevates the stature of the Court as an institution. Justices do not grant interviews very often. Reporters are not allowed to stalk the corridors for a story. Law clerks are expected to keep all memos, draft opinions, and conversations with the justices they work for confidential. Justices are not commonly seen on the frantic Washington, D.C., cocktail party circuit. When meeting in conference to argue and decide cases, the justices meet alone, without secretaries or clerks. Breaches of secrecy have occurred only occasionally. As a result, we know less about the inner workings of the Court than about any other branch of government.

Seniority is another important norm. Seniority determines the assignment of office space, the seating arrangements in open court (the most junior are at

---

standing

Authority to bring legal action because one is directly affected by the issues at hand.

executive privilege

A presidential claim that certain communications with subordinates may be withheld from Congress and the courts.

the ends), and the order of speaking in conference (the chief justice, then the most senior, and so on down the line). Speaking first allows the senior members to set the tone for discussion.

Finally, the justices are expected to stick closely to *precedent* when they decide cases. When the Court departs from a precedent, it is essentially overruling its own past actions, exercising judicial review of itself. In most cases, departures from precedent come in only very small steps over many years. For example, several decisions chipped away at the **separate but equal doctrine** of *Plessy* v. *Ferguson* (1896) before it was decisively reversed in *Brown* v. *Board of Education of Topeka* (1954).

Controlling the Agenda

The Court has a number of screening mechanisms to control what cases it will hear so that it can focus on cases that involve important federal or constitutional questions.

Several technical rules help keep the numbers down. Cases must be *real* and *adverse;* that is, they must involve a real dispute between two parties. The disputants in a case must have *standing;* that is, they must have a real and direct interest in the issues that are raised. The Court sometimes changes the definition of *standing* to make access for **plaintiffs** easier or more difficult. The Warren Court favored an expansive definition; the Rehnquist Court, a restricted one. Cases must also be *ripe;* that is, all other avenues of appeal must have been exhausted, and the injury must already have taken place (the Court will not accept hypothetical cases). Appeals must also be filed within a specified time limit, the paperwork must be correct and complete, and a filing fee of $200 must be paid. The fee may be waived if a petitioner is poor and files an affidavit **in forma pauperis** ("in the manner of a pauper"). One of the most famous cases in American history, *Gideon* v. *Wainwright* (1963), which established the right of all defendants to have lawyers in criminal cases, was submitted in forma pauperis on a few pieces of lined paper by a Florida State Penitentiary inmate named Clarence Earl Gideon. The Rehnquist Court was less friendly to indigent petitions than previous Courts and took several steps to cut down what Chief Justice Rehnquist called "frivolous" suits by "jailhouse lawyers."

The most powerful tool that the Court has for controlling its own agenda is the power to grant or not to grant a **writ of certiorari.** A grant of "cert" is a decision of the Court that an appellate case raises an important federal or constitutional issue that it is prepared to consider.[9] Under the **rule of four,** petitions are granted cert if at least four justices vote in favor. There are several reasons a petition may not command four votes, even if the case involves important constitutional issues: It may involve a particularly controversial issue that the Court would like to avoid, or the Court may not yet have developed a solid majority and may wish to avoid a split decision. Few petitions survive all of these hurdles. Of the almost 8,000 cases that are filed in each session, the Court grants cert for less than 100 (this number varies a bit year to year). In cases denied cert, the decision of the lower court stands.

Deciding how freely to grant cert is a tricky business for the Court. Granted too often, it threatens to inundate the Court with cases. Granted too sparingly, it leaves in place the decisions of 13 different federal appeals courts on substantial federal and constitutional questions, as well as the decisions of state supreme courts, which often leads to inconsistent constitutional interpretations across the country. Because the Court now typically

separate but equal doctrine
The principle articulated in *Plessy* v. *Ferguson* (1896) that laws prescribing *separate* public facilities and services for nonwhite Americans are permissible if the facilities and services are *equal* to those provided for whites.

plaintiff
One who brings suit in a court.

in forma pauperis
Describing a process by which indigents may file a suit with the Supreme Court free of charge.

writ of certiorari
An announcement that the Supreme Court will hear a case on appeal from a lower court; its issuance requires the vote of four of the nine justices.

rule of four
An *unwritten* practice that requires at least four justices of the Supreme Court to agree that a case warrants review by the Court before it will hear the case.

Most major policy and political disputes in the United States eventually make their way to the Supreme Court, so demonstrations at the Supreme Court are common. Here demonstrators ask the Court to affirm the principle of affirmative action in a set of cases involving University of Michigan's undergraduate and law school admissions policies.

hears oral arguments for only about 85 cases a year—compared with roughly 150 in the 1970s and 1980s—more influence than ever is being exercised by the 13 federal circuit courts. For many important cases, the federal circuit courts are becoming the forum of last resort.

Deciding Cases

Cases granted cert are scheduled for oral argument. Lawyers on each side are alerted to the key issues that the justices wish to consider, and new briefs are invited. Briefs are also submitted on most important cases by other parties who may be interested in the disputes. These "friend of the court," or **amicus curiae,** briefs may be submitted by individuals, interest groups, or some agency of the federal government, including the Justice Department or even the president.

amicus curiae
Latin for "a friend of the court"; describes a brief in which individuals not party to a suit may have their views heard.

Each case is argued for one hour, with 30 minutes given to each side in the dispute. Oral argument is not so much a presentation of arguments, however, as it is a give-and-take between the lawyers and the justices and among the justices themselves. When the federal government is a party to the case, the solicitor general or one of his or her deputies presents the oral arguments. Some justices—Antonin Scalia, for instance—are famous for their close grilling of lawyers. Ruth Bader Ginsburg often asks that lawyers skip abstract legal fine points and put the issues in terms of their effect on ordinary people.

After hearing oral arguments and reading the briefs in the case, the justices meet in conference to reach a decision. The custom is for each justice to state his or her position, starting with the chief justice and moving through the ranks in order of seniority. Chief justices of great stature and intellect, such as John Marshall and Charles Evans Hughes, used the opportunity to speak first as a way of structuring the case and of swaying votes. Those who did not command much respect from the other justices (e.g., Warren Burger) were less able to shape the decision process.

Chief Justices of the United States

Political scientists have tried to determine what factors are most important in predicting how the justices will vote. One approach looks at the ideological predilections of the justices and manages to explain a great deal about their voting behavior that way.[10] Another approach focuses on the diaries and personal papers of retired justices and shows that a great deal of negotiating and "horse trading" goes on, with justices trading votes on different cases and joining opinions they do not like so that they can have a hand in modifying them.[11] Another approach tries to link voting behavior to social background, types of previous judicial experience, and the political environment of family upbringing.[12] Still another believes that justices vote strategically, departing from their own policy preferences when they believe a particular decision will enhance the influence of the Court in the federal government and American society.[13] 'None of these approaches has been totally successful because much of what the Court does in conference is secret and can be only imperfectly reconstructed. About all that one can say is that the justices tend to form relatively stable voting blocs over time.[14] Many scholars attribute the change of direction of the Court on civil rights, church–state issues, and state–federal government relations in the 1995 session and after, for example, to the emergence of a strong conservative bloc (Scalia, Thomas, Rehnquist, Kennedy, and O'Connor). This bloc formed the majority in *Gore* v. *Bush* (2000), which effectively determined the outcome of the presidential election, as well as in *Zelman* v. *Simmons-Harris* (2002), upholding Cleveland's school voucher program.

The vote in conference is not final, however. As Justice John Harlan once explained it, "The books on voting are never closed until the decision finally comes down."[15] The justices have an opportunity to change their votes in response to the opinion supporting the majority decision. An opinion is a statement of the legal reasoning that supports the decision of the Court. There are three kinds of opinions. The **opinion of the Court** is the written opinion of the majority. A **concurring opinion** is the opinion of a justice who supports the majority decision but has different legal reasons for doing so. A **dissenting opinion** presents the reasoning of the minority. Dissenting opinions sometimes become the basis for future Court majorities.

If he or she votes with the majority in conference, the chief justice assigns the writing of the opinion. He or she can assign it to any justice in the majority, often to him- or herself. Some jurists and scholars believe that this power to assign is the most important role of the chief justice, and it is guarded jealously. Warren Burger was so eager to play a role in opinion assignments that, much to the distress of his colleagues, he would often delay announcing his vote so that he could place himself with the majority. Justice William Douglas angrily charged that Burger voted with the majority in *Roe* only so that he could assign the case to a justice who was closer to the minority view.[16] If the chief justice's opinion is with the minority, the opinion is assigned by the most senior member of the majority.

The justice assigned to write the opinion does not work in isolation. He or she is assisted not only by law clerks but also by other justices, who helpfully provide memoranda suggesting wording and reasoning. Justices also consider the legal reasoning presented to the Court in amicus curiae briefs.[17] Most opinions go through numerous revisions and are subject to a considerable amount of bargaining among the justices.

Only when an opinion is completed is a final vote taken in conference. The justices are free to change their earlier votes: They may join the majority if they are now persuaded by its reasoning, or a concurring opinion may be so compelling that the majority may decide to replace the original majority opinion with it.

opinion of the Court
The majority opinion that accompanies a Supreme Court decision.

concurring opinion
The opinion of one or more judges who vote with the majority on a case but wish to set out different reasons for their decision.

dissenting opinion
The opinion of the judge or judges who are in the minority on a particular case before the Supreme Court.

 Simulation

You Are a Clerk to Supreme Court Justice Judith Gray

Supreme Court justices here take turns signing opinions that will be published with the Court's decision on a case. Few cases before the Court result in unanimous decisions, so virtually all decisions are announced with attached majority and minority opinions.

The Supreme Court as a National Policymaker

People often say that the Court should settle disputes and not make policy. But because the disputes it settles involve contentious public issues (such as abortion rights and affirmative action) and fundamental questions about the meaning of our constitutional rules, the Court cannot help but make public policy.

It seems likely that the Court recognizes and cultivates its policymaking role. In the main, the Court does not see itself as a court of last resort, simply righting routine errors in the lower courts or settling minor private disputes. It sees itself, instead, as the "highest judicial tribunal for settling policy conflicts" and constitutional issues and chooses its cases accordingly.[18] The fact that decisions are not simply handed down but come with an opinion attached for the purpose of guiding the actions of other courts, litigants, and public officials is another demonstration that the Court recognizes its policymaking role. Let's look at judicial policymaking—which takes the form of the Court's constitutional interpretations as revealed in its decisions—and see how it has evolved over time.

Structural Change and Constitutional Interpretation

Scholars generally identify three periods in the history of constitutional interpretation by the Supreme Court in the United States, one stretching from the founding to the Civil War, the next from the end of the Civil War to the Great Depression, and the last from World War II to the present.[19] We would add a fourth, covering the years from the mid-1980s to the present. We will see how

Under the leadership of Chief Justice John Marshall, the Supreme Court weakened the power of the states to regulate and interfere with interstate commerce, encouraging the emergence of a vital national economy.

changes in constitutional law have been influenced by structural factors, particularly economic change.

Period 1: National Power and Property Rights We saw in Chapter 4 that the United States experienced significant growth and change during the first 75 years of its existence. This growth was accompanied by changes in constitutional law. Chief Justice John Marshall, who presided over the Supreme Court from 1801 to 1835, was the key judicial figure during this important period in our history.[20] Marshall was a follower of the doctrines of Alexander Hamilton, who believed that American greatness depended on a strong national government, a partnership between government and business in which industry and commerce were encouraged, and a national market economy free of the regulatory restraints of state and local governments. In a string of opinions that have shaped the fundamentals of American constitutional law—especially important are *Fletcher* v. *Peck* (1810), *Dartmouth College* v. *Woodward* (1819), *McCulloch* v. *Maryland* (1819), and *Gibbons* v. *Ogden* (1824), discussed elsewhere in this text—Marshall interpreted the Constitution to mean "maximum protection to property rights and maximum support for the idea of nationalism."[21]

Period 2: Government and the Economy The Civil War and the Industrial Revolution triggered the development of a mass-production industrial economy dominated by the business corporation. Determining the role to be played by government in such an economy was a central theme of American political life in the late nineteenth and early twentieth centuries. The courts were involved deeply in this rethinking. At the beginning of this period, the Supreme Court took the position that the corporation was to be protected against regulation by both the state and federal governments; by the end, it

During the crisis of the Great Depression, the federal government took on greater responsibilities for protecting the welfare of the American people. The Supreme Court was slow to endorse the changes but eventually did so under intense political pressure.

laissez-faire

The political-economic doctrine that holds that government ought not interfere with the operations of the free market.

was more sympathetic to the desire of the people and the political branches for the expansion of government regulation and management of the economy during the crisis of the Great Depression.

The main protection for the corporation against this regulation came from the Fourteenth Amendment. This amendment was passed in the wake of the Civil War to guarantee the citizenship rights of freed slaves. The operative phrase was from Section 1: "nor shall any state deprive any person of life, liberty, or property without due process of law"—on its face, hardly relevant to the world of the corporation. But in one of the great ironies of American history, the Court took up this expanded federal power over the states to protect rights and translated it to mean that corporations (considered "persons" under the law) and other forms of business should have increased protection from state regulation.

This reading of **laissez-faire** economic theory into constitutional law made the Supreme Court the principal ally of business in the late nineteenth and early twentieth centuries. Keeping the government out of the economy in general, the Court overturned efforts by both the state and federal governments to provide welfare for the poor; to regulate manufacturing monopolies; to initiate an income tax; to regulate interstate railroad rates; to provide scholarships to students; to regulate wages, hours, and working conditions; and to protect consumers against unsafe or unhealthy products. The Court also supported the use of judicial injunctions to halt strikes by labor unions.

The business–Supreme Court alliance lasted until the Great Depression. Roosevelt's New Deal reflected a new national consensus on the need for a greatly expanded federal government with a new set of responsibilities: to manage the economy; to provide a safety net for the poor, the unemployed, and the elderly; to protect workers' rights to form labor unions; and to regulate business in the public interest. The Supreme Court, however, filled with justices born in the nineteenth century and committed to the unshakable link between the Constitution and laissez-faire economic doctrine, was opposed to the national consensus and in 1935 and 1936 declared unconstitutional several laws that were part of the foundation of the New Deal. In an extraordinary turn of events, however, the Supreme Court reversed itself in 1937, finding the Social Security Act, the Labor Relations Act, and state minimum wage laws acceptable. It is not entirely clear why the so-called switch-in-time-that-saved-nine occurred, but surely Roosevelt's landslide reelection in 1936, the heightening of public hostility toward the Court, and Roosevelt's plan to "pack the Court," all played a role. Whatever the reason, the Court abandoned its effort to prevent the government from playing a central role in the management of the economy and the regulation of business, and it came to defer to the political linkage branches of government on such issues by the end of the 1930s. In doing so, it brought another constitutional era to a close.

Period 3: Individual Rights and Liberties   Three fundamental issues of American constitutional law—the relationship of the states to the nation, the nature and extent of private property rights, and the role of government in the management of the economy—were essentially settled by the time World War II broke out. From then until the mid- to late 1980s, the Court turned its main attention to the relationship between the individual and government.[22]

Most of this story is told in Chapters 15 and 16 on civil rights and civil liberties. For now, it is sufficient to point out that the Court, especially during the tenure of Chief Justice Earl Warren, decided cases that expanded protections for free expression and association, religious expression, fair trials, and civil rights for minorities. In another series of cases dealing with the apportionment of electoral districts, the Court declared for political equality, based on the principle of "one person, one vote." In many of its landmark decisions, the Court applied the Bill of Rights to the states. Although the Court's record was not without blemishes during and after World War II—see the "Using the Framework" feature on *Korematsu* v. *United States* (1944)—it made significant strides in expanding the realm of individual freedom.

Period 4: Conservative Retrenchment   Constitutional law and the Court do not stand still, however; both are responsive to changes in the world around them. A new conservative majority emerged on the Supreme Court in the late 1980s, fashioned by the judicial nominations of Presidents Ronald Reagan and George H. W. Bush. This new majority has moved the Court to reconsider many of the Court's established doctrines in the areas of rights and liberties (see Chapters 15 and 16) and on the relationship between the national and state governments.

Its reconsideration of federalism in favor of "states rights" has been particularly noteworthy (see Chapter 3). In a string of landmark cases, the Court has curtailed national authority in favor of the states. Its main tool has been to strike down federal statutes that, in its view, are based on an overly expansive reading by Congress of the Interstate Commerce Clause. Overturning constitutional doctrine that has been settled since the late 1930s, the Court has not allowed Congress to act with respect to any issue that might be connected—even loosely and indirectly—to the national economy. That is, the present Court is insisting on a much stricter relationship of congressional action to interstate commerce. In 1995, for example, the Court overturned a federal statute that banned guns from the area immediately around public schools,

Using the Framework

Japanese American Internment

If the Supreme Court exists to protect individual rights, why did it allow the military to keep Japanese Americans in internment camps during World War II?

Background: On the advice of the U.S. military, President Franklin Roosevelt signed a series of executive orders in early 1942 authorizing the relocation of 112,000 Japanese Americans living on the West Coast, 70,000 of whom were citizens, into internment camps. In 1944, the Supreme Court in *Korematsu* v. *United States* upheld the legality of the exclusion and confinement orders.

Constitutional scholar Edward Corwin described the internment and the Court's action as "the most drastic invasion of the rights of citizens of the United States by their own government" in modern American history. Taking a broad overview of structural, political linkage, and governmental factors that influenced the Supreme Court's decision will help explain this situation.

Governmental Action

The Supreme Court announces its decision allowing the internment of Japanese Americans in *Korematsu* v. *United States* (1944).

Governmental Level

President Franklin Roosevelt, troubled by the action, but fully aware of the feelings of the public and the wishes of military leaders in wartime, signed the necessary executive orders. → The Supreme Court, unwilling to act against opinion of military leaders that Japanese Americans living on the West Coast posed a national security threat, supported the exclusion order in a case brought by Fred Korematsu.

Military authorities believed that Japanese Americans living on the West Coast posed a national security threat to the United States; asked the President to authorize curfews, relocation, and confinement. → Congress passed supporting legislation making relocation and internment possible.

Political Linkages Level

Anti-Japanese attitudes were widespread among the public, particularly in the West Coast states. → Public opinion strongly supported the war against Japan and whatever military policies were necessary to win it. → The media whipped up hysteria about a possible Japanese invasion.

Structural Level

Japanese immigrants to the United States in the late nineteenth and early twentieth centuries settled mainly in the West Coast states. → The Japanese attack on Pearl Harbor on December 7, 1941, plunged the United States into World War II and helped trigger negative attitudes toward Americans of Japanese descent. → The Constitution vests enormous powers in the president as commander-in-chief during wartime.

saying that Congress had exceeded its powers under the Commerce Clause. Using the same reasoning, it overturned legislation requiring background checks for gun buyers. Recently, the Court used such reasoning to strike down parts of the Violence Against Women Act, the federal law barring age discrimination in employment, and a law that allows citizens to sue state governments that fail to enforce national environmental statutes.

The conservative majority on the Court has also become fond of the notion of "state sovereign immunity," an idea they draw from the Eleventh Amendment that suggests that the states enjoy a broad area of immunity from national government interference. Using this doctrine, the Court ruled in 2001 that states are immune from suits brought by state employees under the Americans with Disabilities Act. Dissenters on the Court expressed concern that this will spell trouble for many federal civil rights laws. The Court ruled in another case in 2002 that states are shielded from rulings by federal agencies acting on complaints from private individuals, a determination that may decrease the powers of agencies such as the Environmental Protection Agency.

In recent years, however, the Supreme Court became more moderate on a significant number of issues—affirmative action, gay rights, the right of individuals to sue states for violations of federal civil rights laws (discussed in more detail in Chapter 16), and the rights of terrorism detainees—mostly because of Justice Sandra Day O'Connor. Between 2001 and 2004, she became the crucial swing vote between the four conservatives on the Court—Kennedy, Rehnquist, Scalia, and Thomas—and the four liberals—Stevens, Ginsburg, Souter, and Breyer. On a Court where many important decisions were decided on the basis of a 5–4 vote, she was increasingly the one who cast the deciding vote. Although she most often voted with the conservatives—note especially her vote with the majority in 2000 in *Bush* v. *Gore* that settled the disputed vote in Florida in favor of Bush and determined the outcome of the presidential election—she surprised many people in 2003 when she joined the majority in the Michigan Law School case that upheld the use of race in law school admissions, the Texas case that banned states from forbidding private gay sexual behavior, and the challenge to the constitutionality of the McCain-Feingold Campaign Finance Reform law (which was rejected). In 2004, she wrote the majority opinion in the decision on the rights of citizens held as "enemy combatants," pointing out that "a state of war is not a blank check for the president when it comes to the rights of the nation's citizens." (*Hamdi* v. *Rumsfeld*, 2004). Some veteran Court observers have suggested that O'Connor's emergence as the swing vote in many crucial cases made her the most important person on the Court during this period and note that briefs submitted to the Court were directed mainly at her.[23]

The Debate Over Judicial Activism

Has the Court become too involved in national policymaking? Many people think so; others think not. Let us examine several of the ways in which what is called **judicial activism** is expressed.

judicial activism
Actions by the courts that go beyond the strict role of the judiciary as interpreter of the law and adjudicator of disputes.

Judicial Review We have already seen how the Court, under John Marshall's leadership, claimed the right of judicial review in the case of *Marbury* v. *Madison* (1803). Still, the power was not exercised by the Court to any great extent until the late nineteenth century. The rate of judicial review picked up during the twentieth century, however, with most of the Court's adverse attention being paid to the states. As described above, however, the present Court has become increasingly aggressive in overturning federal statutes, with an eye toward constraining the power of the national government. Overall, trends in judicial review suggest that the Court has become more willing in modern times to monitor the activities of other governmental entities.

Reversing the Decisions of Past Supreme Courts Despite the norm of precedent that guides judicial decision making, the Warren, Burger, and Rehnquist Courts were not reluctant to overturn previous Court decisions. The most dramatic instance was the reversal of *Plessy* v. *Ferguson* (1896), which endorsed legal segregation in the South, by *Brown* v. *Board of Education* (1954), which removed segregation's legal underpinnings. The Court reversed itself in many other cases as well: the gradual whittling back of abortion protections for women, first enunciated in *Roe* v. *Wade* (1973); the reversal of a range of precedents involving the rights of criminal defendants; and the reconsideration of the nature of federalism and national government power, reviewed earlier.

Deciding "Political" Issues Critics claim that the Court is taking on too many matters that are best left to the elected branches of government. An often-cited example is the Court's willingness to become increasingly involved in the process of drawing congressional electoral district boundaries in the states. Defenders of the Court argue that when such basic constitutional rights as equality of citizenship are at peril, the Court is obligated to protect these rights, no matter what other government bodies may choose to do. The Court's intervention in the 2000 presidential election generated widespread criticism for its meddling in politics, though its many defenders insist that the Court's decision in *Bush* v. *Gore* saved the nation from a constitutional crisis.

Remedies The most criticized aspect of judicial activism is the tendency for federal judges to impose broad remedies on states and localities. A **remedy** is what a court determines must be done to rectify a wrong. Since the 1960s, the Court has been more willing than in the past to impose remedies that require other governmental bodies to take action. Some of the most controversial of these remedies include court orders requiring states to build more prison space and mandating that school districts bus students to achieve racial balance. Such remedies often require that governments spend public funds for things they do not necessarily want to do. Critics claim that the federal judiciary's legitimate role is to prevent government actions that threaten rights and liberties, not to compel government to take action to meet some policy goal.

Original Intention Much of the debate about the role of the Court centers on the issue of **original intention.** Advocates of original intention and its twin, **strict construction,** believe that the Court must be guided by the original intentions of the framers and the words found in the Constitution. They believe that the expansion of rights that has occurred since the mid-1960s—such as the new right to privacy that formed the basis of the *Roe* v. *Wade* decision and rights for criminal defendants—is illegitimate, having no foundation in the framers' intentions or the text of the Constitution. Justices Antonin Scalia and Clarence Thomas are the strongest "originalists" on today's Court.

Opponents of original intention believe that the intentions of the Founders are not only impossible to determine but also unduly constricting. In this view, jurists must try to reconcile the fundamental principles of the Constitution with changing conditions in the United States.

Participation

The Courts and School Vouchers

remedy
An action that a court determines must be taken to rectify a wrong.

original intention
The doctrine that the courts must interpret the Constitution in ways consistent with the intentions of the framers rather than in light of contemporary conditions and needs.

strict construction
The doctrine that the provisions of the Constitution have a clear meaning and that judges must stick closely to this meaning when rendering decisions.

Federal courts often require that states "remedy" a situation found to be in violation of federal standards or constitutional protections. A good example is prison overcrowding, shown here in an Alabama prison. For many years, the courts have insisted that the states do something to end the problem, even if it means spending additional state monies.

When all is said and done, however, it is apparent that the modern Supreme Court is more activist than it was in the past; most justices today hold a more expansive view of the role of the Court in forging national policy than did their predecessors. Because the Court is likely to remain activist—note the present Court's vigorous reinterpretation of the meaning of federalism—the debate about judicial activism is not likely to disappear from American politics.

Outside Influences on the Court

The courts make public policy and will continue to do so, but they do not do so in splendid isolation; many other governmental and political linkage actors and institutions influence what they do. Recall that the influence of structural factors has already been examined at several places in this chapter.

Governmental Factors

The Supreme Court must coexist with other governmental bodies that have their own powers, interests, constituencies, and visions of the public good. Recognizing this, the Court usually tries to stay somewhere near the boundaries of what is acceptable to other political actors. Being without "purse or sword," as Hamilton put it in *The Federalist,* No. 78, the Court cannot force others to obey its decisions. It can only hope that respect for the law and the Court will cause government officials to do what it has mandated in a decision. If the Court fails to gain voluntary compliance, it risks a serious erosion of its influence, for it then appears weak and ineffectual.

Presidential Influence

The president, as chief executive, is supposed to carry out the Court's decrees. However, presidents who have opposed particular decisions or been lukewarm to them have dragged their feet, as President Eisenhower did on school desegregation after the Court's *Brown* decision.

The president has constitutional powers that give him some degree of influence over the Court. In addition to the Court's dependence on the president to carry out its decisions (when the parties to a dispute do not do it voluntarily), for example, the president influences the direction of the Court by his power to appoint judges when there are vacancies. He can also file suits through the Justice Department, try to move public opinion against the Court (as Richard Nixon tried to do), and threaten to introduce legislation to alter the Court's organization or jurisdiction (as Franklin Roosevelt did with his Court-packing proposal).

Congressional Influences

Although Congress can alter the size, organization, and appellate jurisdiction of the federal courts, it rarely does so.[24] The size of the Court, for example, has not changed since 1860. Nor, since that time, has Congress changed its jurisdiction as a reaction to its decisions, despite the introduction of many bills over the years to do so. Congress is more likely to bring pressure to bear by being unsympathetic to pleas from the justices for pay increases or for a suitable budget for clerks or office space. The Senate also plays a role in the appointment process, as we have learned, and can convey its views to the Court during the course of confirmation hearings. Finally, Congress can change statutes or pass new laws that specifically challenge Supreme Court decisions, as it did when it legislated the Civil Rights Act of 1991 to make it easier for people to file employment discrimination suits.

Political Linkage Factors

The Supreme Court is influenced not only by other government officials and institutions but also by what we have termed political linkage factors such as social movements, interest groups, and elections.

Groups and Movements

Interest groups, social movements, and the public not only influence the Court indirectly through the president and Congress but often do so directly. An important political tactic of interest groups and social movements is the **test case.** A test case is an action brought by a group that is designed to challenge the constitutionality of a law or an action by government. Groups wishing to force a court determination on an issue that is important to them will try to find a plaintiff on whose behalf they can bring a suit. When Thurgood Marshall was chief counsel for the NAACP in the 1950s, he spent a long time searching for the right plaintiff to bring a suit that would drive the last nail into the coffin of the *Plessy* separate-but-equal doctrine that was the legal basis for southern segregation. He settled on a fifth-grade girl named Linda Brown who was attending a segregated school in Topeka, Kansas. Several years later, he won the landmark case *Brown* v. *Board of Education of Topeka.*

Many test cases take the form of **class action suits.** These are suits brought by an individual on behalf of a class of people who are in a similar situation. A suit to prevent the dumping of toxic wastes in public waterways, for example, may be brought by an individual in the name of all the people living in the area who are adversely affected by the resulting pollution. Class action suits were invited by the Warren Court's expansion of the definition of stand-

test case
A case brought to force a ruling on the constitutionality of some law or executive action.

class action suit
A suit brought on behalf of a group of people who are in a situation similar to that of the plaintiffs.

Social movements use test cases to challenge the constitutionality of laws and government actions. After a long search, NAACP attorney Thurgood Marshall—shown here in front of the Supreme Court, where he would later sit as a justice—selected Linda Brown, a fifth-grader from Topeka, Kansas, as the principal plaintiff in *Brown* v. *Board of Education of Topeka,* the historic case that successfully challenged school segregation.

ing in the 1960s. The Rehnquist Court later narrowed the definition of standing, making it harder to bring class action suits.

Interest groups often get involved in suits brought by others by filing amicus curiae briefs. Pro-abortion and anti-abortion groups submitted 78 such briefs in *Webster* v. *Reproductive Health Services* (1989), a decision that allowed states to regulate and limit abortion availability.[25] These briefs set out the group's position on the constitutional issues or talk about some of the most important consequences of deciding the case one way or the other. In a sense, this activity is a form of lobbying. Some scholars believe that the Court finds such briefs to be a way to keep track of public and group opinion on the issues before it, which is helpful to its work.[26]

Leaders   The Supreme Court does not usually stray very far from the opinions of public and private sector leaders.[27] Social and economic leaders use their influence in a number of ways. As we learned in earlier chapters, their influence is substantial in the media, the interest group system, party politics, and elections at all levels. It follows, then, that elites play a substantial role in the thinking of presidents and the members of Congress as they, in turn, deal with the Court. In addition to this powerful but indirect influence, the Court is also shaped by developments on issues and doctrine within the legal profession as these are expressed by bar associations, law journals, and law schools. To take but one example, Justice O'Connor, in her opinion in the 2004 Michigan Law School affirmative action case, justified her vote by pointing out that the use of race as one criterion among many in law school admission decisions was now widely accepted in the university and legal communities, as was the legitimacy of the goal of "diversity" in higher education.

Public Opinion   We might think that the Supreme Court is immune from public opinion, since the justices are appointed for life and do not need to face the

How Democratic Are We?

Is the Supreme Court a Democratic or Nondemocratic Institution?

PROPOSITION: The framers intended that Supreme Court be a nondemocratic institution, and it ought to stay that way. It has served us well throughout our history.

AGREE: For a representative democracy to function at all, there must be a referee that stands above the fray, free from the pressure of other elected officials and the public, preserving the rules, overseeing the orderly changing of some rules when the situation demands it, protecting minorities against the potentially tyrannical behavior of the majority, and protecting individuals in the exercise of their constitutionally guaranteed rights. The Supreme Court has done a pretty good job carrying out these responsibilities throughout our history. For example, the Court has been an important factor in the spread and protection of free speech and freedom of the press in the United States, and eventually became a force for ensuring that African Americans would be treated as equal citizens.

DISAGREE: A representative democracy cannot remain democratic if one of its core government institutions, with the power to make binding decisions for the nation as a whole, is neither responsible nor responsive to the people. At some point, the Supreme Court cannot avoid going its own way, sometimes legitimately so—for example, when it has protected the constitutional rights of unpopular individuals and minority groups—and sometimes illegitimately—for example, when it has served as a bulwark against efforts by the people to regulate powerful economic institutions. Especially egregious was the Court's intervention in the 2000 election contest in Florida which decided the outcome of the 2000 presidential election.

CONSIDER: Over the years, public opinion pollsters have consistently reported that the Supreme Court is, along with the military, the most respected institution in the American government—regularly outpacing presidents and Congress—and in American society—higher in the esteem of the public than religious, corporate, labor, or educational institutions. The Supreme Court holds this position despite the fact that its members are not elected, its deliberations are shrouded in mystery, and its decisions are sometimes abstract and complex.

• How would you explain this? • Do you believe the Court has such a high standing with the public because most people don't know much about it and don't see it in operation, with its inevitable disputes among the justices, compromises on decisions, and careful crafting of opinions to gain widespread acceptance—that is, playing politics? • Or is the Court's high standing a product of the valuable role it plays in American democracy, acting as a referee on the rules and settling disputes among contending groups? • How about you? • How would you rate the Supreme Court compared to other governmental and societal institutions and organizations? • Why do you feel this way?

electorate. There is reason to believe, however, that the Court pays attention to public opinion. A substantial amount of research shows that the Court conforms to public opinion about as much as the president and Congress do.[28] It must be noted, on the other hand, that the Court sometimes takes a very long time to move closer to public and elite opinions. For example, during the Great Depression, the Court's strong commitment to laissez-faire economics in the midst of a national economic emergency almost led to a constitutional crisis.

It is important to point out one additional thing as we conclude consideration of outside influences on the Court. Although the Court eventually became an important instrument for the advancement of rights and liberties in the United States, it has not been entirely immune from pressure brought to bear by the public, other government officials, and private-sector leaders to punish suspect groups. For example, the Court went along with local, state, and federal actions to punish dissident voices during the McCarthy era's anti-Communist hysteria of the 1950s. It also approved the forced relocation and internment of Japanese Americans during World War II, as discussed earlier in the "Using the Framework" feature.

Summary

Article III of the Constitution is vague about the powers and responsibilities of the U.S. Supreme Court. Especially noteworthy is the Constitution's silence on the Court's most important power, judicial review. Nevertheless, the Court has fashioned a powerful position for itself in American politics, coequal with the executive and legislative branches.

The federal court system is made up of three parts. At the bottom are 94 federal district courts, in which most cases originate. In the middle are 13 appeals courts. At the top is the Supreme Court, with both original and appellate jurisdiction.

The Supreme Court operates on the basis of several widely shared norms: secrecy, seniority, and adherence to precedent. The Court controls its agenda by granting or not granting certiorari. Cases before the Court wend their way through the process in the following way: submission of briefs, oral argument, initial consideration in conference, opinion writing, and final conference consideration by the justices. Published opinions serve as precedents for other federal courts and future Supreme Court decisions.

The Supreme Court is a national policymaker of considerable importance. Its unelected, life-tenured justices cannot, however, do anything they please, because the Court is significantly influenced by other political linkage and governmental factors. As a result, Court decisions rarely drift very far from public and elite opinion.

Constitutional interpretation by the Supreme Court, heavily influenced by structural changes in American history, has progressed through four stages. In the first, the Court helped settle the question of the nature of the federal union. In the second, it helped define the role of the government in a free enterprise economy. In the third, the Court focused on issues of civil liberties and civil rights. In the fourth, the Court took a more conservative turn in areas such as federalism and the rights of the accused.

The decisions of the Court are influenced by structural, political linkage, and governmental factors. The president and Congress are especially important in this regard, but so too are interest groups and public and elite opinion.

Suggestions for Further Reading

Ackerman, Bruce. *We the People: Transformations.* Cambridge, MA: Harvard University Press, 2000.
> *A compelling interpretation of American constitutional history in which popular pressures are the prime cause for major transformations in the U.S. Supreme Court's approach to major issues.*

Barber, Sotirios A. *The Constitution of Judicial Power.* Baltimore: Johns Hopkins University Press, 1997.
> *A compelling defense of an activist Court.*

Barnett, Randy E. *Restoring the Lost Constitution: The Presumption of Liberty.* Princeton, NJ: Princeton University Press, 2003.
> *A conservative case for understanding the Constitution as a legal framework for the protection of individual rights.*

Clayton, Cornell W., and Howard Gillman, eds. *Supreme Court Decision Making: New Institutionalist Approaches.* Chicago: University of Chicago Press, 1999.
> *An argument by a collection of leading scholars that the most important factor in Supreme Court decision making is neither ideology nor political pressures, but the nature of the law and judicial institutions.*

O'Brien, David M. *Storm Center: The Supreme Court in American Politics,* 6th ed. New York: W. W. Norton, 2002.
> *The leading textbook on the Court and how it operates.*

O'Connor, Sandra Day. *The Majesty of the Law: Reflections of a Supreme Court Justice.* New York: Random House, 2003.
> *Reflections on the law and the Supreme Court by today's most influential justice.*

Randall, Richard S. *American Constitutional Development.* New York: Longman Publishers, 2002.
> *A constitutional law textbook with Supreme Court cases and commentary.*

Schwartz, Bernard. *Decision: How the Supreme Court Decides Cases.* New York: Oxford University Press, 1997.
> *A revealing behind-the-scenes look at how the Supreme Court considers and decides the cases before it.*

Internet Sources

Federal Courts Home Page
www.uscourts.gov
> *Information and statistics about the activities of U.S. District Courts, Circuit Courts of Appeal, and the Supreme Court.*

Find Law.com
www.findlaw.com
> *A treasure trove of links to information about the nation's courts and the legal profession.*

Legal Information Institute, Cornell University Law School
http://www.law.cornell.edu
> *The gateway to a world of information and links to associated law and court sites on the Web. Among its sections you will find the following: the Supreme Court Calendar; Biographies and Opinions of the Justices; Directories of law firms, law schools, and legal associations; Constitutions and Codes, including U.S. statutes, regulations, and judicial rules of procedure; and Court opinions, including those of state supreme courts.*

Senate Judiciary Committee
www.senate.gov/~judiciary/nominations.cfm
> *Track the status of federal judicial nominations and confirmations.*

The Supreme Court
www.supremecourtus.gov/
> *The official Website of the Supreme Court with a wealth of information about the Court's docket and decisions.*

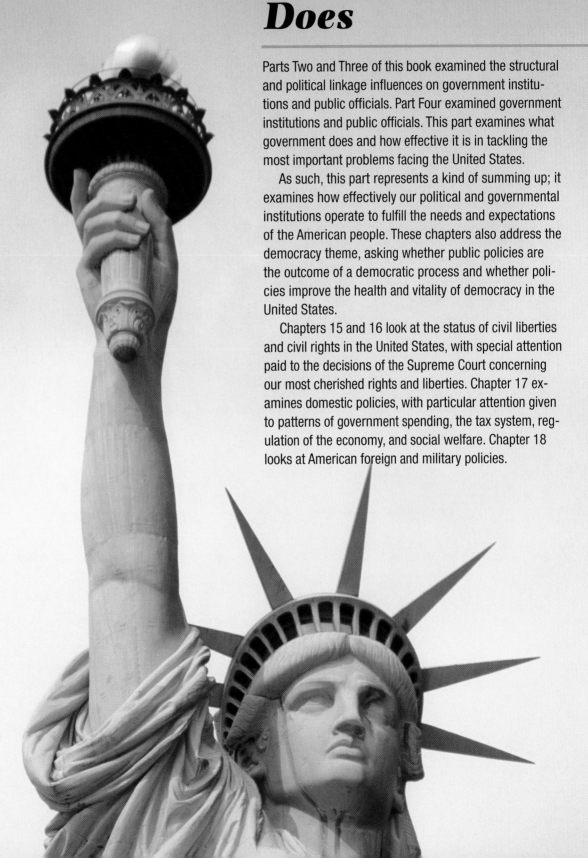

Part Five

What Government Does

Parts Two and Three of this book examined the structural and political linkage influences on government institutions and public officials. Part Four examined government institutions and public officials. This part examines what government does and how effective it is in tackling the most important problems facing the United States.

As such, this part represents a kind of summing up; it examines how effectively our political and governmental institutions operate to fulfill the needs and expectations of the American people. These chapters also address the democracy theme, asking whether public policies are the outcome of a democratic process and whether policies improve the health and vitality of democracy in the United States.

Chapters 15 and 16 look at the status of civil liberties and civil rights in the United States, with special attention paid to the decisions of the Supreme Court concerning our most cherished rights and liberties. Chapter 17 examines domestic policies, with particular attention given to patterns of government spending, the tax system, regulation of the economy, and social welfare. Chapter 18 looks at American foreign and military policies.

Chapter 15
Freedom: The Struggle for Civil Liberties

In This Chapter

- Why liberty is so important in a democracy

- How liberties were gradually applied to the states by the Supreme Court

- How the Supreme Court's interpretation of the meaning of liberties has changed

- How the struggle for democracy has increased the enjoyment of liberties in the United States

- How the war on terrorism may affect civil liberties

Campus Speech Codes and Free Speech

- Campus newspapers across the nation refused to accept a paid advertisement from conservative activist David Horowitz in which he opposed reparations for slavery. Many of the handful of newspapers that ran the ad "Ten Reasons Why Reparations for Slavery is a Bad Idea—and Racist Too" faced angry demonstrations, vandalism of their offices, and theft of the papers containing the offending ads.

- During a class at the University of Michigan, a student argued that homosexuality could be treated with psychotherapy. He was accused of violating a campus rule against victimizing people on the basis of their sexual orientation.

- At Southern Methodist University, a student was sentenced to work for 30 hours with minority organizations because, among other things, he sang "We Shall Overcome" in a sarcastic manner.[1]

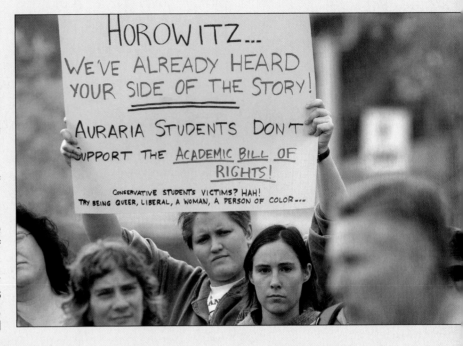

- At the University of Minnesota, four women students brought sexual harassment charges against faculty members in the Scandinavian Studies Department for disagreeing with students about the role of a female character in a story and for greeting a female student in a "nonsupportive" way.[2]

- According to the University of Montana's harassment policy, if a woman "feels" she has been mistreated, that alone proves mistreatment.

- Top officials at the University of Texas, Austin, denounced as abhorrent the statement of law school professor Lino Graglia that black and Hispanic students were not competitive with whites in law school because most of them come from cultures that do not encourage academic achievement or that look upon academic failure as a disgrace. Although Rev. Jesse Jackson joined hundreds of students and faculty members calling for Graglia's dismissal, civil libertarians came to his defense on the grounds of the professor's free speech rights under the Constitution.

- At San Diego State University a student was admonished by school administrators and warned that he might be expelled for getting into a heated argument with four Arab students he encountered in the school's library who had been quietly celebrating the September 11 attacks on the World Trade Center.[3]

- In 2002, a student at California Poly posted fliers for a talk by black conservative C. Mason Weaver, who believes that government assistance programs keep African Americans locked in dependence and poverty. The student was accused by several other students of racial insensitivity, brought before a campus disciplinary board, and found guilty of "disruption" for posting the lecture announcement.[4]

- Stanford University enacted a speech code in 1990 that prohibits "personal vilification of students on the basis of their sex, race, color, handicap, religion, sexual orientation, or national and ethnic origin." The code was pressed by, among others, the African American Law Students Association, the Asian American Law Students Association, and the Jewish Law Students Association. It was strongly opposed by Stanford's eminent constitutional scholar Gerald Gunther, who claimed that hate speech should not be banned but vigorously rejected "with more speech, with better speech, with repudiation and contempt." In 1995, the California Supreme Court agreed with Gunther's position, saying that the Stanford code unconstitutionally restricts free speech rights under the First Amendment to the Constitution.[5]

The college campus has become one of the most visible battlegrounds in the continuing struggle over the meaning of free speech in the United States, as traditional notions of liberty come into conflict with newer notions of equal citizenship (or civil rights, to be discussed in the next chapter). Campus speech codes have been instituted at many colleges and universities across the country in an effort to rid campuses of speech that may offend women and members of various minority groups. Many civil libertarians, like Gerald Gunther, though protective of the rights of minority students to have a supportive learning environment, have fought hard against such codes in the service of free speech and a free society. By and large, the courts have sided with the civil libertarians, as in the Stanford case.

Thinking Critically About This Chapter

Using the Framework   You will see in this chapter how structural, political linkage, and governmental factors influence the meaning and practice of civic freedoms. Although the decisions of the Supreme Court are particularly important in determining the status of civil liberties at any particular moment in American history, you will learn how they are also the product of influences from a wide range of actors, institutions, and social processes.

Using the Democracy Standard   You will see in this chapter how the expansion of the enjoyment of civil liberties in the United States has been a product of the struggle for democracy and how civil liberties are fundamental to the democratic process itself.

Civil Liberties in the Constitution

civil liberties

Freedoms found primarily in the Bill of Rights that are protected from government interference.

We saw in Chapter 2 that the framers were particularly concerned about establishing a society in which liberty might flourish. While government was necessary to protect liberty from the threat of anarchy, the framers believed that government might threaten liberty if it became too powerful. **Civil liberties** are freedoms protected by constitutional provisions, laws, and practices from certain types of government interference. As embodied in the Bill of Rights, civil liberties are protected by prohibitions against government actions that threaten the enjoyment of freedom. These liberties fall into two major groups: first, those associated with freedoms of expression, belief, and association; and second, those involving protections for people accused of committing a crime.

habeas corpus

The legal doctrine that a person who is arrested must have a timely hearing before a judge.

bill of attainder

A governmental decree that a person is guilty of a crime that carries the death penalty, rendered without benefit of a trial.

ex post facto law

A law that retroactively declares some action illegal.

In the Preamble to the Constitution, the framers wrote that they aimed to "secure the Blessings of Liberty to ourselves and our Posterity." But in the original Constitution, they protected few liberties from the national government they were creating and almost none from state governments. To safeguard against tyranny, the framers preferred to give the national government little power with which to attack individual liberties. Rather than listing specific prohibitions against certain kinds of actions, then, they believed that a republican constitutional design that fragmented government power and that included separation of powers, checks and balances, and federalism would best protect liberty. Still, the framers singled out certain freedoms as too crucial to be left unmentioned. For example, the Constitution prohibits Congress and the states from suspending the writ of **habeas corpus,** except when public safety demands it because of rebellion or invasion, and from passing **bills of attainder** or **ex post facto laws** (see Table 15.1 for an enumeration).

TABLE 15.1 • Civil Liberties in the U.S. Constitution

The exact meaning and extent of civil liberties in the Constitution are matters of debate, but here are some freedoms spelled out in the text of the Constitution and its amendments or clarified by early court decisions.

Constitution

Article I, Section 9
Congress may not suspend a writ of habeas corpus.
Congress may not pass bills of attainder or ex post facto laws.

Article I, Section 10
States may not pass bills of attainder or ex post facto laws.
States may not impair obligation of contracts.

Article III, Section 2
Criminal trials in national courts must be jury trials in the state in which the defendant is alleged to have committed the crime.

Article III, Section 3
No one may be convicted of treason unless there is a confession in open court or testimony of two witnesses to the same overt act.

Article IV, Section 2
Citizens of each state are entitled to all privileges and immunities of citizens in the several states.

The Bill of Rights

First Amendment
Congress may not make any law with respect to the establishment of religion.
Congress may not abridge the free exercise of religion.
Congress may not abridge freedom of speech or of the press.
Congress may not abridge the right to assemble or to petition the government.

Second Amendment
Congress may not infringe the right to keep and bear arms.

Third Amendment
Congress may not station soldiers in houses against the owner's will, except in times of war.

Fourth Amendment
Citizens are to be free from unreasonable searches and seizures.
Federal courts may issue search warrants based only on probable cause and specifically describing the objects of search.

Fifth Amendment
Citizens are protected against double jeopardy (being prosecuted more than once for the same crime) and self-incrimination.
Citizens are guaranteed against deprivation of life, liberty, or property without due process of law.
Citizens are guaranteed just compensation for public use of their private property.

Sixth Amendment
Citizens have the right to a speedy and public trial before an impartial jury.
Citizens have the right to face their accuser and to cross-examine witnesses.

Eighth Amendment
Excessive bail and fines are prohibited.
Cruel and unusual punishments are prohibited.

As we saw in Chapter 2, many citizens found the proposed Constitution too stingy in its listing of liberties, so that the Federalists were led to promise a "bill of rights" as a condition for passing the Constitution. The Bill of Rights was passed by the 1st Congress in 1789 and was ratified by the required number of states by 1791. Passage of the Bill of Rights made the constitution more democratic by specifying protections of political liberty and by guaranteeing a context of free political expression that makes popular sovereignty possible.

Reading the Constitution and its amendments, however, reveals how few of our most cherished liberties are to be found in this document. Decisions by government officials and changes brought about by political leaders, interest groups, social movements, and individuals remade the Constitution in the long run; hence many of the freedoms we expect today are not specifically mentioned there. Some extensions of protected liberties were introduced by judges and other officials. Others have evolved as the culture has grown to accept novel and even once-threatening ideas. Still other liberties have secured a place in the Republic through partisan and ideological combat. The key to understanding civil liberties in the United States is to follow their evolution over the course of the nation's history.

Rights and Liberties in the Nineteenth Century

During the nineteenth century, the range of protected civil liberties in the United States was somewhat different from their range today. Especially noteworthy were the special place of **economic liberty** and the understanding that the Bill of Rights did not apply to state governments.

Economic Liberty in the Early Republic

economic liberty
The right to own and use property free from excessive government interference.

Liberty may be understood as protection against government interference in certain kinds of private activities. Among the few such protections mentioned in the original Constitution was one that concerned the use and enjoyment of private property: "No State shall ... pass any ... Law impairing the Obligation of Contracts" (Article I, Section 10). The importance of property rights as a fundamental liberty in the body of the Constitution was reinforced by more than a century of judicial interpretation.

contract clause
The portion of Article I, Section 10, of the Constitution that prohibits states from passing any law "impairing the obligations of contracts."

The Marshall Court (1801–1835)   Although the Supreme Court ruled (in *Barron* v. *Baltimore*, 1833) that the Bill of Rights did not apply to the states, it ruled on several occasions that the **contract clause** in the Constitution directly applied against unwarranted state action. In the hands of Chief Justice John Marshall, the clause became an important defense of property rights against interference by the states. In *Fletcher* v. *Peck* (1810), for example, the Marshall Court upheld a sale of public land, even though almost all of the legislators who had voted for the land sale had been bribed by the prospective purchasers. Chief Justice Marshall argued that even a fraudulent sale created a contract that the state could not void. In *Dartmouth College* v. *Woodward* (1819), Marshall argued that New Hampshire could not modify the charter of Dartmouth College because the original charter constituted a contract, the terms of which could not be changed without impairing the obligations in the original contract. The Founders' attempt to protect the contractual agreements of private parties ballooned in the hands of the Marshall Court to bar virtually any and all changes by the states of established property relations.[6] This expansion of property rights protections made it very difficult for states to regulate business activities.

The Taney Court (1836–1864)   Under the leadership of Chief Justice Roger Taney, the Court began to make a distinction between private property used in ways that encouraged economic growth and private property used for simple enjoyment. In landmark cases, the Taney Court issued rulings favoring the former when the two concepts of property conflicted.[7] In his opinion in *Charles River Bridge* v. *Warren Bridge* (1837), Chief Justice Taney said that Massachusetts, in chartering the Charles River Bridge, had not agreed to create a monopoly that closed off competitors. He ruled that Massachusetts could charter the rival Warren River Bridge because the states should encourage economic competition and technological advances. It did not matter that as a result the stockholders in the Charles River Bridge would lose money. Taney argued that the "creative destruction" of established but idle property in a dynamic market economy is the price of economic and social progress.

Human Property   The defense of property rights was especially and tragically strong when it came to slavery. Until the Civil War, courts in the North and the South consistently upheld the right of slaveholders to recapture fugitive slaves. In his opinion in *Dred Scott* v. *Sandford* (1857)—a case that helped bring on the Civil War—Chief Justice Taney claimed that slaves were not citizens who possessed rights but simply private property belonging to their owners, no different from land or tools.

Economic Liberty After the Civil War

The Fourteenth Amendment, passed after the Civil War, was designed to guarantee the citizenship rights of the newly freed slaves. It included a clause—the **due process clause**—stating that no state "may deprive a person of life, liberty, or property, without due process of law." Strangely, the Supreme Court in the late nineteenth century interpreted this clause as a protection for businesses against the regulatory efforts of the states.

The Court's most famous decision in this regard was *Lochner* v. *New York* (1905). Lochner ran a bakery in Utica, New York. He was convicted of requiring an employee to work more than 60 hours per week, contrary to a New York state maximum-hours statute. But Justice Rufus Peckham wrote for a 5–4 Supreme Court majority that the right of employer and employee to negotiate hours of work was part of the "liberty" of which, under the Fourteenth Amendment, no person could be deprived without due process of law. In other words, New York State had no right to regulate the hours of labor.

The nineteenth century was an era in which the rights of property were expanded, refined, and altered to become consistent with an emerging, dynamic industrial economy. The twentieth century would bring new approaches to property rights and to political liberties in general. These new approaches would be triggered by structural transformations in the economy and culture, the efforts of new political groups and movements, and the actions of government officials, all of which we will examine in greater detail.

due process clause
The section of the Fourteenth Amendment that prohibits states from depriving anyone of life, liberty, or property "without due process of law," a guarantee against arbitrary or unfair government action.

Nationalization of the Bill of Rights

Americans rightly understand the Bill of Rights to be a foundation of American freedom. Until the twentieth century, however, the protections of the Bill of Rights did not apply to the states, only to the national government. The Supreme Court only gradually applied the Bill of Rights to the states through a process known as *selective incorporation*.

Selective Incorporation

The framers were worried more about national government intrusions on individual freedom than about state government intrusions. Most of the states, after all, had bills of rights in their own constitutions, and, being closer to the people, state governments would be less likely to intrude on the people's freedom, or so the framers believed. This reading of the Bill of Rights as a prohibition of certain actions by the national government seems explicit in the language of many of the first 10 amendments. The first, for instance, starts with the words "*Congress shall make no law . . . .*" This understanding of the Bill of Rights as a set of prohibitions against certain actions by the national government and not the states was confirmed by John Marshall in *Barron* v. *Baltimore* (1833). It is apparent that the majority in Congress wanted to change the reach of the Bill of Rights, extending it to the states, however, when it approved the Fourteenth Amendment after the Civil War. Three clauses in this amendment specify that the states cannot violate the rights and liberties of the people living in them:

- The first specifies that all persons born or naturalized in the United States are citizens of both the United States and the states in which they reside.

- The **privileges and immunities clause** specifies that no *state* "shall make or enforce any law which shall abridge the privileges or immunities of citizens of the United States."

- The due process clause specifies that no *state* shall "deprive any person of life, liberty, or property, without due process of law."

Although Congress wrote the Fourteenth Amendment to guarantee that states would protect all of U.S. citizens' rights and liberties, including those found in the Bill of Rights, the Supreme Court was very slow in **nationalizing** or **incorporating** the Bill of Rights, making it binding on the state governments. Indeed, the Supreme Court has not yet fully incorporated or nationalized the Bill of Rights. Rather, it has practiced what constitutional scholars term **selective incorporation,** only slowly adding, step-by-step, even traditional civil liberties to the constitutional obligations of the states.

Standards for Incorporation

How does the Supreme Court decide whether to incorporate some portion of the Bill of Rights? That is, what standard does the Court use to protect a liberty specified in the Bill of Rights from violation by a state government? The answer is quite simple and is spelled out, strange as it may seem, in footnote 4 of the opinion of the Court in *United States* v. *Carolene Products Company* (1938), written by Justice Harlan Fiske Stone. Stone suggested that most legislative enactments by states should be considered constitutional and subject

privileges and immunities clause
The portion of Article IV, Section 2, of the Constitution that states that citizens from out of state have the same legal rights as local citizens in any state.

nationalizing
The process by which provisions of the Bill of Rights become incorporated. See *incorporation*.

incorporation
The gradual use of the Fourteenth Amendment by the Supreme Court to make the Bill of Rights and other constitutional protections binding on the states.

selective incorporation
The U.S. Supreme Court's gradual and piecemeal making of the protections of the Bill of Rights binding on the states.

Whereas the Second Amendment makes it difficult for Congress to pass laws restricting the sale and use of firearms, states can do so more easily because the Second Amendment has not yet been incorporated by the Supreme Court.

only to **ordinary scrutiny** by the Court. However, the footnote declares, three classes of state actions would automatically be presumed unconstitutional, the burden being on the states to prove otherwise. When state actions are presumed to be unconstitutional, the Court is said to be exercising **strict scrutiny.** The three classes of suspect state actions that bring strict scrutiny are those that seem to

- Contradict specific prohibitions in the Constitution, including those of the Bill of Rights.
- Restrict the democratic process.
- Discriminate against racial, ethnic, or religious minorities.

The first of these is the subject matter of this chapter. The second has been addressed at several points in the text. The third is the subject of Chapter 16. In the remainder of this chapter, we focus on specific civil liberties, clarifying their present status in both constitutional law and political practice.

ordinary scrutiny
The assumption that the actions of elected bodies and officials are legal under the Constitution.

strict scrutiny
The assumption that actions by elected bodies or officials violate constitutional rights.

Freedom of Speech

Congress shall make no Law . . . abridging the freedom of speech.
—First Amendment to the U.S. Constitution

Speech can take many forms. The Court has had to consider which forms of speech are protected under the Constitution.

Political Speech For many people, the right to speak one's mind is the first principle of a free and democratic society. Yet the right to free speech was not incorporated (made applicable to state governments) by the Supreme Court until 1925 in *Gitlow* v. *New York* (1925). Benjamin Gitlow had published *The Left Wing Manifesto,* which embraced a militant, revolutionary socialism to mobilize the proletariat to destroy the existing order in favor of communism. Gitlow did not advocate specific action to break the law, but he was nonetheless convicted of a felony under the New York Criminal Anarchy Law (1902).

The Supreme Court majority held that New York State was bound by the First Amendment but then argued that even the First Amendment did not prohibit New York from incarcerating Gitlow for his pamphlet. Said Justice Edward Sanford, "A single revolutionary spark may kindle a fire

Once "free speech" was incorporated by the Supreme Court, states were no longer at liberty to suppress unpopular speech, as many of them had done with some frequency. This radical political rally in Gary, Indiana, in 1919 was broken up by the police soon after this photo was taken.

that, smoldering for a time, may burst into a sweeping and destructive conflagration. It cannot be said that the State is acting . . . unreasonably when . . . it seeks to extinguish the spark without waiting until it has enkindled the flame or blazed into the conflagration." In his famous dissent, Justice Oliver Wendell Holmes said, "Every idea is an incitement . . . Eloquence may set fire to reason. But whatever may be thought of the redundant discourse before us, it had no chance of starting a present conflagration."

Although the *Gitlow* precedent proved to be an important advance for civil liberties in the United States, the Court was still willing to leave Gitlow in jail and allow the states wide latitude in controlling what they considered dangerous speech. For many years, especially during the 1940s and 1950s anti-Communist "Red scare," the Court deferred to political hysteria and allowed the widespread suppression of what we now consider acceptable speech and publication. The Court seldom moved far ahead of the political branches on free speech issues during this period or later.[8]

This early stage of the nationalization of the Bill of Rights by the Court was helped along by a new force, the American Civil Liberties Union (ACLU), which brought the *Gitlow* appeal. Less than 10 years old, the ACLU had little to show for its legal challenges to the suppression of free speech until 1925, when *Gitlow* provided a spark of hope for civil libertarians. The Court's application of the First Amendment to the states provided the ACLU with opportunities to resist censorship and the strangulation of dissent by the states as well as by the national government. Victories remained rare, but the Court's willingness to incorporate free speech encouraged and energized the ACLU.[9]

Freedom of speech has grown in the ensuing years so that far more speech is protected than is not. In general, no U.S. government today may regulate or interfere with the content of speech without a compelling reason. For a reason to be compelling, a government must show that the speech poses a "clear and present danger"—the standard formulated by Holmes in *Schenck* v. *United States* (1919)—that it has a duty to prevent. The danger must be very substantial, and the relationship between the speech and the danger must be direct, such as falsely yelling "Fire!" in a crowded theater. The danger must also be so immediate that the people responsible for maintaining order cannot afford to tolerate the speech. Abstract advocacy of ideas, even ideas considered dangerous by police, politicians, or popular majorities, is protected unless it meets both conditions. Freedom of speech has grown, then, and with it, an important part of democracy in the United States.

For civil libertarians, a disturbing trend is evidence that Americans are becoming increasingly willing to constrain or suppress political speech when it make some members of the larger community uncomfortable. Almost one-third of Americans, for example, "would not allow a rally for a cause or issue that could offend" some members of the community.[10] Two-thirds would be willing to ban speech that was offensive to racial groups; over one-half would forbid speech that offended religious groups.

Actions and Symbolic Speech   Difficult questions about free expression persist, of course. Speech mixed with *conduct* may be restricted if the restrictions are narrowly and carefully tailored to curb the conduct while leaving the speech unmolested. Symbolic expressions (such as wearing armbands or picketing) may also receive less protection from the Court. The use of profanity or words that are likely to cause violence ("fighting words") may be regulated in some cases, as may symbolic actions that prevent others from carrying out legitimate activities. Still, freedom of speech throughout the United States has grown to the point at which contenders wrestle with relatively peripheral issues, leaving a large sphere of expressive freedom. *Texas* v. *Johnson* (1989) shows just how far the protection of free speech has expanded. In this case, Gregory Johnson challenged a Texas state law against flag desecration under which he had been convicted for burning an American flag as part of a demonstration at the 1984 Republican convention. Although dominated by a conservative majority, the Rehnquist Court overturned the Texas law, saying that flag

Visual Literacy

What Speech Is Protected by the Constitution

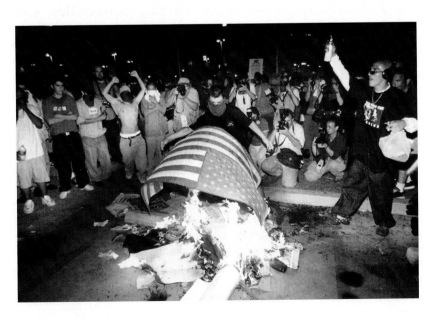

Can state legislatures or Congress pass laws prohibiting flag burning? Although many Americans are infuriated by flag burning, the Supreme Court has ruled that such laws violate freedom of expression.

Senator Joseph McCarthy issues a warning about the "Red tide" of communism sweeping the nation. McCarthy discovered few communists but managed to wreck the lives of many innocent people and created an atmosphere that threatened liberty in the United States for many years in the 1950s.

Timeline

Civil Liberties and
National Security

burning falls under the free expression protections of the Constitution unless imminent incitement or violence is likely.

Suppression of Free Expression   A major exception to the expansion of freedom of expression has been the periodic concern about "internal security." The past century has witnessed several periods when dissenters and radicals were persecuted for their political speech and writings. Censorship of dissent and protests occurring during and after World War I; 32 states enacted laws to suppress dangerous ideas and talk, and local, state, and national officials led raids on the offices of "radicals." Hoping to become president, New York State Attorney General A. Mitchell Palmer conducted raids on the headquarters of suspect organizations in 1919 and 1920, sending the young J. Edgar Hoover out to collect information on radicals and nonconformists.

A similar period of hysteria followed World War II. Its foundations were laid when the Democrat-controlled House of Representatives created the House Committee on Un-American Affairs (generally referred to as the HUAC). When the Republicans won control of the Congress, they professed to see security risks in the Truman administration and Hollywood. Soon Democrats and Republicans alike were exploiting the "Red scare" for political gain. The greatest gain (and, subsequently, the hardest fall) was for Senator Joseph McCarthy (R–WI). McCarthy brandished lists of purported communists and denounced all who opposed him as traitors.[11]

High emotions in the days immediately following the September 11, 2001, terrorist attacks on the United States caused the speech of some dissenters to be quelled temporarily. One professor at the University of New Mexico faced a disciplinary hearing after remarking in class that "anybody who can blow up the Pentagon gets my vote." A librarian at UCLA was suspended after he sent out an e-mail to people on campus decrying American support for Israeli terrorism as the root cause of the terrorist attacks on the United States. Authorities said the views he expressed created a hostile climate for Jewish students.

Many civil libertarians also worry about the possible chilling effect on free speech of new laws—including the 2001 USA Patriot Act—and new administrative procedures for strict treatment outside the normal judicial process of suspected enemy combatants and supporters of terrorist organizations. Will some people be unwilling to criticize government policies regarding the war on terrorism for fear of being brought to the attention of the authorities? Only time will tell.

Balancing Liberty and Security

Freedom of the Press

Congress shall make no law . . . abridging the freedom . . . of the press.
—FIRST AMENDMENT TO THE U.S. CONSTITUTION

In an aside in the opinion of the Court in *Gitlow* v. *New York* (1925), the Supreme Court included freedom of the press as a freedom guaranteed against state interference by the Fourteenth Amendment. Incorporation of this aspect of the Bill of Rights seems reasonable in light of the importance of the free flow of information in a society that aspires to freedom and democracy. In *Near* v. *Minnesota* (1931), the Court made good on the promise of *Gitlow* by invalidating the Minnesota Public Nuisance Law as a violation of freedom of the press.[12] Jay Near published the *Saturday Press,* a scandal sheet that attacked local crime, public officials, and a few other groups that he disliked: Jews, Catholics, blacks, and unions, for example. Near and his associates were ordered by a state court not to publish, sell, or possess the *Saturday Press.* This sort of state action is called **prior restraint,** because it prevents publication before it has occurred. Freedom of the press is not necessarily infringed if publishers are sued or punished for harming others after they have published, but Minnesota was trying to keep Near and his associates from publishing in the future.

prior restraint
The government's power to prevent publication, as opposed to punishment afterward.

Prior Restraint   The prohibition of prior restraint on publication remains the core of freedom of the press. Freedom of the press and freedom of speech tend to be considered together as freedom of expression, so the general principles applicable to free speech apply to freedom of the press as well. Thus, the Court will allow the repression of publication only if the state can show some "clear and present danger" that publication poses, similar to its position on free speech. In *New York Times* v. *United States* (1971), the Court ruled that the U.S. government could not prevent newspapers from publishing portions of the Pentagon Papers, secret government documents revealing the sordid story of how the United States had become involved in the Vietnam War. A major expansion of freedom of the press in *New York Times* v. *Sullivan* (1964) protects newspapers against punishment for trivial or incidental errors when they are reporting on public persons. This limits the use or threat of libel prosecutions by officials because officials can recover damages only by showing that the medium has purposely reported untruths or has made no effort to find out if what is being reported is true.

Offensive Mass Media   The limits of freedom of expression are often tested by media publications that offend many Americans. Pornography, for example, has challenged the ability of citizens, legislatures, and courts to distinguish art from trash that degrades human beings. Typically, communities and legislatures have tried to regulate or eliminate pornography, while civil liberties lawyers and courts have tried to leave choices up to consumers and the market.

Pornography is a nonlegal term for sexual materials: the legal term is **obscenity.** Although the courts have held that *obscenity* is unprotected by the

obscenity
As defined by the Supreme Court, the representation of sexually explicit material in a manner that violates community standards and is without redeeming social importance or value.

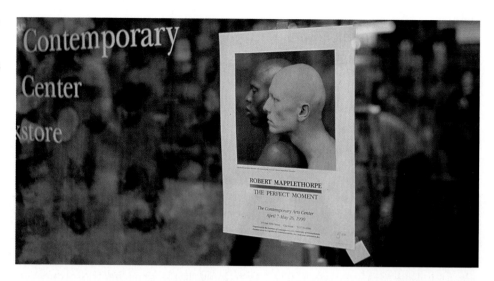

The distinction between art and obscenity can be very difficult to establish, and battles over the banning of controversial works, such as Robert Mapplethorpe's homoerotic photographs, are quite common in American communities.

First Amendment, the definition of obscenity has provoked constitutional struggles for half a century. Early disputes concerned the importation and mailing of works that we regard today as classics: James Joyce's *Ulysses* and D. H. Lawrence's *Lady Chatterley's Lover,* for example.[13] Although the justices admitted that principled distinctions sometimes eluded them (Justice Potter Stewart once said that he did not know how to define hard-core pornography but that he knew it when he saw it), a reasonably clear three-part test emerged from *Miller* v. *California* (1973):

1. The average person, applying contemporary community standards, must find that the work as a whole appeals to the prurient interest (lust).
2. The state law must specifically define what sexual conduct is obscene.
3. The work as a whole must lack serious literary, artistic, political, or scientific value.

If the work survives even one part of this test, it is not legally obscene and is protected by the First Amendment. Community standards, applied by juries, are used to judge whether the work appeals to lust and whether the work is clearly offensive. However, literary, artistic, political, and scientific value (called the *LAPS test,* after the first letter of each of the four values) is *not* judged by community standards but by the jury's assessment of the testimony of expert witnesses. If, and only if, all three standards are met, the Supreme Court will allow local committees to regulate the sale of pornographic materials.

Recently, many Americans have begun to worry about the availability to minors of sexually offensive material on the Internet. Responding to this concern, Congress and President Clinton cooperated in 1996 to pass the Communications Decency Act, which made it a crime to transmit over the Internet or to allow the transmission of indecent materials to which minors might have access. The Supreme Court, in *Reno, Attorney General of the United States* v. *American Civil Liberties Union* (1997), ruled unanimously that the legislation was an unconstitutional violation of the First Amendment, being overly broad and vague and violative of the free speech rights of adults to receive and send information. The strong and unambiguous words of the opinion of the Court make it clear that government efforts to regulate the content of the Internet will not get very far. It may well be the case, however, that Internet-filtering software that allows parents to keep objectionable material from their children will accomplish the same end as government regulation without danger of violating the Constitution.

Free Exercise of Religion

Congress shall make no law . . . prohibiting the free exercise [of religion].
— FIRST AMENDMENT TO THE U.S. CONSTITUTION

For much of our history, Congress did not impede the exercise of religion because it did not legislate much on the subject. Because the states were not covered by the First Amendment, the free exercise of religion was protected by state constitutions or not at all. The Supreme Court was content to defer to the states on issues of religious freedom.

As late as 1940, in *Minersville School District* v. *Gobitis,* the Supreme Court upheld the expulsion of two schoolchildren who refused to salute the flag because it violated their faith as Jehovah's Witnesses. Justice Harlan Stone wrote a stinging dissent:

> *The Constitution expresses more than the conviction of the people that democratic processes must be preserved at all costs. It is also an expression of faith and a command that freedom of mind and spirit must be preserved, which government must obey, if it is to adhere to that justice and moderation without which no free government can exist.*

Stone's dissent, as well as a series of decisions deferring to state restrictions on Jehovah's Witnesses in 1941 and 1942, eventually moved other justices to Stone's side. In *West Virginia* v. *Barnette* (1943), the Court reversed *Gobitis* and firmly established free exercise of religion as protected against the states.

The core of the nationalized **free exercise clause** today is that government may not interfere with religious *beliefs*. This is one of the few absolutes in U.S. constitutional law. Religious *actions,* however, are not absolutely protected. The Court has upheld state laws, for instance, outlawing the use of peyote (an illegal hallucinogen) in Native American religious ceremonies (*Employment Division* v. *Smith,* 1990). Congress and President Clinton tried to overturn this decision with the Religious Freedom Restoration Act in 1993, but the Act was declared unconstitutional in *City of Boerne* v. *Flores* (1997) because the Act, in view of the Court majority, unduly extended national government power over the states.

free exercise clause
That portion of the First Amendment to the Constitution that prohibits Congress from impeding religious observance or impinging upon religious beliefs.

Establishment of Religion

Congress shall make no law respecting an establishment of religion.
— FIRST AMENDMENT TO THE U.S. CONSTITUTION

Freedom of conscience requires that government not favor one religion over another by granting it special favors, privileges, or status. It requires, in Jefferson's famous terms, "a wall of separation between church and state." Nevertheless, incorporation of the **establishment clause** proved to be a particularly messy matter. In *Everson* v. *Board of Education* (1947), Justice Hugo Black for the Supreme Court determined that no state could use revenues to support an institution that taught religion, thus incorporating the First Amendment ban into the Fourteenth Amendment. But the majority in that

establishment clause
The part of the First Amendment to the Constitution that prohibits Congress from establishing an official religion; the basis for the doctrine of the separation of church and state.

case upheld the New Jersey program that reimbursed parents for bus transportation to parochial schools. A year later, Justice Black wrote another opinion incorporating the establishment clause in *McCollum* v. *Board of Education* (1948). This time, a program for teaching religion in public schools was found unconstitutional. In *Zorach* v. *Clauson* (1952), however, the Court upheld a similar program in New York State that let students leave school premises early for religious instruction. The establishment clause had been incorporated, but the justices were having a difficult time determining what "separation of church and state" meant in practice.

The *Lemon* Test   The Warren Court (1953–1969) brought together a solid church–state separationist contingent whose decisions the early Burger Court (1969–1973) distilled into the major doctrine of the establishment clause: the "*Lemon* test." In *Lemon* v. *Kurtzman* (1971), Chief Justice Warren Burger specified three conditions that every law must meet to avoid "establishing" religion:

1. The law must have a secular *purpose*. That secular purpose need not be the only or primary purpose behind the law. The Court requires merely some plausible nonreligious reason for the law.

2. The *primary effect* of the law must be neither to advance nor to retard religion. The Court will assess the probable effect of a governmental action for religious neutrality.

3. Government must never foster *excessive entanglements* between the state and religion.

While lawyers and judges frequently disagree about each of the three "prongs" of the *Lemon* test, the test has erected substantial walls that bar mixing church and state. The Rehnquist Court has been taking many of the bricks out of the walls, however. In *Rosenberger* v. *University of Virginia* (1995), it ruled that the university (a state-supported institution) must provide the same financial subsidy to a student religious publication that it provides to other student publications. In 2002, in *Zelman* v. *Simmons-Harris*, decided by a 5–4 vote, the Court approved Cleveland's program of school vouchers that provides public money to parents who want to send their children to private schools, whether secular or religious. The Court majority based its ruling on the fact that public monies do not go directly to religious schools in the Cleveland program but rather to parents who are free to choose their children's school(s). It remains too early at this writing to know whether this decision will encourage the spread of vouchers, a goal long cherished by conservatives.

Remaining in the wings are a range of issues involving the separation of church and state that the Court will eventually consider, given the number of cases that are working their way up from state courts and federal district courts. These include cases about the display of religious symbols in government buildings, the legitimacy of the words "one nation under God" in the Pledge of Allegiance, the acceptability of the nondenominational prayers that open the daily sessions in Congress, and more. In a 2004 decision, for example, the Court ruled that the state of Washington had done no constitutional harm when it denied a state-funded scholarship to a student studying for the ministry. The point here is fairly straightforward: The debate over where to draw the line that separates church and state is a continuing one in America and is unlikely to be resolved once and for all.

School Prayer   One of the most controversial aspects of constitutional law regarding the establishment of religion concerns school prayer. Although a majority of Americans support allowing a nondenominational prayer or a pe-

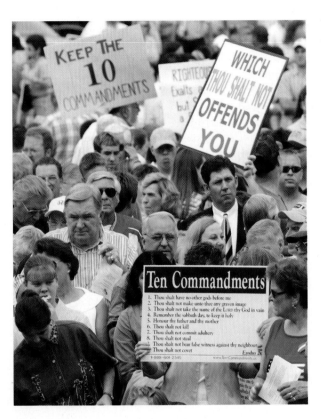

The church–state separation issue continues to generate controversy in American politics. Here, religious protestors in 2004 object to a federal court decree ordering the removal of a large and prominently displayed statue of the Ten Commandments from the Alabama state court house.

riod of silent prayer in the schools, the Court has consistently ruled against such practices since the early 1960s. In *Engel* v. *Vitale* (1962), the Court ordered the state of New York to suspend its requirement that all students in public schools recite a nondenominational prayer at the start of each school day. Writing for the majority, Justice Hugo Black found the prayer requirement

Web Exploration
Disputes About Religious Freedom

Issue: Americans continue to disagree with one another about the meaning of religious freedom.

Site: Access the Christian Coalition and Americans United for the Separation of Church and State on our Website at **www.ablongman.com/ greenberg**. Go to the "Web Explorations" section for Chapter 15. Select "Disputes About . . . ," then "religious freedom." Examine the "press room" section of both organizations.

What You've Learned: Compare which issues each organization focuses on and how the issues are treated by each. Which site is closer to reflecting your own understanding of religious freedom? Do you believe there is common ground upon which the two groups might meet, or do you believe that the differences in view are irreconcilable?

HINT: Your views on religious freedom probably depend not only on your specific religious views but also on your support for the doctrine of "separation of church and state."

to be a state-sponsored religious activity "wholly inconsistent with the establishment clause." In *Stone* v. *Graham* (1980), the Court ruled against posting the Ten Commandments in public school classrooms. In *Lee* v. *Weisman* (1992), it ruled against allowing school-sponsored prayer at graduation ceremonies. In *Santa Fe Independent School District* v. *Doe* (2000), the Court ruled that student-led prayers at school-sponsored events such as football games are not constitutionally permissible because they have the "improper effect of coercing those present to participate in an act of religious worship." In these and other cases the Court has consistently ruled against officially sponsored prayer in public schools as a violation of the separation of church and state. The Court has been willing, however, to allow religious groups to meet in public schools and to allow students to pray on their own or in unofficial study groups while on public school premises.

Returning prayer to the public schools and making schools less secular are very high on the agenda of religious conservatives. Bills supporting voluntary classroom prayer (such as a moment of silent contemplation) are constantly being introduced into Congress and state legislatures, with little success so far. Christian conservatives have also tried without success to pass a school prayer constitutional amendment. In several very religious communities, school officials have simply ignored the Supreme Court and continue to allow prayer in public classrooms.

With no sign that the tide of religious feeling is about to recede in the United States, school prayer, and the question of where to draw the line between church and state in general, are likely to be with us for some time to come.

Privacy

The freedoms addressed so far—speech, press, and religion—are explicitly mentioned in the Bill of Rights. The freedom to be left alone in our private lives—what is usually referred to as the *right to privacy*—is nowhere mentioned. Nevertheless, most Americans consider the right to privacy one of our most precious freedoms; most believe we ought to be spared wire-tapping, e-mail snooping, and the regulation of consensual sexual activities in our own homes, for instance. Many (though not all) constitutional scholars believe, moreover, that a right to privacy is *inherent* (there, but not explicitly stated) in the Bill of Rights; note the prohibitions against illegal searches and seizures and against quartering of troops in our homes, as well as the right to free expression and conscience. Such scholars also point to the Ninth Amendment as evidence that the framers believed in the existence of liberties not specifically mentioned in the Bill of Rights: "The enumeration in the Constitution of certain rights, shall not be construed to deny or disparage others retained by the people." The Supreme Court agreed with this position in *Griswold* v. *Connecticut* (1965), in which it ruled that a constitutional right to privacy exists when it struck down laws making birth control illegal. *Griswold*'s right to privacy doctrine later became an important precedent in *Roe* v. *Wade* (1973), in which the Court ruled in favor of a woman's right to terminate her pregnancy. The right to privacy was also an important component in the Court's decision in 2003 that state anti-sodomy laws prohibiting consensual gay and lesbian sexual relations are unconstitutional.

It is relatively unclear yet whether the courts will support a privacy-based "right to die." So far the Supreme Court has refused to endorse the existence of such a right. Indeed, in *Vacco* v. *Quill* (1997), it threw out two federal circuit court decisions that had overturned state laws in Washington and New York banning doctor-assisted suicide as unconstitutional. The Court majority ruled that states were free to ban doctor-assisted suicide because there is no constitutionally protected right to die. Their ruling did not prohibit states from passing laws establishing such a right, however. Indeed, five of the justices suggested in their written opinions that they might support a claim for the existence of such a right in the future.

In 2004, the Ninth Circuit Court of Appeals upheld Oregon's assisted suicide law passed by voters in 1994. In its opinion the justices strongly criticized Attorney General John Ashcroft's announcement that any doctor prescribing drugs that are used by patients to end their lives would be subject to prosecution under the federal Controlled Substances Act, saying that his action "far exceeds the scope of his authority under federal law."

Rights of the Accused

Five of the 10 amendments that make up the Bill of Rights concern protections for individuals suspected, accused, or convicted of a crime, suggesting that the framers were deeply concerned about this aspect of freedom. Most Americans today treasure the constitutional rights and liberties that protect innocent individuals from wrongful prosecution and imprisonment. But most Americans also want to control crime as much as possible. Balancing the two sentiments is not easy. Those alarmed by lawlessness—actual or imagined—tend to support "whatever it takes" to reduce that lawlessness, even if the rights or liberties of others must be restricted. Others are more alarmed by the lawlessness—real or imagined—of police and prosecutors. These advocates of due process values see violations of rights and liberties as unnecessary and dangerous in a free society. Many due process advocates have become especially concerned about the actions of federal officials that seem to endanger traditional liberties in the name of anti-terrorism and homeland security—issues that we will examine in more detail later.

Participation

Privacy and Rights of the Accused

During the 1950s and 1960s, the Warren Court favored the due process approach and subjected the states' criminal procedures to rigorous interpretations of constitutional guarantees. Increased protections for criminal defendants, however, gave many political candidates an electorally useful explanation for rising crime: Too much regard for "legal technicalities" was "coddling" the guilty and "handcuffing" the police. The backlash led to presidential judicial appointments during the 1970s, 1980s, and 1990s—mainly but not solely by Republican presidents—that favored judges more sympathetic to preserving law and order and less insistent on protecting the rights of suspects and defendants. This led to a gradual change in the law and order/due process balance in the federal courts. We can see these trends in the decisions of the Supreme Court. The Warren Court (1953–1969) expanded due process, preferring constitutional guarantees to efficient law enforcement. The Burger Court (1969–1986) preserved most of the basic due process decisions that the Warren Court had crafted but limited the further growth of protections and introduced many exceptions. The Rehnquist Court that followed has reversed several due process protections.

Unreasonable Searches and Seizures   Consider, for example, the Fourth Amendment, which secures the right of all persons against unreasonable searches and seizures and allows the granting of search warrants only if the police can specify evidence of serious lawbreaking that they reasonably expect to find. Until the Warren Court compelled the states to abide by the Fourth Amendment in 1961, they had frequently used searches and seizures that the federal courts would consider "unreasonable" in an effort to control crime.

The right to due process when accused of a federal crime was part of the Constitution from the outset, but it was the Supreme Court's *Miranda* decision in 1966 that required law enforcement officials in states and localities to inform the accused of their rights at the time of arrest.

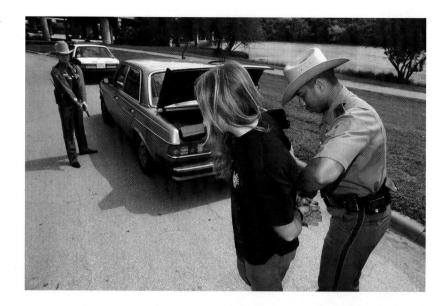

exclusionary rule

A standard promulgated by the Supreme Court that prevents police and prosecutors from using evidence against a defendant that was obtained in an illegal search.

In *Mapp* v. *Ohio* (1961), the Supreme Court enunciated the **exclusionary rule** to prevent the police and prosecutors from using evidence that had been gained through warrantless and unreasonable searches to convict people. In this case, the police forcibly entered the apartment of Dollree Mapp looking for a fugitive. They found no fugitive but decided to search Mapp's apartment anyway, even though they had no search warrant. Finding what they considered obscene photos and books, they arrested Mapp under Ohio's law covering the possession of obscene materials. She was convicted, an action later supported by the Ohio Supreme Court. The conviction was overturned by the U.S. Supreme Court. A majority of the justices believed that the threat of perpetrators' being freed in cases like this would force the police to play by the constitutional rules. The justices did not believe that due process threatened crime control because police lawlessness was not the only way to deal with crime.

The Warren Court demanded that the police get warrants whenever the person to be subjected to a search had a "reasonable expectation of privacy."[14] The Burger Court limited the places in which privacy could be reasonably expected, allowing searches of moving cars stopped even for routine traffic infractions and of garbage cans set out for collection. The Burger Court authorized a "good faith" exception to the exclusionary rule, under which prosecutors may introduce evidence obtained illegally if they can show that the police had relied on a warrant that appeared valid but later proved to be invalid.[15] The Court allowed another exception for illegally gathered evidence that would have been discovered eventually without the illegal search.[16] The Rehnquist Court went well beyond these exceptions. In *Murray* v. *United States* (1988), it allowed prosecutors to use products of illegal searches if other evidence unrelated to the illegal evidence would have justified a search warrant. The combination of "good faith," "inevitable discovery," and "retroactive probable cause" has considerably narrowed the exclusionary rule.

The Rehnquist Court continued to narrow the exclusionary rule when it held in *Minnesota* v. *Carter* (1998) that an officer acting on a drug tip could peer through the gap in Venetian blinds to observe illegal activity without violating the Fourth Amendment. When the Court announced in *Wyoming* v. *Houghton* (1999) that police who have probable cause to search an automobile for illegal substances may also search personal possessions (in this case, a purse) of passengers in the car, the War on Drugs seemed to be trumping privacy. However, the Court also ruled that police could not search every driver or car involved in petty traffic offenses. Thus, a bag of marijuana discovered in a search incident to a speeding ticket in *Knowles* v. *Iowa* (1998) was excluded as the product of an illegal search. Moreover, the Court ruled in *Kyllo* v. *United States* (2001) that police could not use high-technology thermal devices to search through the walls of a house to check for the presence of high-intensity lights used for growing marijuana. Justice Scalia was especially incensed, saying in his opinion that to allow such searches "would leave the homeowner at the mercy of advancing technology . . . ." These four cases show that the fine tuning of the "exclusionary rule" continues.

You Are a Police Officer

Self-Incrimination   Concerning the Fifth Amendment protection against self-incrimination, the Warren Court similarly waxed, the Burger Court waffled, and the Rehnquist Court waned. The Warren Court determined that the privilege not to be forced to incriminate oneself was useless at trial if the police coerced confessions long before the trial took place. To forestall "third-degree" tactics in the station house, the Court detailed a stringent set of procedural guarantees: the famous rights established in *Miranda* v. *Arizona* (1966). Once detained by authorities, all persons had to be informed of their rights to remain silent and to consult with an attorney. Although the Burger Court upheld *Miranda,* it allowed exceptions: It allowed the use of information obtained without "Mirandizing" suspects if the suspects took the stand in their own defense. It also allowed the use of information obtained without *Miranda* warnings if some immediate threat to public safety had justified immediate questioning and postponing warnings.[17] The Rehnquist Court went beyond these exceptions when it held that a coerced confession may be "harmless error" that does not constitute self-incrimination.[18] The main principle of the Miranda decision was upheld by the Rehnquist Court, however, in *Dickerson* v. *United States* (2000) and reaffirmed in three 2004 decisions.

The Right to Counsel   The Sixth Amendment's right to counsel was nationalized—made binding on the states—in two landmark cases. In *Powell* v. *Alabama* (1932)—the famed Scottsboro Boys prosecution—the Court ruled that legal counsel must be supplied to all indigent defendants accused of a **capital crime** (any crime in which the death penalty can be imposed). Before this decision, many poor people in the southern states, especially African Americans, had been tried for and convicted of capital crimes without the benefit of an attorney. Thirty-one years later, in *Gideon* v. *Wainwright* (1963), the Court ruled that defendants accused of any felony in state jurisdictions are entitled to a lawyer and that the states must supply a lawyer when a defendant cannot afford to do so. In this case, Clarence Earl Gideon asked for but was denied a lawyer in a Florida court where he was being tried for having broken into a poolhall. He conducted his own defense and lost. After years of study in his Florida prison's law library and the submission of numerous handwritten appeals to the courts to overturn his conviction, the Supreme Court finally agreed to hear his case, assigning the prominent attorney Abe Fortas (later a Supreme Court justice) to argue for Gideon. Justice Black wrote the following for a unanimous Court:

capital crime
Any crime for which death is a possible penalty.

> *Not only . . . precedents but also reason and reflection require us to recognize that in our adversary system of criminal justice, any person hauled into court, who is too poor to hire a lawyer, cannot be assured of a fair trial unless counsel is provided for him. This seems to be an obvious truth.*

The right to counsel for those accused of a felony crime was not binding on the states until 1963. Here, an attorney vigorously defends her client in a Los Angeles court room.

The Court ordered a new trial. This time, assisted by a public defender supplied by the state of Florida, Gideon was acquitted. By incorporating the Sixth Amendment's guarantee of legal counsel, the Court has ensured that every criminal defendant in the United States can mount a defense regardless of socioeconomic status.

Capital Punishment   The Burger Court examined capital punishment under the Eighth Amendment's prohibition of "cruel and unusual punishment." In *Furman* v. *Georgia* (1972), a split Court found that the death penalty, as used, constituted "cruel and unusual punishment." Congress and 70 percent of the states passed new authorizations of the death penalty, most of which met the Court's objections with procedures to make the infliction of capital punishment less capricious. The Burger Court held in *Gregg* v. *Georgia* (1976) that capital punishment was not inherently cruel or unusual. However, the Court tended to create an "obstacle course" of standards that the states had to meet if they wanted to use the death penalty. Basically, the Court insisted that defendants be given every opportunity to show mitigating circumstances so that as few convicts as possible would be killed.

The Rehnquist Court at first tried to expedite the use of the death penalty. (Some of the reasons are examined in the "Using the Framework" feature.) In *McCleskey* v. *Kemp* (1987), the Court chose to ignore statistical evidence that blacks who kill whites are four times more likely to be sentenced to death than whites who kill blacks. The Court insisted that individual defendants must show that racism played a role in their specific cases. In *Penry* v. *Lynaugh* (1989), the Court allowed the execution of a convicted murderer who had the intelligence of a seven-year-old. In *Stanford* v. *Kentucky* (1989), the Court allowed the execution of a minor who had been convicted of murder. The Court has decided to revisit this issue, however, in a case involving a Missouri man sentenced to death for a murder he committed when he was not yet 18.

The Rehnquist Court also limited avenues of appeal and delay in death penalty cases. In *McCleskey* v. *Zant* (1991), the Court made delays much less likely by eliminating many means of challenging capital convictions. In its 6–3

Using the Framework

The Death Penalty
Why was there such a dramatic increase in executions in the 1990s?

Background: Between the reinstatement of the death penalty by the Supreme Court in 1976 and the end of 2001, 737 inmates were executed in the United States. Of that total, 619 (84 percent) took place in the 1990s. In 1999, 98 executions were carried out, the highest total since 1951, with Texas, Virginia, and Florida leading the way. Although a range of individuals and organizations have been fighting to end the use of the death penalty in the United States, their efforts have been strikingly unsuccessful until quite recently. We can understand better why this is so by looking broadly at how structural, political linkage, and governmental factors have influenced the death penalty issue.

Governmental Action

38 states allow use of the death penalty; of these, 30 have used it since 1976.

The pace of executions increased steadily during the 1990s, though it slowed in 2000 and 2001.

Governmental Level

Since 1976, the Supreme Court has supported most state efforts to reinstate the death penalty and to limit the time and number of appeals for death-row inmates. ➡ The Anti-Terrorism and Effective Death Penalty Act of 1996, passed by a Republican Congress and signed by Democratic president Bill Clinton, placed limits on the appeals process and hastened the execution of many inmates. ➡ Elected on "get tough on crime" platforms, few governors responded favorably to requests for clemency in death penalty cases.

Political Linkages Level

Public opinion has strongly supported the principle of capital punishment. ➡ Fear of crime among the public rose throughout the 1980s and 1990s, contributing to the supportive public climate for use of the death penalty; rising fear was a response to both a real increase in violent crime and to news media sensationalism. ➡ In response to the public mood during this period, most candidates for elected office took a strong "tough on crime" approach. ➡ Opponents of capital punishment were not successful in changing public or leadership attitudes.

Structural Level

The Constitution leaves most of the responsibility for criminal statute writing, prosecution, and punishment to the states. ➡ The Constitution prohibits "cruel and unusual punishment," but there is little evidence that the framers considered the death penalty, as such, "cruel and unusual." ➡ The popular culture has long supported the death penalty. ➡ Violent crime, much of it drug-related, increased during the 1970s, 1980s, and early part of the 1990s.

The execution by the state of Texas of born-again Christian and convicted murderer Karla Faye Tucker in February 1998 brought the issue of capital punishment to the forefront of network news, news magazines, radio talk shows, and newspapers across America. Tucker was the first woman executed in Texas since the Civil War.

decision, the majority reached out to eliminate delays even though no party to the case had requested the Court to do so. In *Keeney* v. *Tamayo-Reyes* (1992), the Court limited the right of "death row" inmates convicted in state courts to appeal to the Supreme Court. The Court is never entirely predictable, however. In *Wright* v. *West* (1992), it rejected Bush administration efforts to sharply restrict appeals by state prisoners to the federal courts.

The environment for the use of the death penalty became steadily more favorable from the middle of the 1960s to the middle of the 1990s. The Court removed most of the obstacles to its use, and public opinion swung solidly in favor. Given this context, it is hardly surprising, then, that the number of people executed in the United States in 1999 reached its highest level (98) since 1976 when the Court reinstated the death penalty, with Texas accounting for more than one-third of the total[19] (see Figure 15.1).

Race and the Death Penalty

Although still strongly in favor of capital punishment in principle, the public and many elected officials seem to be having second thoughts about how fairly it is used in practice. Most of the rethinking about the death penalty seems to be based on rising concerns about executing the mentally retarded, the quality of legal defense for those accused of murder, the fairness of the system toward racial minorities, and the desire to see a wider use of DNA evidence. Interestingly, several committed conservatives, including columnist George Will and Christian conservative Pat Robertson, have expressed reservations about how the death penalty is applied in practice.

The concern about fairness led Governor George Ryan of Illinois in 2002 to impose a moratorium on capital punishment while a state commission studied the fairness of trials and sentencing procedures and, after the commission reported its negative results, to commute the sentences of all death row inmates in Illinois in 2003. Maryland Governor Parris Blendening also imposed a death penalty moratorium in 2002, while legislatures in more than a dozen states began considering the moratorium issue. Eight other states enacted laws guaranteeing DNA testing in capital cases after several high-profile death row inmates were exonerated when new evidence based on DNA was introduced on their behalf.

There is further evidence that the death penalty climate is changing in the United States. For example, since reaching its high point in 1999, annual exe-

FIGURE 15.1 ● **Executions in the United States, 1977–2003**

Fueled by fear of violent crime, executions in the United States increased dramatically from the early 1980s to the late 1990s but declined significantly after that as public concerns rose about how fairly the death penalty is used.

Source: Bureau of Justice Statistics, "Capital Punishment 2001" (December 2001); "Executions in Decline," editorial, *The Boulder Daily Camera* (December 30, 2003), p. A8.

cutions have been falling (see Figure 15.1),[20] the number of inmates on death row has reached its lowest number since 1973,[21] and public support for the death penalty (though still high) has dropped 15 percentage points since its high point in 1994. Moreover, by the end of 2003, federal prosecutors were having trouble convincing juries to impose the death penalty; in federal capital trials, Bush administration prosecutors' death penalty success rate was only about 15 percent through 2003, compared with about 50 percent during the 1988–2000 period.[22]

Much to the surprise of seasoned observers, the Rehnquist Court began in 2002 to pull back from its unstinting support for the death penalty. In *Atkins* v. *Virginia* (2002), the Court followed the lead of 18 states in banning the use of the death penalty for mentally retarded defendants saying, in Justice John Paul Stevens's majority opinion, that "a national consensus now rejects such executions as excessive and inappropriate . . . "and that "society views mentally retarded offenders as categorically less culpable than the average criminal." In *Ring* v. *Arizona* (2002), the Court overruled the death sentences of more than 160 convicted killers, declaring that only juries, and not judges, can decide on the use of the death penalty for those convicted of capital crimes. Taken together, these two Court decisions are likely, over the long term, to decrease the number of people executed each year in the United States.

Civil Liberties and the War on Terrorism

As suggested in Chapter 3, wars shift power to the federal government and encourage feelings of patriotism and national unity. Wars also raise legitimate concerns about public safety and national security. Because of these things,

Comparing Civil Liberties

wars have almost always led to some restrictions on civil liberties in democratic countries, including the United States, particularly for those who vocally dissent from the war effort and for those who seem to be associated with the enemy in one way or another. Note, for example, the Alien and Sedition Acts of 1798, the use of military tribunals for civilians during the Civil War, the Red Scare following World War I, the forced internment of Japanese Americans during World War II, and the McCarthy anti-communist hysteria in the early years of the Cold War with the Soviet Union.

As with past American wars, the war on terrorism and its domestic manifestation, homeland security, have generated significant restrictions on civil liberties. How long these restrictions will remain in place and how widely they will be used in practice by the authorities will probably depend on the length of the war on terrorism and on the degree to which the American public feels threatened by terrorism. Although we are only in the early stages of the war against terrorism, civil libertarians—who include in their ranks not only the usual liberal suspects such as the ACLU, but also conservative libertarians such as the CATO Institute, former Congressman Bob Barr, and *New York Times* columnist William Safire—are already quite alarmed by developments. Here is what has happened at this writing:[23]

- The USA Patriot Act, passed soon after the 9/11 attacks on the United States, gave the federal government expanded powers to use wire-tapping and electronic surveillance, impose stricter penalties for harboring or financing terrorists, monitor the banking accounts and e-mail of suspect individuals and organizations, turn away from our borders anyone who endorses terrorism, and detain any noncitizens living in the United States whom the attorney general deems to be a threat to national security.

- President Bush issued executive orders authorizing the use of military tribunals to try any noncitizen, whether arrested here or abroad, suspected of being tied directly or indirectly to acts of terrorism against the United States. The president also ordered the detention of more than

Pakistani and Saudi men and their families line up at a Los Angeles federal building to verify their legal status in the United States under the National Security Entry-Exit Registration System. This program to increase surveillance of men from selected Muslim countries was instituted in the wake of Nine-Eleven.

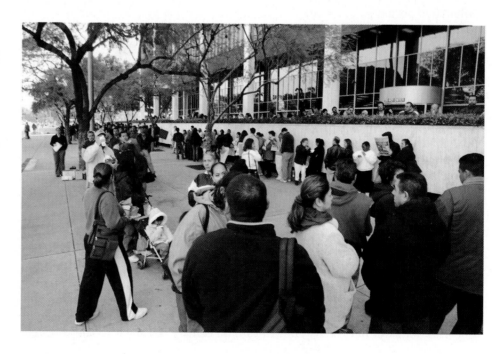

1,200 people for questioning (without releasing their names or specification of crimes purported to have been committed), the questioning of more than 5,000 noncitizens of Middle Eastern and/or Muslim origins about terrorism, the tightening of visa restrictions on people from the Middle East and Muslim countries, and the surveillance of conversations between some suspected terrorists and their attorneys. Claiming extraordinary powers as commander-in-chief in wartime, the president also authorized the indefinite detention of American citizens discovered to have been fighting against U.S. troops in Afghanistan or aiding al Qaeda, designating them "enemy combatants." Finally, the Bush administration instituted secret deportation hearings for detainees held on immigration violations and indefinite detention for people designated "material witnesses" in terrorism cases.

Although Americans have supported most of these homeland security measures—polls show, for example, that strong majorities favor the use of military tribunals, detention of terrorism suspects, restrictions on immigration from the Middle East and other Muslim countries, greater use of electronic surveillance, and more[24]—civil libertarians have won some notable victories in the courts and at other levels of government. City councils in more than 100 cities, including large ones such as Chicago and San Francisco, for example, have passed resolutions of noncooperation with the USA Patriot Act. Some booksellers such as the Tattered Cover in Denver have refused to comply with requests from the FBI to supply lists of customer purchases. A group of former federal prosecutors filed briefs in 2003 challenging the president's authority to jail U.S. citizens as enemy combatants.

Most importantly, perhaps, the courts have begun to look at the issue of the proper balance between security and civil liberties at a time when people feel legitimately threatened by terrorism. For example, the Sixth Circuit Court ruled in 2002 that the government could not hold deportation hearings for Middle Eastern men behind closed doors. Additionally, two federal appeals courts separately ruled in late 2003 that American citizens arrested on U.S. soil could not be held indefinitely simply by designating them "enemy combatants." In early 2004, moreover, a federal district judge invalidated part of the USA Patriot Act, saying that its provision making it a crime to give "expert advice or assistance" is so broad and vague that it threatens the right of free speech. And, in a stunning blow to the Bush administration's claim of extraordinary powers in wartime, the Supreme Court agreed in 2004 that both foreigners and American citizens detained as enemy combatants have a right to contest the bases of their detentions.

The direction that civil liberties will take as a result of the war on terrorism is hard to predict. All we can say with any degree of certainty at this point is that some restrictions will exist for the duration of the war on terrorism and that the severity of these restrictions will be directly related to the degree to which the American people feel afraid that further attacks will occur, and their judgment about how much freedom they are willing to trade for security.

How Democratic Are We?

Civil Liberties and Democracy

PROPOSITION: One reason that democracy is alive and well in the United States is that civil liberties are so well developed and protected.

AGREE: Citizens of the United States live in the freest political society in the world. Powerful constraints prevent government from intruding upon people's ability to believe what they want and to exercise their rights of free expression, association, and petition. Although government has violated several of these rights in the past, political practices and Supreme Court decisions have greatly expanded the domain of political freedom in the current era and made violation of basic civil liberties unlikely in the future. For example, even as the United States fights a war on terrorism and tries to ensure homeland security, the strong tradition of support among elites and the public for civil liberties, and the vigilance of the judiciary, have blocked government officials from going too far in restricting freedom in the name of security.

DISAGREE: This claim cannot be supported for two reasons. First, although freedom exists in theory in the United States, not all people have the capacities and resources to use their liberties effectively. All Americans may enjoy freedom of expression as a formal right, for example, but only a handful can make their voices heard in an effective way. Thus, only a privileged few can make significant campaign contributions; form political lobbying organizations; and run ads for their favorite candidates, parties, and issues. Second, we are in the middle of a war, and we know that civil liberties and war have never comfortably coexisted in the United States. So, we cannot be certain that civil liberties will not be sacrificed for a greater sense of security in a world where terrorists can strike at any time.

CONSIDER: It is important to recognize that the freedoms of speech, association, press, conscience, and religion are far more extensively developed and protected in the United States today than in the past. But we cannot evade the two issues raised in the "disagree" position: the uneven capacity to make use of the available freedoms and the new threat to traditional civil liberties posed by the war on terrorism and homeland security.

- How do you feel about these two "flies in the ointment," as it were?
- Can all Americans avail themselves of the opportunities provided by their civil liberties? • Or are they, in reality, rights whose advantages are useful only to the more educated and economically privileged? • Likewise, do you believe that the war on terrorism and homeland security threaten our freedom? • Or, do you think that this threat has been exaggerated by civil libertarians?

Summary

The formal foundation of American liberties is found in the Constitution and its amendments, particularly the Bill of Rights and the Fourteenth Amendment, but their actual enjoyment depends on the actions of courts, the behavior of government officials, and the struggle for democracy. American history has witnessed an expansion of the boundaries of liberties, especially during the twentieth century, although much remains to be done.

During the nineteenth century, the Supreme Court concerned itself mainly with rights to property. Somewhat belatedly, it nationalized the constitutional protection of civil liberties (i.e., made them applicable to the states) by using the Fourteenth Amendment as its main instrument. The familiar liberties of expression, association, press, and religion, as well as certain due process protections for the accused, were gradually incorporated and guaranteed throughout the nation. The expansion of the rights of the accused was always a hotly disputed political issue, and the conservative orientation of the present Court has resulted in the reversal of many of the due process innovations of the Warren and Burger Courts.

The war on terrorism has resulted in restrictions on the civil liberties of noncitizens living in the United States. How long these restrictions remain in place will depend on the severity and duration of the war on terrorism.

Suggestions for Further Reading

Abraham, Henry J., and Barbara A. Perry. *Freedom and the Court,* 8th ed. Lawrence, KS: University of Kansas Press, 2003.
   A trusted introduction to the study of civil rights and liberties for more than 30 years.

Hentoff, Nat. *Free Speech for Me . . . but Not for Thee: How the American Left and Right Relentlessly Censor Each Other.* New York: HarperPerennial, 1992.
   A disturbing survey of efforts across the nation by both the right and left to censor speech and publications they do not like.

Irons, Peter. *The Courage of Their Convictions.* New York: Free Press, 1988.
   Brief histories of U.S. Supreme Court cases involved in the struggle for civil rights and civil liberties since 1940.

Leone, Richard C., and Greg Anrig, Jr., eds. *The War on Our Freedoms: Civil Liberties in an Age of Terrorism.* New York: Public Affairs Press, 2003.
   A collection of essays decrying the effects of the war on terrorism on American freedoms.

Randall, Richard S. *American Constitutional Development: The Rights of Persons.* New York: Longman, 2003.
   History of, commentary on, and Supreme Court decisions about American liberties.

Walker, Samuel. *In Defense of American Liberties: A History of the ACLU.* New York: Oxford University Press, 1990.
   A comprehensive review of the American Civil Liberties Union, highlighting most major battles for civil liberties in the twentieth century.

Zimring, Franklin. *The Contradictions of American Capital Punishment.* New York: Oxford University Press, 2003.
   Examines the question of why Americans so strongly support the death penalty compared to people in other rich democracies.

Internet Sources

Bureau of Justice Statistics
www.ojp.usdoj.gov/bjs/
   Official statistics on crimes, trials, incarceration rates, executions are available at this site.

The Cato Institute
www.cato.org
   A comprehensive site covering civil liberties issues from the conservative libertarian point of view.

Findlaw Supreme Court Opinions
www.findlaw.com/casecode/supreme.html
   Find historical and contemporary Supreme Court decisions and opinions on civil liberties at this site.

First Amendment Cyber-Tribune
http://w3.trib.com/FACT/index.html
   This comprehensive site is an outstanding gateway to information on the First Amendment freedoms discussed in this chapter and provides links for each freedom to background documents, court cases, breaking news, op-ed pieces, bibliographies, First Amendment Websites, civil liberties organizations, and even an online question-and-answer section.

Chapter 16
Civil Rights: The Struggle for Political Equality

In This Chapter

- Why civil rights are important in a democracy
- Civil rights in the Constitution
- How civil rights protections expanded
- The present status of civil rights protections for racial minorities, women, and gays and lesbians

The Return of Segregated Schools

"I don't know why they left," said one fourth grader at Reid Park Elementary School in Charlotte, North Carolina. "Maybe they didn't like it here."[1] She was referring to the virtual disappearance of white children at her school where, only one year earlier, about one-third of her schoolmates had been white. What was happening at Reid Park Elementary was happening all over the South at the turn of the new century. Fifty years after the Supreme Court had ruled in *Brown* v. *Board of Education* (1954) that "separate but equal" was unconstitutional, schools were becoming more segregated. By 2001, only 30 percent of black children in the South were in schools that were majority white, a decrease from 44 percent as recently as 1988; by 2001, about one-third of black children were in schools that were almost 100 percent black.[2]

For those Americans committed to a racially integrated society, there was much to be proud of in the record of desegregation of public education in the United States after the *Brown* decision, especially in the South where school segregation was official policy from the early twentieth century until the Court's 1954 decision. After a slow start for a few years following *Brown,* school integration took off in the mid-1960s and gained steadily until it reached its peak in the late 1980s. By 1988, only one in four black children were in schools that were 90 to 100 percent black, a far cry from the pre-*Brown* years when virtually all black children were in such schools. During the 1990s, however, the trend reversed all over the South, with more black children going to school where there were few whites or none at all and where white children had less contact with African American children than in many years.[3] (It is worth pointing out, however, that despite the reversal in integration trends in the region, the school integration record of the South remains better than that of any other region of the country; in the Northeast, for example, more than one-half of all African American children are in schools that are 90 to 100 percent black, closely followed by the states in the Midwest. In addition, black children are least exposed to white children in public schools in New York, Illinois, Michigan, California, Maryland, and New Jersey.[4])

So why did the trend in the South toward a more integrated public school system first level off, then recede during the 1990s? The answer is fairly straightforward: The federal courts, following the lead of the Supreme Court in *Dowell* v. *Oklahoma City* (1991)—which ruled that school districts that had made lengthy good-faith efforts to end the effects of pre-

viously legal school segregation in their jurisdictions had fulfilled their constitutional obligations for equal protection of the races in education—began to lift court-ordered desegregation plans that required busing and other methods to integrate schools across local jurisdictions. About 40 school districts over the past 10 years have been relieved of such orders, and it is precisely in these districts where the reversal in school integration trends are most evident.

But that still leaves the question of why lifting federal court orders would lead to such a development. Again, the answer is fairly straightforward: When most whites and most blacks live in racially homogeneous neighborhoods—as they do because of white flight to the suburbs and the existence of informally segregated housing markets—local neighborhood schools, absent busing or other student assignment strategies designed to foster integration, will also be racially homogeneous.

It remains to be seen what the outcomes of these changes will be. Many whites and African Americans believe that integrated schooling, whether achieved voluntarily or under court order, is important for children's educational achievement and for teaching tolerance in a racially diverse society. However, other whites and African Americans believe that integration by itself does little to increase academic achievement, and that court-ordered busing mainly leads to intergroup tensions and wasted tax money. Many African Americans who think this way are becoming attracted to voucher programs that allow children to use public funds to go to either a public or private school as a way to improve schools in predominantly black neighborhoods. The thinking here is that competition for students among schools will force them to offer a better educational product.

Civil rights are government guarantees of political equality and equal treatment—a cornerstone in the promise of equal treatment for all citizens and equal citizenship for all Americans. The expansion of civil rights for African Americans, as well as for other racial, ethnic, and religious minorities and for women, is one of the great achievements of American history. This expansion did not come easily or quickly, however; it took the struggle of millions of Americans to force change from political leaders and government institutions. But change happened, and the result has been the enrichment of American democracy. As this story suggests, however, the expansion of civil rights protections in the United States—as demonstrated by efforts at desegregation begun decades ago—is neither complete nor free of problems, setbacks, and controversy.

Thinking Critically About This Chapter

Using the Framework   In this chapter, you will see that the meaning of civil rights has changed over the course of American history, and you will learn how structural, political linkage, and governmental factors, taken together, explain that change.

Using the Democracy Standard   In this chapter, you will learn how civil rights is at the very center of our understanding of democracy in the United States. You will see, on the one hand, how the struggle for democracy helped expand civil rights protections. You will see, on the other hand, how the expansion of civil rights has enhanced formal political equality in the United States, one of the basic foundations of a democratic political order.

Civil Rights Before the Twentieth Century

civil rights
Government guarantees of political equality and equal treatment.

Concern about **civil rights** protections for women and racial minorities was a comparatively late development in the United States, and most major advances were not evident until well into the twentieth century.

An Initial Absence of Civil Rights

Comparing Civil Rights

Neither the original Constitution nor the Bill of Rights said anything about political equality beyond insisting that all Americans are equally entitled to due process in the courts. Indeed, the word *equality* does not appear in the Constitution at all. Nor did state constitutions offer much in the way of guaranteeing citizenship equality other than equality before the law. Americans in the late eighteenth and early nineteenth centuries seemed more interested in protecting individuals against government (see Chapter 15) than in guaranteeing certain political rights through government.[5] For most racial or ethnic minorities and women, political equality eluded constitutional protection until the twentieth century, although the groundwork was laid earlier.

The political inequality of African Americans and women before the Civil War is quite striking. In the South, African Americans lived in slavery, with no rights at all. Outside the South, although a few states allowed African Americans to vote, the number of states doing so actually declined as the Civil War approached, even as universal white male suffrage was spreading. In

Many African Americans took an active role in fighting for their civil rights before emancipation. Free blacks helped organize the Underground Railroad to smuggle slaves out of the South.

many places outside the slave South, African Americans were denied entry into certain occupations, required to post bonds guaranteeing their good behavior, denied the right to sit on juries, and occasionally threatened and harassed by mobs when they tried to vote or to petition the government. Chief Justice Roger Taney, in *Dred Scott* v. *Sandford* (1857), went so far as to claim that the Founders believed that blacks had no rights that whites or government were bound to honor or respect. As for women, no state allowed them to vote, few allowed them to sit on juries, and a handful even denied them the right to own property or enter into contracts.

Many African Americans and women refused to play a passive political role, however, even though the pre–Civil War period was not conducive to their participation in politics. African Americans, for instance, voted in elections where they were allowed, helped organize the Underground Railroad to smuggle slaves out of the South, and were prominent in the abolitionist movement against slavery. Both black and white women played an important role in the abolitionist movement—the antislavery speaking tours of Angelina and Sarah Grimké caused something of a scandal in the 1840s when women's participation in public affairs was considered improper—and a few began to write extensively on the need for women's emancipation and legal and political equality. In 1848, Elizabeth Cady Stanton issued her call for a convention on women's rights to be held at the village of Seneca Falls, New York. The Declaration of Sentiments and Resolutions issued by the delegates to the convention stands as one of the landmarks in women's struggle for political equality in the United States:

> *All men and women are created equal . . . but the history of mankind is a history of repeated injuries and usurpations on the part of man toward woman, having in direct object the establishment of a direct tyranny over her. . . . [We demand] that women have immediate admission to all the rights and privileges which belong to them as citizens of the United States.*

The Civil War Amendments

After the Civil War, the Thirteenth Amendment to the Constitution outlawed slavery throughout the United States, settling the most divisive issue of the

In 1848, Elizabeth Cady Stanton helped organize the Seneca Falls Convention on women's rights. The resulting Declaration of Sentiments and Resolutions was patterned after the Declaration of Independence, stating that "all men and women are created equal," and included a list of the injustices of men against women.

nineteenth century. The Fourteenth Amendment reversed *Dred Scott* by making all people who are born or naturalized in the United States, black or white, citizens both of the United States and of the states in which they reside. To secure the rights and liberties of recently freed slaves, Article I of the amendment further provided that "no State shall make or enforce any law which shall abridge the privileges or immunities of citizens of the United States" (the *privileges and immunities clause*); "nor shall any State deprive any person of life, liberty, or property, without due process of law" (the *due process clause*); "nor deny to any person within its jurisdiction the equal protection of the laws" (the *equal protection clause*). The Fifteenth Amendment guaranteed African American men the right to vote. Imposing as this constitutional language sounds, the Supreme Court would soon transform it into a protection for property rights, but not for African Americans or women.

Undermining the Civil War Amendments The privileges and immunities clause was rendered virtually meaningless by the *Slaughterhouse Cases* (1873). Writing for the Court, Justice Samuel Miller found that the clause protected only the rights of people as citizens of the United States and were not obligations of state governments. In these cases, the Court denied citizens protection against abuses by state governments, including African Americans disfranchised by state actions. Within five years of its passage, then, the Fourteenth Amendment had been seriously compromised by the Court, which foiled an attempt by the post–Civil War Radical Republican Congress to amend the Constitution in favor of equality.

The equal protection clause survived the *Slaughterhouse Cases* but soon lost all practical meaning. First, the Court said that the Fourteenth Amendment gave Congress no power to prohibit discrimination unless it was practiced by state government. "Equal protection of the laws" did not, therefore, preclude race discrimination by private owners or managers of restaurants, theaters, hotels, and other public accommodations, the Court said in the *Civil Rights Cases* (1883). Then the Court made even state-sponsored discrimination constitutional in *Plessy* v. *Ferguson* (1896). The Court said that the states could separate the races in intrastate railways if they provided "equal" facilities for the races. This doctrine of "separate but equal" would provide the legal foundation for **Jim Crow** segregation in the South and would remain in force until it was overturned in *Brown* v. *Board of Education of Topeka* more than half a century later.

The Fifteenth Amendment's voting guarantees were also rendered ineffectual—this time by a variety of devices invented to prevent African Americans from voting in the former states of the Confederacy. The **poll tax** was a tax required of all voters in many states, and it kept many African Americans away from the polls. Even a small tax was a heavy burden for many to bear, given the desperate economic situation of African Americans in the South in the late nineteenth and early twentieth centuries. Several states required voters to pass a **literacy test** devised and administered by local officials (see Table 16.1). The evaluation of test results was entirely up to local officials, who rarely passed blacks, even those with a college education or a Ph.D. degree. If white voters failed the literacy test, many states allowed them to vote anyway under the **grandfather clause,** which provided that anyone whose ancestors had voted prior to 1867 could vote as well. Since the ancestors of African Americans in the South had been slaves, the grandfather clause was no help to them at all. Several states instituted **white primaries** that excluded African Americans from the process of nominating candidates for local, state,

Jim Crow
Popular term for the system of legal racial segregation that existed in the American South until the middle of the twentieth century.

poll tax
A tax to be paid as a condition of voting; used in the South to keep African Americans away from the polls.

literacy test
A device used by the southern states to prevent African Americans from voting before the passage of the Voting Rights Act of 1965, which banned its use; usually involved interpretation of a section of a state's constitution.

grandfather clause
A device that allowed whites who had failed the literacy test to vote anyway by extending the franchise to anyone whose ancestors had voted prior to 1867.

white primaries
Primary elections open only to whites.

TABLE 16.1 • Selected Items from the Alabama Literacy Test

1. A person appointed to the U.S. Supreme Court is appointed for a term of _____.

2. If a person is indicted for a crime, name two rights which he has.

3. Cases tried before a court of law are of what two types: civil and _____.

4. If no candidate for president receives a majority of the electoral vote, who decides who will become president?

5. If no person receives a majority of the electoral vote, the vice president is chosen by the Senate. True or False?

6. If an effort to impeach the President of the United States is made, who presides at the trial?

7. If the two houses of Congress do not agree to adjournment, who sets the time?

8. A president elected in November takes office the following year on what date?

9. Of the original thirteen states, the one with the largest representation in the first Congress was _____.

10. The Constitution limits the size of the District of Columbia to _____.

These 10 questions are part of the 68-question Alabama Literacy Test used to decide on the eligibility of voters in that state. The test and others like it were declared illegal by the 1965 Voting Rights Act. Most white voters who were unable to pass this or similar tests in the states of the Deep South were protected by a "grandfather clause" allowing people to vote whose grandfathers had done so.

Answers: (1) good behavior; life; (2) jury trial, protection against self incrimination, right to counsel, speedy trial, protection against excessive bail; (3) criminal; (4) the House of Representatives; (5) true; (6) though not stipulated in the Constitution, the House has always turned to its Judiciary Committee to manage the impeachment process; (7) the president; (8) January 20; (9) Virginia; (10) not to exceed 10 miles square.

Lynching was used as a tool well into the twentieth century to intimidate African Americans and keep them from pressing too hard for equal citizenship, mainly in the Deep South, but also at times in other states. This lynching took place in Marion, Indiana, in 1930.

and national offices. The states based these primaries on the argument that political parties were private clubs that could define their own membership requirements, including skin color. For those African Americans who might try to vote anyway in the face of the poll tax, the literacy test, and the white primary, there was always the use of terror as a deterrent: Night riding, bombings, and lynchings were used with regularity, especially during times when blacks showed signs of assertiveness.

The statutory devices for keeping African Americans away from the polls were consistently supported by state and federal courts until well into the twentieth century. Terror as a means of preventing voting remained a factor until the 1960s, when the civil rights movement and federal intervention finally put an end to it.

Women and the Fifteenth Amendment   Politically active women were stung by their exclusion from the Fifteenth Amendment's extension of the right to vote, as the amendment said only that no state could exclude people on the grounds of "race, color, or previous condition of servitude." Thus, they quickly turned their attention to winning the vote for women. Once the Supreme Court had decided, in *Minor* v. *Happersett* (1874), that women's suffrage was not a right inherent in the national citizenship guarantees of the Fourteenth Amendment, women abandoned legal challenges based on their inferior political position and turned to more direct forms of political agitation: petitions, marches, and protests. After many years of struggle, the efforts of the women's suffrage movement bore fruit in the Nineteenth Amendment, ratified in 1920: "The right of citizens of the United States to vote shall not be denied or abridged by the United States or by any State on account of sex."

The Contemporary Status of Civil Rights for Racial Minorities

We saw in Chapter 15 how the Supreme Court, using the guidelines written by Justice Harlan Fiske Stone in *United States* v. *Carolene Products Company* (1938), gradually extended the protections of the Bill of Rights to the states, based on the Fourteenth Amendment. Recall that among the actions by the states that would trigger **strict scrutiny** under the *Carolene* guidelines were those that either "restricted the democratic process" or "discriminated against racial, ethnic, or religious minorities." This reading of the Fourteenth Amendment, particularly the equal protection clause, lent judicial support to the gradual advance of civil rights guarantees for African Americans and other minorities and eventually (though less so) for women. In the following sections, we look at the extension of the civil rights of racial minorities, women, and other groups. Here we concentrate mainly (although not exclusively) on Supreme Court decisions (see Chapter 8 for more information on the civil rights, women's, and other movements).

Two basic issues have dominated the story of the extension of civil rights for African Americans since the mid-1960s:

- The ending of legally sanctioned discrimination, separation, and exclusion from citizenship.
- The debate over what actions to take to remedy the past wrongs done to African Americans.

We examine both in this section.

strict scrutiny
The assumption that actions by elected bodies or officials violate constitutional rights.

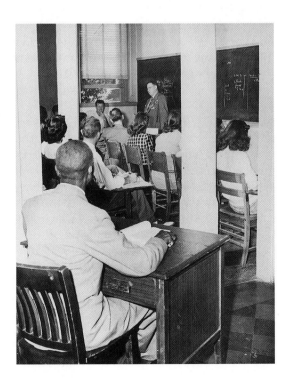

The erosion of official segregation in education came slowly and reluctantly in many parts of the nation. When ordered by a federal court in 1948 to admit a qualified black applicant, the University of Oklahoma law school did so but forced the lone student to sit separated from other students.

Dr. Martin Luther King, Jr., waves to the March on Washington crowd at the Lincoln Memorial after delivering his "I Have a Dream" speech. This event, one of the high points of the civil rights movement, helped convince Congress to pass the Civil Rights Act of 1964.

Ending Government-Sponsored Separation and Discrimination

We reviewed earlier how the Constitution was long interpreted to condone slavery and segregation. In the twentieth century, however, the legal and political battles waged by the civil rights movement eventually pushed the Supreme Court, the president, and Congress to take seriously the equal protection clause of the Fourteenth Amendment.

In 1944, amid World War II (a war aimed in great part at bringing down the racist regime of Adolf Hitler) and the NAACP's campaign to rid the nation of segregation, the Supreme Court finally declared that race was a **suspect classification** that demanded strict judicial scrutiny. This meant that any state or national enactment using racial criteria was presumed to be unconstitutional.

suspect classification

The invidious, arbitrary, or irrational designation of a group for special treatment by government.

Pressed by the legal efforts of the NAACP, the Court gradually chipped away at *Plessy* and the edifice of segregation. In *Smith* v. *Allwright* (1944), the Court declared that the practice of excluding nonwhites from political-party primary elections was unconstitutional. Then the Court ruled that the states' practice of providing separate all-white and all-black law schools was unacceptable. Many of the key cases before the Supreme Court that eroded the official structure of segregation were argued by Thurgood Marshall—later a justice of the Supreme Court—for the NAACP.[6]

The great legal breakthrough for racial equality came in *Brown* v. *Board of Education of Topeka* (1954), also argued by Thurgood Marshall, in which a unanimous Court declared that "separate but equal" was inherently contradictory and that segregation was constitutionally unacceptable in public schools. *Brown* was a constitutional revolution, destined to transform racial relations law and practices in the United States.

The white South did not react violently at first, but it did not desegregate either. Once recognition spread that the Court was going to enforce civil

 Timeline

The Struggle for Equal Protection

rights, however, massive resistance to racial integration gripped the South. This resistance was what Dr. Martin Luther King, Jr., and others had to work (and die) to overcome. The Court—even with many follow-up cases—was able to accomplish little before the president and Congress backed up the justices with the 1964 Civil Rights Act and the 1965 Voting Rights Act. The civil rights movement and supportive changes in American public opinion in favor of protections for blacks helped spur these legislative and judicial actions.

The drive to protect the rights of racial minorities has occupied the nation ever since. The main legal doctrine on racial discrimination is straightforward: Any use of race in law or government regulations to discriminate will trigger strict scrutiny (a presumption of unconstitutionality) by the courts. Recall from our earlier discussion that a state or the federal government can defend its acts under strict scrutiny only if it can produce a *compelling* government interest for which the act in question is a *necessary* means. Almost no law survives this challenge; laws that discriminate on the basis of race are dead from the moment of passage. Needless to say, other racial minority groups in addition to African Americans—Hispanics, Asian Americans, and Native Americans—have benefited from the constitutional revolution that has occurred.

To say that racial discrimination in the law is no longer constitutionally acceptable does not mean that racial discrimination has disappeared from the United States. A *Washington Post*/Kaiser Foundation/Harvard University poll reports, for example, that more than one-third of African Americans and more than one-in-five Latino and Asian men have experienced job discrimination. Overwhelming majorities of African Americans, Latinos, and Asians say they have been subject to poor service in stores and restaurants because of their race and have had disparaging remarks directed at them.[7] All minorities report bad experiences with racial profiling by police. In the same poll, for example, 52 percent of black men and 25 percent of Latino and Asian men claim to have been unfairly stopped by police. Although various police departments have taken steps to stop these practices, the courts have never defined racial profiling as suspect, especially if some important law enforcement need is being met by it.

Affirmative Action

It is now widely accepted that the Constitution protects racial minorities against any discrimination or disadvantage that is sanctioned or protected by law or government action. The issues are not as clear-cut, however, in the area of government actions that *favor* racial minorities (and women) in **affirmative action** programs designed to rectify past wrongs.[8]

affirmative action
Programs of private and public institutions favoring minorities and women in hiring and in admissions to colleges and universities in an attempt to compensate for past discrimination.

Origins of Affirmative Action
The main goal of the civil rights movement of the 1950s and 1960s was to remove barriers to equal citizenship for black Americans. This goal was largely accomplished in the federal courts by passage of the 1964 Civil Rights Act and the Voting Rights Act of 1965 and by broad changes in public attitudes about race. But even with these important changes, the economic and social situations of African Americans did not seem to be improving much. It seemed to an increasing number of people that ending discrimination was a start, but that more proactive government actions would be required if African Americans were to escape the conditions that years of discrimination had put them in. President Lyndon Johnson, Robert Kennedy, and Martin Luther King, Jr., among others, eventually came to believe that the advancement of black Americans could happen only if there was

a broad societal effort to eradicate poverty by equipping the poor, black and white, with the tools for success. This led to the founding of the Johnson administration's Great Society and War on Poverty and programs such as Head Start.

After Martin Luther King's assassination, however, and the urban riots that followed, many people in government, the media, higher education, and the major foundations began to support the notion that progress for African Americans would happen only if government encouraged racial preferences in hiring, contracts, and college admissions. Somewhat surprisingly, it was Richard Nixon, not generally thought of as a booster of civil rights, who took the most important step, requiring in his 1969 Philadelphia Plan that construction companies with federal contracts and the associated construction trade unions hire enough blacks and other minorities to achieve "racial balance" (a proportion roughly equal to the racial balance in the community). Most civil rights organizations opposed the plan, believing that it violated basic civil rights principles and would drive a wedge between African Americans and whites in the labor unions (which it eventually did). When the Philadelphia Plan reached the House of Representatives in 1970, Republicans supported it by a margin of 124–41, while Democrats opposed it, 115–84. The two parties soon switched positions on the issue, however. Nixon himself disavowed it in 1972 when he ordered federal agencies to avoid the use of quotas; meanwhile, the Democrats embraced the principle of racial preferences in their platform at the 1972 party convention.

Although initially skeptical of racial preferences, Justices William Brennan, Byron White, Thurgood Marshall, and Harry Blackmun supported temporary programs to remedy the effects of past discrimination. Joined by Justice Lewis Powell, they formed the majority in *Regents* v. *Bakke* (1978), in which the Court authorized a compromise on affirmative action programs. The Constitution and federal law prohibited employers and admissions committees from using strictly racial quotas, the Court said, but it saw no problem with the use of race as one factor among several in hiring or admissions.

Since *Bakke,* government and higher education racial preference programs have become relatively permanent rather than temporary, and their aim has shifted from providing remedies for past discrimination to enhancing diversity. The proliferation of diversity programs, diversity training, and diversity offices has become commonplace in colleges and universities, in government, and in the corporate world.

Why Affirmative Action?   For the most part, according to proponents, affirmative action programs that promote diversity are needed for the following reasons:

- The effects of past discrimination disadvantage, to one degree or another, all members of discriminated-against groups, so simply removing barriers to advancement is insufficient. The proper remedy is to prefer members of such groups in hiring, contracts, and education until such time as they reach parity with the majority.

- In a diverse society such as the United States, tolerance and a sense of community can develop only if we work together in educational, workplace, and government institutions that are diverse.

- People from disadvantaged and discriminated-against groups will improve themselves only if they have experience with successful role models in important institutions.

Critics of affirmative action are not convinced by these arguments. They believe the following to be true:

- Affirmative action violates one of the most basic American principles: that people be judged, rewarded, and punished as individuals, not because they are members of one group or another.

- Affirmative action benefits those within each preferred group who are already advantaged and need little help. Thus, the main beneficiaries of affirmative action in higher education have been middle-class African Americans, not the poor.

- Affirmative action seeks to remedy the effects of past discrimination by discriminating against others today simply because they belong to non-preferred groups.

- Affirmative action increases intergroup and interracial tension by heightening the saliency of group membership. That is, social friction is increased by encouraging people to think of themselves and others as members of groups and to seek group advantages in a zero-sum game in which one group's gain is another group's loss.

Public Opinion on Affirmative Action　　In survey after survey, a vast majority of Americans say they approve of the diversity goals of affirmative action—special programs to help those who have been discriminated against get ahead; outreach programs to hire minority workers and find minority students—but disapprove of racial preferences in hiring, awarding of government contracts, and admission to colleges.[9] Most polling organizations show the following pattern: When asked whether they generally support affirmative action, about 60 to 65 percent of Americans say they approve;[10] when the survey asks whether they favor affirmative action programs that involve preferential treatment or "set-asides" for racial minorities and women, support erodes dramatically, to no more than 40 percent.[11] Not surprisingly, perhaps, racial differences on the issue of preferential treatment are wide; in 2003, 55 percent of African Americans supported affirmative action programs that involved preferential treatment, whereas only 24 percent of whites did.[12]

To many proponents of affirmative action, this is simply a reflection of the enduring racism of Americans. People oppose affirmative action, in this view, because they are hostile to racial minorities. Political scientists Paul Sniderman and Edward Carmines suggest otherwise. In a series of ingenious studies reported in their book *Reaching Beyond Race,* they set out to unravel the roots of opposition to affirmative action. Their conclusion is that while some people oppose these programs because of their racist attitudes, most do so because they believe that affirmative action is fundamentally unfair and contrary to American values.[13] Judging, rewarding, and punishing people not as individuals but as members of groups does not seem right to many Americans. We can see this in the fact, as sociologist Seymour Martin Lipset reported after examining a wide range of surveys on the issue, that a majority of women and Hispanic Americans, not just white males, oppose affirmative action programs that involve preferential treatment or set-asides of one kind or another.[14]

The Supreme Court on Affirmative Action　　The Supreme Court has been grappling for years with the issue of which forms of affirmative action, if any, are constitutionally permissible. Recall that the prevailing constitutional doctrine on matters of race holds that any mention of race in a government statute, ordinance, or rule is subject to strict scrutiny—that is, unconstitutional—unless the government can show some compelling and necessary reason for it. Historically, of course, there is good reason for the Court to take this position, given the fact that laws mentioning race were usually designed to deny equal protection to African Americans and other racial minorities. But what about government actions meant to compensate African Americans and others for past discriminatory actions?

For most of the last decade, the Supreme Court has been moving toward the position that laws and other government actions that are not colorblind should be subject to strict scrutiny. In *Wygant* v. *Jackson Board of Education* (1986) and *Richmond* v. *Croson Co.* (1989), the Supreme Court said that programs that narrowly redress specific violations will be upheld as constitutional but that broader affirmative action programs that address society's racism will be struck down. In *Adarand Constructors* v. *Peña* (1995), the Court ruled by a 5–4 majority that the federal government must abide by the strict standards for affirmative action programs imposed on the states in the *Richmond* case and could not award contracts using race as the main criterion. In *Miller* v. *Johnson* (1995), the Court ruled, again by a 5–4 majority, that race could not be used as the basis for drawing House district lines in an effort to increase the number of racial minority members in Congress. The Court also refused to overturn a Fifth Circuit Court ruling that race cannot be considered at all in admissions decisions at the University of Texas Law School, seemingly putting the *Bakke* principle in jeopardy. In 1997, the Court refused to overturn a ruling of the Ninth Circuit Court that California's anti–affirmative action Proposition 209 was constitutionally permissible. In 2001, the Court let stand a decision by the Eleventh U.S. Circuit Court of Appeals that disallowed a Fulton County, Georgia, program setting annual goals for awarding county contracts to blacks, Hispanics, Asians, Native Americans, and women.

Given these decisions, civil rights organizations were braced for a decision by the Supreme Court that would render affirmative action admissions policies unconstitutional once and for all. When the Court agreed to hear two admissions cases involving the University of Michigan—one involving its undergraduate program, the other its law school—liberals dreaded the outcome, while conservatives could hardly wait for the ruling. The Court stunned virtually every political observer when it ruled by a 5–4 vote in late June 2003 that universities could take race into consideration when considering applications for admission, so long as the consideration of race was not done in a mechanically quantitative manner or used as part of a racial and ethnic quota system, reaffirming, as it were, its position in the 1978 *Bakke* decision. (See the "Using the Framework" feature for more on why this happened.) In its twin decisions, the Court rejected the University of Michigan's undergraduate admissions affirmative action program—because it automatically assigned extra points to each minority applicant—but accepted the law school's—whose admissions process uses race as but one among several factors in a wholistic examination of each applicant's file. What surprised observers the most, perhaps, was not the decision itself, but the broad language that Justice Sandra Day O'Connor used in her majority opinion, in which she stressed that achieving diversity in universities, and especially in its elite law schools, was indeed a compelling reason for not applying strict scrutiny by the Court:

> *In order to cultivate a set of leaders with legitimacy in the eyes of the citizenry, it is necessary that the path to leadership be visibly open to the talented and qual-*

Using the Framework

Affirmative Action

Why has the Supreme Court narrowed the scope of affirmative action programs?

Background: During the 1990s, the Supreme Court rendered a number of decisions that narrowed the use of racial preferences in the areas of government hiring and contracting, congressional redistricting, and university admissions. It therefore came as a great surprise to both proponents and critics of affirmative action when the Supreme Court ruled by a 5–4 vote in a pair of cases involving the University of Michigan that affirmative action of a certain kind—one that uses race as only one among several factors in a wholistic consideration of each individual's file—is permissible in university admissions. The ruling was made possible by the emergence in the late 1990s of a new Court majority on certain issues led by Sandra Day O'Connor.

Governmental Action

In an exception to the Court's general drift, it rules in 2003 that the use of race in university admissions is permissible if it is not used as part of a mechanical, quantitative formula.

The Supreme Court rejects diversity as a compelling state interest in programs involving government jobs and contracting, and in congressional districting. It also refuses to hear cases from the circuit courts that reject affirmative action in university admissions programs, letting the decisions stand.

Governmental Level

Republican presidents Reagan and Bush nominated conservatives to the Court. → The Senate approved the nominees. → A narrow but firm conservative majority under the leadership of Chief Justice William Rehnquist controls the Court on many issues. → A new majority led by Sandra Day O'Connor appears on a number of issues. She is convinced by briefs from elite universities, major corporations, and former top military officials that affirmative action to increase diversity, if it is done in the right way, is a compelling goal in important institutions.

Political Linkages Level

The Christian conservative movement and other conservative organizations—who are against affirmative action—gained political influence in the 1980s.

The political influence of civil rights organizations declined in the 1980s and 1990s.

→ Republicans, whose platform rejects affirmative action, reached parity with Democrats in national elections.

The majority white population reports in polls that it believes the goals of the civil rights movement have been met.

→ Republicans won control of the Senate from 1981–1986 and from 1995 to 2000.

A substantial majority of Americans report support for nondiscrimination laws but distaste for laws that give minorities and women special advantages in college admissions, jobs, and government contracts.

Structural Level

The Fourteenth Amendment's promise of "equal protection of the laws" clearly bars government discrimination against groups of citizens but is unclear about the need for remedies for past discrimination. → The political culture honors individual rather than group rights and responsibilities. → The white middle and working classes suffered economic reverses during the 1980s and early 1990s, creating a climate that was generally hostile to affirmative action programs.

ified individuals of every race and ethnicity . . . Access to legal education (and thus the legal profession) must be inclusive of talented and qualified individuals of every race and ethnicity so that all members of our heterogeneous society may participate in the educational institutions that provide the training and education necessary to succeed in America. . . . Cross-racial understanding helps to break down racial stereotypes and better prepares graduates for the working world . . . The law school's educational judgment that such diversity is essential to its educational mission is one to which we defer.[15]

After the University of Michigan cases, here is where affirmative stands at the present time:

- Any program by a government entity that uses race to define who receives or does not receive benefits is subject to strict scrutiny—that is, considered unconstitutional unless compelling and necessary reasons for the program are proved. This holds whether or not such programs are designed to discriminate against or favor racial minorities.

- With respect to the award of government contracts and government hiring—whether federal, state, or local—affirmative action programs are acceptable only if they are narrowly tailored to rectify past discriminatory actions by that particular government agency. In the view of the Court, rectifying past racist actions by a particular government agency is a compelling reason. Such programs, however, must be temporary efforts to transcend past practices and not a permanent feature of hiring and contracting. Affirmative action in hiring and contracting is not

Demonstrators celebrate after learning that the Supreme Court had decided in favor of the University of Michigan Law School's affirmative action policies.

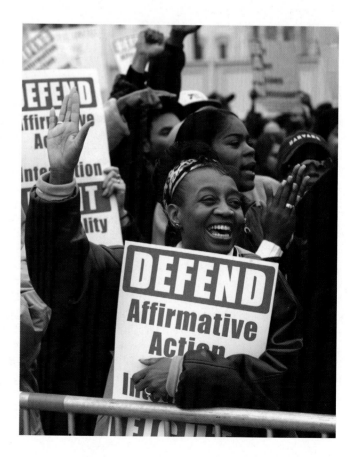

valid if it is designed simply to increase diversity or to decrease racism in society.

- With respect to admission to educational institutions—into undergraduate and graduate programs, law schools, and medical schools—actions to rectify past discriminatory admissions policies by a particular higher education institution are compelling and necessary, and are permitted.

- With respect to higher education admissions, the goal of achieving a diverse student body is a compelling reason to have affirmative action programs. However, race can only be used if it is one among several factors considered in a wholistic consideration of each applicant's file; quantitative formulas in which students of a particular race or ethnicity automatically receive a set number of points is not permissible.

Affirmative action programs in the United States have been designed to help not only African Americans, of course, but other racial and ethnic minorities as well, including Hispanics, Asian Americans, and Native Americans. Most of the programs also include women as beneficiaries. The present Supreme Court guidelines on affirmative action described here apply to all of these groups, not only African Americans.

The Contemporary Status of Civil Rights for Women

The expansion of civil rights protections for women has taken a decidedly different path from that of civil rights protections for African Americans.

Intermediate Scrutiny

For all its egalitarian reputation, the Warren Court did not significantly advance the cause of women's rights. Once the Burger Court seriously looked at sex discrimination laws, it had to decide whether to apply ordinary scrutiny (the presumption of constitutionality that almost all laws survive) or strict scrutiny (the presumption of unconstitutionality that dooms almost all laws). The Burger Court opted for a new position, called **intermediate scrutiny,** but not before coming to the very brink of declaring gender a suspect classification demanding strict scrutiny.

By 1976 the proposed **Equal Rights Amendment (ERA)** to the Constitution to guarantee full legal equality for women had stalled, falling short of the required three-fourths of the states. Moreover, the Supreme Court did not have the necessary votes for a strict scrutiny interpretation of gender classification. There was support, however, for the new doctrine that came to be called intermediate scrutiny. In *Craig* v. *Boren* (1976), six justices supported Justice William Brennan's compromise, which created a more rigorous scrutiny of gender as a *somewhat* suspect classification. This intermediate scrutiny provided a compromise solution to the problem of choosing between strict and ordinary scrutiny. In the view of the justices, the use of strict scrutiny would endanger traditional sex roles, while the use of ordinary scrutiny would allow blatant sex discrimination to survive. The Burger Court defined a test that it believed to be "just right." Under intermediate scrutiny, government enactments that relied on gender would be constitutional if the

intermediate scrutiny
A legal test falling between ordinary and strict scrutiny relevant to issues of gender; under this test, the Supreme Court will allow gender classifications in laws if they are *substantially* related to an *important* government objective.

Equal Rights Amendment (ERA)
Proposed amendment to the U.S. Constitution stating that equality of rights shall not be abridged or denied on account of a person's sex.

use of gender were *substantially related* to an *important objective.* Intermediate scrutiny defines a legal test, then, somewhere between strict and lax. Thus, for example, certain laws protecting pregnant women from dangerous chemicals in the workplace have passed this test.

The improvement of women's rights under the doctrine of intermediate scrutiny is less than what many in the women's movement wanted. While the new standard has allowed the courts to throw out some laws based on degrading stereotypes of women, it was used in *Craig* v. *Boren* to justify invalidating an Oklahoma law that discriminated against young *men.* Similarly, the beneficiaries of intermediate scrutiny decisions in *Wengler* v. *Druggists Mutual Insurance Company* (1980) and *Mississippi University for Women* v. *Hogan* (1982) were also men.

Thus, women's rights have not followed the path of other rights and liberties. The nation has not restructured civil rights for women based on an expansive reading of the equal protection clause of the Fourteenth Amendment by the courts. Rather, advances have come by virtue of changing societal attitudes about the role of women in society, increased involvement of women in politics, and new statutes designed to equalize women's opportunities. In the private sector, women have made important advances in the corporate world and in the professions. In the public sector, more and more women hold important elected and appointed positions in all levels of government and serve in all branches of the armed services. Women also have successfully pushed for laws that compensate for past injustices. One example of such a law is Title IX of the Civil Rights Act of 1964, which prohibits discrimination against women at federally funded institutions, including universities. Title IX is generally credited with enhancing funding for women's sports programs in colleges and dramatically improving the quality of women's athletics in the United States.

Title IX had the effect of increasing funding for women's sports in American colleges and universities and encouraging more women to participate in sports. One result was a dramatic improvement in the quality of America's national teams. Here members of the U.S. Women's Soccer Team celebrate their victory in the Women's World Cup in 1999.

Abortion Rights

One of the most controversial decisions of the Burger Court was *Roe* v. *Wade* (1973). Two recent graduates of the University of Texas Law School, Linda Coffee and Sarah Weddington, were looking for a client who would challenge a Texas statute that prohibited physicians from performing abortions except to save the life of the pregnant woman.[16] They found a client in Norma "Pixie" McCorvey, a 21-year-old divorcee who had already given birth to a child. McCorvey claimed that she had been gang raped, but her attorneys doubted her story. They argued instead for a general constitutional right to decide not to complete a pregnancy.

For women's rights activists Coffee and Weddington, the federal courts offered an alternative to the Texas legislature. The case transformed abortion from a legislative issue into a constitutional issue, from a matter of policy into a matter of rights. Eleven states had reformed their statutes to allow women to have abortions when the woman's health, fetal abnormalities, or rape or incest were involved. Four more states (Alaska, Hawaii, Washington, and New York) went further and repealed prohibitions of abortion. In most states, however, progress was slow or nonexistent.

The litigation over abortion reflected changes in public opinion, pressure by interest groups, and persisting inequities against women. Disapproval of abortion decreased and discussion of abortion increased during the 1960s, even among Roman Catholics.[17] Numerous groups worked to reform or to eliminate abortion laws before *Roe* was decided.[18] Norma McCorvey's case relied greatly on the money of supporters of women's rights. The pro-choice team benefited from 42 amicus curiae briefs. The medical profession, which had been instrumental in making abortion a crime in the nineteenth century,[19] supported reform in the 1960s. Justice Harry Blackmun's opinion for the majority prohibited the states from interfering with a woman's decision to have an abortion in the first two trimesters of her pregnancy. He based his opinion

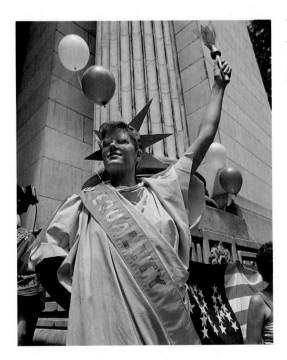

The women's movement helped raise Americans' awareness of the issue of "equal pay for equal work" and contributed to improvements in pay equity for women in both the public and private sectors. Here, a demonstrator in New York presses for pay equity.

on the right to privacy, first given constitutional protection in *Griswold* v. *Connecticut* (1965), even though no such right is mentioned in the Constitution.

The Court's decision hardly resolved matters. Anti-abortion groups, energized by the repeal of abortion laws, struck back after *Roe*. Single-issue anti-abortion politics surfaced in the 1976 and subsequent elections and became an important pillar of the conservative Reagan movement. The pro-life forces that helped elect Ronald Reagan insisted that he appoint anti-abortion judges to the federal courts. He did so with great effectiveness. In the end, the Supreme Court responded to anti-abortion politics by deciding two cases, *Webster* v. *Reproductive Health Services* (1989) and *Planned Parenthood* v. *Casey* (1992), that gave considerable latitude to the states in restricting abortions. Many states have acted. In 1996, nine states enacted 14 measures restricting abortion in one way or another: mandating parental notification, waiting periods, counseling against abortion, and/or prohibiting using public money for the procedure. In 1997, 31 states enacted 44 such measures. In 1998, 22 states passed 46 restrictive bills. And, in 1999, pro-choice New Jersey Governor Christine Todd Whitman signed a bill requiring teenage girls to notify their parents before getting an abortion.[20]

To the surprise of many observers, however, the Court majority, despite the appointment of new conservative justices by Presidents Reagan and Bush, affirmed its support of the basic principles of *Roe* in the *Planned Parenthood* opinion. Also surprising was the Court's decision, in *National Organization for Women* v. *Scheidler* (1994), that abortion clinics could sue anti-abortion groups for damages under the federal racketeering law. And, during its 2000 session, the Court ruled that states could not ban so-called late-term abortions and said that state laws and local ordinances keeping anti-abortion demonstrators away from clinic entrances were constitutional.

Abortion has been an important issue in recent judicial confirmations. Judge Robert Bork ascribed his own defeat to the issue,[21] and hearings on Judge David Souter in 1990 and Clarence Thomas in 1992 raised the issue repeatedly. Ruth Bader Ginsburg took a Solomonic position: Like conservative pro-lifers, she opposed the reasoning of *Roe* v. *Wade,* but like liberal pro-choicers, she insisted that some abortion rights are essential to women's equality.

Sexual Harassment

Another issue of concern to many women (and many men) is sexual harassment in the workplace. One poll reports that 21 percent of women say they have experienced sexual harassment at work.[22] The Equal Employment Opportunity Commission (EEOC) reports that 35 percent of female federal employees have been subjected to unwelcome sexual remarks and that 26 percent have experienced unwelcome touching.[23]

People disagree, of course, about what kinds of behavior constitute sexual harassment, although the courts, regulatory agencies, and legislative bodies are gradually defining the law in this area. In 1980, the EEOC ruled that making sexual activity a condition of employment or promotion violates the 1964 Civil Rights Act, a ruling upheld by the Supreme Court. The EEOC also ruled that creating "an intimidating, hostile, or offensive working environment" is contrary to the law. State courts have begun to fill in the meaning of "intimidating, hostile, or offensive." The Florida Supreme Court ruled in 1991, for instance, that an open display of nude pinups in a mixed-gender workplace fits the definition. A California court ruled that unwelcome love letters from a

Professor Anita Hill's dramatic testimony before the Senate Judiciary Committee considering the nomination of Clarence Thomas to the Supreme Court raised the visibility in American politics of the issue of sexual harassment.

supervisor constitute harassment. The U.S. Supreme Court took a major step in defining sexual harassment when it ruled unanimously, in *Harris* v. *Forklift Systems, Inc.* (1993), that workers do not have to prove that offensive actions make them unable to do their jobs or cause them psychological harm, only that the work environment is hostile or abusive. In a pair of rulings in June 1998, the Court broadened the definition of sexual harassment by saying that companies were liable for the behavior of supervisors even if top managers were unaware of harassing behavior. However, companies were offered a measure of protection by the Court when it ruled that companies with solid and well-communicated harassment policies could not be held liable if victims failed to report harassment in a reasonable period of time.

An increase in public awareness about sexual harassment has triggered an increase in lawmaking by state legislatures to erase sexual harassment in the workplace. Many private companies have also begun to specify appropriate behavior on the job for their employees.

Broadening the Civil Rights Umbrella

The expansion of civil rights protections for women and racial minorities encouraged other groups to press for expanded rights protections.

The Elderly and the Disabled

Interest groups for the elderly have pressed for laws barring age discrimination and have enjoyed some success in recent years. Several federal and state laws, for instance, now bar mandatory retirement. And, the Age Discrimination in Employment Act passed in 1967 prohibits employers from discriminating against employees over the age of 40 in pay, benefits, promotions, and working conditions. The courts have also begun to strike down hiring practices based on age unless a compelling reason for such age requirements can be demonstrated. But problems persist; downsizing companies often lay off older

You Are the Mayor

workers first, because the pay and benefits of older workers are almost always higher than those of younger workers.

Disabled Americans have also pushed for civil rights and other protections and have won some notable victories, including passage of the Americans with Disabilities Act of 1990. The act prohibits employment discrimination against the disabled and requires that reasonable efforts be made to make places of employment and public facilities (such as concert halls, restaurants, retail shops, schools, and government offices) accessible to them. The proliferation of wheelchair ramps and wheelchair-accessible toilet facilities is a sign that the legislation is having an important effect. Several advocates for the disabled, however, claim that the act depends too much on voluntary compliance.

In 2001, the Supreme Court dramatically narrowed the reach of the Disabilities Act, saying that state employees could not sue states for damages arising from violations of the Act, as provided for in the legislation. Advocates for the rights of the disabled worried that this judicial ruling expanding the scope of state immunity from congressional actions means that other sections of the Disabilities Act are doomed, including the requirement that state governments make their services and offices accessible to people with disabilities. Others worried that a wide range of civil rights laws that require nondiscriminatory behavior by state agencies—schools and hospitals, for example—may be at risk, as well, because the basis of the Court's decision was that Congress had gone beyond its authority in telling the states what to do under the interstate commerce clause.[24] If the states are immune from the requirements of the Americans with Disabilities Act, the reasoning goes, why should it not be immune from the provisions of other civil rights laws passed by Congress? In 2004, the Court ruled that the disabled could sue a state for money damages in federal court if the state fails to make its courts fully accessible. The Supreme Court was silent, however, on whether this right to sue extends to other areas where states have not fully complied with other federal civil rights requirements, so the issue still remains unsettled.

Gays and Lesbians

The gay and lesbian civil rights movements began in earnest in the late 1960s following the 1969 "Stonewall rebellion": three days of rioting set off by police harassment of the patrons of a popular gay bar in Greenwich Village in New York. The movements picked up steam as the gay community reacted to the powerful inroads of AIDS, and in response to the Supreme Courts decision in *Bowers* v. *Hardwick* (1986) upholding Georgia's ban against homosexual sexual relations. The movements were also inspired by and borrowed many of the tactics of the civil rights and women's movements. Their goal was to gain the same civil rights protections under the law enjoyed by African Americans and other minority groups and to gain respect from the public. Their tactics have ranged from patient lobbying and voting to mass demonstrations and deliberately shocking actions by groups such as ACT-UP. While some important gains have been made by the gay and lesbian movements, their open advocacy for civil rights for homosexuals has suffered strong counterattacks by groups strongly opposed to their objectives, such as the Christian Coalition and Focus on the Family.

Gays and lesbians have moved toward equal treatment in a variety of settings in the private sector. Gains in the areas of high culture and mass entertainment have been important. Sympathetic gay and lesbian characters appear regularly on network and cable television and in the movies, for example, and plays such as *Angels in America* are regularly staged.[25] Many gays and lesbians have "come out of the closet," as it were, and the number of Americans who are aware of gay and lesbian relatives, friends, and coworkers has increased. Many private corporations, including Coors and Disney, universities, labor unions, and nonprofits have instituted same-sex partner health care and retirement benefits.

Not surprisingly, given the advances they have made in the arts and mass entertainment, public attitudes about gays and lesbians are growing steadily more tolerant. Fewer Americans today than in the past think that gay and lesbian relationships are wrong. Substantial majorities, moreover, favor ending discrimination against gays and lesbians in jobs, housing, and education and favor passing hate-crime legislation. Americans still strongly oppose the idea of same-sex marriage, however, though 44 percent of 18- to 29-year-olds favor it.[26]

The gay and lesbian movement's political efforts have had mixed success. On the legislative front, there has not been much success at the national level. Civil rights legislation has not made much headway in Congress. Indeed, Congress passed the Defense of Marriage Act in 1996, trying to preserve marriage as a union of man and woman. Gays and lesbians have had more success at the local level in places such as Boulder, Aspen, New York City, and San Francisco, where ordinances have been passed protecting them against discrimination in jobs and housing. Eight states ban discrimination against gay people, and seven other states operate under executive orders that prohibit such discrimination.[27]

In presidential politics, partial advances also have been the order of the day. When Bill Clinton was a presidential candidate, for example, he promised to lift the ban on gay people in the military, but as president he was forced in 1993 to reverse his course in light of the hostile reaction from Congress and the armed services. The resulting "don't ask, don't tell, don't pursue" policy satisfied very few people, and the U.S. Navy has routinely flouted the policy. Democratic presidential candidate John Kerry endorsed same-sex civil unions, but opposed same-sex marriage. President Bush, however, strongly opposed both **civil unions** and marriages for gays, using part of his 2004 State of the Union address to attack judges for their support of

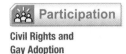

Civil Rights and
Gay Adoption

civil union

A status in which same-sex couples have the same legal rights, benefits, and protections as married couples.

Web Exploration
Same-Sex Marriage

Issue: Passions run high on the issue of same-sex marriages.

Site: Access two sites that take contrasting positions on the issue of same-sex marriage: the Family Research Council and TurnOut. Go to our Website at **www.ablongman.com/greenberg**. Go to the "Web Explorations" section for Chapter 16, select and open "same-sex marriage." At the Family Research Council site, select "Policy Areas," then look at both "marriage and family" and "human sexuality." At the TurnOut site, select "issues," and then "the right to marry."

What You've Learned: Compare the coverage of the issue of same-sex marriage at each site. Is each telling the full story? Are there areas of agreement between the two sides, or is the gap between them a yawning one?

HINT: On issues involving conflicts over fundamental values, agreement and compromise are often very difficult to achieve.

Gay activists celebrate the decision of the state supreme court permitting same-sex marriage in Massachusetts. The ruling not only encouraged gay activists to push for same-sex marriage in other cities and states, but sparked a powerful political response from religious conservatives across the country.

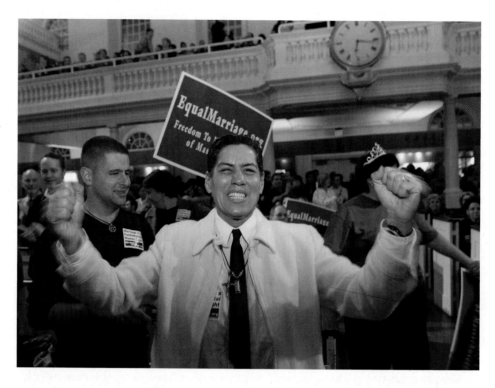

such arrangements and hinting that a constitutional amendment might be needed to rectify the situation.

It is in the courts, however, where gays and lesbians have made the biggest advances. At the state level, Vermont's high court ruled in 2003 that same-sex couples must be granted the same legal rights, protections, and benefits as heterosexual married couples, including such matters as joint tax returns, insurance benefits, and medical decisions involving a spouse. In 2004, Massachusetts's high court ruled that same-sex couples must be granted the opportunity to marry, citing the state's constitutional provision for equal rights for all citizens. It is worth noting that the Massachusetts decision sparked action in several other states to amend their constitutions to say that marriage is confined to a union between a man and a woman.

Although gays and lesbians recently lost an important case before the U.S. Supreme Court—it ruled that the Boy Scouts of America, and by implication, other private "expressive or advocacy" organizations whose association was protected by the First Amendment, were within their rights to exclude gays from leadership positions—they won important victories as well. The Court ruled in *Romer* v. *Evans* (1996), for example, that state laws designed to deny basic civil rights to gays and lesbians are unconstitutional. In this case, the Court looked at Colorado's provision (known as Amendment 2) prohibiting local communities from passing gay anti-discrimination ordinances. In declaring the law constitutionally unacceptable because of its denial of equal protection, Justice Anthony Kennedy declared in his opinion that "a state cannot so deem a class of persons [gays and lesbians] a stranger to its laws." And, in a stunning and highly unexpected decision in 2003, the Supreme Court overturned its own *Bowers* decision from 1986 and ruled in *Lawrence* v. *Texas* that state anti-sodomy laws designed to make homosexual sexual relations were unconstitutional. Justice Kennedy again gave the ruling a very expansive

How Democratic Are We?

Civil Rights in the United States

PROPOSITION: Civil rights were not a prominent feature of the original Constitution nor has the promise of equal citizenship (which goes hand-in-hand with political equality) been realized over the course of our history.

AGREE: There is no provision in the original Constitution ensuring equality of citizenship for women, African Americans, and Native Americans. Women were denied the vote well into the twentieth century; most African Americans were slaves until passage of the Thirteenth Amendment and were not admitted into full citizenship across the nation until at least 1965 after passage of the Civil Rights Act and the Voting Rights Act. Even today, women, racial and ethnic minorities, and gays and lesbians continue to be discriminated against in a wide range of institutions and fail to play a role in the political process commensurate with their numbers in the population. This is still a political system run by and for the benefit of white men.

DISAGREE: While it is true that the framers largely ignored the issue of equal citizenship, the story of the United States is the story of the gradual inclusion of all identifiable groups into the political process as equal citizens. To be sure, though discrimination has not been eliminated in all areas of American life, it is now no longer constitutionally possible for government and other public institutions such as universities to discriminate against women and racial and ethnic minorities. Barriers to discrimination are also falling for gays and lesbians. And, not only has government discrimination against these groups ended, but many new affirmative action programs are in place to make up for past discrimination and to increase the diversity in the country's most important institutions. As to the issue of participation and power, though it is true that levels of political participation and political power are not the same for all groups in American society, this has more to do with inequalities in the distribution of income, wealth, and education than with formal mechanisms of exclusion.

CONSIDER: Political equality is one of the three pillars of democracy, equal in importance to popular sovereignty and political liberty. Consequently, to evaluate "how democratic" we are, we need to know if equal citizenship is a goal we are about to reach, or whether it is one receding into the distance.

• What do you think? • In your view, have women, racial and ethnic minorities, and members of other historically discriminated-against groups become equal citizens? • If so, have they become equal citizens in both legal terms and political influence? • Or, on the other hand, do you believe, as some Americans do, that these groups have become more than equal to others, that government officials pay them too much heed and do too much for them at the expense of others? • If you believe this, how would you explain the influence of such groups, given shortages of the usual currency of political influence? • Why do political leaders pay attention to their demands at all?

reading in his majority opinion, declaring that gay people "were entitled to freedom, dignity, and respect for their private lives."

It is evident that the struggle over gay and lesbian civil rights will remain an important part of the American political agenda for a long time to come. The eventual outcome remains very much in doubt, however. While gays and lesbians have made important advances, to be sure, many conservatives have been politically mobilized by the possibility that state courts and the U.S. Supreme Court might eventually sanction same-sex marriage as a basic civil right.

Summary

The Constitution and the Bill of Rights are relatively silent on political equality, other than providing for equality before the law. Important advances for civil rights were the passage of the Thirteenth, Fourteenth, and Fifteenth Amendments after the Civil War. The Fourteenth Amendment, with its specification that all persons born or naturalized in the United States are citizens of both the nation and the states in which they live and that federal and state governments must provide for "equal protection of the laws," was a particularly important civil rights milestone, even though the Supreme Court was slow to act on its promise.

The Court paid little attention during the nineteenth century to the issue of political equality for racial minorities and women. Under the pressure of structural changes in society, the transformation of attitudes about race and gender, and the political efforts of racial and ethnic minority group members and women of all races, the Court slowly began to pay attention by the middle of the twentieth century. Important advances toward equality have been made by both racial minorities and women. Although constitutional law now fully protects both racial minorities and women against discrimination sanctioned by law or government action, the status of affirmative action programs meant to rectify past wrongs and to compensate for institutional barriers to equality remains unsettled. The question of whether lesbians and gay men can be discriminated against in housing, employment, and education has been largely settled, although the issues of gays and lesbians in the military and same-sex marriages remain the subject of considerable political debate.

Suggestions for Further Reading

Barry, Brian. *Culture and Equality*. Cambridge, MA: Harvard University Press, 2001.

An assault on multiculturalism in the name of liberal egalitarianism by a distinguished political philosopher.

Bowen, William G., and Derek C. Bok. *The Shape of the River: Long-Term Consequences of Considering Race in College and University Admissions.* Princeton, NJ: Princeton University Press, 1998.

Based on surveys of more than 60,000 white and African American students at highly selective colleges and universities, Bowen and Bok argue that affirmative action in college and university admissions has had substantial and widespread positive effects on American society.

Burns, James MacGregor, and Stewart Burns. *A People's Charter: The Pursuit of Rights in America.* New York: Knopf, 1991.

A magisterial survey of the history of civil rights and liberties in the United States.

Evans, Sarah M. *Born for Liberty: A History of Women in America.* New York: Free Press, 1997.

A compelling history of women's struggle for civil rights.

Gates, Henry Louis, Jr. *America Behind the Color Line.* New York: Warner Books, 2004.

An examination of the legacy of the civil rights movement for African Americans.

Gerstmann, Evan. *Same-Sex Marriage and the Constitution.* New York: Cambridge University Press, 2003.

A careful examination of the constitutional issues at the root of this contemporary controversy.

Sniderman, Paul M., and Edward G. Carmines. *Reaching Beyond Race.* Cambridge, MA: Harvard University Press, 1997.

A brilliant examination of what Americans really mean when they answer survey questions about race.

Internet Sources

Civil Rights Project
www.civilrightsproject.harvard.edu

Cutting-edge research on race in America.

Cornell Law Library/Civil Rights
http://www.law.cornell.edu

Links to the Constitution, landmark and recent Supreme Court civil rights decisions, international treaties on human rights, the Civil Rights Division of the Justice Department, and more.

Issues: Gay Rights
www.politics1.com/issues-gay.htm

Links to organizations in favor of and opposed to advancing gay and lesbian civil rights.

Martin Luther King, Jr., Home Page
http://www.seattletimes.com/mlk/

Created by the Seattle Times, *the site includes study guides on King and the civil rights movement, interactive exercises, audios of King speeches, and links to other King and civil rights Websites.*

Yahoo/Civil Rights
http://www.yahoo.com/Society_and_Culture/Issues_ and_Causes/Civil_Rights/

Linkages to a vast compendium of information on civil rights and to organizations devoted to the protection and expansion of domestic and international rights.

Chapter 17
Domestic Policy: The Economy and Social Welfare

In This Chapter

- Why and how government manages the economy and provides social welfare
- What tools government uses to manage the economy
- The federal budget, the deficit, and the national debt
- Why government subsidizes some business activities and regulates others
- Why the American welfare state is the way it is
- How interest groups, parties, social movements, and public opinion affect economic and social welfare policy

Whatever Happened to the Budget Surplus?

When asked to comment on the dramatic downturn in the nation's budget outlook, former Congressional Budget Office Robert Reischauer invoked John Milton's epic work *Paradise Lost,* which described a dramatic fall from grace, from heaven to hell. He said "It really has been a Miltonian experience, from the heights to the depths."[1]

Paradise Lost indeed! In early 2001, federal officials and private economists issued confident predictions that the government's budget would be in the black by more than $230 billion in 2002, and that total cumulative surpluses over a 10-year period would be about $5.6 trillion. For elected officials in Washington, the news could not have been better. As officeholders who must periodically face the voters, elected officials of both parties were delighted with the prospect of an ever-growing budget cornucopia that could be used to safeguard Social Security and Medicare, pay down the national debt, and pay for new educational and drug benefit programs—with ample room left over for tax cuts.

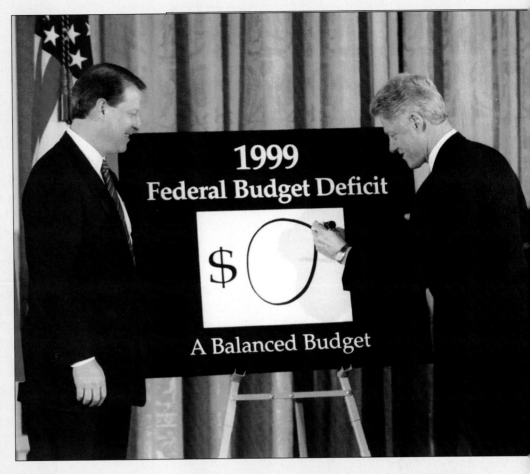

All this changed dramatically in 2002. The Bush White House announced that the federal budget was going to be at least $106 billion in the red for 2002 and would remain in deficit until at least 2005, perhaps longer. The Congressional Budget Office (CBO) estimated that the 10-year accumulated deficit would be $1.6 trillion. The change from an estimated surplus of $5.6 trillion to a deficit of $1.6 trillion represented the most dramatic reversal of the fiscal health of the nation in more than 50 years.

However, the worst was yet to come. By the time President Bush submitted his fiscal year 2005 Budget to Congress in early February 2004, the CBO was predicting that annual budget deficits would not disappear for a long time and that the accumulated national debt would grow even more than it had predicted just two years earlier. It now put the 10-year accumulated annual deficits—what would be added to the national debt—at $1.9 trillion. If tax breaks that are set to expire during this period are made permanent, as President Bush asked Congress to do, an additional $2 trillion would get tacked on to the national debt, for a total of almost $4 trillion.

How had things changed so dramatically in so short a time? How had paradise been lost in the space of only two or three years? What caused the deficits to reappear is fairly obvious, though Democrats, Republicans, economists, and budget analysts disagree about how much weight to give to each factor. First, budget estimates did not accurately predict the troubles that would visit the American economy: the 2001 economic recession, the 2002 stock market collapse, and 2003's jobless recovery. Thus, the unsustainable "go-go" economy of the late 1990s slowed down sharply in late 2000 and 2001, with GDP contracting sharply. Then, in 2002, an overvalued stock market lost almost 20 percent of its value, and previously hot dot-com companies folded by the dozens. Telecommunications and computer companies reported huge losses, as did most of the nation's airlines. Most remarkably, the energy trading company Enron collapsed early in 2002, leaving stockholders and employees in the lurch. WorldCom reported that it had failed to report $5 billion in expenses, and other accounting and reporting failures rocked Wall Street. Finally, even when the economy began to accelerate again in late 2002 and 2003, companies hesitated to hire new people. Taken together, these developments put a serious dent in government receipts; with individuals and companies earning less and capital gains falling, fewer taxes were flowing into the federal treasury.

Second, congressional and executive branch budget officials in early 2001 could not have foreseen the terrorist attacks on the United States and the tremendous costs that eventually would be associated with rebuilding and recovering from them. Nor could they have anticipated the occurrence or the cost of the subsequent war on terrorism—including the conflicts in Afghanistan and Iraq—and homeland security. In 2003, for example, President Bush convinced Congress to appropriate an additional $87 billion for war and occupation in Iraq and proposed very large increases for national defense and homeland security in his fiscal year 2005 budget.

Third, there is no gainsaying the effect of President Bush's three massive tax cuts—the first was for $1.35 trillion over 10 years—on the shrinking long-term surplus. While the rebates to taxpayers in 2001 and the reductions in certain taxes in 2002 probably kept the recession from becoming more serious than it was—because the returned taxes acted as an economic stimulant—budget officials were eventually forced to take account of substantially reduced federal revenues caused by the massive tax cuts over the next 10 years when thinking about the eventual size of long-term surpluses.

Finally, in 2003, President Bush successfully pushed a complex and expensive Medicare prescription drug benefit through Congress that the administration and the CBO esti-

mated would add $534 billion in accumulated deficits over 10 years. To be sure, virtually everyone thought that such a program was long overdue—seniors wanted it, and both Al Gore and George W. Bush promised during the 2000 election campaign to get them this benefit if elected (though Gore and the Democrats did not like the form the drug benefit eventually took). Nevertheless, the cost of the program will be considerable as it phases in over the next few years.

Annual decisions about taxes and federal government spending are among the most important decisions that presidents and members of Congress make. These decisions determine in broad outline what activities and programs the federal government will undertake and how the government will go about paying for them. They affect how the national economy works and who in society will benefit or lose from government activities. Finally, budget policies are not made in a vacuum; these decisions are profoundly affected by what is going on in the nation and in the world outside of Washington.

In this chapter and the next, we turn our attention to an examination of a broad range of these federal government activities and programs and the effect they have on the American people. Obviously, we cannot cover every policy area in the allotted space. We focus, instead, on policy areas we consider most important for protecting the security of American citizens and ensuring their economic and social well-being. In Chapter 18, we look in detail at U.S. foreign and military policy. In this chapter, we look at two broad areas of domestic policy: (1) federal government activities related to the U.S. economy, including the budget, fiscal and monetary policies, subsidies, and regulation; and (2) social welfare programs, including Social Security, Medicare, and public assistance.

Thinking Critically About This Chapter

Using the Framework   You will see in this chapter how the framework can be used to explain why government does what it does in the areas of economic and social welfare policies. You will use what you learned in previous chapters about structural, political linkage, and government factors to better understand what government does in terms of spending, taxing, regulating, and providing income support and social services.

Using the Democracy Standard   In previous chapters, you used the democracy standard to examine the extent to which American political and government institutions enhanced popular sovereignty, political equality, and liberty. You will use the democracy standard in this chapter to ask whether the American people get the sorts of policies and performance they want from government.

Why Government Is Involved in the Economy and Social Welfare

Governments in all modern capitalist societies play a substantial role in managing their national economies and providing social welfare for their citizens. Let's see why they do so.

Economic Management

No government today would dare leave problems such as stagnant economic growth, unemployment, international trade imbalances, or inflation to work themselves out "naturally." Citizens and political leaders in the Western democracies have learned that free market economies, left to themselves, are subject to periodic bouts of **inflation** and unemployment, as well as occasional collapses of employment and economic output (called **depressions**). The worldwide trauma of the Great Depression in the 1930s was the event that etched this lesson into the minds of virtually everyone and forever changed the role of government in economic affairs.

Government responsibility for the state of the national economy is now so widely accepted that national elections are often decided by the voters' judgment of how well the party in power is carrying out this responsibility. When times are good, the party or president in power is very likely to be reelected; when times are bad, those in power have an uphill battle staying in office.

inflation
A condition of rising prices.

depression
A severe and persistent drop in economic activity.

 Comparative

Comparing Economic Policy

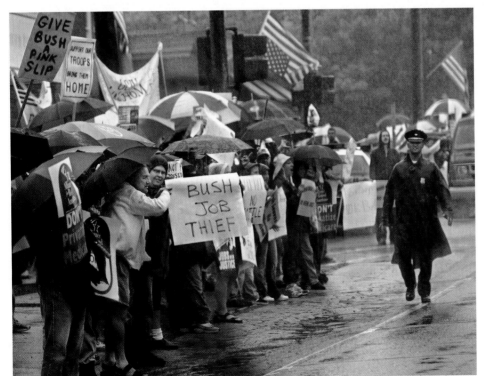

The government is regularly held accountable for economic hardships. Here demonstrators in Ohio protest President George W. Bush's inability to stop the outsourcing of manufacturing jobs. Outsourcing and what to do about it became an important issue in the 2004 presidential campaign.

Social Welfare

welfare state
The set of government programs that protects the minimum standard of living of families and individuals against loss of income.

All rich democracies have programs that protect the minimum standards of living of families and individuals against loss of income due to economic instability, old age, illness and disability, and family disintegration.[2] Nations that provide such a range of programs are often called **welfare states**. All rich democracies are also social welfare states, and the reason is simple: Their citizens have demanded it. They have apparently recognized that market economies, even when working at peak efficiency, do not guarantee a minimum decency of living for all or offer protection against economic dislocations even for people making their best efforts.[3]

Economic Policy

Government economic policies have a number of objectives; all have consequences for the American people.

The Goals of Economic Policy

Although economic policy goals sometimes conflict, and involve important trade-offs,[4] they are consistently driven by five key themes, which we will explore next.

gross domestic product (GDP)
Monetary value of all goods and services produced in a nation each year, excluding income residents earn abroad.

The quintessential goal of economic policymakers is sustained economic growth—defined here as an annual increase in the **gross domestic product (GDP)**. A growing economy generally means more jobs, more products, and higher incomes, so most Americans support this goal. Economic growth is also the basis for increased profits, so business tends to support it as well. For political leaders, economic growth, accompanied by rising standards of living, brings public popularity and heightened prospects for reelection, as well as more revenues for government programs.

In addition to having economic growth, most people want to avoid inflation, a condition in which the purchasing power of money declines. With serious inflation, people's wages, salaries, savings accounts, and retirement pensions diminish in value. So, too, do the holdings of banks and the value of their loans. Economists point out that inflation also brings uncertainty and erratic economic behavior as consumers and businesses try to protect themselves from the effects of future price changes. To nobody's surprise, political leaders seek policies that dampen inflation and provide stable prices. Their problem is that such policies often require slower economic growth, with lower wages and higher levels of unemployment, and these conditions are harmful to broad sectors of the population, usually the most vulnerable sectors.

balance of payments
The annual difference between payments and receipts between a country and its trading partners.

All nations, including the United States, strive to keep their **balance of payments** in positive territory, that is, to export more manufactured goods and services—things such as insurance and banking—than they import. They do so because sustained negative trade balances lead to a decline in the value of a nation's currency in international markets, as more money leaves the country than is brought in. In this situation, businesses and consumers find that their dollars buy less, and they must either do without or borrow to make up the difference.

externalities
The positive and negative effects of economic activities on third parties.

Most people also want to avoid what are called **negative externalities**, the bad side-effects that often accompany normal economic activity. A growing manufacturing economy, for example, often produces things such as air and

Before government regulation, industries were allowed to dump hazardous wastes into the environment without threat of financial or legal repercussions. Here, waste from a copper smelter is dumped into a river.

water pollution, toxic wastes, and workplace injuries and health hazards. In response to these negative externalities, the public over the years has pressed the government to take compensatory action—for example, to prosecute polluters and hold them responsible for cleanups.

Finally, there is a range of economic activities that is essential for the health of the national economy but which is unlikely to be provided by private firms. Almost without exception, governments in the Western democracies, including the United States, have stepped into the breach and provided support for such vital activities and services, either by direct subsidy and tax incentives or by public ownership (although not in the United States). For example, the United States and all European countries subsidize farmers, who are vital to the nation's food chain. Also, the federal government encourages business activity in America's inner cities by using enterprise zone tax incentives; supports the defense industry by directly purchasing weapons systems and subsidizing research; and pays for essential infrastructure such as airports, harbors, and highways.

Farm Subsidies and Domestic Policy

The Tools of Macroeconomic Policy

Government actions affect (but do not solely determine) the rate of inflation, the level of unemployment, and the growth of income and output in the national economy. This always has been so. What is new since the end of World War II is that government leaders, economists, and citizens know this to be true and insist that government use whatever means it has available to ensure good economic outcomes.

Government efforts to encourage economic growth, low unemployment, and stable prices fall under the heading of **macroeconomic policy**, or policy that affects the performance of the economy as a whole. The main tools of macroeconomic policy are **fiscal policy** (having to do with government spending and taxes) and **monetary policy** (having to do with the supply and cost of money).

macroeconomic policy
Having to do with the performance of the economy as a whole.

fiscal policy
Government's actions affecting spending and taxing levels; affects overall output and income in the economy.

monetary policy
Government's actions affecting the supply of money and the level of interest rates in the economy.

Federal Reserve monetary polices have an important impact on the U.S. and global economies. Here, Fed Chairman Alan Greenspan testifies before the House Banking Committee.

Fiscal Policy   In theory, fiscal policy is a flexible tool for stimulating the economy when it is underperforming and for slowing down the economy when it is getting too hot—that is, growing so fast that it triggers inflation. The president and Congress can increase government spending or decrease taxes when economic stimulation is required (one of the arguments George W. Bush made in favor of his proposed tax cut in 2003), thus getting more money into circulation; they can cut spending or increase taxes when the economy needs a cooling-off period.

Fiscal tools are not easy to use, however. Decisions about how much government should spend or what level and kinds of taxes ought to be levied are not made simply on the basis of their potential effects on economic stability and growth. The elderly want Social Security and Medicare benefits to keep pace with inflation, for example, regardless of their effect on the overall economy.

Monetary Policy   The Federal Reserve Board (commonly known as the Fed) is responsible for monetary policy. It is made up of seven members (called governors) who serve overlapping 14-year terms and a chair who serves a renewable four-year term. Each is appointed by the president. Alan Greenspan has been Chairman of the Federal Reserve since 1987. The Fed is closely connected with, and very solicitous of, the needs of commercial and investment bankers and generally prefers to control inflation as a first order of business to protect the value of financial assets. The Fed is relatively independent; aggressive actions by Congress or the president to pressure the Fed would surely trigger adverse reactions on Wall Street and in the financial community at home and abroad—reactions that neither the president nor Congress is eager to confront.

The Fed makes decisions that affect how much money is available to businesses and individuals from banks, savings and loans, and credit unions. The more money that is available and the lower the interest rates at which money can be borrowed, the higher overall consumer and business spending are likely to be. For example, if the Fed wants to increase total spending in the economy (called *aggregate demand*), it increases the money supply (by having its *open market committee* buy back government securities from the private sector) and lowers the **discount rate,** or the cost member banks pay to borrow money from the Fed. If it wants to slow down the economy, it decreases the money supply and increases interest rates.

The Debate About the Proper Role of Government in the Economy   People may agree that government has a role to play in the management of the economy, but they disagree about how it should be done. **Keynesians**—who trace their roots to English economist John Maynard Keynes's classic work, *The General Theory of Employment, Interest, and Money*—have one view. They believe that in an economy where the tools of production (labor, tools, factories, and the like) are not being used to full capacity, which they believe is the case most of the time, government must stimulate economic activity by increasing government spending or by cutting taxes (or both). Most Keynesians would prefer to see increased spending rather than lower taxes, and they are associated with an activist conception of the role of government most favored by liberal Democrats.

Monetarists, such as Nobel Prize-winning economist Milton Friedman, believe that government (the Federal Reserve in particular) should confine its activity to managing the growth in the supply of money and credit so that it closely tracks the growth in productivity in the economy as a whole. In the monetarist view, this will stimulate private investment, which in turn will allow slow but steady economic growth without inflation. Balanced federal budgets are essential in the monetarist position because unbalanced budgets, in their view, make it difficult for central banks to control the money supply properly. Monetarism is the economic policy, then, of those who believe in a minimal federal government and the virtues of the free market most associated with conservatives and Republicans.

Supply-siders believe that the economy works best when the reins on the free market and individual initiative are loosened, and advocate that government be radically reduced by cutting taxes—even if this unbalances the budget—and lightening the regulatory load on business. This belief formed the core of Ronald Reagan's economic policy as well as George W. Bush's.

discount rate
The interest rate the Federal Reserve charges member banks to cover short-term loans.

Keynesians
Advocates of government programs to stimulate economic activity through tax cuts and government spending.

monetarists
Advocates of a minimal government role in the economy, limited to managing the growth of the money supply.

supply-siders
Advocates of steep tax cuts and regulatory relief for business as a way to stimulate economic growth.

The Federal Budget and Fiscal Policy

Decisions by the president and Congress on spending and taxes in the federal budget constitute America's fiscal policy. As "The Rise of Partisan Conflict" feature points out, these decisions are being made in an increasingly partisan environment.

Spending, Taxes, and Debt

Spending   The federal government spent about $2.32 trillion in 2004, roughly 20 percent of GDP. Figure 17.1 on page 514 shows the change over time in federal outlays as a percentage of GDP. Several things are immediately apparent.

First, the most dramatic increases in federal government spending are associated with involvement in major wars; note the big spikes in the graph for the years associated with World War I, World War II, and the Korean War. Second, the relative spending level of the federal government increased steadily from the early 1930s to the early 1980s, then leveled off and declined

Visual Literacy

Evaluating Federal Spending and Economic Policy

The Rises of Partisan Conflict

Spending Like Drunken Sailors: Bush Spending Surplus on Tax Cut Binge

The Story: Democrats were contemptuous of President George W. Bush's proposed $2.4 trillion budget for fiscal 2005. The budget included an estimated deficit of $521 billion and projected annual deficits well into the future, as well as below-inflation budget increases for domestic social programs. Republicans claimed the deficits were unavoidable, as was the modest funding for many domestic programs, caused by the need to fight terrorism and provide security on the homefront. Most Democrats acknowledged the need for an expanded defense and homeland security budget, but blamed the massive Bush tax cuts for the deteriorating budget situation. One Democratic National Committee press release had this to say about the budget proposal: "President Bush has released his budget for the fiscal year 2005, and it spells disaster for America. His failed economic policies are saddling the nation with enormous budget deficits as far as the eye can see. Working families will be paying off the Bush debts for generations." Noting that the new budget included deep cuts in job training programs that the president had praised in his state of the union address two weeks earlier, Democratic National Committee Chairman Terry McAuliffe had this to say: "Just like President Bush's claim about Iraq and nuclear weapons in last year's address, his claims about more funding for job training is directly contradicted by the facts. Most Americans probably believed the president when he talked about the importance of job training,

but they also believed him when he made untrue claims about Iraq seeking nuclear weapons in his 2003 address. These deep cuts to vocational education programs will be disastrous to job creation, and this time the President has only himself—not the British government—to blame for another misleading statement in his State of the Union address."

Noting that the Democrats wanted to solve the deficit problem by raising taxes on upper income groups, Republican Chairman Ed Gillespie had this to say in a speech before the Conservative Political Action Committee in February 2004: "Their desire to raise taxes—under the guise of class warfare—will only reverse the economic gains we're experiencing now. And let's be clear, what Democrats today call tax reform is really just class warfare. They all promise to "soak the rich"—but whenever a Democrat calls for soaking the rich, the middle class needs to grab an umbrella."

The Background: President Bush presented his fiscal 2005 budget in February 2004 to a Congress in which bitter partisan conflict and incivility between Republicans and Democrats had been building for years. Matters worsened in 2003, as Democrats found themselves virtually frozen out of the deliberations

after that. This decrease was caused, in large part, by a substantial decrease in the relative size of the national defense budget after the end of the Cold War environment. Fourth and finally, the costs of recovery from the terrorist attacks on the United States and the subsequent war on terrorism and homeland security pushed up federal spending once more, primarily for national defense.

In 2004, 19.6 percent of federal government expenditures was for *national defense,* a big increase from the 16.4 percent spent in 2001, the budget year immediately preceding the post–9/11 defense buildup. Defense expenditures that led to passage of the Medicare prescription drug program and consideration of President Bush's energy bill. With majorities in both houses of Congress, and with strong party discipline in the House of Representatives, Republicans felt free to fashion what they wanted on both bills in the conference committees, confident that the Democrats could not stop the conference report on either bill once each reached the floor of the House and the Senate. Republicans added insult to injury during this period by throwing Democrats out of a library in the House of Representatives where they had been meeting and extending the customary time limit for casting a vote—in this case, on the Medicare bill—from 15 minutes to three hours so that a few more votes could be rounded up.

Democrats in Congress and the National Committee saw the 2005 budget proposal as an irresistible opportunity to highlight their differences with the Republican Bush administration. Partly, their animus toward the budget proposal was based on what they considered to be their shabby treatment by majority Republicans in Congress. Partly it was anger at a president whose election in 2000 they considered illegitimate and whose overly generous tax cuts heavily favored high-income and wealthy Americans. But most of all, Democrats were angry about what they thought was a well-thought-out plan by the president to engineer a fiscal crisis so that Republicans could roll back a wide range of domestic programs dear to the hearts of Democrats and their constituents. It is, of course, not possible to prove such a charge, but it is interesting to note that the staid *Financial Times* of London wondered if "...the more extreme Republicans actually want a fiscal train wreck ... Proposing to slash federal spending, particularly on social programs ... offers the tantalizing prospect of forcing such cuts through the back door." Republican representative Mike Pence of Indiana, while denying that such a conspiracy exists, acknowledged that "there's no question that annual federal deficits have been the only effective check on congressional spending in the modern era."

What's at Stake: Fashioning the annual federal budget—deciding what programs will be funded and by how much, how revenues will be raised to support these programs, and which individuals and groups in society will foot the bill—is among the most important things that presidents and members of Congress do. It is never easy, even in the best of times, when revenues are plentiful, economic prospects are good, and Republicans and Democrats are willing to settle their differences through compromise. Absent these conditions, the processes by which 14 or 15 separate annual appropriations bills work their way through Congress and by which new tax legislation is considered every now and then becomes a torturous, conflict-laden, blame-apportioning business, filled with anger and vituperation. In recent years, as partisanship has increased, the budget process has become particularly slow, with appropriations bills not passed by the dates specified in the rules of each house, leading either to the shutdown of the government—as happened twice during the Clinton administration—or use of continuing resolutions to allow various government agencies to function temporarily. Needless to say, these outcomes make it exceedingly difficult for agencies to plan and execute policy on a rational and consistent basis. And, the partisan heat generated by budget battles makes it even more difficult for Congress to fulfill its many other legislative responsibilities.

Is This Good for Democracy? It is no doubt a good thing when parties take clear stands on spending and tax policies. When parties do so, it is easier for voters to choose between them, and by so doing, have an important say in determining what government does.

● However, is there a point at which the differences between the parties become so wide and the animosity so deep that the normal give and take of politics can no longer function properly? ● Is a stable form of democracy possible in an environment where elections put one party into power to dismantle the policies of the other party? ● What do you think?

Sources: Title from the Democratic National Committee Website (February 4, 2004), **www.dnc.org**. See also David Firestone, "Dizzying Dive to Red Ink Poses Stark Choices for Washington," *The New York Times* (September 14, 2003), p. A1; Greg Hitt and John D. McKinnon, "Bush Unveils Budget Package of $2.4 Trillion," *The Wall Street Journal* (February 3, 2004); Sheryl Gay Stolberg, "The High Costs of Rising Incivility on Capitol Hill," *The New York Times* (November 30, 2003), Week In Review, p. 10.

are much lower today, however, than at the height of the Cold War; in 1960, for example, national defense consumed more than half of all federal government spending. Spending for *human resources,* including welfare, health, veterans' benefits, and education and training, have grown considerably since 1980, accounting for around 65 percent of federal spending. Most of the growth is accounted for by just two programs: Social Security and Medicare. Outlays for *physical resources,* including transportation, energy, and the environment, accounted for 5.5 percent of federal dollars in 2004, a considerable drop from

Visual Literacy

Where the Money Goes . . .

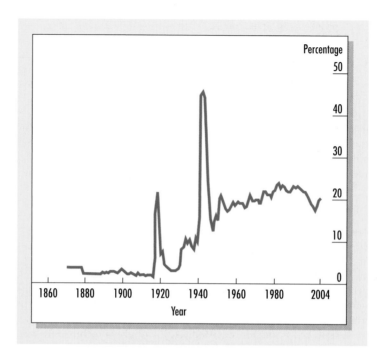

FIGURE 17.1 ● Federal Government Spending as a Percentage of GDP, 1869–2004

This graph shows the scale of federal government spending relative to the size of the U.S. economy. We see that the increase in the relative size of the federal government is a twentieth-century phenomenon. We also see that involvement in major wars has been an important factor in the growth in federal spending, with the major spikes coming during World Wars I and II. The permanent change in the role of the federal government in American society is also seen in the steady rise in spending triggered by the Great Depression during the 1930s. Also noteworthy was the decline of relative federal spending through the 1980s and 1990s and the recent upsurge.

Source: Office of Management and Budget, *Budget of the United States, Historical Tables, Fiscal 2005.*

1980. Other federal, nondefense outlays, which support programs ranging from housing to agriculture, national parks, science and technology, international affairs, and the administration of justice, attracted six cents of every federal dollar spent. Interest payments on the national debt were substantial in 2004, accounting for 7 percent of federal expenditures (down considerably from its modern high point of 15.9 percent in 1996).

Taxes   Government can spend money, of course, only if it has a stream of revenues coming in. Such revenues are raised by various kinds of taxes. Although the American system of taxation shares some features with those of other countries, it is unique in a number of ways.

First, though Americans from all walks of life report feeling squeezed by taxes, the total of all taxes levied by all government jurisdictions in the United States as a proportion of GDP is relatively low, at 32 percent, when compared with the tax bite in the other rich democracies (see Figure 17.2). And, on average, what Americans pay in taxes as a percentage of their incomes has stayed about the same for the past 25 years.[5] Second, reflecting the fact that ours is a federal system, states and localities levy their own taxes. The national government depends primarily on individual income taxes (personal and corporate) and payroll taxes to fund its activities (see Figure 17.3). Other rich democracies depend more on national sales and consumption taxes. In the United States, the states get most of their revenues from sales taxes, although many

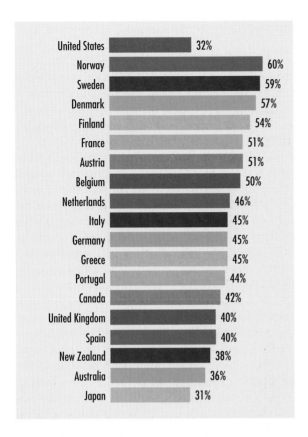

FIGURE 17.2 • Tax Receipts as a Percentage of GDP in the United States and the OECD Countries, 2002

The total tax burden of the United States is lighter than that of most other rich democracies.

Source: U.S. Bureau of the Census, *Statistical Abstract of the United States, 2003.*

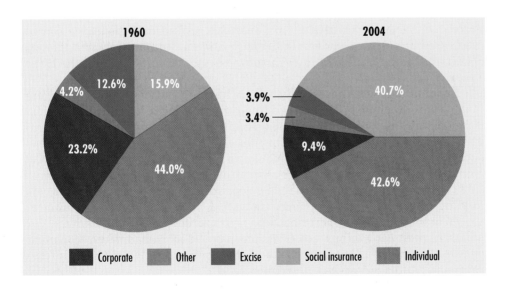

FIGURE 17.3 • Sources of Federal Tax Revenues, 1960 and 2004

The source of federal tax receipts has shifted over the years. Most notable have been the increase in the share of taxes accounted for by social insurance payroll taxes and the shrinking share shouldered by corporations.

Source: Office of Management and Budget, *Budget of the United States, Fiscal 2005.*

have income taxes as well. Local governments depend most heavily on property taxes.

Also, the American tax system is uniquely complex. The U.S. Tax Code is a voluminous document, filled with endless exceptions to the rules and special treatment for individuals, companies, and communities, usually the product of political influence of one kind or another. Few people besides accountants and tax attorneys fully understand the Code, and their services are available mainly to those who can afford them.

Perhaps most interesting of all, though the federal income tax looks to be quite progressive—a system in which tax rates increase as income and wealth increase—in actuality it is only mildly progressive; high-income individuals pay only a slightly higher percentages of their income than others, after all deductions, exclusions, credits, and tax shelters are taken into account. Other federal taxes, such as Social Security and Medicare payroll taxes, and excise taxes on alcohol and cigarettes, are regressive—that is, they take a higher proportion of income in taxes from those lower in the income scale. The result is an overall federal tax system that is relatively flat, meaning that most people in the United States pay about the same percentage of their income in taxes, leaving the highly unequal income distribution of Americans relatively untouched.[6] Critics of the Bush tax cuts, which heavily favored the wealthiest Americans, will actually make income and wealth distribution in the United States even more unequal than it has been; an estimated 38 percent of the long-term benefits of the 10-year, $1.35 trillion tax bill passed in 2001 will go to the top 1 percent of income earners in the United States.[7] A noteworthy feature of the tax cut bill was the elimination of the estate tax on the wealthiest Americans.

The Deficit and the National Debt

As we showed in the opening story, annual budget and the national debt are back in the news. Like any other person, organization, or institution that spends more than it makes, the federal government must borrow from others to cover the shortfall and must pay interest to those from whom it borrows. The **national debt** is the total of what the government owes in the form of treasury bonds, bills, and notes to American citizens and institutions (financial institutions, insurance companies, corporations, etc.), foreign individuals and institutions (including foreign governments and banks), and even to itself (i.e., to units such as the Social Security Trust Fund).

Are annual deficits necessarily bad? Is having a national debt a bad thing? It depends. Economists generally agree that running a **budget deficit** in a slow economy is a good thing because it helps stimulate economic activity. They also agree that a national debt that grows larger to meet emergencies—such as waging a war—is unavoidable and that borrowing to make investments that will have positive long-term impacts on society and the economy—such as building schools and roads, modernizing ports and airports, and funding research and development—is a good thing. However, going into further debt to pay current operating costs is dangerous, something akin to living on one's credit card to buy groceries and pay the mortgage. Most economists believe that running annual deficits of this sort generally drives up interest rates and crowds out private investment.

Before the 1980s, the national debt grew mainly because of deficit spending to wage war. After each war, the debt, relative to GDP, gradually declined.[8] This pattern changed dramatically during the 1980s, however, when the size of annual federal budget deficits escalated, despite the absence of a major war (see Figure 17.4). The national debt as a percentage of GDP began to decline

You Are Trying to Get a Tax Cut

national debt

The total outstanding debt of the federal government; the sum total of all annual budget deficits and surpluses.

budget deficit

The amount by which annual government expenditures exceed revenues.

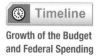

Growth of the Budget and Federal Spending

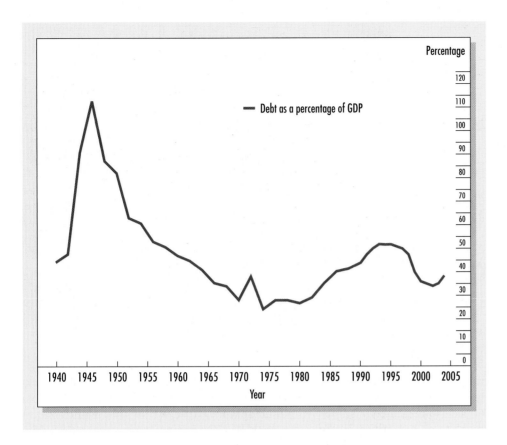

FIGURE 17.4 ● The National Debt as a Percentage of GDP

In strictly dollar terms, the national debt grew steadily from the early 1970s until 1997, when it began to shrink. It rose again after 2001 as budget deficits returned. The relative national debt—that is, the debt compared with the total size of the American economy (GDP)—also grew from the early 1970s but fell after 1993. The relative size of the debt is again increasing. Even at its worst, however, the size of the relative national debt in recent decades was nowhere near the historic high point it reached during World War II.
Source: Office of Management and Budget, *Budget of the United States, Historical Tables, Fiscal 2005.*

in the 1990s, as annual budget deficits turned into annual (and growing) surpluses caused by changes in federal fiscal policies and by the tax windfalls from a booming economy. As suggested in the chapter-opening story, however, deficits returned with a vengeance in 2002, and the budget is likely to stay in deficit for years.

Regulation

Regulation is one of the most visible and important activities of the federal government. For example, federal agencies issue rules that private businesses must follow. These rules may involve how a company treats its toxic wastes, what hiring procedures it practices, or how it reports its profits and losses.

regulations
The issuing of rules by government agencies with the aim of reducing the scale of negative externalities produced by private firms.

Why Government Regulates   A free market economy, even when it is working optimally, produces a range of negative externalities that cannot be or are unlikely to be solved by private businesses on their own. These problems include, among others, air and water pollution, inadequate information for investors,

The stock market crash in 1929 convinced many Americans, including the financial community, that the federal government had an important role to play in regulating and protecting the securities industry against some of its worst excesses. The result was creation of the Securities and Exchange Commission.

unsafe products, unsafe and unwholesome workplaces, toxic wastes, and reckless financial practices. The American people have demonstrated on a number of occasions and consistently in public opinion surveys that they want government to do something about these problems. At various times, elected leaders have acted democratically by responding to these demands and increasing regulation. As odd as it may seem, however, business leaders also have advocated government regulation to meet one problem or another. The *economic theory of regulation* holds that regulation is caused by the political efforts of powerful businesses that turn to government for protection against competitors. This theory argues that regulation allows firms to restrict overall output, to deny entry to business competitors, and to maintain above-market prices.[9]

A History of American Regulation   A brief review of the history of regulation illustrates how the interaction of democratic and nondemocratic factors has produced today's regulatory agencies and policies.[10]

Between 1900 and World War I, laws were passed to regulate activities of powerful new corporations. These progressive era reforms were pushed by labor unions, the Populists, and middle-class Americans anxious about the conditions reported by muckraking journalists. Landmark regulatory measures included the Federal Trade Commission Act, the Meat Inspection Act, the Pure Food and Drug Act, and the Federal Reserve Act. These measures dealt with problems such as monopolies, unstable financial institutions, unwholesome products, and unsafe working conditions.

Some scholars believe, however, that large corporations were major players in the conception, formulation, and enactment of regulatory legislation.[11] Seen in this light, the Federal Reserve Act was primarily a government response to the entreaties of the American Bankers Association, which worried that financial panics would destroy its business.

Roosevelt's New Deal in the 1930s focused on speculative and unsafe practices in the banking and securities industries that had contributed to the onset of the Great Depression. The goal was to restore stability to financial markets and important industries. Legislation focused on such issues as federal bank inspection, federal deposit insurance, the prohibition of speculative investments by banks, and the creation of the Securities and Exchange Commission to regulate stock market operations. Again, the political sources of New Deal regulation were mixed. Some came from popular pressures,[12] but some also came from the business community, seeking stability in its various industries.[13]

The successes of the consumer, environmental, and civil rights movements from the late 1960s to the late 1970s resulted in a substantial increase in the federal government's regulation of business. The aim of these regulatory efforts was to protect against health and environmental hazards, to provide equal opportunity, and to allow more public access to regulatory rule making. Under the authority of new laws, agencies such as the Environmental Protection Agency, the Equal Opportunity Employment Agency, and the Federal Drug Administration issued numerous rules that affected business operations and decisions. It was one of the only times in our history when business was almost entirely on the defensive, unable to halt the imposition of laws and regulations to which it was strongly opposed.[14]

By the end of the 1970s, the mood of opinion leaders both inside and outside the government had turned against regulation in the name of economic efficiency. Many blamed excessive regulation for forcing inefficient practices on American companies, contributing to sluggish economic growth, slow productivity gains, and disappointing competitiveness in the global economy. And many found fault with the government for imposing uniform national standards, strict deadlines for compliance with regulations, and detailed instructions.[15] The deregulatory mood was spurred by a business political offensive that funded think tanks, journals of opinion, foundations favorable to the business point of view, and electoral campaigns of sympathetic candidates.[16] From then until today, the watchword has been **deregulation,** the attempt to loosen the hand of government in a variety of economic sectors including banking and finance, transportation, and telecommunications.

deregulation
The process of diminishing regulatory requirements for business.

President George W. Bush is an enthusiastic deregulator. His administration supported rule changes to allow more road building in national forests, to restore snowmobile use in national parks (eventually blocked by the courts), to allow developers more freedom to build in wetlands, and to exempt some power plants from clean air rules. He also appointed several critics of regulation to important regulatory bodies.[17] The position of administration supporters is that more sensible and economically efficient ways of regulating business are possible, but only after the heavy hand of government is removed.

The Future of Regulation　While deregulation may mean that especially egregious, unfair, and inefficient regulations will be erased from the books, the regulatory state is likely here to stay, mainly because the public supports most existing regulatory programs, especially those aimed at environmental and consumer protection.

The regulatory state is here to stay, moreover, because economic activity and technological change bring new problems and demands for government intervention to protect the public. The ready availability of pornography on the Internet, for example, has triggered efforts by Christian conservatives and others to regulate its content. Unraveling the human genome has led to calls for regulating how this new knowledge will be used. When people become ill from E.coli microbes in ground beef, the public demands higher standards of meat inspection and tracking. When mergers threaten competition, most consumers welcome government intervention. And when companies such as Enron collapse, taking with them the retirement savings of their employees, or when accounting firms and investment banks allow companies such as WorldCom to mislead investors, Americans demand that government protect them against similar behavior by other companies.

While strong environmental policies are supported by a majority of Americans, business and industry as well as their employees often exert strong pressure to reduce government action in this area.

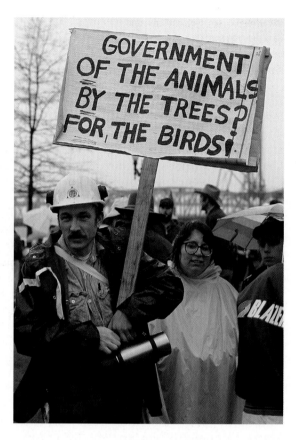

Also, business itself will continue to turn to government for regulation when it suits the purpose of a particular industry. Thus, in 2004, after the discovery of mad cow disease in the United States, the National Cattlemen's Beef Association, the main trade association of the beef industry, asked political leaders to institute regulations that would restore consumer confidence in beef products and reopen foreign markets, where U.S. beef exports had been banned. Ironically, perhaps, the American Cattlemen's Association had lobbied for years against such regulation.

Social Welfare

Timeline

The Evolution of Social Welfare Policy

social insurance
Government programs that provide services or income support in proportion to the amount of mandatory contributions made by individuals to a government trust fund.

means-tested
Meeting the criterion of demonstrable need.

Another important domain of domestic policy in the United States is social welfare, a broad range of programs that protects the minimum standards of living of families and individuals against some of life's unavoidable circumstances: unemployment, income loss and poverty, physical and mental illness and disability, family disintegration, and old age. Such programs account for the largest share of the annual federal budget.

Outline of the American Welfare State

Social welfare in the United States is provided by a complex mix of programs, but we can distinguish two basic kinds. The first is **social insurance,** in which individuals contribute to an insurance trust fund by way of a payroll tax on their earnings and receive benefits based on their lifetime contributions. Social Security is an example of social insurance. The second kind is **means-tested,** meaning that benefits are distributed on the basis of need to

When companies such as Enron and WorldCom collapse because of legal but ethically suspect and financially dangerous actions by their executives, lawyers, and accountants, many people are hurt, including employees like these at Enron. Not surprisingly, when this happens, pressure builds on elected officials to protect the public by regulating such corporate practices.

those who can prove that their income is low enough to qualify. These programs are funded by general income tax revenues, rather than by payroll taxes. The food stamp program is an example.

Some social welfare programs are administered directly from Washington, while others are jointly administered by federal and state governments. Social Security is an example of a program run from the nation's capital. Taxes for Social Security are levied directly on wages and salaries by the federal government, and benefit checks are issued to the elderly and the disabled by the Social Security Administration. By contrast, Medicaid is jointly funded and administered by state and federal governments. One result of such mixed programs is wide variation in benefit levels across the states.

Some welfare state programs are **entitlement** programs; that is, payments are made automatically to people who meet certain eligibility requirements. All Americans over the age of 65, for example, are covered by Medicare, and most citizens whose income is under a certain limit are entitled to food stamps. Because payments are made automatically, these expenditures are locked into the federal budget, and Congress can only tinker around the margins of the budget.

entitlements
Government benefits that are distributed automatically to citizens who qualify on the basis of a set of guidelines set by law; for example, Americans over the age of 65 are entitled to Medicare coverage.

Social Security and Other Social Insurance Programs

Social insurance programs that guard against loss of income due to old age, disability, and illness are the largest, most popular, and fastest-growing parts of the American welfare state[18] (see Figure 17.5). Such programs account for about one-third of annual federal government expenditures. In the next sections, we'll explore each of them.

Old Age, Survivors, and Disability Insurance (OASDI)   This is the largest of the social insurance programs and the full, technical name of Social Security. OASDI is funded by a payroll tax on employees and employers under the Federal

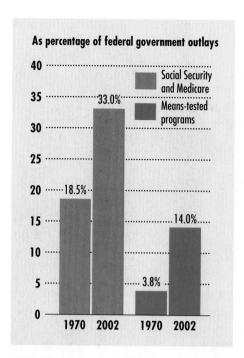

As percentage of federal government outlays

FIGURE 17.5 ● **Comparing the Size of Social Insurance and Means-Tested Programs, 2002**

Social insurance programs, such as Social Security and Medicare, receive many more federal dollars than means-tested programs, such as public assistance, food stamps, and Medicaid. Social insurance now accounts for one-third of federal government spending.

Source: Office of Management and Budget, *The Budget of the United States, 2003.*

Insurance Contributions Act (the familiar FICA on your weekly or monthly pay stub). Theoretically, these tax revenues are deposited in a Social Security trust fund; in fact, this is a paper transaction only, with payroll taxes treated as simply another component of the government's general revenue stream. Because the program is paid for to a substantial degree by those who are currently working, the net effect is to redistribute income across generations.

Many Americans worry that Social Security funds will run out before they can begin collecting benefits. Presently, Social Security takes in more in payroll taxes than it pays out in benefits each year, so its trust fund shows a strong positive balance. However, because the population is aging—meaning there will be fewer working people paying taxes to pay the benefits for additional elderly recipients—a time will come when the fund will be paying out at a faster clip than it is being replenished. Especially troublesome to many is the sizable baby-boom generation, whose first members will reach retirement age in 2010. According to recent estimates by the actuary of the Social Security trust fund, the fund will not move into the red until the year 2042. Of course, long before then, Americans can decide to solve the trust fund problem by raising payroll taxes, cutting back benefit levels, or raising the retirement age.[19] Policymakers can also decide, as some have suggested, to fully or partially privatize the system, having individuals manage their own stock market accounts.

Generally, Democrats think the system is in good health, and requires only some tinkering to solve emerging problems. Republicans, on the other hand, believe the system is seriously flawed and that the only way to save it is with major overhauls such as individual investment accounts.

Medicare This program, also for older Americans, pays for a substantial portion of the hospital and doctor bills of retirees and the disabled. A partial prescription drug benefit program goes into effect in 2006. Since Medicare was created in 1965, it has grown into one of the largest federal programs in total dollar expenditures; more than $271 billion was spent in 2004, almost 12 percent of the annual federal budget. The prescription drug benefit will add about $534 billion over 10 years to Medicare expenditures.

Paying for Medicare is a recurring problem. Outlays grew at about 10 percent a year over the past 15 years, much faster than those for other federal programs and much faster than Medicare revenues are coming in. And waiting in the wings, again, is the baby-boom generation and the drug prescription program. Medicare fund trustees reported in 2004 that the fund will be depleted by 2019 unless changes are made. It is no wonder, then, that the issue of controlling Medicare costs has become one of the constants of recent American politics.

Do Social Insurance Programs Work? In an era when it is fashionable to deride the ability of government to do anything well, it is important to recognize how successful America's social insurance programs have been. There is no doubt that Social Security and Medicare work beyond the wildest dreams of their founders. Although the benefits do not allow people to live luxuriously, they provide an income floor for the retired and pay for costly medical services that, before 1965, were as likely as not to impoverish those who had serious illnesses and long hospital stays.

The effectiveness of Social Security and Medicare was shown in a 1989 Census Bureau study on the effects of government taxing and spending programs on income inequality and poverty. The principal finding was that Social Security (including Medicare) "is the Federal government's most effective weapon against poverty and reduces the inequality of Americans' income more than the tax system and more than recent social welfare [means-tested] programs."[20] In fact, Social Security and Medicare have helped reduce the elderly poverty rate from about 48 percent in the mid-1950s to about 10 percent today.[21]

To be sure, there are problems as well. Social Security and Medicare have remained viable, for instance, only because Congress has steadily raised payroll taxes to pay for them. FICA and Medicare taxes now take a larger bite out of the paychecks of a majority of Americans than the personal income tax. For those who generally oppose taxes, this trend is cause for concern. Whether taxes are too high cannot be answered objectively or scientifically, of course, although it is worth repeating that our overall effective tax rates remain well below those of most other Western countries.

Many also worry about the fiscal viability of Social Security and Medicare, as discussed earlier. The problem is serious, to be sure, but it is certainly solvable, as we also suggested earlier. Still others believe that Medicare coverage is insufficient and that it should cover people under the age of 65 as well as those 65 and older, while others regard the prescription drug benefit as too skimpy.

Means-Tested Programs (Welfare)

Means-tested programs, popularly called *welfare*, account for only a small part of the annual federal budget but have attracted more popular discontent than virtually anything else government does. While Social Security and Medicare enjoy widespread support, means-tested welfare programs have long been an object of scorn.

Most Americans say they want government to help the poor, but almost everyone disliked the now-defunct Aid to Families with Dependent Children

By the Numbers

How many Americans are poor?

Although the Bible says, "For you will have the poor with you always" (Matthew 26:11), it does not tell us how many of the poor will be with us at any given time.

Why It Matters: Knowing how many poor there are, and being relatively confident in the validity and reliability of that number, is extremely important for a number of reasons:

- Comparing the number who are poor in the United States over time gives us an indication of how well we are doing as a society.
- Comparing the number who are poor in the United States over time lets us know the dimensions of a serious social problem that may require government action or the mobilization of private charities, or both.
- The number of people living in poverty helps determine the size (and thus the cost) of many government programs, including food stamps, Medicaid, rent supplements, and the Earned Income Tax Credit.

Interestingly, if the numbers are to be believed, we made good progress during the 1990s—the poverty rate fell to 11.3 in 2000, its lowest point in 21 years—but increased again between then and 2002 as the United States went through a recession and then a jobless recovery. In 2003, 12.5 percent of Americans—around 35.9 million people—were below the poverty line, according to the Census Bureau.

The Story Behind the Poverty Measure: But what is poverty and how can we measure it? Most would probably agree that poverty involves living in dire circumstances; that is, being poorly housed, un-

derfed, and without adequate medical care. But we might have a harder time agreeing on the exact dividing line between adequate and inadequate living standards. To get around this, government statisticians use *income* as a proxy for calculating poverty. Rather than collect information about how people live—what their homes and apartments are like, for example—the Census Bureau collects information about how much money they earn. The assumption, of course, is that in an economy such as ours, what one earns is directly related to how one lives and consumes.

Calculating the Poverty Line: The poverty line was first calculated in 1964 by Census Bureau statisticians. They started with the Department of Agriculture's determination of what it would cost a family of four to buy enough food to survive (called the "emergency food budget"). Then, because it had been determined that the average American family in 1964 spent one-third of its after-tax income on food, the statisticians multiplied the Agricultural Department's emergency food budget figure by three to determine the official government poverty line. They then adjusted this income number for family size, creating poverty line numbers for single persons living alone, two-person families, and so on.

This 1964 baseline figure is used to the present day. Starting in 1965, and every year since then, the poverty line from the previous year is adjusted for inflation, taking into account different family sizes. The accompanying table shows the official poverty line thresholds for 2003. To be under the line is to be officially poor.

Criticisms of the Poverty Line Measure: As with most official statistics, the poverty line calculation has its critics:

- Because the typical American household today spends a much lower proportion of its income on food than in 1964, the "emergency food budget" figure from the Agriculture Department should

(AFDC) program—not only conservatives, but liberals as well; not only average citizens, but also welfare recipients; and not only voters and political leaders, but people who work for welfare agencies. A consensus long existed that something was wrong with AFDC.[22] For most Americans, AFDC and other be multiplied not by three, as has been since the beginning, but by five or six, to calculate the poverty threshold, say some critics. This would result in a substantial increase in the number of people officially designated as poor.

- If poverty is really about lifestyles and consumption patterns, argue conservatives, then household income calculations should include the income equivalents of noncash government benefits such as public housing, rent supplements, Medicaid support, and food stamps. Doing this would reduce the number of people officially living in poverty.

- By calculating a single, national poverty threshold, the Census Bureau fails to take into account the substantial differences in the cost of living that exist across states and communities. A family of four earning $17,000, for example, could no doubt stretch its dollars farther in rural Alabama than in San Francisco.

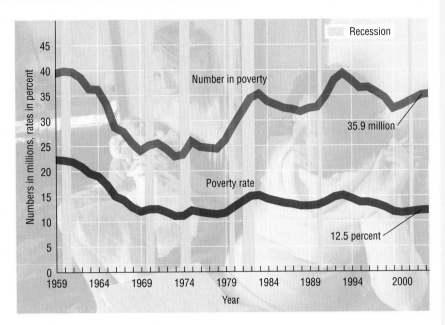

Poverty in the United States

What to Watch For: All government statistics are built on a set of assumptions, some of which are sensible and some of which defy common sense. Be aware of such assumptions when you use official statistics. Luckily, every government agency describes in detail how it collects and calculates statistics, so you can figure it out once you read the documentation.

What Do You Think?   With all its problems, should we continue to depend on the Census Bureau's poverty line calculation? Do the virtues of simplicity, consistency, and comparability across the years of the present way of calculating poverty trump its several problems? Or would you rather see poverty rates calculated in some other way? What do you think should be included and excluded from such a calculation?

Poverty in the United States

1 Person	2 People	3 People	4 People	5 People	6 People	7 People	8 People	9 or More People
$9,393	$12,015	$14,680	$18,801	$22,245	$25,122	$28,554	$31,589	$37,656

means-tested programs seemed to contradict such cherished cultural values as independence, hard work, stable families, and responsibility for one's own actions. Public opinion polls consistently showed that Americans believed that welfare kept people dependent; didn't do a good job of helping people stand on

Because of limits on how many years people can be on welfare under the 1996 welfare reform legislation, many families, including this one, will soon find their benefits running out.

their own two feet; and encouraged divorce, family disintegration, and out-of-wedlock births.[23] (See the "By the Numbers" feature to learn more about the number of poor people in the United States.)

The government offers several means-tested programs designed to assist low-income Americans. Let us look at the five most important ones.

Food Stamps   This program is available to most Americans who fall below a certain income line. About 8 percent of Americans presently receive food stamps. Food stamp benefit levels are set by the individual states under general federal guidelines, and states vary substantially in their generosity. Stamps can be used only for food; they cannot be used for alcohol, cigarettes, beauty care products, or gambling, despite rumors to the contrary. The program seems to have made a significant dent in the prevalence of malnutrition in the United States, even though the average benefit has never exceeded 80 cents per person per meal.[24]

Medicaid   The federal government allocates matching funds to the states to provide medical assistance for their indigent citizens in this rapidly growing program. Except for having to follow the requirement to provide Medicaid for all public assistance recipients, the states formulate their own eligibility requirements and set their own benefit levels. The eligibility rules are complex and tend to exclude those who are not extremely poor, blind, disabled, or children of out-of-work parents. The problem of noninclusion is serious; only about 40 percent of the nation's officially designated poor are covered by Medicaid, and the remainder are without medical benefits or protection.

Supplemental Security Income   Created in 1974, Supplemental Security Income (SSI) is a program that provides cash benefits to the elderly, blind, and disabled poor when social insurance programs are insufficient to elevate them above the poverty line. The program is relatively small and getting smaller.

The Earned Income Tax Credit   The working poor benefit greatly from a provision in the U.S. Tax Code that allows low-income individuals with at least one child to claim a credit against taxes owed or, for some, to receive a direct cash transfer from the IRS. This provision of the Tax Code benefits more than 56 million low-income Americans without much bureaucratic fuss.[25]

Welfare Block Grants   The Temporary Assistance to Needy Families (TANF) Act, passed in 1996, replaced AFDC with an entirely new system of public assistance. (See the "Using the Framework" feature on why the change happened.) Its major features are as follows:

- The status of welfare assistance as a federal entitlement was ended. The families of poor children are no longer guaranteed assistance by the federal government.
- The design and administration of welfare programs have been turned over to the states, meaning there are 50 different welfare systems in the United States.
- States receive block grants from the federal government to help them finance the welfare systems they devise. States add their own money in varying amounts, with some states, such as New York, much more generous than others.
- States use these combined funds to give both direct cash assistance to families—usually, a monthly welfare check—and money for child care, education and training, and other services to encourage recipients to enter paid employment. By 2003, the states were putting more money into noncash assistance than into cash assistance.[26]

Web Exploration
Making It on Welfare

Issue: Is it possible to live a decent life under the new welfare system? Find out by preparing your own family budget and comparing it with the welfare benefits available in your state.

Site: Access the Green Book of the House Ways and Means Committee and look at the maximum TANF family payment for your state on our Website at **www.ablongman.com/greenberg**. Go to the "Web Explorations" section for Chapter 17, select "making it on welfare," then "benefits." In Section 7, look carefully at Table 7.9 on "maximum benefits" for each state.

What You've Learned: Imagine you are a welfare recipient living in your present community. Pretend that you have two children. Prepare a monthly budget for what it would cost you to live at a minimum level of decency. Be sure to account for housing costs, including utilities, food (you will pay about half, with food stamps covering the other half), transportation (used car, with insurance and gas, or public transportation), school supplies for your children, some modest entertainment, some clothes, personal hygiene and beauty care products, and whatever else you believe to be essential. Don't worry about medical care; you'll be covered by Medicaid.

How does your budget compare with the maximum monthly benefit paid in your state? Do you believe it is possible for you and your hypothetical family to live a decent life under TANF? Is there anything you could eliminate from your budget to make it leaner?

Hint: Most students find that what they consider to be necessary for minimum decency is far above what is allowed to welfare families.

Using the Framework

Welfare Reform

Why did our welfare system change so drastically in 1996?

Background: America's traditional welfare system, created in 1935 almost as an afterthought to Social Security, had grown to the point that it provided cash payments to families of one in nine children in the United States by 1995. Although it did not pay very much to individual families, and represented but a tiny portion of the federal government's budget, the program was never very popular with the public, grew even less popular in recent decades, and was replaced by a radically new program in 1996. Examining structural, political linkage, and governmental factors that contributed to a dramatic change in welfare policy will make the story clearer.

Governmental Action

The Temporary Assistance to Needy Families Act becomes law in 1996.

Governmental Level

The Republican-controlled Congress delivered on its promise in the Republican Contract with America to pass a bill to radically transform welfare.

President Clinton, a member of the DLC and a believer in welfare reform (he had promised to "end welfare as we know it"), signed the bill into law near the beginning of the 1996 presidential campaign.

Political Linkages Level

The Democratic Party lost a substantial number of blue-collar, unionized workers, concerned about "wasteful spending" on welfare, from their electoral base.

Moderate Democrats of the Democratic Leadership Council (DLC) also embraced welfare reform.

Republican consevatives won control of the House and Senate in the 1994 elections.

Conservative intellectuals and think tanks attacked the AFDC welfare system during the 1980s on the grounds that it killed individual initiative and created dependency, destroyed families, and rewarded immorality.

Public opinion became more critical of welfare in the 1970s and 1980s.

The Republican Party used the "welfare mess" issue with great effect in election campaigns, winning the presidency in 1980, 1984, and 1988 and the Senate for much of the 1980s.

Structural Level

The American political culture celebrates competitive individualism, small government, and self-reliance, and denigrates handouts to the "undeserving" poor.

Competitive pressures from the global economy in the 1990s pushed governments in all of the rich democracies to make their welfare states more efficient.

The fall of communism and the post–Cold War boom in the United States enhanced the attractiveness of conservative ideas in America.

Federalism allowed states to experiment with alternative modes of welfare delivery.

- The head of every family receiving welfare is required to work within two years of receiving benefits and is limited to a total of five years of benefits. States are allowed to impose even more stringent time requirements. Connecticut, for example, has set the limit at 21 months. States are also allowed to use their own funds (not federal block grant money) to extend the two-year and five-year limits.

- Unmarried teenage parents can receive welfare benefits only if they stay in school and live with an adult.

- States must provide Medicaid to all who qualify under current law.

Proponents of welfare reform believed the new welfare system would end welfare dependence, reestablish the primacy of the family in poor communities, improve the income situation of the poor as they enter the job market, and help balance the federal budget. Opponents of welfare reform believed the legislation would lead to more poverty, homelessness, and hunger—especially among children—once recipients reached their five-year time limit.

Participation

Making a Difference:
Welfare Reform

Only time will tell which of these scenarios will prevail over the long run. In the short run, however, some results are encouraging. Welfare rolls have diminished in every state, many people have been trained for jobs and have entered the paid workforce, and many have raised their incomes.[27] For example, about two-thirds of those who left welfare between 1996 and 2001 were working at least 20 hours per week.[28] But, say critics, there is a hidden and darker story: 20 percent of those who left the welfare roles between 1997 and 2001, for example, eventually returned to them. And, because pay levels for entry-level jobs are so low, only a handful of former welfare recipients were able to cross the official **poverty-line** threshold during this period.[29] Worse yet, according to critics, things became worse for welfare people when economic hard times returned between 2001 and 2003. Many of those who had used up their five years of lifetime welfare eligibility were without jobs and suffering the consequences. Urban Institute researchers reported in 2003, for example, that 48 percent of unemployed former welfare recipients report that they and their family have skipped meals for lack of food, 63 report that they often or sometimes run out of money to buy food, while 46 percent report that they have sometimes been unable to pay the rent or mortgage, or utilities.[30]

poverty line
The federal government's calculation of the amount of income families of various sizes need to stay out of poverty.

How the American Welfare State Compares with Others

Although all the world's rich democracies are also social welfare states, not all social welfare states are alike. Welfare states range from minimalist—where benefits are low and are narrowly targeted (e.g., to the poor and the elderly)—to highly developed, social democratic types—where benefits are generous and include most people in the society.[31] The United States is very close to the minimalist end of the spectrum. For those who believe that small government is always better than big government, this is a very good thing. Others disagree, believing that government should play a more significant role in protecting and sustaining its citizens, and they admire the more comprehensive programs of other countries such as Sweden and Germany.

What are the differences between our welfare state and those of the other rich democracies?

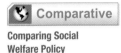

Comparative

Comparing Social
Welfare Policy

- *The American welfare state is much less costly.* Despite complaints about its overall cost, ours is among the least costly of the social welfare states.[32] Among the rich democracies, only Japan and Australia spend relatively less than we do on social welfare, and Japan is well known for the generosity of company benefits to workers.

- *The American welfare state covers fewer people than other welfare states.* Most of western European nations blanket their entire populations with benefits. Family allowances in places such as Austria, the Netherlands, Norway, and Sweden, for instance, go to all citizens who have children. In the United States, in contrast, social welfare provision is a patchwork, and many citizens are not protected or covered.

- *The American welfare state favors the elderly, while other welfare states distribute benefits more equitably.* Medicare and Social Security, already the largest parts of social welfare in the United States, continue to outstrip the rate of growth of programs that benefit the nonelderly poor, especially children. In most other welfare states, family allowances and universal medical coverage keep benefit distributions more balanced.[33] One result is a significant decrease in the poverty rate among the elderly over the past two decades and an increase in the poverty rate among children.[34]

- *The American welfare state is less redistributive.* The degree of income equality in the OECD nations (with the exception of Japan) is a function of the amount of money they spend on social welfare programs and the degree to which program coverage is universal. The United States ranks very low on both, so our social welfare state does not make much of a dent in the degree of income and wealth inequality in comparison with those of other nations.[35]

- *The American welfare state requires less of private employers.* All western European countries require that employers help employees with their parenting obligations. For example, all require employers to offer maternity and parenting leaves (now required for workers in firms with 50 or more employees in the United States under the Family and Medical Leave Act), with pay (not required here), and all require that work schedules be adjusted for parenting needs. German mothers receive six weeks' paid leave before giving birth and eight weeks' after. Further, all western European governments mandate four to six weeks of paid vacation.

Medicare pays for a substantial portion of the health care costs of elderly Americans. Before Medicare, those over 65 depended on private health insurance or paid out-of-pocket for medical care.

- *The American welfare state does not include universal health care.* The OECD countries either provide health services directly (the National Health Service in Great Britain is an example), offer universal health insurance coverage (e.g., the Canadian system), or use some combination of the two. In the United States, Medicare provides health insurance coverage for the elderly and a prescription drug benefit (starting in 2006), Medicaid provides coverage for the poor, and the Veterans Administration covers costs for veterans of the military and their dependents. Other Americans must depend on private insurance, pay out-of-pocket, or do without. Almost 44 million Americans, for example, have no health insurance coverage at all.[36]

Why the American Welfare State Is Different

How to explain the special character of the American welfare state? Here we identify structural and political linkage factors that influence the kind of social welfare state we have.

Constitutional Rules   Federalism is one reason social welfare programs were introduced here so late. Until the 1930s, it was not clear where the main responsibility for social welfare was constitutionally lodged. In fact, it was not generally accepted that the national government had any authority at all on social welfare matters until the U.S. Supreme Court belatedly relented and accepted the New Deal. Federalism is also responsible for the incredible administrative complexity of our social welfare state and for the great unevenness in program coverage. Because of federalism, that is, our system takes into account the needs and interests of each state. The result is great variation among the states in benefits, eligibility requirements, and rules. The only large-scale programs that are universal in the European sense (uniform, comprehensive, and administered and funded by the national government) are Social Security and Medicare.

Racial and Ethnic Diversity   It is often argued that Europe's greater propensity toward welfare states with universal coverage is a result of the ethnic and racial homogeneity of their societies. In homogeneous societies, the argument goes, voters are willing to support generous welfare programs because recipients are believed to be very much like themselves—neighbors, down on their luck.[37]

Whether or not this argument is valid—the growing diversity within European countries will eventually make it possible to test this idea—it is apparent that racial and ethnic tensions influence the shape of the American welfare state. Some of the hostility toward AFDC, for instance, was probably related to the fact that African Americans made up a disproportionately large share of AFDC recipients (although less than a majority of all recipients), and that media stories about welfare recipients focused almost entirely on African Americans.[38] Politicians such as former senator Jesse Helms of North Carolina built long and successful careers by tapping into resentments built on the purported tie between race and welfare.

Political Culture   Almost every aspect of the American political culture works against a generous and comprehensive welfare state. The belief in competitive individualism is especially important. Voters who believe that people should stand on their own two feet and take responsibility for their

How Democratic Are We?

Economic and Social Policy and the American People

PROPOSITION: The economic and social policies that the government in Washington produces are a far cry from what the people want. Americans don't get the kinds of economic and social policies that satisfy them.

AGREE: The discontent expressed by the public about government—it's too big, spends and taxes too much, and cannot be trusted to do the right thing—is largely related to the fact that government actions do not come close to what the public wants. Once elected, our leaders are largely unaffected by elections and focus on what special interests want, so our economic and social policies are tilted in ways that satisfy those special interests. For example, people told pollsters for years that they wanted a prescription drug benefit, but it took roughly three decades to get it. Worse yet, the final program seemed to channel most of its dollars to drug and insurance companies. Another example is a tax code that heavily rewards upper-income and wealthy Americans.

DISAGREE: In broad outline, the American public gets what it wants from government in terms of economic and social policy, although, to be sure, they continue to complain about government. Even though current economic and social policies do not satisfy many conservative or liberal critics, democracy is served to the extent that policies closely match what the majority wants from government. For example, Americans want a level of government spending and taxing that is lower than that of the other rich democracies, which it gets. It wants a government that provides only minimal cash support and services for people who seem able but unwilling to help themselves, which it also gets. In the post–Cold War arena, it wants funds shifted from the defense sector to domestic needs, which elected leaders have done, until forced to change course after the September 11, 2001, attacks on the United States. The public wants a government that mostly allows the free market to operate on its own but that also pays attention to issues of consumer safety and environmental protection. Economic policies reflect these seemingly contradictory desires.

CONSIDER: The complexity and range of current economic and social welfare policies in the United States make it difficult to reach a simple verdict about how democratic public policy is in the United States.

• What overall conclusion would you make about it? • Do the American people get what they want from government? • How about you? • Are you satisfied with the federal government's economic and social welfare policies? • Which policies do you support? • Which ones would like to see changed? • And, if you want things changed, do either of the two major political parties seem willing or capable of changing them?

lives are not likely to be sympathetic to appeals for helping able-bodied, working-age people.[39]

Anti-government themes in the political culture also play a role. Generous and comprehensive welfare states, such as those in Europe, are almost always large and centralized states supported by high taxes. Being deeply suspicious of politicians, centralized government, and taxes, Americans strongly resist welfare state appeals.

Business Power   Business plays a disproportionately powerful role in American politics (see Chapter 7). Almost without exception, the business community has opposed the creation of a welfare state along European lines. It has been a voice for low taxes and limited benefits and for voluntary efforts over government responsibility. This stance is most obvious in the area of medical care. Ours is a patchwork quilt that combines social insurance for the elderly (Medicare), a means-tested program (Medicaid) for *some* of the poor, private insurance (Blue Cross/Blue Shield, Prudential, etc.) for many Americans, and a multitude of for-profit hospitals and nursing homes. Doctors, hospital corporations, insurance companies, and nursing home owners are major players in the American system of interest group politics, and they continuously press politicians to maintain this system of mixed government–private enterprise medical care.

Weak Labor Unions   Countries in which the working class is organized and exercises significant political power have extensive welfare states; countries in which the working class is not well organized and fails to exercise significant political power have minimal welfare states.[40] American labor unions have never been very strong or influential when compared with labor unions in other Western capitalist countries. And the proportion of American workers who join labor unions has always been lower in the United States than in other capitalist countries. Moreover, neither one of our political parties defines itself as a working-class or labor party committed to using government as an instrument of equality. We have no party equivalent, for example, to the labor-backed Social Democratic party that has dominated Swedish politics since the mid-1930s.

Summary

The federal government plays an important role in national economic affairs and in providing social welfare for its citizens. Both roles arise from problems created by a dynamic free enterprise market economy and the demand by people in a democratic society that government lend a helping hand.

   With respect to macroeconomic policy, the government uses both fiscal and monetary tools to try to encourage economic growth and low inflation. The annual budget fashioned by the president and Congress is the main tool of fiscal policy; decisions by the Federal Reserve Board that affect the supply of money in the economy serve as the main tool of monetary policy. Monetary policy has become increasingly important as problems in controlling the budget deficit have made fiscal policy less effective and less attractive.

   The federal government also subsidizes essential infrastructure that would otherwise not be made available by private enterprise and plays an important regulatory role. The origins of the government's role may be found in market failures and diseconomies that triggered popular and business pressures on government. Despite the deregulation efforts of recent years, the regulatory responsibilities of the federal government are likely to remain substantial.

   Economic policies are fashioned by the president, Congress, and the Federal Reserve Board. But others are involved as well. Interest groups play a particularly central role. Political parties are also important: Democrats and Republicans take different approaches to economic questions and support different policies when in power.

The social welfare commitment of the federal government has grown substantially since the 1930s, with the most important recent growth occurring in social insurance programs such as Social Security and Medicare. Public assistance grew less slowly and accounted for a much smaller portion of the federal government's social welfare budget. Public assistance was unpopular, however, and in 1996, it was replaced by a block grant program in which the states were given wide latitude to design their own programs.

The American welfare state is very different from others. Ours is smaller, less comprehensive, less redistributive, and more tilted toward the benefit of the elderly. Structural and political linkage factors explain most of the differences.

Suggestions for Further Reading

Eisner, Marc Allen. *Regulatory Politics in Transition,* 2nd ed. Baltimore: Johns Hopkins University Press, 2000.
Argues that regulatory policies are best understood in terms of the historical periods in which they were introduced.

Gilens, Martin. *Why Americans Hate Welfare.* Chicago: University of Chicago Press, 1999.
A very provocative book that suggests that low popular support for welfare is based on unflattering stereotypes about African Americans.

Howard, Christopher. *The Hidden Welfare State.* Princeton, NJ: Princeton University Press, 2001.
Argues that the American welfare state is every bit as big and comprehensive as those of western Europe, but that they take a different form: public-private partnerships, indirect subsidies and loan guarantees, and the like.

Noble, Charles. *Welfare as We Know It: A Political History of the American Welfare State.* New York: Oxford University Press, 1997.
A comprehensive, sophisticated, and lively discussion of why we have the kind of welfare state we have in the United States and why the establishment of a European-style welfare state remains out of the question here.

Page, Benjamin I., and James R. Simmons. *What Government Can Do: Dealing with Poverty and Inequality.* Chicago: University of Chicago Press, 2000.
A passionate, articulate, and empirically supported argument in favor of a larger role for government in alleviating poverty and making the United States a more equal society.

Peters, Guy B. *American Public Policy: Promise and Performance,* 6th ed. Washington, DC: CQ Press, 2004.
A comprehensive examination of the formation and content of American public policies.

Weidenbaum, Murray. *Business and Government in the Global Marketplace,* 7th ed. New York: Prentice-Hall, 2003.
A comprehensive examination of how government actions and policies affect business.

Internet Sources

American Enterprise Institute
www.aei.org
A prominent conservative think tank with information about social policy.

Budget of the United States
www.whitehouse.gov/omb/budget/index.html
The budget of the United States, with numbers, documentation, and analyses.

Electronic Policy Network
www.epn.org/
Reports from liberal think tanks on social welfare issues.

Fedstats
www.fedstats.gov
Links to statistics and data from a broad range of federal government agencies, including those most relevant for economic and social welfare policy in the United States. These include the Federal Reserve Board, the Bureau of Labor Statistics, the Social Security Administration, the Bureau of the Census, the Bureau of Economic Analysis, and Administration for Children and Families.

Public Agenda Online
www.publicagenda.org/
A nonpartisan site with comprehensive information about government policies, alternative proposals to solve societal problems, and what the public thinks about existing and alternative policies.

Chapter 18
Foreign Policy and National Defense

In This Chapter

- Why the U.S. is a superpower
- What new problems are emerging in the post–Cold War world
- What national security means today
- How foreign and defense policies are made
- How the political process affects foreign and defense policies

Unilateralism or Multilateralism?

In his "State of the Union" address on January 29, 2002, President George W. Bush announced a dramatic shift in American foreign policy. In addition to the war on terrorism, which he vowed to continue regardless of duration or cost, the president also indicated that the United States was committed to an even more ambitious foreign policy goal:

> Our . . . goal is to prevent regimes that sponsor terror from threatening America or our friends and allies with weapons of mass destruction. . . . States like these [Iraq, Iran, and North Korea], and their terrorist allies, constitute an **axis of evil** [emphasis added], arming to threaten the peace of the world. . . . The United States of America will not permit the world's most dangerous regimes to threaten us with the world's most destructive weapons.[1]

If these countries failed to dismantle their weapons of mass destruction programs, and if others were not prepared to help, said the president, then the United States was prepared to act militarily on its own.

> My hope is that all nations will heed our call. . . . But some governments will be timid in the face of terror. And make no mistake about it: If they do not act, America will.[2]

Barely eight months later, President Bush's report to Congress, "The National Security Strategy of the United States of America," put flesh on the skeletal framework set out in his "axis of evil" speech, setting out a new grand strategy for the future. At the center of the new strategy was "preemption," the idea that in a dangerous world where terrorists and tyrants consort, and where weapons of mass destruction are increasingly likely to get into the wrong hands, the United States will reserve the right to "strike first"—that is, before it absorbs a punishing attack. In the words of the document: "We must be prepared to stop rogue states and their terrorist clients before they are able to threaten or use weapons of mass destruction against the United States and our allies and friends." And, if necessary, the document announces, we might need to act unilaterally: "The United States will constantly strive to enlist the support of the international community . . . [But] we will not hesitate to act alone . . . to exercise our right of self-defense by acting preemptively."[3]

Although talk of "axis of evil" and preemptive intervention generally played well in the United States, American allies expressed alarm. None had been consulted. None thought that lumping these three countries into a single axis made intel-

lectual or policy sense. None thought it would work. None were happy. The German Foreign Minister complained that Bush was treating the allies like mere "satellites" and warned that "success of future actions . . . will not lie in . . . policies of lonely decision making"; the French Foreign Minister dismissed Bush's goals as "simplistic"; Christopher Patten, the foreign affairs minister of the European Union, worried aloud about the "absolutist" nature of the president's thinking and protested that allies were being treated as "an optional extra."[4]

The new strategic orientation of the Bush administration was put into practice in March 2003 when the president ordered U.S. armed forces to attack Iraq and remove the

Saddam Hussein regime from power. Bush had tired of the U.N. weapons inspection process in Iraq, as well as the determined opposition of France, Germany, and Russia to U.S. military action. Unable to convince a majority in the United Nations Security Council to back the United States's call for the use of force, the president claimed that it was the duty of the United States to protect world peace and enforce U.N. resolutions—in this case, Resolution 1441 demanding that Iraq disarm and rid itself of weapons of mass destruction—when the United Nations was unable or unwilling to act on its own. In his speech on March 17, 2003, moreover, the president showed that disarmament was not all that was on his mind concerning the coming war; regime change was a coequal objective of the American invasion. Addressing himself to Iraq's citizens, he declared that "the tyrant will soon be gone. The day of your liberation is near."

Bush administration actions in Afghanistan and Iraq, and the articulation of the doctrine of preemption regarding the **"axis of evil"** and other countries and groups that might threaten the United States, triggered a debate in the United States and among our traditional allies about whether unilateralism had become the guiding principle of American foreign policy, and, if it had, whether this was a good thing. Advocates of unilateralism, such as Bush's Defense Secretary Donald Rumsfeld and Vice President Richard Cheney, argued that the United States must be engaged in the world to protect its security, its interests, and its values—it cannot be isolationist, that is to say—but it must do so on its own terms, without asking leave of international organizations or allies. To critics both here and abroad, only "multilateralism"—that is, a foreign and military policy based on consultation and cooperation with a broad range of allied countries and the United Nations—could protect the interests of both the United States and the world community.

The debates in the United States and abroad about whether American foreign policy *is* unilateralist or multilateralist in character, and whether it *should be* unilateralist or multilateralist, will be with us for some time to come. So too will the debates about preemption and regime change as the centerpieces of U.S. doctrine. How we ultimately choose to deal with other peoples and countries as we try to protect our security, interests, and values in the world will be enormously consequential for us and for others. We can only hope that our political system operates in a fashion that allows a wide range of Americans to be engaged in the deliberations that decide the issue.

---

axis of evil
Three countries—Iraq, Iran, and North Korea—named by President Bush in 2002 as significant threats to the security of the United States because of their purported ties to terrorism and weapons of mass destruction.

Thinking Critically About This Chapter

This chapter is about American foreign and military policies, how these policies are made, and how they affect Americans and others.

Using the Framework　You will see in this chapter how foreign and military policies are the product of the interaction of structural factors (such as American economic and military power, the collapse of the Soviet Union, and "globalization"), political linkage factors (such as the choices the media make about foreign news coverage, public opinion about what the U.S. role in the world ought to be, and what various interest groups want the government to do), and governmental factors (such as the objectives and actions of presidents, members of Congress, and important executive branch agencies such as the Central Intelligence Agency and the Joint Chiefs of Staff).

Using the Democracy Standard　Using the evaluative tools you learned in Chapter 1, you will see that foreign policy is not always made with the public as fully informed or as involved as they are in domestic affairs. You will see why this is so, ask whether policies would be better if they were made more democratically, and investigate how the public might play a larger role.

Foreign Policy and Democracy: A Contradiction in Terms?

Making U.S. foreign and military policy has traditionally been different from making domestic policy. For one thing, presidents and the executive branch tend to play a much more important part than they do on domestic issues, primarily because the Constitution lodges most responsibilities and powers for foreign and military affairs there rather than in Congress. Most importantly, the Constitution makes the president commander-in-chief of the nation's armed forces as well as its chief diplomat, as described in Chapter 12 on the presidency. In the perpetual tug-of-war between presidents and Congress, presidents usually prevail in the midst of diplomatic or military crises. Also, the ordinary political factors, such as public opinion and interest groups, are sometimes set aside in favor of considerations of the **national interest,** as defined by a small number of national security advisers and other executive branch officials.

national interest
What is of benefit to the nation as a whole.

Other factors also explain why ordinary citizens play a smaller role in the formation of foreign and military policy than they do in the formation of domestic policy. Public opinion, for example, is sometimes reshaped or ignored by government leaders, partly because the public tends to pay more attention to domestic issues than foreign policy matters. In crisis situations, moreover, the public often "rallies 'round the flag," accepting the president's actions, at least as long as the results seem good and there is little dissent among political leaders. (When things go wrong, however, domestic politics can return with a vengeance, as it did in the case of the Vietnam War.) Also, much of foreign policy is influenced by fundamental factors such as the power and resources of the United States and its economic interests abroad.

Involvement by ordinary citizens is also diminished by the sheer complexity of international matters, their remoteness from day-to-day life, and the unpredictability of other countries' actions; all of these tend to make the public's convictions about foreign policy less certain and more subject to revision in the light of events. In military matters, the need for speed, unity, and secrecy in decision making and the concentration of authority in the executive branch mandated by the Constitution mean that the public may be excluded and that government policy sometimes shapes public opinion rather than being shaped by it.

At the same time, however, the exclusion of the public is far from total. The American public has probably always played a bigger part in the making of foreign policy than some observers have imagined, and its role has become increasingly important in such foreign policy issues as trade, immigration, global environmental protection, and corporate behavior abroad. Note, for example, the very high involvement of the public in general, and interest groups in particular (labor unions, environmental organizations, corporations, business trade associations, and the like), in the struggle over ratification of the North American Free Trade Agreement (NAFTA) and in the debate over granting China normal trade status and membership in the World Trade Organization (WTO). Public involvement was high because what was decided in these cases was certain to have important effects on jobs, wages, and environmental quality.

The Superpower Status of the United States

In the autumn of 1990, the United States sent more than half a million troops, 1,200 warplanes, and six aircraft carriers to the Persian Gulf region to roll back Iraq's invasion of Kuwait. In 1996, U.S. troops were deployed in Bosnia as part of a NATO peacekeeping operation. The warring parties signed the peace agreement in Bosnia only after the United States consented to be the guarantor of the agreement, backed by troops on the ground. In 1999, the United States supplied almost all the pilots, airplanes, ordinance, supplies, and intelligence for the NATO bombing campaign to force the Serb military out of Kosovo province. In less than three months following 9/11, American armed forces overwhelmed the Taliban and al Qaeda in Afghanistan. In 2003, the United States invaded Iraq, and in less than four weeks had routed Iraq's regular army and its Republican Guard, gained nominal control of all its major cities, including Baghdad, and removed the Saddam Hussein regime from power. These examples reflect the status of the United States as the world's **superpower,** the only nation strong enough militarily and economically to project its power into any area of the globe. In this section, we will examine the foundations of this superpower status.

superpower

A nation armed with nuclear weapons and able to project force anywhere on the globe.

The Collapse of the Soviet Union and the Warsaw Pact

For most of the second half of the twentieth century, the United States and its NATO (North Atlantic Treaty Organization) allies in western Europe faced off against the Soviet Union and its Warsaw Pact allies in eastern and central Europe. For much of this period, a nuclear standoff existed between the United States and the U.S.S.R., so the struggle between them, and between liberal capitalism and communism more generally, played themselves out in what has come to be called the **Cold War** (referred to as *cold* because the adversaries never actually fought each other during these years). The Cold War was defined by alliance building by each side, small but hot wars fought by

Cold War

The period of tense relations between the United States and the Soviet Union from the late 1940s to the late 1980s.

The collapse of the Soviet Union triggered the withdrawal of Soviet forces from the satellite nations of eastern Europe. Here, Soviet tanks are loaded on a train for shipment out of Germany.

surrogates, counterinsurgency and terror directed against the opposing alliance, and efforts to win over Third World nations.

In the late 1980s and early 1990s, however, communism in eastern Europe collapsed, followed by the dissolution of the Soviet Union itself. Much of the change had to do with Mikhail Gorbachev, who came to power as head of the Soviet Union in 1985. In a desperate attempt to catch up to the West, he introduced policies to foster greater use of the "market" in economic affairs (*perestroika,* or "restructuring") and more political freedom (*glasnost,* or "openness"). Not wanting to get bogged down in efforts to occupy rebellious former satellites, he also refused to intervene militarily, as the Soviet Union had done on numerous occasions in the past, when anti-communist regimes came to power in Poland, Czechoslovakia, and Hungary and asked the Soviets to withdraw behind their own borders. In November 1989, Berliners tore down the wall that had long separated them from their friends, family, and countrymen, and the process was under way that eventually led to the absorption of the former communist East Germany into the German Federal Republic.

The final collapse of the Soviet Union followed a failed coup against Gorbachev in August 1991 by hard-line communists. Boris Yeltsin, president of the Russian Republic—the first popularly elected official in Russian history—led the resistance to the coup in Moscow and Leningrad. The coup plotters, winning little popular or military support, quickly gave up, and Gorbachev was restored to office. But the central government rapidly disintegrated. The Communist party, which Gorbachev had tried to reform, lost all legitimacy and was temporarily banned in most of the Soviet Union. The Soviet Union itself fell apart, as member republics became independent—first the Baltic republics (Estonia, Latvia, and Lithuania), then the other 12 republics, and eventually even the crucial Ukraine and Russia.

Although historians will argue for years about why the Soviet Union and its empire in eastern and central Europe collapsed, it is at least plausible to suggest that the economic inefficiencies of the Soviet Union's and Warsaw Pact countries' centrally planned economies played a role, as did rising aspirations for democracy in police states newly penetrated by global mass culture and alternative sources of information. Because of their creaking economies, neither the U.S.S.R. nor its allies could provide a standard of living for its people that could match that found in the United States and western Europe; nor could they match the quality of NATO's military forces. And, because they allowed few freedoms to their people at a time when their citizens were increasingly aware of how other people lived, the governments of the Soviet Union and their Warsaw Pact allies lost popular credibility and legitimacy.

Whatever the causes of these developments, however, what is undeniable is that the collapse of the Soviet Union and the unraveling of its empire removed from the stage America's most formidable and threatening adversary. It is one of the reasons the United States has emerged as the world's single superpower. But it is not the only reason. In the next section, we look at some of the structural foundations of the United States' superpower status.

**You Are President
John F. Kennedy**

**From Stand-Alone to
Superpower: The
Evolution of U.S.
Foreign Policy**

The Structural Bases of American Superpower Status

In addition to the power of its real and potential rivals, a nation's place in the international system is largely determined by its relative economic, military, and cultural power. At the beginning of the twenty-first century, the United States is particularly advantaged in all three areas. Together, they make the United States the world's only superpower, so preeminent that leaders and commentators are searching for new language to describe it. The French, for

By the Numbers

How many voting-eligible Americans live abroad?

Many Americans who are eligible to vote in national, state, and local elections live outside of the United States, but we don't really know how many of them there are. They include active-duty military personnel, federal government employees, students, retirees, teachers, employees of NGOs (such as Greenpeace or Amnesty International), employees of U.S.-headquartered multinational firms, independent businesspeople, and more. Estimates of the numbers of these folks range from as low as 3 million to as high as 7 million. But the truth is, we don't know exactly.

Why It Matters: If voting-eligible citizens living abroad were to cast absentee ballots in U.S. elections, how they apportion their votes might determine the outcome of important elections. After all, if we accept the 7 million estimate, then Americans living abroad form a larger population than that of any of the 24 smallest states. Their impact is potentially so important that Republican and Democratic party leaders are starting to pay attention to them, trying to figure out how to advertise to them, how to encourage them to vote, and how to induce them to vote the "right way." Party leaders are no doubt mindful of the fact that late overseas absentee ballots—63 percent of which were cast for George W. Bush—swung the election in Florida to Bush, according to the count certified by the Florida Secretary of State.

Knowing how many eligible voters live abroad raises other important issues for American politics. For example, should federal campaign finance rules on contributions and party and candidate expenditures hold for campaigns that target Americans abroad? Should citizens living abroad be counted toward the population totals in each of the states for purposes of apportioning seats in the House of Representatives? After the 2000 census was completed, the state of Utah claimed that its state population count ought to have included in it the thousands of Mormon missionaries who were working abroad. Had the courts agreed—which they didn't—Utah would have picked up an additional seat in Congress at the expense of North Carolina.

Calculating the Number: When it comes to Americans living abroad, the only numbers we are sure about concern active-duty military personnel and employees of the federal government and their family members. The Defense Department keeps track of its people, as do civilian agencies such as the State and Commerce Departments. In 2000, this amounted to almost 576,000 people. For the remainder of the people living abroad, all we have are estimates. In 1960 and 1970, the Census Bureau took a count, which depended on people coming to U.S. embassies or consulates to fill out census forms. This didn't work very well, and the effort was abandoned. The State Department has tried to make educated guesses, depending on embassy personnel in each country to use their judgment in coming up with a number. You can see their estimate by country for 1999 in the accompanying graph. The State Department has tried to estimate long-term residents living abroad by counting the number of passports issued to American citizens already located overseas. The total came to about 7 million in 2003.

As inaccurate as these numbers are, they do tell us something very important. Perhaps reflecting the very large role the United States plays in the world today, a considerable number of Americans live outside the country. Further, given the United States's position as the world's superpower, there is no reason to believe that this number will get smaller any time soon.

Criticisms of the Existing Counts: The basic problem in counting those living abroad is that no federal government agency is charged with making

example, have started to use the term "hyperpower," while talk of a new American empire is widespread in Europe and elsewhere.[5] (One mark of the reach of America's global presence is the number of its citizens who live, work, and fight abroad, an issue that is explored in the "By the Numbers" feature.)

Top 15 countries where Americans lived in 1999, excluding military personnel and their dependents and federal government employees and their dependents.

*Estimates by the Bureau of Consular Affairs, U.S. Department of State.

such a count, nor has any agency the capability to do so. Furthermore, no requirement says that Americans living abroad must register with the U.S. government in any way. What we are left with are two unsatisfactory methods: dependence on people voluntarily coming to U.S. embassies or consulates to fill out census forms or counting the number of passports applied for by Americans abroad. Both methods surely miss large numbers of people: those who do not appear to fill out census forms and those who obtain their passports in the United States then go abroad for an extended stay.

What to Watch For: There may be an attempt to include overseas Americans in the 2010 census, using much more aggressive ways to find out where they are living and getting census forms to them. Census officials will probably ask corporations,

NGOs, and educational institutions to provide names of their people working abroad. Census officials have announced test censuses of Americans in France, Kuwait, and Mexico in 2004 and 2005 to see if they can get reasonably reliable results.

What Do You Think? How important do you think this issue is? Should people living abroad be counted by the Census Bureau? If so, should the numbers be used in figuring out how many congressional seats each state gets and what portion of federal grant money the state is entitled to? Do you think political parties trying to convince people to cast absentee ballots should be subject to the same spending limitations that exist here?

Source: Taylor E. Dark III, "Americans Abroad: The Challenge of a Globalized Electorate," *PS* (October 2003), pp. 733–740.

Economic Power In 2003, the United States had a population of about 290 million people—considerably fewer than China's 1.3 billion or India's roughly 1 billion—but enough to support the world's largest economy, with an annual gross domestic product (GDP) of more than $10.9 trillion. The GDP of the United States in 2003 was about $2 trillion more than the combined GDPs of

American invasion forces took less than four weeks to defeat Iraq armed forces, capture its major cities, and remove the regime of Saddam Hussein from power. Here, marines battle for a key bridge leading to the center of Baghdad.

France, Great Britain, Germany, and Japan. The United States's GDP, moreover, is almost double that of fast-rising China (but seven times larger on a per-capita basis). The United States also ranks first in the world in total exports and imports.[6]

By all indications, the relative strength of the American economy has been increasing, even taking into consideration the 2001–2003 economic doldrums and stock market decline, with GDP growing at much faster rates than in any of the major western European nations or Japan. Throughout the 1990s especially, but also in the opening years of the twenty-first century, U.S.-headquartered companies have established preeminence in the economic sectors that count the most in the new global economy: telecommunications, mass entertainment, biotechnology, software, finance, e-commerce, business services, transportation, and computer chips.

American corporations also are increasingly global, a fact that affects U.S. foreign policy. For the largest of them, a substantial portion of their revenues comes from sales abroad, much of their manufacturing takes place in other countries, and many of the parts for items manufactured domestically are imported. And in industries such as oil and petrochemicals, many of the sources of raw materials are outside our borders. Because American businesses can be found almost anywhere, American national interests can be said to exist almost anywhere as well. It follows that American officials must be attentive to potential trouble spots around the globe. Today, they are especially attentive to the problem of terrorism, whether the threat is to government installations, such as embassies and bases, or to private American companies and their employees, thus protecting U.S. economic power.

Military Power   This enormous economic strength enables the United States to field the most powerful armed forces in the world. The scale of military American superiority, as well as the nation's ability to deploy and use these resources, is orders of magnitude beyond any rival or potential rival. Here are a few indicators of this disproportionality of U.S. military power:[7]

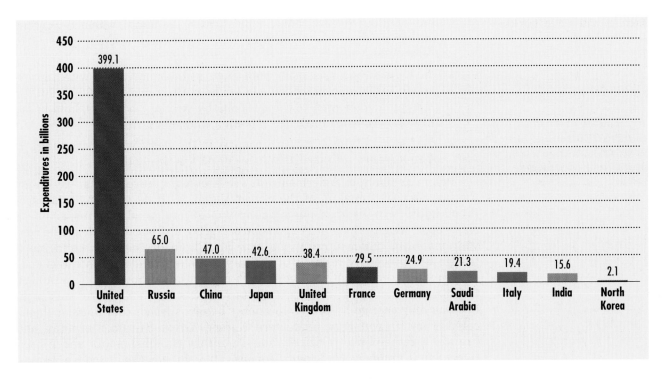

FIGURE 18.1 • **Expenditures for National Defense, 2003**

The national defense budget of the United States is orders of magnitude higher than those of friends and foes alike. The continuing war on terrorism is likely to push U.S. defense spending even higher in the years ahead.

Source: Center for Defense Information, Washington, D.C., 2004.

Evaluating Defense
Spending

- In 2003, the United States's defense budget exceeded those of all other NATO countries (including Great Britain, France, Germany, Italy, and more), Russia, China, Japan, and North Korea combined (see Figure 18.1).

- The United States's naval power is unrivaled. It has nine supercarrier battle groups, with another on the way; no other country has even one supercarrier vessel, let alone full battlegroups. It has more modern submarines, moreover, than the rest of the world combined, including the stealthy Seawolf-class, nuclear-powered submarine.

- The United States's airpower is unrivaled. It has more advanced fighter aircraft and bombers, many of the stealth variety, than the rest of the world combined. Its aerial tanker fleet allows these aircraft to reach any target in the world. These aircraft also have the advantage of carrying a varied arsenal of "smart" munitions.

- The United States's ground warfare capabilities are unrivaled. While China has a large standing army, it is not as well armed as U.S. ground forces and lacks many of the logistical and technological capabilities of American forces. In addition, no other nation comes even close to matching America's armored forces, which includes approximately 9,000 M1 Abrams tanks, firing smart munitions.

- The United States's electronic warfare capabilities are unrivaled. These capabilities include, among other things, global positioning systems to guide smart weapons to their targets, self-guided anti-tank missiles that seek out enemy tanks, sophisticated jamming system to confuse anti-aircraft guns and missiles, and underwater sensing systems to track submarines.

- The United States's strategic nuclear arsenal is unrivaled, with approximately 6,000 nuclear warheads—to be cut to roughly 2,000 by 2012—that can be delivered to their targets by strategic bombers, land-based **intercontinental ballistic missiles,** and submarines.

- The United States is the only country in the world with permanent and often sizeable military bases in every part of the world.[8]

intercontinental ballistic missiles (ICBMs)
Guided missiles capable of carrying nuclear warheads across continents.

Potential rivals to American military hegemony have a long way to go. Russia, after the breakup of the Soviet Union, with its economy and once-proud military in disarray, has renounced most foreign adventures, given up on its opposition to eastward expansion of NATO, and cut its nuclear and conventional arms under international treaties. China, on the other hand, has a fast-growing economy, millions of military personnel, and some strategic nuclear missiles, but most of China's arms consist of old Soviet-style weapons. China's recent effort at modernizing its weapons has not progressed much, but this may change as China's economy becomes richer and more sophisticated. The rich countries of western Europe (Great Britain, Germany, and France) together have relatively small military establishments and a relatively small number of nuclear weapons. They do, however, produce, deploy, and operate very sophisticated military technologies, usually under the umbrella of NATO, in which the United States plays the leading role. Acutely aware of their military inferiority to the United States, France, Germany, and Belgium recently proposed that a joint European military force independent of NATO—and of the United States—be created, but the idea has not gotten very far. Most observers, in fact, believe the western European nations are unlikely to make the budgetary commitments necessary for such an enhanced military capability.[9]

Although powerful, the United States is not omnipotent. Its resources, for example, are not unlimited. Americans discovered this in the war with and occupation of Iraq, in which its ground forces were stretched to the limit, requiring extended deployments of regular troops and a heavy reliance on reserve and National Guard forces. Moreover, the nation's extensive conventional and strategic military power may not be terribly useful in the war against terrorism—a war in which the enemy is not a country, but rather loosely organized and shadowy cells that may best be uprooted by police investigations and intelligence-gathering operations in cooperation with other countries.

"Soft Power"   Although critics here and abroad often decry "Americanization"—by which they generally mean the spread of McDonald's, Kentucky Fried Chicken, Disney theme parks, Hollywood movies, and television sitcoms and dramas—one should not underestimate the influence of what some have called America's "soft power," the attractiveness of its culture, ideology, and way of life for many people living in other countries. As political scientist Joseph Nye has pointed out, it is important for the U.S. position in the world that more than half a million foreign students study in American colleges and universities; that people in other countries flock to American entertainment and cultural products; that English has become the language of the Internet, business, science, and technology; and that the openness and opportunity of American society are admired by many people around the world.[10] And, if it is this very openness and opportunity that allow the United States to be in the best position to prosper in the new global, information-based economy—which

In March 2003, hundreds of thousands of people in the United States, Latin America, Asia, and Europe joined anti-war demonstrations to protest Bush administration plans to invade Iraq. The demonstrations failed to convince the president to alter his plans.

many believe to be the case—then the United States's soft power enhances its harder economic and military powers.[11]

However, a strong and growing anti-American sentiment also exists in the world. Although unfavorable views of the United States have always existed, they rose dramatically after the invasion of Iraq in spring 2003. Although the increase in anti-Americanism was most pronounced in the Arab and Muslim worlds, it also intensified in western Europe, Latin America, and Russia.[12]

How to explain these developments? Some observers suggest that the war in Iraq—which was opposed almost everywhere—accounts for the rise in anti-Americanism. Even in those countries allied at the time with the United States, including Great Britain, Italy, and Spain,[13] public opinion was strongly against the action. Some suggest that rising anti-Americanism is tied to the growing concern that the United States has become so powerful that it can act on its own in pursuit of its own interests, without consultations with other countries or the United Nations and without attending to the values and wishes of others. Europeans seem especially alarmed by America's rejection of a multitude of international treaties and agreements and by President Bush's policy of pre-emption.[14] Still others suggest that anti-Americanism is rampant among those whose ways of life and well-being are threatened by economic and cultural globalization or who have been left behind in the global race for development—especially in the Arab world—and who simply resent the dynamism, wealth, and power of the United States.[15]

All of this suggests that America's soft power advantages are not as solid and as unchallenged as its advantages with respect to military and economic power. Growing anti-Americanism is troubling and is something that American presidents and other foreign policymakers increasingly must take into account.

Problems of the Post–Cold War World

During the Cold War, oddly enough, the standoff between the Soviet Union and the United States, and between capitalism and communism, made matters relatively simple for policymakers on both sides of the conflict. Foreign policy issues—including relationships with allies; efforts to win the support of newly independent poor countries in Africa, Asia, and Latin America; and decisions regarding which weapons systems to develop—were all measured against what the other side was doing or was likely to do. American policy during the Cold War was based on the doctrine of **containment,** meaning that foreign and military policy was designed to halt the spread of the Soviet state and the influence of communism.[16] When the Soviet Union and communism collapsed, the world became a much more confusing and complex place for American policymakers, who have been trying to come up with a new doctrine to guide foreign and military policies ever since.

As the country struggles with this issue, debate tends to be organized around two views about what America's role in the world should be and how it should conduct its affairs:

- **Unilateralists** would have the United States act on the international stage on its own terms, without asking the permission of others, binding itself under restrictive international agreements, or following the lead of international organizations such as the United Nations. The existence of this theme in American foreign policy may explain, for example, the United States's unwillingness to sign treaties to establish an international criminal court and ban land mines. Unilateralists are also interested in using American power unilaterally, if it comes to that, to spread American values such as liberty, free enterprise, and democracy, believing these values to be universally valid and appealing. Unilateralists do not see a contradiction between power and principle. Indeed, they believe that one depends inextricably on the other.[17]

  As the chapter-opening story suggests, President George Bush is a strong advocate of unilateralism, as are many in the Bush administration, including Secretary of State Condoleezza Rice, Defense Secretary Donald Rumsfeld, and Vice President Richard Cheney. Each of them, for example, advised the president to go it alone in disarming Iraq if the United Nations failed to authorize strong measures against Saddam Hussein. Some conservative commentators have taken unilateralism to its logical end point: empire. Charles Krauthammer, Max Boot, and Robert Kaplan, among many others, have celebrated the emergence of a new and benevolent American empire,[18] though the cost—in lives and treasury—of war and occupation in Iraq has dampened some of the initial enthusiasm.

- **Multilateralists** believe that American interests are compatible with the interests of others in the world and that protecting these interests requires cooperation and collaboration with other nations and international organizations. Although the United States is undeniably the most powerful nation in the world, it cannot solve all important problems on its own. Problems such as global warming, pollution, the wider availability of the means to make weapons of mass destruction, the spread of AIDs and other infectious diseases—SARS, bird flu, and Mad Cow come to mind—and terrorism threaten virtually every country in

containment

The policy of resisting expansion of the Soviet Union's influence by diplomatic, economic, and military means.

unilateralists

Those who believe the United States should vigorously use its military and diplomatic power to pursue American national interests in the world, but on a "go it alone" basis.

multilateralists

Those who believe the United States should use its military and diplomatic power in the world in cooperation with other nations and international organizations.

the world, and solving these problems, insist multilateralists, will require broad cooperation and collaboration by many countries and international organizations. Interestingly, while much of the thrust of his foreign policy has been unilateralist in character, President Bush also moved in a multilateralist direction when needed. For example, he forged a multilateral coalition and gained U.N. support for the attack on the Taliban and al Qaeda in Afghanistan following 9/11. He also pushed a multinational effort to control North Korea's and Iran's nuclear arms programs. And, he eventually turned to the United Nations to help install a new Iraqi government and give it a sense of legitimacy in the eyes of the world.

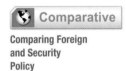

Comparing Foreign and Security Policy

Central to the debate between unilateralists and multilateralists is the nature of our relationships with western Europe and its two most powerful countries, France and Germany, and what role we want the United Nations to play in global security issues. It is no secret that European-American relations are at a post–World War II low. Public opinion polls in virtually every western European country report concerns about growing American power and how it is used and decreasing regard for the United States and its leaders. It has become even more fashionable than in the past, moreover, for intellectuals in Great Britain, France, Spain, Italy, and Germany to disparage American actions, motives, and way of life. And, the leaders of Germany and France, Gehardt Schroeder and Jacques Chirac, not only opposed the American invasion of Iraq but insisted that the United Nation's Security Council was the only body that could legitimately make such a decision. It is no secret that President Chirac has been trying to fashion a united European foreign policy and an enhanced European military capability to balance the awesome power of the United States.

What is to be done? Some Americans are happy to return European enmity with our own—thus the talk of "old Europe" from Bush's Defense Secretary Donald Rumsfeld and quixotic efforts by others to rename French fries "freedom fries." Other Americans believe we can change European attitudes about

Web Exploration
What Direction for U.S. Foreign Policy?

Issue: Although the United States is unequaled in military and economic power, Americans are not entirely sure how they want to use that power.

Site: Access Public Agenda Online on our Website at **www.ablongman.com/greenberg**. Go to the "Web Explorations" section for Chapter 18. Select "what direction for U.S. foreign policy," then "U.S. role." Select "America's global role" in the "issue guides" section. Then look in the section "Bills and Proposals."

What You've Learned: See what the public thinks about the United Nations, humanitarian intervention, and foreign assistance. After looking at the poll results, would you conclude that Americans are isolationists, unilateralists, or multilateralists?

HINT: You might be surprised to learn how many Americans lean in a multilateral direction.

the United States by using our power more carefully, consulting with our allies, and giving more authority to the United Nations, a position taken by John Kerry during the 2004 presidential campaign. Still others believe that nothing can be done, that differences of world view between Europe and the United States are caused by the great disproportionality in power between the two. According to several scholars, European regard for international collaboration, international law, and the United Nations is rooted less in abstract principles than in recognition by Europeans that it is only these institutions that can help them constrain the powerful United States and ensure that their interests and values will be taken into account in the international system.[19]

With the end of the Cold War, the main concerns of that era—the possibility of global thermonuclear war, a land war in Europe against the Soviet Union, and communist takeovers of Third World countries—have disappeared from the list of foreign policy problems that concern Americans and their leaders. But a host of problems remain. We review these in the next several sections, keeping in mind that the debate among unilateralists and multilateralists will help shape our response to each one, as will the nature of our long-term relationships with Europe.

New Security Issues

Although the security threat represented by the Soviet Union has disappeared, many threats to American security remain.

Terrorism   The issue of terrorism moved front-and-center on the American political agenda after the September 11, 2001, attacks on the World Trade Center and the Pentagon. The retaliatory U.S. attacks on the Taliban regime and al Qaeda in Afghanistan are likely to be but the opening rounds in a long war on terrorism. This war is likely to involve a wide range of activities, some undertaken in cooperation with others, some undertaken unilaterally, no matter who is president. At a minimum, American policymakers will try to improve intelligence gathering (sharply criticized by the 9/11 Commission in 2004), create rapid-strike armed forces to attack terrorist cells, and fashion

The fight against terrorism is likely to be a major element of American foreign policy for a long time to come. Here, people in Nairobi, Kenya, haul away victims of the 1998 bombing of the U.S. Embassy by elements of the al Qaeda terrorist organization.

credible policies that will make other countries less likely to offer aid and sanctuary to terrorist organizations. Their job will likely be complicated by the bitter feelings felt by many in the Arab and Muslim worlds as a result of the invasion and occupation of Iraq and American support for Israel.

Weapons of Mass Destruction   As the chapter-opening story related, President Bush designated Iraq, Iran, and North Korea as nations both capable of creating weapons of mass destruction—chemical, biological, and/or nuclear—and using them against neighbors, American allies, or the United States. The problem of the spread and use of weapons of mass destruction, whether by axis or other so-called rogue nations, by factions within disintegrating nations, by terrorists, by nuclear scientists in places such as Pakistan seeking financial gain, is surely real, though how to go about addressing this danger is not entirely obvious. With respect to Iraq, President Bush chose direct military action. With respect to North Korea, Iran, and Libya, some mix of diplomatic pressure, multilateral-organized sanctions, International Atomic Energy Agency inspections, and threats of force have all been used.

The collapse of the centralized communist regime in the Soviet Union in the early 1990s and its breakup into several independent counties threw into question the fate of the vast Russian and former Soviet armed forces, with their millions of troops and many nuclear weapons—more than 10,000 of them. Could these weapons fall into the hands of warring ethnic factions, criminal organizations, terrorist groups, or rogue states such as Iran, creating new dangers and instability? The United States worked out agreements for drastic reductions in Russian, Ukrainian, and Kazakh nuclear weaponry. Ukraine and Kazakhstan have renounced nuclear weapons altogether, but their stockpiles of weapons remain large, and central control appears shaky. There is some evidence of Russian nuclear materials showing up on the international black market, raising dangers of **nuclear proliferation,** or the spread of nuclear weapons. A high-priority task for American foreign policy has been to prevent proliferation.

nuclear proliferation
The spread of nuclear weapons to additional countries or to terrorist groups.

The Middle East   The Middle East is home to some of the least developed nations in the world in terms of economic development, democracy and freedom, women's rights, and education.[20] It is also a veritable tinderbox, as evidenced by the seemingly unending conflict between Israel and the Palestinians, which stirs passions in the Arab and Muslim worlds and feeds anti-Americanism. What to do about this conflict is a matter of intense debate. Although groups such as Hamas and Hezbollah are committed to the destruction of Israel, most others support some sort of two-state solution in which Israel and Palestine live side-by-side as independent countries. The United States, as well as the European Union, are committed to this outcome, as is the majority of the Israeli public. The sticking point is how to move the parties involved to take the steps necessary to reach this broadly agreed-upon goal. What can be done, for example, to reach an agreement on Jewish settlers in the occupied territories and, at the same time, deal with the Palestinians' insistence on the right of Palestinians to return to what is now Israel? What can be done to stop the violence of terrorist attacks on Israel and the often-violent occupation by Israel of the West Bank and Gaza? What can be done to reach an agreement on the boundaries of the two states?

As if the Israel-Palestinian conflict weren't enough to render the Arab Middle East a tinderbox, it is also a place where people are saddled with un-elected and corrupt governments, near-useless educational systems, stagnant

Winning over the "Arab street" will be an enduring problem for American foreign policy in the years ahead. As this demonstration in Lebanon suggests, this will not be an easy task.

economies, and mass unemployment. And, according to some scholars, it is a place where people are deeply resentful of the non-Muslim West's economic, military, and cultural dominance of the region.[21] These circumstances inevitably feed popular discontent and threaten instability in a region that is vital to the world's energy supply. (Saudi Arabia, for example, sits on 25 percent of the world's known oil reserves.) Such populations, it must be said, also provide many of the foot soldiers and much of the financial support for terrorism.

The Indian Subcontinent   U.S. policymakers must also be concerned about the possible outbreak of war between India and Pakistan, each armed with nuclear weapons. The issues between the two will not be easily resolved, given the history of enmity between them, past military conflicts, and the struggle over the fate of the future of Muslim-majority Kashmir. The situation is complicated for the United States by the fact that Pakistan is crucial in the fight against terrorism and al Qaeda in Afghanistan, and India has appropriated American rhetoric on terrorism to excoriate Pakistan for support of terrorism in Kashmir.

China   With its huge population, fast-growing economy, and modernizing military, China may pose a long-term threat to the United States. Some Americans have warned of a great "clash of civilizations" between the West and "Confucian" China.[22] Disputes over fair trade, alleged nuclear spying, threats against Taiwan, and human rights disputes periodically cloud U.S.–Chinese relations. In addition, China opposed the United States on the invasion of Iraq. But China also joined the anti-terrorism coalition that George W. Bush created in the wake of September 11, 2001, and the United States and China cooperated on anti-terrorist intelligence gathering during and after the Afghanistan conflict. The United States also supported China's successful effort to join the World Trade Organization. And, perhaps most importantly, China and the United States have become strong trading partners.

Ethnic Conflicts in the Developing World   American policymakers and the public must decide how large a role the United States wants to play in reducing conflicts in the developing world, even when it is not directly threatened by them. One example concerns humanitarian intervention. When the government of a country is violating the basic human rights and taking the lives of segments of its own population—Rwanda, Sudan, and Chechnya come to mind—should the United States intervene or stay out? If it intervenes, should it do so on its own or under the auspices of the United Nations or NATO?

Economic and Social Dilemmas

In addition to national security concerns, a number of other international issues have drawn the attention of American policymakers and the public.

Globalization   Globalization, or the integration of much of the world into a single market and production system, with the United States playing the leading role, has raised a number of new issues for American policymakers and American citizens to address.

Trade   At the peak of its economic dominance after World War II, the United States presided over a world regime of free trade in which many countries negotiated lower tariff barriers through the **General Agreement on Tariffs and Trade (GATT).** Because the United States was the world's most powerful trading state, these reduced rates were very advantageous for U.S. exports and investments, which continued to grow.

By the late 1960s, however, the rebuilt economies of Germany and Japan began to turn out goods that challenged American products abroad and in the United States, beginning with automobiles and moving on to consumer electronics. Additional competition came from newly industrialized countries (NICs), such as South Korea, Taiwan, Singapore, and Hong Kong, and from the increasingly integrated Economic Community (EC) of Europe. By the mid-1980s, Americans were importing many more goods than they were exporting, creating a multibillion-dollar **trade deficit.**

Reacting to this competitive pressure, the United States pressured other countries during the 1980s—especially Japan and the EC, now known as the **European Union (EU)**—to lower hidden barriers and subsidies that hurt American exports while arranging voluntary quotas and other policies to control their own exports to the United States. Next, U.S. policymakers negotiated the **North American Free Trade Agreement (NAFTA)** with Canada and Mexico, which was finally implemented in 1993 after a vote in Congress resolved a bitter political conflict over its implications for U.S. jobs.[23] The Clinton administration also concluded a comprehensive free trade agreement with 116 countries, under the Uruguay Round of GATT. The agreement, signed in 1994, set up the **World Trade Organization (WTO)** for enforcement. U.S. negotiators hoped that the new agreement would open more markets to American agricultural products and halt the piracy of patented and copyrighted goods such as software and films. The massive anti-WTO demonstrations in Seattle in late 1999, and others that followed, helped focus public attention on the WTO and the world trading system.

A crucial question about growing international trade, and about the increased ability of firms from the United States and other countries to produce goods cheaply abroad, is whether it brings prosperity to all Americans. Does freer trade produce lower wages for American workers? Does it lead to

General Agreement on Tariffs and Trade (GATT)
An international agreement that requires the lowering of tariffs and other barriers to free trade.

trade deficit
An excess of the value of the goods a country imports over the value of the goods it exports.

European Union (EU)
A common market formed by western European nations, with free trade and free population movement among them.

North American Free Trade Agreement (NAFTA)
An agreement among the United States, Canada, and Mexico to eliminate nearly all barriers to trade and investment among the three countries.

World Trade Organization (WTO)
An agency designed to enforce the provisions of the General Agreement on Tariffs and Trade and to resolve trade disputes between nations.

The outsourcing of high-tech jobs to other countries has become worrisome for many Americans. Here, software engineers at INFOSYS, an Indian company located in Bangalore, work on a complex problem for an American client.

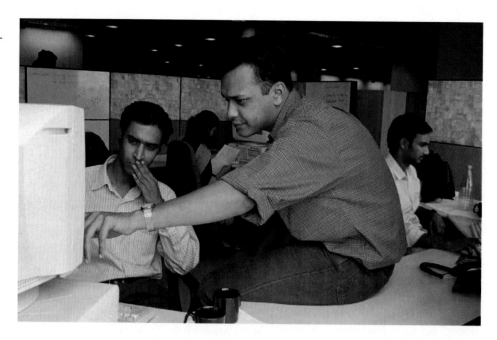

the export of jobs? If free trade does hurt U.S. wages and jobs—matters about which economists are deeply divided[24]—what can be done, short of reintroducing economically inefficient protectionism? And what about poorer countries that trade with us? Are the lives of their people made better or worse? Again, this is a question about which economists are deeply divided.[25]

Corporate Behavior Abroad   U.S.-based corporations operating abroad find themselves being scrutinized for their behavior on a variety of fronts.[26] Some activists, NGOs (nongovernmental organizations), journalists, and government officials have focused the international spotlight on matters of pay and working conditions, including such issues as "sweatshop" production, child labor, the absence of labor rights in many places, and gender inequities. Others have focused on the effects of corporate production practices on local environments. Still others have focused on the purported homogenizing effects of global products on local cultures—think here of McDonald's and Hollywood—among others.

Intellectual Property Rights   How strongly should our foreign policy attempt to protect the intellectual property rights—patents and copyrights—of American companies and citizens? The issue is fairly straightforward when it comes to the "piracy" of movies, music tapes and CDs, and software in places such as China; Americans generally support policies that are aimed at ending these practices. Protection of patents for life-saving drugs is another matter—anti-malarial and anti-AIDS medications, for example. Many Americans believe companies ought to provide such drugs at low prices or allow poor countries to find or produce generic substitutes despite the patent protections of Western pharmaceutical companies. There has been some movement on this front in the last several years. Companies have lowered prices on a range of drugs, and the U.S. government signed an agreement in 2003 to suspend the normal trade rules of the WTO and allow the production and use of certain

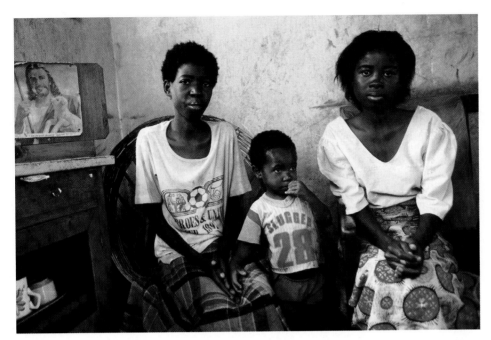

AIDS is devastating many countries of Sub-Sahara Africa. After years of pressure from anti-AIDS activists there and in the West, several global pharmaceutical firms lowered prices for AIDS drugs, and the United States increased that part of its foreign aid devoted to AIDS eradication.

critical generic drugs. In terms of AIDS drugs, assistance cannot come too soon; in 2002, 2.4 million people died of the disease, with an additional 3.5 million adults and children newly infected.[27]

Global Economic Instability   What role should the United States play in stabilizing global financial markets and in rescuing countries on the verge of economic collapse? A strong American role is probably inevitable, as we are the leading player and financial supporter of the International Monetary Fund and the World Bank, and as our own economy is affected by what happens elsewhere. But precisely how to respond to crises is not clear. No consensus has emerged among American leaders. In 1982 and 1995, for example, the United States helped Mexico emerge from its debt crisis and financial collapse; in 2001–2002, however, the United States offered only modest assistance to Argentina (in the form of an IMF loan) as that country tried to recover from a devastating financial collapse.

Foreign Aid   The world is divided rather sharply into rich and poor nations. Rich nations, whether for humanitarian or security reasons, have given assistance to poor countries for many years in an effort to improve living standards. Although the United States contributes to World Bank developmental loans for poor countries and has programs such as Food for Peace, the Peace Corps, and technical and educational assistance programs, our spending for foreign aid is very low and has been declining relative to the size of the total federal budget and the size of the American economy. Spending for foreign aid now stands at less than 1.0 percent of the federal budget and less than 0.1 percent of U.S. GDP.[28] Although we spend more dollars on foreign assistance than any other country, relative to the size of our economy we spend the least (see Figure 18.2). Moreover, only about two-thirds of U.S. foreign aid goes toward economic development and humanitarian relief; the remainder is linked

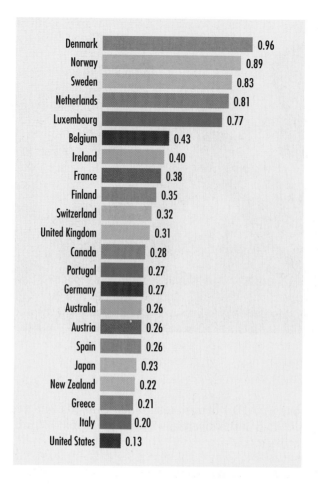

FIGURE 18.2 • Foreign Aid as a Percentage of GDP, 2002

Although Americans often complain about how much aid we give to other countries, a comparison with other donor countries shows that we give very little as a percentage of GDP.

Source: Organization for Economic Cooperation and Development, 2004.

to military and security objectives or to encourage sale of American goods and services abroad. To the surprise of many, President Bush announced in 2002 that he would ask Congress to increase the American foreign aid budget by $5 billion over three years starting in 2004, with the bulk of the additional money going to poor countries willing to reform their governments and economies and to help in the war against terrorism.

The Global Environment Increasingly, Americans realize that environmental problems cross national borders. Thus, the United States and Canada have worked out a joint approach to reduce acid rain; and the United States has signed on to agreements on oil spills, the exploitation of Antarctica, the protection of fish species, and the protection of the ozone layer. The United States is also a signatory to the biodiversity treaty. Global warming is a different story, however. Although the Clinton administration was involved in hammering out the details of the Kyoto Protocol to limit greenhouse gases, George W. Bush refused to join the agreement; the president was concerned that the treaty imposed no pollution controls on large, fast-growing economies among the developing countries, such as China and India, and would do irreparable harm to the American economy.

The Drug Trade   U.S. relations with nations south of its border are complicated by the flow of enormous amounts of marijuana and cocaine into the United States from Peru, Bolivia, Haiti, Colombia, and Mexico and by the inability or unwillingness of those countries to stop the profitable drug trade. U.S. responses have included assistance with law enforcement (not always fully welcomed), crop eradication (bitterly resented by poor peasant farmers), and crop replacement (very costly). Some military strategists have proposed using U.S. armed forces to seize drug shipments and eradicate production, but that would threaten other countries' sovereignty and raise the specter of Vietnam-like drug wars in which the United States might be pitted against local populations. The United States is now heavily involved, for example, in a program to train and equip the Colombian military to wage war on drugs in its country.

Part of the problem in eradicating the drug trade is that demand for drugs is very high in the rich countries, including the United States. Additionally, many of the technologies and organizational strategies that make it possible for corporations to operate on a global scale also help criminal drug organizations do the same thing. Such organizations have easy access to e-mail, express package service, air freight, global banking services, and high-speed telecommunications to enhance the efficiency of their operations.

Immigration   Throughout history, people have migrated to other lands, seeking a better way of life for themselves and their families. In the emerging global economy, where manufacturing and associated jobs are highly mobile, and where the revolution in transportation makes movement of people easier, cheaper, and more efficient, people seeking to improve their standards of living are increasingly mobile. Especially noteworthy is the migration of people from poor Third World countries to the rich democracies of the West. Where poor countries lie adjacent to rich countries—for example, Mexico and Central America are close to the United States, the world's richest country—immigration pressures are especially strong.

In recent years, immigration from abroad—especially illegal immigration—has become a major political issue in the United States, because many Americans perceive pressure on their jobs, wages, and tax-supported social benefits, and they worry about cultural conflict.[29] Post–9/11, many also worry that loose immigration controls will allow terrorists to enter the country. Government leaders have responded by tightening the borders, aggressively seeking out and deporting illegal immigrants, and denying certain government benefits to them. This has contributed, however, to worsening relations with Mexico.

Who Makes Foreign Policy?

We pointed out in Chapter 12 and at the outset of this chapter, that the president is the key player in making foreign and national security policies and is especially powerful during international crises and in times of war—recently in Afghanistan and Iraq and in the war on terrorism. But Congress has always been involved in decisions about international trade, foreign aid, military

Although presidents are the main decision makers regarding American foreign policy and national defense, they depend on a wide range of experts and advisers for information and advice. Here President Bush confers with top military, intelligence, and foreign policy members of the National Security Council and the Cabinet regarding the military campaign against the Taliban regime in Afghanistan.

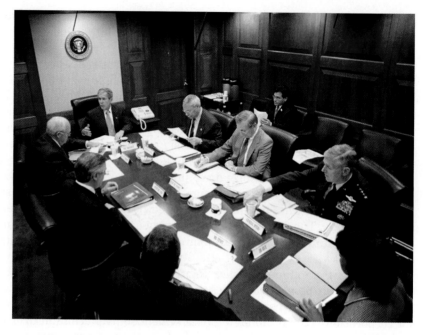

spending, immigration, and other matters that clearly and directly touch constituents' local interests, and it is seeking a larger voice in diplomatic and military affairs. Public opinion, the mass media, the parties, and organized interest groups affect what both Congress and the executive branch do.

Different types of foreign policy are made in very different ways. Crisis decision making, for example, involving sudden threats, high stakes, quick action, or **covert operations,** belongs mostly to the executive branch—often, just a small, unified group of top national security officials. The major decisions on the military response to the September 11 terrorist attacks on the United States, for example, were made by the president in consultation with a small handful of staffers and executive branch officials, including Vice President Cheney, Defense Secretary Rumsfeld, National Security Adviser Rice, CIA chief George Tenet, and Secretary of State Colin Powell.[30] Congress, the public, interest groups, and others usually do not play much part, except to the extent that executive decision makers consulted a few key members of Congress and tried to anticipate the public's reactions.

Broader issues of defense policy—including treaties on arms control or military alliances, participation in major wars, and the amount of money spent on defense—involve much greater participation by Congress, the general public, interest groups, and others. Here, too, the executive branch ordinarily takes the lead, but it must be attentive to the public and interest groups as well. Decisions about opening and closing military bases and procurement contracts involve congressional committees and interest groups, especially local businesspeople dependent on bases and weapon-producing corporations. Foreign trade, international economic policy, and immigration also sometimes provoke substantial political conflict.

The President and the Executive Branch

Presidents rely on many people and several government agencies to help them make military and foreign policy decisions. Vice President Cheney and

---

covert operations

Secret or semisecret activities abroad, often involving intelligence gathering, influence on other countries' politics, or the use of force.

You Are the President

Defense Secretary Rumsfeld have been particularly important players in the Bush administration. Condoleezza Rice, his first national security adviser, then Secretary of State, has played a big role, too. The national security adviser plays a prominent role in every administration, advising the president on a daily basis on foreign and national security matters.[31]

The State Department, headed by the Secretary of State, is the president's chief arm for carrying out diplomatic affairs. Some secretaries of state have been extremely important in helping the president make foreign policy—Henry Kissinger in the Nixon and Ford administrations comes to mind—though others have not been among the key players in the inner circle around the president. It was widely reported, for example, that Colin Powell was less influential with President Bush, for example, than Cheney, Rumsfeld, and Rice. The department itself is organized along both functional lines—economic affairs, human rights, counterterrorism, and refugees—and geographic lines, with "country desks" devoted to each nation of the world. The State Department has 180 embassies and 90 other missions around the world that carry out policy and advise the department on new developments.[32] Attached to the State Department are the Arms Control and Disarmament Agency, the U.S. Information Agency, and the Agency for International Development, which oversees foreign economic aid. As issues of trade, U.S. corporate investment in other countries, and protection of intellectual property rights (patents and copyrights) become more important in the global economy, both the Department of Commerce, another cabinet department, and the Office of the U.S. Trade Representative, part of the Executive Office of the President, have become more important in foreign policy making.

The Department of Defense (DOD), housed in the **Pentagon,** is also influential in shaping foreign and military policies. The DOD is headed by a civilian secretary of defense, who has authority over the entire department and reports directly to the president. Civilian secretaries are also in charge of the Departments of the Army, Navy, and Air Force and report to the secretary of defense. Each service also has a military command structure headed by people in uniform: the army and air force chiefs of staff, the chief of naval operations, the commandant of the marine corps, and their subordinates. The uniformed chiefs of each branch serve together in the **Joint Chiefs of Staff (JCS),** headed by the chairman of the Joint Chiefs, who reports not only to the secretary of defense but also directly to the president. The organization of the Defense Department often leads to a certain degree of tension between civilian control and military hierarchy and rivalries between the services over missions, weapons systems, and budgets. Defense Secretary Rumsfeld and the military services were often at loggerheads during the first years of the Bush administration. At issue were Rumsfeld's plans to turn the U.S. military into a lighter, more mobile, and high-tech-oriented set of organizations, capable of speed, surprise, and innovation in combat in many locations, rather than a large and immobile force designed to fight a massive land war on the plains of Europe.

A large intelligence community is also involved in the fashioning and implementation of foreign and military policy. This community is made up of a number of specific agencies. The **National Security Agency (NSA)** is responsible for intercepting and monitoring electronic messages from around the world, and the **National Reconnaissance Office (NRO)** is responsible for satellite reconnaissance. Each of the armed services also has a separate tactical intelligence unit. Most important is the **Central Intelligence Agency (CIA),** which was established in 1947 to advise the National Security

Pentagon

The building in Arlington, Virginia, that contains the offices of the military chiefs and top officials of the Defense Department.

Joint Chiefs of Staff (JCS)

The military officers in charge of each of the armed services.

National Security Agency (NSA)

The federal government agency that intercepts and decodes electronic messages and secures U.S. communications around the world.

National Reconnaissance Office (NRO)

The government agency in charge of surveillance by satellite photography and other technological means.

Central Intelligence Agency (CIA)

The organization that coordinates all U.S. intelligence agencies; it also gathers and evaluates intelligence itself and carries out covert operations.

These B-52 bombers, destroyed by the United States as part of the Strategic Arms Limitations Treaty, must be left in their dismembered state for 90 days so that Russia can confirm their destruction with satellite photos. Satellite photography is used by the United States and other nations to confirm arms control measures and as a strategic device to monitor activities around the world.

Council, to coordinate all U.S. intelligence agencies, to gather and evaluate intelligence information, and to carry out such additional functions as the NSC directs. Congress, the press, and the public subjected the CIA to intense scrutiny in 2004 because of its failure to alert the nation to the September 11 terrorist attacks, and its apparent misreading of the existence of weapons of mass destruction in Iraq prior to the U.S. invasion.

Also in 2004, the 9/11 Commission issued its final report on the terrorist attacks on the United States, focusing on the continuing failures of the American intelligence community in the area of counterterrorism intelligence. The Commission, comprised of five Democrats and five Republicans with broad experience in foreign and military affairs, unanimously recommended that a new agency be created to facilitate both the sharing of information from various agencies (who, more often than not, are reluctant to share their information with others in the government) and the comprehensive evaluation of streams of intelligence from inside and outside the United States. The proposed National Counterterrorism Center, headed by a National Intelligence Director, with power to set budgets for the various intelligence agencies and power to hire and fire, would be responsible for "connecting the dots" and for joint operational planning of counterterrorism efforts. It remains to be seen whether these and other recommendations will be implemented by the president and Congress.

Congress

Congress has generally played a less active role in foreign than domestic policy. Members of Congress believe that their constituents care more about policies that are close to home than those that are far away. Moreover, the executive branch, with its vast intelligence and national security apparatus, has far more information, expertise, and control of events. Still, Congress has shown signs of increased activity since the end of the Cold War. Because the military threat to the United States seemed to have declined with the collapse of the Soviet Union, members of Congress during the 1990s did not feel as compelled as before to defer to the commander-in-chief on any but the most dangerous situations. Also, on a range of foreign policy issues that now directly affect the everyday lives of their constituents—immigration, drug trafficking, and corporate investment abroad—members of Congress are less willing than in the past to leave matters to the president. Congress became especially assertive on foreign affairs during Bill Clinton's second term, when animosity between the president and the Republican-controlled Congress was intense and no apparent foreign military threat was evident. For example, in early 2000 the House of Representatives passed a bill that mandated more direct ties between the United States and the Taiwan military, much to the dismay of President Clinton, who was trying to forge stronger relations with China, whose leadership sees Taiwan as one of its own provinces.

In the immediate aftermath of the terrorist attacks on the United States in 2001, however, Congress took a back seat to the president on foreign and military policy. None of its leaders was about to take on George W. Bush, given the crisis situation and the president's extraordinary popularity. However, Congress reasserted itself after information about CIA, FBI, and NSA intelligence failures surrounding September 11 became public in 2002. Various committees held hearings to get to the bottom of intelligence gathering, coordination, and interpretation problems in the executive branch, especially in 2004 after the publication of former White House intelligence staffer Richard Clarke's explosive book *Against All Enemies: Inside America's War on Terrorism* Congress also launched a series of investigations in 2004 and 2005 on the progress of the Iraq occupation and the handover of power to a new Iraqi government. Not surprisingly, the congressional inquiries brought out sharp Republican and Democratic differences, an issue explored further in "The Rise of Partisan Conflict" feature.

The Constitution gives Congress the power to declare war—which it has not been asked to do since the beginning of World War II—and to decide about any spending of money. It also gives the Senate the power to approve or disapprove treaties and the appointment of ambassadors. At times, Congress has used its treaty or spending powers to challenge the president on important issues: trying to force an end to the Vietnam War, trying to gain some influence on the presidential use of American armed forces abroad (the War Powers Act of 1973 as described in Chapter 12), creating difficulties over the Panama Canal treaty and the SALT II arms control treaty, defeating the Nuclear Test Ban Treaty, resisting the Reagan administration's aid to the Nicaraguan Contras, and barely acquiescing to military and peacekeeping operations in Bosnia and Kosovo.

Congress has probably exerted its greatest foreign policy influence on issues that involve spending money, all of which must pass through the regular congressional appropriations process. Congress has tended to reduce foreign aid appropriations, for example. And military bases and contracts are a special focus of attention because each has a great economic effect on congressional districts and powerful interest groups. Because of congressional pressure, for

The Rise of Partisan Conflict

The President and His Senior Aides Began the March to War in Iraq in the Earliest Days of the Administration, Long Before the Terrorists Struck the Nation on 9/11

The Story: Many Democrats are convinced that President Bush's invasion of Iraq was not simply a bad policy decision, or a well-intentioned policy decision made on the basis of faulty intelligence about weapons of mass destruction programs in Iraq, but a decision made with nefarious objectives in mind. Depending on which Democrat you listen to— Kennedy, Democratic National Chairman Terry McAuliffe, or shrill Websites such as Democrats.com—the Iraq war was waged to avenge the Iraqi attempt to kill the president's father (George H. W. Bush) af-

ter the 1991 Gulf War, seize control of Iraqi Oil for American oil interests, help Israel in the unending Israeli-Palestinian struggle in the Middle East, spread America's imperial power or help the GOP retain power in Congress in the 2002 elections, or detract attention from corporate corruption scandals. In the minds of many Democrats, the war was a fraud, and Bush administration efforts to justify it in terms of weapons of mass destruction or the war on terrorism were not exaggerations or well-intentioned justifications, but knowingly made lies and fabrications designed to mislead the American people.

The Background: Many Democrats felt that the harsh criticisms of President Bush's invasion and occupation of Iraq were not much different than the GOP's harsh attacks on Democratic president Bill Clinton's foreign policy decisions during his term. Similar to Democratic attacks on Bush, Republican attacks on Clinton seemed less about honest disagreements over policies than about finding ulterior and nefarious motives. For example, regarding Clinton's decision to attack a chemical weapons plant in Sudan with cruise missiles—the plant,

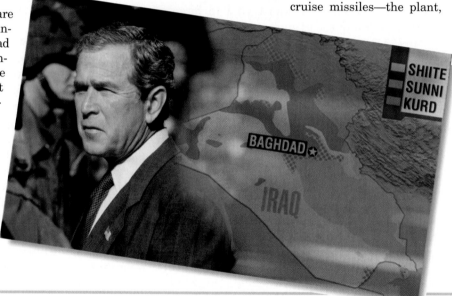

example, the commission on base closings and the Clinton administration decided to keep open several bases despite the fact that the military said it did not need them.

Public Opinion and the News Media

It was once thought that public opinion on foreign policy was so uninformed, unstable, and weak that it could not possibly have much effect on policymaking. As we saw in Chapter 5, however, that picture is not correct. It is now clear that public opinion can have substantial effects. Historical studies of issues such as arms control and foreign aid indicate that policymakers have often taken public opinion into account in making their decisions.[33]

it turns out, was not manufacturing deadly chemicals at all—many Republican politicians and commentators suggested that the attack was a cynical "wag-the-dog" strategy (named after the Robert DiNiro–Dustin Hoffman film of the same name) to distract the news media and the American people from the mounting scandals surrounding the president, not a genuine attempt to neutralize a perceived terrorist threat. Republicans were also exceedingly harsh with Clinton on the NATO-backed air war in Yugoslavia to stop Serbian forces from ethnically cleansing Muslims from Kosovo. Several Republican members of the House and Senate explained their refusal to vote for a resolution authorizing Clinton to conduct an air war in Kosovo by claiming that the president was attempting to distract attention from his troubles in the Paula Jones lawsuit. Other Republicans suggested that opposing the war was a great electoral strategy, as well, arguing that "the best strategy is to keep Republican fingerprints off this war, call it the 'Clinton-Gore' war, wait for it to fail, and then blame the administration for the whole debacle." As GOP Senator Richard Lugar put it, "This is President Clinton's war, and when he falls flat on his face, that's his problem."

What's at Stake?

During the long Cold War with the Soviet Union, Democrats and Republicans generally lived by the dictum that "politics stops at the water's edge," meaning that disagreements over foreign policy ought to be kept within bounds in order to present a united front against the communist enemy. Although it was understood during this period that Republicans and Democrats might have genuine disagreements over foreign and national security policies, these disagreements were not to be about basic goals—the containment of communism—nor were they to become so heated that they would weaken the hand of the president as he dealt with friends and foes abroad. Although partisan leaders didn't always follow the dictum—note Republican attacks on Truman's war in Korea and disagreements over "who lost China" to the communists—it was followed most of the time. Even when it wasn't, the debate between the parties rarely descended to the depths it has reached today, in which the opposing party accuses the president of lies and hidden evil motives and genuinely hopes that the president's foreign policy will fail so its own party might gain in the next national election. What's at stake, then, is whether American politics can encompass genuine debate about foreign policy objectives and methods without crippling the president's ability to effectively carry out foreign policy.

Is it Good for Democracy?

Senator Arlan Specter (R–PA), for one, apparently supports the idea that the "politics stops at the water's edge." Note his statement regarding Iraq: "We think the president has the strongest hand in international affairs if we don't voice doubts." However, such a dictum may lead to a situation where honest policy differences are not debated at all, leaving the people with little insight into the alternative foreign policy options. In reality, the very opposite dictum seems to have taken hold in recent years—that is, do whatever it takes to discredit the foreign and national security policy of the opposition-party president.

- Do you think democracy can work well if either dictum prevails? • Is it helpful to you, in figuring out which are the best policies, that parties vigorously, even viciously expose the errors of the other side? • Or, in a dangerous world with many enemies, should politics stop at "the water's edge"?

Sources: The Democratic National Committee Website (**www.democrats. org**); The Republican National Committee Website (**www.rnc.org**); Democrats.Com (**www.democrats.com**); Tim weiner, "Crisis in the Balkans: The Debate," *New York Times* (May 4, 1999), p. A1.

Still, the executive branch has considerable leeway. Seldom does public opinion demand that particular actions be taken abroad. More often, the public more or less goes along with what the president does, at least until the results begin to come in. If the results look bad (as in the Vietnam War), the public tends to punish the administration with low popularity ratings and rejection at the polls. If the results look good, as in the Persian Gulf War and in the Afghanistan conflict, the public rewards the administration. In the run-up to the 2004 presidential election, troubles with the occupation in Iraq played a role in the erosion of president Bush's historically high ratings with the public.

As Chapter 10 explained, this system of electoral reward and punishment creates incentives for presidents to do things that will please the public in the long run, but there is leeway in the short run, and presidents

News media reporting of foreign events can often sway public opinion about distant places. Here, a horde of television cameras document the plight of Muslim refugees fleeing ethnic cleansing in Kosovo. This news coverage helped pressure American and NATO leaders to initiate military action against the Serb-dominated Yugoslav government of Slobodan Milosevic as a way to halt the expulsion of Kosovars from their homes.

sometimes miscalculate how things will work out, as Lyndon Johnson did in Vietnam. Moreover, with many foreign policies that are secret or barely visible, the moment for reward or punishment never comes, and the administration can act without being called to account.

According to political scientist V. O. Key, Jr., public opinion mainly sets up "dikes" that confine policy to certain broad channels. Within those channels, the president and the executive branch largely determine the flow.[34] This view may have to be altered slightly to take account of the increasingly important role the mass media play in placing issues on the agenda and framing the debate about them. When the plight of Kosovar Muslims at the hands of the Serbs dominated the news broadcasts, the president, the executive branch, and Congress were forced to pay attention. Other human rights tragedies receiving less attention—as in the early stages of the Rwanda atrocities—did not lead to significant U.S. intervention. (See the "Using the Framework" feature for more on the conflict in Kosovo.)

Corporations, Interest Groups, and Social Movements

American corporations are among the most active players in the global economy, producing, marketing, and selling goods and services around the world. Naturally, these corporations with a considerable global presence have good reasons to care about U.S. foreign policy. Companies such as Microsoft, for example, want the government to aggressively fight software piracy in places such as China and Russia. And many multinational firms seek free trade policies and diplomatic or military protection abroad. Other firms, especially those relying on U.S. markets but threatened by foreign competition (e.g., in automobiles, steel, clothing, and consumer electronics), have sought government subsidies, tariffs, or quotas against foreign goods.

The defense budget involves big money interests as well. Arms manufacturers such as Lockheed Martin, Boeing, Raytheon, BAE Systems, Northrop Grumman, and General Dynamics play a significant part in decisions about

Using the Framework

Air War in Kosovo

Why did we depend entirely on air power in Kosovo? Why no ground forces?

Background: Americans strongly supported the use of American ground forces in Afghanistan following the September 11, 2001, terrorist attacks on the United States, and tell pollsters they are willing to have ground forces used in a widened war against terrorism. They supported President Bush's decision to invade Iraq in 2003 because he convinced them that Iraqi weapons of mass destruction posed an imminent threat to the United States. Apparently, the American people are willing to use troops and to accept casualties when threats to the national security of the United States are clear. This has not been the case in other recent conflicts.

Announcing his plan to rely solely on an air bombing campaign to try to halt the Serb "ethnic cleansing" campaign in the Yugoslavian province of Kosovo in 1999, President Clinton renounced the use of ground combat troops. Many critics, including several of our NATO allies, believed that only troops on the ground could protect Kosovar Muslims from being forced from their homes. Air power eventually prevailed, forcing a Serb withdrawal, but it took time, and the human toll was high. Why, then, did President Clinton avoid sending ground troops? Taking a broader look at how structural, political linkage, and governmental factors affected President Clinton's decision to only use air power in Kosovo will help explain the situation.

Governmental Action

President Clinton orders air strikes against Serb forces in Yugoslavia and Kosovo.

Governmental Level

The president and his advisers believed that Serb aggression threatened the stability of the Balkans and that some form of military intervention in Kosovo was essential.

Congress was uneasy about the use of ground troops and voted a (nonbinding) resolution against their use.

The Joint Chiefs and other military leaders did not want to get bogged down in a Balkan quagmire.

Political Linkages Level

Recently, the news media have "individualized" and "personalized" American military action so that virtually every American combat death receives extensive coverage.

The public was not inclined to accept American casualties in humanitarian interventions where the perceived threat to the United States was low.

The public came to believe that air power was both effective and saved American lives.

Structural Level

As commander-in-chief, the president had the constitutional power to put American military forces into action.

As the leading military power in the world, the United States had the resources to wage any form of military campaign in Kosovo it wished.

The United States had, near at hand, especially at various locations in Europe, sufficient air assets to wage a bombing campaign.

How Democratic Are We?

The American Public and the Making of Foreign Policy

PROPOSITION: Foreign and national security policymaking is not and should not be very democratic.

AGREE: Americans care more about what is going on in the United States that affects them directly than they do about issues and developments in distant places. They also know more about what is going on in the United States—whether health care, living standards, or the environment—than they do about what is happening elsewhere, particularly in the poor countries that get very little media news coverage. Additionally, to be effective, many foreign and military policies must be made in secret, so citizens often do not have the information that is necessary to be politically effective. Given all of this, it is clear that Americans are more competent as citizens when faced with domestic matters than with military and foreign affairs. Therefore, for the most part, Americans give political, diplomatic, and military leaders a relatively free hand in making foreign and military policy, as well they should.

DISAGREE: While it is true that citizens play a smaller role in deciding foreign policies compared with domestic policies, they are not powerless. Citizens do, in fact, give their leaders a great deal of freedom in deciding what to do in foreign and military affairs, but these leaders are ultimately answerable to the people, and they know it. Presidents and members of Congress pay very close attention to public opinion and worry about the next election, so they are careful to avoid actions that may eventually prove unpopular. In addition, if Americans play a lesser role than required by democratic theory, it is something we ought to work on improving. If we are to be a democracy at all, citizens must be engaged in helping to decide all important policies, whether these policies are about health care or war in Iraq.

CONSIDER: It is true that Americans know less and care less about foreign affairs than they do about domestic affairs. It is also true that some secrecy is required in fashioning and conducting foreign and military policies and that speed is sometimes of the essence.

• But does this mean that ordinary Americans should have little say in what goes on in foreign and national security affairs? • Can we really be a democracy if such an important part of public affairs is off-limits to citizens. • What do you think? • And, if you believe that citizens should play an important role in this area, how competent do you feel to take part? • How well informed are you about these things? • When you read a newspaper or watch TV news, are you more interested in stories about domestic issues or foreign affairs? • About which do you feel more confident to offer an opinion?

the development and selection of weapons systems, and are major contributors to congressional and presidential campaigns. As the military subcontracts many of its logistical and support functions to companies such as Halliburton—providing food and housing for troops in combat zones, training private security forces to protect military facilities, building military bases in the United States and abroad—these companies come to have a say in policies and budgets and can also be counted upon for campaign contributions. In addition, lobbyists representing defense contractors have a major presence on Capitol Hill.

Ethnic groups also can affect U.S. foreign policy. This is most obvious in the case of U.S. policy toward Israel, in which widespread public sympathy toward that country is reinforced by the efforts of the American-Israel Public Affairs Committee (AIPAC) and by various organized groups representing Jewish Americans. Palestinian American and Arab American organizations are now becoming more active in an effort to counteract this tendency in U.S. foreign policy. Similarly, African American groups strongly opposed apartheid in South Africa and military rule in Haiti, and Cuban American groups have insisted on tough policies against Fidel Castro's Cuba.

Global NGOs (nongovernmental organizations) also try to influence American foreign and national security policy. Greenpeace, for example, uses public relations campaigns and stages dramatic events—such as trying to block whaling vessels—to swing U.S. and world public opinion in favor of environmental protection. Amnesty International and Human Rights Watch try to get the governments of the rich democracies to live up to their own professed beliefs and to intervene to protect human rights in other countries.

As the single-minded focus on the Cold War has receded and other foreign policy issues with domestic implications come to the fore, an increasing number of public and private interest groups have been drawn into the politics of foreign policymaking. Labor unions, for example, have become very active in the politics of trade agreements, pushing hard for wage guarantees and worker safety provisions so that jobs at home are not lost to cheap labor abroad. In addition, in 2000, farm organizations successfully lobbied Congress to allow food exports to Cuba.

Participation

Economic Sanctions and Cuba

Summary

The United States has become the world's only military superpower, with a much larger economy and much more powerful armed forces than any other nation. The United States's advantages in high-tech and smart weapons, aerial reconnaissance, and the ability to deploy large forces to world trouble-spots are particularly important.

For more than 40 years, American foreign policy was focused around the tense Cold War with the Soviet Union, competing for influence in Europe, fighting Soviet allies in Korea and Vietnam, and skirmishing over the Third World. When the Soviet Union collapsed, attention turned to other issues, including regional and ethnic conflicts, international economic competition, efforts at transition to democracy and free markets in Russia and eastern Europe, terrorism, problems of world poverty, and the global environment.

Foreign policy has traditionally been made mostly in the executive branch, where the president is assisted by a large national security bureaucracy, including the National Security Council, the Department of Defense, the Department of State, and various intelligence agencies. Congress has been little involved in crises or covert actions and has generally gone along with major decisions on defense policy; it has asserted itself chiefly on matters of foreign trade and aid, military bases, and procurement contracts. Public opinion affects policy, perhaps increasingly so, but this influence is limited by the executive branch's centralization of decision making, secrecy, and control of information. How large a part interest groups and corporations play is disputed, but it is probably substantial. Structural factors, including U.S. economic and military strength and the nature of the international system, strongly affect what policies seem feasible or desirable.

Suggestions for Further Reading

Ambrose, Stephen. *Rise to Globalism,* rev. ed. New York: Penguin Books, 1997.
> *Describes the rise of the U.S. military, economic, and political power in the twentieth century.*

Daalder, Ivo H., and James M. Lindsay. *America Unbound: The Bush Revolution in Foreign Policy.* Washington, D.C.: Brookings Institution Press, 2003.
> *A balanced examination of the foreign policy innovations of President George W. Bush and how they happened.*

Greider, William. *One World, Ready or Not: The Manic Logic of Global Capitalism.* New York: Simon & Schuster, 1997.
> *A pessimistic analysis of trends in global capitalism; describes the future as one of economic instability, growing inequality, and corporate control.*

Huntington, Samuel P. *The Clash of Civilizations: Civilizations and the Remaking of World Order.* New York: Simon & Schuster, 1997.
> *Suggests that the post–Cold War world will be organized along the lines of competing civilizations and that one of these civilizations, Islam, presents the greatest danger to a stable world order.*

Johnson, Chalmers. *The Sorrows of Empire: Militarism, Secrecy, and the End of the Republic.* New York: Metropolitan Books, 2004.
> *Argues that the emergence of militarism in the United States threatens American democracy and individual rights.*

Kagan, Robert. *Of Paradise and Power: America and Europe in the New World Order.* New York: Random House, 2003.
> *Suggests that the deepening split between the United States and Europe is based on dramatic and growing disproportionalities of power between the two.*

Nye, Joseph. *The Paradox of American Power: Why the World's Only Superpower Can't Go It Alone.* Oxford: Oxford University Press, 2002.
> *A passionate argument for a multilateral rather than a unilateral foreign policy.*

Sen, Amartya Kumar. *Development as Freedom.* New York: Knopf, 1999.
> *The Nobel Prize winner in economics argues that freedom is the basis for the development of poor countries, a fact that should inform the foreign policies of the rich countries.*

Internet Sources

Amnesty International
www.amnesty.org
> *Reports and documents from the international human rights organization.*

Center for Defense Information
www.cdi.org
> *Analyses of the defense budget, weapons systems, and national security threats.*

Defense Link
www.defenselink.mil/
> *The home page of the Department of Defense.*

Fedworld
www.fedworld.gov
> *Links to the home pages of all federal departments and agencies involved in foreign affairs and national defense, including the State Department, the Central Intelligence Agency, the Commerce Department, and the Defense Department.*

International Herald Tribune Online
http://www.iht.com/
> *Complete international news with a much broader perspective than that found in most U.S. newspapers and other media outlets.*

National Security Website
www.nationalsecurity.org
> *Essays and news about foreign and military policy, sponsored by the Heritage Foundation, from a conservative point of view.*

Peacenet
http://www.peacenet.apc.org
> *A Website devoted to peace, social and economic justice, and human rights; information on all of these subjects as well as links to organizations working in these fields.*

Statistical Resources on the Web: Military and Defense
www.lib.umich.edu/govdocs/stats.html
> *A vast statistical and information compendium on military and national security issues; covers the United States and other countries.*

United Nations
www.un.org
> *Home page of the United Nations; links to a wealth of statistics, documents and reports, U.N. departments and conferences, and information on reaching U.N. officials.*

Appendix

The Declaration of Independence

When in the Course of human events, it becomes necessary for one people to dissolve the political bands which have connected them with another, and to assume among the Powers of the earth, the separate and equal station to which the Laws of Nature and of Nature's God entitle them, a decent respect to the opinions of mankind requires that they should declare the causes which impel them to the separation.

We hold these truths to be self-evident, that all men are created equal, that they are endowed by their Creator with certain unalienable Rights, that among these are Life, Liberty and the pursuit of Happiness. That to secure these rights, Governments are instituted among Men, deriving their just powers from the consent of the governed, That whenever any Form of Government becomes destructive of these ends, it is the Right of the People to alter or to abolish it, and to institute new Government, laying its foundation on such principles and organizing its powers in such form, as to them shall seem most likely to effect their Safety and Happiness. Prudence, indeed, will dictate that Governments long established should not be changed for light and transient causes; and accordingly all experience hath shown, that mankind are more disposed to suffer, while evils are sufferable, than to right themselves by abolishing the forms to which they are accustomed. But when a long train of abuses and usurpations, pursuing invariably the same Object evinces a design to reduce them under absolute Despotism, it is their right, it is their duty, to throw off such Government, and to provide new Guards for their future security.—Such has been the patient sufferance of these Colonies; and such is now the necessity which constrains them to alter their former Systems of Government. The history of the present King of Great Britain is a history of repeated injuries and usurpations, all having in direct object the establishment of an absolute Tyranny over these States. To prove this, let Facts be submitted to a candid world.

He has refused his Assent to Laws, the most wholesome and necessary for the public good.

He has forbidden his Governors to pass Laws of immediate and pressing importance, unless suspended in their operation till his Assent should be obtained; and when so suspended, he has utterly neglected to attend to them.

He has refused to pass other Laws for the accommodation of large districts of people, unless those people would relinquish the right of Representation in the Legislature, a right inestimable to them and formidable to tyrants only.

He has called together legislative bodies at places unusual, uncomfortable, and distant from the depository of their Public Records, for the sole purpose of fatiguing them into compliance with his measures.

He has dissolved Representative Houses repeatedly, for opposing with manly firmness his invasions on the rights of the people.

He has refused for a long time, after such dissolutions, to cause others to be elected; whereby the Legislative Powers, incapable of Annihilation, have returned to the People at large for their exercise; the State remaining in the mean time exposed to all the dangers of invasion from without, and convulsions within.

He has endeavoured to prevent the population of these States; for that purpose obstructing the Laws of Naturalization of Foreigners; refusing to pass others to encourage their migration hither, and raising the conditions of new Appropriations of Lands.

He has obstructed the Administration of Justice, by refusing his Assent to Laws for establishing Judiciary Powers.

He has made Judges dependent on his Will alone, for the tenure of their offices, and the amount and payment of their salaries.

He has erected a multitude of New Offices, and sent hither swarms of Officers to harass our People, and eat out their substance.

He has kept among us, in times of peace, Standing Armies without the Consent of our legislature.

He has affected to render the Military independent of and superior to the Civil Power.

He has combined with others to subject us to a jurisdiction foreign to our constitution, and unacknowledged by our laws; giving his Assent to their acts of pretended legislation:

For quartering large bodies of armed troops among us:

For protecting them, by a mock Trial, from Punishment for any Murders which they should commit on the Inhabitants of these States:

For cutting off our Trade with all parts of the world:

For imposing taxes on us without our Consent:

For depriving us in many cases, of the benefits of Trial by Jury:

For transporting us beyond Seas to be tried for pretended offences:

For abolishing the free System of English Laws in a neighbouring Province, establishing therein an Arbitrary government, and enlarging its Boundaries so as to render it at once an example and fit instrument for introducing the same absolute rule into these Colonies:

For taking away our Charters, abolishing our most valuable Laws, and altering fundamentally the Forms of our Governments:

For suspending our own Legislature, and declaring themselves invested with Power to legislate for us in all cases whatsoever.

He has abdicated Government here, by declaring us out of his Protection and waging War against us.

He has plundered our seas, ravaged our Coasts, burnt our towns, and destroyed the lives of our people.

He is at this time transporting large armies of foreign mercenaries to compleat the works of death, desolation and tyranny, already begun with circumstances of Cruelty & perfidy scarcely paralleled in the most barbarous ages, and totally unworthy the Head of a civilized nation.

He has constrained our fellow Citizens taken Captive on the high Seas to bear Arms against their Country, to become the executioners of their friends and Brethren, or to fall themselves by their Hands.

He has excited domestic insurrections amongst us, and has endeavoured to bring on the inhabitants of our frontiers, the merciless Indian Savages, whose known rule of warfare, is an undistinguished destruction of all ages, sexes and conditions.

In every stage of these Oppressions We have Petitioned for Redress in the most humble terms: Our repeated Petitions have been answered only by repeated injury. A Prince, whose character is thus marked by every act which may define a Tyrant, is unfit to be the ruler of a free People.

Nor have We been wanting in attention to our British brethren. We have warned them from time to time of attempts by their legislature to extend an unwarrantable jurisdiction over us. We have reminded them of the circumstances of our emigration and settlement here. We have appealed to their native justice and magnanimity, and we have conjured them by the ties of our common kindred to disavow these usurpations, which, would inevitably interrupt our connections and correspondence. They too have been deaf to the voice of justice and of consanguinity. We must, therefore, acquiesce in the necessity, which denounces our Separation, and hold them, as we hold the rest of mankind, Enemies in War, in Peace Friends.

We, therefore, the Representatives of the united States of America, in General Congress, Assembled, appealing to the Supreme Judge of the world for the rectitude of our intentions, do, in the Name, and by Authority of the good People of these Colonies, solemnly publish and declare, That these United Colonies are, and of Right ought to be Free and Independent States; that they are Absolved from all Allegiance to the British Crown, and that all political connection between them and the State of Great Britain, is and ought to be totally dissolved; and that as Free and Independent States, they have full Power to levy War, conclude Peace, contract Alliances, establish Commerce, and to do all other Acts and Things which Independent States may of right do. And for the support of this Declaration, with a firm reliance of the Protection of Divine Providence, we mutually pledge to each other our Lives, our Fortunes and our sacred Honor.

John Hancock,

Josiah Bartlett, Wm Whipple, Saml Adams, John Adams, Robt Treat Paine, Elbridge Gerry, Steph. Hopkins, William Ellery, Roger Sherman, Samel Huntington, Wm Williams, Oliver Wolcott, Matthew Thornton, Wm Floyd, Phil Livingston, Frans Lewis, Lewis Morris, Richd Stockton, Jno Witherspoon, Fras Hopkinson, John Hart, Abra Clark, Robt Morris, Benjamin Rush, Benja Franklin, John Morton, Geo Clymer, Jas Smith, Geo. Taylor, James Wilson, Geo. Ross, Caesar Rodney, Geo Read, Thos M:Kean, Samuel Chase, Wm Paca, Thos Stone, Charles Carroll of Carrollton, George Wythe, Richard Henry Lee, Th. Jefferson, Benja Harrison, Thos Nelson, Jr., Francis Lightfoot Lee, Carter Braxton, Wm Hooper, Joseph Hewes, John Penn, Edward Rutledge, Thos Heyward, Junr., Thomas Lynch, Junor., Arthur Middleton, Button Gwinnett, Lyman Hall, Geo Walton.

The Constitution of the United States

We the people of the United States, in Order to form a more perfect Union, establish Justice, insure domestic Tranquility, provide for the common defence, promote the general Welfare, and secure the Blessings of Liberty to ourselves and our Posterity, do ordain and establish this constitution for the United States of America.

Article I

Section 1 All legislative Powers herein granted shall be vested in a Congress of the United States, which shall consist of a Senate and House of Representatives.

Section 2 The House of Representatives shall be composed of Members chosen every second Year by the People of the several States, and the Electors in each State shall have the Qualifications requisite for Electors of the most numerous Branch of the State Legislature.

No person shall be a Representative who shall not have attained to the Age of twenty-five Years, and been seven Years a Citizen of the United States, and who shall not, when elected, be an Inhabitant of that State in which he shall be chosen.

Representatives and direct Taxes shall be apportioned among the several States which may be included within this Union, according to their respective Numbers, which shall be determined by adding to the whole Number of free Persons, including those bound to Service for a Term of Years, and excluding Indians not taxed, three fifths of all other Persons. The actual Enumeration shall be made within three Years after the first Meeting of the Congress of the United States, and within every subsequent Term of ten Years, in such Manner as they shall by Law direct. The Number of Representatives shall not exceed one for every thirty Thousand, but each State shall have at Least one Representative; and until such enumeration shall be made, the State of New Hampshire shall be entitled to chuse three, Massachusetts eight, Rhode-Island and Providence Plantations one, Connecticut five, New-York six, New Jersey four, Pennsylvania eight, Delaware one, Maryland six, Virginia ten, North Carolina five, South Carolina five, and Georgia three.

When vacancies happen in the Representation from any State, the Executive Authority thereof shall issue Writs of Election to fill such Vacancies.

The House of Representatives shall chuse their Speaker and other Officers; and shall have the sole Power of Impeachment.

Section 3 The Senate of the United States shall be composed of two Senators from each State, chosen by the Legislature thereof, for six Years; and each Senator shall have one Vote.

Immediately after they shall be assembled in Consequence of the first Election, they shall be divided as equally as may be into three Classes. The Seats of the Senators of the first Class shall be vacated at the Expiration of the second Year, of the second Class at the Expiration of the fourth Year, and of the third Class at the Expiration of the sixth Year, so that one-third may be chosen every second Year; and if Vacancies happen by Resignation, or otherwise, during the Recess of the Legislature of any State, the Executive thereof may make temporary Appointments until the next Meeting of the Legislature, which shall then fill such Vacancies.

No Person shall be a Senator who shall not have attained to the Age of thirty Years, and been nine Years a Citizen of the United States, and who shall not, when elected, be an Inhabitant of that State in which he shall be chosen.

The Vice President of the United States shall be President of the Senate, but shall have no vote, unless they be equally divided.

The Senate shall chuse their other Officers, and also a President pro tempore, in the absence of the Vice President, or when he shall exercise the Office of the President of the United States.

The Senate shall have the sole Power to try all Impeachments. When sitting for that purpose, they shall be on Oath or Affirmation. When the President of the United States is tried, the Chief Justice shall preside: And no person shall be convicted without the Concurrence of two thirds of the Members present.

Judgment in Cases of Impeachment shall not extend further than to removal from Office, and disqualification to hold and enjoy any Office of honor, Trust, or Profit under the United States: but the Party convicted shall nevertheless be liable and subject to Indictment, Trial, Judgment, and Punishment, according to Law.

Section 4 The Times, Places and Manner of holding Elections for Senators and Representatives, shall be prescribed in each state by the Legislature thereof; but the Congress may at any time by Law make or alter such Regulations, except as to the Places of Chusing Senators.

The Congress shall assemble at least once in every Year, and such Meeting shall be on the first Monday in December, unless they shall by Law appoint a different Day.

Section 5 Each House shall be the Judge of the Elections, Returns and Qualifications of its own Members, and a Majority of each shall constitute a Quorum to do Business; but a smaller number may adjourn from day to day, and may be authorized to compel the Attendance of absent Members, in such Manner, and under such Penalties, as each House may provide.

Each House may determine the Rules of its Proceedings, punish its Members for disorderly Behavior, and, with the Concurrence of two thirds, expel a Member.

Each House shall keep a Journal of its Proceedings, and from time to time publish the same, excepting such Parts as may in their Judgment require Secrecy; and the Yeas and Nays of the Members of either House on any question shall, at the Desire of one fifth of those Present, be entered on the Journal.

Neither House, during the Session of Congress, shall, without the Consent of the other, adjourn for more than three days, nor to any other Place than that in which the two Houses shall be sitting.

Section 6 The Senators and Representatives shall receive a Compensation for their Services, to be ascertained by Law, and paid out of the Treasury of the United States. They shall in all Cases, except Treason, Felony, and Breach of the Peace, be privileged from arrest during their Attendance at the Session of their respective Houses, and in going to and returning from the same; and for any Speech or Debate in either House, they shall not be questioned in any other Place.

No Senator or Representative shall, during the Time for which he was elected, be appointed to any civil Office under the Authority of the United States, which shall have been created, or the Emoluments whereof shall have been increased, during such time; and no Person holding any Office under the United States shall be a Member of either House during his continuance in Office.

Section 7 All Bills for raising Revenue shall originate in the House of Representatives; but the Senate may propose or concur with Amendments as on other bills.

Every Bill which shall have passed the House of Representatives and the Senate, shall, before it become a Law, be presented to the President of the United States; If he approve he shall sign it, but if not he shall return it, with his Objections, to that House in which it shall have originated, who shall enter the Objections at large on their Journal, and proceed to reconsider it. If after such Reconsideration two thirds of that House shall agree to pass the bill, it shall be sent, together with the objections, to the other House, by which it shall likewise be reconsidered, and if approved by two thirds of that House, it shall become a Law. But in all such Cases the Votes of both Houses shall be determined by Yeas and Nays, and the Names of the Persons voting for and against the Bill shall be entered on the Journal of each House respectively. If any Bill shall not be returned by the President within ten Days (Sundays excepted) after it shall have been presented to him, the Same shall be a Law, in like Manner as if he had signed it, unless the Congress by their Adjournment prevent its Return, in which Case it shall not be a Law.

Every Order, Resolution, or Vote to which the Concurrence of the Senate and House of Representatives may be necessary (except on a question of Adjournment) shall be presented to the President of the United States; and before the Same shall take Effect, shall be approved by him, or being disapproved by him, shall be repassed by two thirds of the Senate and House of Representatives, according to the Rules and Limitations prescribed in the Case of a Bill.

Section 8 The Congress shall have Power

To lay and collect Taxes, Duties, Imposts and

Excises, to pay the Debts and provide for the common Defence and general Welfare of the United States; but all Duties, Imposts and Excises shall be uniform throughout the United States;

To borrow money on the credit of the United States;

To regulate Commerce with foreign Nations, and among the several States, and with the Indian Tribes;

To establish a uniform Rule of Naturalization, and uniform Laws on the subject of Bankruptcies throughout the United States;

To coin Money, regulate the Value thereof, and of foreign Coin, and fix the Standard of Weights and Measures;

To provide for the Punishment of counterfeiting the Securities and current Coin of the United States;

To establish Post offices and post Roads;

To promote the Progress of Science and useful Arts, by securing for limited Times to Authors and Inventors the exclusive Right to their respective Writings and Discoveries;

To constitute Tribunals inferior to the Supreme Court;

To define and punish Piracies and Felonies committed on the high Seas, and Offences against the Law of Nations;

To declare War, grant Letters of Marque and Reprisal, and make Rules concerning Captures on Land and Water;

To raise and support Armies, but no Appropriation of Money to that Use shall be for a longer Term than two Years;

To provide and maintain a Navy;

To make Rules for the Government and Regulation of the land and naval forces;

To provide for calling forth the Militia to execute the Laws of the Union, suppress Insurrections and repel Invasions;

To provide for organizing, arming, and disciplining the Militia, and for governing such Part of them as may be employed in the Service of the United States, reserving to the States respectively, the Appointment of the Officers, and the Authority of training the Militia according to the discipline prescribed by Congress;

To exercise exclusive Legislation in all Cases whatsoever, over such District (not exceeding ten Miles square) as may, by Cession of particular States, and the acceptance of Congress, become the Seat of Government of the United States, and to exercise like Authority over all Places purchased by the Consent of the Legislature of the State in which the Same shall be, for the Erection of Forts, Magazines, Arsenals, dock-Yards, and other needful Buildings;—And

To make all Laws which shall be necessary and proper for carrying into Execution the foregoing Powers, and all other Powers vested by this Constitution in the government of the United States, or in any Department or Officer thereof.

Section 9 The Migration or Importation of such Persons as any of the States now existing shall think proper to admit, shall not be prohibited by the Congress prior to the Year one thousand eight hundred and eight, but a tax or duty may be imposed on such Importation, not exceeding ten dollars for each Person.

The privilege of the Writ of Habeas Corpus shall not be suspended, unless when in Cases of Rebellion or Invasion the public Safety may require it.

No Bill of Attainder or ex post facto Law shall be passed.

No capitation, or other direct, Tax shall be laid unless in Proportion to the Census or Enumeration herein before directed to be taken.

No Tax or Duty shall be laid on Articles exported from any State.

No Preference shall be given by any Regulation of Revenue to the Ports of one State over those of another: nor shall Vessels bound to, or from, one state, be obliged to enter, clear, or pay Duties in another.

No Money shall be drawn from the Treasury, but in Consequence of Appropriations made by Law; and a regular Statement and Account of the Receipts and Expenditures of all public Money shall be published from time to time.

No Title of Nobility shall be granted by the United States: And no Person holding any Office of Profit or Trust under them, shall, without the Consent of the Congress, accept of any present, Emolument, Office, or Title, of any kind whatever, from any King, Prince, or Foreign State.

Section 10   No state shall enter into any Treaty, Alliance, or Confederation; grant Letters of Marque and Reprisal; coin Money; emit Bills of Credit; make any Thing but gold and silver Coin a Tender in Payment of Debts; pass any Bill of Attainder, ex post facto Law, or Law impairing the Obligation of Contracts, or grant any Title of Nobility.

No State shall, without the Consent of the Congress, lay any Imposts or Duties on Imports or Exports, except what may be absolutely necessary for executing its inspection Laws: and the net Produce of all Duties and Imposts, laid by any State on Imports or Exports, shall be for the Use of the Treasury of the United States; and all such Laws shall be subject to the Revision and Control of the Congress.

No State shall, without the Consent of Congress, lay any duty of Tonnage, keep Troops, or Ships of War in time of Peace, enter into any Agreement or Compact with another State, or with a foreign Power, or engage in War, unless actually invaded, or in such imminent Danger as will not admit of delay.

Article II

Section 1   The executive Power shall be vested in a President of the United States of America. He shall hold his Office during the Term of four years, and, together with the Vice President, chosen for the same Term, be elected, as follows:

Each State shall appoint, in such Manner as the Legislature thereof may direct, a Number of Electors, equal to the whole Number of Senators and Representatives to which the State may be entitled in the Congress; but no Senator or Representative, or Person holding an Office of Trust or Profit under the United States, shall be appointed an Elector.

The Electors shall meet in their respective States, and vote by Ballot for two persons, of whom one at least shall not be an Inhabitant of the same State with themselves. And they shall make a List of all the Persons voted for, and of the Number of Votes for each; which List they shall sign and certify, and transmit sealed to the Seat of the Government of the United States, directed to the President of the Senate. The President of the Senate shall, in the Presence of the Senate and House of Representatives, open all the Certificates, and the Votes shall then be counted. The Person having the greatest Number of Votes shall be the President, if such Number be a Majority of the whole Number of Electors appointed; and if there be more than one who have such Majority, and have an equal Number of Votes, then the House of Representatives shall immediately chuse by Ballot one of them for President; and if no Person have a Majority, then from the five highest on the List the said House shall in like Manner chuse the President. But in chusing the President, the votes shall be taken by States, the Representation from each State having one Vote; a quorum for this Purpose shall consist of a Member or Members from two-thirds of the States, and a Majority of all the States shall be necessary to a Choice. In every Case, after the Choice of the President, the Person having the greatest Number of Votes of the Electors shall be the Vice President. But if there should remain two or more who have equal votes, the Senate shall chuse from them by Ballot the Vice President.

The Congress may determine the time of chusing the Electors, and the Day on which they shall give their Votes; which Day shall be the same throughout the United States.

No person except a natural-born Citizen, or a Citizen of the United States, at the time of the Adoption of this Constitution, shall be eligible to the Office of President; neither shall any Person be eligible to that Office who shall not have attained to the Age of thirty-five years, and been fourteen Years a Resident within the United States.

In Case of the Removal of the President from Office, or of his Death, Resignation, or Inability to discharge the Powers and Duties of the said Office, the same shall devolve on the Vice President, and the Congress may by Law provide for the Case of Removal, Death, Resignation, or Inability, both of the President and Vice President, declaring what Officer shall then act as President, and such Officer shall act accordingly, until the disability be removed, or a President shall be elected.

The President shall, at stated Times, receive for his Services a Compensation, which shall neither be increased nor diminished during the Period for which he shall have been elected, and he shall not receive within that Period any other Emolument from the United States, or any of them.

Before he enter on the execution of his Office, he shall take the following Oath or Affirmation:—"I do solemnly swear (or affirm) that I will faithfully execute the Office of President of the United States, and will, to the best of my Ability, preserve, protect, and defend the Constitution of the United States."

Section 2 The President shall be Commander in Chief of the Army and Navy of the United States, and of the Militia of the several States, when called into the actual Service of the United States; he may require the Opinion, in writing, of the principal Officer in each of the executive Departments, upon any subject relating to the Duties of their respective Offices, and he shall have Power to Grant Reprieves and Pardons for Offences against the United States, except in Cases of Impeachment.

He shall have Power, by and with the Advice and Consent of the Senate, to make Treaties, provided two thirds of the Senators present concur; and he shall nominate, and by and with the Advice and Consent of the Senate, shall appoint Ambassadors, other public Ministers and Consuls, Judges of the supreme Court, and all other Officers of the United States, whose Appointments are not herein otherwise provided for, and which shall be established by Law: but the Congress may by Law vest the Appointment of such inferior Officers, as they think proper, in the President alone, in the Courts of Law, or in the Heads of Departments.

The President shall have Power to fill up all Vacancies that may happen during the Recess of the Senate, by granting Commissions which shall expire at the End of their next Session.

Section 3 He shall from time to time give to the Congress Information of the State of the Union, and recommend to their Consideration such Measures as he shall judge necessary and expedient; he may, on extraordinary occasions, convene both Houses, or either of them, and in Case of Disagreement between them, with respect to the Time of Adjournment, he may adjourn them to such Time as he shall think proper; he shall receive Ambassadors and other public Ministers; he shall take Care that the Laws be faithfully executed, and shall Commission all the Officers of the United States.

Section 4 The President, Vice President and all civil Officers of the United States, shall be removed from Office on Impeachment for, and Conviction of, Treason, Bribery, or other high Crimes and Misdemeanors.

Article III

Section 1 The judicial Power of the United States, shall be vested in one supreme Court, and in such inferior Courts as the Congress may from time to time ordain and establish. The Judges, both of the supreme and inferior Courts, shall hold their Offices during good Behaviour, and shall, at stated Times, receive for their Services, a Compensation, which shall not be diminished during their Continuance in Office.

Section 2 The judicial Power shall extend to all Cases, in Law and Equity, arising under this Constitution, the Laws of the United States, and treaties made, or which shall be made, under their Authority;—to all Cases affecting ambassadors, other public ministers and consuls;—to all cases of admiralty and maritime Jurisdiction;—to Controversies to which the United States shall be a Party;—to Controversies between two or more States;—between a State and Citizens of another State;—between Citizens of different States,—between Citizens of the same State claiming Lands under Grants of different States, and between a State, or the Citizens thereof, and foreign States, Citizens or Subjects.

In all Cases affecting Ambassadors, other public Ministers and Consuls, and those in which a State shall be Party, the supreme Court shall have original Jurisdiction. In all the other Cases before mentioned, the supreme Court shall have appellate Jurisdiction, both as to Law and Fact, with such Exceptions, and under such Regulations as the Congress shall make.

The trial of all Crimes, except in Cases of Impeachment, shall be by Jury; and such Trial shall be held in the State where the said Crimes shall have been committed; but when not committed within any State, the Trial shall be at such Place or Places as the Congress may by Law have directed.

Section 3 Treason against the United States, shall consist only in levying War against them, or in adhering to their Enemies, giving them Aid and Comfort. No Person shall be convicted of Treason unless on the testimony of two Witnesses to the same overt Act, or on Confession in open Court.

The Congress shall have power to declare the Punishment of Treason, but no Attainder of Treason shall work Corruption of Blood, or Forfeiture except during the Life of the Person attained.

Article IV

Section 1 Full Faith and Credit shall be given in each State to the public Acts, Records, and judicial Proceedings of every other State. And the Congress may by general Laws prescribe the Manner in which such Acts, Records and Proceedings shall be proved, and the Effect thereof.

Section 2 The Citizens of each State shall be entitled to all Privileges and Immunities of Citizens in the several States.

A Person charged in any State with Treason, Felony, or other Crime, who shall flee from Justice, and be found in another State, shall on demand of the executive Authority of the State from which he fled, be delivered up, to be removed to the State having Jurisdiction of the crime.

No Person held to Service or Labour in one State, under the Laws thereof, escaping into another, shall, in

Consequence of any Law or Regulation therein, be discharged from such Service or Labour, but shall be delivered up on Claim of the Party to whom such Service or Labour may be due.

Section 3   New States may be admitted by the Congress into this Union; but no new State shall be formed or erected within the Jurisdiction of any other State; nor any State be formed by the Junction of two or more States, or parts of States, without the Consent of the Legislatures of the States concerned as well as of the Congress.

The Congress shall have Power to dispose of and make all needful Rules and Regulations respecting the Territory or other Property belonging to the United States; and nothing in this Constitution shall be so construed as to Prejudice any Claims of the United States, or of any particular State.

Section 4   The United States shall guarantee to every State in this Union a Republican Form of Government, and shall protect each of them against Invasion; and on Application of the Legislature, or the Executive (when the Legislature cannot be convened) against domestic Violence.

Article V

The Congress, whenever two-thirds of both Houses shall deem it necessary, shall propose Amendments to this Constitution, or, on the Application of the Legislatures of two-thirds of the several States, shall call a Convention for proposing Amendments, which, in either Case, shall be valid to all Intents and Purposes, as part of this Constitution, when ratified by the Legislatures of three-fourths of the several States, or by Conventions in three-fourths thereof, as the one or the other Mode of Ratification may be proposed by the Congress; Provided that no Amendment which may be made prior to the Year One thousand eight hundred and eight shall in any Manner affect the first and fourth Clauses in the Ninth Section of the first Article; and that no State, without its Consent, shall be deprived of its equal Suffrage in the Senate.

Article VI

All Debts contracted and Engagements entered into, before the Adoption of this Constitution, shall be as valid against the United States under this Constitution, as under the Confederation.

This Constitution, and the Laws of the United States which shall be made in Pursuance thereof; and all Treaties made, or which shall be made, under the Authority of the United States, shall be the supreme Law of the Land; and the Judges in every State shall be bound thereby, any Thing in the Constitution or Laws of any State to the Contrary notwithstanding.

The Senators and Representatives before mentioned, and the Members of the several State Legislatures and all executive and judicial Officers, both of the United States and of the several States, shall be bound by Oath or Affirmation to support this Constitution; but no religious Test shall ever be required as a qualification to any Office or public Trust under the United States.

Article VII

The Ratification of the Conventions of nine States shall be sufficient for the Establishment of this Constitution between the States so ratifying the same.

Done in Convention by the Unanimous Consent of the States present the Seventeenth Day of September in the Year of our Lord one thousand seven hundred and Eighty seven, and of the Independence of the United States of America the Twelfth. In Witness whereof We have hereunto subscribed our Names.

Go. Washington, President and deputy from Virginia; Attest William Jackson, Secretary; Delaware: Geo. Read,* Gunning Bedford, Jr., John Dickinson, Richard Basset, Jaco. Broom; Maryland: James McHenry, Daniel of St. Thomas' Jenifer, Danl. Carroll; Virginia: John Blair, James Madison, Jr.; North Carolina: Wm. Blount, Richd. Dobbs Spaight, Hu Williamson; South Carolina: J. Rutledge, Charles Cotesworth Pinckney, Charles Pinckney, Pierce Butler; Georgia: William Few, Abr. Baldwin; New Hampshire: John Langdon, Nicholas Gilman; Massachusetts: Nathaniel Gorham, Rufus King; Connecticut: Wm. Saml. Johnson, Roger Sherman,* New York: Alexander Hamilton; New Jersey: Wil. Livingston, David Brearley, Wm. Paterson, Jona. Dayton; Pennsylvania: B. Franklin,* Thomas Mifflin, Robt. Morris,* Geo. Clymer,* Thos. FitzSimons, Jared Ingersoll, James Wilson, Gouv. Morris.

Articles in Addition to, and Amendment of, the Constitution of the United States of America, Proposed by Congress, and Ratified by the Legislatures of the Several States, Pursuant to the Fifth Article of the Original Constitution.

Amendment I [1791]

Congress shall make no law respecting an establishment of religion, or prohibiting the free exercise thereof; or abridging the freedom of speech, or of the press; or the right of the people peaceably to assemble, and to petition the Government for a redress of grievances.

Amendment II [1791]

A well regulated Militia, being necessary to the security of a free State, the right of the people to keep and bear Arms shall not be infringed.

Amendment III [1791]

No Soldier shall, in time of peace, be quartered in any house, without the consent of the Owner, nor in time of war, but in a manner to be prescribed by law.

Amendment IV [1791]

The right of the people to be secure in their persons, houses, papers, and effects, against unreasonable searches and seizures, shall not be violated, and no Warrants shall issue, but upon probable cause, supported by Oath or affirmation, and particularly describing the place to be searched, and the persons or things to be seized.

Amendment V [1791]

No person shall be held to answer for a capital or otherwise infamous crime, unless on a presentment or indictment of a Grand Jury, except in cases arising in the land or naval forces, or in the Militia, when in actual service in time of War or public danger; nor shall any person be subject for the same offence to be twice put in jeopardy of life or limb; nor shall be compelled in any criminal case to be a witness against himself, nor be deprived of life, liberty, or property, without due process of law; nor shall private property be taken for public use, without just compensation.

Amendment VI [1791]

In all criminal prosecutions, the accused shall enjoy the right to a speedy and public trial, by an impartial jury of the State and district wherein the crime shall have been committed, which district shall have been previously ascertained by law, and to be informed of the nature and cause of the accusation; to be confronted with the witnesses against him; to have compulsory process for obtaining witnesses in his favor, and to have the Assistance of Counsel for his defence.

Amendment VII [1791]

In suits at common law, where the value in controversy shall exceed twenty dollars, the right of trial by jury shall be preserved, and no fact tried by a jury, shall be otherwise reexamined in any Court of the United States, than according to the rules of the common law.

Amendment VIII [1791]

Excessive bail shall not be required, nor excessive fines imposed, nor cruel and unusual punishments inflicted.

Amendment IX [1791]

The enumeration in the Constitution, of certain rights, shall not be construed to deny or disparage others retained by the people.

Amendment X [1791]

The powers not delegated to the United States by the Constitution, nor prohibited by it to the States, are reserved to the States respectively, or to the people.

Amendment XI [1798]

The Judicial power of the United States shall not be construed to extend to any suit in law or equity, commenced or prosecuted against one of the United States by Citizens of another State, or by Citizens or Subjects of any Foreign State.

Amendment XII [1804]

The Electors shall meet in their respective States and vote by ballot for President and Vice President, one of whom, at least, shall not be an inhabitant of the same State with themselves; they shall name in their ballots the person voted for as President, and in distinct ballots the person voted for as Vice President, and they shall make distinct lists of all persons voted for as President, and of all persons voted for as Vice President, and of the number of votes for each, which lists they shall sign and certify, and transmit sealed to the seat of the government of the United States, directed to the President of the Senate;—The President of the Senate shall, in the presence of the Senate and House of Representatives, open all the certificates and the votes shall then be counted;— The person having the greatest number of votes for President, shall be the President, if such number be a majority of the whole number of Electors appointed; and if no person have such majority, then from the persons having the highest numbers not exceeding three on the list of those voted for as President, the House of Representatives shall choose immediately, by ballot, the President. But in choosing the President, the votes shall be taken by states, the representation from each state having one vote; a quorum for this purpose shall consist of a member or members from two-thirds of the states, and a majority of all the states shall be necessary to a choice. And if the House of Representatives shall not choose a President whenever the right of choice shall devolve upon them, before the fourth day of March next following, then the Vice President shall act as President, as in the case of the death or other constitutional disability of the President.—The person having the greatest number of votes as Vice President, shall be the Vice President, if such number be a majority of the whole number of Electors appointed, and if no person have a majority, then from the two highest numbers on the list, the Senate shall choose the Vice President; a quorum for the purpose shall consist of two-thirds of the whole number of Senators, and a majority of the whole number shall be necessary to a choice. But no person constitutionally ineligible to the office of President shall be eligible to that of Vice President of the United States.

Amendment XIII [1865]

Section 1 Neither slavery nor involuntary servitude, except as a punishment for crime whereof the party shall have been duly convicted, shall exist within the United States, or any place subject to their jurisdiction.

Section 2 Congress shall have power to enforce this article by appropriate legislation.

Amendment XIV [1868]

Section 1 All persons born or naturalized in the United States, and subject to the jurisdiction thereof, are citizens of the United States and of the State wherein they reside. No State shall make or enforce any law which shall abridge the privileges or immunities of citizens of the United States; nor shall any State deprive any person of life, liberty, or property, without due process of law; nor deny to any person within its jurisdiction the equal protection of the laws.

Section 2 Representatives shall be apportioned among the several States according to their respective numbers, counting the whole number of persons in each State, excluding Indians not taxed. But when the right to vote at any election for the choice of electors for President and Vice President of the United States, Representatives in Congress, the Executive and Judicial officers of a State, or the members of the Legislature thereof, is denied to any of the male inhabitants of such State, being twenty-one years of age, and citizens of the United States or in any way abridged, except for participation in rebellion, or other crime, the basis of representation therein shall be reduced in the proportion which the number of such male citizens shall bear to the whole number of male citizens twenty-one years of age in such State.

Section 3 No person shall be a Senator or Representative in Congress, or elector of President and Vice President, or hold any office, civil or military, under the United States, or under any State, who, having previously taken an oath, as a member of Congress, or as an officer of the United States, or as a member of any State legislature, or as an executive or judicial officer of any State, to support the Constitution of the United States, shall have engaged in insurrection or rebellion against the same, or given aid or comfort to the enemies thereof. But Congress may by a vote of two-thirds of each House, remove such disability.

Section 4 The validity of the public debt of the United States, authorized by law, including debts incurred for payment of pensions and bounties for services in suppressing insurrection or rebellion, shall not be questioned. But neither the United States nor any State shall assume or pay any debt or obligation incurred in aid of insurrection or rebellion against the United States, or any claim for the loss or emancipation of any slave; but all such debts, obligations, and claims shall be held illegal and void.

Section 5 The Congress shall have the power to enforce, by appropriate legislation, the provisions of this article.

Amendment XV [1870]

Section 1 The right of citizens of the United States to vote shall not be denied or abridged by the United States

or by any State on account of race, color, or previous condition of servitude—

Section 2 The Congress shall have power to enforce this article by appropriate legislation.

Amendment XVI [1913]

The Congress shall have power to lay and collect taxes on incomes, from whatever source derived, without apportionment among the several States, and without regard to any census or enumeration.

Amendment XVII [1913]

The Senate of the United States shall be composed of two Senators from each State, elected by the people thereof, for six years; and each Senator shall have one vote. The electors in each State shall have the qualifications requisite for electors of the most numerous branch of the State legislatures.

When vacancies happen in the representation of any State in the Senate, the executive authority of such State shall issue writs of election to fill such vacancies: Provided, That the legislature of any State may empower the executive thereof to make temporary appointments until the people fill the vacancies by election as the legislature may direct. This amendment shall not be so construed as to affect the election or term of any Senator chosen before it becomes valid as part of the Constitution.

Amendment XVIII [1919]

Section 1 After one year from the ratification of this article the manufacture, sale, or transportation of intoxicating liquors within, the importation thereof into, or the exportation thereof from the United States and all territory subject to the jurisdiction thereof for beverage purposes is hereby prohibited.

Section 2 The Congress and the several States shall have concurrent power to enforce this article by appropriate legislation.

Section 3 This article shall be inoperative unless it shall have been ratified as an amendment to the Constitution by the legislatures of the several States, as provided in the Constitution, within seven years from the date of the submission hereof to the States by the Congress.

Amendment XIX [1920]

The right of citizens of the United States to vote shall not be denied or abridged by the United States or by any State on account of sex.

Congress shall have power to enforce this article by appropriate legislation.

Amendment XX [1933]

Section 1 The terms of the President and Vice President shall end at noon on the 20th day of January, and the terms of Senators and Representatives at noon on the 3d day of January, of the years in which such terms would have ended if this article had not been ratified; and the terms of their successors shall then begin.

Section 2 The Congress shall assemble at least once in every year, and such meeting shall begin at noon on the 3d day of January, unless they shall by law appoint a different day.

Section 3 If, at the time fixed for the beginning of the term of the President, the President elect shall have died, the Vice President elect shall become President. If a President shall not have been chosen before the time fixed for the beginning of his term, or if the President elect shall have failed to qualify, then the Vice President elect shall act as President until a President shall have qualified; and the Congress may by law provide for the case wherein neither a President elect nor a Vice President elect shall have qualified, declaring who shall then act as President, or the manner in which one who is to act shall be selected, and such person shall act accordingly until a President or Vice President shall have qualified.

Section 4 The Congress may by law provide for the case of the death of any of the persons from whom the House of Representatives may choose a President whenever the right of choice shall have devolved upon them, and for the case of the death of any of the persons from whom the Senate may choose a Vice President whenever the right of choice shall have devolved upon them.

Section 5 Sections 1 and 2 shall take effect on the 15th day of October following the ratification of this article.

Section 6 This article shall be inoperative unless it shall have been ratified as an amendment to the Constitution by the legislatures of three-fourths of the several States within seven years from the date of its submission.

Amendment XXI [1933]

Section 1 The eighteenth article of amendment to the Constitution of the United States is hereby repealed.

Section 2 The transportation or importation into any State, Territory, or possession of the United States for delivery or use therein of intoxicating liquors, in violation of the laws thereof, is hereby prohibited.

Section 3 This article shall be inoperative unless it shall have been ratified as an amendment to the Constitution by conventions in the several States, as provided in the Constitution, within seven years from the date of the submission hereof to the States by the Congress.

Amendment XXII [1951]

No person shall be elected to the office of the President more than twice, and no person who has held the office of President, or acted as President, for more than two years of a term to which some other person was elected President shall be elected to the office of the President more than once.

But this Article shall not apply to any person holding the office of President when this Article was proposed by the Congress, and shall not prevent any person who may be holding the office of President or acting as President, during the term within which this Article becomes operative from holding the office of President or acting as President during the remainder of such term.

Amendment XXIII [1961]

Section 1 The District constituting the seat of Government of the United States shall appoint in such manner as the Congress may direct:

A number of electors of President and Vice President equal to the whole number of Senators and Representatives in Congress to which the District would be entitled if it were a State, but in no event more than the least populous State; they shall be in addition to those appointed by the States, but they shall be considered, for the purposes of the election of President and Vice President, to be electors appointed by a State; and they shall meet in the District and perform such duties as provided by the twelfth article of amendment.

Section 2 The Congress shall have power to enforce this article by appropriate legislation.

Amendment XXIV [1964]

Section 1 The right of citizens of the United States to vote in any primary or other election for President or Vice President, for electors for President or Vice President, or for Senator or Representative in Congress, shall not be denied or abridged by the United States or any State by reason of failure to pay any poll tax or other tax.

Section 2 The Congress shall have the power to enforce this article by appropriate legislation.

Amendment XXV [1967]

Section 1 In case of the removal of the President from office or his death or resignation, the Vice President shall become President.

Section 2 Whenever there is a vacancy in the office of the Vice President, the President shall nominate a Vice President who shall take the office upon confirmation by a majority vote of both houses of Congress.

Section 3 Whenever the President transmits to the President pro tempore of the Senate and the Speaker of the House of Representatives his written declaration that he is unable to discharge the powers and duties of his office, and until he transmits to them a written declaration to the contrary, such powers and duties shall be discharged by the Vice President as Acting President.

Section 4 Whenever the Vice President and a majority of either the principal officers of the executive departments, or of such other body as Congress may by law provide, transmit to the President pro tempore of the Senate and the Speaker of the House of Representatives their written declaration that the President is unable to discharge the powers and duties of his office, the Vice President shall immediately assume the powers and duties of the office as Acting President.

Thereafter, when the President transmits to the President pro tempore of the Senate and the Speaker of the House of Representatives his written declaration that no inability exists, he shall resume the powers and duties of his office unless the Vice President and a majority of either the principal officers of the executive departments, or of such other body as Congress may by law provide, transmit within four days to the President protempore of the Senate and the Speaker of the House of Representatives their written declaration that the President is unable to discharge the powers and duties of his office. Thereupon Congress shall decide the issue, assembling within 48 hours for that purpose if not in session. If the Congress, within 21 days after receipt of the latter written declaration, or, if Congress is not in session, within 21 days after Congress is required to assemble, determines by two-thirds vote of both houses that the President is unable to discharge the powers and duties of his office, the Vice President shall continue to discharge the same as Acting President; otherwise, the President shall resume the powers and duties of his office.

Amendment XXVI [1971]

Section 1 The right of citizens of the United States, who are 18 years of age or older, to vote shall not be denied or abridged by the United States or any state on account of age.

Section 2 The Congress shall have the power to enforce this article by appropriate legislation.

Amendment XXVII [1992]

No law varying the compensation for the service of Senators and Representatives shall take effect until an election of Representatives shall have intervened.

The Federalist Papers

The Federalist Papers is a collection of 85 essays written by Alexander Hamilton, John Jay, and James Madison under the pen name Publius. They were published in New York newspapers in 1787 and 1788 to support ratification of the Constitution. Excerpts from Federalist Nos. 10, 51, and 78 are reprinted here.

James Madison: Federalist No. 10

Among the numerous advantages promised by a well constructed Union, none deserves to be more accurately developed than its tendency to break and control the violence of faction. The friend of popular governments never finds himself so much alarmed for their character and fate as when he contemplates their propensity to this dangerous vice. He will not fail, therefore, to set a due value on any plan which, without violating the principles to which he is attached, provides a proper cure for it. The instability, injustice, and confusion, introduced into the public councils, have, in truth been the mortal diseases under which popular governments have everywhere perished; as they continue to be the favorite and fruitful topics from which the adversaries to liberty derive their most specious declamations. The valuable improvements made by the American constitutions on the popular models, both ancient and modern, cannot certainly be too much admired; but it would be an unwarrantable partiality, to contend that they have as effectually obviated the danger on this side, as was wished and expected. Complaints are everywhere heard from our most considerate and virtuous citizens, equally the friends of public and private faith, and of public and personal liberty, that our governments are too unstable; that the public good is disregarded in the conflicts of rival parties; and that measures are too often decided, not according to the rules of justice, and the rights of the minor party, but by the superior force of an interested and overbearing majority. However anxiously we may wish that these complaints had no foundation, the evidence of known facts will not permit us to deny that they are in some degree true. It will be found, indeed, on a candid review of our situation, that some of the distresses under which we labor, have been erroneously charged on the operation of our governments; but it will be found, at the same time, that other causes will not alone account for many of our heaviest misfortunes; and, particularly, for the prevailing and increasing distrust of public engagements, and alarm for private rights, which are echoed from one end of the continent to the other. These must be chiefly, if not wholly, effects of the unsteadiness and injustice, with which a factious spirit has tainted our public administrations.

By a faction, I understand a number of citizens, whether amounting to a majority or minority of the whole, who are united and actuated by some common impulse of passion, or of interest, adverse to the rights of other citizens, or to the permanent and aggregate interests of the community.

There are two methods of curing the mischiefs of faction: The one, by removing its causes; the other, by controlling its effects.

There are again two methods of removing the causes of faction: the one, by destroying the liberty which is essential to its existence; the other, by giving to every citizen the same opinions, the same passions, and the same interests.

It could never be more truly said, than of the first remedy, that it was worse than the disease. Liberty is to faction what air is to fire, an aliment, without which it instantly expires. But it could not be a less folly to abolish liberty, which is essential to political life because it nourishes faction, than it would be to wish the annihilation of air, which is essential to animal life, because it imparts to fire its destructive agency.

The second expedient is as impracticable, as the first would be unwise. As long as the reason of man continues fallible, and he is at liberty to exercise it, different opinions will be formed. As long as the connection subsists between his reason and his self-love, his opinions and his passions will have a reciprocal influence on each other; and the former will be objects to which the latter will attach themselves. The diversity in the faculties of men, from which the rights of property originate, is not less an insuperable obstacle to a uniformity of interests. The protection of those faculties is the first object of government. From the protection of different and unequal faculties of acquiring property, the possession of different degrees and kinds of property immediately results; and from the influence of these on the sentiments and views of the respective proprietors, ensues a division of the society into different interests and parties.

The latent causes of faction are thus sown in the nature of man; and we see them everywhere brought into different degrees of activity, according to the different circumstances of civil society. A zeal for different opinions concerning religion, concerning government, and many other points, as well of speculation as of practice; an attachment to different leaders, ambitiously contending for preeminence and power; or to persons of other descriptions, whose fortunes have been interesting to the human passions, have, in turn, divided mankind into parties, inflamed them with mutual animosity, and rendered them much more disposed to vex and oppress each other, than to cooperate for their common good. So strong is this propensity of mankind, to fall into mutual animosities, that where no substantial occasion presents itself, the most frivolous and fanciful distinctions have been sufficient to kindle their unfriendly passions, and excite their most violent conflicts. But the most common and durable source of factions has been the various and unequal distribution of property. Those who hold, and those who are without property, have ever formed distinct interests in society. Those who are creditors, and those who are debtors, fall under a like discrimination. A landed interest, a manufacturing interest, a mercantile interest, a moneyed interest, with many lesser interests, grow up of necessity in civilized nations, and divide them into different classes, actuated by different sentiments and views. The regulation of these various and interfering interests forms the principle task of modern legislation, and involves the spirit of party and faction in the necessary and ordinary operations of government.

No man is allowed to be a judge in his own cause; because his interest will certainly bias his judgment, and, not improbably, corrupt his integrity. With equal, nay, with greater reason, a body of men are unfit to be both judges and parties at the same time; yet what are many of the most important acts of legislation, but so many judicial determinations, not indeed concerning the rights of single persons, but concerning the rights of large bodies of citizens? And what are the different classes of legislators, but advocates and parties to the cause which they determine? Is a law proposed concerning private debts? It is a question to which the creditors are parties on one side, and the debtors on the other. Justice ought to hold the balance between them. Yet the parties are, and must be, themselves the judges; and the most numerous party, or, in other words, the most powerful faction, must be expected to prevail. Shall domestic manufactures be encouraged, and in what degree, by restrictions on foreign manufactures? are questions which would be differently decided by the landed and the manufacturing classes; and probably by neither with a sole regard to justice and the public good. . . .

It is in vain to say, that enlightened statesmen will be able to adjust these clashing interests, and render them all subservient to the public good. Enlightened statesmen will not always be at the helm; nor, in many cases, can such an adjustment be made at all, without taking into view indirect and remote considerations, which will rarely prevail over the immediate interest which one party may find in disregarding the rights of another, or the good of the whole.

The inference to which we are brought is, that the causes of faction cannot be removed; and that relief is only to be sought in the means of controlling its effects.

If a faction consists of less than a majority, relief is supplied by the republican principle, which enables the majority to defeat its sinister views, by regular vote. It may clog the administration, it may convulse the society; but it will be unable to execute and mask its violence under the forms of the constitution. When a majority is included in a faction, the form of popular government, on the other hand, enables it to sacrifice to its ruling passion or interest, both the public good and the rights of other citizens. To secure the public good, and private rights, against the danger of such a faction, and at the same time to preserve the spirit and the form of popular government, is then the great object to which our inquiries are directed. Let me add, that it is the great desideratum, by which alone this form of government can be rescued from the opprobrium under which it has so long labored, and be recommended to the esteem and adoption of mankind.

By what means is this object attainable? Evidently by one of two only. Either the existence of the same passion or interest in a majority, at the same time must be prevented; or the majority, having such coexistent passion or interest, must be rendered, by their number and local situation, unable to concert and carry into effect schemes of oppression. If the impulse and the opportunity be suffered to coincide, we well know, that neither moral nor religious motives can be relied on as an adequate control. They are not found to be such on the injustice and violence of individuals, and lose their efficacy in proportion to the number combined together; that is in proportion as their efficacy becomes needful.

From this view of the subject, it may be concluded, that a pure democracy, by which I mean a society consisting of a small number of citizens, who assemble and administer the government in person, can admit of no cure from the mischiefs of faction. A common passion or interest will, in almost every case, be felt by a majority of the whole; a communication and concert, results from the form of government itself; and there is nothing to check the inducements to sacrifice the weaker party, or an obnoxious individual. Hence it is, that such democracies have ever been spectacles of turbulence and contention; have ever been found incompatible with personal security, or the rights of property; and have, in general been as short in their lives, as they have been violent in their deaths. Theoretic politicians, who have patronized this species of government, have erroneously supposed that by reducing mankind to a perfect equality in their political rights, they would, at the same time, be perfectly equalized and assimilated in their possessions, their opinions, and their passions.

A republic, by which I mean a government in which the scheme of representation takes place, opens a different prospect, and promises the cure for which we are seeking. Let us examine the points in which it varies from pure democracy, and we shall comprehend both the nature of the cure and the efficacy which it must derive from the union.

The two great points of difference, between a democracy and a republic, are, first, the delegation of the government, in the latter, to a small number of citizens elected by the rest; secondly, the greater number of citizens, and greater sphere of country, over which the latter may be extended.

The effect of the first difference is on the one hand, to refine and enlarge the public views, by passing them through the medium of a chosen body of citizens, whose wisdom may best discern the true interest in their country, and whose patriotism and love of justice, will be least likely to sacrifice it to temporary or partial considerations. Under such a regulation, it may well happen, that the public voice, pronounced by the representatives of the people, will be more consonant to the public good, than if pronounced by the people themselves, convened for the purpose. On the other hand, the effect may be inverted. Men of factious tempers, of local prejudices, or of sinister designs, may by intrigue, by corruption, or by other means, first obtain the suffrages, and then betray the interests, of the people. The question resulting is, whether small or extensive republics are most favorable to the election of proper guardians of the public weal; and it is clearly decided in favor of the latter by two obvious considerations.

In the first place, it is to be remarked, that however small the republic may be, the representatives must be raised to a certain number, in order to guard against the cabals of a few; and that however large it may be, they must be limited to a certain number, in order to guard against the confusion of a multitude. Hence, the number of representatives in the two cases not being in proportion to that of the constituents, and being proportionally greatest in the small republic, it follows that if the proportion of fit characters be not less in the large than in the small republic, the former will present a greater option, and consequently a greater probability of a fit choice.

In the next place, as each representative will be chosen by a greater number of citizens in the large than in the small republic, it will be more difficult for unworthy candidates to practice with success the vicious arts, by which elections are too often carried; and the suffrages of the people being more free, will be more likely to center in men who possess the most attractive merit, and the most diffusive and established characters. . . .

The other point of difference is, the greater number of citizens, and extent of territory, which may be brought within the compass of republican, than of democratic government; and it is this circumstance principally which renders factious combinations less to be dreaded in the former, than in the latter. The smaller the society, the fewer probably will be the distinct parties and interests composing it; the fewer the distinct parties and interests, the more frequently will a majority be found of the same party; and the smaller the number of individuals composing a majority, and the smaller the compass within which they are placed, the more easily they will concert and execute their plans of oppression. Extend the sphere, and you take in a greater variety of parties and interests; you make it less probable that a majority of the whole will have a common motive to invade the rights of other citizens; or if such a common motive exists, it will be more difficult for all who feel it to discover their own strength, and to act in unison with each other. . . .

Hence, it clearly appears, that the same advantage, which a republic has over a democracy, in controlling the effects of faction, is enjoyed by a large over a small republic—is enjoyed by the union over the states composing it. Does this advantage consist in the substitution of representatives, whose enlightened views and virtuous sentiments render them superior to local prejudices, and to schemes of injustice? It will not be denied, that the representation of the union will be most likely to possess these requisite endowments. Does it consist in the greater security afforded by a greater variety of parties, against the event of any one party being able to outnumber and oppress the rest? In an equal degree does the increased variety of parties, comprised within the union, increase this security? Does it, in fine, consist in the greater obstacles opposed to the concert and accomplishment of the secret wishes of an unjust and interested majority? Here, again, the extent of the union gives it the most palpable advantage. The influence of factious leaders may kindle a flame within their particular states, but will be unable to spread a general conflagration through the other states; a religious sect may degenerate into a political faction in a part of the confederacy; but the variety of sects dispersed over the entire face of it, must secure the national councils against any danger from that source; a rage for paper money, for an abolition of debts, for an equal division of property, or for any other improper or wicked project, will be less apt to pervade the whole body of the union, than a particular member of it; in the same proportion as such a malady is more likely to taint a particular country or district, than an entire state.

In the extent and proper structure of the union, therefore, we behold a republican remedy for the diseases most incident to republican government. And according to the degree of pleasure and pride we feel in being republicans, ought to be our zeal in cherishing the spirit, and supporting the character of Federalists.

James Madison: Federalist No. 51

To what expedient then shall we finally resort, for maintaining in practice the necessary partition of power among the several departments, as laid down in the constitution? The only answer that can be given is, that as all these exterior provisions are found to be inadequate, the defect must be supplied, by so contriving the interior structure of the government, as that its several constituent parts may, by their mutual relations, be the means of keeping each other in their proper places. . . .

In order to lay a due foundation for that separate and distinct exercise of the different powers of government, which, to a certain extent, is admitted on all hands to be essential to the preservation of liberty, it is evident that each department should have a will of its own; and consequently should be so constituted, that the members of each should have as little agency as possible in the appointment of the members of the others. . . .

It is equally evident, that the members of each department should be as little dependent as possible on those of the others, for the emoluments annexed to their offices. Were the executive magistrate, or the judges, not independent of the legislature in this particular, their independence in every other would be merely nominal.

But the great security against a gradual concentration of the several powers in the same department, consists in giving to those who administer each department, the necessary constitutional means, and personal motives, to resist encroachments of the others. The provision for defense must in this, as in all other cases, be made commensurate to the danger of attack. Ambition must be made to counteract ambition. The interest of the man must be connected with the constitutional rights of the place. It may be a reflection on human nature, that such devices should be necessary to control the abuses of government. But what is government itself, but the greatest of all reflections on human nature? If men were angels, no government would be necessary. If angels were to govern men, neither external nor internal controls on government would be necessary. In framing a government, which is to be administered by men over men, the great difficulty lies in this: You must first enable the government to control the governed; and in the next place, oblige it to control itself. A dependence on the people is, no doubt, the primary control on the government; but experience has taught mankind the necessity of auxiliary precautions.

This policy of supplying by opposite and rival interests, the defect of better motives, might be traced through the whole system of human affairs, private as well as public. We see it particularly displayed in all the subordinate distributions of power; where the constant aim is, to divide and arrange the several offices in such a manner, as that each may be a check on the other; that the private interest of every individual, may be a sentinel over the public rights. These interventions of prudence cannot be less requisite to the distribution of the supreme powers of the state.

But it is not possible to give to each department an equal power of self-defense. In republican government, the legislative authority necessarily predominates. The remedy for this inconvenience is, to divide the legislature into different branches; and to render them by different modes of election, and different principles of action, as little connected with each other, as the nature of their common functions, and their common dependence on the society will admit. It may even be necessary to guard against dangerous encroachments, by still further precautions. As the weight of the legislative authority requires that it should be thus divided, the weakness of the executive may require, on the other hand, that it should be fortified. An absolute negative on the legislature, appears, at first view, to be the natural defense with which the executive magistrate should be armed. But perhaps it would be neither altogether safe, nor alone sufficient. On ordinary occasions, it might not be exerted with the requisite firmness; and on extraordinary occasions, it might be perfidiously abused. May not this defect of an absolute negative be supplied by some qualified connection between this weaker department, and the weaker branch of the stronger department, by which the latter may be led to support the constitutional rights of the former, without being too much detached from the rights of its own department?

There are, moreover, two considerations particularly applicable to the federal system of America, which place that system in a very interesting point of view.

First. In a single republic, all the power surrendered by the people is submitted to the administration of a single government, and the usurpations are guarded against by a division of the government into distinct and separate departments. In the compound republic of America, the power surrendered by the people is first divided between two distinct governments, and then the portion allotted to each subdivided among distinct and separate departments. Hence a double security arises to the rights of the people. The different governments will control each other, at the same time that each will be controlled by itself.

Second. It is of great importance in a republic not only to guard the society against the oppression of its rulers, but to guard one part of the society against the injustice of the other part. Different interests necessarily exist in different classes of citizens. If a majority be united by a common interest, the rights of the minority will be insecure. There are but two methods of providing against this evil: the one by creating a will in the community independent of the majority—that is, of the society itself; the other, by comprehending in the society so many separate descriptions of citizens as will render an unjust combination of a majority of the whole very probable, if not impracticable. The first method prevails in all governments possessing an hereditary or self-appointed authority. This, at best, is but a precarious security; because a power independent of the society may as well espouse the unjust views of the major, as the rightful interests of the minor party, and may possibly be turned against both parties. The second method will be exemplified in the federal republic of the United States. Whilst all authority in it will be derived from and dependent on the society, the society itself will be broken into so many parts, interests and classes of citizens, that the rights of individuals, or of the minority, will be in little danger from interested combinations of the majority. In a free government the security for civil rights must be the same as that for religious rights. It consists in the one case in the multiplicity of interests, and in the other in the multiplicity of sects. The degree of security in both cases will depend on the number of interests and sects; and this may be presumed to depend on the extent of country and number of people comprehended under the same government. This view of the subject must particularly recommend a proper federal system to all the sincere and considerate friends of republican government, since it shows that in exact proportion as the territory of the Union may be formed into more circumscribed Confederacies, or States, oppressive combinations of a majority will be facilitated; the best security, under the republican forms, for the rights of every class of citizens, will be diminished; and consequently the stability and independence of some member of the government, the only other security, must be proportionately increased. Justice is the end of the government. It is the end of civil society. It ever has been and ever will be pursued until it be obtained, or until liberty be lost in the pursuit. In a society under the forms of which the stronger faction can readily unite and oppress the weaker, anarchy may as truly be said to reign as in a state of nature, where the weaker individual is not secured against the violence of the stronger; and as, in the latter state, even the stronger individuals are prompted, by the uncertainty of their condition, to submit to a government which may protect the weak as well as themselves; so, in the former state, will the more powerful factions or parties be gradually induced, by a like motive, to wish for a government which will protect all parties, the weaker as well as the more powerful. It can be little doubted that if the State of Rhode Island was separated from the Confederacy and left to itself, the insecurity of rights under the popular form of government within such narrow limits would be displayed by such reiterated oppressions of factious majorities that some power altogether independent of the people would soon be called for by the voice of the very factions whose misrule had proved the necessity of it. In the extended republic of the United States, and among the great variety of interests, parties, and sects which it embraces, a coalition of a majority of the whole society could seldom take place on any other principles than those of justice and the general good; whilst there being thus less danger to a minor from the will of a major party, there must be less pretext, also, to provide for the security of the former, by introducing into the government a will not dependent on the latter, or, in other words, a will independent of the society itself. It is no less certain than it is important, notwithstanding the contrary opinions which have been entertained, that the larger the society, provided it lie within a practical sphere, the more duly capable it will be of self-government. And happily for the republican cause, the practicable sphere may be carried to a very great extent, by a judicious modification and mixture of the federal principle.

Alexander Hamilton: Federalist No. 78

We proceed now to an examination of the judiciary department of the proposed government.

In unfolding the defects of the existing confederation, the utility and necessity of a federal judicature have been clearly pointed out. It is the less necessary to recapitulate the considerations there urged; as the propriety of the institution in the abstract is not disputed; the only questions which have been raised being relative to the manner of constituting it, and to its extent. To these points, therefore, our observations shall be confined.

The manner of constituting it seems to embrace these several objects: 1st. The mode of appointing the judges; 2nd. The tenure by which they are to hold their places; 3rd. The partition of the judiciary authority between courts, and their relations to each other.

First. As to the mode of appointing the judges: This is the same with that of appointing the officers of the union in general, and has been so fully discussed . . . that nothing can be said here which would not be useless repetition.

Second. As to the tenure by which the judges are to hold their places: This chiefly concerns their duration in office; the provisions for their support; the precautions for their responsibility.

According to the plan of the convention, all the judges who may be appointed by the United States are to hold their offices during good behavior; which is conformable to the most approved of the state constitutions. . . . The standard of good behavior for the continuance in office of the judicial magistracy is certainly one of the most valuable of the modern improvements in the practice of government. In a monarchy, it is an excellent barrier to the despotism of the prince; in a republic, it is a no less excellent barrier to the encroachments and oppressions of the representative body. And it is the best expedient which can be devised in any government, to secure a steady, upright, and impartial administration of the laws.

Whoever attentively considers the different departments of power must perceive, that, in a government in which they are separated from each other, the judiciary, from the nature of its functions, will always be the least dangerous to the political rights of the constitution; because it will be at least in a capacity to annoy or injure them. The executive not only dispenses the honors, but holds the sword of the community. The legislature not only commands the purse, but prescribes the rules by which the duties and rights of every citizen are to be regulated. The judiciary, on the contrary, has no influence over either the sword or the purse; no direction either of the strength or of the wealth of the society; and can take no active resolution whatever. It may truly be said to have neither force nor will, but merely judgment; and must ultimately depend upon the aid of the executive arm for the efficacious exercise even of this faculty.

This simple view of the matter suggests several important consequences: It proves incontestably, that the judiciary is beyond comparison, the weakest of the three departments of power, that it can never attack with success either of the other two: and that all possible care is requisite to enable it to defend itself against their attacks. It equally proves, that, though individual oppression may now and then proceed from the courts of justice, the general liberty of the people can never be endangered from that quarter; I mean so long as the judiciary remains truly distinct from both the legislature and executive. For I agree, that "there is no liberty, if the power of judging be not separated from the legislative and executive powers." It proves, in the last place, that as liberty can have nothing to fear from the judiciary alone, but would have everything to fear from its union with either of the other departments; that, as all the effects of such a union must ensue from a dependence of the former on the latter, notwithstanding a nominal and apparent separation; that as, from the natural feebleness of the judiciary, it is in continual jeopardy of being overpowered, awed or influenced by its coordinate branches; that, as nothing can contribute so much to its firmness and independence as permanency in office, this quality may therefore be justly regarded as an indispensable ingredient in its constitution; and, in a great measure, as the citadel of the public justice and the public security.

The complete independence of the courts of justice is peculiarly essential in a limited constitution. By a limited constitution, I understand one which contains certain specified exceptions to the legislative authority; such, for instance, as that it shall pass no bills of attainder, no ex post facto laws, and the like. Limitations of this kind can be preserved in practice no other way than through the medium of the courts of justice, whose duty it must be to declare all acts contrary to the manifest tenor of the constitution void. Without this, all the reservations of particular rights or privileges would amount to nothing.

Some perplexity respecting the right of the courts to pronounce legislative acts void, because contrary to the constitution, has arisen from an imagination that the doctrine would imply a superiority of the judiciary to the legislative power. It is urged that the authority which can declare the acts of another void, must necessarily be superior to the one whose acts may be declared void. As this doctrine is of great importance in all the American constitutions, a brief discussion of the grounds on which it rests cannot be unacceptable.

There is no position which depends on clearer principles than that every act of a delegated authority, contrary to the tenor of the commission under which it is exercised, is void. No legislative act, therefore, contrary to the constitution, can be valid. To deny this would be to affirm, that the deputy is greater then his principal; that the servant is above his master; that the representatives of the people are superior to the people themselves; that men, acting by virtue of powers, may do not only what their powers do not authorize, but what they forbid.

If it be said that the legislative body are themselves the constitutional judges of their own powers, and that the construction they put upon them is conclusive upon the other departments, it may be answered, that this cannot be the natural presumption, where it is not to be collected from any particular provisions in the constitution. It is not otherwise to be supposed that the constitution could intend to enable the representatives of the people to substitute their will to that of their constituents. It is far more rational to suppose that the courts were designed to be an intermediate body between the people and the legislature, in order, among other things, to keep the latter within the limits assigned to their authority. The interpretation of the laws is the proper and peculiar province of the courts. A constitution is, in fact, and must be, regarded by the judges as a fundamental law. It must therefore belong to them to ascertain its meaning, as well as the meaning of any particular act proceeding from the legislative body. If there should happen to be an irreconcilable variance between the two, that which has the superior obligation and validity ought, of course, to be preferred; in other words, the constitution ought to be preferred to the statute, the intention of the people to the intention of their agents.

Nor does this conclusion by any means suppose a superiority of the judicial to the legislative power. It only supposes that the power of the people is superior to both; and that where the will of the legislature declared in its statutes, stands in opposition to that of the people declared in the constitution, the judges ought to be governed by the latter, rather than the former. They ought to regulate their decisions by the fundamental laws, rather than by those which are not fundamental. . . .

It can be of no weight to say, that the courts, on the pretense of a repugnancy, may substitute their own pleasure to the constitutional intentions of the legislature. This might as well happen in the case of two contradictory statutes; or it might as well happen in every adjudication upon any single statute. The courts must declare the sense of the law; and if they should be disposed to exercise will instead of judgment, the consequence would equally be the substitution of their pleasure to that of the legislative body. The observation, if it proved anything, would prove that there ought to be no judges distinct from the body.

If then the courts of justice are to be considered as the bulwarks of a limited constitution, against legislative encroachments, this consideration will afford a strong argument for the permanent tenure of judicial officers, since nothing will contribute so much as this to that independent spirit in the judges, which must be essential to the faithful performance of so arduous a duty.

This independence of the judges is equally requisite to guard the constitution and the rights of individuals, from the effects of those ill-humors which are the arts of designing men, or the influence of particular conjunctures, sometimes disseminate among the people themselves, and which, though they speedily give place to better information, and more deliberate reflection, have a tendency, in the meantime, to occasion dangerous innovations in the government, and serious oppressions of the minor party in the community. . . . Until the people have, by some solemn and authoritative act, annulled or changed the established form, it is binding upon themselves collectively, as well as individually; and no presumption, or even knowledge of their sentiments, can warrant their representatives in a departure from it, prior to such an act. But it is easy to see, that it would require an uncommon portion of fortitude in the judges to do their duty as faithful guardians of the constitution, where legislative invasions of it had been instigated by the major voice of the community.

But it is not with a view to infractions of the constitution only, that the independence of the judges may be an essential safeguard against the effects of occasional ill-humors in the society. These sometimes extend no farther than to the injury of the private rights of particular classes of citizens, by unjust and partial laws. Here also the firmness of the judicial magistracy is of vast importance in mitigating the severity, and confining the operation of such laws. It not only serves to moderate the immediate mischiefs of those which may have been passed, but it operates as a check upon the legislative body in passing them; who, perceiving that obstacles to the success of an iniquitous intention are to be expected from the scruples of the courts, are in a manner compelled by the very motives of the injustice they meditate, to qualify their attempts. . . .

That inflexible and uniform adherence to the rights of the constitution, and of individuals, which we perceive to be indispensable in the courts of justice, can certainly not be expected from judges who hold their offices by a temporary commission. Periodical appointments, however regulated, or by whomsoever made, would, in some way or other, be fatal to their necessary independence. If the power of making them was committed either to the executive or legislature, there would be danger of an improper compliance to the branch which possessed it; if to both, there would be an unwillingness to hazard the displeasure of either; if to the people, or to persons chosen by them for the special purpose, there would be too great a disposition to consult popularity to justify a reliance that nothing would be consulted but the constitution and the laws.

There is yet a further and a weighty reason for the permanency of judicial offices, which is deducible from the nature of the qualifications they require. It has been frequently remarked, with great propriety, that a voluminous code of laws is one of the inconveniences necessarily connected with the advantages of a free government. To avoid an arbitrary discretion in the courts, it is indispensable that they should be bound down by strict rules and precedents, which serve to define and point out their duty in every particular case that comes before them; and it will readily be conceived, from the variety of controversies which grow out of the folly and wickedness of mankind, that the records of those precedents must unavoidably swell to a very considerable bulk, and must demand long and laborious study to acquire a competent knowledge of them. Hence it is, that there can be but few men in the society, who will have sufficient skill in the laws to qualify them for the stations of judges. And making the proper deductions for the ordinary depravity of human nature, the number must be still smaller, of those who unite the requisite integrity with the requisite knowledge. . .

Presidents and Congresses, 1789–2009

Year	President and Vice President	Party of President	Congress	Majority Party	
				House	Senate
1789–1797	**George Washington** John Adams	None	1st 2nd 3rd 4th	Admin. Supporters Federalist Democratic-Republican Federalist	Admin. Supporters Federalist Federalist Federalist
1797–1801	**John Adams** Thomas Jefferson	Federalist	5th 6th	Federalist Federalist	Federalist Federalist
1801–1809	**Thomas Jefferson** Aaron Burr (to 1805) George Clinton (to 1809)		7th 8th 9th 10th	Democratic-Republican Democratic-Republican Democratic-Republican Democratic-Republican	Democratic-Republican Democratic-Republican Democratic-Republican Democratic-Republican
1809–1817	**James Madison** George Clinton (to 1813) Elbridge Gerry (to 1817)	Democratic-Republican	11th 12th 13th 14th	Democratic-Republican Democratic-Republican Democratic-Republican Democratic-Republican	Democratic-Republican Democratic-Republican Democratic-Republican Democratic-Republican
1817–1825	**James Monroe** Daniel D. Tompkins	Democratic-	15th 16th 17th 18th	Democratic-Republican Democratic-Republican Democratic-Republican Democratic-Republican	Democratic-Republican Democratic-Republican Democratic-Republican Democratic-Republican
1825–1829	**John Quincy Adams** John C. Calhoun	National-Republican	19th 20th	Admin. Supporters Jacksonian Democrats	Admin. Supporters Jacksonian Democrats
1829–1837	**Andrew Jackson** John C. Calhoun (to 1833) Martin Van Buren (to 1837)	Democratic	21st 22nd 23rd 24th	Democratic Democratic Democratic Democratic	Democratic Democratic Democratic Democratic
1837–1841	**Martin Van Buren** Richard M. Johnson	Democratic	25th 26th	Democratic Democratic	Democratic Democratic
1841	**William H. Harrison** (died a month after inauguration) John Tyler	Whig			
1841–1845	**John Tyler** (VP vacant)	Whig	27th 28th	Whig Democratic	Whig Whig
1845–1849	**James K. Polk** George M. Dallas	Democratic	29th 30th	Democratic Whig	Democratic Democratic
1849–1850	**Zachary Taylor** (died in office) Millard Fillmore	Whig	31st	Democratic	Democratic
1850–1853	**Millard Fillmore** (VP vacant)	Whig	32nd	Democratic	Democratic

Year	President and Vice President	Party of President	Congress	Majority Party House	Senate
1853–1857	**Franklin Pierce** William R. King	Democratic	33rd 34th	Democratic Republican	Democratic Democratic
1857–1861	**James Buchanan** John C. Breckinridge	Democratic	35th 36th	Democratic Republican	Democratic Democratic
1861–1865	**Abraham Lincoln** (died in office) Hannibal Hamlin (to 1865) Andrew Johnson (1865)	Republican	37th 38th	Republican Republican	Republican Republican
1865–1869	**Andrew Johnson** (VP vacant)	Republican	39th 40th	Unionist Republican	Unionist Republican
1869–1877	**Ulysses S. Grant** Schuyler Colfax (to 1873) Henry Wilson (to 1877)	Republican	41st 42nd 43rd 44th	Republican Republican Republican Democratic	Republican Republican Republican Republican
1877–1881	**Rutherford B. Hayes** William A. Wheeler	Republican	45th 46th	Democratic Democratic	Republican Democratic
1881	**James A. Garfield** (died in office) Chester A. Arthur	Republican	47th	Republican	Republican
1881–1885	**Chester A. Arthur** (VP vacant)	Republican	48th	Democratic	Republican
1885–1889	**Grover Cleveland** Thomas A. Hendricks	Democratic	49th 50th	Democratic Democratic	Republican Republican
1889–1893	**Benjamin Harrison** Levi P. Morton	Republican	51st 52nd	Republican Democratic	Republican Republican
1893–1897	**Grover Cleveland** Adlai E. Stevenson	Democratic	53rd 54th	Democratic Republican	Democratic Republican
1897–1901	**William McKinley** (died in office) Garret A. Hobart (to 1901) Theodore Roosevelt (1901)	Republican	55th 56th	Republican Republican	Republican Republican
1901–1909	**Theodore Roosevelt** (VP vacant, 1901–1905) Charles W. Fairbanks (1905–1909)	Republican	57th 58th 59th 60th	Republican Republican Republican Republican	Republican Republican Republican Republican
1909–1913	**William Howard Taft** James S. Sherman	Republican	61st 62nd	Republican Democratic	Republican Republican

Year	President and Vice President	Party of President	Congress	House	Senate
1913–1921	**Woodrow Wilson** Thomas R. Marshall	Democratic	63rd 64th 65th 66th	Democratic Democratic Democratic Republican	Democratic Democratic Democratic Republican
1921–1923	**Warren G. Harding** (died in office) Calvin Coolidge	Republican	67th	Republican	Republican
1923–1929	**Calvin Coolidge** (VP vacant, 1923–1925) Charles G. Dawes (1925–1929)	Republican	68th 69th 70th	Republican Republican Republican	Republican Republican Republican
1929–1933	**Herbert Hoover** Charles Curtis	Republican	71st 72nd	Republican Democratic	Republican Republican
1933–1945	**Franklin D. Roosevelt** (died in office) John N. Garner (1933–1941) Henry A. Wallace (1941–1945) Harry S Truman (1945)	Democratic	73rd 74th 75th 76th 77th 78th	Democratic Democratic Democratic Democratic Democratic Democratic	Democratic Democratic Democratic Democratic Democratic Democratic
1945–1953	**Harry S Truman** (VP vacant, 1945–1949) Alben W. Barkley (1949–1953)	Democratic	79th 80th 81st 82nd	Democratic Republican Democratic Democratic	Democratic Republican Democratic Democratic
1953–1961	**Dwight D. Eisenhower** Richard M. Nixon	Republican	83rd 84th 85th 86th	Republican Democratic Democratic Democratic	Republican Democratic Democratic Democratic
1961–1963	**John F. Kennedy** (died in office) Lyndon B. Johnson	Democratic	87th	Democratic	Democratic
1963–1969	**Lyndon B. Johnson** (VP vacant, 1963–1965) Hubert H. Humphrey (1965–1969)	Democratic	88th 89th 90th	Democratic Democratic Democratic	Democratic Democratic Democratic
1969–1974	**Richard M. Nixon** (resigned office) Spiro T. Agnew (resigned office) Gerald R. Ford (appointed vice president)	Republican	91st 92nd	Democratic Democratic	Democratic Democratic
1974–1977	**Gerald R. Ford** Nelson A. Rockefeller (appointed vice president)	Republican	93rd 94th	Democratic Democratic	Democratic Democratic
1977–1981	**Jimmy Carter** Walter Mondale	Democratic	95th 96th	Democratic Democratic	Democratic Democratic

Year	President and Vice President	Party of President	Congress	Majority Party House	Majority Party Senate
1981–1989	**Ronald Reagan** George H. W. Bush	Republican	97th 98th 99th 100th	Democratic Democratic Democratic Democratic	Republican Republican Republican Democratic
1989–1993	**George H. W. Bush** J. Danforth Quayle	Republican	101st 102nd	Democratic Democratic	Democratic Democratic
1993–2001	**Bill Clinton** Albert Gore Jr.	Democratic	103rd 104th 105th 106th	Democratic Republican Republican Republican	Democratic Republican Republican Republican
2001–2009	**George W. Bush** Richard Cheney	Republican	107th 108th 109th	Republican Republican Republican	Democratic Republican Republican

Notes

1. During the entire administration of George Washington and part of the administration of John Quincy Adams, Congress was not organized in terms of parties. This table shows that during these periods the supporters of the respective administrations maintained control of Congress.

2. This table shows only the two dominant parties in Congress. Independents, members of minor parties, and vacancies have been omitted.

Chief Justices of the Supreme Court, 1789–2005

Chief Justice	Appointing President	Dates of Service
John Jay	Washington	1789–1795
John Rutledge	Washington	1795–1795
Oliver Ellsworth	Washington	1796–1800
John Marshall	J. Adams	1801–1835
Roger Brooke Taney	Jackson	1836–1864
Salmon Portland Chase	Lincoln	1864–1873
Morrison Remick Waite	Grant	1874–1888
Melville Weston Fuller	Cleveland	1888–1910
Edward Douglass White	Taft	1910–1921
William Howard Taft	Harding	1921–1930
Charles Evans Hughes	Hoover	1930–1941
Harlan Fiske Stone	F. Roosevelt	1941–1946
Frederick Moore Vinson	Truman	1946–1953
Earl Warren	Eisenhower	1953–1969
Warren Earl Burger	Nixon	1969–1986
William Hubbs Rehnquist	Reagan	1986–

Glossary

affirmative action Programs of private and public institutions favoring minorities and women in hiring and in admissions to colleges and universities in an attempt to compensate for past discrimination.

agenda setting Influencing what people consider important.

amicus curiae Latin for "a friend of the court"; describes a brief in which individuals not party to a suit may have their views heard.

Anti-Federalists Opponents of the Constitution during the fight over ratification.

appellate courts Courts that hear cases on appeal from other courts.

appropriation Legal authority for a federal agency to spend money from the U.S. Treasury.

axis of evil Three countries—Iraq, Iran, and North Korea—named by President Bush in 2002 as significant threats to the security of the United States because of their purported ties to terrorism and weapons of mass destruction.

balance of payments The annual difference between payments and receipts between a country and its trading partners.

beat The assigned location where a reporter regularly gathers news stories.

bias Deviation from some ideal standard, such as representativeness or objectivity.

bicameral As applied to a legislative body, consisting of two houses or chambers.

bill of attainder A governmental decree that a person is guilty of a crime that carries the death penalty, rendered without benefit of a trial.

Bill of Rights The first ten amendments to the U.S. Constitution, concerned with basic liberties.

block grants Federal grants to the states to be used for general activities.

blue-collar worker A skilled, semiskilled, or unskilled worker in industry.

briefs Documents setting out the arguments in legal cases, prepared by attorneys and presented to courts.

budget deficit The amount by which annual government expenditures exceed revenues.

bundling A practice in which an interest group asks its supporters to write checks for a preferred list of candidates; the group then sends the checks in a bundle to each of the candidates.

bureaucracy A large, complex organization characterized by a hierarchical set of offices, each with a specific task, controlled through a clear chain of command, and where appointment and advancement of personnel is based on merit.

bureaucrat A person who works in a bureaucratic organization.

capital crime Any crime for which death is a possible penalty.

capture A situation in which a regulated industry exercises substantial influence on the government agency regulating it.

casework Services performed by members of Congress for constituents.

categorical grants Federal aid to states and localities clearly specifying what the money can be used for.

caucus nominating system A system for selecting delegates to the national party conventions characterized by neighborhood and areawide meetings of party supporters and activists; used in only a handful of states.

Central Intelligence Agency (CIA) The organization that coordinates all U.S. intelligence agencies; it also gathers and evaluates intelligence itself and carries out covert operations.

checks and balances The constitutional principle that government power shall be divided and that the fragments should balance or check one another to prevent tyranny.

chief of staff A top adviser to the president who also manages the White House staff.

circuits The 12 geographical jurisdictions and one special court that hear appeals from the federal district courts.

civil disobedience Intentionally breaking a law and accepting the consequences as a way to publicize the unjustness of the law.

civil liberties Freedoms found primarily in the Bill of Rights that are protected from government interference.

civil rights Government guarantees of political equality and equal treatment.

civil servants Government workers employed under the merit system; not political appointees.

civil service Federal government jobs held by civilian employees, excluding political appointees.

civil union A status in which same-sex couples have the same legal rights, benefits, and protections as married couples.

Civil War Amendments The Thirteenth, Fourteenth, and Fifteenth Amendments to the Constitution adopted immediately after the Civil War.

class action suit A suit brought on behalf of a group of people who are in a situation similar to that of the plaintiffs.

cloture A vote to end a filibuster or a debate; requires the votes of three-fifths of the membership of the Senate.

Cold War The period of tense relations between the United States and the Soviet Union from the late 1940s to the late 1980s.

collective public opinion The political attitudes of the public as a whole, expressed as averages, percentages, or other summaries of many individuals' opinions.

concurring opinion The opinion of one or more judges who vote with the majority on a case but wish to set out different reasons for their decision.

conditions Provisions in federal assistance requiring that state and local governments follow certain policies in order to obtain federal funds.

confederation A loose association of states or territorial divisions in which very little power is lodged in the central government.

conference committees Ad hoc committees, made up of members of both the Senate and the House of Representatives, set up to reconcile differences in the provisions of bills.

Connecticut Compromise Also called the Great Compromise; the compromise between the New Jersey and Virginia plans formulated by the Connecticut delegates at the Constitutional Convention; called for a lower legislative house based on population size and an upper house based on equal representation of the states.

conservative The political position that holds that the federal government ought to play a very small role in economic regulation, social welfare, and overcoming racial inequality.

constituency The district of a legislator.

constituent A citizen who lives in the district of an elected official.

constitution The basic framework of law that prescribes how government is to operate.

constitutional courts Federal courts created by Congress under the authority of Article III of the Constitution.

containment The policy of resisting expansion of the Soviet Union's influence by diplomatic, economic, and military means.

contract clause The portion of Article, Section 10, of the Constitution that prohibits states from passing any law "impairing the obligations of contracts."

convention A gathering of delegates who nominate a party's presidential candidate.

conventional participation Political activity related to elections (voting, persuading, and campaigning) or to contacting public officials.

cooperative federalism Federalism in which the powers of the states and the national government are so intertwined that public policies can happen only if the two levels of government cooperate.

core beliefs Individual's views about the fundamental nature of human beings, society, and economy; taken together, they comprise the political culture.

cost-benefit analysis A method of evaluating rules and regulations by weighing their potential costs against their potential benefits to society.

Council of Economic Advisers (CEA) An organization in the Executive Office of the President made up of a small group of economists who advise on economic policy.

covert operations Secret or semisecret activities abroad, often involving intelligence gathering, influence on other countries' politics, or the use of force.

dealignment A gradual reduction in the dominance of one political party without another party supplanting it.

delegate According to the doctrine articulated by Edmund Burke, an elected representative who acts in perfect accord with the wishes of his or her constituents.

democracy A system of rule by the people, defined by the existence of popular sovereignty, political equality, and political liberty.

depression A severe and persistent drop in economic activity.

deregulation The process of diminishing regulatory requirements for business.

descriptive representation Sometimes called statistical representation; means that the composition of a representative body reflects the demographic composition of the population as a whole.

devolution The delegation of power by the central government to state or local bodies.

direct democracy A form of political decision making in which the public business is decided by all citizens meeting in small assemblies.

discharge petition A petition signed by 218 House members to force a bill that has been before a committee for at least 30 days while the House is in session out of the committee and onto the floor for consideration.

discount rate The interest rate the Federal Reserve charges member banks to cover short-term loans.

dissenting opinion The opinion of the judge or judges who are in the minority on a particular case before the Supreme Court.

disturbance theory A theory that locates the origins of interest groups in changes in the economic, social, or political environment that threaten the well-being of some segment of the population.

divided government Control of the executive and the legislative branches by different political parties.

dual federalism An interpretation of federalism in which the states and the national government have separate jurisdictions and responsibilities.

due process clause The section of the Fourteenth Amendment that prohibits states from depriving anyone of life, liberty, or property "without due process of law," a guarantee against arbitrary or unfair government action.

economic conservatives People who favor private enterprise and oppose government regulations on spending.

economic liberals People who favor government regulation of business and government spending for social programs.

economic liberty The right to own and use property free from excessive government interference.

elastic clause Article I, Section 8, of the Constitution, also called the necessary and proper clause; gives Congress the authority to make whatever laws are necessary and proper to carry out its enumerated responsibilities.

Electoral College Elected representatives of the states whose votes formally elect the president; the number of electors in each state is equal to the total number of its senators and representatives in the House.

electoral competition model A form of election in which parties seeking votes move toward the median voter or the center of the political spectrum.

electoral reward and punishment The tendency to vote for the incumbents when times are good and against them when times are bad.

electors Representatives who are elected in the states to formally choose the U.S. president.

entitlements Government benefits that are distributed automatically to citizens who qualify on the basis of a set of guidelines set by law; for example, Americans over the age of 65 are entitled to Medicare coverage.

enumerated powers Powers of the federal government specifically mentioned in the Constitution.

equal protection clause The section of the Fourteenth Amendment that provides equal protection of the laws to all citizens.

Equal Rights Amendment (ERA) Proposed amendment to the U.S. Constitution stating that equality of rights shall not be abridged or denied on account of a person's gender.

equal time provision The former requirement that television stations give or sell the same amount of time to all competing candidates.

establishment clause The part of the First Amendment to the Constitution that prohibits Congress from establishing an official religion; the basis for the doctrine of the separation of church and state.

European Union (EU) A common market formed by western European nations, with free trade and free population movement among them.

ex post facto law A law that retroactively declares some action illegal.

exclusionary rule A standard promulgated by the Supreme Court that prevents police and prosecutors from using evidence against a defendant that was obtained in an illegal search.

executive agreement An agreement with another country signed by the president that has the force of law, like a treaty; does not require Senate approval; originally used for minor technical matters, now an important tool of presidential power in foreign affairs.

Executive Office of the President (EOP) A group of organizations that advise the president on a wide range of issues; includes the Office of Management and Budget, the National Security Council, and the Council of Economic Advisers.

executive order A rule or regulation issued by the president that has the force of law, based either on the constitutional powers of the presidency or on congressional statutes.

executive privilege A presidential claim that certain communications with subordinates may be withheld from Congress and the courts.

externalities The positive and negative effects of economic activities on third parties.

faction James Madison's term for groups or parties that try to advance their own interests at the expense of the public good.

fairness doctrine The former requirement that television stations present contrasting points of view.

federal Describing a system in which significant governmental powers are divided between a central government and smaller territorial units, such as states.

federal bureaucracy The totality of the departments and agencies of the executive branch of the national government.

federalism A system in which significant governmental powers are divided between a central government and smaller units, such as states.

Federalists Proponents of the Constitution during the ratification fight; also the political party of Hamilton, Washington, and Adams.

filibuster A parliamentary device used in the Senate to prevent a bill from coming to a vote by "talking it to death," made possible by the norm of unlimited debate.

fiscal policy Government's actions affecting spending and taxing levels; affects overall output and income in the economy.

framing Providing a context for interpretation.

franchise The right to vote.

franking privilege Public subsidization of mail from the members of Congress to their constituents.

free exercise clause That portion of the First Amendment to the Constitution that prohibits Congress from impeding religious observance or impinging upon religious beliefs.

free rider One who gains a benefit without contributing; explains why it is so difficult to form social movements and noneconomic interest groups.

General Agreement on Tariffs and Trade (GATT) An international agreement that requires the lowering of tariffs and other barriers to free trade.

general revenue sharing Federal aid to the states without any conditions on how the money is to be spent.

gerrymandering Redrawing electoral district lines to give an advantage to a particular party or candidate.

grand juries Groups of citizens who decide whether there is sufficient evidence to bring an indictment against accused persons.

grandfather clause A device that allowed whites who had failed the literacy test to vote anyway by extending the franchise to anyone whose ancestors had voted prior to 1867.

grants-in-aid Funds from the national government to state and local governments to help pay for programs created by the national government.

grassroots The constituents, voters, or rank-and-file of a party.

Great Depression The period of economic crisis in the United States that lasted from the stock market crash of 1929 to America's entry into World War II.

gross domestic product (GDP) Monetary value of all goods and services produced in a nation each year, excluding income residents earn abroad.

habeas corpus The legal doctrine that a person who is arrested must have a timely hearing before a judge.

hearings The taking of testimony by a congressional committee or subcommittee.

hopper The box in the House of Representatives in which proposed bills are placed.

horizontal federalism Term used to refer to relationships among the states.

in forma pauperis Describing a process by which indigents may file a suit with the Supreme Court free of charge.

incorporation The gradual use of the Fourteenth Amendment by the Supreme Court to make the Bill of Rights and other constitutional protections binding on the states.

independent expenditures Money spent on behalf of candidates by interest groups and individuals who are not connected to a candidate's campaign organization.

Industrial Revolution The period of transition from predominantly agricultural to predominantly industrial societies in the Western nations in the nineteenth century.

inflation A condition of rising prices.

infotainment The merging of hard news and entertainment in news presentations.

initiatives Procedures available in some states for citizens to put proposed laws and constitutional amendment on the ballot for voter approval or rejection.

institutional presidency The permanent bureaucracy associated with the presidency, designed to help the incumbent of the office carry out his responsibilities.

integration Policies encouraging the interaction between different races in schools or public facilities.

intercontinental ballistic missiles (ICBMs) Guided missiles capable of carrying nuclear warheads

interest group Any private organization or association that seeks to influence public policy as a way to protect or advance some interest.

interest group liberalism A political regime in which interest groups help formulate and carry out government policies.

intermediate scrutiny A legal test falling between ordinary and strict scrutiny relevant to issues of gender; under this test, the Supreme Court will allow gender classifications in laws if they are *substantially* related to an *important* government objective.

interstate compacts Agreements among states to cooperate on solving mutual problems; requires approval by Congress.

iron triangle An enduring alliance of common interest among an interest group, a congressional committee, and a bureaucratic agency.

isolationism The policy of avoiding involvement in foreign affairs.

Jim Crow Popular term for the system of legally sanctioned racial segregation that existed in the American South until the middle of the twentieth century.

Joint Chiefs of Staff (JCS) The military officers in charge of each of the armed services.

joint committees Congressional committees with members from both the House and the Senate.

judicial activism Actions by the courts that go beyond the strict role of the judiciary as interpreter of the law and adjudicator of disputes.

judicial review The power of the Supreme Court to declare actions of the other branches and levels of government unconstitutional.

Keynesians Advocates of government programs to stimulate economic activity through tax cuts and government spending.

laissez-faire The political-economic doctrine that holds that government ought not interfere with the operations of the free market.

legislative courts Highly specialized federal courts created by Congress under the authority of Article I of the Constitution.

liberal The political position that holds that the federal government has a substantial role to play in economic regulation, social welfare, and overcoming racial inequality.

literacy test A device used by the southern states to prevent African Americans from voting before the passage of the Voting Rights Act of 1965, which banned its use; usually involved interpretation of a section of a state's constitution.

lobby An interest or pressure group that seeks to convey the group's interest to government decision makers.

macroeconomic policy Having to do with the performance of the economy as a whole.

majority rule The form of political decision making in which policies are decided on the basis of what a majority of the people want.

majority tyranny Suppression of the rights and liberties of a minority by the majority.

majority-minority districts Districts drawn to ensure that a racial minority makes up the majority of voters.

mandate A formal order from the national government that the states carry out certain policies.

markup The process of revising a bill in committee.

mass mobilization The process of involving large numbers of people in a social movement.

means-tested Meeting the criterion of demonstrable need.

median household income Household income number at which one-half of all households have more income and one-half have less income; the midpoint of all households ranked by income.

median voter Refers to the voter at the exact middle of the political spectrum.

monetarists   Advocates of a minimal government role in the economy, limited to managing the growth of the money supply.

monetary policy   Government's actions affecting the supply of money and the level of interest rates in the economy.

multilateralist   The stance toward foreign policy that suggests that the United States should seek the cooperation of other nations and multilateral institutions in pursuing its goals.

national debt   The total outstanding debt of the federal government; the sum total of all annual budget deficits and surpluses.

national interest   What is of benefit to the nation as a whole.

National Reconnaissance Office (NRO)   The government agency in charge of surveillance by satellite photography and other technological means.

national security adviser   A top foreign policy and defense adviser to the president who heads the National Security Council.

National Security Agency (NSA)   The federal government agency that intercepts and decodes electronic messages and secures U.S. communications around the world.

National Security Council (NSC)   An organization in the Executive Office of the President made up of officials from the State and Defense Departments, the CIA, and the military, who advise on foreign and security affairs.

nationalist position   The view of American federalism that holds that the Constitution created a system in which the national government is supreme, relative to the states, and that granted to it a broad range of powers and responsibilities.

nationalizing   The process by which provisions of the Bill of Rights become incorporated. See *incorporation.*

nativist   Anti-foreign; applied to political movements active in the nineteenth century.

necessary and proper clause   Article I, Section 8, of the Constitution, also known as the *elastic clause;* gives Congress the authority to make whatever laws are necessary and proper to carry out its enumerated responsibilities.

New Deal   The programs of the administration of President Franklin D. Roosevelt.

New Deal coalition   The informal electoral alliance of working-class ethnic groups, Catholics, Jews, urban dwellers, racial minorities, and the South that was the basis of the Democratic party dominance of American politics from the New Deal to the early 1970s.

New Jersey Plan   Proposal of the smaller states at the Constitutional Convention to create a government based on the equal representation of the states in a unicameral legislature.

newsworthy   Worth printing or broadcasting as news, according to editors' judgments.

normal vote   The proportion of the votes that each party would win if party identification alone affected voting decisions.

North American Free Trade Agreement (NAFTA)   An agreement among the United States, Canada, and Mexico to eliminate nearly all barriers to trade and investment among the three countries.

nuclear proliferation   The spread of nuclear weapons to additional countries or to terrorist groups.

nullification   An attempt by states to declare national laws or actions null and void.

objective journalism   News reported with no evaluative language and with any opinions quoted or attributed to a specific source.

obscenity   As defined by the Supreme Court, the representation of sexually explicit material in a manner that violates community standards and is without redeeming social importance or value.

Office of Management and Budget (OMB)   An organization within the Executive Office of the President that advises on the federal budget, domestic legislation, and regulations.

open-seat election   An election in which there is no incumbent officeholder.

opinion   The explanation of the majority's reasoning that accompanies a court decision.

opinion of the Court   The majority opinion that accompanies a Supreme Court decision.

ordinary scrutiny   The assumption that the actions of elected bodies and officials are legal under the Constitution.

original intention   The doctrine that the courts must interpret the Constitution in ways consistent with the intentions of the framers rather than in light of contemporary conditions and needs.

original jurisdiction   The authority of a court to be the first to hear a particular kind of case.

participation   Political activity, including voting, campaign activity, contacting officials, and demonstrating.

partisan   A committed member of a party; seeing issues from the point of view of the interests of a single party.

party caucus   An organization of the members of a political party in the House or Senate.

party identification   The sense of belonging to one or another political party.

party platform   A party's statement of its positions on the issues of the day.

patronage   The practice of distributing government offices and contracts to the supporters of the winning party; also called the spoils system.

Pentagon   The building in Arlington, Virginia, that contains the offices of the military chiefs and top officials of the Defense Department.

petit (trial) juries   Juries that hear evidence and sit in judgment on charges brought in civil or criminal cases.

plaintiff   One who brings suit in a court.

pluralist   A political scientist who views American politics as best understood in terms of the interaction, conflict, and bargaining of groups.

plurality More votes than any other candidate but less than a majority of all votes cast.

pocket veto Rejection of a bill if the president takes no action on it for 10 days and Congress has adjourned during that period.

policy preferences Citizens' preferences concerning what policies they want government to pursue.

political action committee (PAC) An entity created by an interest whose purpose is to collect money and make contributions to candidates in federal elections.

political attitudes Individual's views about public policies, political parties, candidates, government institutions, and public officials.

political efficacy The sense that an individual can affect what government does.

political equality The principle that says that each person carries equal weight in the conduct of the public business.

political ideology A system of interrelated and coherently patterned beliefs and attitudes.

political liberty The principle that citizens in a democracy are protected from government interference in the exercise of a range of basic freedoms, such as the freedoms of speech, association, and conscience.

political socialization The process by which individuals come to have certain core beliefs and political attitudes.

poll tax A tax to be paid as a condition of voting; used in the South to keep African Americans away from the polls.

popular sovereignty The basic principle of democracy that the people ultimately rule.

pork Also called *pork barrel;* projects designed to bring to the constituency jobs and public money for which the members of Congress can claim credit.

poverty line The federal government's calculation of the amount of income families of various sizes need to stay out of poverty.

precedents Rulings by courts that guide judicial reasoning in subsequent cases.

preemption Exclusion of the states from actions that might interfere with federal authority or statutes.

presidential approval rating A president's standing with the public, indicated by the percentage of Americans who tell survey interviewers that they approve a president's "handling of his job."

presidential popularity The percentage of Americans who approve a president's handling of his job.

pressure group An interest group or lobby; a group that brings pressure to bear on government decision makers.

primary election Statewide elections in which voters choose delegates to the national party conventions; virtually all delegates are pledged to a specific candidate for the party's nomination.

prior restraint The government's power to prevent publication, as opposed to punishment afterward.

private interest group An interest group that seeks to protect or advance the material interests of its members.

privatization The process of turning over certain government functions to the private sector.

privileges and immunities clause The portion of Article IV, Section 2, of the Constitution that states that citizens from out of state have the same legal rights as local citizens in any state.

proportional representation The awarding of legislative seats to political parties to reflect the proportion of the popular vote each party receives.

prospective voting model A theory of democratic elections in which voters decide what government will do in the near future by choosing one or another responsible party.

public interest group An interest group that advocates for a cause or an ideology.

public opinion Political attitudes expressed by ordinary citizens.

pundits Somewhat derisive term for print, broadcast, and radio commentators on the political news.

random sampling The selection of survey respondents by chance, with equal probability, to ensure their representativeness of the whole population.

realignment The process by which one party supplants another as the dominant party in a political system.

reapportionment The reallocation of House seats among the states, done after each national census, to ensure that seats are held by the states in proportion to the size of their populations.

reciprocity Deferral by members of Congress to the judgment of subject-matter specialists, mainly on minor technical bills.

red tape Overbearing bureaucratic rules and procedures.

redistricting The redrawing of congressional district lines within a state to ensure roughly equal populations within each district.

referenda Procedures available in some states by which proposed state laws or constitutional amendments are submitted to the voters for approval or rejection.

regulations The issuing of rules by government agencies with the aim of reducing the scale of negative externalities produced by private firms.

remedy An action that a court determines must be taken to rectify a wrong.

representative democracy Indirect democracy, in which the people rule through elected representatives.

republicanism, eighteenth century A political doctrine advocating limited government based on popular consent, protected against majority tyranny.

reservation clause The Tenth Amendment to the Constitution, reserving powers to the states or the people.

responsible party A political party that takes clear, distinct stands on the issues and enacts them as policy when in office.

retrospective voting A form of election in which voters look back at the performance of a party in power and cast ballots on the basis of how well it did in office.

rule of four An unwritten practice that requires at least four justices of the Supreme Court to agree that a case warrants review by the Court before it will hear the case.

sample survey An interview study asking questions of a set of people who are chosen as representative of the whole population.

scope of conflict The number of groups involved in a political conflict; few groups mean a narrow scope of conflict, and many groups mean a wide scope of conflict.

secularization The spread of nonreligious values and outlooks.

select committees Temporary committees in Congress created to conduct studies or investigations; they have no power to report bills.

selective incorporation The U.S. Supreme Court's gradual and piecemeal making of the protections of the Bill of Rights binding on the states.

senatorial courtesy The tradition that judicial nominations for federal district court appointments be cleared by the senior senator of the president's party from the relevant state.

seniority Length of service.

separate but equal doctrine The principle articulated in *Plessy* v. *Ferguson* (1896) that laws prescribing *separate* public facilities and services for nonwhite Americans are permissible if the facilities and services are equal to those provided for whites.

separation of powers The distribution of government legislative, executive, and judicial powers to separate branches of government.

sit-down strike A form of labor action in which workers stop production but do not leave their job site.

social (lifestyle) conservatives People who favor traditional social values; they tend to support strong law-and-order measures and oppose abortion and gay rights.

social (lifestyle) liberals People who favor civil liberties, abortion rights, and alternative lifestyles.

social insurance Government programs that provide services or income support in proportion to the amount of mandatory contributions made by individuals to a government trust fund.

soft money Unregulated expenditures by political parties on general public education, voter registration, and voter mobilization; often used to indirectly influence campaigns for elective office, until banned after 2002.

spoils system The practice of distributing government offices and contracts to the supporters of the winning party; also called *patronage.*

standing Authority to bring legal action because one is directly affected by the issues at hand.

standing committees Relatively permanent congressional committees that address specific areas of legislation.

stare decisis The legal doctrine that says precedent should guide judicial decision making.

states' rights position The view of American federalism that holds that the Constitution created a system of dual sovereignty in which the national government and the state governments are sovereign in their own spheres.

stay acts Enactments postponing the collection of taxes or mortgage payments

strict construction The doctrine that the provisions of the Constitution have a clear meaning and that judges must stick closely to this meaning when rendering decisions.

strict scrutiny The assumption that actions by elected bodies or officials violate constitutional rights.

subgovernment Alliances among interest groups, institutions within each house of Congress, and an executive branch agency that work to advance a particular agenda; can take various forms.

suffrage The right to vote.

Sun Belt States of the Lower South, Southwest, and West, where sunny weather and often conservative politics prevail.

superpower A nation armed with nuclear weapons and able to project force anywhere on the globe.

supply-siders Advocates of steep tax cuts and regulatory relief for business as a way to stimulate economic growth.

supremacy clause The provision in Article VI of the Constitution that states that the Constitution and the laws and treaties of the United States are the supreme law of the land, taking precedence over state laws and constitutions.

suspect classification The invidious, arbitrary, or irrational designation of a group for special treatment by government.

test case A case brought to force a ruling on the constitutionality of some law or executive action.

think tanks Nonprofit organizations that do research on public policy issues and distribute their findings through a variety of outlets. Although formally nonpartisan, most have an identifiable ideological stance.

trade deficit An excess of the value of the goods a country imports over the value of the goods it exports.

trustee According to the doctrine articulated by Edmund Burke, an elected representative who believes that his or her own best judgment, rather than instructions from constituents, should be used in making legislative decisions.

trusts Large combinations of business corporations.

turnout The proportion of eligible voters who actually vote in a given election.

tyranny The abuse of power by a ruler or a government.

unanimous consent Legislative action taken "without objection" as a way to expedite business; used to conduct much of the business of the Senate.

unconventional participation   Political activity in the form of demonstrations or protests.

unilateralist   The stance toward foreign policy that suggests that the United States should "go it alone," pursuing its national interests without seeking the cooperation of other nations or multilateral institutions.

unitary system   A system in which a central government has complete power over its constituent units or states.

veto   Presidential disapproval of a bill that has been passed by both houses of Congress. The president's veto can be overridden by a two-thirds vote in each house.

War Powers Act   A resolution passed by Congress in 1973 in an effort to constrain presidential war-making powers because of excesses during the Vietnam War; requires the president to consult with Congress before committing troops and to report to Congress within 48 hours when he has done so, and to terminate the use of U.S. armed forces within 60 days unless Congress gives approval for an extension.

watchdog   The role of the media in scrutinizing the actions of government officials.

welfare state   The set of government programs that protects the minimum standard of living of families and individuals against loss of income.

whip   A political party member in Congress charged with keeping members informed of the plans of the party leadership, counting votes before action on important issues, and rounding up party members for votes on bills.

whistle-blowers   People who bring official misconduct in their agencies to public attention.

white primaries   Primary elections open only to whites.

white-collar worker   A person working at a service, sales, or office job.

World Trade Organization (WTO)   An agency designed to enforce the provisions of the General Agreement on Tariffs and Trade and to resolve trade disputes between nations.

writ of certiorari   An announcement that the Supreme Court will hear a case on appeal from a lower court; its issuance requires the vote of four of the nine justices.

writ of mandamus   A court order that forces an official to act.

yellow journalism   Sensational newspaper stories with large headlines and, in some cases, color

Endnotes

Chapter 1

1. William H. Chafe, *The Unfinished Journey: America Since World War II* (New York: Oxford University Press, 1986), p. 304; Howard Zinn, *SNCC: The New Abolitionists* (Boston: Beacon Press, 1964), p. 64.

2. Chafe, *Unfinished Journey*, p. 305.

3. For a fuller treatment of these claims, as well as supporting evidence for them, see Robert A. Dahl, *Democracy and Its Critics* (New Haven, CT: Yale University Press, 1989); Robert A. Dahl, *On Democracy* (New Haven, CT: Yale University Press, 1998). Also see Benjamin Radcliff, "Politics, Markets, and Life Satisfaction: The Political Economy of Human Happiness," *American Political Science Review*, 95, (December 2001), pp. 939–952.

4. John Dewey, *The Public and Its Problems* (New York: Holt, 1927).

5. Dahl, *Democracy and Its Critics*, pg. 13.

6. See Robert A. Dahl, *After the Revolution: Authority in the Good Society* (New Haven, CT: Yale University Press, 1970); Dahl, *Democracy and Its Critics;* Jane Mansbridge, *Beyond Adversary Democracy* (New York: Basic Books, 1980).

7. See Benjamin Barber, *Strong Democracy: Participatory Democracy for a New Age* (Berkeley, CA: University of California Press, 1984); Peter Bachrach, *The Theory of Democratic Elitism* (Boston: Little, Brown, 1967); Robert A. Dahl, *A Preface to Economic Democracy* (Berkeley, CA: University of California Press, 1985); Edward S. Greenberg, *Workplace Democracy: The Political Effects of Participation* (Ithaca, NY: Cornell University Press, 1986); C. B. MacPherson, *Democratic Theory: Essays in Retrieval* (Oxford, U.K.: Clarendon Press, 1973); Carole Pateman, *Participation and Democratic Theory* (London: Cambridge University Press, 1970).

8. Esther Dyson, *Release 2.0* (New York: Broadway Books, 1997); Lawrence K. Grossman, *The Electronic Republic: Reshaping Democracy in the Information Age* (New York: Viking Press, 1995).

9. On deliberation and democracy, see Seyla Benhabib, "Toward a Deliberative Model of Democratic Legitimacy," in Seyla Benhabib, ed., *Democracy and Difference* (Princeton, NJ: Princeton University Press, 1996); John Dryzek, *Discursive Democracy* (Cambridge: Cambridge University Press, 1990); Nancy Fraser, "Rethinking the Public Sphere," in Craig Calhoun, ed., *Habermas and the Public Sphere* (New Brunswick, NJ: Rutgers University Press, 1992), pp. 109–142; Amy Guttman and Dennis Thompson, *Democracy and Disagreement* (Cambridge, U.K.: Belknap Press, 1996); Jurgen Habermas, *The Structural Transformation of the Public Sphere* (Cambridge, MA: MIT Press, 1989).

10. Kenneth May, "A Set of Independent, Necessary, and Sufficient Conditions for Simple Majority Decision," *Econometrical*, 20 (1952), pp. 680–684, shows that only majority rule can guarantee popular sovereignty, political equality, and neutrality among policy alternatives. See also Douglas W. Rae, "Decision Rules and Individual Values in Constitutional Choice," *American Political Science Review*, 63 (1969), pp. 40–53; Phillip D. Straffin, Jr., "Majority Rule and General Decision Rules," *Theory and Decision*, 8 (1977), pp. 351–360.

11. Dahl, *A Preface to Economic Democracy*, p. 68.

12. Robert A. Dahl, "On Removing Certain Impediments to Democracy in the United States," *Political Science Quarterly*, 92, No. 1 (Spring 1977), p. 14; Elaine Spitz, *Majority Rule* (Chatham, NJ: Chatham House, 1984), p. 83; Dahl, *Democracy and Its Critics*, p. 170.

13. See Marc Plattner, "Liberalism and Democracy," *Foreign Affairs* (March–April 1998), pp. 171–180.

14. David Caute, *The Great Fear* (New York: Simon & Schuster, 1978); Victor Navasky, *Naming Names* (New York: Viking, 1980); Michael Rogin, *The Intellectuals and McCarthy* (Cambridge, MA: MIT Press, 1967).

15. See Bernard R. Berelson, Paul F. Lazarsfeld, and William N. McPhee, *Voting* (Chicago: University of Chicago Press, 1954); V. O. Key, Jr., *Public Opinion and American Democracy* (New York: Knopf, 1961); Herbert McClosky and Alida Brill, *Dimensions of Tolerance* (New York: Russell Sage Foundation, 1983). But see, in rebuttal, James L. Gibson, "Political Intolerance and Political Repression During the McCarthy Red Scare," *American Political Science Review*, 82 (1988), pp. 511–529; Benjamin I. Page and Robert Y. Shapiro, *The Rational Public: Fifty Years of Trends in Americans' Policy Preferences* (Chicago: University of Chicago Press, 1992). See a summary of the debate and the supporting evidence in Carroll J. Glynn et al., *Public Opinion* (Boulder, CO: Westview Press, 1999).

16. Dahl, *Democracy and Its Critics*, p. 161.

17. Philip A. Klinkner with Rogers M. Smith, *The Unsteady March: The Rise and Decline of Racial Equality in America* (Chicago: The University of Chicago Press, 1999).

Chapter 2

1. Page Smith, *A People's History of the Young Republic: Vol. 3. The Shaping of America* (New York: McGraw-Hill, 1980), p. 25.

2. Quoted in Jackson Turner Main, *The Anti-Federalists* (Chapel Hill, NC: University of North Carolina Press, 1961), p. 62.

3. Richard Bushman, "Revolution," in Eric Foner and John A. Garraty, eds., *The Reader's Companion to American History* (Boston: Houghton Mifflin, 1991), p. 936; Gordon S. Wood, *The Creation of the American Republic* (New York: Norton, 1972), p. 12.

4. Joseph J. Ellis, *Founding Brothers: The Revolutionary Generation* (New York: Alfred A. Knopf, 2001), pp. 212–213.

5. Sarah M. Evans, *Born for Liberty: A History of Women in America* (New York: Free Press, 1997); John Hope Franklin and Alfred A. Moss, Jr., *From Slavery to Freedom* (New York: Knopf, 1967).

6. See Hannah Arendt, *On Revolution* (New York: Viking, 1965).

7. Smith, *Shaping of America,* pp. 8–9.

8. Richard Hofstadter, *The American Political Tradition* (New York: Vintage Books, 1948), p. 4.

9. Alexander Hamilton, James Madison, and John Jay, *The Federalist Papers,* ed. Clinton Rossiter (New York: New American Library, 1961), No. 10. (Originally published 1787–1788.)

10. See Gordon S. Wood, *The Radicalism of the American Revolution* (New York: Knopf, 1992).

11. Wood, *Creation of the American Republic,* pp. 311–318.

12. Ibid., ch. 8.

13. Samuel Elliot Morison, *The Oxford History of the American People* (New York: Oxford University Press, 1965), p. 274.

14. See Wood, *Creation of the American Republic,* p. 400.

15. Melvin I. Urofsky, *A March of Liberty* (New York: Knopf, 1988), p. 89.

16. Quoted in *The Washington Post* (May 7, 1987). Also see Lee Epstein and Thomas G. Walker, *Constitutional Law for a Changing America* (Washington, D.C.: CQ Press, 2000), p. 6.

17. Charles Beard, *An Economic Interpretation of the Constitution* (New York: Macmillan, 1913).

18. See Robert Brown, *Charles Beard and the Constitution* (Princeton, NJ: Princeton University Press, 1956); Hofstadter, *The American Political Tradition;* Leonard Levy, *Constitutional Opinions* (New York: Oxford University Press, 1986); Robert A. McGuire and Robert L. Ohsfeldt, "An Economic Model of Voting Behavior over Specific Issues at the Constitutional Convention of 1787," *Journal of Economic History,* 66 (March 1986), pp. 79–111; James A. Morone, *The Democratic Wish* (New York: Basic Books, 1990); Forrest McDonald, *We the People: The Economic Origins of the Constitution* (Chicago: University of Chicago Press, 1958); Gordon S. Wood, *The Convention and the Constitution* (New York: St. Martin's Press, 1965); Wood, *Creation of the American Republic.*

19. Quoted in Wood, *Creation of the American Republic,* p. 473.

20. Ibid., p. 432.

21. Ellis, *Founding Brothers,* p. 110.

22. Max Farrand, *The Records of the Federal Convention of 1787* (New Haven, CT: Yale University Press, 1937).

23. "The Invention of Centralized Federalism," in William H. Riker, ed., *The Development of Centralized Federalism* (Boston: Kluwer Academic, 1987).

24. Robert A. Dahl, "On Removing the Impediments to Democracy in the United States," *Political Science Quarterly,* 92 (Spring 1977), p. 5.

25. Hamilton, Madison, and Jay, *The Federalist Papers,* No. 51.

26. Thomas Jefferson, *Notes on the State of Virginia,* ed. Thomas Perkins Abernathy (New York: Harper & Row, 1964), p. 120.

27. See Main, *The Anti-Federalists;* Wood, *Creation of the American Republic;* Smith, *Shaping of America,* p. 99; Herbert Storing, *What the Anti-Federalists Were For* (Chicago: University of Chicago Press, 1981), p. 71.

Chapter 3

1. "Enemy of the States," *The Economist,* September 6, 2003, pp. 53–54; "In Spitzer's Sights," *The Economist,* September 13, 2003, pp. 65–66; Editorial, *BusinessWeek* (June 17, 2002), p. 108.

2. William H. Riker, *The Development of American Federalism* (Boston: Kluwer Academic, 1987), pp. 56–60.

3. Kay Lawson, *The Human Polity* (Boston: Houghton Mifflin, 2003), p. 467.

4. Rodney Hero, *Faces of Inequality: Social Diversity in American Politics* (New York: Oxford University Press, 1998).

5. The study of the complex constitutional, legal, fiscal, and political links states and the national government is often called the study of *intergovernmental relations* (the ever-changing constitutional, legal, fiscal, and political linkages among the states and the national government). For more on this, see David B. Walker, *Toward a Functioning Federalism* (Cambridge, MA: Winthrop, 1981).

6. Hero, *Faces of Inequality,* pp. 31–34.

7. Robert G. McCloskey, *American Supreme Court,* 2nd ed., ed. Sanford Levinsonn (Chicago: University of Chicago Press, 1994), pp. 43–45.

8. McCloskey, *American Supreme Court,* pp. 97–100, 111–112.

9. John D. Donahue, *Disunited States* (New York: Basic Books, 1997). pp. 11–12.

10. Ibid., p. 13.

11. Ann O. M. Bowan and George A. Krause, "Power Shift: Measuring Policy Centralization in U.S. Intergovernmental Relations, 1947–1998," *American Politics Research,* 31, no. 3 (May 2003), pp. 301–313; B. Guy Peters, *American Public Policy: Promise and Performance* (Washington, D.C.: CQ Press, 2004), pp. 22–27; Robert Nagel, *The Implosion of American Federalism* (New York: Oxford University Press, 2002).

12. Morton Grodzins, *The American System* (New Brunswick, NJ: Transaction Books, 1983).

13. Walker, *Toward a Functioning Federalism,* pp. 60–63.

14. Paul E. Peterson, Barry G. Rabe, and Kenneth Wong, *When Federalism Works* (Washington, D.C.: Brookings Institution, 1986), p. 2.

15. Ed Gillespie and Bob Schellhas, eds., *Contract with America: The Bold Plan by Rep. Newt Gingrich, Rep. Dick Armey and the House Republicans to Change the Nation* (New York: Random House, 1994), p. 125.

16. William H. Riker, *Federalism: Origin, Operation, Significance* (Boston: Little, Brown, 1964), ch. 6.

17. Jack Walker, "The Diffusion of Innovations Among the American States," *American Political Science Review,* 63 (1969), p. 883.

18. Paul E. Peterson, *City Limits* (Chicago: University of Chicago Press, 1981); Paul E. Peterson, *The Price of*

Federalism (Washington, D.C.: Brookings Institution, 1995).

Chapter 4

1. Bureau of the Census, *Statistical Abstract of the United States, 2001,* table 5.

2. For data on the foreign-born population, see Bureau of the Census press releases of March 10 and September 3, 2003.

3. Daniel J. Tichenor, *Dividing Lines: The Politics of Immigration Control in the United States* (Princeton, NJ: Princeton University Press, 2002), p. 284.

4. National Public Radio/the Kaiser Family Foundation/the Kennedy School of Government, "Security and Civil Liberties Poll Results" (November 30, 2001).

5. Michael Powell, "Brooklyn's Exodus," *The Washington Post National Weekly Edition* (June 9–15, 2003), pp. 8–9; "Arab Americans: Under Suspicion," *The Economist* (March 29, 2003), p. 31.

6. Michael Reich, "The Proletarianization of the Workforce," in Richard Edwards, Michael Reich, and Thomas A. Weisskopf, eds., *The Capitalist System* (Englewood Cliffs, NJ: Prentice Hall, 1966), p. 125.

7. Stanley Lebergott, "The American Labor Force," in Lance E. Davis, ed., *American Economic Growth* (New York: Harper & Row, 1972), pp. 124, 187.

8. William Julius Wilson, *When Work Disappears: The World of the New Urban Poor* (New York: Knopf, 1996).

9. *Human Development Report, 2003* (New York: The United Nations, 2004).

10. U.S. Bureau of the Census, 2004; David Cay Johnston, "IRS Says Americans' Income Shrank for 2 Consecutive Years," *The New York Times* (July 29, 2004), p. A1.

11. Stanley B. Greenberg, *Middle-Class Dreams* (New York: Times Books, 1995); Susan J. Tolchin, *The Angry American* (Boulder, CO: Westview Press, 1999).

12. Peter Gottschalk, "Inequality, Income Growth and Mobility," *Journal of Economic Perspectives,* 11, no. 2 (Spring 1997): 13–19; and the U.S. Bureau of the Census, 2004.

13. U.S. Bureau of the Census, 2004.

14. Wilson, *When Work Disappears.*

15. Edward Wolff, "International Comparisons of Wealth Inequality," *Review of Income and Wealth,* 42, no. 4 (December 1996).

16. Kevin Phillips, *Wealth and Democracy: How Great Fortunes and Government Created America's Aristocracy* (New York: Broadway Books, 2002).

17. From Edward Wolff's *Top Heavy,* reported in Alexander Stille, "Grounded by Income Gap," *The New York Times* (December 15, 2001), p. A15.

18. The numbers are from various federal government reports, reported in "Inequality: Would You Like Your Class War Shaken or Stirred, Sir?" *The Economist* (September 6, 2003), p. 28.

19. From the Federal Reserve Board, reported in Edmund L. Andrews, "Economic Inequality Grew in the 90's Boom, Fed Reports," *The New York Times* (January 22, 2003), p. 1.

20. See Edward S. Greenberg, *Capitalism and the American Political Ideal* (Armonk, NY: Sharpe, 1985), ch. 4.

21. On this history, see Thomas C. Cochran and William Miller, *The Age of Enterprise* (New York: Harper & Row, 1961); Louis M. Hacker, *American Economic Growth and Development* (New York: Wiley, 1970); Robert Wiebe, *The Search for Order* (New York: Hill & Wang, 1967).

22. U.S. Department of Commerce, *International Direct Investment* (Washington, D.C.: U.S. Government Printing Office, 1984), p. 1.

23. Jennifer L. Hochschild, *Facing Up to the American Dream* (Princeton, NJ: Princeton University Press, 1995), ch. 1. For a contrary view—namely, that America is divided into distinct political cultural traditions—see Rogers M. Smith, *Civic Ideals: Conflicting Visions of Citizenship in American* (New Haven, CT : Yale University Press, 1997).

24. See Jennifer L. Hochschild, *What's Fair? American Beliefs about Distributive Justice* (Cambridge, MA: Harvard University Press, 1981); Herbert McClosky and John R. Zaller, *The American Ethos: Public Attitudes Toward Capitalism and Democracy* (Cambridge, MA: Harvard University Press, 1984); Sidney Verba and Gary R. Orren, *Equality in America* (Cambridge, MA: Harvard University Press, 1985).

25. Verba and Orren, *Equality in America,* p. 255.

26. Alexis de Tocqueville, *Democracy in America* (1845).

27. On the domination of classical liberalism in America, see Louis Hartz, *The Liberal Tradition in America* (New York: Harcourt, Brace, 1955). But also see Rogers M. Smith, "Beyond Tocqueville, Myrdal, and Hartz: The Multiple Traditions of America," *American Political Science Review,* 87, no. 3 (September 1993), pp. 549–566.

28. John Kenneth Galbraith, *American Capitalism* (Boston: Houghton Mifflin, 1956); see also McClosky and Zaller, *The American Ethos,* pp. 270–271; John Micklethwait and Adrian Wooldridge, *The Right Nation* (New York: Penguin, 2004).

29. Russell Hanson, *The Democratic Imagination in America* (Princeton, NJ: Princeton University Press, 1985).

30. McClosky and Zaller, *The American Ethos,* p. 18.

31. Gary Wills, *Under God: Religion and American Politics* (New York: Simon and Schuster, 1991); Micklethwait and Wooldridge, *The Right Nation.*

32. Micklethwait and Wooldridge, *The Right Nation.*

Chapter 5

1. Joseph C. Goulden, *Truth Is the First Casualty: The Gulf of Tonkin Affair—Illusion and Reality* (Chicago: Rand McNally, 1969).

2. All public opinion polls cited in this chapter-opening story are from John E. Mueller, *War, Presidents and Public Opinion* (New York: Wiley, 1973).

3. U.S. Department of Defense, OASD (Comptroller), *Selected Manpower Statistics* (Washington, D.C.: Government Publications, June 1976), pp. 59–60.

4. Alexander Hamilton, James Madison, and John Jay, *The Federalist Papers,* ed. Clinton Rossiter (New York: New American Library, 1961; originally published 1787–1788). See Benjamin I. Page and Robert Y. Shapiro, *The Rational Public: Fifty Years of Trends in Americans' Policy Preferences* (Chicago: University of Chicago Press, 1992), chs. 1 and 2.

5. Walter Lippmann, *Public Opinion* (New York: Macmillan, 1922), p. 127.

6. Philip E. Converse, "The Nature of Belief Systems in Mass Publics," in David Apter, ed., *Ideology and Discontent* (New York: Free Press, 1964), pp. 206–261; Philip E. Converse, "Attitudes and Non-Attitudes: Continuation of a Dialogue," in Edward R. Tufte, ed., *The Quantitative Analysis of Social Problems* (Reading, MA: Addison-Wesley, 1970), pp. 168–189.

7. Pew Research Center for the People and the Press, *That Year: A Look Back at 1998* (Washington, D.C, 1999), p. 8.

8. Lawrence R. Jacobs and Robert Y. Shapiro, *Politicians Don't Pander: Political Manipulation and the Loss of Democratic Responsiveness* (Chicago: University of Chicago Press, 2000), p. 301.

9. Times Mirror Center for the People and the Press, "The Vocal Minority in American Politics," press release (July 16, 1993).

10. Robert S. Erikson and Kent L. Tedin, *American Public Opinion: Its Origins, Content, and Impact,* 6th ed. (New York: Longman, 2003), tells much more about the techniques and the results of polling. Also see Carroll J. Glynn, Susan Herbst, Garrett J. O'Keefe, and Robert Y. Shapiro, *Public Opinion* (Boulder, CO: Westview Press, 1999), ch. 3.

11. Elizabeth Kolber, "Public Opinion Polls Swerve with the Turns of a Phrase," *The New York Times* (June 5, 1995), pp. A1, C11.

12. For a review of the research literature on political socialization see Erikson and Tedin, *American Public Opinion,* ch. 5.

13. Paul Sniderman and Thomas Piazza, *Black Pride and Black Prejudice* (Princeton, NJ: Princeton University Press, 2002), pp. 175–179.

14. Robert C. Smith and Richard Seltzer, *Contemporary Controversies and the American Racial Divide* (Lanham, MD: Rowman and Littlefield, 2000).

15. This and the votes of other democratic groups reported in this section are from "Edison/Mitofsky Exit Poll, 2004 Presidential Election," CNN.com, **www.cnn.com/ELECTION/2004,** November 2, 2004.

16. General Social Survey, 2002.

17. Stanley B. Greenberg, *The Two Americas: Our Current Political Deadlock and How to Break It* (New York: Thomas Dunne Books, St. Martins Press, 2004).

18. *American National Election Studies,* 1998.

19. Gallup Poll Report, August 22, 2003.

20. John A. Garcia, *Latino Politics in America: Community, Culture, and Interests* (Lanham, MD: Rowman and Littlefield Publishers, 2003), chs. 6 and 7.

21. U.S. Bureau of the Census, press release, June 18, 2003.

22. For a summary of statistics on how adherents of different religious traditions divide on party identification and on a range of policy issues, see Erikson and Tedin, *American Public Opinion,* pp. 189–197.

23. "Portrait of the Electorate," *The New York Times* (November 13, 1994), p. 15.

24. "Edison/Mitofsky Exit Poll."

25. General Social Survey, 2002.

26. Earl Black and Merle Black, *The Rise of Southern Republicans* (Cambridge, MA: Harvard University Press, 2002); The Pew Research Center for the People and the Press, *Evenly Divided: The 2004 Political Landscape* (Washington, D.C, 2003), ch. 1.

27. General Social Survey, 2002.

28. *American National Election Studies,* 2000.

29. Bernadette C. Hayes, "The Impact of Class on Political Attitudes," *European Journal of Political Research,* 27 (1995), p. 76.

30. Thomas B. Edsall, "The Shifting Sands of America's Political Parties," *The Washington Post, National Edition* (April 9–15, 2001), p. 11. For a contrary view see Jeffrey M. Stonecash, *Class and Party in American Politics* (Boulder, CO: Westview, 2000).

31. Brigid C. Harrison, *Women in American Politics* (Belmont, CA: Thomson/Wadsworth Publishing, 2003), pp. 40–45.

32. M. Margaret Conway, Gertrude A. Steuernagel, and John R. Terocik, *Women and Political Participation* (Washington, D.C.: Congressional Quarterly Press, 1997).

33. Karen M. Kaufmann and John R. Petrocik, "The Changing Politics of American Men," *The American Journal of Political Science,* 43 (July 1999), pp. 864–887.

34. Mark Schlesinger and Caroline Heldman, "Gender Gap or Gender Gaps?" *The Journal of Politics,* 63, no. 1 (February 2001), pp. 59–92; Robert Y. Shapiro and Harpreet Mahajan, "Gender Differences in Policy Preferences: A Summary of Trends from the 1960s to the 1980s," *Public Opinion Quarterly,* 50 (1986), pp. 42–61; Glynn et al., *Public Opinion,* pp. 235–238; American National Election Studies, 2003.

35. Richard Morin, "Defense Tops the List," *The Washington Post National Edition* (November 26–December 2, 2001), p. 34; General Social Survey, 2002.

36. Pew Research Center, *Evenly Divided,* p. 30.

37. Albert H. Cantril and Susan Davis Cantril, *Reading Mixed Signals: Ambivalence in American Public Opinion about Government* (Baltimore, MD: Johns Hopkins University Press, 1999), Table 2.4, p. 22.

38. Michael X Delli Carpini and Scott Keeter, *What Americans Know About Politics and Why It Matters* (New Haven, CT: Yale University Press, 1996).

39. Erikson and Tedin, *American Public Opinion;* Page and Shapiro, *The Rational Public,* pp. 9–14. We also calculated some percentages from the National Opinion Research Center's General Social Survey.

40. Glynn et al, *Public Opinion,* Table 8.1, p. 252.

41. Paul M. Sniderman, Richard A. Brody, and Philip E. Tetlock, *Reasoning and Choice: Explorations in Political Psychology* (New York: Cambridge University Press, 1991);

see also Delli Carpini and Keeter, *Information and Empowerment;* Samuel Popkin, *The Reasoning Voter* (Chicago: University of Chicago Press, 1991).

42. Robert E. Lane, *Political Ideology: Why the American Common Man Believes What He Does* (New York: Free Press, 1962); Jennifer L. Hochschild, *What's Fair? American Beliefs about Distributive Justice* (Cambridge, MA: Harvard University Press, 1986); Glynn et al., *Public Opinion,* ch. 8.

43. Page and Shapiro, *The Rational Public.* Also see Taeku Lee, *Mobilizing Public Opinion: Black Insurgency and Racial Attitudes in the Civil Rights Era* (Chicago: University of Chicago Press, 2002).

44. General Social Survey, 2002.

45. Allensbach Opinion Research Institute, reported in *The Economist* (November 8, 2003), p. 4.

46. Derek Bok, *The Trouble with Government* (Cambridge, MA: Harvard University Press, 2001); Joseph S. Nye, Jr., Philip D. Zelikow, and David C. King, eds., *Why People Don't Trust Government* (Cambridge, MA: Harvard University Press, 1997).

47. Robert Putnam, "Bowling Together: The United State of America," *The American Prospect* (February 11, 2002), pp. 20–22.

48. Pew Research Center, *Evenly Divided,* ch. 6.

49. *American National Election Studies, 1948–2002* (Ann Arbor, MI: University of Michigan, 2003).

50. Samuel Kernell, "Explaining Presidential Popularity," *American Political Science Review,* 72 (June 1978), pp. 506–522; Richard A. Brody, *Assessing the President: The Media, Elite Opinion, and Public Support* (Stanford, CA: Stanford University Press, 1991).

51. All material is from Pew Research Center, *Evenly Divided.,* ch. 2.

52. Bruce E. Keith, David B. Magleby, Candice J. Nelson, Elizabeth Orr, Mark C. Westlye, and Raymond E. Wolfinger, *The Myth of the Independent Voter* (Berkeley, CA: University of California Press, 1992). Also see Marjorie Randon Hershey and Paul Allen Beck, *Party Politics in America,* 10th ed. (New York: Longman, 2003), pp. 120–121.

53. Walter Dean Burnham, "The Appearance and Disappearance of the American Voter," in Richard Rose, ed., *Electoral Participation: A Comparative Analysis* (Beverly Hills, CA: Sage, 1980), pp. 35–73; Jeffrey E. Cohen, *American Political Parties: Decline or Resurgence?* (Washington, D.C.: CQ Press, 2001); Michael B. MacKuen, Robert S. Erikson, and James A. Stimson, "Macropartisanship," *American Political Science Review,* 83 (1989), pp. 1125–1143.

54. Pew Research Center, *Evenly Divided,* ch. 2.

55. Princeton Survey Research Associates/Pew Research Center, April 2001.

56. Steven Kull, *Americans and Foreign Aid: A Study of American Public Attitudes* (Washington, D.C.: Program on International Policy Attitudes, 1995).

57. Gallup Poll, conducted for CNN and *USA Today,* February 2001.

58. Lawrence R. Jacobs and Benjamin I. Page, *Who Influences Foreign Policy?* unpublished manuscript, 2004; William

Caspary, "'The Mood Theory': A Study of Public Opinion and Foreign Policy," *American Political Science Review,* 64 (1970), pp. 536–547; John E. Rielly, ed., *American Public Opinion and U.S. Foreign Policy, 1995* (Chicago: Chicago Council on Foreign Relations, 1995), p. 13; Princeton Survey Associates/Pew Research Center, October 1999.

59. *Time*/CNN Survey, December 7, 1994.

60. Gallup Poll, conducted for CNN and *USA Today,* September 2001.

61. Summary of polls on American foreign policy reported at *The Public Agenda On-Line* at **www.publicagenda.org/**; Jacobs and Page, *Who Influences Foreign Policy?*

62. For a summary of the evidence see Paul Burstein, "The Impact of Public Opinion on Public Policy: A Review and an Agenda," *Political Research Quarterly,* 56, no. 1 (March 2003), pp. 29–40.

63. Alan D. Monroe, "Consistency Between Public Preferences and National Policy Decisions," *American Politics Quarterly,* 7 (January 1979), pp. 3–19; Benjamin I. Page and Robert Y. Shapiro, "Effects of Public Opinion on Policy," *American Political Science Review,* 77 (1983), pp. 175–190.

64. James A. Stimson, *Public Opinion in America: Moods, Cycles and Swings* (Boulder, CO: Westview Press, 1991).

65. Summarized in Benjamin I. Page, "The Semi-Sovereign Public," in Jeff Manza, Fay Lomax Cook, and Benjamin I. Page, eds., *Navigating Public Opinion: Polls, Policy, and the Future of American Democracy* (New York: Oxford University Press, 2002).

66. Jacobs and Shapiro, *Politicians Don't Pander;* John Zaller, *The Nature and Origins of Mass Opinion* (New York: Cambridge University Press, 1992).

Chapter 6

1. Doris Graber, *Mass Media and American Politics,* 4th ed. (Washington, D.C.: Congressional Quarterly Press, 1993), p. 35.

2. See Suzanne Garment, *Scandal: The Crisis of Mistrust in American Politics* (New York: Random House, 1991); Larry J. Sabato, Mark Stencel, and S. Robert Lichter, *Peepshow: Media and Politics in an Age of Scandal* (Boulder, CO: Rowman & Littlefield Publishers, 2000).

3. Bill Kovach and Tom Rosenstiel, *Warp Speed: America in the Age of Mass Media* (New York: The Century Fund Press, 1999).

4. Diana Owen, "Talk Radio and Evaluations of President Clinton," *Political Communications,* 14 (1997), pp. 333–353.

5. *Talkers Magazine Online,* **www.talkers.com**, Fall 2003.

6. Kenneth Dautrich and Thomas H. Hartley, *How the News Media Fail American Voters* (New York: Columbia University Press, 1999).

7. National Election Studies, University of Michigan, *Post-Election Surveys, 1996 and 2000.*

8. Regis McKenna, *Real Time* (Cambridge, MA: Harvard University Press, 1997).

9. Kovach and Rosensteil, *Warp Speed,* pp. 52–57.

10. Erik P. Bucy et al., "The Engaged Electorate: New Media Use as Political Participation," in Lynda Lee Kaid and Dianne G. Bystrom, eds., *The Electronic Election* (Mahwah, NJ: Lawrence Erlbaum and Associates, 1997).

11. Ben H. Bagdikian, *The New Media Monopoly* (Boston: Beacon Press, 2004); "Who Owns What?" *Columbia Journalism Review Online,* **www.cjr.org,** 2004.

12. Symposium, "The Real Dangers of Conglomerate Control," *Columbia Journalism Review* (March–April 1997), pp. 47–51.

13. W. Lance Bennett, *News: The Politics of Illusion,* 5th ed. (New York: Longman, 2003), pp. 104–106.

14. Ibid., pp. 13–15, Doug Underwood, "Market Research and the Audience for Political News," in Graber, McQuail, and Norris, eds., *The Politics of News* (Washington, D.C.: CQ Press, 1998), p. 171.

15. Edward Jay Epstein, *News from Nowhere: Television and the News* (New York: Vantage, 1973), p. 142.

16. Leon V. Sigal, *Reporters and Officials: The Organization and Politics of News Reporting* (Lexington, MA: Heath, 1973), p. 124. Also see Bennett, *News,* pp. 124–125, for recent research confirming these findings.

17. Mark Hertsgaard, *On Bended Knee* (New York: Farrar, Straus & Giroux, 1988), p. 5.

18. David Murray, Joel Schwartz, and S. Robert Lichter, *It Ain't Necessarily So: How Media Make and Unmake the Scientific Picture of Reality* (Lanham, MD: Rowan and Littlefield Publishers, 2001), pp. 29–30.

19. Lawrence C. Soley, *The News Shapers: The Sources Who Explain the News* (New York: Praeger, 1992); Eric Alterman, *Sound and Fury: The Washington Punditocracy and the Collapse of American Politics* (New York: HarperCollins, 1992).

20. G. William Domhoff, *Who Rules America: Power and Politics,* 4th ed. (Boston: Mayfield Publishing Company, 2001), p. 115.

21. William Schneider and I. A. Lewis, "Views on the News," *Public Opinion,* 8 (August–September 1985), p. 7; Karlyn Keene et al., "Monitoring Media Attitudes," *American Enterprise* (July–August 1990), p. 95; S. Robert Lichter, Stanley Rothman, and L. S. Lichter, *The Media Elite* (Bethesda, MD: Adler & Adler, 1986); David Weaver and G. Cleveland Wilhoit, *The American Journalist* (Mahwah, NJ: Lawrence Erlbaum, 1996).

22. Howard Kurtz, "Acid Rain on the Media Parade: A Big Report Pooh-Poohing the Danger Gets Scant Press," *Washington Post Weekly Edition* (January 21–27, 1991), p. 38.

23. Thomas E. Patterson and Wolfgang Donsbach, "News Decisions: Journalists as Partisan Actors," *Political Communications,* 13 (October–December 1996).

24. *Editorials on File,* 19 (November 1–15, 1988), p. 1272.

25. Calculated by the authors from periodic reports in *Editor and Publisher* magazine.

26. Kim Fridkin Kahn and Patrick J. Kenney, "The Slant of the News: How Editorial Endorsements Influence Campaign Coverage and Citizens' Views of Candidates," *American Political Science Review,* 96, no. 2 (June 2002), pp. 381–394.

27. Fred Kaplan, *The Wizards of Armageddon* (New York: Simon & Schuster, 1983); Tom Gervasi, *The Myth of Soviet Military Supremacy* (New York: Harper & Row, 1986).

28. Thomas E. Patterson, *Out of Order* (New York: Knopf, 1993); Steven Ansolabehere and Shanto Iyengar, *Going Negative: How Attack Ads Shrink and Polarize the Electorate* (New York: Free Press, 1996).

29. Kovach and Rosenstiel, *Warp Speed,* p. 66.

30. Bennett, *News,* pp. 13–16; and Kovach and Rosenstiel, *Warp Speed.*

31. David L. Paletz, "The Media and Public Policy," in Graber et al., *The Politics of News.*

32. Shanto Iyengar and Donald R. Kinder, *News That Matters* (Chicago: University of Chicago Press, 1987).

33. G. Ray Funkhauser, "The Issues of the Sixties: An Exploratory Study in the Dynamics of Public Opinion," *Public Opinion Quarterly,* 37 (Spring 1973), pp. 62–75.

34. George C. Edwards, "Who Influences Whom? The President, Congress and the Media," *The American Political Science Review,* 93 (June 1999), pp. 327–344.

35. Shanto Iyengar, *Is Anyone Responsible? How Television News Frames Political Issues* (Chicago: University of Chicago Press, 1991); Kathleen Hall Jamieson and Paul Waldman, *The Press Effect* (Washington, D.C.: CQ Press, 2002).

36. Benjamin I. Page, Robert Y. Shapiro, and Glenn R. Dempsey, "What Moves Public Opinion?" *American Political Science Review,* 81 (1987), pp. 23–43.

37. David L. Protess, Fay Lomax Cook, Jack C. Doppelt, James S. Ettema, Margaret T. Gordon, Donna R. Leff, and Peter Miller, *The Journalism of Outrage: Investigative Reporting and Agenda Building in America* (New York: Guilford Press, 1991).

38. Stephen C. Craig, ed., *Broken Contract: Changing Relations Between Americans and Their Government* (Boulder, CO: Westview Press, 1996); Bennett, *News;* Thomas E. Patterson, "Bad News, Period," *PS* (March 1996), pp. 17–20.

39. Daniel C. Hallin, *The "Uncensored War": The Media and Vietnam* (Berkeley, CA: University of California Press, 1989).

40. W. Lance Bennett and David L. Paletz, eds., *Taken by Storm: The Media, Public Opinion, and U.S. Foreign Policy in the Gulf War* (Chicago: University of Chicago Press, 1994).

41. "Views of a Changing World 2003: War with Iraq Further Divides Global Publics," The Pew Research Center for the People and the Press (June 3, 2003).

42. Doris Graber, *Mass Media and American Politics,* 4th ed. (Washington, D.C.: Congressional Quarterly Press, 1993), pp. 67–68.

43. Federal Communications Commission, press release, July 8, 2003.

44. Dan Schiller, *Digital Capitalism: Networking in the New Global Market System* (Cambridge, MA: MIT Press, 1999).

45. Lawrence Lessig, *Code and Other Laws of Cyberspace* (New York: Basic Books, 1999).

Chapter 7

1. The Center for Responsive Politics, based on Federal Election Commission reports.

2. Ibid.

3. Joel Brinkley, "Energy Bill Draws a Deeply Split Utilities Lobby," *The New York Times,* August 23, 2003, p. A10.

4. Alexander Hamilton, James Madison, and John Jay, *The Federalist Papers,* ed. Clinton Rossiter (New York: New American Library, 1961), No. 10. (Originally published 1787–1788.)

5. Arthur F. Bentley, *The Process of Government* (Chicago: University of Chicago Press, 1908); David Truman, *The Governmental Process* (New York: Knopf, 1951); V. O. Key, Jr., *Politics, Parties, and Pressure Groups* (New York: A. Crowell, 1952); Robert A. Dahl, *A Preface to Democratic Theory* (Chicago: University of Chicago Press, 1956); Robert A. Dahl, *Who Governs?* (New Haven, CT: Yale University Press, 1961). See also Jeffrey M. Berry, *The New Liberalism: The Rising Power of Citizen Groups* (Washington, D.C.: Brookings, 1999).

6. Roger H. Davidson and Walter J. Oleszek, *Congress and Its Members* (Washington, D.C.: CQ Press, 2004), p. 367.

7. The Center for Responsive Politics, based on required reports to the House and Senate, 2003.

8. Kay Lehman Schlozman and John T. Tierney, *Organized Interests and American Democracy* (New York: Harper & Row, 1986), pp. 77–78.

9. Berry, *The New Liberalism,* pp. 20–21.

10. Anne Costain, *Inviting Women's Rebellion* (Baltimore: Johns Hopkins University Press, 1992).

11. Truman, *The Governmental Process.*

12. Mancur Olson, *The Logic of Collective Action* (Cambridge, MA: Harvard University Press, 1965).

13. On Olson's theory, see Brian Barry and Russell Hardin, eds., *Rational Man and Irrational Society?* (Newbury Park, CA: Sage, 1982); Dennis Chong, *Collective Action and the Civil Rights Movement* (Chicago: University of Chicago Press, 1991); Russell Hardin, *Collective Action* (Baltimore: Johns Hopkins University Press); Terry Moe, *The Organization of Interests* (Chicago: University of Chicago Press, 1980).

14. E. E. Schattschneider, *The Semi-Sovereign People* (New York: Holt, Rinehart & Winston, 1960).

15. Berry, *The New Liberalism;* Thomas Byrne Edsall, *The New Politics of Inequality* (New York: Norton, 1984); Michael Goldfield, *The Decline of Organized Labor in the United States* (Chicago: University of Chicago Press, 1987); Edward S. Greenberg, *Capitalism and the American Political Ideal* (Armonk, NY: Sharpe, 1985); David Vogel, *Fluctuating Fortunes: The Political Power of Business in America* (New York: Basic Books, 1989), ch. 8.

16. U.S. Bureau of Labor Statistics, 2004.

17. Jeffrey M. Berry, *Lobbying for the People* (Princeton, NJ: Princeton University Press, 1977), p. 7; Berry, *The New Liberalism,* p. 2.

18. Berry, *Lobbying for the People;* David Broder, *Changing the Guard* (New York: Simon & Schuster, 1980); Hugh Heclo, "Issue Networks and the Executive Establishment," in Anthony King, ed., *The New American Political System* (Washington, D.C.: American Enterprise Institute, 1978); Schlozman and Tierney, *Organized Interests;* Jack L. Walker, Jr., "The Origins and Maintenance of Interest Groups in America," *American Political Science Review,* 77 (1983), pp. 390–406.

19. Theda Skocpol, "Associations Without Members," *The American Prospect,* 10, no. 4 (July/August 1999), pp. 66–73.

20. Jack L. Walker, Jr., *Mobilizing Interest Groups in America* (Ann Arbor, MI: University of Michigan Press, 1991).

21. Leslie Wayne and Melody Petersen, "A Muscular Lobby Rolls Up Its Sleeves," *The New York Times* (November 4, 2001), Section 3, p. 1.

22. Mark A. Smith, *Business and Political Power: Public Opinion, Elections and Democracy* (Chicago: University of Chicago Press, 2000).

23. Jeffrey M. Berry, *The Interest Group Society* (Glenview, IL: Scott, Foresman, 1989), p. 141.

24. Susan Glasser and Ben White, "The Dashing Life of Washington Lobbyists," *The Washington Post National Edition* (July 12, 1999), p. A13.

25. Kenneth M. Goldstein, *Interest Groups, Lobbying and Participation in America* (New York: Cambridge University Press, 1999), ch. 2; Kenneth Kollman, *Outside Lobbying* (Princeton, NJ: Princeton University Press, 1998).

26. E. E. Schattschneider, *The Semi-Sovereign People.*

27. Berry, *The New Liberalism.*

28. Schlozman and Tierney, *Organized Interests,* p. 175.

29. Steven Greenhouse, "Labor Marshalls Resources to Unseat the President," *The New York Times* (February 15, 2003), p. A7.

30. Berry, *The New Liberalism.*

31. Wendy L. Hansen and Neil J. Mitchell, "Money and Power" (unpublished manuscript, 2001), p. 9.

32. Leslie Wayne and Melody Petersen, "A Muscular Lobby Rolls Up Its Sleeves," *The New York Times* (November 4, 2001), Section 3, p. 1.

33. Federal Election Commission.

34. "Money Talks, Congress Listens," *The Boston Globe* (December 12, 1982), p. A24.

35. Federal Election Commission, *Soft Money Expenditures* (Washington, D.C.: U.S. Government Printing Office, 2003).

36. Derek Bok, *The Trouble with Government* (Cambridge, MA: Harvard University Press, 2001), pp. 81–94.

37. Marver Bernstein, *Regulating Business by Independent Commission* (Princeton, NJ: Princeton University Press, 1955).

38. Theodore J. Lowi, *The End of Liberalism* (New York: Norton, 1969).

39. Berry, *The New Liberalism;* Allan J. Cigler, "Interest Groups," in William Crotty, ed., *Political Science: Looking to the Future,* Vol. 4 (Evanston, IL: Northwestern University Press, 1991); Robert H. Salisbury et al., "Who Works with Whom? Interest Group Alliances and Opposition," *American Political Science Review,* 81 (1987), pp. 1217–1234.

40. Jeffrey M. Berry, "Citizen Groups and the Changing Nature of Interest Group Politics in America," *The Annals,* 528 (1993), pp. 16–23; Heclo, "Issue Networks"; Robert H. Salisbury, John P. Heinz, Edward O. Laumann, and Robert L. Nelson, "Triangles, Networks, and Hollow Cores," and Mark P. Petracca, "The Rediscovery of Interest Group Politics," in Mark P. Petracca, ed., *The Politics of Interests: Interest Groups Transform* (Boulder, CO: Westview Press, 1992); Robert M. Stein and Kenneth Bickers, *Perpetuating the Pork Barrel: Policy Subsystems and American Democracy* (Cambridge, UK: Cambridge University Press, 1995).

41. Richard Smith, "Interest Group Influence in Congress," *Legislative Studies Quarterly,* 20 (1995), pp. 89–139.

42. Charles Lindblom, *Politics and Markets* (New York: Basic Books, 1977), p. 356. For criticisms from the left, see John Manley, "Neo-Pluralism: A Class Analysis of Pluralism I and Pluralism II," *American Political Science Review,* 77 (1983), pp. 368–383. For criticisms from the right, see Irving Kristol, *Two Cheers for Capitalism* (New York: Basic Books, 1977); James Q. Wilson, "Democracy and the Corporation," in Robert Sessen, ed., *Does Big Business Rule America?* (Washington, D.C.: Ethics and Public Policy Center, 1987). For a recent dissent, see Mark Smith, "Public Opinion, Elections, and Representation Within a Market Economy," *American Journal of Political Science,* 43, no. 3 (1999), p. 842.

43. Neil J. Mitchell, *The Conspicuous Corporation: Business, Public Policy and Representative Democracy* (Ann Arbor, MI: University of Michigan Press, 1997), p. 167.

44. Dan Clawson, Alan Neustadt, and Mark Weller, *Dollars and Votes* (Philadelphia: Temple University Press, 1998), pp. 26–28, 64–71, 97–99.

45. Vogel, *Fluctuating Fortunes.*

46. Ibid.

47. Ibid, p. 291.

48. Jeffrey Berry disagrees in *The New Liberalism.*

49. Davidson and Oleszek, *Congress and Its Members,* p. 366.

50. Walter Dean Burnham, *Critical Elections and the Mainsprings of American Politics* (New York: Norton, 1970), p. 133.

51. John E. Chubb and Paul E. Peterson, "American Political Institutions and the Problem of Governance," in John E. Chubb and Paul E. Peterson, eds., *Can the Government Govern?* (Washington, D.C.: Brookings Institution, 1989).

Chapter 8

1. James MacGregor Burns and Stewart Burns, *A People's Charter: The Pursuit of Rights in America* (New York: Knopf, 1991), ch. 5; E. McGlen and Karen O'Connor, *Women's Rights* (New York: Praeger, 1983), ch. 3.

2. Joyce Gelb, *Feminism and Politics: A Comparative Perspective* (Berkeley, CA: University of California Press, 1989), pp. 14, 30. See also Doug McAdams, *Political Process and the Development of Black Insurgency* (Chicago: University of Chicago Press, 1982); David Plotke, "Citizenship and Social Movements," paper delivered at the annual meetings of the American Political Science Association, Washington, D.C., September 2–5, 1993.

3. Sidney Tarrow, "Social Movements as Contentious Politics," *American Political Science Review,* 90 (1996), pp. 853–866.

4. CBS News telecast, February 16, 2003.

5. E. E. Schattschneider, *The Semi-Sovereign People* (New York: Holt, Rinehart & Winston, 1960), p. 142.

6. Richard Polenberg, *One Nation Divisible* (New York: Penguin, 1980), p. 268; Craig A. Rimmerman, *From Identity to Politics: The Lesbian and Gay Movements in the United States* (Philadelphia: Temple University Press, 2002), ch. 1.

7. Theodore J. Lowi, *The Politics of Disorder* (New York: Basic Books, 1971), p. 54.

8. Doug McAdams, John D. McCarthy, and Mayer N. Zald, "Social Movements," in Neil J. Smelser, ed., *Handbook of Sociology* (Newbury Park, CA: Sage, 1994); McAdams, *Political Process;* Sidney Tarrow, *Social Movements, Collective Action, and Politics* (New York: Cambridge University Press, 1994).

9. Neil J. Smelser, *Theory of Collective Behavior* (New York: Free Press, 1962).

10. Barbara Sinclair Deckard, *The Women's Movement* (New York: Harper & Row, 1983); Ethel Klein, *Gender Politics: From Consciousness to Mass Politics* (Cambridge, MA: Harvard University Press, 1984), ch. 2.

11. Donald P. Haider-Markel, "Creating Change—Holding the Line," in Ellen D. B. Riggle and Barry L. Tadlock, eds., *Gays and Lesbians in the Political Process* (New York: Columbia University Press, 1999).

12. William Gamson, *The Strategy of Social Protest* (Homewood, IL: Dorsey, 1975); John D. McCarthy and Mayer N. Zald, "Resource Mobilization and Social Movements: A Partial Theory," *American Journal of Sociology,* 82 (1977), pp. 1212–1241.

13. Jo Freeman, *The Politics of Women's Liberation* (New York: McKay, 1975); Nancy Burns, "Gender: Public Opinion and Political Action," in Ira Katznelson and Helen V. Milner, eds., *Political Science: The State of the Discipline* (New York: W.W. Norton, 2002), pp. 472–476.

14. McAdams, *Political Process;* Peter K. Eisenger, "The Conditions of Protest Behavior in American Cities," *American Political Science Review,* 67 (1973), pp. 11–28.

15. Frances Fox Piven and Richard A. Cloward, *Poor People's Movements* (New York: Vintage, 1979), ch. 3.

16. Klein, *Gender Politics,* pp. 90–91.

17. National Opinion Research Center, General Social Survey, 1972.

18. The Pew Research Center for the People and the Press, *Evenly Divided and Increasingly Polarized: The 2004 Political Landscape* (Washington, D.C., 2003).

19. Rimmerman, *From Identity to Politics.*

20. Jane Mansbridge, *Why We Lost the ERA* (Chicago: University of Chicago Press, 1986).

21. See David Caute, *The Great Fear* (New York: Simon & Schuster, 1978); Robert Justin Goldstein, *Political Repression in Modern America* (Cambridge, MA: Schenkman, 1978); Alan Wolfe, *The Seamy Side of Democracy* (New York: McKay, 1978).

22. Edward S. Greenberg, *Capitalism and the American Political Ideal* (Armonk, NY: Sharpe, 1985).

23. William H. Chafe, *The Unfinished Journey: America Since World War II* (New York: Oxford University Press, 1986); Deckard, *The Women's Movement;* Klein, *Gender Politics,* ch. 2; Freeman, *Politics of Women's Liberation.*

Chapter 9

1. Glen Justice, "Court Ruling Affirms New Landscape of Campaign Finance," *The New York Times* (December 11, 2003), p. A1.

2. Ibid.

3. "N.R.A.'s New Ad Idea," *The New York Times* (December 12, 2003), p. A16.

4. David Menefee-Libey, *The Triumph of Campaign-Centered Politics* (New York: Chatham House Publishers, 2000); and Daniel M. Shea, "The Passing of Realignment and the Advent of the 'Baseless' Party System," *American Politics Quarterly,* 27 (January 1997), pp. 33–57.

5. Robert A. Dahl, *On Democracy* (New Haven, CT: Yale University Press, 1998).

6. E. E. Schattschneider, *Party Government* (New York: Holt, Rinehart & Winston, 1942), p. 208.

7. Ibid.

8. See A. James Reichley, *The Life of the Parties: A History of American Political Parties* (New York: Free Press, 1992), ch. 1.

9. Steven J. Rosenstone and John Mark Hansen, *Mobilization, Participation, and Democracy in America* (New York: Macmillan, 1993).

10. E. E. Schattschneider, *The Semi-Sovereign People* (New York: Holt, Rinehart & Winston, 1960).

11. On realignment, see Walter Dean Burnham, *Critical Elections and the Mainsprings of American Politics* (New York: Norton, 1970); Walter Dean Burnham, "Critical Realignment Lives: The 1994 Earthquake," in Colin Campbell and Bert A. Rockman, eds., *The Clinton Presidency* (Chatham, NJ: Chatham House, 1996); William Nisbet Chambers and Walter Dean Burnham, eds., *The American Party Systems* (New York: Oxford University Press, 1967); Jerome Clubb, William H. Flanigan, and Nancy H. Zingale, *Partisan Realignment* (Newbury Park, CA: Sage, 1980); V. O. Key, Jr., "A Theory of Critical Elections," *Journal of Politics,* 17 (1955), pp. 3–18; David R. Mayhew, *Electoral Realignments* (New Haven, CT: Yale University Press, 2004); James L. Sundquist, *Dynamics of the Party System* (Washington, D.C.: Brookings Institution, 1973).

12. C. Vann Woodward, *The Strange Career of Jim Crow* (New York: Oxford University Press, 1966).

13. John Aldrich and Richard Niemi, "The Sixth American Party System," in Stephen C. Craig, *Broken Contract: Changing Relationships Between Americans and Their Government* (Boulder, CO: Westview Press, 1996); Walter J. Stone and Ronald B. Rapoport, "It's Perot Stupid! The Legacy of the 1992 Perot Movement in the Major-Party System, 1994–2000," *PS: Political Science and Politics,* XXXIV, No. 1 (March 2001), pp. 49–56.

14. Thomas Byrne Edsall and Mary D. Edsall, *Chain Reaction: the Impact of Race, Rights and Taxes on American Politics,* (New York: Norton, 1991); Stanley B. Greenberg, *Middle Class Dreams: The Politics and Power of the New American Majority* (New Haven, CT: Yale University Press, 1996).

15. Helmut Norpoth and Jerrold Rusk, "Partisan Dealignment in the American Electorate," *American Political Science Review* 76 (September 1982), pp. 719–736. Also see Larry Sabato, *The Party's Just Begun* (Glenview, IL: Scott, Foresman, 1988); Sundquist, *Dynamics of the Party System;* Martin P. Wattenberg, *The Decline of American Political Parties* (Cambridge, MA: Harvard University Press, 1994); Greenberg, *Middle-Class Dreams;* Everett C. Ladd, "The 1994 Congressional Elections," *Political Science Quarterly* 110, pp. 1–23.

16. Stanley B. Greenberg, *The Two Americas: Our Current Political Deadlock and How to Break It* (New York: Thomas Dunn Books, 2004)

17. The classic statement on electoral rules is Maurice Duverger, *Political Parties* (New York: Wiley, 1954).

18. Much of this discussion is drawn from Steven J. Rosenstone, Roy L. Behr, and Edward H. Lazarus, *Third Parties in America* (Princeton, NJ: Princeton University Press, 1984).

19. Marjorie Randon Hershey and Paul Allen Beck, *Party Politics in America,* 10th ed. (New York: Longman Publishers, 2003), pp.102–104.

20. Roger H. Davidson and Walter J. Oleszek, *Congress and Its Members* (Washington, D.C.: CQ Press, 2002), chs. 3 and 4; and Shea, "The Passing of Realignment and the Advent of the 'Baseless' Party System."

21. Jill Abramson, "A Law Survives. Now Let's Subvert It," *The New York Times* (December 14, 2003), Week in Review, p. 1.

22. Menefee-Libey, *The Triumph of Candidate-Centered Politics.*

23. J. A. Schlesinger, "The New American Political Party," *American Political Science Review* 79 (1985), pp. 1152–1169; John Aldrich, *Why Parties?* (Chicago: University of Chicago Press, 1995).

24. Greenberg, *The Two Americas;* Morris P. Fiorino, "Parties, Participation, and Representation in America," in Ira Katznelson and Helen V. Milner, eds., *Political Science: the State of the Discipline* (New York: W.W. Norton, 2002); Hershey and Beck, *Party Politics in America,* ch. 15; Marc J. Hetherington, "Resurgent Mass Partisanship: The Role of Elite Polarization," *The American Political Science Review,* 95, No. 1 (September 2001), pp. 619–632; J. L. Jackson, N. Clayton, and J. C. Green, "Issue Networks and Party Elites in 1996," in J. C. Green and D. M. Shea, eds.,

The State of the Parties (Lanham, MD: Rowman and Littlefield, 1999); Gerald Pomper, "Parliamentary Government in the United States," in Green and Shea, eds., *The State of the Parties*.

25. *National Election Studies* (Ann Arbor: University of Michigan, 2001).

26. Hetherington, "Resurgent Mass Partisanship," p. 624.

27. Pew Research Center for the People and the Press, *Evenly Divided and Increasingly Polarized* (Washington, D.C., 2003).

28. Alan D. Monroe, "American Party Platforms and Public Opinion," *American Journal of Political Science*, 27 (February 1983), p. 35; Gerald M. Pomper, *Elections in America* (New York: Longman, 1980), p. 169.

29. *New York Times*/CBS News, "Convention Delegate Polls," June 16–July 17, 2004, and August 3–23, 2004.

30. Douglas Hibbs, *The American Political Economy* (Cambridge, MA: Harvard University Press, 1987); Dennis P. Quinn and Robert Shapiro, "Business Political Power: The Case of Taxation," *American Political Science Review* 85 (1991), pp. 851–874.

31. Thomas Byrne Edsall, *The New Politics of Inequality* (New York: Norton, 1984); Kevin P. Phillips, *Boiling Point: Democrats, Republicans, and the Decline of Middle-Class Prosperity* (New York: Random House, 1993); David Vogel, *Fluctuating Fortunes: The Political Power of Business in America* (New York: Basic Books, 1989); Davidson and Oleszek, *Congress and Its Members*, pp. 190–192.

32. Nils Gilman, "What the Rise of the Republicans as America's First Ideological Party Means for the Democrats," *The Forum*, 2, No. 1 (2004), pp. 1–5.

33. James MacGregor Burns, *Deadlock of Democracy* (Englewood Cliffs, NJ: Prentice Hall, 1967).

34. Morris P. Fiorina, *Divided Government* (New York: Macmillan, 1992); Gary Jacobson, *The Electoral Origins of Divided Government: Competition in U.S. House Elections* (Boulder, CO: Westview Press, 1990); David R. Mayhew, *Divided We Govern: Party Control, Lawmaking, and Investigations, 1946–1990* (New Haven, CT: Yale University Press, 1991).

35. Hedrick Smith, *The Power Game* (New York: Random House, 1988), p. 652.

36. Benjamin Ginsberg and Martin Shefter, *Politics by Other Means: The Declining Significance of Elections in America* (New York: Basic Books, 1990).

37. Mayhew, *Divided We Govern*.

Chapter 10

1. Campaign finance figures for this opening story are from Glen Justice, "Even with Campaign Finance Law, Money Talks Louder Than Ever," *The New York Times* (November 8, 2004), p. A16; and Sharon Theimer, "Million Dollar-Plus Political Donors Rise," The Associated Press, October 29, 2004.

2. "'04 Elections Expected to Cost Nearly $4 Billion; Presidential Race to Top $1.2 Billion," The Center for Responsive Politics, **www.opensecrets.org/pressreleases/ 2004/04spending.asp,** October 21, 2004.

3. For further discussion, see Benjamin I. Page, *Choices and Echoes in Presidential Elections: Rational Man and Electoral Democracy* (Chicago: University of Chicago Press, 1978), ch. 2; Robert A. Dahl, *Democracy and Its Critics* (New Haven, CT: Yale University Press, 1989).

4. See Austin Ranney, *The Doctrine of Responsible Party Government: Its Origins and Present State* (Urbana, IL: University of Illinois Press, 1962); E. E. Schattschneider, *Party Government* (New York: Holt, Rinehart & Winston, 1942).

5. Anthony Downs, *An Economic Theory of Democracy* (New York: Harper & Row, 1957); Otto Davis, Melvin Hinich, and Peter Ordeshook, "An Expository Development of a Mathematical Model of the Electoral Process," *American Political Science Review*, 64 (1970), pp. 426–448.

6. Lawrence R. Jacobs and Robert Y. Shapiro, *Politicians Don't Pander: Political Manipulation and the Loss of Democratic Responsiveness* (Chicago: University of Chicago Press, 2000).

7. See V. O. Key, Jr., *Public Opinion and American Democracy* (New York: Knopf, 1961); Morris P. Fiorina, *Retrospective Voting in American National Elections* (Cambridge, MA: Harvard University Press, 1981).

8. Katharine Q. Seelye, "Study Says 2000 Election Missed Millions of Votes," *The New York Times* (August, 10, 2001), p. A17.

9. David Stout, "Study Finds Ballot Problems Are More Likely for Poor," *The New York Times* (July 9, 2001), p. A9.

10. Chilton Williamson, *American Suffrage* (Princeton, NJ: Princeton University Press, 1960), pp. 223, 241, 260. More precisely, there was universal suffrage for white male taxpayers.

11. See John Hope Franklin, *From Slavery to Freedom* (New York: Knopf, 1967); Leon Litwack, *North of Slavery* (Chicago: University of Chicago Press, 1961); and Alexander Keyssar, *The Right to Vote: The Contested History of Democracy in the United States* (New York: Basic Books, 2001).

12. Keyssar, *The Right to Vote*.

13. Walter Dean Burnham, "The Turnout Problem," in A. James Reichley, ed., *Elections, American Style* (Washington, D.C.: Brookings Institution, 1987), pp. 113–114.

14. Martin P. Wattenberg, *Where Have All the Voters Gone?* (Cambridge, MA: Harvard University Press, 2002), p. 120.

15. Kay Lehman Schlozman, "Citizen Participation in America: What Do We Know? Why Do We Care?" in Ira Katznelson and Helen V. Milner, eds., *Political Science: The State of the Discipline* (New York: W. W. Norton, 2002), pp. 439–443.

16. *The New York Times* (November 21, 1988), p. B16.

17. Nelson W. Polsby and Aaron Wildavsky, *Presidential Elections*, 11th ed. (Lanham, MD: Rowman and Littlefield, 2003), p. 17.

18. Ibid.; U.S. Bureau of the Census, 2002.

19. Wattenberg, *Where Have All the Voters Gone?* ch. 6.

20. Polsby and Wildavsky believe that barriers to registration are more important than alienation in explaining nonvoting. See *Presidential Elections*, p. 9.

21. Joseph S. Nye, Jr., Philip D. Zelikow, and David C. King, eds., *Why People Don't Trust Government* (Cambridge, MA: Harvard University Press, 1997).

22. "Forum" in *The American Political Science Review,* 93 (December 1999), pp. 851–910; Richard R. Lau and Gerald M. Pomper, "Effects of Negative Campaigning on Turnout in U.S. Senate Elections, 1988–1998, *The Journal of Politics,* 63, no. 3 (August 2001), pp. 804–819.

23. Morris P. Fiorina, "Parties, Participation, and Representation in American: Old Theories Face New Realities," in Katznelson and Milner, *Political Science.*

24. Steven J. Rosenstone and John Mark Hansen, *Mobilization, Participation, and Democracy in American* (New York: Macmillan, 1993).

25. Alan S. Gerber and Donald M. Green, "The Effects of Canvassing, Telephone Calls, and Direct Mail on Voter Turnout," *American Political Science Review,* 94 (2000), pp. 653–663.

26. Russell Dalton, *Citizen Politics in Western Democracies* (Chatham, NJ: Chatham House, 1988), p. 42.

27. National Opinion Research Center, *The General Social Survey,* 1999.

28. Sidney Verba, Kay Lehman Schlozman, and Henry E. Brady, *Voice and Equality: Civic Volunteerism in American Politics* (Cambridge, MA: Harvard University Press, 1995), pp. 51, 56.

29. Jack C. Doppelt and Ellen Shearer, *Non-Voters: America's No-Shows* (New York: Sage, 1999); Jeffrey Berry, *The New Liberalism* (Washington, D.C.: Brookings, 1999), pp. 39–40.

30. Verba, Schlozman, and Brady, *Voice and Equality,* ch. 7; Sidney Verba and Norman H. Nie, *Participation in America* (New York: Harper & Row, 1972).

31. Susan A. MacManus, *Young v. Old* (Boulder, CO: Westview Press, 1996), ch. 2.

32. Margaret M. Conway, *Political Participation in the United States,* 3rd ed, (Washington, D.C.: CQ Press, 2000), p. 37.

33. E. J. Dionne, "If Nonvoters Had Voted: Same Winner, but Bigger," *The New York Times* (November 21, 1988), p. B16.

34. Sidney Verba, Kay Lehman Schlozman, Henry E. Brady, and Norman H. Nie, "Citizen Activity: Who Participates? What Do They Say?" *American Political Science Review,* 87 (1993), pp. 303–318.

35. Polsby and Wildavsky, *Presidential Elections,* pp. 53–55, 57.

36. Ibid., pp. 92–93, 143–147.

37. Larry Bartels, *Presidential Primaries and the Dynamics of Public Choice* (Princeton, NJ: Princeton University Press, 1988); John H. Aldrich, *Before the Convention* (Chicago: University of Chicago Press, 1980).

38. Stephen J. Wayne, *The Road to the White House, 1992* (New York: Worth, 2000).

39. William G. Mayer, "Forecasting Presidential Nominations or, My Model Worked Just Fine, Thank You," *PS* (April 2003), pp. 153–157.

40. Polsby and Wildavsky, *Presidential Elections,* pp. 143–147.

41. Ibid., pp. 62–67.

42. On this research see Thomas E. Mann, "Linking Knowledge and Action: Political Science and Campaign Finance Reform," *Perspectives on Politics,* 1, no. 1 (2003), pp. 69–83.

43. See Verba, Schlozman, and Brady, *Voice and Equality.*

44. Efforts to sort out their relative contributions include Benjamin I. Page and Calvin Jones, "Reciprocal Effects of Policy Preferences, Party Loyalties, and the Vote," *American Political Science Review,* 73 (1979), pp. 1071–1089; Gregory B. Markus and Philip E. Converse, "A Dynamic Simultaneous Equation Model of Public Choice," *American Political Science Review,* 73 (1979), pp. 1066–1070.

45. Carlos Elordi, "Ideology: Assessing Its Impact on Political Choices," *Public Perspective* (March/April 2000), pp. 34–35.

46. Larry M. Bartels, "Partisanship and Voting Behavior, 1952–1996," *American Journal of Political Science,* 44 (January 2000), pp. 35–50.

47. Donald E. Stokes, "Some Dynamic Elements of Contests for the Presidency," *American Political Science Review,* 60 (1966), pp. 19–28.

48. Fiorina, *Retrospective Voting.*

49. Thomas B. Edsall, "The Shifting Sands of America's Political Parties," *The Washington Post National Edition* (April 9–15, 2001), p. 11.

50. Polsby and Wildavsky, *Presidential Elections,* p. 137.

51. James E. Campbell, *The American Campaign: U.S. Presidential Elections and the National Vote* (College Station, TX: Texas A&M Press, 2000). Also see Marjorie Randon Hershey and Paul Allen Beck, *Party Politics in America* (New York: Longman, 2003), pp. 216–219.

52. Campbell, *The American Campaign,* p. 189.

Chapter 11 Notes

1. "'04 Elections Expected to Cost Nearly $4 Billion; Presidential Race to Top $1.2 Billion," The Center for Responsive Politics, **www.opensecrets.org/pressreleases/ 2004/04spending.asp,** October 21, 2004; and "CFI's Post-Election Analysis of the 2004 Battle of Congress," press release, The Campaign Finance Institute, The George Washington University (November 5, 2004).

2. Alexandra Starr, "In Congress, a Vanishing Center," *BusinessWeek,* November 15, 2004, pp. 46–47.

3. Roger H. Davidson and Walter J. Oleszek, *Congress and Its Members,* 9th ed. (Washington, D.C.: Congressional Quarterly Press, 2004), pp. 17–18.

4. Ibid., pp. 25–26.

5. Quoted in Charles Warren, *The Supreme Court in U.S. History* (Boston: Little, Brown, 1919), p. 195.

6. Walter J. Oleszek, *Congressional Procedures and the Policy Process,* 5th ed. (Washington, D.C.: Congressional Quarterly Press, 2001), p. 4.

7. On this general question, see Jane Mansbridge, "Rethinking Representation," *American Political Science Review,* 97, no.4 (2003), pp. 515–528.

8. Quoted in Charles Henning, *The Wit and Wisdom of Politics* (Golden, CO: Fulcrum, 1989), p. 235.

9. Abraham Lincoln, announcement in the *Sagamo Journal,* New Salem, Illinois (June 13, 1836).

10. The Inter-Parliamentary Union, 2003, reported in *The Economist* (March, 22, 2003), p. 98.

11. Davidson and Oleszek, *Congress and Its Members,* pp. 120–121.

12. Arturo Vega and Juanita Firestone, "The Effects of Gender on Congressional Behavior and the Substantive Representation of Women," *Legislative Studies Quarterly,* 20 (May 1995), pp. 213–222. Also see Michele L. Swers, *The Difference Women Make* (Chicago: University of Chicago Press, 2002); and the collection of research on women's impact on the legislative process in Cindy Simon Rosenthal, ed., *Women Transforming Congress* (Norman, OK: University of Oklahoma Press, 2002).

13. Gary W. Cox and Jonathan Katz, "The Reapportionment Revolution and Bias in U.S. Congressional Elections," *American Journal of Political Science,* 43 (1999), pp. 812–840.

14. Davidson and Oleszek, *Congress and Its Members,* pp. 51–56.

15. Charles Cameron, David Epstein, and Sharon O'Halloran, "Do Majority-Minority Districts Maximize Black Representation in Congress?" *American Political Science Review,* 90 (1996), pp. 794–812; David Epstein and Sharon O'Halloran, "A Social Science Approach to Race, Districting and Representation," *American Political Science Review,* 93 (1999), pp. 187–191; David Lublin, *The Paradox of Representation: Racial Gerrymandering and Minority Interests* (Princeton, NJ: Princeton University Press, 1997).

16. Federal Election Commission, 2003; and Davidson and Oleszek, *Congress and Its Members,* pp. 68–75.

17. Ibid.

18. Gary W. Cox and Eric Magar, "How Much Is Majority Status in the U.S. Congress Worth?" *American Political Science Review,* 93 (1999), pp. 299–309.

19. Richard Hall and Frank W. Wayman, "Buying Time: Moneyed Interests and the Mobilization of Bias in Congressional Committees," *American Political Science Review,* 84 (1990), pp. 797–820.

20. David R. Mayhew, *Congress: The Electoral Connection* (New Haven, CT: Yale University Press, 1974).

21. Malcolm Jewell, "Legislators and Their Districts," *Legislative Studies Quarterly,* 13 (1988), pp. 403–412.

22. Richard F. Fenno, Jr., *Senators on the Home Trail* (Norman, OK: University of Oklahoma Press, 1996).

23. Bruce Cain, John A. Ferejohn, and Morris P. Fiorina, *The Personal Vote: Constituency Service and Electoral Independence* (Cambridge, MA: Harvard University Press, 1987); Glenn Parker, *Homeward Bound: Explaining Change in Congressional Behavior* (Pittsburgh: University of Pittsburgh Press, 1986).

24. Robert S. Erikson, "Constituency Opinion and Congressional Behavior," *American Journal of Political Science,* 22 (1978), pp. 511–535; Robert S. Erikson and Gerald C. Wright, "Voters, Candidates, and Issues in Congressional Elections," in Lawrence C. Dodd and Bruce I. Oppenheimer, eds., *Congress Reconsidered,* 4th ed. (Washington, D.C.: Congressional Quarterly Press, 1989), pp. 91–116.

25. Alan Monroe, "Consistency Between Public Preferences and National Policy Decisions," *American Politics Quarterly,* 7 (1979), pp. 3–19; Benjamin I. Page and Robert Y. Shapiro, "Effects of Public Opinion on Policy," *American Political Science Review,* 77 (1983), pp. 175–190.

26. Davidson and Oleszek, *Congress and Its Members,* p. 274.

27. Ibid., p. 276.

28. Ibid., pp. 278–279.

29. Alan I. Abramowitz and Kyle L. Saunders, "Ideological Realignment in the U.S. Electorate," *Journal of Politics,* 60 (1998), pp. 634–652; Keith T. Poole and Howard Rosenthal, *Congress: A Political-Economic History of Roll-Call Voting* (New York: Oxford University Press, 1997).

30. Mickey Edwards, "Political Science and Political Practice," *Perspectives on Politics,* 1, no. 2 (June 2003), p. 352.

31. See John J. Kornacki, ed., *Leading Congress: New Styles, New Strategies* (Washington, D.C.: Congressional Quarterly Press, 1990); David W. Rohde, *Parties and Leaders in the Postreform Congress* (Chicago: University of Chicago Press, 1991).

32. Alan A. Abramowitz, " 'Mr. Mayhew, Meet Mr. DeLay,' or the Electoral Connection in the Post-Reform Congress," *PS,* 34, no. 2 (June 2001), pp. 257–258.

33. Oleszek, *Congressional Procedures and the Policy Process,* p. 33.

34. Melinda Henneberger, "DeLay Holds No Gavel, But Firm Grip on Reins," *The New York Times* (June 21, 1999), p. 1, Carl Hulse, "In New G.O.P. Era, DeLay Drives Agenda for Congress," *The New York Times* (January 4, 2003), p. 1.

35. Eric S. Heberlig, "Congressional Parties, Fundraising, and Committee Ambition," *Political Research Quarterly,* 56, no. 2 (June 2003), pp. 151–161.

36. David A. Rohde and Kenneth A. Shepsle, "Democratic Committee Assignments in the House of Representatives: Strategic Aspects of a Social Choice Process," in Matthew D. McCubbins and Terry Sullivan, eds., *Congress: Structure and Policy* (New York: Cambridge University Press, 1987).

37. Lawrence C. Dodd and Bruce I. Oppenheimer, "Revolution in the House: Testing the Limits of Party Government," in Lawrence C. Dodd and Bruce I. Oppenheimer, eds., *Congress Reconsidered,* 4th ed. (Washington, D.C.: Congressional Quarterly Press, 1989).

38. Davidson and Oleszek, *Congress and Its Members,* ch. 8; Donald R. Matthews, *U.S. Senators and Their World* (Chapel Hill, NC: University of North Carolina Press, 1960).

39. Eric M. Uslaner, *The Decline of Comity in Congress* (Ann Arbor, MI: University of Michigan Press, 1996).

40. Robert Bendiner, *Obstacle Course on Capitol Hill* (New York: McGraw-Hill, 1964), p. 15.

41. Garry Young and Joseph Cooper, "Multiple Referral and the Transformation of House Decision Making," in Lawrence C. Dodd and Bruce I. Oppenheimer, eds., *Congress Reconsidered,* 5th ed. (Washington, D.C.: Congressional Quarterly Press, 1993).

42. Morris P. Fiorina, *Congress: Keystone of the Washington Establishment,* 2nd ed. (New Haven, CT: Yale University Press, 1989); Mayhew, *Congress;* Gary C. Jacobson, *Politics of Congressional Elections,* 2nd ed. (Boston: Little, Brown, 1987).

43. Morris P. Fiorina, "The Decline of Collective Responsibility," *Daedalus* (Summer 1980), pp. 24–37; Cain, Ferejohn, and Fiorina, *The Personal Vote.*

44. Davidson and Oleszek, *Congress and Its Members,* pp. 455–457; John R. Hibbing and Elizabeth Theiss-Morse, *Congress as Public Enemy: Public Attitudes Toward American Political Institutions* (New York: Cambridge University Press, 1995).

45. Hibbing and Theiss-Morse, *Congress as Public Enemy,* p. 147.

Chapter 12

1. Robin Toner and Neil A. Lewis, "White House Push on Security Steps Bypasses Congress," *The New York Times* (November 14, 2001), p. A1.

2. U.S. Department of Commerce, *Historical Statistics of the United States, Colonial Times to 1970* (Washington, D.C.: U.S. Government Printing Office, 1971), pp. 8, 1143.

3. U.S. Bureau of the Census.

4. Quoted in Laurence J. Peter, *Peter's Quotations* (New York: Morrow, 1977), p. 405.

5. *United States* v. *Curtiss-Wright* (1936).

6. Arthur Schlesinger, Jr, *The Imperial Presidency* (New York: Popular Library, Atlantic Monthly Press, 1973).

7. James P. Pfiffner, *The Modern Presidency* (New York: St. Martin's Press, 1998), ch. 4.

8. Nathan Miller, *FDR: An Intimate History* (Lanham, MD: Madison Books, 1983), p. 276.

9. Thomas E. Cronin and Michael A. Genovese, *The Paradoxes of the American Presidency* (New York: Oxford University Press, 1998), ch. 10; Joseph A. Pika, "The Vice-Presidency: New Opportunities, Old Constraints," in Michael Nelson, ed., *The Presidency and the Political System,* 4th ed. (Washington, D.C.: Congressional Quarterly Press, 1995), pp. 496–528.

10. Benjamin Bradlee, *Conversations with Kennedy* (New York: Norton, 1975), p. 38.

11. Richard E. Neustadt, *Presidential Power and the Modern Presidents: The Politics of Leadership from Roosevelt to Reagan* (New York: Free Press, 1990).

12. William G. Howell, *Power Without Persuasion: The Politics of Direct Presidential Action* (Princeton, N.J.: Princeton University Press, 2003).

13. Graham T. Allison, *Essence of Decision: Explaining the Cuban Missile Crisis* (Boston: Little, Brown, 1971), pp. 141–142.

14. Neustadt, *Presidential Power and the Modern Presidents,* ch. 2.

15. Charles O. Jones, *Separate but Equal: Congress and the Presidency* (New York: Chatham House, 1999).

16. For the view that divided government affects the content of public policy, see James L. Sundquist, "Needed: A Political Theory for the New Era of Coalition Government in the U.S.," *Political Science Quarterly,* 103 (1988), pp. 613–635; L. Mezey, "The Legislature, the Executive and Public Policy," and N. Pfiffner, "Divided Government and the Problems of Governance," in James Thurber, ed., *Divided Democracy* (Washington, D.C.: Congressional Quarterly Press, 1991). For the view that divided government doesn't matter much, see David R. Mayhew, *Divided We Govern: Party Control, Lawmaking, and Investigations, 1946–1990* (New Haven, CT: Yale University Press, 1991); Charles Jones, *The Presidency in a Separated System* (Washington, D.C.: Brookings Institution, 1994). It may be that divided government matters for some issue areas and not others; for this view, see Martha Gibson, "Issues, Coalitions, and Divided Government," *Congress and the Presidency,* 22 (1995), pp. 155–165.

17. George C. Edwards III, *Presidential Influence in Congress* (San Francisco: Freeman, 1980); Jon R. Bond and Richard Fleischer, *The President in the Legislative Arena* (Chicago: University of Chicago Press, 1990); Mark A. Peterson, *Legislating Together* (Cambridge, MA: Harvard University Press, 1990). For a contrary view suggesting that an ideologically cohesive majority is what matters, not the actual size of the majority, see Jon R. Bond and Richard Fleischer, eds., *Polarized Politics: Congress and the President in a Partisan Era* (Washington, D.C.: CQ Press, 2000).

18. Terry Sullivan, "Headcounts, Expectations and Presidential Coalitions in Congress," *American Journal of Political Science,* 32 (1988), pp. 657–689.

19. Aaron Wildavsky, "The Two Presidencies," in Aaron Wildavsky, ed., *Perspectives on the Presidency* (Boston: Little, Brown, 1975), pp. 448–461.

20. Edwards, *Presidential Influence in Congress,* pp. 90–100; Bond and Fleischer, *The President in the Legislative Arena.*

21. Richard Brody, *Assessing the President: The Media, Elite Opinion, and Public Support* (Stanford, CA.: Stanford University Press, 1991).

22. Jeffrey K. Tulis, *The Rhetorical Presidency* (Princeton, NJ: Princeton University Press, 1987), chs. 2 and 3, esp. p. 64.

23. Woodrow Wilson, *Leaders of Men,* ed. T. H. Vail Motter (Princeton, NJ: Princeton University Press, 1952), p. 39; quoted in Tulis, *The Rhetorical Presidency,* ch. 4, which analyzes Wilson's theory at length and expresses some skepticism about it.

24. Tulis, *The Rhetorical Presidency,* pp. 138, 140.

25. Samuel Kernell, *Going Public: Strategies of Presidential Leadership,* 2nd ed. (Washington, D.C.: Congressional Quarterly Press, 1993), p. 92 and ch. 4.

26. Benjamin I. Page and Robert Y. Shapiro, "Presidents as Opinion Leaders: Some New Evidence," *Policy Studies Journal,* 12 (1984), pp. 649–661; Benjamin I. Page, Robert Y. Shapiro, and Glenn R. Dempsey, "What Moves Public Opinion," *American Political Science Review,* 81 (1987), pp. 23–43; but see Donald L. Jordan, "Newspaper Effects on Policy Preferences," *Public Opinion Quarterly,* 57 (1993), pp. 191–204.

27. Lawrence R. Jacobs and Robert Y. Shapiro, *Politicians Don't Pander: Political Manipulation and the Loss of Democratic Responsiveness* (Chicago: University of Chicago Press, 2000).

28. Benjamin I. Page and Mark P. Petracca, *The American Presidency* (New York: McGraw-Hill, 1983), p. 122. Also see Benjamin I. Page and Robert Y. Shapiro, "Effects of Public Opinion on Policy," *American Political Science Review,* 77 (1983), pp. 175–190.

29. Lawrence Jacobs and Robert Y. Shapiro, "The Rise of Presidential Polling: The Nixon White House in Historical Perspective," *Public Opinion Quarterly,* 59 (1995), pp. 163–195.

30. Brody, *Assessing the President.* See also John E. Mueller, "Presidential Popularity from Truman to Johnson," *American Political Science Review,* 64 (1970), pp. 18–34; Samuel Kernell, "Explaining Presidential Popularity," *American Political Science Review,* 72 (1978), pp. 506–522.

31. See Mark P. Petracca, ed., *The Politics of Interests* (Boulder, CO: Westview Press, 1992).

32. Alexander Heard, *The Costs of Democracy* (Chapel Hill, NC: University of North Carolina Press, 1960); Thomas Ferguson and Joel Rogers, *Right Turn: The Decline of the Democrats and the Future of American Politics* (New York: Hill and Wang, 1987); Thomas Ferguson, *Golden Rule* (Chicago: University of Chicago Press, 1995).

33. Howard Fineman and Michael Isikoff, "Big Energy at the Table," *Newsweek* (May 14, 2001), pp. 19–22.

34. Douglas A. Hibbs, Jr., "Partisan Theory After Fifteen Years," *European Journal of Political Economy,* 8 (1992), pp. 361–373.

Chapter 13

1. David S. Broder, "So, Now Bigger Is Better," *The Washington Post National Weekly Edition* (January 20–26, 2003), p. 21.

2. Wallace Sayre, "Bureaucracies: Some Contrasts in Systems," *Indian Journal of Public Administration,* 10 (1964), p. 223.

3. Richard J. Stillman II, *The American Bureaucracy* (Chicago: Nelson-Hall, 1987), p. 18.

4. Stephen Skowronek, *Building a New American State: The Expansion of National Administrative Capacities, 1877–1920* (New York: Cambridge University Press, 1982), pp. 19–46.

5. See Edward S. Greenberg, *Capitalism and the American Political Ideal* (Armonk, NY: Sharpe, 1985); Samuel P. Hays, *The Response to Industrialization* (Chicago: University of Chicago Press, 1957); Gabriel Kolko, *The Triumph of Conservatism* (Chicago: Quadrangle, 1967); Robert Wiebe, *The Search for Order, 1877–1920* (New York: Hill & Wang, 1967); James Weinstein, *The Corporate Ideal in the Liberal State* (Boston: Beacon Press, 1968).

6. Matthew A. Crenson and Francis E. Rourke, "American Bureaucracy Since World War II," in Louis Galambos, ed., *The New American State* (Baltimore: Johns Hopkins University Press, 1987).

7. *The 9/11 Commission Report* (New York: W. W. Norton, 2004), pp. 406–415.

8. B. Guy Peters, *American Public Policy: Policy and Performance,* 6th ed. (New York: CQ Press, 2004), pp. 97–98).

9. Theodore J. Lowi, *The End of Liberalism,* 2nd ed. (New York: Norton, 1979).

10. Christopher Lee, "An Overhaul, Not a Tuneup," *The Washington Post National Edition* (June 22, 2003), p. 30.

11. See Samuel Krislov and David H. Rosenbloom, *Representative Bureaucracy and the American Political System* (New York: Praeger, 1981); Charles T. Goodsell, *The Case for Bureaucracy,* 4th ed. (Washington, D.C.: CQ Press, 2003).

12. Goodsell, *The Case for Bureaucracy,* pp. 84–90; Stanley Rothman and S. Robert Lichter, "How Liberal Are Bureaucrats?" *Regulation* (November–December 1983), pp. 35–47.

13. Office of Personnel Management, 2004.

14. See Goodsell, *The Case for Bureaucracy,* p. 85; Kenneth J. Meier, "Representative Bureaucracy: An Empirical Analysis," *American Political Science Review* 69 (June 1975), pp. 537–539.

15. Richard P. Nathan, *The Administrative Presidency* (New York: Wiley, 1983).

16. Hugh Heclo, *A Government of Strangers* (Washington, D.C.: Brookings Institution, 1977), p. 103.

17. Cornelius M. Kerwin, *Rulemaking: How Government Agencies Write Law and Make Policy* (Washington, DC: CQ Press, 2003), p. 183.

18. Richard E. Neustadt, *Presidential Power* (New York: Wiley, 1960).

19. Terry M. Moe, "Control and Feedback in Economic Regulation," *American Political Science Review,* 79 (1985), pp. 1094–1116; Richard W. Waterman, *Presidential Influence and the Administrative State* (Knoxville, TN: University of Tennessee Press, 1989).

20. Roger H. Davidson and Walter J. Oleszek, *Congress and Its Members,* 9th ed. (Washington, D.C.: CQ Press, 2004), pp. 336–343; Matthew D. McCubbins, "The Legislative Design of Regulatory Structure," *American Journal of Political Science,* 29 (1985), pp. 421–438.

21. Nolan McCarty and Rose Razaghian, "Advice and Consent: Senate Responses to Executive Branch Nominations, 1885–1996," *American Journal of Political Science,* 43 (October 1999), pp. 1122–1143.

22. Richard Fenno, *The Power of the Purse* (Boston: Little, Brown, 1966); Aaron Wildavsky, *The Politics of the Budgetary Process* (Boston: Little, Brown, 1964).

23. John A. Ferejohn and Charles R. Shipan, "Congressional Influence on Administrative Agencies: A Case Study of Telecommunications Policy," in Lawrence C. Dodd and Bruce I. Oppenheimer, eds., *Congress Reconsidered,* 4th ed. (Washington, D.C.: Congressional Quarterly Press, 1989).

24. See Derek Bok, *The Trouble with Government* (Cambridge, MA: Harvard University Press, 2001), ch. 9; Emanuel S. Savas, *Privatization: The Key to Better Government* (Chatham, NJ: Chatham House, 1987); Sheila B. Kamerman and Alfred J. Kahn, eds., *Privatization and the Welfare State* (Princeton, NJ: Princeton University Press, 1989); Lester M. Salamon, ed., *The Tools of Government: A Guide to the New Governance* (Oxford: Oxford University Press, 2002).

25. Bok, *The Trouble with Government,* p. 233–234; Roberta Lynch and Ann Markusen, "Can Markets Govern?" *American Prospect* (Winter 1994), pp. 125–134.

26. David Osborne and Ted Gaebler, *Reinventing Government* (Reading, MA: Addison-Wesley, 1992).

27. Bok, *The Trouble with Government,* pp. 234–239; Joel D. Aberbach and Bert A. Rockman, eds., *In the Web of Politics: Three Decades of the U.S. Federal Executive* (Washington, D.C.: Brookings Institution Press, 2000); Lester M. Salamon, "The New Governance and the Tools of Public Administration," in Salamon, ed., *The Tools of Government.*

28. Al Gore, Jr., *From Red Tape to Results: Creating a Government That Works Better and Costs Less* (Washington, D.C.: U.S. Government Printing Office, 1993).

29. Jim Collins, "Turning Goals Into Results: The Power of Catalytic Mechanisms," *Harvard Business Review* (July–August 1999), pp. 13–17.

30. Terry M. Moe, "The Politics of Bureaucratic Structure," in John E. Chubb and Paul E. Peterson, eds., *Can the Government Govern?* (Washington, D.C.: Brookings Institution, 1989), p. 280; John E. Chubb and Paul E. Peterson, "American Political Institutions and the Problem of Governance," in Chubb and Peterson, eds., *Can the Government Govern?*, p. 41; James L. Sundquist, *Constitutional Reform and Effective Government* (Washington, D.C.: Brookings Institution, 1986).

Chapter 14

1. J. M. Sosin, *The Aristocracy of the Long Robe: The Origins of Judicial Review in America* (Westport, CT: Greenwood Press, 1989).

2. Robert G. McCloskey, *The American Supreme Court* (Chicago: University of Chicago Press, 1960), pp. 12–13.

3. On *Marbury,* see Sylvia Snowmiss, *Judicial Review and the Law of the Constitution* (New Haven, CT: Yale University Press, 1990).

4. Richard S. Randall, *American Constitutional Development* (New York: Longman, 2002), pp. 488–489.

5. Neil Lewis, "An Appeals Court That Always Veers to the Right," *The New York Times* (May 24, 1999), p. A.1.

6. David M. O'Brien, *Storm Center: The Supreme Court in American Politics,* 3rd ed. (New York: Norton, 1993), p. 68.

7. Robert A. Carp and Ronald Stidham, *Judicial Process in America,* 3rd ed. (Washington, D.C.: Congressional Quarterly Press, 1996), ch. 8; Sheldon Goldman, "Federal Judicial Recruitment," in John B. Gates and Charles Johnson, eds., *The American Courts: A Critical Assessment* (Washington, D.C.: Congressional Quarterly Press, 1991), pp. 195, 199.

8. Lawrence Baum, "The Supreme Court in American Politics," in Nelson W. Polsby, ed., *Annual Review of Political Science* (Palo Alto, CA: Annual Reviews, 2003), pp. 161–180; Robert Dahl, "Decision-Making in a Democracy: The Supreme Court as a National Policy-Maker," *Journal of Public Law,* 6 (1957), pp. 279–295; Ronald Stidham and Robert A. Carp, "Judges, Presidents, and Policy Choices," *Social Science Quarterly,* 68 (1987), pp. 395–404; Carp and Stidham, *Judicial Process in America,* ch. 9.

9. For details, see H. W. Perry, Jr., *Deciding to Decide: Agenda Setting in the United States Supreme Court* (Cambridge, MA: Harvard University Press, 1991).

10. David Adamany, "The Supreme Court," in Gates and Johnson, eds., *The American Courts,* pp. 111–112; Baum, "The Supreme Court in U.S. Politics," pp. 162–168; Glendon Schubert, *The Judicial Mind* (Evanston, IL: Northwestern University Press, 1965); Jeffrey A. Segal and Harold J. Spaeth, *The Supreme Court and the Attitudinal Model* (New York: Cambridge University Press, 1993);

John D. Sprague, *Voting Patterns of the United States Supreme Court* (Indianapolis: Bobbs-Merrill, 1968).

11. Walter Murphy, *Elements of Judicial Strategy* (Princeton, NJ: Princeton University Press, 1964).

12. Joel B. Grossman, "Social Backgrounds and Judicial Decision-Making," *Harvard Law Review,* 79 (1966), pp. 1551–1564; S. Sidney Ulmer, "Dissent Behavior and the Social Background of Supreme Court Justices," *Journal of Politics,* 32 (1970), pp. 580–589.

13. L. Epstein, J. Knight, and J. Martin, "The Supreme Court as a Strategic National Policy-Maker," *Emory Law Review,* 50 (2001), pp. 583–610.

14. Nicholas Wade, "A Mathematician Crunches the Supreme Court's Numbers," *The New York Times* (August 4, 2003), p. A.21.

15. John Harlan, "A Glimpse of the Supreme Court at Work," *University of Chicago Law School Record,* 1, no. 7 (1963), pp. 35–52.

16. Bob Woodward and Scott Armstrong, *The Brethren: Inside the Supreme Court* (New York: Simon & Schuster, 1979).

17. Lee Epstein and Jack Knight, "Mapping Out the Strategic Terrain: The Informational Role of Amici Curiae," in Cornell Clayton and Howard Gillman, eds., *Supreme Court Decision-Making* (Chicago: University of Chicago Press, 1999).

18. Herbert Jacob, *Justice in America,* 3rd ed. (Boston: Little, Brown, 1978), p. 245.

19. McCloskey, *The American Supreme Court.*

20. Carp and Stidham, *Judicial Process in America,* p. 28.

21. McCloskey, *The American Supreme Court,* p. 57.

22. Ibid. Also see H. W. Perry, Jr., *The Transformation of the Supreme Court's Agenda: From the New Deal to the Reagan Administration* (Boulder, CO: Westview Press, 1991).

23. Charles Lane, "A Mirror on the Nation's Mood," *The Washington Post National Edition* (July 14–20, 2003), p. 29; Linda Greenhouse, "In a Momentous Term, Justices Remake the Law, and the Court," *The New York Times* (July 1, 2003), p. A1; "Affirmative Action," *The Economist* (June 28, 2003), 28.

24. Baum, "The Supreme Court in American Politics," p. 167.

25. Edward Lazarus, *Closed Chambers* (New York: Penguin, 1999), pp. 373–374.

26. Epstein and Knight, "Mapping Out the Strategic Terrain."

27. Dahl, "Decision Making in a Democracy," pp. 279–295; Thomas R. Marshall, "Public Opinion, Representation, and the Modern Supreme Court," *American Politics Quarterly,* 16 (1988), pp. 296–316; McCloskey, *The American Supreme Court,* p. 22; O'Brien, *Storm Center,* p. 325.

28. G. Caldeira, "Courts and Public Opinion," in Gates and Johnson, eds., *The American Courts;* Jay Casper, "The Supreme Court and National Policy Making," *American Political Science Review,* 70 (1976), pp. 50–63; Marshall, "Public Opinion, Representation, and the Modern Supreme Court"; William Mishler and Reginald S. Sheehan, "The Supreme Court as a Counter-Majoritarian Institution: The Impact of Public Opinion on Supreme Court Decisions," *American Political Science Review,* 87 (1993), pp. 87–101; Benjamin I. Page and Robert Y. Shapiro, "Effects of Public

Opinion on Policy," *American Political Science Review,* 77 (1983), p. 183.

Chapter 15

1. The first three examples were cited in George F. Will, "Compassion on Campus," *Newsweek* (May 31, 1993), p. 66.

2. Kenneth Lasson, "Political Correctness," *Tennessee Law Review,* 63 (Spring, 1996), p. 32.

3. Diana Jean Schemo, "New Battles in Old War Over Freedom of Speech," *New York Times* (November 21, 2001), p. B6.

4. Harvey A. Silverglate and Greg Lukianoff, "Speech Codes Alive and Well at Colleges," *The Chronicle of Higher Education* (August 1, 2003), p. 1.

5. Nat Hentoff, "Chilling Codes," *Washington Post,* Nexis: LEGI-SLATE Article No. 225/226.

6. Laurence H. Tribe, *American Constitutional Law,* 3rd ed. (New York: Foundation Press, 2000), ch. 9.

7. Morton J. Horwitz, *The Transformation of American Law, 1780–1860* (Cambridge, MA: Harvard University Press, 1977); J. Willard Hurst, *Law and the Conditions of Freedom in the Nineteenth-Century United States* (Madison, WI: University of Wisconsin Press, 1956).

8. Robert A. Dahl, "Decision-Making in a Democracy: The Supreme Court as National Policy-Maker," *Journal of Public Law,* 6 (1967), pp. 279–295.

9. Samuel Walker, *In Defense of American Liberties: A History of the ACLU* (New York: Oxford University Press, 1990).

10. Richard Morin, "The High Price of Free Speech," *The Washington Post Weekly Edition* (January 8–14, 2001), p. 34.

11. See Stanley I. Kutler, *The American Inquisition: Justice and Injustice in the Cold War* (New York: Hill & Wang, 1982).

12. See Fred W. Friendly, *Minnesota Rag* (New York: Vintage, 1981).

13. See Charles Rembar, *The End of Obscenity* (New York: Harper & Row, 1968).

14. *Katz* v. *United States* (1967).

15. *United States* v. *Leon* (1984); *Massachusetts* v. *Sheppard* (1984).

16. *Nix* v. *Williams* (1984).

17. *Harris* v. *New York* (1971); *New York* v. *Quarles* (1984).

18. *Arizona* v. *Fulminate* (1991).

19. Jim Yardley, "A Role Model for Executions," *The New York Times* (January 9, 2000), p. A1, IV–5.

20. Jim Yardley, "Number of Executions Falls for Second Year in a Row," *The New York Times* (December 13, 2001), p. A13.

21. Adam Liptak, "Death Row Numbers Decline as Challenges to System Rise," *The New York Times* (January 11, 2003), p. A1.

22. Adam Liptak, "Juries Reject Death Penalty in Nearly All Federal Trials," *The New York Times* (November 21, 2003), p. A1.

23. Much of the following is based on Harold Hongju Koh, "Rights to Remember," *The Economist* (November 1, 2003), pp. 24–25.

24. "Security Trumps Civil Liberties," a report of a poll conducted by National Public Radio, the Kennedy School of Government of Harvard University, and the Kaiser Family Fund, November 30, 2001.

Chapter 16

1. Greg Winter, "Schools Resegregate, Study Finds," *The New York Times* (January 21, 2003), p. A14.

2. Gary Orfield and Chungmei Lee, *Brown at 50: King's Dream or Plessy's Nightmare?* (Cambridge, MA: Harvard University—The Civil Rights Project, 2004), p. 1.

3. Ibid., p. 20.

4. Ibid., p. 27.

5. James MacGregor Burns and Stewart Burns, *A People's Charter: The Pursuit of Rights in America* (New York: Knopf, 1991), p. 37.

6. William H. Chafe, *The Unfinished Journey: America Since World War II* (New York: Oxford University Press, 1986), p. 149.

7. Richard Morin and Michael H. Cottman, "The Invisible Slap," *The Washington Post National Edition* (July 2–8, 2001), p. 5.

8. This section is based on Richard D. Kahlenberg, *The Remedy: Class, Race, and Affirmative Action* (New York: Basic Books, 1996).

9. Sam Howe Verhovek, "In Poll, Americans Reject Means But Not the Ends of Racial Diversity," *The New York Times* (December 14, 1997), p. A1; Martin Gilens, Paul M. Sniderman, and James H. Kuklinski, "Affirmative Action and the Politics of Realignment," *British Journal of Political Science,* 28 (January 1998), pp. 159–184; Jack Citrin, David O. Sears, Christopher Muste, and Cara Wong, "Multiculturalism in American Public Opinion," *British Journal of Political Science* 31 (2001), pp. 247–275.

10. The Gallup Survey (August 2001); CNN/USA Today poll (January 2000).

11. The Pew Research Center for the People and the Press, "Evenly Divided and Increasingly Polarized" (Washington, D.C., 2003), p. 45; "Conflicted Views of Affirmative Action" (Washington, D.C, 2004), p. 1.

12. Ibid., p. 46.

13. Paul M. Sniderman and Edward G. Carmines, *Reaching Beyond Race* (Cambridge, MA: Harvard University Press, 1997).

14. Seymour Martin Lipset, *American Exceptionalism* (New York: Norton, 1996), ch. 4.

15. Opinion of the Court, *Grutter* v. *Bollinger* (2003).

16. See Marian Faux, *Roe* v. *Wade* (New York: Macmillan, 1988).

17. Ibid., p. 45.

18. Eva R. Rubin, *Abortion, Politics, and the Courts* (Westport, CT: Greenwood Press, 1982), ch. 2.

19. Kristen Luker, *Abortion and the Politics of Motherhood* (Berkeley: University of California Press, 1984), ch. 2.

20. Katharine Q. Seelye, "Advocates of Abortion Rights Report a Rise in Restrictions," *The New York Times* (January 15, 1998), p. A1; David Kocieniewski, "Abortion Rights Movement Stunned by Whitman," *The New York Times* (June 15, 1999), p. A29.

21. Robert Bork, *The Tempting of America: The Political Seduction of the Law* (New York: Free Press, 1990), p. 281.

22. *Newsweek* (October 21, 1991), p. 34.

23. Ibid., p. 36.

24. Linda Greenhouse, "Justices Give the States Immunity from Suits by Disabled Workers," *The New York Times* (February 22, 2001), p. A1.

25. Kenneth Sherrill and Alan Yang, "From Outlaws to In-Laws," *Public Perspectives* (January/February 2000), pp. 20–23.

26. ABC News/*Washington Post* Poll (January 15–18, 2004); CBS News/*New York Times* Poll (December 10–13, 2003); *The Los Angeles Times* Poll (November 15–18, 2003); *Time*/CNN Poll conducted by Harris Interactive (November 18–19, 2003); *The Los Angeles Times* Poll (May 2004), reported in "Another Thirty Years War in the Makeup?" *The Economist* (May 2004), p. 24.

27. Lisa Keen, "Referendums and Rights: Across the Country, Battles Over Protection for Gays and Lesbians," *Washington Post* (October 31, 1993), p. C3.

Chapter 17

1. David Firestone, "Dizzying Dive to Red Ink Poses Stark Choices for Washington," *The New York Times* (September 14, 2003), p. A1.

2. Fred C. Pampel, *Age, Class, Politics, and the Welfare State* (New York: Cambridge University Press, 1989), p. 16; Harold Wilensky, *The Welfare State and Equality* (Berkeley, CA: University of California Press, 1975).

3. Robert E. Goodin, "Reasons for Welfare," in J. Donald Moon, ed., *Responsibility, Rights, and Welfare: The Theory of the Welfare State* (Boulder, CO: Westview Press, 1988); and Wilensky, *The Welfare State and Equality.* See also Clark Kerr, John T. Dunlop, Fredrick H. Harbison, and Charles A. Myers, *Industrialism and Industrial Man* (New York: Oxford University Press, 1964).

4. This discussion is based largely on B. Guy Peters, *American Public Policy: Promise and Performance,* 6th ed. (New York: CQ Press, 2003), pp. 193–203.

5. *The Budget of the United States, Fiscal 2005.*

6. Peters, *American Public Policy,* pp. 234–35.

7. David Cay Johnston, *Perfectly Legal: The Covert Campaign to Rig Our Tax System to Benefit the Super Rich—and Cheat Everybody Else* (New York: Penguin, 2003), pp. 309–311; Richard W. Stevenson, "Fed Chairman Says Tax Cuts Should Follow Debt Reduction," *The New York Times* (January 25, 2002), p. A1. (Data on tax effects in the article are from Citizens for Tax Justice).

8. Benjamin Friedman, *Day of Reckoning: The Consequences of American Economic Policy Under Reagan and After* (New York: Random House, 1989), p. 90.

9. George J. Stigler, "The Theory of Economic Regulation," *Bell Journal,* 2 (Spring 1971), pp. 3–21. Also see Gabriel Kolko, *The Triumph of Conservatism* (Chicago: Quadrangle, 1967); James Weinstein, *The Corporate Ideal in the Liberal State* (Boston: Beacon Press, 1968).

10. See Richard Harris and Sidney Milkis, *The Politics of Regulatory Change* (New York: Oxford University Press, 1989); Marc Allen Eisner, *Regulatory Politics in Transition* (Baltimore: Johns Hopkins University Press, 2000).

11. See G. William Domhoff, *The Higher Circles* (New York: Random House, 1970); Edward S. Greenberg, *Capitalism and the American Political Ideal* (Armonk, NY: Sharpe, 1985); Kolko, *The Triumph of Conservatism;* Weinstein, *The Corporate Ideal in the Liberal State.*

12. Frances Fox Piven and Richard A. Cloward, *Poor People's Movements* (New York: Vintage, 1979).

13. Marver Bernstein, *Regulation by Independent Commission* (Princeton, NJ: Princeton University Press, 1955); Grant McConnell, *Private Power and American Democracy* (New York: Vintage Books, 1966); Theodore J. Lowi, *The End of Liberalism,* 2nd ed. (New York: Norton, 1979).

14. David Vogel, *Fluctuating Fortunes: The Political Power of Business in the United States* (New York: Basic Books 1989), pp. 59, 112.

15. James Buchanan and Gordon Tullock, "Polluters, Profits and Political Responses: Direct Control versus Taxes," *American Economic Review,* 65 (1975), pp. 139–147; L. Lave, *The Strategy of Social Regulation* (Washington, D.C.: Brookings Institution, 1981); Murray Weidenbaum, *The Costs of Government Regulation of Business* (Washington, D.C.: Joint Economic Committee of Congress, 1978).

16. See Thomas Byrne Edsall, *The New Politics of Inequality* (New York: Norton, 1984); Vogel, *Fluctuating Fortunes;* Kevin P. Phillips, *The Politics of Rich and Poor: Wealth and the American Electorate in the Reagan Aftermath* (New York: Random House, 1990); Thomas Ferguson and Joel Rogers, *Right Turn: The Decline of the Democrats and the Future of American Politics* (New York: Farrar, Straus & Giroux, 1986).

17. Stephen Labaton, "Bush Is Putting Team in Place for a Full-Bore Assault on Regulation," *The New York Times* (May 22, 2001), p. A1; Joel Brinkley, "Out of Spotlight, Bush Overhauls U.S. Regulations," *The New York Times* (August 14, 2004), p. A1.

18. See Merton C. Bernstein and Joan Brodshaug Bernstein, *Social Security: The System That Works* (New York: Basic Books, 1988), pp. 13–14; Peters, *American Public Policy,* ch. 11.

19. Benjamin I. Page and James R. Simmons, *What Government Can Do: Dealing with Poverty and Inequality* (Chicago: University of Chicago Press, 2000), ch. 3.

20. "U.S. Pensions Found to Lift Many of the Poor," *The New York Times* (December 28, 1989), p. A1. See also Theodore R. K. Marmor, Jerry L. Mashaw, and Philip L. Harvey, *America's Misunderstood Welfare State* (New York: HarperCollins, 1990), ch. 4.

21. U.S. Bureau of the Census, *Statistical Abstracts of the United States, 2003.*

22. Hugh Heclo, "The Political Foundations of Anti-Poverty Policy," in Sheldon Danziger and Daniel Weinberg, eds., *Fighting Poverty: What Works and What Doesn't?*

(Cambridge, MA: Harvard University Press, 1986); Fay Lomax Cook and Edith J. Barrett, *Support for the American Welfare State: The Views of Congress and the Public* (New York: HarperCollins, 1990), ch 4.

23. David T. Ellwood, *Poor Support: Poverty in the American Family* (New York: Basic Books, 1988); Martin Gilens, *Why Americans Hate Welfare: Race, Media, and the Politics of Antipoverty Policy* (Chicago: The University of Chicago Press, 1999).

24. John E. Schwarz, *America's Hidden Success: A Reassessment of Public Policy from Kennedy to Reagan* (New York: Norton, 1988), p. 37.

25. Peters, *American Public Policy,* p. 314; Christopher Howard, *The Hidden Welfare State* (Princeton, NJ: Princeton University Press, 1999), ch. 3.

26. Robert Pear, "Welfare Spending Shows Huge Shift," *The New York Times* (October 12, 2003), p. A1.

27. Leslie Kaufman, "Millions Have Left Welfare, but Are They Better Off? Yes, No and Maybe," *The New York Times* (October 20, 2003), p. A16.

28. Carey Goldberg, "Most Get Work After Welfare," *The New York Times* (April 16, 1999), p. 1.

29. Jared Bernstein and Mark Greenberg, "Reforming Welfare Reform," *The American Prospect* (January 1–15, 2001), pp. 10–16; Robin H. Rogers-Dillon, "What Do We Really Know About Welfare Reform?" *Society,* 38, no. 2 (January/February 2001), pp. 7–15.

30. Kaufman, "Millions Have Left Welfare," p. A16.

31. Gosta Esping-Andersen, "The Three Political Economies of the Welfare State," *Canadian Review of Sociology and Anthropology,* 26 (1989), pp. 10–36; Norman Furniss and Timothy Tilton, *The Case for the Welfare State* (Bloomington, IN: Indiana University Press, 1977); Walter Korpi, *Democratic Class Struggle* (New York: Routledge, 1983).

32. Vincent A. Mahler and Claudio J. Katz, "Social Benefits in Advanced Capitalist Countries: A Cross-National Assessment," *Comparative Politics,* 21 (1988), pp. 37–50. See also Arnold J. Heidenheimer, Hugh Heclo, and Carolyn Teich Adams, *Comparative Public Policy: The Politics of Social Choice in America, Europe, and Japan,* 3rd ed. (New York: St. Martin's Press, 1990); Stein Ringen, *The Possibility of Politics: A Study in the Political Economy of the Welfare State* (New York: Clarendon Press, 1987).

33. Fred C. Pampel and Paul Adams, "Demographic Change and Public Support for Children: Family Allowance Expenditures in Advanced Industrial Democracies," working paper, Department of Sociology, University of Colorado, Boulder, 1990.

34. Eugene Smolensky, Sheldon Danziger, and Peter Gottschalk, "The Declining Significance of Age in the United States: Trends in the Well-Being of Children and the Elderly Since 1939," in John L. Palmer, Timothy Smeedling, and Barbara Boyle Torrey, eds., *The Vulnerable* (Washington, D.C.: Urban Institute, 1988); U.S. Bureau of the Census, *Poverty in the United States, 1998.*

35. Mahler and Katz, "Social Benefits in Advanced Capitalist Countries"; John Freeman, *Democracy and Markets* (Ithaca, NY: Cornell University Press, 1989); Ringen, *The Possibility of Politics,* ch. 7.

36. Robert Pear, "Big Increase Seen in People Lacking Health Insurance," *The New York Times* (September 29, 2003), p. A1.

37. Nathan Glazer, *The Limits of Social Policy* (Cambridge, MA: Harvard University Press, 1988), pp. 187–188. See also W. Sombart, *Why There Is No Socialism in the United States* (Armonk, NY: Sharpe, 1976).

38. Gilens, *Why Americans Hate Welfare;* Jeff Manza, "Race and Underdevelopment of the American Welfare State," *Theory and Society,* 29 (2000), pp. 819–832.

39. See Louis Hartz, *The Liberal Tradition in America* (New York: Harcourt Brace, 1955); G. V. Rimlinger, *Welfare Policy and Industrialization in Europe, America and Russia* (New York: Wiley, 1971); Marmor, Marshaw, and Harvey, *America's Misunderstood Welfare State;* Wilensky, *The Welfare State and Equality.*

40. See David Cameron, "Social Democracy, Corporatism, Labor Quiescence, and the Representation of Interests in Advanced Capitalist Society," in John H. Goldthorpe, ed., *Order and Conflict in Contemporary Capitalism* (New York: Clarendon Press, 1984); Francis G. Castles, *The Impact of Parties: Politics and Policies in Democratic Capitalist States* (Newbury Park, CA: Sage, 1982); Gosta Esping-Andersen, *Politics Against Markets* (Princeton, NJ: Princeton University Press, 1985); Korpi, *Democratic Class Struggle;* John Stephens, *The Transition from Capitalism to Socialism* (London: Macmillan, 1979).

Chapter 18

1. President George W. Bush, The State of the Union Address, The United States Capitol, Washington, D.C. (January 29, 2002).

2. Ibid.

3. Both quotations are from *The National Security Strategy of the United States* (Washington, D.C.: The White House, September, 2003), ch. V, p. 1.

4. Steven Erlanger, "Europe Seethes as the U.S. Flies Solo in World Affairs," *The New York Times* (February 22, 2002), p. A10; David E. Sanger, "Allies Hear Sour Notes in 'Axis of Evil' Chorus," *The New York Times* (February 17, 2002), p. A1.

5. Niall Ferguson, *Colossus: The Price of America's Empire* (New York: Pengum, 2004); William E. Odom and Robert Dujarric, *America's Inadvertent Empire* (New Haven: Yale University Press, 2004); Chalmers Johnson, *The Sorrows of Empire* (New York: Metropolitan Books, 2004).

6. Statistics are from the *CIA World Factbook, 2004.*

7. Gregg Easterbrook, "American Might Moves Beyond Superpower," *The New York Times* (April 27, 2003), Week in Review Section, p. 1; The Center for Defense Information, **www.cdi.org** (2003).

8. Johnson, *The Sorrows of Empire.*

9. Laurent Cohen-Tanugi, *An Alliance at Risk: The United States and Europe Since September 11* (Baltimore, MD: John Hopkins University Press, 2003); Ferguson, *Colossus;* Robert-Kagan, *of Paradise and Power: America and Europe in the New World Order* (New York: Knopf, 2003).

10. Joseph S. Nye, Jr., "Redefining the National Interest," *Foreign Affairs* (July/August 1999), pp. 22–35.

11. Thomas L. Friedman, *The Lexus and the Olive Tree* (New York: Farrar, Straus, Giroux, 1999).

12. Pew Research Center for the People and the Press, "War with Iraq Further Divides Global Publics" (June 3, 2003), "A Year After Iraq War: Mistrust of America in Europe Ever Higher, Muslim Anger Persists" (March 16, 2004).

13. Ibid.

14. Kagan, *Of Paradise and Power;* Richard Bernstein, "Foreign Views of U.S. Darken After Sept. 11," *The New York Times* (September, 2003), p. A1.

15. Fouad Ajami, "The Falseness of Anti-Americanism," *Foreign Policy* (September/October 2003), pp. 52–61; Dominique Moisi and Hubert Vedrine, *France in an Age of Globalization* (Washington, D.C.: Brookings Institution Press, 2001); Bernard Lewis, *What Went Wrong? Western Impact and Middle Eastern Response* (Oxford: Oxford University Press, 2001).

16. "X" (George F. Kennan), "The Sources of Soviet Conduct," *Foreign Affairs,* 25 (1947), pp. 566–582; Lawrence S. Wittner, *American Intervention in Greece, 1943–1949* (New York: Columbia University Press, 1982).

17. John Lewis Gaddis, "A Grand Strategy," *Foreign Policy* (November/December 2002), pp. 50–57; Ivo H. Daalder and James M. Lindsay, *America Unbound: The Bush Revolution in Foreign in Policy* (Washington, D.C.: Brookings Institution Press, 2003).

18. Emily Eakin, "All Roads Lead to D.C.," *The New York Times* (March 31, 2002), Week in Review, p. 3.

19. Cohen-Tanugi, *An Alliance at Risk;* Kagan, *Of Paradise and Power;* Robert Jervis, "The Compulsive Empire," *Foreign Policy* (July/August 2003), pp. 83–87.

20. Arab Human Development Report 2003, *Building a Knowledge Society* (New York: The United Nations, 2003).

21. Lewis, *What Went Wrong?*

22. Samuel P. Huntington, "The Clash of Civilizations," *Foreign Affairs,* 72 (1993).

23. Mario F. Bognanno and Kathryn J. Ready, eds., *The North American Free Trade Agreement: Labor, Industry, and Government Perspectives* (Westport, CT: Praeger, 1993).

24. Jagdish Bhagwati and Marvin H. Kosters, eds., *Trade and Wages: Leveling Down Wages?* (Washington, D.C.: AEI Press, 1994); Jagdish Bhagwati, *In Defense of Globalization* (New York: Oxford University Press, 2004); Dani Rodrik, Robert Z. Lawrence, and Scott Bradford, *Has Globalization Gone Too Far?* (Washington, D.C.: Institute for International Economics, 1997); Joseph E. Stiglitz, *Global-ization and Its Discontents* (New York: W. W. Norton and Company, 2003).

25. Ibid.; Arvind Panagariya, "International Trade," *Foreign Policy* (November/December 2003), pp. 20–28.

26. Jerry Mander and Edward Goldsmith, eds., *The Case Against the Global Economy* (San Francisco: Sierra Club Books, 1996).

27. World Health Organization, 2003.

28. *Budget of the United States, 2005;* Organization for Economic Cooperation and Development (OECD), *International Development Statistics, 2004.*

29. Samuel P. Huntington, *Who Are We? The Challenges of America's National Identity* (New York: Simon and Schuster, 2004).

30. Bob Woodward, *Plan of Attack* (New York: Simon and Schuster, 2004).

31. Charles W. Kegley, Jr., and Eugene R. Wittkopf, *American Foreign Policy: Pattern and Process,* 6th ed. (Belmont, CA: Wadsworth Publishing, 2002), p. 387.

32. Donald M. Snow and Eugene Brown, *Puzzle Palaces and Foggy Bottom: U.S. Foreign and Defense Policy-Making in the 1990s* (New York: St. Martin's Press, 1994), p. 96.

33. Bruce M. Russett, *Controlling the Sword: The Democratic Governance of National Security* (Cambridge, MA: Harvard University Press, 1990); Richard Sobel, ed., *Public Opinion in U.S. Foreign Policy: The Controversy over Contra Aid* (Lanham, MD: Rowman & Littlefield, 1993).

34. V. O. Key, Jr., *Public Opinion and American Democracy* (New York: Knopf, 1961), p. 552.

Credits

Text, Figures, and Tables

Page 69: From Morris P. Fiorina and Paul E. Peterson, *New American Democracy*, 2nd edition (New York: Longman Publishers, 2001), p. 81. Reprinted by permission of Pearson Education, Inc.; **p. 73**: Box map, "Educated Guesses: Sampling Is Taboo, But the Census Does Plenty of 'Imputing'—It Fills in Missing Answers on Race, Sex, Age—Even Postulates Whole People—Whatever the Neighbors Say," by Glenn R. Simpson, *The Wall Street Journal*, August 30, 2001. Copyright © 2001 Dow Jones & Company, Inc. Reproduced by permission of Dow Jones & Company, Inc. in the format Textbook via Copyright Clearance Center; **p. 77**: Figure 3.5, used with the permission of the Center for American Women and Politics (CAWP), Eapleton Institute of Politics, Rutgers University; **p. 227**: Table 8.1, Percent of Whites Giving Pro-Integration Responses, 1942–1963 from *America in Black and White* by Stephan Thernstrom and Abigail Thernstrom. Copyright © 1997 by Stephan and Abigail Thernstrom. Reprinted with the permission of Simon & Schuster Adult Publishing Group; **p. 289**: Table 10.1, "Comparing Major Party Convention Delegates to Other Americans" from *The New York Times*/CBS News poll, *The New York Times*, August 14, 2000. Reprinted by permission of *The New York Times*.; **p. 427**: Figure 14.3, From *Storm Center: The Supreme Court in American Politics*, Third Edition, by David M. O'Brien. Copyright © 1993, 1990, 1986 by David M. O'Brien. Used by permission of W. W. Norton & Company, Inc.; and **p. 514**: Figure 17.1, "American GDP Change on Previous Quarter" (10/28/95). Copyright © 1995 The Economist Newspaper Ltd. All rights reserved. Reprinted with permission. Further reproduction prohibited. www.economist.com.

Photos

Page v: Eliot Crowley/Index Stock Imagery; **part openers:** Gail Mooney/CORBIS; **chapter openers:** Bill Ross/CORBIS; **p. 4:** AP/Wide World Photos; **p. 7:** The Granger Collection, New York; **p. 8:** Alan Diaz/AP/Wide World Photos; **p. 9:** Bob Daemmrich/The Image Works; **p. 10:** Image Bank/ITTC Productions/Getty Images; **p. 12:** The Granger Collection; **p. 14:** The Granger Collection; **p. 18:** AP/Wide World Photos; **p. 25:** The Granger Collection; **p. 28 (left):** The Granger Collection; **p. 28 (right):** Library of Congress; **p. 31:** Scala/Art Resource, NY; **p. 34:** Art Resource, NY; **p. 37:** © The Illustrated London News/February 16, 1861; **p. 47:** Rick Reinard; **p. 51:** James Leynse/CORBIS; **p. 53:** AP/Wide World Photos; **p. 53:** Tony Freeman/PhotoEdit Inc.; **p. 56:** Brooks Kraft/CORBIS; **p. 60:** David Turnley/CORBIS; **p. 63:** Timothy O. Sullivan/Library of Congress; **p. 65:** Franklin Delano Roosevelt Library; **p. 67:** Tyrone Turner/STOCK-PHOTO—Black Star; **p. 70:** CORBIS; **p. 71:** P. Jorden/Corbis Sygma; **p. 72:** Comstock Royalty Free; **p. 74:** AP/Wide World Photos; **p. 79:** Anneal Vohra; **p. 83:** Reuters/CORBIS; **p. 87:** S. Kelly, © 1995 San Diego Union-Tribune, Copley News Service; **p. 91:** Ariel Skelley/CORBIS; **p. 92:** Karin Slade/Getty Images; **p. 94:** Joe Sohm/Chromosohm; **p. 98:** Bettmann/CORBIS; **p. 99:** Forrest Anderson/Getty Images; **p. 101:** AP/Wide World Photos; **p. 102:** Enrico Dagnino/Stockphoto – Black Star; **p. 104:** Diego Goldberg; **p. 115:** C. Simonpietri/Corbis Sygma; **p. 118:** Billy E. Barnes/PhotoEdit Inc.; **p. 120:** Bettmann/UPI/Corbis; **p. 121:** Kent Meireis/The Image Works; **p. 122:** FireFly Productions/CORBIS; **p. 126:** Bob Daemmrich/PhotoEdit Inc.; **p. 127:** Tony Freeman/PhotoEdit Inc.; **p. 130:** Charlie Archambault/Folio, Inc.; **p. 132:** Flip Schulke/CORBIS; **p. 134:** Wally McNamee/Corbis Sygma; **p. 136:** Doug Mills/AP/Wide World Photos; **p. 140:** Ron Edmonds/AP/Wide World Photos; **p. 145:** Mark Mainz/Getty Images; **p. 153:** HO/AFP/Getty Images; **p. 155:** MacNelly, © Copyright, 2005, Newsday. Reprinted with permission; **p. 156:** © New York Journal, February 7, 1898; **p. 157:** Colorado Historical Society; **p. 159:** Mark Peterson/CORBIS; **p. 160:** SuperStock; **p. 162:** AP/Wide World Photos; **p. 163:** Richard Drew/AP/Wide World Photos; **p. 166:** Time Life Pictures/Getty Images; **p. 167:** Brendan McDermid/Reuters/Landov; **p. 169:** Alex Wong/Getty Images; **p. 173:** CNN; **p. 178:** © By permission of Mike Luckovich and Creators Syndicate; **p. 179:** The Image Works; **p. 182:** Rick Wilking/AP/Wide World Photos; **p. 184:** Michael L. Abramson/Time Life Pictures/Getty Images; **p. 187:** David Frazier/The Image Works; **p. 189:** Library of Congress; **p. 192:** Chris Hondros/Getty Images; **p. 195:** Bob Child/AP/Wide World Photos; **p. 196:** Dennis Brack/Stockphoto – Black Star; **p. 198:** Paul Conklin/PhotoEdit; **p. 200:** Allan Tannenbaum; **p. 202:** Ted Spiegel/CORBIS; **p. 210:** AP/Wide World Photos; **p. 217:** The Granger Collection; **p. 220:** David Butow/ Corbis Saba Press; **p. 221:** Elaine Thompson/AP/Wide World Photos; **p. 225:** McCartney/Photo Researchers, Inc.; **p. 226:** Ramin Talaie/CORBIS; **p. 228:** Peter Lennihan/AP/Wide World Photos; **p. 230:** Bettmann/Corbis; **p. 231:** AP/Wide World Photos; **p. 234:** Stephen Morton/AP/Wide World Photos; **p. 239:** AP/Wide World Photos; **p. 241:** Edward Greenberg; **p. 244:** Pearson Education U.S. ELT/Scott Foresman; **p. 246:** Bettmann/CORBIS; **p. 250:** Image Bank/Yellow Dog Productions/Getty Images; **p. 252:** William Waldron/The Image Works; **p. 253:** AP/Wide World Photos; **p. 255:** Mark Peterson/Corbis Saba Press; **p. 257:** Mathieu/Corbis Sygma; **p. 258:** Bush-Cheney '04/AP/Wide World Photos; **p. 261:** Mark Wilson/Newsmakers/Getty Images; **p. 269 (left):** Ed Reinke/AP/Wide World Photos; **p. 269 (right):** Gerald Herbert/AP/Wide World Photos; **p. 274:** David Burnett/Contact Press Images; **p. 277:** Rob Crandall/The Image Works; **p. 279:** The St. Louis Art Museum. Gift of Bank of America; **p. 282:** AP/Wide World Photos; **p. 286:** Lonny Shavelson/Zuma Press; **p. 289:** Tannen Maury/The Image Works; **p. 290:** Mike Segar/Reuters/CORBIS; **p. 291 (left):** Bettmann/Corbis; **p. 291 (right):** Arnold Zann/Stockphoto

Index